D1277311

INTRODUCTION TO LITERATURE

GINN
LITERATURE SERIES
Edward J. Gordon
SENIOR AUTHOR

INTRODUCTION TO LITERATURE
THE STUDY OF LITERATURE
UNDERSTANDING LITERATURE
TYPES OF LITERATURE
AMERICAN LITERATURE
ENGLISH LITERATURE

WILLIAM ELLER

State University of New York at Buffalo

BETTY YVONNE WELCH

Smiley Junior High School, Denver

INTRODUCTION
TO
LITERATURE

EDWARD J. GORDON

Yale University

BAPTIST BIBLE COLLEGE EAST
BOX 458 STONEY ST.
SHRUB OAK, NEW YORK 10588

GINN AND COMPANY

OCT 1 0 1980

© Copyright, 1967, 1964, by Ginn and Company
All Rights Reserved
Library of Congress Catalog Card Number: 67-11780
Home Office, Boston, Massachusetts 02117

WILLIAM ELLER is professor of education, department of language arts education, at the State University of New York at Buffalo. Dr. Eller is a past president of the National Reading Conference and a member of the Committee on Secondary School Reading of NCTE.

BETTY YVONNE WELCH, formerly an English teacher at both the junior and senior high school levels in Denver, Colorado, is now the dean of girls at Smiley Junior High School in Denver. Mrs. Welch is an active member of the Denver Area English Council and of the NCTE.

EDWARD J. GORDON, assoicate professor of English at Yale University, is director of Yale's Office of Teacher Training. He was head of the English department of Germantown Friends School in Philadelphia before going to Yale. He has been chairman of and the motivating force behind the annual Yale Conference on the teaching of English. Mr. Gordon is a director of the School and College Conference on the Teaching of English and a director of the NCTE.

Acknowledgments

Grateful acknowledgment is due to the following publishers, authors, and other holders of copyright material for permission to use selections from their publications.

APPLETON-CENTURY-CROFTS: "Onawandah," by Louisa May Alcott, from *St. Nicholas Magazine*. Reprinted by permission of Appleton-Century-Crofts; "Roland Sees the King," "Roland Becomes a Knight," from *Famous Legends Adapted for Children* by Emeline G. Crommelin; "Bill," from *Yellow Gentians and Blue*, by Zona Gale. Copyright, 1927, by D. Appleton and Company; renewed, 1955. By permission of Appleton-Century; "The Reef," by Samuel Scoville, Jr., from *St. Nicholas Magazine*. Copyright, 1923, The Century Company. Reprinted by permission of the publishers Appleton-Century-Crofts.

MRS. GEORGE BAMBRIDGE: "Tommy," from *Barrack Room Ballads*, by Rudyard Kipling.

THE BODLEY HEAD LTD.: "Our Lady's Juggler," from *Mother of Pearl*, by Anatole France.

BOY'S LIFE MAGAZINE: "Patrol at Valley Forge," by Russell Gordon Carter. By permission of the author and *Boy's Life*, published by the Boy Scouts of America.

BRANDT & BRANDT: "Crazy Horse," "Lewis and Clark," "Thomas Jefferson," from *A Book of Americans*, by Rosemary and Stephen Vincent Benét, Holt, Rinehart and Winston, Inc. Copyright, 1933 by Rosemary and Stephen Vincent Benét. Copyright renewed 1961 by Rosemary Carr Benét.

CURTIS BROWN, LTD.: "Death at Suppertime," by Phyllis McGinley. Reprinted by permission of the author. Copyright 1948 by The New Yorker Magazine, Inc.

MRS. RUSSELL GORDON CARTER: "Patrol at Valley Forge," by Russell Gordon Carter.

THE CLARENDON PRESS: "Robin Hood and Alan a Dale," from *The Oxford Book of Ballads*, edited by Sir Arthur Quiller-Couch.

FRANK MARSHALL DAVIS: "Rain," by Frank Marshall Davis.

DODD, MEAD & COMPANY: "Our Lady's Juggler," reprinted by permission of Dodd, Mead & Company from *Mother of Pearl*, by Anatole France; "The Cremation of Sam McGee," reprinted by permission of Dodd, Mead & Company from *Collected Poems of Robert Service*.

DOUBLEDAY & COMPANY, INC.: "Good-by, Grandma," by Ray Bradbury, copyright © 1957 by The Curtis Publishing Company, from *Dandelion Wine*. Reprinted by permission of Doubleday & Company, Inc.; "The Gift of the Magi," from *The Four Million*, by O. Henry; "Tommy," by Rudyard Kipling, from the book *Collected Verse by Rudyard Kipling*. Reprinted by permission of Mrs. George Bambridge and Doubleday & Company, Inc.

CONSTANCE GARLAND DOYLE AND ISABEL GARLAND LORD: "A Day's Pleasure," from *Main-Travelled Roads*, by Hamlin Garland.

E. P. DUTTON & CO., INC.: "Young Washington, The Embassy to the French Forts, 1753," from the book *I Sing the Pioneer*, by Arthur Guiterman. Copyright, 1926, by E. P. Dutton & Co., Inc. Renewal, 1954, by Mrs. Vida Lindo Guiterman. Reprinted by permission of the publishers.

FARRAR, STRAUS & COMPANY, INC.: "Where Are the Children?" Reprinted, in slightly adapted form, by permission of Farrar, Straus & Company, Inc. from *My Mother's House and Sido* by Colette, translated by Una Vicenzo Troubridge and Enid McLeod. Copyright 1953 by Farrar, Straus & Young, Inc.

AMBROSE FLACK: "The Strangers That Came to Town," by Ambrose Flack. © Copyright 1952 by Crowell Collier Publishing Co.; appeared originally in *Woman's Home Companion*. Reprinted by permission of the author.

HOLT, RINEHART AND WINSTON, INC.: "A Wild Strain," from *Great River*, by Paul Horgan. Copyright 1954 by Paul Horgan. Reprinted by permission of Holt, Rinehart and Winston, Inc.; "Oh, when I was in love with you," from *A Shropshire Lad*–Authorised Edition–from *Complete Poems*, by A. E. Housman. Copyright © 1959 by Holt, Rinehart and Winston, Inc. Reprinted by permission of Holt, Rinehart and Winston, Inc.

HOUGHTON MIFFLIN COMPANY: "How We Astonished the Rivermouthians," from *The Story of a Bad Boy*, by Thomas Bailey Aldrich; "The Apples of Idun," from *Legends of the North*, by Olivia E. Coolidge; "Daedalus," "Phaethon, Son of Appollo," from *Greek Myths*, by Olivia E. Coolidge; "Curfew," from *The Complete Poetical Works by Henry Wadsworth Longfellow*; "The First Snowfall," from *The Complete Poetical Works of James Russell Lowell;* "Homer, The Great Storyteller," from *Old World Hero Stories*, by Eva March Tappan.

ALFRED A. KNOPF, INC.: "The Noblest Instrument," reprinted from *Life with Father and Mother*, by Clarence Day, by permission of Alfred A. Knopf, Inc. Copyright, 1924, 1935 by Clarence Day; "Watch America,"—copyright, 1945, 1950 by Robert Nathan—"Dunkirk,"—copyright, 1941, 1950 by Robert Nathan. Reprinted from *The Green Leaf*, by Robert Nathan, by permission of Alfred A. Knopf, Inc.; "The Idealist," reprinted from *The Stories of Frank O'Connor*, by Frank O'Connor, by permission of Alfred A. Knopf, Inc.

MacEDWARD LEACH: "Bonny Barbara Allan," "The Crafty Farmer,' "Lord Randal," from *The Ballad Book*.

LITTLE, BROWN AND COMPANY: "Elysium," "I like to see it lap the Miles," from *The Complete Poems of Emily Dickinson*, ed. by Thomas H. Johnson, by permission of Little, Brown and Co.; excerpts from *The Fables of India* ("The Monkey Gardeners," "The Fox in Saint's Clothing," "The Talkative Tortoise"), by Joseph Gaer. Copyright 1955, by Joseph Gaer. Reprinted by permission of Little, Brown and Co.; "Demeter (Ceres)," "Hercules," "The Judgment of Paris" (including an excerpt from "The Trojan War"), from *Mythology*, by Edith Hamilton. Copyright 1940, 1942, by Edith Hamilton. Reprinted by permission of Little, Brown and Co.; "First Crossing of the Atlantic," from *Christopher Columbus, Mariner*, by Samuel Eliot Morison. Copyright 1942, 1955 by Samuel Eliot Morison. Reprinted by permission of Little, Brown and Co. and Atlantic Monthly Press; "Song of the Open Road," from *Verses from 1929 On* by Ogden Nash. Copyright 1932 by Ogden Nash; originally appeared in *The New Yorker*. Reprinted by permission of Little, Brown and Co.

GEORGE P. (PATRICK) McCALLUM: "The Song Caruso Sang," from *The American Magazine*. Reprinted by permission of the author.

THE MACMILLAN COMPANY: "The Building of the Wall," reprinted with permission of the publisher from *The Children of Odin*, by Padraic Colum. Copyright 1920 by The Macmillan Company, renewed 1948 by Padraic Colum; "Abraham Lincoln Walks at Midnight," reprinted with permission of the publisher from *Collected Poems*, by Vachel Lindsay. Copyright 1914 by The Macmillan Company, renewed 1942 by Elizabeth C. Lindsay; "Prometheus and Pandora," reprinted with permission of the publisher from *A Book of Myths, Selections from Bulfinch's Age of Fable*, by Helen Sewell. Copyright 1942 by The Macmillan Company; "The Coin," reprinted with permission of the publisher from *Collected Poems*, by Sara Teasdale. Copyright 1920 by The Macmillan Company, renewed 1948 by Mamie T. Wheless; "He Wishes for the Cloths of Heaven," reprinted with the permission of the publisher from *Collected Poems*, by William Butler Yeats. Copyright 1906 by The Macmillan Company, renewed 1934 by William Butler Yeats.

THE MACMILLAN CO. OF CANADA, LTD.: "Tommy," from *Barrack Room Ballads*, by Rudyard Kipling; "He Wishes for the Cloths of Heaven," reprinted by permission of the publisher from *Collected Poems*, by William Butler Yeats.

HAROLD MATSON COMPANY, INC.: "The Idealist," reprinted from *The Stories of Frank O'Connor*, by Frank O'Connor by permission of Harold Matson Co., Inc.; "Top Man," from *Island of the Blue Macaws*, by James Ramsey Ullman. Copyright 1940 by the Curtis Publishing Company. Reprinted with permission of Harold Matson Co., Inc.

WILLIAM MORROW AND COMPANY, INC.: excerpt from *That Lively Man, Ben Franklin*, by Jeanette Eaton, copyright 1948 by William Morrow and Company, Inc., reprinted by permission of William Morrow and Company, Inc.

JOHN MURRAY: "The Redheaded League," from *The Complete Sherlock Holmes*, by Sir Arthur Conan Doyle. Reprinted by permission of the Trustees of the Estate of Sir Arthur Conan Doyle and the publisher, John Murray.

HAROLD OBER ASSOCIATES, INCORPORATED: "City: San Francisco," by Langston Hughes reprinted by permission of Harold Ober Associates, Incorporated. Copyright © 1958 by Langston Hughes.

PUTNAM & CO. LTD.: "A Night at an Inn," by Lord Dunsany.

RANDOM HOUSE, INC.: "Perseus," from *Bulfinch's Mythology*, by Thomas Bulfinch.

THE RYERSON PRESS: "The Cremation of Sam McGee," reprinted from *The Complete Poems of Robert Service*, by Robert Service, by permission of the Ryerson Press, Toronto.

CHARLES SCRIBNER'S SONS: "How Roland Slew a Sea Monster" is reprinted by permission of Charles Scribner's Sons from *The Story of Roland*, by James Baldwin. (Charles Schribner's Sons, 1883); "The Open Road" is reprinted by permission of Charles Scribner's Sons from *The Wind in the Willows*, by Kenneth Grahame; "You Never Know" ("The Year I Had the Colds"), (Copyright © 1955 Nancy Hale) is reprinted by permission of Charles Scribner's Sons from *The Empress's Ring*, by Nancy Hale; "Robin Hood and Little John" and "King Richard Cometh to Sherwood Forest" are reprinted by permission of Charles Scribner's Sons from *The Merry Adventures of Robin Hood*, by Howard Pyle. (Charles Scribner's Sons, 1883); "The Wind," from *The Complete Poems of Robert Louis Stevenson*, reprinted by permission of Charles Scribner's Sons.

MARTIN SECKER & WARBURG LIMITED: "Where Are the Children?" from *My Mother's House and Sido*, by Colette; "Before the Squall," "The Loom of Dreams," from *Silhouettes*, by Arthur Symons.

THE SOCIETY OF AUTHORS: "Oh, when I was in love with you," from *A Shropshire Lad*, in *The Collected Poems of A. E. Housman*. Reprinted by the permission of The Society of Authors as the literary representative of the Estate of the late A. E. Housman, and Messrs. Jonathan Cape, Ltd., publishers of A. E. Housman's *Collected Poems*.

TWAYNE PUBLISHERS, INC.: "The Tropics in New York," by Claude McKay from *Selected Poems of Claude McKay*, published by Bookman Associates.

A. P. WATT & SON: "Tommy," from *Barrack Room Ballads*, by Rudyard Kipling; "He wishes for the Cloths of Heaven," from *Collected Poems*, by William Butler Yeats.

WELLS GARDNER DARTON & CO. LTD.: Stories of King Arthur ("How Arthur Was Crowned King," "The Marvel of the Sword," "The Sword Excalibur"), from *The Book of King Arthur and His Noble Knights* by Mary Macleod.

MRS. W. B. YEATS: "He Wishes for the Cloths of Heaven," from *Collected Poems* by William Butler Yeats.

MARY YOST ASSOCIATES: "The Redheaded League," from *The Complete Sherlock Holmes*, by Sir Arthur Conan Doyle. Reprinted by permission of the Estate of Sir Arthur Conan Doyle.

Contents

Building America

Myths, Fables, and Legends

The One-Act Play 357

Poetry 410

Famous Characters in Literature 500

Preface

Introduction to Literature is designed to further a student's enjoyment and understanding of literature in two ways: first, to increase the student's awareness of his world by presenting him with new ideas to consider; and second, to give the student some of the basic means of analyzing ideas in literature.

This anthology contains eight units which, through their varying organizations, show the student some of the more important approaches to literature. The opening units, for example, emphasize plot and characterization, two fundamental aspects of nearly all literary works. Other units emphasize special characteristics of a particular literary form (such as poetry) or use a thematic approach (as in the unit "Building America").

Each unit begins by explaining its purpose and some of the ideas or techniques which are presented in more detail throughout the unit. Each of the selections is then introduced by a headnote which discusses a key literary technique used in the selection. The questions that follow the selections reinforce the material in the headnotes and help the student respond fully to the ideas in the selection. Further activities are often suggested. Attention is also given to increasing vocabulary and to vocabulary-building techniques, such as use of contexts, connotations, prefixes, and suffixes.

Several supplementary aids are included at the end of the book. Biographical sketches of the authors of the selections are useful for giving students additional background and further reading suggestions. Definitions of literary terms used in the book, as well as additional terms some teachers may wish to introduce, follow the biographical sketches. Each definition also refers the reader to pages on which the term is further discussed. Unfamiliar words which students will encounter often in reading, as well as all vocabulary exercise words, are defined in a glossary. Difficult words which are rarely used, proper names, and allusions are footnoted in the text.

By reading the selections, studying the material in the unit introductions and headnotes, and discussing the questions which follow the selections, the student should greatly increase both his understanding and his enjoyment of the world of literature.

Plot

THE BEGINNINGS of literature grew from man's desire to tell and to hear a good story. The storyteller, whose main object is to entertain you, tries to take you out of your world into his. He tries to convince you that something is happening (plot) to someone (character) somewhere (setting). Over the thousands of years that men have spent as tellers of tales, they have invented ways of putting a story together so that it will convince you of its reality. That last word—reality—is a complicated one. It does not mean that the story is really happening; it means that while you read, you believe that it is. And this makes all the difference.

Some people are so dull that they could not convince anyone that the sun will rise tomorrow morning. But good writers have convinced many children, during a story, that a cow could jump over the moon, that the Pied Piper of Hamelin could lead all the children away from their parents, or that Alice could have fallen down a rabbit hole. Give the writer a chance and he will take you into many new places and adventures.

The storyteller usually creates his story by organizing a series of related incidents into a plot. The good writer does not just tell you what happens; if he did that, he would be merely reporting. He has to select from what happened those moments that are the most significant for his purpose. And the incidents which make up the plot are related to one another. Because the character in the story is in a particular situation, he does something; he may be led then to do something else. You can think of a plot as a chain of incidents, each link joined to the next. When you read a short story, therefore, the first question you should ask is: What happens? And then: How is each event related to the one before it?

It is believed that when the author of this story, Zona Gale, was working for the news-paper *New York World*, she was asked by the editor to check up on this advertisement which had appeared in the paper:

> A man with a few months to live would
> like nice people to adopt his little girl,
> six, blue eyes, curls. References required.

The following short story is based on what Zona Gale found out.

Bill

Zona Gale

IMPROVING YOUR READING: A writer has to interest you early in the story. He does this through the use of *suspense*, usually by setting a question in the reader's mind. The question is not openly stated, but is suggested by the action of the story. In this story Miss Gale begins: "Bill was thirty when his wife died, and little Minna was four. Bill's carpenter shop was in the yard of his house, so he thought that he could keep up his home for Minna and himself." The question, then, that causes the suspense is: Will Bill be able to take care of his daughter until she is old enough to take care of herself? You read on then to find the answer.

BILL WAS THIRTY when his wife died, and little Minna was four. Bill's carpenter shop was in the yard of his house, so he thought that he could keep up his home for Minna and himself. All day while he worked at his bench, she played in the yard, and when he was obliged to be absent for a few hours, the woman next door looked after her. Bill could cook a little, coffee and bacon and fried potatoes and flapjacks, and he found bananas and sardines and crackers useful. When the woman next door said this was not the diet for four-year-olds, he asked her to teach him to cook oatmeal and vege-tables, and though he always burned the dishes in which he cooked these things, he cooked them every day. He swept, all but the corners, and he dusted, dabbing at every object; and he complained that after he had cleaned the windows he could not see out as well as he could before. He washed and patched Minna's little garments and mended her doll. He found a kitten for her so that she wouldn't be lonely. At night he heard her say her prayer, kneeling in the middle of the floor with her hands folded, and speaking like lightning. If he forgot the prayer, he either woke her up, or else he made her say it the first thing next morning. He himself used to try to

2

pray: "Lord, make me do right by her if you see me doing wrong." On Sundays he took her to church and sat listening with his head on one side, trying to understand, and giving Minna peppermints when she rustled. He stopped work for a day and took her to the Sunday-school picnic. "Her mother would of," he explained. When Minna was old enough to go to kindergarten, Bill used to take her morning or afternoon, and he would call for her. Once he dressed himself in his best clothes and went to visit the school. "I think her mother would of," he told the teacher, diffidently.[1] But he could make little of the colored paper and the designs and the games, and he did not go again. "There's some things I can't be any help to her with," he thought.

Minna was six when Bill fell ill. On a May afternoon he went to a doctor. When he came home he sat in his shop for a long time and did nothing. The sun was beaming through the window in bright squares. He was not going to get well. It might be that he had six months. . . . He could hear Minna singing to her doll.

When she came to kiss him that night, he made an excuse, for he must never kiss her now. He held her at arm's length, looked in her eyes, said: "Minna's a big girl now. She doesn't want Papa to kiss her." But her lip curled and she turned away sorrowful, so the next day Bill went to another doctor to make sure. The other doctor made him sure.

1 diffidently: shyly.

He tried to think what to do. He had a sister in Nebraska, but she was a tired woman. His wife had a brother in the city, but he was a man of many words. And little Minna . . . there were things known to her which he himself did not know—matters of fairies and the words of songs. He wished that he could hear of somebody who would understand her. And he had only six months. . . .

Then the woman next door told him bluntly that he ought not to have the child there, and him coughing as he was; and he knew that his decision was already upon him.

One whole night he thought. Then he advertised in a city paper:

A man with a few months more to live would like nice people to adopt his little girl, six, blue eyes, curls. References required.

They came in a limousine, as he had hoped that they would come. Their clothes were as he had hoped. They had with them a little girl who cried: "Is this my little sister?" On which the woman in the smart frock said sharply:

"Now then, you do as Mama tells you and keep out of this or we'll leave you here and take this darling little girl away with us."

So Bill looked at this woman and said steadily that he had now other plans for his little girl. He watched the great blue car roll away. "For the land sake!" said the woman next door when she heard. "You done her out of a fortune. You hadn't the right—a man in your health." And when other cars came, and he let them go, this woman told her husband that Bill ought to be reported to the authorities.

The man and woman who walked into Bill's shop one morning were still mourning their own little girl. The woman was not sad—only sorrowful, and the man, who was tender of her, was a carpenter. In a blooming of his hope and his dread, Bill said to them: "You're the ones." When they asked: "How long before we can have her?" Bill said: "One day more."

That day he spent in the shop. It was summer and Minna was playing in the yard. He could hear the words of her songs. He cooked their supper and while she ate, he watched. When he had tucked her in her bed, he stood in the dark hearing her breathing. "I'm a little girl tonight— kiss me," she had said, but he shook his head. "A big girl, a big girl," he told her.

When they came for her the next morning, he had her ready and her little garments were ready, washed and mended, and he had mended her doll. "Minna's never been for a visit!" he told her buoyantly. And when she ran toward him, "A big girl, a big girl," he reminded her.

He stood and watched the man and woman walking down the street with Minna between them. They had brought her a little blue parasol in case the parting should be hard. This parasol Minna held bobbing above her head, and she was so absorbed in looking up at the blue silk that she did not remember to turn and wave her hand.

Understanding Literature

1. What do you learn, in the first paragraph, of the situation in which Bill and Minna find themselves at the opening of the story?
2. What change in the situation is described in the second paragraph? How does the change increase the suspense?
3. What drives Bill to put the advertisement in the paper?
4. How does he treat the woman in the limousine? Why does he treat her this way?
5. Why does he approve of the man and woman who came? How does the author contrast the attitude of the first woman toward her daughter with the attitude of the couple toward Minna?
6. The author never says how Bill feels toward Minna; instead, she has him act out his attitude. The reader has to draw his own conclusion. How does Bill feel toward his daughter? How does he feel in the last paragraph? How does Minna feel at the end?

Further Activity

When an author writes a story, a poem, or a play, he expects the reader to have an emotional reaction to it. In this story he wants the reader to feel a sense of pity.

Write a paragraph that begins with the following sentence: "A reader of 'Bill' finishes with a feeling of pity." In the second sentence tell for whom you had a sense of pity. In the next few sentences point out two incidents in the story that aroused this feeling in you.

Have you ever wanted to conquer a mountain? This challenge is difficult for many people to understand, but one purpose of literature is to help you better understand other people, their desires, ideals, and ways of living. As you read the adventure "Top Man," try to predict the ending. It is an unusual one.

Top Man

James Ramsey Ullman

IMPROVING YOUR READING: In every story there must first be a *conflict* which needs to be resolved. Otherwise, there would be no story. In "Top Man" there are two problems: one is the conflict of man against man, and the other is the conflict of man against nature. Notice how the story develops around these two conflicts.

FOCUSING ON WORDS: Unless you are familiar with climbing, you will need to learn the following words in order to enjoy and understand this story fully: *gorge, summit, avalanche, precipices, glacier, reconnaissance, crevasse, outcroppings, traverse, rarefied, pinnacle, chimney.* If you need to use the glossary, be sure to find the definition which fits the word as it would be used in a story about mountain climbing.

THE GORGE BENT. The walls fell steeply away, and we came out on the edge of a bleak boulder-strewn valley.

And there it was.

Osborn saw it first. He had been leading the column, threading his way slowly among the huge rock-masses of the gorge's mouth. Then he came to the first flat bare place and stopped. He neither pointed nor cried out, but every man behind him knew instantly what it was. The long file sprang taut, like a jerked rope. As swiftly as we could, but in complete silence, we came out one by one into the open space where Osborn stood and raised our eyes with his.

In the records of the Indian Topographical Survey it says: "Kalpurtha: altitude 27,930 ft. The highest peak in the Garhwal Himalayas. Also known as K₃. A Tertiary formation of sedimentary limestone . . ."

There were men among us who had spent months of their lives—in some cases years—reading, thinking, planning about what now lay before us; but at that moment statistics and geology, knowledge, thought and plans, were as remote and forgotten as the far-away western cities from which we had come. We were men bereft of everything but eyes, everything but the single electric perception: *there it was!*

Before us the valley stretched into miles of rocky desolation. To right and left it was bounded by low ridges, which, as the eye followed them, slowly mounted and drew closer together, until the valley was no longer a valley at all, but a narrowing, rising corridor between the cliffs. What happened then I can describe only as a stupendous crash of music. At the end of the corridor and above it—so far above it that it shut out half the sky—hung the blinding white mass of K_3.

It was like the many pictures I had seen, and at the same time utterly unlike them. The shape was there, and the familiar distinguishing features: the sweeping skirt of glaciers; the monstrous vertical precipices of the face and the jagged ice line of the east ridge; finally the symmetrical summit pyramid that transfixed the sky. But whereas in the pictures the mountain had always seemed unreal —a dream-image of cloud, snow and crystal—it was now no longer an image at all. It was a mass: solid, palpable,[1] appalling. We were still too far away to see the windy whipping of its snowplumes or to hear the cannonading of its avalanches, but in that sudden silent moment every man of us was for the first time aware of it not as a picture in his mind, but as a thing, an antagonist. For all its twenty-eight thousand feet of lofty grandeur it seemed, somehow, less to tower than to crouch—a white-hooded giant, secret and remote, but living. Living and on guard.

I turned my eyes from the dazzling glare and looked at my companions. Osborn still stood a little in front of the others. He was absolutely motionless, his young face tense and shining, his eyes devouring the mountain as a lover's might devour the form of his beloved. One could feel in the very set of his body the overwhelming desire that swelled in him to act, to come to grips, to conquer. A little behind him were ranged the other white men of the expedition: Randolph, our leader, Wittmer and Johns, Dr. Schlapp and Bixler. All were still, their eyes cast upward. Off to one side a little stood Nace, the Englishman, the only one among us who was not staring at K_3 for the first time. He had been the last to come up out of the gorge and stood now with arms folded on his chest, squinting at the great peak he had known so long and fought so tirelessly and fiercely. His lean British face, under its mask of stubble and windburn, was expressionless. His lips were a thin line, and his eyes seemed almost shut. Behind the sahibs[2] ranged the porters, bent forward over their staffs, their brown seamed faces straining upward from beneath their loads.

For a long while no one spoke or moved. The only sounds were the soft hiss of our breathing and the pounding of our hearts.

Through the long afternoon we wound slowly between the great boulders of the valley and at sundown pitched camp in the bed of a dried-up stream. The porters ate their rations in silence, wrapped themselves in their blankets and fell asleep under the stars. The rest of

1 **palpable:** easily seen.

2 **sahibs:** masters.

us, as was our custom, sat close about the fire that blazed in the circle of tents, discussing the events of the day and the plans for the next. It was a flawlessly clear Himalayan night, and K₃ tiered up into the blackness like a gigantic beacon lighted from within. There was no wind, but a great tide of cold air crept down the valley from the ice fields above, penetrating our clothing, pressing gently against the canvas of the tents.

"Another night or two and we'll be needing the sleeping bags," commented Randolph.

Osborn nodded. "We could use them tonight would be my guess."

Randolph turned to Nace. "What do you say, Martin?"

The Englishman puffed at his pipe a moment. "Rather think it might be better to wait," he said at last.

"Wait? Why?" Osborn jerked his head up.

"Well, it gets pretty nippy high up, you know. I've seen it thirty below at twenty-five thousand on the east ridge. The longer we wait for the bags, the better acclimated[3] we'll get."

Osborn snorted. "A lot of good being acclimated will do, if we have frozen feet."

"Easy, Paul, easy," cautioned Randolph. "It seems to me Martin's right."

Osborn bit his lip, but said nothing. The other men entered the conversation, and soon it had veered to other matters: the weather, the porters and pack animals, routes, camps and strategy, the inevitable inexhaustible topics of the climber's world.

There were all kinds of men among the eight of us, men with a great diversity of background and interest. Sayre Randolph whom the Alpine Club had named leader of our expedition, had for years been a well-known explorer and lecturer. Now in his middle fifties, he was no longer equal to the grueling physical demands of high climbing, but served as planner and organizer of the enterprise. Wittmer was a Seattle lawyer, who had recently made a name for himself by a series of difficult ascents in the Coast Range of British Columbia. Johns was an Alaskan, a fantastically strong able sourdough,[4] who had been a ranger in the U.S. Forestry Service and had accompanied many famous Alaskan expeditions. Schlapp was a practicing physician from Milwaukee, Bixler a government meteorologist with a talent for photography. I, at the time, was an assistant professor of geology at an eastern university.

Finally, and pre-eminently,[5] there were Osborn and Nace. I say "pre-eminently," because even at this time, when we had been together as a party for little more than a month, I believe all of us realized that these were the two key men of our venture. None, to my knowledge, ever expressed it in words, but the conviction was none the less there that if any of us were eventually to stand on the summit of K₃, it would be one of

---

3 **acclimated** (ăk′lə māt′ĭd): used to the climate.

4 **sourdough:** Alaskan prospector or explorer.
5 **pre-eminently** (prĭ ĕm′ə nənt lĭ): above all others.

PLOT

them, or both. They were utterly dissimilar men. Osborn was twenty-three and a year out of college, a compact buoyant mass of energy and high spirits. He seemed to be wholly unaffected by either the physical or mental hazards of mountaineering and had already, by virtue of many spectacular ascents in the Alps and Rockies, won a reputation as the most skilled and audacious of younger American climbers. Nace was in his forties—lean, taciturn, introspective.[6] An official in the Indian Civil Service, he had explored and climbed in the Himalayas for twenty years. He had been a member of all four of the unsuccessful British expeditions to K_3, and in his last attempt had attained to within five hundred feet of the summit, the highest point which any man had reached on the unconquered giant. This had been the famous tragic attempt in which his fellow climber and lifelong friend, Captain Furness, had slipped and fallen ten thousand feet to his death. Nace never mentioned his name, but on the steel head of his ice ax were engraved the words: *TO MARTIN FROM JOHN.* If fate were to grant that the ax of any one of us should be planted upon the summit of K_3, I hoped it would be this one.

Such were the men who huddled about the fire in the deep still cold of a Himalayan night. There were many differences among us, in temperament as well as in background. In one or two cases, notably that of

Osborn and Nace, there had already been a certain amount of friction, and as the venture continued and the struggles and hardships of the actual ascent began, it would, I knew, increase. But differences were unimportant. What mattered—all that mattered—was that our purpose was one: to conquer the monster of rock and ice that now loomed above us in the night; to stand for a moment where no man, no living thing, had ever stood before. To that end we had come from half a world away, across oceans and continents to the fastnesses[7] of inner Asia. To that end we were prepared to endure cold, exhaustion and danger, even to the last extremity of human endurance. . . . Why? . . . There is no answer, and at the same time every man among us knew the answer; every man who has ever looked upon a great mountain and felt the fever in his blood to climb and conquer knows the answer. George Leigh Mallory, greatest of mountaineers, expressed it once and for all when he was asked why he wanted to climb unconquered Everest.

"I want to climb it," said Mallory, "because it is there."

Day after day we crept on and upward. Sometimes the mountain was brilliant above us, as it had been when we first saw it; sometimes it was partially or wholly obscured by tiers of clouds. The naked desolation of the valley was unrelieved by any motion, color or sound, and, as we progressed, the great rock walls

6 taciturn, introspective (tăs′ə tûrn′, ĭn′trə spĕkt′ĭv): silent, thoughtful.

7 fastnesses: strongholds; fortresses.

that enclosed it grew so high and steep that its floor received the sun for less than two hours each day. The rest of the time it lay in ashen half-light, its gloom intensified by the dazzling brilliance of the ice slopes above. As long as we remained there we had the sensation of imprisonment; it was like being trapped at the bottom of a deep well or in a sealed court between tall skyscrapers. Soon we were thinking of the ascent of the shining mountain not only as an end in itself, but as an escape.

In our nightly discussions around the fire our conversation narrowed more and more to the immediate problems confronting us, and during them I began to realize that the tension between Osborn and Nace went deeper than I had at first surmised.[8] There was rarely any outright argument between them—they were both far too able mountain men to disagree on fundamentals—but I saw that at almost every turn they were rubbing each other the wrong way. It was a matter of personalities, chiefly. Osborn was talkative, enthusiastic, optimistic, always chafing to be up and at it, always wanting to take the short straight line to the given point. Nace, on the other hand, was matter-of-fact, cautious, slow. He was the apostle of trial and error and watchful waiting. Because of his far greater experience and intimate knowledge of K_3 Randolph almost invariably followed his advice, rather than Osborn's, when a

difference of opinion arose. The younger man usually capitulated[9] with good grace, but I could tell that he was irked.

During the days in the valley I had few occasions to talk privately with either of them, and only once did either mention the other in any but the most casual manner. Even then, the remarks they made seemed unimportant and I remember them only in view of what happened later.

My conversation with Osborn occurred first. It was while we were on the march, and Osborn, who was directly behind me, came up suddenly to my side. "You're a geologist, Frank," he began without preamble.[10] "What do you think of Nace's theory about the ridge?"

"What theory?" I asked.

"He believes we should traverse under it from the glacier up. Says the ridge itself is too exposed."

"It looks pretty mean through the telescope."

"But it's been done before. He's done it himself. All right, it's tough —I'll admit that. But a decent climber could make it in half the time the traverse will take."

"Nace knows the traverse is longer," I said. "But he seems certain it will be much easier for us."

"Easier for *him* is what he means." Osborn paused, looking moodily at the ground. "He was a great climber in his day. It's a shame a man can't be honest enough with himself to know when he's through." He fell

8 **surmised:** guessed; imagined.

9 **capitulated** (kə pĭch′ə lāt′): yielded; agreed.
10 **preamble:** introduction.

silent and a moment later dropped back into his place in line.

It was that same night, I think, that I awoke to find Nace sitting up in his blanket and staring at the mountain.

"How clear it is," I whispered.

The Englishman pointed. "See the ridge?"

I nodded, my eyes fixed on the great twisting spine of ice that climbed into the sky. I could see now, more clearly than in the blinding sunlight, its huge indentations and jagged wind-swept pitches.[11] "It looks impossible," I said.

"No, it can be climbed. Trouble is, when you've made it you're too done in for the summit."

"Osborn seems to think its shortness would make up for its difficulty."

Nace was silent a long moment before answering. Then for the first and only time I heard him speak the name of his dead companion. "That's what Furness thought," he said quietly. Then he lay down and wrapped himself in his blanket.

For the next two weeks the uppermost point of the valley was our home and workshop. We established our base camp as close to the mountain as we could, less than half a mile from the tongue of its lowest glacier, and plunged into the arduous tasks of preparation for the ascent. Our food and equipment were unpacked, inspected and sorted, and finally repacked in lighter loads for transportation to more advanced camps. Hours were spent poring over maps and charts and studying the intricate heights above us through telescope and binoculars. Under Nace's supervision, a thorough reconnaissance of the glacier was made and the route across it laid out; then began the backbreaking labor of moving up supplies and establishing the chain of camps.

Camps I and II were set up on the glacier itself, in the most sheltered sites we could find. Camp III we built at its upper end, as near as possible to the point where the great rock spine of K_3 thrust itself free of ice and began its precipitous[12] ascent. According to our plans, this would be the advance base of operations during the climb. The camps to be established higher up, on the mountain proper, would be too small and too exposed to serve as anything more than one or two nights' shelter. The total distance between the base camp and Camp III was only fifteen miles, but the utmost daily progress of our porters was five miles, and it was essential that we should never be more than twelve hours' march from food and shelter. Hour after hour, day after day, the long file of men wound up and down among the hummocks and crevasses of the glacier, and finally the time arrived when we were ready to advance.

Leaving Dr. Schlapp in charge of eight porters at the base camp, we proceeded easily and on schedule, reaching Camp I the first night, Camp II the second and the advance

---

11 **pitches:** slopes.

12 **precipitous** (prĭ sĭp′ə təs)**:** steep.

base the third. No men were left at Camps I and II, inasmuch as they were designed simply as caches[13] for food and equipment; and furthermore we knew we would need all the man power available for the establishment of the higher camps on the mountain proper.

For more than three weeks now the weather had held perfectly, but on our first night at the advance base, as if by malignant[14] prearrangement of nature, we had our first taste of the fury of a high Himalayan storm. It began with great streamers of lightning that flashed about the mountain like a halo; then heavily through the weird glare snow began to fall. The wind rose. At first it was only sound—a remote, desolate

moaning in the night high above us —but soon it descended, sucked down into the deep valley as if into an enormous funnel. Hour after hour it howled about the tents with hurricane frenzy, and the wild flapping of the canvas dinned in our ears like machine-gun fire.

There was no sleep for us that night or the next. For thirty-six hours the storm raged without lull, while we huddled in the icy gloom of the tents, exerting our last ounce of strength to keep from being either buried alive or blown into eternity. At last, on the third morning, it was over, and we came out into a world transformed by a twelve-foot cloak of snow. No single landmark remained as it had been before, and our supplies and equipment were in the wildest confusion. Fortunately

13 **caches** (kăsh′əz): hiding places.
14 **malignant**: evil.

PLOT

there had not been a single serious injury, but it was another three days before we had regained our strength and put the camp in order.

Then we waited. The storm did not return, and the sky beyond the ridges gleamed flawlessly clear; but night and day we could hear the thunder of avalanches on the mountain above us. To have ventured so much as one step into that savage vertical wilderness before the new-fallen snow froze tight would have been suicidal. We chafed[15] or waited patiently, according to our individual temperaments, while the days dragged by.

It was late one afternoon that Osborn returned from a short reconnaissance up the ridge. His eyes were shining and his voice jubilant.

"It's tight," he cried. "Tight as a drum. We can go!" All of us stopped whatever we were doing. His excitement leapt like an electric spark from one to another. "I went about a thousand feet, and it's sound all the way. What do you say, Sayre? Tomorrow?"

Randolph hesitated, then looked at Nace.

"Better give it another day or two," said the Englishman.

Osborn glared at him. "Why?" he challenged.

"It's generally safer to wait until—"

"Wait! Wait!" Osborn exploded. "Don't you ever think of anything but waiting? Man, the snow's firm, I tell you!"

"It's firm down here," Nace replied

quietly, "because the sun hits it only two hours a day. Up above it gets the sun for twelve hours. It may not have frozen yet."

"The avalanches have stopped."

"That doesn't necessarily mean it will hold a man's weight."

"It seems to me that Martin's point—" Randolph began.

Osborn wheeled on him. "Sure," he snapped. "I know. Martin's right. The cautious bloody English are always right. Let him have his way, and we'll be sitting here chewing our nails until the mountain falls down on us." His eyes flashed to Nace. "Maybe with a little less of that bloody cautiousness you English wouldn't have made such a mess of Everest. Maybe your pals Mallory and Furness wouldn't be dead."

"Osborn!" commanded Randolph sharply.

The youngster stared at Nace for another moment, breathing heavily. Then abruptly he turned away.

The next two days were clear and windless, but we still waited, following Nace's advice. There were no further brushes between him and Osborn, but an unpleasant air of restlessness and tension hung over the camp. I found myself chafing almost as impatiently as Osborn himself for the moment when we would break out of that maddening inactivity and begin the assault.

At last the day came. With the first paling of the sky a roped file of men, bent almost double beneath heavy loads, began slowly to climb the ice slope, just beneath the jagged line of the east ridge. In accordance

15 **chafed** (chāft): became irritated; fretted.

with prearranged plan, we proceeded in relays, this first group consisting of Nace, Johns, myself and eight porters. It was our job to ascend approximately two thousand feet in a day's climbing and establish Camp IV at the most level and sheltered site we could find. We would spend the night there and return to the advance base next day, while the second relay, consisting of Osborn, Wittmer and eight more porters, went up with their loads. This process was to continue until all necessary supplies were at Camp IV, and then the whole thing would be repeated between Camps IV and V and V and VI. From VI, at an altitude of about 26,000 feet, the ablest and fittest men —presumably Nace and Osborn— would make the direct assault on the summit. Randolph and Bixler were to remain at the advance base throughout the operations, acting as directors and co-ordinators. We were under the strictest orders that any man—sahib or porter—who suffered illness or injury should be brought down immediately.

How shall I describe those next two weeks beneath the great ice ridge of K_3? In a sense there was no occurrence of importance, and at the same time everything happened that could possibly happen, short of actual disaster. We established Camp IV, came down again, went up again, came down again. Then we crept laboriously higher. With our axes we hacked uncountable thousands of steps in the gleaming walls of ice. Among the rocky outcroppings of the cliffs we clung to holds and strained at ropes until we thought our arms would spring from their sockets. Winds swooped down on us, battered us and passed, and the air grew steadily colder and more difficult to breathe. One morning two of the porters awoke with their feet frozen black; they had to be sent down. A short while later Johns developed an uncontrollable nosebleed and was forced to descend to a lower camp. Wittmer was suffering from racking headaches and I from a continually dry throat. But providentially,[16] the one enemy we feared the most in that icy gale-lashed hell did not again attack us. No snow fell. And day by day, foot by foot, we ascended.

It is during ordeals like this that the surface trappings of a man are shed and his secret mettle[17] laid bare. There were no shirkers or quitters among us—I had known that from the beginning—but now, with each passing day, it became more manifest[18] which were the strongest and ablest among us. Beyond all argument, these were Osborn and Nace.

Osborn was magnificent. All the boyish impatience and moodiness which he had exhibited earlier were gone, and, now that he was at last at work in his natural element, he emerged as the peerless mountaineer he was. His energy was inexhaustible, his speed, both on rock and ice, almost twice that of any other man in the party. He was always discovering new routes and short cuts.

16 **providentially:** luckily; miraculously.
17 **mettle:** spirit; disposition.
18 **more manifest:** plainer; more obvious.

PLOT

Often he ascended by the ridge itself, instead of using the traverse beneath it, as had been officially prescribed; but his craftsmanship was so sure and his performance so brilliant that no one ever thought of taking him to task. Indeed, there was such vigor, buoyancy and youth in everything he did that it gave heart to all the rest of us.

In contrast, Nace was slow, methodical, unspectacular. Since he and I worked in the same relay, I was with him almost constantly, and to this day I carry in my mind the clear image of the man: his tall body bent almost double against shimmering slopes of ice; his lean brown face bent in utter concentration on the problem in hand, then raised searchingly to the next; the bright prong of his ax rising, falling, rising, falling with tireless rhythm, until the steps in the glassy incline were so wide and deep that the most clumsy of the porters could not have slipped from them had he tried. Osborn attacked the mountain head on. Nace studied it, sparred with it, wore it down. His spirit did not flap from his sleeve like a pennon;[19] it was deep inside him—patient, indomitable.[20]

The day soon came when I learned from him what it is to be a great mountaineer. We were making the ascent from Camp IV to V, and an almost perpendicular ice wall had made it necessary for us to come out for a few yards on the exposed crest of the ridge. There were six of us in the party, roped together, with Nace leading, myself second and four porters bringing up the rear. The ridge at this particular point was free of snow, but razor-thin, and the rocks were covered with a smooth glaze of ice. On either side the mountain dropped away in sheer precipices of five thousand feet.

Suddenly the last porter slipped. I heard the ominous scraping of boot nails behind me and, turning, saw a gesticulating[21] figure plunge sideways into the abyss. There was a scream as the next porter was jerked off too. I remember trying frantically to dig into the ridge with my ax, realizing at the same time it would no more hold against the weight of the falling men than a pin stuck in a wall. Then I heard Nace shout, "Jump!" As he said it, the rope went tight about my waist, and I went hurtling after him into space on the opposite side of the ridge. After me came the nearest porter. . . .

What happened then must have happened in five yards and a fifth of a second. I heard myself cry out, and the glacier, a mile below, rushed up at me, spinning. Then both were blotted out in a violent spasm,[22] as the rope jerked taut. I hung for a moment, an inert mass, feeling that my body had been cut in two, then I swung in slowly to the side of the mountain. Above me the rope lay tight and motionless across the crest of the ridge, our weight exactly counterbalancing that of the men who had fallen on the far slope.

19 **pennon:** flag; banner.
20 **indomitable:** unconquerable.

21 **gesticulating:** gesturing; suddenly motioning.
22 **spasm:** sudden movement; convulsion.

Nace's voice came up from below. "You chaps on the other side!" he shouted. "Start climbing slowly. We're climbing too."

In five minutes we had all regained the ridge. The porters and I crouched panting on the jagged rocks, our eyes closed, the sweat beading our faces in frozen drops. Nace carefully examined the rope that again hung loosely between us.

"All right men," he said presently. "Let's get on to camp for a cup of tea."

Above Camp V the whole aspect of the ascent changed. The angle of the ridge eased off, and the ice, which lower down had covered the mountain like a sheath, lay only in scattered patches between the rocks. Fresh enemies, however, instantly appeared to take the place of the old. We were now laboring at an altitude of more than 25,000 feet—well above the summits of the highest surrounding peaks—and day and night, without protection or respite,[23] we were buffeted[24] by the fury of the wind. Worse than this was that the atmosphere had become so rarified it could scarcely support life. Breathing itself was a major physical effort, and our progress upward consisted of two or three painful steps followed by a long period of rest in which our hearts pounded wildly and our burning lungs gasped for air. Each of us carried a small cylinder of oxygen in his pack, but we used it only in emergencies and

found that, while its immediate effect was salutary,[25] it left us later even worse off than before. My throat dried and contracted until it felt as if it were lined with brass. The faces of all of us, under our beards and windburn, grew haggard and strained.

But the great struggle was now mental as much as physical. The lack of air induced a lethargy[26] of mind and spirit; confidence and the powers of thought and decision waned, and dark foreboding crept out from the secret recesses of the subconscious. The wind seemed to carry strange sounds, and we kept imagining we saw things which we knew were not there. The mountain, to all of us, was no longer a mere giant of rock and ice; it had become a living thing, an enemy, watching us, waiting for us, hostile, relentless and aware. Inch by inch we crept upward through that empty forgotten world above the world, and only one last thing remained to us of human consciousness and human will: to go on. To go on.

On the fifteenth day after we had first left the advance base we pitched Camp VI at an altitude of almost 26,000 feet. It was located near the uppermost extremity of the east ridge, directly beneath the so-called shoulder of the mountain. On the far side of the shoulder the vast north face of K_3 fell sheer to the glaciers, two miles below. And above it and to the left rose the symmetrical bulk of the summit pyramid. The top-

---

23 **respite** (rĕs′pĭt): relief; time of rest.
24 **buffeted**: struck repeatedly.

25 **salutary** (săl′yə tĕr′ĭ): helpful; beneficial.
26 **lethargy** (lĕth′ər jĭ): inaction.

most rocks of its highest pinnacle were clearly visible from the shoulder, and the intervening two thousand feet seemed to offer no insuperable obstacles.

Camp VI, which was in reality no camp at all, but a single tent, was large enough to accommodate only three men. Osborn established it with the aid of Wittmer and one porter; then, the following morning, Wittmer and the porter descended to Camp V, and Nace and I went up. It was our plan that Osborn and Nace should launch the final assault —the next day, if the weather held— with myself in support, following their progress through binoculars and going to their aid or summoning help from below if anything went wrong. As the three of us lay in the tent that night, the summit seemed already within arm's reach, victory securely in our grasp.

Then the blow fell. With malignant timing, which no power on earth could have made us believe was a simple accident of nature, the mountain hurled at us its last line of defense. It snowed.

For a day and a night the great flakes drove down upon us, swirling and swooping in the wind, blotting out the summit, the shoulder, everything beyond the tiny white-walled radius of our tent. Hour after hour we lay in our sleeping bags, stirring only to eat or to secure the straining rope and canvas. Our feet froze under their thick layers of wool and rawhide. Our heads and bodies throbbed with a dull nameless aching, and time crept over our numbed

minds like a glacier. At last, during the morning of the following day, it cleared. The sun came out in a thin blue sky, and the summit pyramid again appeared above us, now whitely robed in fresh snow. But still we waited. Until the snow either froze or was blown away by the wind it would have been the rashest courting of destruction for us to have ascended a foot beyond the camp. Another day passed. And another.

By the third nightfall our nerves were at the breaking point. For hours on end we had scarcely moved or spoken, and the only sounds in all the world were the endless moaning of the wind outside and the harsh sucking noise of our breathing. I knew that, one way or another, the end had come. Our meager food supply was running out; even with careful rationing there was enough left for only two more days.

Presently Nace stirred in his sleeping bag and sat up. "We'll have to go down tomorrow," he said quietly.

For a moment there was silence in the tent. Then Osborn struggled to a sitting position and faced him.

"No," he said.

"There's still too much loose snow above. We can't make it."

"But it's clear. As long as we can see—"

Nace shook his head. "Too dangerous. We'll go down tomorrow and lay in a fresh supply. Then we'll try again."

"Once we go down we're licked. You know it."

Nace shrugged. "Better to be

licked than—" The strain of speech was suddenly too much for him and he fell into a paroxysm[27] of coughing. When it had passed there was a long silence.

Suddenly Osborn spoke again. "Look, Nace," he said, "I'm going up tomorrow."

The Englishman shook his head.

"I'm going—understand?"

For the first time since I had known him I saw Nace's eyes flash in anger. "I'm the senior member of this group," he said. "I forbid you to go!"

Osborn jerked himself to his knees, almost upsetting the tiny tent. "You forbid me? This may be your fifth time on the mountain, and all that, but you don't *own* it! I know what you're up to. You haven't got it in you to make the top yourself, so you don't want anyone else to make it. That's it, isn't it? Isn't it?" He sat down again suddenly, gasping for breath.

Nace looked at him with level eyes. "This mountain has beaten me four times," he said softly. "It killed my best friend. It means more to me to climb it than anything else in the world. Maybe I'll make it and maybe I won't. But if I do, it will be as a rational intelligent human being—not as a fool throwing my life away."

He collapsed into another fit of coughing and fell back in his sleeping bag. Osborn, too, was still. They lay there inert,[28] panting, too exhausted for speech.

27 **paroxysm** (păr′ək sĭz′əm): fit; attack.
28 **inert:** motionless; inactive.

It was hours later that I awoke from dull uneasy sleep. In the faint light I saw Nace fumbling with the flap of the tent.

"What is it?" I asked.

"Osborn. He's gone."

The words cut like a blade through my lethargy. I struggled to my feet and followed Nace from the tent.

Outside, the dawn was seeping up the eastern sky. It was very cold, but the wind had fallen and the mountain seemed to hang suspended in a vast stillness. Above us the summit pyramid climbed bleakly into space, like the last outpost of a spent and lifeless planet. Raising my binoculars, I swept them over the gray waste. At first I saw nothing but rock and ice; then, suddenly, something moved.

"I've got him," I whispered.

As I spoke, the figure of Osborn sprang into clear focus against a patch of ice. He took three or four slow upward steps, stopped, went on again. I handed the glasses to Nace.

The Englishman squinted through them, returned them to me and re-entered the tent. When I followed he had already laced his boots and was pulling on his outer gloves.

"He's not far," he said. "Can't have been gone more than half an hour." He seized his ice ax and started out again.

"Wait," I said. "I'm going with you."

Nace shook his head. "Better stay here."

"I'm going with you," I said.

He said nothing further, but waited while I made ready. In a few moments we left the tent, roped up and started off.

Almost immediately we were on the shoulder and confronted with the paralyzing two-mile drop of the north face; but we negotiated[29] the short exposed stretch without mishap and in ten minutes were working up the base of the summit pyramid. The going here was easier, in a purely climbing sense: the angle of ascent was not steep, and there was firm rock for hand- and foot-holds between the patches of snow and ice. Our progress, however, was creepingly slow. There seemed to be literally no air at all, and after almost every step we were forced to rest, panting and gasping as we leaned forward against our axes. My heart swelled and throbbed with every movement until I thought it would explode.

The minutes crawled into hours, and still we climbed. Presently the sun came up. Its level rays streamed across the clouds, far below, and glinted from the summits of distant peaks. But, although the pinnacle of K_3 soared a full three thousand feet above anything in the surrounding world, we had scarcely any sense of height. The wilderness of mountain valley and glacier that spread beneath us to the horizon was flattened and remote, an unreal insubstantial landscape seen in a dream. We had no connection with it, or it with us. All living, all awareness, purpose and will, were concentrated in the next step, and the next; to put one foot before the other; to breathe; to ascend. We struggled on in silence.

I don't know how long it was since we had left the camp—it might have been two hours, it might have been six—when we suddenly sighted Osborn. We had not been able to find him again since our first glimpse through the binoculars; but now, unexpectedly and abruptly, as we came up over a bulge of rock, there he was. He was at a point, only a few yards above us, where the mountain steepened into an almost vertical wall. The smooth surface directly in front of him was obviously unclimbable, but two alternate routes were presented. To the left, a chimney cut obliquely[30] across the wall, forbiddingly steep, but seeming to offer adequate holds. To the right was a gentle slope of snow that curved upward and out of sight behind the rocks. As we watched, Osborn ascended to the edge of the snow, stopped and probed it with his ax. Then, apparently satisfied that it would bear his weight he stepped out on the slope.

I felt Nace's body tense. "Paul!" he cried out.

His voice was too weak and hoarse to carry. Osborn continued his ascent.

Nace cupped his hands and called his name again, and this time Osborn turned. "Wait!" cried the Englishman.

Osborn stood still, watching us, as we struggled up the few yards to the

29 **negotiated:** passed (as an obstacle).

30 **obliquely** (ə blēk′lĭ): in a sloping or slanting line.

edge of the snow slope. Nace's breath came in shuddering gasps, but he climbed faster than I had ever seen him climb before.

"Come back!" he called. "Come off the snow!"

"It's all right. The crust is firm," Osborn called back.

"But it's melting. There's—" Nace paused, fighting for air. "There's nothing underneath!"

In a sudden sickening flash I saw what he meant. Looked at from directly below, at the point where Osborn had come to it, the slope on which he stood appeared as a harmless covering of snow over the rocks. From where we were now, however, a little to one side, it could be seen that it was in reality no covering at all, but merely a cornice or unsupported platform clinging to the side of the mountain. Below it was not rock, but ten thousand feet of blue air.

"Come back!" I cried. "Come back!"

Osborn hesitated, then took a downward step. But he never took the next. For in that same instant the snow directly in front of him disappeared. It did not seem to fall or to break away. It was just soundlessly and magically no longer there. In the spot where Osborn had been about to set his foot there was now revealed the abysmal drop of the north face of K_3.

I shut my eyes, but only for a second, and when I reopened them Osborn was still, miraculously, there. Nace was shouting, "Don't move! Don't move an inch!"

"The rope—" I heard myself saying.

The Englishman shook his head. "We'd have to throw it, and the impact would be too much. Brace yourself and play it out." As he spoke, his eyes were traveling over the rocks that bordered the snow bridge. Then he moved forward.

I wedged myself into a cleft in the wall and let out the rope which extended between us. A few yards away Osborn stood in the snow, transfixed, one foot a little in front of the other. But my eyes now were on Nace. Cautiously, but with astounding rapidity, he edged along the rocks beside the cornice. There was a moment when his only support was an inch-wide ledge beneath his feet, another where there was nothing under his feet at all, and he supported himself wholly by his elbows and hands. But he advanced steadily, and at last reached a shelf wide enough for him to turn around on. At this point he was perhaps six feet away from Osborn.

"It's wide enough here to hold both of us," he said in a quiet voice. "I'm going to reach out my ax. Don't move until you're sure you have a grip on it. When I pull, jump."

He searched the wall behind him and found a hold for his left hand. Then he slowly extended his ice ax, head foremost, until it was within two feet of Osborn's shoulder. "Grip it!" he cried suddenly. Osborn's hands shot out and seized the ax. "Jump!"

There was a flash of steel in the sunlight and a hunched figure hurtled inward from the snow to the ledge. Simultaneously another figure hurtled out. The haft of the ax jerked suddenly from Nace's hand, and he lurched forward and downward. A violent spasm convulsed my body as the rope went taut. Then it was gone. Nace did not seem to hit the snow; he simply disappeared through it, soundlessly. In the same instant the snow itself was gone. The frayed, yellow end of broken rope spun lazily in space. . . .

Somehow my eyes went to Osborn. He was crouched on the ledge, where Nace had been a moment before, staring dully at the ax he held in his hands. Beyond his head, not two hundred feet above, the white untrodden pinnacle of K_3 stabbed the sky.

Perhaps ten minutes passed, perhaps a half hour. I closed my eyes and leaned forward motionless against the rock, my face against my arm. I neither thought nor felt; my body and mind alike were enveloped in a suffocating numbness. Through it at last came the sound of Osborn moving. Looking up, I saw he was standing beside me.

"I'm going to try for the top," he said tonelessly.

I merely stared at him.

"Will you come?"

"No," I said.

Osborn hesitated; then turned and began slowly climbing the steep chimney above us. Halfway up he paused, struggling for breath. Then he resumed his laborious upward progress and presently disappeared beyond the crest.

I stayed where I was, and the hours passed. The sun reached its zenith above the peak and sloped away behind it. And at last I heard above me the sound of Osborn returning. As I looked up, his figure appeared at the top of the chimney and began the descent. His clothing was in tatters, and I could tell from his movements that only the thin flame of his will stood between him and collapse. In another few minutes he was standing beside me.

"Did you get there?" I asked dully.

He shook his head. "I couldn't make it," he answered. "I didn't have what it takes."

We roped together silently and began the descent to the camp.

There is nothing more to be told of the fifth assault on K₃—at least not from the experiences of the men who made it. Osborn and I reached Camp V in safety, and three days later the entire expedition gathered at the advance base. It was decided, in view of the tragedy that had occurred, to make no further attempt on the summit, and by the end of the week we had begun the evacuation of the mountain.

It remained for another year and other men to reveal the epilogue.[31]

The summer following our attempt a combined English-Swiss expedition stormed the peak successfully. After weeks of hardship and struggle they attained the topmost pinnacle of the giant, only to find that what should have been their great moment of triumph was, instead, a moment of the bitterest disappointment. For when they came out at last upon the summit they saw that they were *not* the first. An ax stood there. Its haft was embedded in rock and ice and on its steel head were the engraved words: *TO MARTIN FROM JOHN.*

They were sporting men. On their return to civilization they told their story, and the name of the conqueror of K₃ was made known to the world.

31 **epilogue** (ĕp′ə lôg′): conclusion to the story.

Understanding Literature

1. What are the two kinds of conflict in this story?
2. A person's character is usually revealed through what he says and what he does. What do the statements and actions of Osborn and Nace reveal about their characters? In what ways are the two men alike? In what ways are they different?
3. What details in the story indicate that its author knows what mountain climbing is like?
4. Summarize the story of the ice ax on which was engraved: *To Martin from John.* Who was John? What had happened to him?
5. Randolph, the leader of the expedition, usually followed the advice of Nace. Why?

JAMES RAMSEY ULLMAN

6. Which character in "Top Man" tells the story? Why did the author use this character instead of Nace or Osborn to tell the story?

7. Although this story is probably not true, it is related very convincingly. How does the use of "I" to tell the story help to make it seem true? How does the author keep the "I," the narrator of the story, on the scene?

8. What incidents suggest the struggle going on inside of the men? What details suggest the physical strain they undergo? What are the signs of growing danger in the story?

9. After the descent the narrator says, "It remained for another year and other men to reveal the epilogue." What was the epilogue? Why had Osborn not told the others that he had reached the top? Why had he placed Nace's ice ax there?

Further Activities

1. After the men on the expedition first see the towering Kalpurtha, each feels that the mountain is an *antagonist* (par. 7). *Antagonist* is a key word, one you must know before you will fully understand the story and the men. Notice the way *antagonist* is explained and defined in the remainder of the paragraph. Define *antagonist* in your own words. Then look up the word in the glossary. Why is the mountain described as an antagonist?

2. When you are writing, it is best to choose a topic about which you have definite understanding or experience. James Ullman's writing skill, for example, is due partly to his extensive travels (Brazil, Hawaii, Russia, Africa, the Alps, and the Andes) and to his experience in mountain climbing. *The White Tower*, a best-selling novel, also illustrates Ullman's knowledge of mountains and mountain climbing.

   Select a topic about which you have some special knowledge, such as photography, cooking, chemistry, building models, or any one of a number of possibilities. Your special knowledge might be the outgrowth of some type of lesson—music, dance, horseback riding. Or perhaps you are particularly interested and skilled in a certain sport.

   After you have decided on a topic, write two or three paragraphs in which you describe this special interest, including those details which are most important. Plan your beginning sentence most carefully so that it will immediately arouse the reader's interest. Remember that this beginning sentence will probably be your *topic sentence*, although a topic sentence can occur any place within the paragraph.

Before copying your rough draft, rework and proofread it carefully. Will it make sense to a reader who does not have your background about the subject? Have you said exactly what you want to say? Are all the words spelled correctly? Are your punctuation, grammar, and capitalization correct?

3. Why do men climb mountains? dive to the bottom of the sea? go into outer space? In the story Ullman quotes the famous mountaineer, George Leigh Mallory, who, when asked why he wanted to climb Mount Everest, answered, "I want to climb it because it is there."

Write a paragraph in which you explain what you think Mallory meant by his statement, and indicate why you feel that his answer is a good one or a poor one.

Mark Twain, whose real name was Samuel Clemens, is known to everyone as the author of *Tom Sawyer* and *Huckleberry Finn*. He was a newspaperman in California when, in 1865, he wrote "The Celebrated Jumping Frog of Calaveras County." When the story was printed in the East, it made Twain a national celebrity. Suddenly it seemed that everyone was reading and talking about the famous frog which could jump so well "that he'd nail a fly every time as fur as he could see him."

The Celebrated Jumping Frog of Calaveras County

Mark Twain

IMPROVING YOUR READING: The first question you ask of a story is: What happens? In answering the question, you are talking about *plot*, the connected incidents leading to a *climax*, the point of highest interest. In the following story you see a man tricked. If Mark Twain had described the trick alone, he would have been writing an anecdote instead of a short story. Instead, he describes a series of connected incidents; he shows you what led up to the trick, how it came about. The trick itself is the climax.

IN COMPLIANCE with the request of a friend of mine, who wrote me from the East, I called on good-natured, garrulous[1] old Simon Wheeler, and inquired after my friend's friend, Leonidas W. Smiley, as requested to do, and I hereunto append[2] the result. I have a lurking suspicion that *Leonidas W.* Smiley is a myth; that my friend never knew such a personage; and that he only conjectured[3] that if I asked old Wheeler about him, it would remind him of his infamous *Jim* Smiley, and he would go to work and bore me to death with some exasperating reminiscence[4] of him as long and as tedious as it should be useless to me. If that was the design, it succeeded.

I found Simon Wheeler dozing comfortably by the barroom stove of the dilapidated tavern in the decaying mining camp of Angel's, and I noticed that he was fat and bald-headed, and had an expression of winning gentleness and simplicity upon his tranquil countenance.[5] He roused up, and gave me good day. I told him a friend of mine had commissioned me to make some inquiries about a cherished companion of his boyhood named *Leonidas* W. Smiley —Rev. *Leonidas* W. Smiley, a young

1 **garrulous** (găr′ə ləs): talkative.
2 **append**: attach.
3 **conjectured**: guessed.
4 **reminiscence** (rĕm′ə nĭs′əns): remembered experience.

5 **countenance**: face.

minister of the Gospel, who he had heard was at one time a resident of Angel's Camp. I added that if Mr. Wheeler could tell me anything about this Rev. Leonidas W. Smiley, I would feel under many obligations to him.

Simon Wheeler backed me into a corner and blockaded me there with his chair, and then sat down and reeled off the monotonous narrative which follows this paragraph. He never smiled, he never frowned, he never changed his voice from the gentle-flowing key to which he tuned his initial sentence, he never betrayed the slightest suspicion of enthusiasm; but all through the interminable[6] narrative there ran a vein of impressive earnestness and sincerity, which showed me plainly that, so far from his imagining that there was anything ridiculous or funny about his story, he regarded it as a really important matter, and admired its two heroes as men of transcendent genius in *finesse*.[7] I let him go on in his own way, and never interrupted him once.

"Rev. Leonidas W. H'm, Reverend Le—well, there was a feller here once by the name of *Jim* Smiley, in the winter of '49—or maybe it was the spring of '50—I don't recollect exactly, somehow, though what makes me think it was one or the other is because I remember the big flume[8] warn't finished when he first come to the camp; but anyway, he was the curiosest man about always betting on anything that turned up you ever see, if he could get anybody to bet on the other side; and if he couldn't he'd change sides. Any way that suited the other man would suit *him*—any way just so's he got a bet, *he* was satisfied. But still he was lucky, uncommon lucky; he most always come out winner. He was always ready and laying for a chance; there couldn't be no solit'ry thing mentioned but that feller'd offer to bet on it, and take ary side you please, as I was just telling you. If there was a horse race, you'd find him flush or you'd find him busted at the end of it; if there was a dog fight, he'd bet on it; if there was a cat fight, he'd bet on it; if there was a chicken fight, he'd bet on it; why, if there was two birds setting on a fence, he would bet you which one would fly first; or if there was a camp meeting, he would be there reg'lar to bet on Parson Walker, which he judged to be the best exhorter[9] about here, and so he was, too, and a good man. If he even see a straddlebug start to go anywheres, he would bet you how long it would take him to get to—to wherever he was going to, and if you took him up, he would foller that straddlebug to Mexico but what he would find out where he was bound for and how long he was on the road. Lots of the boys here has seen that Smiley, and can tell you about him. Why, it never made no difference to *him*—he'd bet on *any* thing—the dangdest feller. Parson Walker's

6 **interminable** (ĭn tûr′mə nə bəl): endless.
7 **transcendent . . .** *finesse*: exceptional talent in strategy.
8 **flume**: channel for carrying water.

9 **exhorter**: one who advises or urges.

wife laid very sick once, for a good while, and it seemed as if they warn't going to save her; but one morning he come in, and Smiley up and asked him how she was, and he said she was considable better—thank the Lord for his inf'nite mercy—and coming on so smart that with the blessing of Prov'dence she'd get well yet; and Smiley, before he thought, says: 'Well, I'll resk two-and-a-half she don't anyway.'

"Thish-yer Smiley had a mare—the boys called her the fifteen-minute nag, but that was only in fun, you know, because, of course, she was faster than that—and he used to win money on that horse, for all she was so slow and always had the asthma, or the distemper, or the consumption, or something of that kind. They used to give her two or three hun-

dred yards start, and then pass her under way; but always at the fag end of the race she'd get excited and desperate like, and come cavorting and straddling up, and scattering her legs around limber, sometimes in the air, and sometimes out to one side among the fences, and kicking up m-o-r-e dust and raising m-o-r-e racket with her coughing and sneezing and blowing her nose—and *always* fetch up at the stand just about a neck ahead, as near as you could cipher it down.

"And he had a little small bull pup, that to look at him you'd think he warn't worth a cent but to set around and look ornery and lay for a chance to steal something. But as soon as money was up on him he was a different dog; his underjaw'd begin to stick out like the fo'castle of a steam-

28   PLOT

boat, and his teeth would uncover and shine like the furnaces. And a dog might tackle him and bullyrag him, and bite him, and throw him over his shoulder two or three times, and Andrew Jackson—which was the name of the pup—Andrew Jackson would never let on but what *he* was satisfied, and hadn't expected nothing else—and the bets being doubled and doubled on the other side all the time, till the money was all up; and then all of a sudden he would grab that other dog jest by the j'int of his hind leg and freeze to it—not chaw, you understand, but only just grip and hang on till they throwed up the sponge, if it was a year. Smiley always come out winner on that pup, till he harnessed a dog once that didn't have no hind legs, because they'd been sawed off in a circular saw, and when the thing had gone along far enough, and the money was all up, and he come to make a snatch for his pet holt, he see in a minute how he'd been imposed on,[10] and how the other dog had him in the door, so to speak, and he 'peared surprised, and then he looked sorter discouraged-like and didn't try no more to win the fight, and so he got shucked out bad. He give Smiley a look, as much as to say his heart was broke, and it was *his* fault, for putting up a dog that hadn't no hind legs for him to take holt of, which was his main dependence in a fight, and then he limped off a piece and laid down and died. It was a good pup, was that Andrew Jackson, and would have made a name for hisself if he'd lived, for the stuff was in him and he had genius—I know it, because he hadn't no opportunities to speak of, and it don't stand to reason that a dog could make such a fight as he could under them circumstances if he hadn't no talent. It always makes me feel sorry when I think of that last fight of his'n, and the way it turned out.

"Well, thish-yer Smiley had rat-tarriers, and chicken cocks, and tomcats and all them kind of things, till you couldn't rest, and you couldn't fetch nothing for him to bet on but he'd match you. He ketched a frog one day, and took him home, and said he cal'lated[11] to educate him; and so he never done nothing for three months but set in his back yard and learn that frog to jump. And you bet you he *did* learn him, too. He'd give him a little punch behind, and the next minute you'd see that frog whirling in the air like a doughnut—see him turn one summerset, or maybe a couple, if he got a good start, and come down flat-footed and all right, like a cat. He got him up so in the matter of ketching flies, and kep' him in practice so constant, that he'd nail a fly every time as fur as he could see him. Smiley said all a frog wanted was education, and he could do 'most anything—and I believe him. Why, I've seen him set Dan'l Webster down here on this floor—Dan'l Webster was the name of the frog—and sing out, 'Flies, Dan'l, flies!' and quicker'n you could wink he'd spring straight up and snake a fly off'n the

---

10 **imposed on:** here, tricked; cheated.   11 **cal'lated:** calculated.

counter there, and flop down on the floor ag'in as solid as a gob of mud, and fall to scratching the side of his head with his hind foot as indifferent as if he hadn't no idea he'd been doin' any more'n any frog might do. You never see a frog so modest and straightfor'ard as he was, for all he was so gifted. And when it come to fair and square jumping on a dead level, he could get over more ground at one straddle than any animal of his breed you ever see. Jumping on a dead level was his strong suit, you understand; and when it come to that, Smiley would ante up money on him as long as he had a red. Smiley was monstrous proud of his frog, and well he might be, for fellers that had traveled and been everywheres all said he laid over any frog that ever *they* see.

"Well, Smiley kep' the beast in a little lattice box, and he used to fetch him down town sometimes and lay for a bet. One day a feller—a stranger in the camp, he was—come acrost him with his box, and says:

" 'What might it be that you've got in the box?'

"And Smiley says, sorter indifferent-like: 'It might be a parrot, or it might be a canary, maybe, but it ain't —it's only just a frog.'

"And the feller took it, and looked at it careful, and turned it round this way and that, and says: 'H'm—so 'tis. Well, what's *he* good for?'

" 'Well,' Smiley says, easy and careless, 'he's good enough for *one* thing, I should judge—he can out-jump any frog in Calaveras county.'

"The feller took the box again, and took another long, particular look, and give it back to Smiley, and says, very deliberate, 'Well,' he says, 'I don't see no p'ints about that frog that's any better'n any other frog.'

" 'Maybe you don't,' Smiley says. 'Maybe you understand frogs and maybe you don't understand 'em; maybe you've had experience, and maybe you ain't only a amature,[12] as it were. Anyways, I've got *my* opinion, and I'll resk forty dollars that he can outjump any frog in Calaveras county.'

"And the feller studied a minute, and then says, kinder sad like, 'Well, I'm only a stranger here, and I 'ain't got no frog; but if I had a frog, I'd bet you.'

"And then Smiley says, 'That's all right—that's all right—if you'll hold my box a minute, I'll go and get you a frog.' And so the feller took the box, and put up his forty dollars along with Smiley's, and set down to wait.

"So he set there a good while thinking and thinking to hisself, and then he got the frog out and prized his mouth open and took a teaspoon and filled him full of quail shot— filled him pretty near up to his chin— and set him on the floor. Smiley he went to the swamp and slopped around in the mud for a long time, and finally he ketched a frog, and fetched him in, and give him to this feller, and says:

" 'Now, if you're ready, set him alongside of Dan'l, with his forepaws just even with Dan'l's, and I'll give

12 amature: amateur.

the word.' Then he says, 'One—two —three—*git!*' and him and the feller touched up the frogs from behind, and the new frog hopped off lively, but Dan'l give a heave, and hysted up his shoulders—so—like a Frenchman, but it warn't no use—he couldn't budge; he was planted as solid as a church, and he couldn't no more stir than if he was anchored out. Smiley was a good deal surprised, and he was disgusted too, but he didn't have no idea what the matter was, of course.

"The feller took the money and started away; and when he was going out at the door, he sorter jerked his thumb over his shoulder—so—at Dan'l, and says again, very deliberate, 'Well,' he says, '*I* don't see no p'ints about that frog that's any better'n any other frog.'

"Smiley he stood scratching his head and looking down at Dan'l a long time, and at last he says, 'I do wonder what in the nation that frog throw'd off for—I wonder if there ain't something the matter with him —he 'pears to look mighty baggy, somehow.' And he ketched Dan'l by the nap of the neck, and hefted him, and says, 'Why, blame my cats if he don't weigh five pound!' and turned him upside down and he belched out a double handful of shot. And then he see how it was, and he was the maddest man—he set the frog down and took out after that feller, but he never ketched him. And—"

Here Simon Wheeler heard his name called from the front yard, and got up to see what was wanted. And turning to me as he moved away, he said: "Just set where you are, stranger, and rest easy—I ain't going to be gone a second."

But, by your leave, I did not think that a continuation of the history of the enterprising vagabond *Jim* Smiley would be likely to afford me much information concerning the Rev. *Leonidas W.* Smiley, and so I started away.

At the door I met the sociable Wheeler returning, and he buttonholed me and recommenced:

"Well, thish-yer Smiley had a yaller one-eyed cow that didn't have no tail, only just a short stump like a bannanner, and—"

However, lacking both time and inclination, I did not wait to hear about the afflicted cow, but took my leave.

Understanding Literature

1. In this story there is a double plot: the story of the "I" who is telling the whole tale, and the story told by Simon Wheeler. What do you learn in the opening paragraphs about the "I"? about Simon Wheeler?
2. In the fourth paragraph Wheeler begins telling the story of Jim Smiley. How does Smiley spend his time? Tell in your own words the anecdotes about Smiley described in the fourth paragraph.

MARK TWAIN

3. Tell the stories of Smiley and his mare and of Smiley and his bull pup. How is the story of the bull pup like the story of the frog?
4. Repeated phrases are always important in a story. Twice "the feller" in the story says, "I don't see no p'ints about that frog that's any better'n any other frog." How does Smiley react the first time it is said? How does he react the second time?
5. Look back at the first three paragraphs and at the ending (after Smiley's story). What is the "I" in the story like? What is his reaction to the story? What is your reaction to the story?
6. Find examples of Mark Twain's use of exaggeration or over-statement.

Edgar Allan Poe, one of America's greatest writers, was a master of the short horror story. Here he is concerned not so much with a murder as with a man's reaction to it. What is going on inside the mind of the narrator, the teller of the tale?

The Telltale Heart

Edgar Allan Poe

IMPROVING YOUR READING: A writer establishes the *mood* of his story by the way he describes how different things look, feel, and sound. A dark, empty house at night is quite different from a pond in bright sunlight; each scene creates a different mood. Thus an author can change the mood by the way he uses light or dark and sound or silence, and by shifting from one scene to another. How does Poe build the mood, or atmosphere, in this story?

TRUE!—NERVOUS—very, very dreadfully nervous I had been and am; but why *will* you say that I am mad? The disease had sharpened my senses —not destroyed—not dulled them. Above all was the sense of hearing acute. I heard all things in the heaven and in the earth. I heard many things in hell. How, then, am I mad? Hearken! and observe how healthily—how calmly I can tell you the whole story.

It is impossible to say how first the idea entered my brain; but once conceived, it haunted me day and night. Object there was none. Passion there was none. I loved the old man. He had never wronged me. He had never given me insult. For his gold I had no desire. I think it was his eye! yes, it was this! One of his eyes resembled that of a vulture—a pale blue eye, with a film over it. Whenever it fell upon me, my blood ran cold; and so by degrees—very gradually—I made up my mind to take the life of the old man, and thus rid myself of the eye forever.

Now this is the point. You fancy me mad. Madmen know nothing. But you should have seen *me*. You should have seen how wisely I proceeded—with what caution—with what foresight—with what dissimulation[1] I went to work! I was never kinder to the old man than during the whole week before I killed him. And every night, about midnight, I turned the latch of his door and opened it—oh, so gently! And then, when I had made an opening sufficient for my head, I put in a dark lantern, all closed, closed, so that no light shone out, and then I thrust in my head. Oh, you would have laughed to see how cunningly I

1 **dissimulation** (dǐ sǐm'yə lā'shən): pretense; deception.

thrust it in! I moved it slowly—very, very slowly, so that I might not disturb the old man's sleep. It took me an hour to place my whole head within the opening so far that I could see him as he lay upon his bed. Ha!—would a madman have been so wise as this? And then, when my head was well in the room, I undid the lantern cautiously—oh, so cautiously—cautiously (for the hinges creaked)—I undid it just so much that a single thin ray fell upon the vulture eye. And this I did for seven long nights—every night just at midnight—but I found the eye always closed; and so it was impossible to do the work; for it was not the old man who vexed me, but his Evil Eye. And every morning, when the day broke, I went boldly into the chamber, and spoke courageously to him, calling him by name in a hearty tone, and inquiring how he had passed the night. So you see he would have been a very profound old man, indeed, to suspect that every night, just at twelve, I looked in upon him while he slept.

Upon the eighth night I was more than usually cautious in opening the door. A watch's minute hand moves more quickly than did mine. Never before that night had I *felt* the extent of my own powers—of my sagacity.[2] I could scarcely contain my feelings of triumph. To think that there I was, opening the door, little by little, and he not even to dream of my secret deeds or thoughts. I fairly chuckled at the idea; and perhaps he

heard me; for he moved on the bed suddenly, as if startled. Now you may think that I drew back—but no. His room was as black as pitch with the thick darkness (for the shutters were close fastened, through fear of robbers), and so I knew that he could not see the opening of the door, and I kept pushing it on steadily, steadily.

I had my head in, and was about to open the lantern, when my thumb slipped upon the tin fastening, and the old man sprang up in the bed, crying out—"Who's there?"

I kept quite still and said nothing. For a whole hour I did not move a muscle, and in the meantime I did not hear him lie down. He was still sitting up in the bed listening—just as I have done, night after night, hearkening to the death watches in the wall.

Presently I heard a slight groan, and I knew it was the groan of mortal terror. It was not a groan of pain or of grief—oh, no!—it was the low stifled sound that arises from the bottom of the soul when overcharged with awe. I knew the sound well. Many a night, just at midnight, when all the world slept, it has welled up from my own bosom, deepening, with its dreadful echo, the terrors that distracted me. I say I knew it well. I knew what the old man felt, and pitied him, although I chuckled at heart. I knew that he had been lying awake ever since the first slight noise, when he had turned in the bed. His fears had been ever since growing upon him. He had been trying to fancy them causeless, but could not. He had been saying to

2 **sagacity** (sə găs′ə tĭ): shrewdness; cunning.

himself—"It is nothing but the wind in the chimney—it is only a mouse crossing the floor," or "it is merely a cricket which has made a single chirp." Yes, he has been trying to comfort himself with these suppositions; but he had found all in vain. *All in vain;* because Death, in approaching him, had stalked with his black shadow before him, and enveloped the victim. And it was the mournful influence of the unperceived[3] shadow that caused him to feel—although he neither saw nor heard—to *feel* the presence of my head within the room.

When I had waited a long time, very patiently, without hearing him lie down, I resolved to open a little—a very, very little crevice in the lantern. So I opened it—you cannot imagine how stealthily, stealthily—until, at length, a single dim ray, like the thread of the spider, shot from out of the crevice and full upon the vulture eye.

It was open—wide, wide open—and I grew furious as I gazed upon it. I saw it with perfect distinctness—all a dull blue, with a hideous veil over it that chilled the very marrow in my bones; but I could see nothing else of the old man's face or person: for I had directed the ray as if by instinct, precisely upon the damned spot.

And now have I not told you that what you mistake for madness is but over-acuteness of the senses?—now, I say, there came to my ears a low, dull, quick sound, such as a watch makes when enveloped in cotton. I knew *that* sound well too. It was the beating of the old man's heart. It increased my fury, as the beating of a drum stimulates the soldier into courage.

But even yet I refrained and kept still. I scarcely breathed. I held the lantern motionless. I tried how steadily I could maintain the ray upon the eye. Meantime the hellish tattoo[4] of the heart increased. It grew quicker and quicker, and louder and louder every instant. The old man's terror *must* have been extreme! It grew louder, I say, louder every moment!—do you mark me well? I have told you that I am nervous: so I am. And now at the dead hour of the night, amid the dreadful silence of that old house, so strange a noise as this excited me to uncontrollable terror. Yet, for some minutes longer I refrained and stood still. But the beating grew louder, louder! I thought the heart must burst. And now a new anxiety seized me—the sound would be heard by a neighbor! The old man's hour had come! With a loud yell, I threw open the lantern and leaped into the room. He shrieked once—once only. In an instant I dragged him to the floor, and pulled the heavy bed over him. I then smiled gaily, to find the deed so far done. But, for many minutes, the heart beat on with a muffled sound. This, however, did not vex me; it would not be heard through the wall. At length it ceased. The old man

---

3 **unperceived:** unseen.

4 **tattoo:** here, beating; drumming.

was dead. I removed the bed and examined the corpse. Yes, he was stone, stone dead. I placed my hand upon the heart and held it there many minutes. There was no pulsation. He was stone dead. His eye would trouble me no more.

If still you think me mad, you will think so no longer when I describe the wise precautions I took for the concealment of the body. The night waned, and I worked hastily, but in silence. First of all I dismembered the corpse. I cut off the head and the arms and the legs.

I then took up three planks from the flooring of the chamber, and deposited all between the scantlings. I then replaced the boards so cleverly, so cunningly, that no human eye—not even *his*—could have detected anything wrong. There was nothing to wash out—no stain of any kind—no blood spot whatever. I had been too wary for that. A tub had caught all —ha! ha!

When I had made an end of these labors, it was four o'clock—still dark as midnight. As the bell sounded the hour, there came a knocking at the street door. I went down to open it with a light heart—for what had I *now* to fear? There entered three men, who introduced themselves, with perfect suavity,[5] as officers of the police. A shriek had been heard by a neighbor during the night; suspicion of foul play had been aroused; information had been lodged at the police office, and they (the officers) had been deputed[6] to search the premises.

I smiled—for *what* had I to fear? I bade the gentlemen welcome. The shriek, I said, was my own in a dream. The old man, I mentioned, was absent in the country. I took my visitors all over the house. I bade them search—search *well*. I led them, at length, to *his* chamber. I showed them his treasures, secure, undisturbed. In the enthusiasm of my confidence, I brought chairs into the room, and desired them *here* to rest from their fatigues, while I myself, in the wild audacity of my perfect triumph, placed my own seat upon the very spot beneath which reposed the corpse of the victim.

The officers were satisfied. My *manner* had convinced them. I was singularly at ease. They sat, and while I answered cheerily, they chatted familiar things. But, ere long, I felt myself getting pale and wished them gone. My head ached, and I fancied a ringing in my ears: but still they sat and still chatted. The ringing became more distinct:— it continued and became more distinct: I talked more freely to get rid of the feeling: but it continued and gained definitiveness—until, at length, I found that the noise was *not* within my ears.

No doubt I now grew *very* pale;— but I talked more fluently,[7] and with a heightened voice. Yet the sound increased—and what could I do? It was *a low, dull, quick sound—such a*

---

5 **suavity** (swăv′ə tĭ): here, smooth politeness.

6 **deputed:** assigned.

7 **more fluently:** more easily; faster.

sound as a watch makes when enveloped in cotton. I gasped for breath—and yet the officers heard it not. I talked more quickly—more vehemently; but the noise steadily increased. I arose and argued about trifles, in a high key and with violent gesticulations,[8] but the noise steadily increased. Why *would* they not be gone? I paced the floor to and fro with heavy strides, as if excited to fury by the observation of the men—but the noise steadily increased. Oh God! what *could* I do? I foamed—I raved—I swore! I swung the chair upon which I had been sitting, and grated it upon the boards, but the noise arose over all and continually increased. It grew louder—louder—

louder! And still the men chatted pleasantly, and smiled. Was it possible they heard not? Almighty God! —no, no! They heard!—they suspected!—they *knew!*—they were making a mockery of my horror!—this I thought, and this I think. But anything was better than this agony! Anything was more tolerable than this derision! I could bear those hypocritical smiles no longer! I felt that I must scream or die!—and now —again!—hark! louder! louder! louder! *louder!*—

"Villains!" I shrieked, "dissemble[9] no more! I admit the deed!—tear up the planks!—here, here!—it is the beating of his hideous heart!"

---

8 gesticulations (jĕs tĭk′yə lā′shənz): gestures.

9 dissemble (dĭ sĕm′bəl): pretend.

Understanding Literature

1. What is the setting of the story? Point out specific phrases that show where the story takes place.
2. Why does the narrator take the police to the old man's chamber?
3. The narrator of the story states several times that the reader may think that he is a madman, but that he is not. Is he a madman? What evidence can you find for your answer?
4. In what manner does the murderer reveal the hiding place of the body to the police?
5. Where do you suppose the narrator, the "I," is when he tells the story?
6. What use is made of sound or lack of sound in the events of the story? If you read aloud a section of the story, following the rhythm of the lines, you will find that the author tries to imitate the beating of a heart. Note especially the paragraph beginning "No doubt I now grew *very* pale. . . ." In what way does the sound of this paragraph differ from the sound of the earlier ones?
7. Point out places where Poe uses light and dark to create a particular mood.

Further Activities

1. Write a one-paragraph report on the murder as it might have been written by one of the policemen.
2. At some time in your life you have probably felt fear or fright. When you got over this fear, you might have found that it was quite ridiculous; you may have even laughed about it. Prepare a short talk in which you describe a time when you were frightened. Perhaps you will want to use some of the words Poe used to establish a mood of fear.

   Think through your talk so that you can be brief and to the point. Probably more time should be spent on planning your beginning sentence than on any other. Your first sentence should immediately arouse the interest of your listeners. The closing sentence is next in importance.

   If you are called upon to tell about your experience, work to appear poised, look at your audience so that everyone feels included, and be enthusiastic and expressive about what you have to tell.

Focusing on Words

A suffix is a letter or group of letters added to the end of a word or to the root of a word. The suffix *phobia* signifies fear or dislike of something. For example, *claustrophia* is fear of being enclosed in a small area. *Acrophobia* is a fear of high places. If you see, therefore, the suffix -*phobia* added to the stem word, you will know it means a fear of something. Often *phobia* is used alone in a sentence as in "He has a phobia about lightning." Find and define five other words ending in -*phobia*.

Poor Sam McGee loves gold, but he cannot stand cold weather. How can he survive in the Yukon?

Poems that tell a story are called *narrative poems.* They use the same devices, such as setting, exposition, and mood, that you find in short stories.

The Cremation
of
Sam McGee

Robert W. Service

There are strange things done in the midnight sun
   By the men who moil[1] for gold;
The Arctic trails have their secret tales
   That would make your blood run cold;
The Northern Lights have seen queer sights,   5
   But the queerest they ever did see
Was that night on the marge[2] of Lake Lebarge
   I cremated Sam McGee.

Now Sam McGee was from Tennessee, where the cotton blooms and blows.
Why he left his home in the South to roam 'round the Pole, God only knows.   10
He was always cold, but the land of gold seemed to hold him like a spell;
Though he'd often say in his homely way that "he'd sooner live in hell."

On a Christmas Day we were mushing our way over the Dawson trail.
Talk of your cold! through the parka's fold it stabbed like a driven nail.
If our eyes we'd close, then the lashes froze till sometimes we couldn't see;   15
It wasn't much fun, but the only one to whimper was Sam McGee.

And that very night, as we lay packed tight in our robes beneath the snow,

---

1 **moil:** work; toil.   2 **marge:** here, shore.

And the dogs were fed, and the stars o'erhead were dancing heel and toe,
He turned to me, and "Cap," says he, "I'll cash in this trip, I guess;
And if I do, I'm asking that you won't refuse my last request."   20

Well, he seemed so low that I couldn't say no; then he says with a sort of moan:
"It's the cursèd cold, and it's got right hold till I'm chilled clean through to the bone.
Yet 'taint being dead—it's my awful dread of the icy grave that pains;
So I want you to swear that, foul or fair, you'll cremate my last remains."

A pal's last need is a thing to heed, so I swore I would not fail;   25
And we started on at the streak of dawn; but God! he looked ghastly pale.
He crouched on the sleigh, and he raved all day of his home in Tennessee;
And before nightfall a corpse was all that was left of Sam McGee.

There wasn't a breath in that land of death, and I hurried, horror-driven,
With a corpse half hid that I couldn't get rid, because of a promise given;   30
It was lashed to the sleigh, and it seemed to say: "You may tax your brawn and brains,
But you promised true, and it's up to you to cremate those last remains."

Now a promise made is a debt unpaid, and the trail has its own stern code.
In the days to come, though my lips were dumb, in my heart how I cursed that load.
In the long, long night, by the lone firelight, while the huskies, round in a ring,   35
Howled out their woes to the homeless snows—O God! how I loathed the thing.

And every day that quiet clay seemed to heavy and heavier grow;
And on I went, though the dogs were spent and the grub was getting low;
The trail was bad, and I felt half mad, but I swore I would not give in;
And I'd often sing to the hateful thing, and it hearkened with a grin.   40

Till I came to the marge of Lake Lebarge, and a derelict[3] there lay;

3 **derelict:** abandoned vessel.

It was jammed in the ice, but I saw in a trice it was called the "Alice
  May."
And I looked at it, and I thought a bit, and I looked at my frozen chum;
Then "Here," said I, with a sudden cry, "is my cre-ma-tor-eum."

Some planks I tore from the cabin floor, and I lit the boiler fire;   45
Some coal I found that was lying around, and I heaped the fuel higher;
The flames just soared, and the furnace roared—such a blaze you seldom
  see;
And I burrowed a hole in the glowing coal, and I stuffed in Sam McGee.

Then I made a hike, for I didn't like to hear him sizzle so;
And the heavens scowled, and the huskies howled, and the wind began
  to blow.   50
It was icy cold, but the hot sweat rolled down my cheeks, and I don't
  know why;
And the greasy smoke in an inky cloak went streaking down the sky.

I do not know how long in the snow I wrestled with grisly fear;
But the stars came out and they danced about ere again I ventured
  near;
I was sick with dread, but I bravely said: "I'll just take a peep inside.   55
I guess he's cooked, and it's time I looked;" . . . then the door I opened
  wide.

And there sat Sam, looking cool and calm, in the heart of the furnace
  roar;
And he wore a smile you could see a mile, and he said: "Please close
  that door.
It's fine in here, but I greatly fear you'll let in the cold and storm—
Since I left Plumtree, down in Tennessee, it's the first time I've been
  warm."   60

> There are strange things done in the midnight sun
>   By the men who moil for gold;
> The Arctic trails have their secret tales
>   That would make your blood run cold;
> The Northern Lights have seen queer sights,   65
>   But the queerest they ever did see
> Was that night on the marge of Lake Lebarge
>   I cremated Sam McGee.

Understanding Literature

1. What is the setting of the poem?
2. What is Sam's predicament, his unfortunate situation, as described in stanzas 4 and 5? Why does he want to be cremated?
3. How does the narrator try to cremate Sam? How does it affect Sam? Where is the climax of the poem?
4. What is the mood of the poem? How does the author create this mood?

Jimmy Tom's skill as a swimmer and diver is tested by the dangers of the reef. As he attempts to find the treasures hidden beneath the water, Jimmy Tom is daring—perhaps too daring—but he knows the treasure would enable him to buy the boat he wants so much.

The Reef

Samuel Scoville, Jr.

IMPROVING YOUR READING: *Setting*, the time and place of the action, is very important in this story. The author adds contrast to the setting by comparing what is above the water to what lies beneath it. To test the importance of setting in a story, ask yourself: Could the story take place in another setting?

LUNE-GREEN AND amber, a strip of fading sky glowed across the trail of the vanished sun. Far below, the opal sea paled to mother-of-pearl. Then, over sea and sky, strode the sudden dark of the tropics and in an instant the southern stars flamed and flared through the violet night. A long, tense moment, with sea and sky waiting, and a rim of raw gold thrust itself above the horizon as the full moon of midsummer climbed toward the zenith.[1] Rising, its light made a broad causeway across the sea clear to the dark reef which lurked in the shimmering water.

Suddenly, inked black against the moonpath, showed the lean shape of a canoe. All the way from Carib Island, a day and a night away, Jim Tom, who in his day had been a famous sponge diver, had brought his grandson Jimmy Tom for a first visit to the reef. Both had the cinnamon-red skins of the Red Caribs, who once had ruled mightily the whole Caribbean. Jim Tom's hair was cut to an even edge all the way around his neck; his small, deep-set eyes were like glittering crumbs of black glass, and ever since a day when he dived below the twenty-five-fathom mark both of his legs had been paralyzed.

Swiftly the little craft neared the reef, and only the plash of the paddles broke the stillness. Then in an instant the molten gold of the water was shattered by a figure like a vast bat, with black wings which measured all of thirty feet from tip to tip, a spiked tail, and long antennæ streaming out beyond a huge, hooked mouth. Like a vampire from the pit, it rose into the air, blotting out the moon with its monstrous bulk, and then dropped back with a crash, raising a wave which nearly swamped the canoe. As it disappeared beneath the water, Jimmy Tom turned and looked questioningly at the

1 zenith (zē′nĭth): high point of the heavens.

old man. The latter laughed silently.

"Only a manta ray," he said at last. "They like to fly around in the moonlight and frighten untried young men," he added slyly.

For answer his grandson stretched out his paddle at full length. It showed in the air rigid and motionless as an iron bar. The old man grunted approvingly.

"You may tremble yet before you are through with the reef," was all that he said however, as he steered toward the circle of coral which separated the lagoon from the ocean, which beat against the barrier in a crashing surf. Waiting until several of the great rollers had passed, the paddlers caught the crest of a huge wave and in an instant were swept ten feet in the air toward the patch of beach which showed beyond the little lagoon. Just as the wave broke, the canoe tilted and rushed down its long slope like a toboggan, clearing the rim of sharp coral and leaping into the still lagoon beyond.

All the rest of that glorious night, as the moon went westering down the sky, the two slept on the rose-bed, honey-brown sand, until, without any dawn, the sun suddenly rose above a heliotrope[2] horizon. Then they breakfasted, and Jim Tom became quite talkative—for a Carib.

"We must not waste a moment of this day," he said. "Perhaps before night we may make the hundred of dollars you need for that sloop about which you have been bothering me so long. In my day," he went on severely, "boys were glad enough to have a good canoe."

Jimmy Tom grunted.

"Whoever heard," he said at last, "of making a hundred of dollars in one day?"

"It has been done—and here," returned his grandfather, positively; "but it takes good lungs and—a brave heart."

As they talked, the canoe reached a point where the reef sloped away in a series of terraces to unfathomable depths. There they stopped paddling and stared down through the water which lay before them like a thick sheet of plate glass. The great ledge over which they floated was dotted with thickets of colored corals and purple and gold sea fans, among which schools of brilliant fish sped and lazed and drifted like birds in the air. Molten-silver tarpon shot through shoals of chubby cow pilots, all green and gold and indigo, while turquoise-blue parrot fish raced here and there, and crimson cardinal fish crept in and out of crevices in the rocks. There were angelfish in gorgeous robes of emerald and scarlet, and jet-black butterfly fish with golden fins, orange gills, and vivid blue mouths, while warty purple sea cucumbers showed among clumps of yellow sea anenomes.

"This is the treasure-ledge of the reef," said Jim Tom, suddenly. "Here too," he went on, "death hides and waits," and he paused for a moment.

Jimmy's answer was to slip out of his unbleached cotton shirt and trousers and stand poised like a red-bronze statue of speed with the long,

2 **heliotrope** (hē′lǐ ə trōp′): blue-red.

PLOT

flat muscles rippling over his lithe[3] body and graceful limbs.

"It was here that your father died," said Jim Tom again. "I was lying watching him search among the sponges," he went on after a pause, "when before my very eyes he was gone. My only son," he went on his voice rising as he harked back over forgotten years, "in the jaws of one of those accursed sculpins of the deep water, a *tonu* ten feet long."

"And then," asked Jimmy Tom, very softly, as the old man stopped.

"And then," went on the old man, fiercely, "everything went red around me. I gripped my spike and dove and swam, as I never swam before, down to that lurking, ugly demon. In a second I was on him and stabbed him with all my might—once, twice, three times—until, dying, he went off the ledge into the depths below and I followed him beyond, to where no man may dare to swim. There he died. As his hateful mouth gaped I dragged out your father by the arm and brought him back to the top; but when I climbed with him into the canoe he was dead, and I was as you see me now—dead too from the waist down. All the rest of that day and all the night beyond and the next day I paddled and paddled until we came home—my dead son and I. No, no," went on the old man, "let us try the safer side of the reef."

For answer, Jimmy Tom quickly fastened in place the outriggers on either side of the canoe, which made it firm and safe to dive from. Around

his neck he slipped the *"toa,"* the wide-mouthed bag with a drawstring into which a sponge diver thrusts his findings. Around his neck, too, he hung the "spike," a double-pointed stick two feet long of black palm-wood, hard and heavy as iron. Then, standing on the bow seat, he filled his great lungs again and again until every air cell was opened. The old man looked at him proudly.

"You are of my blood," he said softly. "Go with God. I will watch above you and be your guard. Forget not to look up at me, and, if I signal, come back to me fast—for I cannot go to you," he finished sadly.

The young man gave a brief nod and, filling his lungs until his chest stood out like a square box, dived high into the air with that jackknife dive which was invented by sponge divers and, striking the water clean as the point of a dropped knife, he shot down toward the beautiful depths below. Into his lithe body rushed and pulsed the power and energy of the great swinging sea as he swam through the air-clear water toward a thicket of gorgonias, which waved against the white sand like a bed of poppies. In thirty seconds he was twenty fathoms down, where the pressure of seventy pounds to the square inch would have numbed and crippled an ordinary swimmer, but meant nothing to his steel-strong body, hardened to the depths by years of deep diving. Even as he reached the gleaming thicket he saw, with a great throb of delight, a soft, golden-brown tuft of silk sponge hidden beneath the living branches. The silk

---

3 **lithe** (līth): limber; relaxed.

sponge is to spongers in the sea what the silver fox is to trappers on the land, and the whole year's output from all seas is only a few score.

With a quick stroke, Jimmy Tom reached the many-colored sea shrub. The moving branches had to be parted carefully with the spike, lest they close and hide, beyond finding, the silky clump growing within their depths. Even as the boy started to slip over his head the cord from which swung the pointed stick, he looked up to see Jim Tom beckoning frantically for him to return. Yet nowhere in the near-by water could he see anything unusual, except a little fish some eight inches long marked with alternate bands of blue and gold, which came close to him and then turned and swam out to sea. Still his grandfather beckoned, his face con-

torted with earnestness.

The boy hesitated. An arm's length away lay a fortune. It might well be that never again could he find that exact spot if he went back to the surface now. All this passed through his mind in the same second in which he suddenly plunged his bare arm into the center of the gorgonia clump without waiting to use the spike, as all cautious sponge divers do. Following the clue of the waving silken end, he grasped a soft mass. Even as he pulled out a silk sponge, worth more than its weight in gold, something sharp as steel and brittle as ice pierced his hand deep, and he felt a score of spines break and rankle in his flesh like splinters of broken glass. By an ill chance he had thrust his hand against one of those chestnut burs of the ocean, a purple-black sea urchin, whose villainous spines, like those of a porcupine, pierce deep and break off. Setting his teeth against the pain, the boy shifted the silky clump of sponge to his other hand and swam for the canoe with all his might. As he rose he saw his grandfather mouthing the word "Hurry!" every line on his tense face set in an agony of pleading.

Even as the boy shot toward the surface, he caught sight once again of the same brilliant little fish returning from deep water. Close behind it, dim at first, but growing more and more distinct as it came, showed a sinister shape, slate-gray, with yellow-brown stripes, the dreaded tiger shark of deep water, convoyed by that little jackal of the sea, the pilot fish. It was fortunate for Jimmy Tom that the tiger shark is not among the swiftest of its family and that he was halfway to the surface before the cold deadly eyes of that one caught sight of his ascending body. With a rush like a torpedo boat, the thirty-foot shark shot toward the straining, speeding figure, and reached it just as, with a last desperate effort, Jimmy Tom broke water by the canoe. Only the fact that a shark has to be on its back to bring into play its seven rows of triangular, saw-edged teeth saved the boy's life. The tiny tick of time which the fish took in turning enabled the old man, with a tremendous heave of his powerful arms, to drag Jimmy Tom bodily over the gunwale just as the fatal jaws snapped shut below him.

For a long minute the sea-tiger circled the canoe with hungry speed. Then, seeing that his prey had escaped, he swam away, guided, as always, by the strange pilot fish, which feeds on the scraps of the feasts which it finds for its companion.

As the shark turned toward deep water Jimmy Tom sat up from where he had been lying at the bottom of the canoe and grinned cheerfully after his disappearing foe. Then, without a word, he handed Jim Tom the clump of sponge which, throughout his almost dead-heat with death, he had held clutched tightly in his left hand. With the same motion, he stretched out his other hand, filled like a pincushion with keen, glassy spines from the sea urchin.

"Not twice in a long lifetime," said his grandfather, "have I seen a finer silk sponge. Already that sloop is half paid for."

Without further words, he drew from his belt a sharp-pointed knife and began the painful process of removing one by one the embedded spines from the boy's right hand before they should begin to fester. He finished this bit of rough-and-ready surgery by washing out each deep puncture with stinging salt water. When he had entirely finished, Jimmy Tom carefully tucked away the sponge in a pocket fastened to the inside of the canoe and, slipping the wide-mouthed bag again over his neck, stood on the thwart ready for another dive.

"Try to remember with your thick head," said his grandfather, severely, "all that I have told you, and if I signal you to come back, you *come*."

The boy nodded briefly, took several deep breaths, and again shot down through the water, directing his course toward another part of the reef, where the white sand was dotted with shells, all hyaline or clouded with exquisite colors. As he reached the bottom, the boy's swift, supple fingers searched among crystal-white, purple and rose and gold olivellas, dosinias, and tellinas which, in spite of their beauty, had no special value. Just as he was about to return to the surface empty-handed, his eye caught the gleam of several spires of the rare, sky-white coral showing among the waving waterweed. A hasty look aloft showed no signal of danger from his sentinel, and he still had nearly three minutes before water would exact her toll of oxygen from him. A swift stroke brought him to the edge of the weed bed. Just as he was about to reach for the coral, his trained eye caught sight of a gleaming white, beautifully shaped shell nearly as large as the palm of his hand. With a quick motion, he reached under the wavering leaves and, even as his fingers closed on its corrugated surface, realized that he had found at last a perfect specimen of the royal wentletrap, among the rarest and most beautiful of shells.

In the collections of the world, there are perhaps not six perfect specimens, and sponge divers and shell gatherers along a thousand lonely coasts are ever on the lookout for this treasure of the sea. The pure white rounded whorls[4] of this one were set off with wide, frilled varices,[5] each ending in a point above, the whole forming a perfect crown of snow and crystal indescribably airy and beautiful. The sight and feeling of this treasure put every thought out of Jimmy Tom's mind save to reach the surface with it as soon as possible. The coral could wait. For that shell any one of the collectors who called at Carib Island would gladly pay him twice the hundred dollars he needed.

Suddenly, even as he turned toward the surface, from a deep crevice in the coral close to his side, shot a fierce and hideous head, like that of some monstrous snake, ridged with a fin which showed like a crest. Before the boy could move, two long jaws filled with curved teeth snapped shut on his right hand and wrist, and he realized with a dreadful pang of fear and pain that he had been gripped by one of the great conger eels which lurk in the crevices of the reef. Eight feet in length and as large around as a man's leg, they are among the most fearsome of all the sea-folk which a diver must brave. For a second, Jimmy Tom tugged with all his strength, but with no result except that the greenish-gray body retreated deeper into its cave. Then it was that he remembered what his grandfather had told him was the only way to escape from the deadly jaws of a conger eel. Relaxing every muscle, he allowed his hand to lie limp in the great fish's teeth. Sooner or later, if he kept

---

4 **whorls**: turns.

5 **varices** (vâr′ə sēz′): ridges.

quiet, the monster would open its jaws for a better grip.

As the cold, deadly eyes stared implacably[6] into his, the beating of his laboring heart sounded in his ears like a drum of doom. If so be that the fierce fish did not relax his grip within the next thirty seconds, the boy knew that his life would go out of him in a long stream of silvery air bubbles. By a tremendous effort of will he strove against the almost irresistible impulse to do something, to pull, to struggle, to slash with his knife at the horrid head. Yet, clinching his teeth grimly, he set himself to that hardest of all tasks—to wait and wait. His eyes, hot and dim with suffused blood, fell on the crowned shell which he held in his free hand, that shell which was to win for him the sloop, and suddenly through the luminous, gleaming water he seemed to see his cabin on far-away Carib Island and his mother's face looking into his.

As the vision faded he felt a slight shifting and loosening of the grim jaws. With a last effort of his will, dimming before the flood of unconsciousness creeping up to his brain, he allowed his body to float limp, and relaxed every straining muscle. Even as he did so, the great jaws gaped apart for an instant and the fierce head thrust itself toward him for a fresh grip. Fighting back the waves of blackness which swept across his eyes, by a quick turn and wrench he freed his imprisoned hand and, with a tremendous scissors-kick of his

6 **implacably** (Ĭm plăk′ə blĭ): ruthlessly; heartlessly.

powerful legs, shot away just as the curved teeth struck, empty, together.

Up and up and up he sped, swimming as he had never swum before, yet seeming to himself, under the desperate urge of his tortured lungs, to move slow as the hour hand of a clock. The sunlit surface seemed to move away and away and recede to an immeasurable distance. Just as he felt despairingly that he could no longer resist the uncontrollable desire of his anguished lungs to act, even if they drew in the waters of death, his head shot above the surface. There was a sudden roaring in his ears as the strong arms of Jim Tom pulled him into the canoe. Too weak to speak or move, he lay experiencing the utter happiness there is in breathing, which only the half-drowned may know.

All the rest of that day the boy lay in the shade of the towering coral wall, while old Jim Tom dressed his gashed and pierced hand. As the calm weather still held, the old man decided to spend the night in the canoe just outside the sheer wall of the reef, where the water stretched away to unknown depths. Toward evening the boy's strength came back; and after eating and drinking ravenously, he showed but little effect of the strain to which he had been subjected.

"When the moon rises," said his grandfather at length, "we will start for home."

The boy shook his head obstinately.

"Tomorrow, as soon as it is light," he said, "I dive again to bring up

such white coral as has not been seen on Carib Island in my day."

"In your day!" exclaimed old Jim Tom, much incensed.[7] "In your minute—for that is all you have lived. Never has any man made a better haul than you. Be satisfied. The reef is not fortunate for the greedy."

"My silk sponge was won from the jaws of a shark and my shell from the conger eel," returned the boy, doggedly. "I ask no favors of the reef."

The old man glanced around apprehensively, while the water seemed to chuckle as it lapped against the coral.

"It is not lucky to talk that way," he said softly. "Sleep now," he went on after a pause. "When morning comes, perhaps there will be a better spirit in you and we will go home."

A little later, while the great moon climbed the sky and the golden sea stretched away unbroken, the two slept. Hours later, Jim Tom awoke with a start. Through his sleep had penetrated the sharp sinister scent of musk, and, even before he opened his eyes, he felt some hostile living presence near him. As he raised his head above the side of the canoe, the still surface of the sea beyond was all a-writhe with what seemed a mass of white sea snakes. Suddenly from out of the livid tangle shot toward the boat two thirty-foot tentacles larger around than a man's body, tapering to a point and covered with round, sucking discs armed with claws of black horn, sharp and curved as those of a tiger. The great white squid, the devil-fish of unknown depths, which hardly once or twice in a generation comes

7 **incensed:** enraged; angered.

to the surface, was before him.

For a moment the old man stared in horror at the twisting, fatal tentacles. Then, with a hoarse cry, he roused Jimmy Tom, who started up, grasping the keen machete which always lay in a sheath at the bottom of the canoe. Even as he unsheathed the curved blade, one of the vast, pale streamers reached the canoe, flowed over its side, and licked around the waist of the old man. On the instant, red stains showed through his thin shirt where the armed discs sank deep into his flesh as the horrid arm dragged his helpless body toward the water. Just in time, the boy swung the machete over his head and severed the clutching streamer, and then, with a return stroke, cut through another that licked out toward him across the boat.

As he turned, the old man stretched his arm out toward the sea with a gasp of horror. Up through the water came a vast cylindrical shape of livid flesh, many times the size of the canoe, from which long tentacles radiated like a wheel. In the middle of the shapeless mass was set a head of horror, with a vast parrot-like beak which gnashed over a mouth like a cavern. On either side of the demon jaws glared two lidless eyes, each larger than a barrel, rimmed around with white. Of an inky, unfathomable black, they stared at the boat with a malignancy[8] which

no earthborn creature could equal or endure. Unable to sustain their appalling glare, both of the Caribs thrust their arms before their faces, expecting every second to feel the deadly touch of the armed tentacles.

It was the boy who recovered himself first. Setting his teeth grimly, he suddenly raised his head to face again this demon of the lowest depths. At his exclamation of surprise, the old man forced himself to look up. The water stretched before them empty and unbroken. Only the scent of musk and grisly fragments of the death-pale tentacles in the bottom of the canoe were there to prove that the monster had not been a ghastly dream of the night. Without a word, Jimmy Tom shipped the outriggers and, gripping his paddle, took his place in the bow. All the rest of that night and far into the next day they paddled, until at last Carib Island loomed up on the horizon.

From the sale of the wentletrap and the silk sponge Jimmy Tom bought not only his sloop and a new canoe for Jim Tom, but still had the hundred of dollars which makes a man rich on Carib Island. Yet in spite of the fortune he brought back from the reef, he has never returned to it again. When urged by friends or collectors, he only shakes his head and says oracularly,[9] "Enough is plenty."

---

8 **malignancy** (mə lĭg′nənt sĭ): hatred.   9 **oracularly:** wisely; profoundly.

SAMUEL SCOVILLE, JR.

51

1. What is the setting of "The Reef"? What does the setting contribute to the meaning of the story?
2. How does the author create suspense in the early part of the story? What details do you learn from the conversation between Jimmy Tom and his grandfather? Why does the old man talk about the death of Jimmy Tom's father?
3. After seeing the manta ray fly through the air, Jimmy Tom "stretched out his paddle at full length." What was he trying to prove to his grandfather?
4. Describe briefly each of the three encounters Jimmy Tom has with dangerous sea life. What skill or knowledge does he need in each situation? Why is the order in which these situations happen of importance?
5. What kind of person is Jimmy Tom? In what ways is he like his grandfather? In what ways is he different from him?
6. What does Jimmy Tom mean by saying that "Enough is plenty"?
7. In many places in the story, the author speaks to the reader directly to explain something that the reader might not know. Find at least three of these places.

Further Activity

Look up the definitions for *courage* and *daring* in the glossary. Can you be courageous without being daring? Or can you be daring without being courageous? Think about this; then discuss how these two words fit Jimmy Tom and his adventures.

Characterization

YOU READ literature partly to learn more about how people act and why they act that way. Reading, then, is important because it helps you to understand other people and to understand yourself.

In literature you judge a character in much the same way that you judge people in real life. Ordinarily you decide on a person's character by observing what he says, what he does, and, sometimes, by what others say about him. When John asks you about Joe, he says, "What's he like?" You base your answer on how you have seen Joe act and from what you have heard him say. In literature the author presents a person in action, and expects you to draw the conclusions which will answer the question, "What's he like?" Your answer will be determined by how thoughtfully you read.

In the following selections the characterization is very carefully done. The emphasis is on *motivation*, on why people act as they do.

One of the important things you need to understand in dealing with other people is that you seldom really know them. You get quick impressions of new people and then cling to those impressions. You do not know, at first, *why* they do what they do. As you get to know people better, you should be willing to change your mind. In the following story is an expression of an important idea: To know all is to forgive all. What does this statement mean? How does it relate to the story?

The Strangers That Came to Town

Ambrose Flack

IMPROVING YOUR READING: As a story begins and people move onto the scene, you should ask, "What are they like?" When you answer this question, you have judged the characters of the people; you speak of them as honest, cruel, or generous, for example. You are able to make this judgment because of the *characterization*. The author does not usually tell you what people are like; he lets them act out their characters. When Andy, who tells the following story, drops a cake of soap in the tub of fish, he shows a streak of cruelty. When his father carries out a series of acts, you see that he is fair. As you read, observe what people do and say, and then draw conclusions about what kinds of people they are.

THE FIRST OF April came dark and stormy, with silver whips of lightning cracking open the lowering clouds that seemed to skim the treetops. My brother Tom and I, recovering from chest colds, tired of reading and listening to the radio, turned to the big living-room window of our house on Syringa Street.

"Here they come, Mother," cried Tom when a big truck drove up in the teeming rain and stopped in front of the empty cottage across the street.

Mother hurried in from the kitchen and we three looked out. That truck, we knew, contained the Duvitch family and all their earthly possessions.

Mr. Duvitch and the biggest boy carefully helped Mrs. Duvitch from the seat and walked her into the house, supporting her all the way. Another big boy, carrying a well-bundled baby, followed. A stream of young Duvitches, accompanied by a big brown houndlike dog, poured out of the back of the truck and stood in a huddle in the rain.

The barnyard sounds we heard escaped from two crates of hens the Duvitches had fetched along and from a burlap bag in which a small flock of ducks had been stowed. While the livestock made noises according to its kind, the Duvitches were quiet—almost solemn. They showed no elation at finding them-

54   CHARACTERIZATION

selves in a new neighborhood and a very pretty neighborhood at that.

All afternoon Mother, Tom and myself had been watching out for them, with rather mixed emotions. For the Duvitches were immigrants and the first of their nationality to settle in our small smug town. Coming to our obscure part of the state a year before, they had moved into a rotting old farmhouse two miles north of town, long abandoned. After the slashing hurricane of mid-March, the moss-rotten dwelling looked like the house in the fairy tale that remained standing only because it did not know which way to fall and the Duvitches were forced to give it up.

"I wonder if Mrs. Duvitch is ill," murmured Mother, looking through the rain at the dreary street scene.

"She must be," said Tom. "I wonder if it'll be all right for Andy and me to help 'em move in their stuff."

This request, as Mother well knew, was not inspired by genuine feeling for the Duvitches but by curiosity and she shook her head. It was a strict family rule that any illness which kept us out of school would automatically keep us indoors.

But the Duvitches got along very well without help from us. As it turned out, they were old hands at moving. For years before coming to America they had been on the move, to escape starvation, separation, possible assassination. Every child capable of two-legged locomotion pitched in and helped carry the things from the truck. In no time at all, it seemed, the truck was empty

and the Duvitches were shut up tight in their new home.

That was the signal for Mother to step into the kitchen. She returned swathed[1] in her hooded raincoat, carrying a basket containing a vacuum jug of chicken soup, a baked tuna-fish dish, steaming hot; a loaf of fresh bread and a chocolate cake. These she took to the house across the street and gave basket and all to the boy who answered her knock. It wasn't her plan to stop for a visit that day but to wait a week or so and call when the Duvitches were all settled.

The next day when the three of us —Mother, Tom and myself—were having lunch, we heard a faint tap at the back door. I answered it and there stood a pale dark-eyed boy, looking very solemn, holding our basket. It contained the empty vacuum jug, casserole dish and cake plate, all of which shone, and a tiny very shapely potted rose tree, in exquisite pink-tipped bud, the handsomest plant—and the only plant of its kind—ever seen in that neighborhood.

"I send them a few scraps of food," murmured Mother, a few seconds later, deeply touched, "and get this queenly gift!"

That was our last traffic with the Duvitch family for over two years. When Mother stopped to visit them a week after their coming, the little girl who opened the door a few inches said, "Mamma sick; she stay in bed today." Mrs. Duvitch never crossed the street to our house and Mother, a

1 swathed: wrapped.

rather formal woman, made no further attempts to see the family. But Father disagreed when she remarked that she thought the Duvitches probably wished to be left alone.

Syringa Street seemed to be a friendly street. It was a crooked maple-shady country lane that wound through the town without losing its charm. The sidewalk here and there was almost lost in weeds and the ditches, in places, were brightened by clumps of orange day lilies. Widely spaced cottages, some of them smothered in vines, only seemed to make the neighborhood more rural. There were brilliant flower gardens, vegetable plots, fruit trees—and a few henhouses. The children, who enjoyed all the benefits of country life while actually living in town, were quite numerous. Behind the façades of the street's dwellings there was probably no more greed, envy, superstition or intolerance than lurked behind the doors of any average dwelling in any average American town. The cardinal[2] virtues, no doubt, were all represented. Yes, Syringa Street seemed to be a friendly street.

But the Duvitches were marked people. They were the one struggling family in a prosperous community—and poverty, amid prosperity, is often embarrassing and irritating to the prosperous. They were considered unattractive physically. They were so meek! The Duvitches never fought back.

The women started in on Mrs. Du-

vitch because she "never showed her face." It is true, she was rarely if ever seen in the daytime, emerging from her dwelling only after dark in warm weather, to sit on the veranda, where she found privacy behind the ragged trumpet creeper.[3] But this gave rise to the rumor that she was the victim of an obscure skin disease and that every morning she shook scales out of the bed sheet. (When my father heard that one, he went out to the pantry and mixed himself a tall drink.)

Mr. Duvitch, too, was classified as an untouchable. His job, a rather malodorous[4] one, was with the local rendering plant[5] as a laborer. It followed that the Syringa Street young, meeting him on the street, sometimes stopped their noses as they passed him by—a form of torment all the more acute when Mr. Duvitch had to share it with the children that happened to be with him.

Black hard luck seemed to be their lot.

A few weeks after they moved to Syringa Street they suffered a tragedy they were all summer in recovering from—Mr. Duvitch lost two weeks' pay while gathering mushrooms in Tamarack Swamp. Inside of a year and a half, three Duvitch boys had lost, among them, by various mishaps, two fingers, one eye and an ear lobe. They were forever being cut up, bruised, mutilated by things falling, breaking, cracking and exploding.

A mild case of typhoid, mass cases

2 **cardinal:** chief; most important.

3 **trumpet creeper:** a climbing plant with trumpet-shaped flowers.
4 **malodorous:** ill-smelling.
5 **rendering plant:** a plant which makes industrial fats and oils from livestock carcasses.

CHARACTERIZATION

of whooping cough and measles—all plagued the family within a year of their arrival. Their only bright spot here was Dr. Switzer, one of the town's kindliest souls. He declined to accept fees, but was several times seen leaving the Duvitch cottage, carrying off a handsome house plant and looking very pleased. The Duvitches' dog, Kasimar, acted just like the family to which he belonged—like one of the world's poorest canine relations. He seemed to be afraid of his own shadow and no one had ever heard him bark or growl.

Because they cast their eyes on the sidewalk as one passed them by and spoke only when spoken to, the young Duvitches, like their parents, were considered antisocial. They were regarded as born scavengers too, for they spent hours foraging[6] in the town dump, where they often picked up their footgear, some of their pants and shirts and furnishings for the house as well. They went on country excursions to gather watercress, dandelion greens, mushrooms and wild berries; and the few apples and tomatoes they occasionally concealed under their blouses didn't make the farmers on whom they poached much poorer. Tom and I raided tomato patches and robbed apple trees just for the fun of it.

That first September four Duvitches—Irving, Benny, Abe and Esther—registered at the local grammar school. Mrs. Lovejoy, the principal, said they were bright, conscientious, pathetically eager but almost pathologically[7] shy. Before she could put a stop to it, some of their classmates scoffed at the leaf-lard-and-black-bread sandwiches they ate for lunch, huddled in one corner of the recreation room, dressed in their boiled-out ragpickers' clothes. After school they headed straight for home, never lingering on the playground.

Even the tradesmen to whom the Duvitches gave good money were either curt[8] with them or downright rude. Mrs. Frithjof Kinsella, the proprietor of the general store and a big jolly Viking who could be heard two blocks away, extended credit to almost everybody in town and had a way of insulting her customers so heartily that they all loved her for it. The Duvitches, however, Mrs. Kinsella very carefully *did not insult* (a form of insult in itself) and neither did she extend them credit.

But Mother, remembering the potted rose tree, always had a friendly word and a smile for the young Duvitches when she saw them and a bone for Kasimar when he found courage to venture across the road. Father was the only man on Syringa Street who tipped his hat to sixteen-year-old pock-marked Maria Duvitch, otherwise quite pretty, when he met her coming home from her piece-work job in Miller's Box Factory. It may have been that their European travail[9] made it easy for them to endure such a trifle as humiliation in America.

"I think," said Father one fine Sat-

---

6 **foraging:** searching for provisions.

7 **pathologically:** abnormally.
8 **curt:** short in language.
9 **travail:** torment.

urday morning in July two years after the Duvitches had come to Syringa Street, "that it would be very pleasant for Andy, Tom and myself to pitch our tent out at Durston's Pond and spend the night. We could fish and swim. That is," he added, "if Mother can spare us."

"I can spare you very well," Mother said cheerfully.

She had a notion it did menfolk good to get away from their women occasionally and in this instance the sacrifice came easily, because camp life was little to her liking. She packed a hamper of food, Tom and I fetched the tent from the attic and Father looked over his fishing tackle. An hour after lunch we were driving through rolling farm country out to Durston's Pond, four miles north of town.

We often had the serene little lake all to ourselves but on our arrival that afternoon we found half a dozen male Duvitches in possession. They had been fishing for several hours, casting from the shore, dropping their lines over the wooden bridge that spanned Cat Creek where it flowed into the pond and trolling for bass from a flat-bottomed rowboat.

Tom and I, Philistines[10] like our friends, ignored the Duvitch boys but Father went up to Mr. Duvitch, who was fishing from the shore, and put out his hand.

"Good afternoon, Mr. Duvitch! It's nice to see you and the boys here. What a beautiful day! Are Mrs. Duvitch and the girls all well?"

10 **Philistines:** here, insensitive people.

Mr. Duvitch was a little fellow, a lean starveling of a man with watery blue eyes and a kicked-about look. Gratitude for being agreeably noticed showed in his mosquito-bitten face as he took Father's hand and his tremulous smile showed broken teeth.

"I know the mosquitoes are biting," Father went on pleasantly, "but are the fish?"

Proudly, oh, so proudly, Mr. Duvitch exhibited the catch that would probably feed his family for the better part of a week: a fine mess of bass, perch and sunfish, all of them alive, as far as I could see, and swimming around in the oaken washtub in which they had been dropped. Father gave Mr. Duvitch hearty congratulations and said we couldn't hope to do as well but that we'd try.

We three pitched the tent on a little knoll over the pond, and then Father, with a happy sigh, lay down on the blanket for a nap in the sun. Tom and I played a game of chew-the-peg on the grassy bank above the water and, later on, made several trips to the tent, for the camera, the field glasses, the sun lotion. On a trip for a cold drink from the vacuum jug and to fetch towels and soap, we stopped to look again at the Duvitches' catch of fish.

Mr. Duvitch and the boys had moved away and were fishing in a a small arm of the pond below us. None of them seemed visible. Tom and I, our glances meeting over the big cake of soap in my hand, were similarly and wickedly inspired—the thing was irresistible. We held a brief whispering conversation; and then, egged on[11] by him and quite willing on my own, I played a shameful trick on the Duvitches, the memory of which will come back to the end of my days to plague me. Without considering further, I dropped the cake of soap into the tub of fish.

"Let's go," whispered Tom after we had watched the soap sink to the bottom.

We swam out to the raft, diving and frolicking in the deep water. After a while the Duvitches, calling it a day, assembled at a spot on the shore below our tent, happy in the knowledge of a good catch to take home.

In a little while Tom and I could hear their muffled exclamations of disbelief and dismay. Father woke up and joined our neighbors in a conclave,[12] looking down at the tub of fish near his feet. After a few moments he produced the whistle he carried on all our country excursions and blew it piercingly three times, the proclamation of emergency. This meant that Tom and I must come at once.

Looking as guilty as we felt, we swam in and joined the group gathering around the tub. In the midst of our stricken neighbors stood Father, holding the half-melted cake of soap in his palm silently but accusingly, for the fish had perished miserably in the soapy water and were unfit to eat. Not only had Tom and I snatched precious food from their mouths but we had brazenly[13] advertised the contempt[14] in which we held them.

Father's eyes were narrow slits of blue fire in his white face. I had never seen him so angry. One look at Tom and me told him everything. Words would have been superfluous[15] and my brother and I bowed our heads in acknowledgment of our guilt.

"You will begin," Father said in a voice I didn't recognize, "by saying you're sorry."

Our stunned neighbor wiped his blinking eyes as he listened to our mumbled words, which Father made us repeat when they were inaudible. But there was no hostility, no animosity[16] toward us in the man and it was obvious also that he considered himself too humble to receive an apology, finding it, like most of life's troubles, a mockery to be endured without protest. His sons showed no resentment, either, only a kind of resignation in their minds, which carried almost atavistic memories[17] of century-old oppression by country barons and landed gentry.

One-eyed Manny Duvitch, as it turned out, had told Father he had seen me drop something in the tub of fish (before he learned that it had been a cake of soap). Now he looked guiltier than Tom and I. Because he had been the witness and accuser, it was as if he considered himself to be the trouble-maker, deserving the punishment. The two real culprits were the young lords of the ruling manor,

---

11 **egged on:** encouraged.
12 **conclave:** private meeting.
13 **brazenly:** boldly; impudently.

14 **contempt:** scorn.
15 **superfluous:** unnecessary.
16 **animosity:** ill-will; resentment.
17 **atavistic memories:** memories inherited from ancestors.

with unlimited license, exempt from chastisement.[18] To Manny, the fortunate, the well-to-do, were also the privileged.

"Do you realize," said Father coldly, looking from Tom to me, "that in certain primitive communities the sort of stunt you've pulled would be punishable by death?"

Tom and I did not reply.

"Turn over the tub," said Father abruptly, addressing us as if we were strangers.

We turned it over. The gray soapy water ran away in bubbly rivulets, disappearing in the coarse mat of turf, and the poisoned fish lay exposed on the grass—quiet, strangled, open-mouthed—and somehow looking as if they were mutely[19] protesting their horrid unnatural fate.

"Count the fish," Father ordered us, his voice like steel.

Tom and I got down on our knees.

"How many are there?" demanded Father.

"Sixty-one," I said.

"How many bass?"

"Twelve."

Father handed Mr. Duvitch two dollars, the price of a day's rental of the rowboat. Then, looking both the avenging angel and executioner, he ordered Tom and me, with our tackle and bait, off the land we had disgraced—into exile, out on Durston's Pond.

"And you are not to come back," he gave out in the same steely tones,

<hr>

18 **exempt from chastisement:** not subject to punishment.

19 **mutely:** soundlessly.

CHARACTERIZATION

"until you've caught sixty-one fish to repay Mr. Duvitch. See to it that among them you bring in at least a dozen bass."

Father stepped up to the tent on the knoll to fetch our shirts and dungarees. These he rolled into a tight ball and shot like a bolt into the rowboat. He then turned his back to us and, thus disowned, Tom and I lost no time in rowing out on the pond. Father's decisions, even with Mother present, were never reversed and swift execution, from which there was no appeal, followed his sentences.

Out in the middle of the big pond we dropped anchor, threaded our steel rods and, baiting our hooks, began to fish. I knew that if it took us all summer to catch them, we dared not set foot ashore without sixty-one fish. Almost at once Tom pulled in a good-sized bass and ten minutes later two yellow perch were added to our string. The crestfallen Duvitches went home. Father threw himself on the blanket, furiously smoking a cigar. That was about four in the afternoon.

Oh, the mosquitoes! They were bad enough at the time, and while the light held, but after we had been fishing for three hours and had caught eight fish, they swarmed out of the dark Hades of swampland surrounding the pond like Lucifer's[20] angels, in legions.

After an hour of it we wanted to leap overboard. They got in our ears, our noses, our eyes, even in our mouths, and nestling in our hair, they bit through to our scalps. I remembered tales of Indian prisoners in Alaska, stripped by their captors and turned loose on the tundra,[21] where they died of the mosquitoes in two hours. Several times we slipped over the side of the boat, immersing ourselves in the water to escape the bloodthirsty clouds. The night dragged on while the whining swarms grew thicker.

"Andy, what time is it?"

"Ten o'clock, Tom."

"Is that all?" Tom groaned and pulled in another bass and killed six or eight mosquitoes in one slap. Two hours passed and midnight was ghostly on Durston's Pond.

The moon, bright as day, sailed high in the purple sky, dimming the starfire, casting a great white shaft of quivering radiance on the water, but it was all hideous. The big yellow disk sank in a gauzy cloudbank, then disappeared for good and the stars shone out with renewed splendor.

"Andy, what *time* is it?"

"Two o'clock, Tom."

The treetops whispered as if in conspiracy against us. Owls hooted —mockingly we thought—and bats circled over our heads, making us feel thoroughly damned. Our only solace[22] was the campfire Father kept burning near the tent, which flared like a beacon light in the dark. We went on fishing as our tormentors bit and sang. Each hour was an eternity of frenzy and I fairly panted for the light of dawn to come, but even now

20 Lucifer's: the Devil's.

21 tundra: treeless plain.
22 solace: comfort.

I cannot decide which was worse, that night with the mosquitoes on Durston's Pond or the following day in the blistering heat.

"Andy—"

"It's four o'clock, Tom, and we've got sixteen fish."

Dawn came but even I, a highly impressionable youngster of seventeen, did not enjoy that calm effulgent[23] majesty of daybreak. A long stretch on Durston's Pond, under the July sun, still faced us.

The rising sun was red, casting glimmering circles of rose-colored light on the windless surface of the pond. The mosquitoes thinned, the fish continued to bite. But as we fished the sun mounted steadily and by eleven it had fulfilled its awful prophecy and became a ball of fire in the cloudless skies. Tom and I began to bake in the heat waves that shimmered over the pond and we were steamed in the scalding vapory mist.

"I wish it was night again, Andy," groaned Tom after sweating out two hours of it. "This is worse than the mosquitoes."

"At least we won't get any infections from our bites, Tom," I said feebly. "The sun's cauterizing[24] them."

"We might get sunstrokes, though. We're liable to, without our hats. But I don't care if I do. I'd rather be unconscious."

Tom was only fifteen and I think he hated me that day. I, the older, should have been his protector against participation in crime, not his accomplice. I wanted to row him in, then come back to finish the business alone, but there on the green Eden-like shore stood Father—the archangel bearing the fiery sword, stationed by the Lord at the gates of Paradise to bar the way.

Tom and I weighed our hooks down to the deep cold water. We caught two more bass and half a dozen sunfish.

By one o'clock groups of people gathered on the shore, for word of the drama that was being enacted on Durston's Pond had spread through the town. Some of the visitors praised Father for his stern discipline; others berated[25] him. He went right on reading his magazine and smoking his cigar, as indifferent to their praise as he was to their criticism.

Local fishermen who knew the lake and something about the angling ability of the average youngster made gloomy estimates as to the possible length of our exile on the water. A few had us fishing until the snow flew. They made bets too. Would Tom and I have the guts to stick it out? Most of the bets were against us.

But we sat there in the rowboat, without food, through the hottest day of the summer.

No breeze stirred. No cloud obscured the sun. Even the bird life of the swamp, usually a medley of song, was silent and dead. Tom was drooping visibly in the glare and I tried hard not to look at his scorched face.

23 **effulgent:** radiant; brightly shining.
24 **cauterizing:** burning; searing.

25 **berated:** criticized.

CHARACTERIZATION

Between three and four we dropped lines in a school of yellow perch and pulled up no less than twenty. The bass continued to bite in the deep black holes off the swamp, which bristled with tree trunks. Benumbed, half-blinded, moving like automatons,[26] Tom and I geared ourselves for the home stretch.

When the sun, dropping low, had lost its fury and the hard blue enamel of the sky began to pale, I pulled up the thirteenth bass, which was our sixty-first fish.

Turned lobster-red, fairly devoured, famished and drooping from lack of sleep, we put together our rods and with our remaining strength rowed to where Father was waiting.

He received us coolly, making no comment on our condition. At once he asked to see the fish and we held them up by the strings.

"Count them," he said.

Obviously we would receive permission to land only when we had produced the required number, which was the price of our freedom.

"Sixty-one," said Tom.

"Including thirteen bass," I added.

"Very good," said Father in businesslike tones. "We will now restore to Mr. Duvitch his rightful property."

Tom and I took care not to play the part of triumphant heroes, even of redeemed sinners—that would not have suited our parent. Certainly, in appearance, we were more damned than redeemed. But when we tottered out of the rowboat something in me was quietly rejoicing. I guessed

that Father was secretly proud of our fortitude and I realized, too, that all through the night he had suffered with us.

We walked through the crowd of visitors on the lake shore, climbed into the car and silently drove to the Duvitch cottage. Mrs. Duvitch and the children were not visible but we found Mr. Duvitch sitting on the porch.

When he saw Tom and me and we silently handed him the strings of fish, he gulped and swallowed hard. For a moment he could not speak. Then, in a voice that was raw with emotion, he protested that he had not wished us to suffer so. Suppose we had fallen overboard in the dark?

"Will you shake hands with the boys?" asked Father.

Instead, Mr. Duvitch broke down. My brother and I did not know where to look and during those moments we suffered more acutely than we had suffered in the clouds of mosquitoes and under the broiling sun. After our neighbor had composed himself, he seized our hands and bowed his head over them. There was something Biblical, like a picture in the Old Testament, in the man's gesture. Anyway, it was my greatest lesson in humility.

When Mother, who had heard about our exile on the pond from a neighbor, saw us she burst into tears. She tried to embrace us but we drew back painfully. While she was rubbing salves and ointments on our seared backs and necks, somebody knocked at the kitchen door and Father opened it to find Mrs. Duvitch

26 **automatons** (ô tŏm′ə tŏnz′): automatic machines; robots.

standing there, her face and skin as undefiled as the Virgin's—the first time she had crossed the street to our house.

In her pale swaying hand Mrs. Duvitch held a porcelain teacup, ornamented with pink rosebuds and golden leaves—a relic from the old country and, as it turned out, her most cherished possession.

Her voice, thin and wispy from fright and shock, was difficult to follow. But we gathered that she had brought the teacup over as a peace offering and as a plea for our forgiveness to her family for the living purgatory,[27] no matter whose fault, through which my brother and I had passed. When Mother declined the teacup and assured Mrs. Duvitch that she would not have it otherwise with Tom and me, our neighbor, unable to find her tongue, made a little eloquent sign with her hands that was for thanks and that looked like a silent blessing. She quietly turned and went away; and again I felt that I had witnessed a scene from the Old Testament.

Mother continued her ministrations[28] to Tom and me and put us to bed. Despite our skin, which stuck to sheet and pillowcase, we slept like creatures drugged.

"It is high time," Tom and I heard Father say calmly, sanely, to Mother around noon next day when we woke up, "for this senseless feeling against the Duvitches to stop and I'm willing to do still more to stop it. Tonight we are having supper with them.

I've just seen Mr. Duvitch and he remarked that since Andy and Tom caught the fish, he'd feel better if we all shared in them. I suggested a fish-fry picnic supper and with a few hints from me, and some encouragement, he invited us over. It may be an ordeal but we ought to be able to bear it."

We walked across the street at six o'clock, not knowing what to expect. All the Duvitches, dressed in their Sunday best, bright and flushed and shining as we had never seen them, received us at the door as if we had been royalty. They looked at Tom and me and delicately looked away— I shuddered when I thought of what my brother and I would have had to endure had this been any other family.

Instead of a wretched abode we found a scantily furnished home that shone with cleanliness and smelled of spicy garden pinks. In its almost barren simplicity there was something comely.[29] A few of the stands, chairs and tables had the intimate quality of what is fashioned by the human hand. These, together with odds and ends the family had brought from the old country and others resurrected from the town dump and mended, painted, waxed and polished, made for a kind of native household harmony. The house plants (no window was without several) delighted Mother. Mrs. Duvitch was raising little orange and lemon trees from seed and experimenting with a pine-

27 **purgatory:** prolonged punishment.
28 **ministrations:** actions of aid and comfort.

29 **comely:** pleasant; attractive.

CHARACTERIZATION

apple plant growing in a butter tub.

At once we were conscious of a remarkable difference in the demeanor[30] of the family. The children, thrilled by their first party, by the family's first recognition in this country, kept showing their pleasure in wide delighted smiles. I couldn't believe they were the same timid downcast youngsters one met on the street and saw in school; they seemed to have been touched by a wand. The Duvitches' home was their castle: sustained and animated[31] by the security of its four walls, shut away from a world of contempt and hostility, they were complete human beings. In their own house their true personalities emerged.

As the host Mr. Duvitch was a man we were seeing for the first time. Overjoyed to have neighbors in his house, he was so full of himself that I was conscious of an invisible stature in him which made him seem quite as tall as Father. He beamed and feasted his eyes on us. Saying very little, he managed to make us feel a great deal and he constantly sought his wife's eyes with glances of delight over the wonder of what was happening.

David, the oldest boy, helped his father serve a bottle of homemade blackberry wine.

We ate fried fish and good food of the American picnic variety at a long plank table set out in the back yard under an apple tree. The young Duvitches passed things politely, never helping themselves first: and their thanks upon receiving a dish were almost ceremonial. They waited patiently for their plates and ate every scrap of food.

Father kept the conversation going. His every word was listened to, every childish eye riveted on him while he spoke.

Tom and I, fascinated by the family's metamorphosis,[32] almost forgot about our blisters and our stings. As Father told stories and jokes, we discovered that the Duvitches had a gift for gaiety, for laughter, all but extinguished but still capable of resurrection. They were merry people who had suffered too much. How strange to see the boys and girls throw back their heads and laugh when Father said something that was funny, but not terribly funny.

After supper we were ushered to the open summer kitchen, the coolest room in the house, for entertainment.

David played folk songs on his accordion. Mr. Duvitch turned out to be an amateur ventriloquist; he made the dog Kasimar talk Polish, the cat Jan talk Russian and a doll named Sophia talk English. Mrs. Duvitch read aloud to us, translating as she went along, a letter her mother had received from the great actress Modjeska, whom her family had known long ago.

I could tell that the Duvitches were a great revelation to Father and that he had enjoyed the evening tremendously.

"To think," he murmured as if talking to himself, while we were cross-

30 **demeanor:** behavior.
31 **sustained and animated:** supported and strengthened.

32 **metamorphosis:** transformation.

ing the street, "that they should turn out to be gentle people of cultivation and accomplishment. Looked down on and ignored by their inferiors!"

I like to believe that the oil paintings of George Washington, Abraham Lincoln and Thomas Jefferson, which hung in our living room, helped to establish the Duvitches in our community. Even the fountain tinkling in the lily pool in our garden might have helped. In that town, oil paintings and flowing fountains were the symbols of wealth and aristocracy. Only a few mansions on Sycamore Hill were adorned with such.

Because our home was graced with these symbols, we had always been classified with the town's great, which gave us such prestige in the neighborhood that people often followed our lead. Obviously the Duvitches were important in Father's eyes, shown by the rigorous sentence he had imposed on Tom and me for our misuse of them. Added to that, we had recognized the family by taking a meal with them in their own house. People, often persuaded to accept what we accepted, to believe what we believed, began to think the Duvitches must really count, after all. Most of our neighbors decided that if they were good enough for a highly educated man like Father (the only college graduate on Syringa Street), they were good enough for them. The galvanized[33] community began to look upon things in a different light and it soon became the fashion to give the Duvitches the favorable nod.

33 galvanized: stimulated; aroused.

Mother invited Mrs. Duvitch to a tea party, where her delicate manners, and the fine needlework which engaged her, won the approval of the local housewives who were present. On hot days our neighbor asked one of her big boys to carry the pineapple plant (which Mother had advertised well), into the back yard; and since botanical rarities were irresistible in that town of gardens, people were soon stopping by the fence for a look at the tropical specimen. After a while Mrs. Duvitch found courage to ask these people into her house and, if Mr. Duvitch was at home, he told the visitors stories about life in the old country. It was then that the neighborhood learned about the family's European past.

The children ceased stopping their noses when Mr. Duvitch passed them by and it wasn't long before the young Duvitches were able to enjoy outside companionship when they found time to play. They blossomed out in school and they were soon shining in school plays and festivals. Even Kasimar began to take on the ways of an American dog, daring to bark and growl on occasion.

Nathan Duvitch, who was seventeen, could throw and hit a baseball as far as anybody his age in town. When I learned this, and let it be known, he was asked to join one of the local ball clubs. David, invited to play his accordion at a country dance, turned out to be a magician with the instrument and ended up being one of the community's most popular players. Mrs. Frithjof Kinsella gave One-eyed Manny an after-school job in her store and later on told Mother he was worth three boys put together.

The community presently had reason to be grateful for Mrs. Duvitch's presence. It turned out that she had a great gift for nursing, and no fear of death, no fear of disease, contagious or otherwise. In times of severe illness Dr. Switzer often suggested that she be sent for—her own girls could take over at home. There were almost no nurses in town and the nearest hospital was over a hundred miles away. When Mrs. Duvitch quietly slipped into a sickroom, she never failed to bring along a sedative[34] influence, a kind of sanity. After an hour or two of her serene presence, the patient was calmed and comforted and the family reassured.

People began to turn to the Duvitches in all kinds of trouble. A boy who got in a bad scrape, a bitter family quarrel, a baby who had come into the world deformed—the elder Duvitches, with their old-world wisdom and gift for accepting the inevitable, could sit by the hour and argue gently and convincingly against disgrace, false pride, grief, fear.

Most surprising of all, Mr. Duvitch, in one respect, turned out to be characteristically American. One Saturday afternoon when my ball team was playing Nathan's, Father met him in the local ball park.

"Chust like de American boy," Mr. Duvitch exploded when Nathan made a timely hit that drove in two runs. Our neighbor choked with pride and went on: "Nathan's battering averich three hunnert twenty-sevened!"

On a cold snowy afternoon in winter Mr. Duvitch stopped at our house and presented Father (who had enormous hands, much bigger than any of the Duvitches') with a handsome pair of leather mittens, lined with fur, which had a slightly acrid[35] ashy odor.

"No doubt one of the boys resurrected them from a heap of ashes in the dump," remarked Father, drawing on the mittens, which fitted perfectly. "Why should I value them any the less? *Who* would have dreamed that the Duvitches would have so much more to offer us than we have to offer them?"

34 **sedative:** quieting; calming.

35 **acrid:** bitter.

Understanding Literature

1. The story begins with a description of the weather. How does it reflect the way people feel? Where else in the story does the weather have a connection with what is happening in the minds of the characters?
2. How does the author introduce the two families in the story? What details does he give you of what they say and do? At the beginning of the story in what respect are the families alike? How are they different?

3. Two years after the Duvitches move to Syringa Street, they still have no friends in the neighborhood. In what ways do the Duvitches limit their opportunities to make friends? How do the neighborhood children and adults treat the Duvitches? Why?
4. Point out the steps by which the author presents new evidence about what the Duvitch family is like. In your answer cite specific incidents in the story.
5. How does the author show that Tom and Andy are suffering during the fishing scene?
6. Is Tom and Andy's father justified in what he does to the boys? Explain. Why are the Duvitches so moved by the presentation of the fish?
7. What change takes place in the Duvitch family? Is the change justified by what happens in the story? Explain.
8. How is Andy different at the end of the story from the way he was at the beginning? Why is the story told from Andy's point of view?

Further Activities

1. Write a paragraph describing how you changed your mind about what someone was like. Give your first impression of the person and then show how, as you got to know the person better, you changed your mind about him or her. Make very clear what the new evidence was that changed your mind.
2. It is very important for an author to pick the right person to tell his story. In one or two paragraphs discuss how the story would be different if one of the other characters had told it. For example, how different would the story be if it were told from the point of view of Tom and Andy's father?

Focusing on Words

1. *Anti-* is a prefix which you see quite often. According to the dictionary, *anti-* is defined as *opposite, against, contrary, reverse*. This story states that "the young Duvitches, like their parents, were considered antisocial." What does *antisocial* mean? Think of other words which begin with the prefix *anti-*. Can you explain what they mean? Look in a dictionary to see whether or not you are correct.
2. Another prefix is *mal-*. Mr. Duvitch's job at the rendering plant is described as being "a rather malodorous one." What does the dictionary indicate *mal-* means? Find and define other words beginning with *mal-*.

The Espositos are people who enjoy each other and their Sunday evenings of good music. Their favorite record is *"Celeste Aïda,"*[1] which the great singer Enrico Caruso has given to Mr. Esposito. This story is built on a problem—will the family sell the record?

The Song Caruso Sang

Patrick McCallum

IMPROVING YOUR READING: Here is another story in which you should look closely at the characterization. The father looks at life differently from the way his children do. This difference causes disagreement or a *conflict* which must be resolved. Is the resolution of the conflict real? Does it, in other words, grow out of the characters of the people? Would you expect them to act the way they do?

WELL, IT'S ALL over now and everything is okay again, although not very long ago it looked like the whole Esposito family was going to bust right up. That would have been pretty bad, because we're a big family—Mamma and Papa and six kids, counting Beppe, who is married now and last year made me an uncle.

My name is George Washington Esposito because I was born the day Papa became an American citizen. He was so proud that he named me after our first President. I sort of think he hoped some day I might be a President, too. But that was fourteen years ago, and so far there's been no sign of me heading in that direction.

What I want to tell you about is the record, and what happened to it and to the Espositos because of it. I

know it sounds crazy when I tell you all the things that a recording of *"Celeste Aïda"* by Enrico Caruso did to us, but it's the truth, all of it.

As long as I can remember anything at all, I remember the Sunday evenings in our parlor, even when I was little and we lived on the East Side of Manhattan. It's gone on the same right here in Brooklyn, too.

The whole family was always together then—Papa and Mamma, of course, and Angelina, Beppe (now with Rosa and little Peppino), Enrico, Giovanni, Mary Alice, and me, George Washington. We last two are the only Espositos who have real American names, though Mamma calls us "Maria" and "Giorgio."

Let me tell you it was a roomful, especially when the Pezzullos from next door came over. You can imagine how we squeezed together on the horsehair sofa and filled all the chairs, the straight-backed ones with

1 *Celeste Aïda:* "Heavenly Aïda." Aïda (ä ē′dä) is the heroine in the opera of the same name by Verdi.

the round knobs that pressed against our spines when we sat up straight like we ought to in them, as well as the ones from the kitchen; and still some of us had to sit on the floor. But we didn't mind. What did it matter where you sat when you were listening to beautiful music? That's something to be enjoyed anywhere.

You see, Papa had this job at Sheeler's, the big music store just off Times Square. It wasn't much of a job in those days, but even if he was only a janitor, it paid enough for him to take care of his family, and he could be near music. Before he came to America, Papa played the violincello in the string quartet at the Ristorante Ricco, one of the best places to eat in Naples in case you ever go there. But after the first big war, when times got bad, Papa wrote to Uncle Guido in America, and Uncle Guido said to come over, so he and Mamma and Beppe came to New York. That was clear back in 1920.

I was telling you about Papa's job. Like I said, he didn't mind being a janitor, because it meant he was where he could hear music all day. Mr. Sheeler took a liking to Papa and let him bring records home over the weekend, so we could all hear the wonderful music that Papa listened to every day at the store as he swept and mopped the floors.

So that's the way the Sunday evenings began. We had a phonograph, a second-hand one that Papa got at the store real cheap; not the latest model, of course, but it had a clear tone, and that's what counts. It was my job to wind it up between rec-ords, but that's as much as Papa would let any of us do; he always changed the records himself. In all the years he brought records home only one was broken and two scratched. That's pretty good, I'd say.

We all love music. From the very beginning, even back in Italy before my oldest brother, Beppe, was born, the Esposito house had music in it. And after Mamma and Papa got to America and could afford it, there was a piano, and Angelina and Beppe took lessons. Later there was a violin for Giovanni; and Mamma, who had done some singing herself before she got married, taught Enrico to sing, because he had the best voice, and maybe just a little because his name was Enrico. As for me, I'm learning to play the piccolo in the school band.

There was more than music to our Sundays in the parlor. There was the being together, and for me that was best of all. During the week we were all running in and out of the house to and from school and work; only at supper could we be together, and then only for a little while, because Angelina had her night classes at business college, and Beppe and Giovanni were turning out for basketball at the YMCA, and Enrico practiced his singing in the bedroom with the door closed, and Mary Alice and I had our homework. So it was really only Sunday in the evening that we could gather in the parlor with the lights dim and listen while Papa played the operas of Verdi and the symphonies of Beethoven.

CHARACTERIZATION

For over an hour we would listen. Then Papa would say, "That's all tonight," and start to close down the top of the phonograph.

"But the record, Papa!" Everyone in the room chimed in. "We want to hear the record!"

Papa would look mystified, as though he didn't know what we were talking about. "The record? What record?"

"The Caruso record, Papa!" we would come back at him, everyone grinning. "You know which one we mean!"

"Ah!" He would nod as though just barely remembering. "The Caruso record." He would smile then. "Well, *bambini,* if you insist." He would shake his head. "But I do not understand why you want every time this same record."

Papa knew his part in the game. He would pick up the record, the one I mentioned before, *"Celeste Aïda,"* from the table, where he had placed it, knowing that we would demand to hear it.

To me, it is the best recording Caruso ever made of that lovely aria of Verdi's. Maybe it's because I've heard it almost every Sunday since I can remember; maybe it's because this is the only one of its kind, since no other copies were made, and it is ours.

Well, here is how it came to be: You see, long ago Papa had known Caruso in Naples, because sometimes the great tenor would come to Ricco's for a late supper when he was singing at the San Carlo. He even sang with the quartet when he felt like it —just got up in the middle of supper and sang. It was really something to hear, Papa says.

Papa had written Caruso that he and Mamma and Beppe would soon be in New York. The great man had made him promise to write if ever the Espositos came to America. He was not one to forget his old friends. If he had been, there wouldn't have been the record nor the thing that happened to us because of it.

I've heard so many times the story of Papa's meeting in New York with the man my brother Enrico was named after that now I almost feel I was there, myself, that day when Papa, following Caruso's instructions, went to the recording studio where the famous tenor was making an album of opera selections.

It was while he was singing into the big, flower-shaped horn of the recording machine that Papa entered the studio, having been permitted with the card that Caruso had sent him.

The aria was nearly over, the high, clear notes of that difficult solo going onto the soft wax disc so easily. *Ay! Mamma mia!* There was a voice straight out of heaven!

He turned away from the horn as he let go of the last note, and it was then he saw Papa through the glass and waved and smiled, crying out, *"Eh, Pasqualino, cumme stai?"*[2] and even before Papa could answer that he was fine, Caruso came rushing out of the studio and embraced him joyfully. "Come!" he said in Italian— this was before Papa knew any Eng-

lish. "We shall hear the record and then have some lunch. A feast it shall be! A feast to welcome my old friend to his new home!" Then he laughed and embraced Papa again.

They sat down to listen to the record.

The last note of *"Celeste Aïda"* faded away. There was a pause, then *"Eh, Pasqualino, cumme stai?"* came out of the loud-speaker as clearly as the aria just finished.

Papa said Caruso turned speechlessly and pointed his finger at Papa and then at himself in astonishment.

The engineers in the recording room had funny looks on their faces as they hurried out. "I'm afraid you'll have to do it over, Mr. Caruso," one of them said. "It'd be pretty hard to cut out that last part without ruining the music; there isn't enough of a pause between the last note of the singing and the words you spoke afterward."

Caruso shrugged his shoulders. "Okay," he said, and grinned. "Then we do it over." He got up and started into the studio again. "I will not be long, Pasqualino," he promised. "Then we go eat."

Papa says his heart seemed to quiver and his voice would hardly come as he stopped the singer. "Enrico," he said, "what is to become of the one you just made?"

Caruso went through the motions of breaking an invisible record over his knee, grinning as he did so.

Papa nodded gravely, his voice trembling as he continued. "Enrico, may I have it?" he asked, almost in a whisper.

2 *cumme stai:* "How are you?"

CHARACTERIZATION

The tenor did not seem to understand. "You want that record, Pasqualino?" he asked. "But why? It is no good. I can make you a better one right now."

"No, no, my friend!" Papa begged. "Please, I want only that one, the one where you speak to me and call my name."

Caruso laughed and slapped Papa on the back. "Ah, now I see!" he said. "Of course you may have it! One 'Celeste Aïda' just for you!" And he added, "With my special autograph!"

So, nearly every Sunday since, we have heard the golden voice of Enrico Caruso singing "Celeste Aïda," then felt proud and happy as we heard this greatest tenor of all time call out joyfully to our own father, "Eh, Pasqualino, cumme stai?" as if he were right in our parlor with us.

You can understand now why we all thought so much of the record. It was more than just a recording of "Celeste Aïda" by Enrico Caruso. Yet, I don't think I could tell you all the things it was to us. Like red wine on the table, the smell of garlic in the kitchen, early Mass on Sunday, and the sound of Neapolitan Italian being spoken, it was just part of our lives; we never knew any different. It isn't easy to explain things like that. . . .

Well, the years passed and we all grew older. The big boys began to shave and the girls to round out their figures. Beppe got married, and Angelina got a secretarial position, a good one with an import-export firm because she knew both English and

Italian and was a good secretary besides.

The Sunday evenings continued through all these changes in our lives. By now Papa had a better job at Sheeler's and no longer had to sweep and mop the floors; he didn't have to borrow records, either. We saved our money through the years and bought our own. One Christmas we all put together, my brothers and sisters and I, and bought Papa and Mamma a new radio-phonograph, the best there is; they were so surprised and happy that they both cried when they saw it under the tree.

Papa's record by Caruso, though, was still the prize possession of the Espositos, and it never seemed to get scratched or worn. Of course, no one touched it but Papa, and he was very careful, playing it only once a week, and always with a new needle.

It was after that first Sunday when my sister Angelina brought Dick Mantini, her boss, home to supper and our concert afterward, that things began to change. Dick's just a young guy, but he's got a swell position in this export outfit, and Angelina is his secretary. He sure got a funny look on his face when we began our act of "The record, Papa! Let us hear the record!" Then Angelina explained what it was all about, and Dick smiled politely as Papa carefully lowered the needle onto the whirling disc.

I never saw anyone spring to life as quickly as Dick when he realized that "Eh, Pasqualino, cumme stai?" was on the record.

"Hey, that's terrific!" Dick exclaimed. "There's a real collector's item, I'd say. Ought to be worth a lot of money." The parlor got real quiet when he asked Papa, "Have you ever tried to sell it?"

Papa didn't seem to understand. "Sell? What you mean, sell?"

"Why, there are people would pay you a lot of money for that record, Mr. Esposito; I couldn't say how much, but plenty, I'll bet. The singing alone, this being the only copy, would be worth a lot." He shook his head in amazement. "And with that business at the end, you could make a small fortune on it."

The room became awfully quiet, a different quiet than when we were listening to the music.

"Well," Papa sighed, "it's not for sale. It is mine, given by my friend Enrico Caruso. I will sell first my right arm."

Beppe, on the horsehair sofa with Rosa and Peppino, started to speak. "But, Papa," he began—only, when Papa looked in his direction he didn't finish what he started to say.

There was an atmosphere of uneasiness in the parlor that night and I had a feeling that Dick's idea would not just fade away by itself. . . .

The following Sunday, Beppe got up after we had heard the record and made a little speech. "Papa," he began, and everyone in the parlor knew what he was going to say.

"This week I have been thinking, and I have talked with Dick and with Enrico and Giovanni."

Papa sat up stiff but didn't say anything. Mamma looked like she'd rather be out in the kitchen making *lasagne.*

"Papa," Beppe went on, "for a long time now you've dreamed of owning a little piece of land out in Jersey, where you could have a garden and grow some grapes and fruit trees. You and Mamma have worked hard, and now it is time you took life easy. You owe it to yourselves."

Papa still did not speak. Beppe looked around him like maybe he wished Enrico or Giovanni was doing the talking.

"Well, Papa," he continued, after a pause that was nearly a sigh, "we think you ought to sell the record. Dick says he knows a man who is interested in such things and probably would give you plenty of money for it. Maybe a thousand dollars, even."

We all blinked our eyes at Beppe's words. A thousand dollars! For a record? Even if it is by Caruso? Not possible! Yet I'd never seen Beppe with a more serious expression on his face. Believe me, he wasn't kidding.

Papa spoke at last. "My record is not for sale," he said quietly but firmly. "I said before, I say again, not for a thousand or five thousand. We talk about it no more." He got up and left the parlor.

Beppe and Rosa and the baby went home, and the rest of us went to bed. I thought the talk of the record was finished and, without knowing why, I was kind of relieved. Still, letting myself dream for a minute, it would be nice to have a little farm in New Jersey. We often talked about it and dreamed of our own grapes and a few apple and cherry trees. But to sell the record? Somehow, even the little farm we wanted so much didn't seem worth that sacrifice.

It was the next day, just as I was sure the matter was closed, that Beppe came to the house all excited; while we were eating supper it was.

Beppe's eyes were bright as he told Papa about the new idea. "You wouldn't even have to sell the record, Papa!" he said breathlessly. "I talked to Dick about it again today. He says he thinks you could just sell the rights to it; you'd only have to let one of the big companies borrow the record and make a copy of it. You might get even more money than from a private collector. Think of it, Papa!" He leaned clear across the table and looked into Papa's face, waiting for him to say something.

Papa kept right on eating his supper. Then he took a sip of Chianti from the glass beside his plate, and after what seemed a long, long time, said, "I will think." But there was not even a trace of a smile on his face when he said it.

"Can I find out how to get in touch with the right party at the recording company, just in case?" Beppe asked, still leaning across the table.

Papa took another sip of wine, then nodded slowly. I could tell he wanted to forget the whole business.

Speaking of forgetting, I'd be just as glad to forget that next couple of weeks after Papa said okay to Beppe. For the first time in my memory we didn't even have the music in the parlor. You see, except for Papa and Mamma, nobody was speaking to anybody.

After Papa had agreed to Beppe's suggestion, my oldest brother contacted someone who was interested in the record and wanted to hear it. "The way they talk," Beppe explained, "I think they might give even more than a thousand for the record."

Papa finally agreed that the people from the recording company could hear the Caruso record, but they'd have to come to our house to do so; he wouldn't let the record out of the house.

It was then the unhappiness began. All my brothers and sisters, and with shame I must include myself, began thinking of the different ways we could spend the money, even before we had any idea how much it would be. Only Papa and Mamma said nothing. They were like two lost children who didn't know which way to turn; they would sit and listen to Angelina and Enrico and Giovanni and Mary Alice and me, and Beppe when he came from his house, quarreling about the money.

Giovanni wanted us to have a car, a big, new one. We'd never had a car, but he could think of all the reasons why we really needed one.

Angelina said that it would be nice to have a home out on Long Island and commute to work on the train.

Enrico thought we should all take a trip back to Italy, and he could study voice there.

Beppe and Rosa still held out for the farm in New Jersey, as it would be a good place to bring the baby on sunny weekends.

I don't think Mary Alice and I knew what we wanted, because we changed our minds every day. All of us were guilty of stretching the amount we thought we'd get for the record to cover whatever it was we wanted. . . .

The man from the recording company was coming on Sunday evening to listen to the record and decide whether or not it was what his company wanted. By that Sunday our house was not a place to be in if you were in a good mood and wanted to stay that way. Once, when I looked into Mamma's face I could tell she'd been crying, and Papa, who was always cheerful, never smiled any more.

Mamma had insisted that everybody come to dinner that Sunday, just like always, even if we were all mad at each other.

"Such faces," Papa said with a sigh as we all sat down at the table. "Only Peppino looks happy."

The little boy laughed when he heard his name. The rest of us looked down at our plates, just as we had when we were little and Papa scolded us for fighting.

"It is over two weeks now," Papa went on, "that the boss of Angelina tells us maybe we can get much money for our record. I feel this is not good, but as to give only the use of the record does not really seem bad I say nothing."

Papa sighed and shook his head sadly. "But, *si*, it is bad, very bad. I know this now. Ever since we think to sell I watch this family, and I see it is no more a family. Before, it is happy, and this house is filled with love and much laughing. Now there is only angry faces and fighting. Always before this time I hurry home from my work at night; now I stay away."

I could hear Mamma beginning to sniffle at the other end of the table.

"Why is this?" Papa continued. "It is because of a record, a record by my dear friend Enrico Caruso which for many years brings much joy to the Espositos." His voice sounded strange, not Papa's voice at all. "Now the thing that for many years is happiness for Pasqualino Esposito is unhappiness. I ask myself can I buy with money this happiness once again, and I find the only answer is *No*."

You could almost hear the silence in the room. Finally Giovanni spoke. "But, Papa," he reminded, "you'd still have your record and the little farm in Jersey with the apples and grapes . . ."

"Apples and grapes I can buy at the fruit stand of Pezzullo," Papa interrupted. "A family I cannot buy in any place." He left the room.

Mamma got up, too, and looked at us as though to say something, but then she turned without saying it and followed Papa into the parlor and closed the door.

Beppe was the first to speak after they had gone. "Papa's right," he said. "It's all my fault."

"Your fault?" Giovanni asked.

Beppe nodded. "I insisted that Papa consider selling after he'd said he didn't want to. If only I'd—"

"Don't be stupid, Beppe!" Giovanni interrupted. "You were right to insist. You were just thinking of the good of the family. Once this is all over and the record is sold, Papa will see it is right. Like you said just now, he'll have his record and the money, too."

"But the family?" Beppe asked. "Didn't you hear Papa and see his face just now? And Mamma, too? That's what made me realize it. We stand a chance of losing more than we could ever gain in dollars."

They argued on, everybody pitching in, until finally Beppe banged his fist on the table and said, "We're not going to sell the record, so what's the use of arguing?"

The others stopped talking, although Giovanni did remind Beppe that in any case it was too late to call up Mr. Kamp, the man from the recording company, and tell him not to bother to come.

I found myself awfully glad about what Beppe had said. I knew now that the last thing I wanted was for us to sell the Caruso record. If it went out of our house, then something awfully important would be gone out of our family, perhaps forever. . . .

The recording-company representative, Mr. Kamp, a bald-headed little man, came on the dot of seven-thirty, just as he was supposed to. We all went into the parlor and sat down. Mr. Kamp sat alone on the horsehair sofa. The room was deadly quiet, like just before a thunderstorm.

Papa picked up the record from its place among the others on the table and put it on the turntable. It began to turn, and he lowered the needle carefully into the outside groove.

His hand was shaking noticeably.

We all looked at each other in surprise. It wasn't "Celeste Aïda" at all! In confusion, Papa had put on "Vesti la giubba," instead. Both records, the big, thick kind they used to make before I was born, looked exactly alike.

Papa asked Mr. Kamp's pardon for the mistake and took "Celeste Aïda" from the table and put it on the machine.

The little man from the recording company leaned forward and stared at the floor as he listened to the record. When it was finished he merely nodded and asked to hear it again.

Papa sat by the phonograph looking intently at each of us as Caruso sang of his love for Aïda. Following Papa's gaze, I saw Angelina and Beppe and Enrico and Giovanni and Mary Alice all with the same worried expression, one just like the next. They were not like my brothers and sisters at all, nor was this the happy time of those other Sundays.

"Best 'Celeste Aïda' ever recorded by Caruso, I'm convinced," Mr. Kamp said in a businesslike tone after hearing it the second time. He was the authority on Caruso for his company, he told us, and had heard all the great tenor's records, "but none quite like this." He was smiling for the first time. "That little personal touch at the end would make it a record seller, too," he told us, and laughed as though he thought he'd said something funny.

He got up off the sofa and, jamming his hands down into his pockets, paced across the parlor twice, his

bald head almost glowing. He seemed very excited. "Mr. Esposito," he said in an even more businesslike tone than before, "my company will pay you five thousand dollars for all rights to the use of this recording if it's what we want, and I do not hesitate to assure you that it is." He began to explain the details.

There were little gasps all over the room. Five thousand dollars! We had never really dreamed of so much!

Papa nodded, but looked as though he weren't even listening to Mr. Kamp.

It was then that Beppe stood up and told Mr. Kamp the record was not for sale.

"Sorry you had to come out to Brooklyn for nothing," Beppe apologized. "We just this afternoon decided not to sell the record or the rights to it."

Both Papa and Mamma just sat looking at Beppe as though they couldn't believe what they were hearing.

Enrico and Giovanni didn't just sit there, though. They both began talking at once, each having forgotten that it would be better for the whole family, as they'd agreed, if we didn't sell our record. The offer of five thousand dollars had been too much for them. I began to tremble, and wanted to speak but couldn't.

Mr. Kamp stood up, too, as Beppe, his arms folded across his chest, stood facing Enrico and Giovanni defiantly, shaking his head. "If I might get a word in here," the record-company representative said, "I would like to tell you I have been authorized to go as high as six thousand if necessary."

"Six thousand!" Enrico and Giovanni shouted together. Angelina and Mary Alice looked as though they might weaken, but Beppe stood his ground.

I still could not speak, and there were tears in my eyes which almost blinded me. I turned my head away so no one could see that I was crying. Through a blur I could see the record on the table.

I'll never be able to explain, not even to myself, just how it happened, but, with a sob of "No! No!" I grabbed the record from off the table and slammed it onto the floor, breaking it into a thousand pieces.

Everything in the room stopped dead-still where it was. Giovanni's hands hovered above Beppe's shoulders, where they were about to grab and shake him good. Papa's face had an expression of sorrow and joy and relief all at once as he took my hand. Mamma broke the silence sobbing and saying over and over in Italian, "Good son!" The others just stood staring at me in disbelief.

Mr. Kamp finally grabbed his hat and left, muttering to himself, "Crazy as loons, all of them!"

I ran into the kitchen, no longer able to control my sobs. The others followed, all except Beppe, and they were crying and hugging me and saying I had done the right thing, that it was the only way to bring them to their senses. Papa, his arm around my shoulder, assured me, "This is a family again, and nothing else matters.".

Mamma began pouring wine and passing it around, stopping only to brush away a tear from time to time; she was smiling for the first time in two weeks.

We became conscious of the sound of music drifting in from the parlor. A few seconds later Beppe appeared at the kitchen door. "Listen," he said.

We could hardly believe our ears. It was *"Celeste Aïda!"*

Beppe grinned at me. "I guess we'll have to get a new 'Vesti la giubba,'" he said. "It seems like our old one got broken somehow."

In my rush I had grabbed the wrong record from off the table!

"Celeste Aïda" never sounded so beautiful as it did then. We listened as though for the first time. When it was over and Caruso called out, *"En, Pasqualino, cumme stai?"* Papa answered, "Happy again, my friend, very happy." He spoke for all of us. . . .

Well, that's all there is. We're a family again and still have the record. Maybe someday we'll save enough money to move to that farm in Jersey. Right now it's just something nice to dream about.

The Sunday evenings are once again as before, except that Angelina has married Dick, and now he also is with us every Sunday. Maybe sometime you would like to come hear the record with us, too. Caruso never sang *"Celeste Aïda"* better, and we all still get a big kick out of *"Eh, Pasqualino, cumme stai?"* at the very end.

Understanding Literature

1. Which character tells the story? Why did the author choose this character to tell the story?
2. What kind of job does Papa have so that he can hear music all day? How does this job benefit the Espositos in their Sunday evening music sessions?
3. Describe the scene between Papa and Enrico Caruso at the recording studio. Why is this scene necessary to the story?
4. What is the major conflict in the story?
5. You can often tell what people are like by the kinds of things they desire. What do the various members of the Esposito family want to buy with the money? What do their plans show about their characters?
6. The record has become a part of the lives of the Esposito family. George compares the record with other things which are just naturally a part of their lives. What are they?
7. Why does George break the record? Why is the discovery of the undamaged record important to the conclusion of the story? How would the conclusion be different if the broken record had been "*Celeste Aïda*"? Would that ending be more satisfying? Why?
8. What idea does the record stand for?

Further Activity

Perhaps there is a special ceremony or tradition which is important to your family. Or maybe there is a piece of jewelry, a photograph, a book, or some other item which your family is particularly proud of or fond of. In two or three carefully planned paragraphs, tell about this tradition or item. The first paragraph should describe it. The second paragraph should probably give the background of the tradition or item, and the third paragraph could show in what ways it is precious to your family. Give your paper a title that is fitting and interesting. Be sure to proofread your paper before it is handed in. Is the spelling perfect? Are you satisfied with the punctuation? Have you used the exact word you wanted for each description?

Focusing on Words

Because the Esposito children love music, they would be able to explain the meaning of these words. With the aid of the glossary for those you do not know, define: *opera, symphony, aria, tenor, quartet.*

The loyal friendship of a person whom we love and admire is precious to all of us. We all need someone whom we can count on. This story takes us back to the early 18th century, when one of America's frontiers was the Connecticut River where it passes through Massachusetts. Frequent Indian raids made the settlers believe that all Indians were bad. Louisa May Alcott, who also wrote *Little Women* and *Little Men*, here poses the problem of whether an Indian boy can justify the faith a frontier family places in him.

Onawandah

Louisa May Alcott

IMPROVING YOUR READING: This story is based largely on *conflict*. People have problems and either solve them or not. Conflict is what makes a story; you read to find out how the problem gets solved. If you do not become interested in the problem, or conflict, you may not like the story. The main conflict in this story comes from the fact that people do not understand the character of Onawandah.

LONG AGO, WHEN hostile Indians haunted the great forests, and every settlement had its fort for the protection of the inhabitants, in one of the towns on the Connecticut River lived Parson Bain and his little son and daughter. The wife and mother was dead; but an old servant took care of them, and did her best to make Reuben and Eunice good children. Her direst[1] threat, when they were naughty, was, "The Indians will come and fetch you, if you don't behave." So they grew up in great fear of the red men. Even the friendly Indians, who sometimes came for food or powder, were regarded with suspicion by the people. No man went to work without his gun nearby. On Sundays, when they trudged to the rude meeting house, all carried the trusty rifle on the shoulder, and while the pastor preached, a sentinel mounted guard at the door, to give warning if canoes came down the river or a dark face peered from the wood.

One autumn night, when the first heavy rains were falling and a cold wind whistled through the valley, a knock came at the minister's door and, opening it, he found an Indian boy, ragged, hungry, and footsore, who begged for food and shelter. In his broken way, he told how he had fallen ill and been left to die by enemies who had taken him from his own people, months before; how he had wandered for days till almost sinking; and that he had come now to ask for help, led by the hospitable light in the parsonage window.

1 direst: most terrible.

LOUISA MAY ALCOTT

81

"Send him away, Master, or harm will come of it. He is a spy, and we shall all be scalped by the murdering Injuns who are waiting in the wood," said old Becky, harshly; while little Eunice hid in the old servant's ample skirts, and twelve-year-old Reuben laid his hand on his crossbow, ready to defend his sister if need be.

But the good man drew the poor lad in, saying, with his friendly smile: "Shall not a Christian be as hospitable as a godless savage? Come in, child, and be fed; you sorely need rest and shelter."

Leaving his face to express the gratitude he had no words to tell, the boy sat by the comfortable fire and ate like a famished wolf, while Becky muttered her forebodings[2] and the children eyed the dark youth at a safe distance. Something in his pinched face, wounded foot, and eyes full of dumb pain and patience, touched the little girl's tender heart, and, yielding to a pitiful impulse, she brought her own basin of new milk and, setting it beside the stranger, ran to hide behind her father, suddenly remembering that this was one of the dreaded Indians.

"That was well done, little daughter. Thou shalt love thine enemies, and share thy bread with the needy. See, he is smiling; that pleased him, and he wishes us to be his friends."

But Eunice ventured no more that night, and quaked in her little bed at the thought of the strange boy sleeping on a blanket before the fire below. Reuben hid his fears better, and resolved to watch while others slept; but was off as soon as his curly head touched the pillow, and dreamed of tomahawks and war whoops till morning.

Next day, neighbors came to see the waif, and one and all advised sending him away as soon as possible, since he was doubtless a spy, as Becky said, and would bring trouble of some sort.

"When he is well, he may go whithersoever he will; but while he is too lame to walk, weak with hunger, and worn out with weariness, I will harbor him. He cannot feign[3] suffering and starvation like this. I shall do my duty, and leave the consequences to the Lord," answered the parson, with such pious firmness that the neighbors said no more.

But they kept a close watch upon Onawandah, when he went among them, silent and submissive,[4] but with the proud air of a captive prince, and sometimes a fierce flash in his black eyes when the other lads taunted him with his red skin. He was very lame for weeks, and could only sit in the sun, weaving pretty baskets for Eunice, and shaping bows and arrows for Reuben. The children were soon his friends, for with them he was always gentle, trying in his soft language and expressive gestures to show his good will and gratitude; for they defended him against their ruder playmates, and, following their father's example, trusted and cherished the homeless youth.

When he was able to walk, he

---

2 **forebodings:** forewarnings.

3 **feign** (fān): pretend.
4 **submissive:** meek.

CHARACTERIZATION

taught the boy to shoot and trap the wild creatures of the wood, to find fish where others failed, and to guide himself in the wilderness by star and sun, wind and water. To Eunice he brought little offerings of bark and feathers; taught her to make moccasins of skin, belts of shells, or pouches gay with porcupine quills and colored grass. He would not work for old Becky—who plainly showed her distrust—saying: "A brave does not grind corn and bring wood; that is squaw's work. Onawandah will hunt and fish and fight for you, but no more." And even the request of the parson could not win obedience in this, though the boy would have died for the good man.

"We cannot tame an eagle as we can a barnyard fowl. Let him remember only kindness of us, and so we turn a foe into a friend," said Parson Bain, stroking the sleek, dark head, that always bowed before him, with a docile reverence[5] shown to no other living creature.

Winter came, and the settlers fared hardly through the long months, when the drifts rose to the eaves of their low cabins, and the stores, carefully harvested, failed to supply even their simple wants. But the minister's family never lacked wild meat, for Onawandah proved himself a better hunter than any man in the town, and the boy of sixteen led the way on his snowshoes when they went to track a bear to its den, chase the deer for miles, or shoot the wolves that howled about their homes in the winter nights.

5 **docile reverence:** obedient respect.

But he never joined in their games, and sat apart when the young folk made merry, as if he scorned such childish pastimes and longed to be a man in all things. Why he stayed when he was well again, no one could tell, unless he waited for spring to make his way to his own people. But Reuben and Eunice rejoiced to keep him; for while he taught them many things, he was their pupil also, learning English rapidly, and proving himself a very affectionate and devoted friend and servant, in his own quiet way.

"Be of good cheer, little daughter; I shall be gone but three days, and our brave Onawandah will guard you well," said the parson, one April morning, as he mounted his horse to visit a distant settlement, where the bitter winter had brought sickness and death to more than one household.

The boy showed his white teeth in a bright smile as he stood beside the children, while Becky croaked, with a shake of the head:

"I hope you mayn't find you've warmed a viper in your bosom, Master."

Two days later, it seemed as if Becky was a true prophet, and that the confiding minister *had* been terribly deceived; for Onawandah went away to hunt, and, that night, the awful war whoop woke the sleeping villagers to find their houses burning, while the hidden Indians shot at them by the light of the fires kindled by dusky scouts. In terror and confusion the whites flew to the fort; and, while the men fought bravely, the

women held blankets to catch arrows and bullets, or bound up the hurts of their defenders.

It was all over by daylight, and the red men sped away up the river, with several prisoners, and such booty as they could plunder from the deserted houses. Not till all fear of a return of their enemies was over, did the poor people venture to leave the fort and seek their ruined homes. Then it was discovered that Becky and the parson's children were gone, and great was the bewailing, for the good man was much beloved by all his flock.

Suddenly the smothered voice of Becky was heard by a party of visitors, calling dolefully:

"I am here, betwixt the beds. Pull me out, neighbors, for I am half dead with fright and smothering."

The old woman was quickly extricated[6] from her hiding place, and with much energy declared that she had seen Onawandah, disguised with war paint, among the Indians, and that he had torn away the children from her arms before she could fly from the house.

"He chose his time well, when they were defenseless, dear lambs! Spite of all my warnings, Master trusted him, and this is the thanks we get. Oh, my poor Master! How can I tell him this heavy news?"

There was no need to tell it; for, as Becky sat moaning and beating her breast on the fireless hearth, and the sympathizing neighbors stood about her, the sound of a horse's hoofs was heard, and the parson came down the

6 extricated: freed.

84   CHARACTERIZATION

hilly road like one riding for his life. He had seen the smoke afar off, guessed the sad truth, and hurried on, to find his home in ruins and to learn by his first glance at the faces around him that his children were gone.

When he had heard all there was to tell, he sat down upon his doorstone with his head in his hands, praying for strength to bear a grief too deep for words. The wounded and weary men tried to comfort him with hope, and the women wept with him as they hugged their own babies closer to the hearts that ached for the lost children. Suddenly a stir went through the mournful group, as Onawandah came from the wood with a young deer upon his shoulders, and amazement in his face as he saw the desolation before him. Dropping his burden, he stood an instant looking with eyes that kindled fiercely; then he came bounding toward them, undaunted by the hatred, suspicion, and surprise plainly written on the countenances[7] before him. He missed his playmates, and asked but one question:

"The boy? the little squaw?—where gone?"

His answer was a rough one, for the men seized him and poured forth the tale, heaping reproaches[8] upon him for such treachery and ingratitude. He bore it all in proud silence till they pointed to the poor father whose dumb sorrow was more eloquent than all their wrath. Onawandah looked at him, and the fire died

out of his eyes as if quenched by the tears he would not shed. Shaking off the hands that held him, he went to his good friend, saying with passionate earnestness:

"Onawandah is *not* traitor! Onawandah remembers. Onawandah grateful! You believe?"

The poor parson looked up at him, and could not doubt his truth; for genuine love and sorrow ennobled the dark face, and he had never known the boy to lie.

"I believe and trust you still, but others will not. Go, you are no longer safe here, and I have no home to offer you," said the parson, sadly, feeling that he cared for none, unless his children were restored to him.

"Onawandah has no fear. He goes; but he comes again to bring the boy, the little squaw."

Few words, but they were so solemnly spoken that the most unbelieving were impressed; for the youth laid one hand on the gray head bowed before him, and lifted the other toward heaven, as if calling the Great Spirit to hear his vow.

A relenting murmur went through the crowd, but the boy paid no heed, as he turned away, and with no arms but his hunting knife and bow, no food but such as he could find, no guide but the sun by day, the stars by night, plunged into the pathless forest and was gone.

Then the people drew a long breath, and muttered to one another:

"He will never do it, yet he is a brave lad for his years."

"Only a shift to get off with a whole skin, I warrant you. These varlets

7 **countenances:** faces.
8 **reproaches:** accusations.

are as cunning as foxes," added Becky, sourly.

The parson alone believed and hoped, though weeks and months went by, and his children did not come.

Meantime, Reuben and Eunice were far away in an Indian camp, resting as best they could, after the long journey that followed that dreadful night. Their captors were not cruel to them, for Reuben was a stout fellow and, thanks to Onawandah, could hold his own with the boys who would have tormented him if he had been feeble or cowardly. Eunice also was a hardy creature for her years, and when her first fright and fatigue were over, made herself useful in many ways among the squaws, who did not let the pretty child suffer greatly; though she was neglected, because they knew no better.

Life in a wigwam was not a life of ease, and fortunately the children were accustomed to simple habits and the hardships that all endured in those early times. But they mourned for home till their young faces were pathetic with the longing, and their pillows of dry leaves were often wet with tears in the night. Their clothes grew ragged, their hair unkempt, their faces tanned by sun and wind. Scanty food and exposure to all weathers tried the strength of their bodies, and uncertainty as to their fate saddened their spirits; yet they bore up bravely, and said their prayers faithfully, feeling sure that God would bring them home to father in His own good time.

One day, when Reuben was snaring birds in the wood—for the Indians had no fear of such young children venturing to escape—he heard the cry of a quail, and followed it deeper and deeper into the forest, till it ceased, and, with a sudden rustle, Onawandah rose up from the brakes,[9] his finger on his lips to prevent any exclamation that might betray him to other ears and eyes.

"I come for you and little Laraka," (the name he gave Eunice, meaning "Wild Rose"). "I take you home. Not know me yet. Go and wait."

He spoke low and fast; but the joy in his face told how glad he was to find the boy after his long search, and Reuben clung to him, trying not to disgrace himself by crying like a girl, in his surprise and delight.

Lying hidden in the tall brakes they talked in whispers, while one told of the capture, and the other of a plan of escape; for, though a friendly tribe, these Indians were not Onawandah's people, and they must not suspect that he knew the children, else they might be separated at once.

"Little squaw betray me. You watch her. Tell her not to cry out, not speak me any time. When I say come, we go—fast—in the night. Not ready yet."

These were the orders Reuben received, and, when he could compose himself, he went back to the wigwams, leaving his friend in the wood, while he told the good news to Eunice, and prepared her for the part she must play.

9 **brakes:** bushes.

CHARACTERIZATION

Fear had taught her self-control, and the poor child stood the test well, working off her relief and rapture by pounding corn in the stone mortar till her little hands were blistered, and her arms ached for hours afterward.

Not till the next day did Onawandah make his appearance, and then he came limping into the village, weary, lame, and half starved after his long wandering in the wilderness. He was kindly welcomed, and his story believed, for he told only the first part, and said nothing of his life among the white men. He hardly glanced at the children when they were pointed out to him by their captors, and scowled at poor Eunice, who forgot her part in her joy, and smiled as she met the dark eyes that till now had always looked kindly at her. A touch from Reuben warned her, and she was glad to hide her confusion by shaking her long hair over her face, as if afraid of the stranger.

Onawandah took no further notice of them, but seemed to be very lame with the old wound in his foot, which prevented his being obliged to hunt with the men. He was resting and slowly gathering strength for the hard task he had set himself, while he waited for a safe time to save the children. They understood, but the suspense proved too much for little Eunice, and she pined[10] with impatience to be gone. She lost appetite and color, and cast such appealing glances at Onawandah that he could not seem quite indifferent, and gave

10 **pined:** lost strength.

her a soft word now and then, or did such acts of kindness as he could perform unsuspected. When she lay awake at night thinking of home, a cricket would chirp outside the wigwam, and a hand slip in a leaf full of berries, or a bark-cup of fresh water for the feverish little mouth. Sometimes it was only a caress or a whisper of encouragement, that reassured the childish heart, and sent her to sleep with a comfortable sense of love and protection, like a sheltering wing over a motherless bird.

Reuben stood it better, and entered heartily into the excitement of the plot, for he had grown tall and strong in these trying months, and felt that he must prove himself a man to sustain and defend his sister. Quietly he put away each day a bit of dried meat, a handful of parched corn, or a well-sharpened arrowhead, as provision for the journey; while Onawandah seemed to be amusing himself with making moccasins and a little vest of deerskin for an Indian child about the age of Eunice.

At last, in the early autumn, all the men went off on the warpath, leaving only boys and women behind. Then Onawandah's eyes began to kindle, and Reuben's heart to beat fast, for both felt that their time for escape had come.

All was ready, and one moonless night the signal was given. A cricket chirped shrilly outside the tent where the children slept with one old squaw. A strong hand cut the skin beside their bed of fir boughs, and two trembling creatures crept out to follow the tall shadow that flitted noiselessly before them into the darkness of the wood. Not a broken twig, a careless step, or a whispered word betrayed them, and they vanished as swiftly and silently as hunted deer flying for their lives.

Till dawn they hurried on, Onawandah carrying Eunice, whose strength soon failed, and Reuben manfully shouldering the hatchet and the pouch of food. At sunrise they hid in a thicket by a spring and rested, while waiting for the friendly night to come again. Then they pushed on, and fear gave wings to their feet, so that by another morning they were far enough away to venture to travel more slowly and sleep at night.

If the children had learned to love and trust the Indian boy in happier times, they adored him now, and came to regard him as an earthly Providence, so faithful, brave, and tender was he; so forgetful of himself, so bent on saving them. He never seemed to sleep, ate the poorest morsels, or went without any food when provisions failed; let no danger daunt him, no hardship wring complaint from him; but went on through the wild forest, led by guides invisible to them, till they began to hope that home was near.

Twice he saved their lives. Once, when he went in search of food, leaving Reuben to guard his sister, the children, being very hungry, ignorantly ate some poisonous berries which looked like wild cherries, and were deliciously sweet. The boy generously gave most of them to Eunice, and soon was terror-stricken to see her grow pale and cold and deathly ill. Not knowing what to do, he could only rub her hands and call wildly for Onawandah.

The name echoed through the silent wood, and, though far away, the keen ear of the Indian heard it, his fleet feet brought him back in time, and his knowledge of wild roots and herbs made it possible to save the child when no other help was at hand.

"Make fire. Keep warm. I soon come," he said, after hearing the story and examining Eunice, who could only lift her eyes to him, full of childish confidence and patience.

Then he was off again, scouring the woods like a hound on the scent, searching everywhere for the precious little herb that would counteract the poison. Anyone watching him would have thought him crazy as he rushed hither and thither, tearing up the leaves, creeping on his hands and knees that it might not escape him, and when he found it, springing up with a cry that startled the birds, and carried hope to poor Reuben, who was trying to forget his own pain in his anxiety for Eunice, whom he thought dying.

"Eat, eat, while I make drink. All safe now," cried Onawandah, as he came leaping toward them with his hands full of green leaves, and his dark face shining with joy.

The boy was soon relieved, but for hours they hung over the girl, who suffered sadly, till she grew unconscious and lay as if dead. Reuben's courage failed then, and he cried bitterly, thinking how hard it would be

CHARACTERIZATION

to leave the dear little creature under the pines and go home alone to father. Even Onawandah lost hope for a while, and sat like a bronze statue of despair, with his eyes fixed on his Wild Rose, who seemed fading away too soon.

Suddenly he rose, stretched his arms to the west, where the sun was setting splendidly, and in his own musical language prayed to the Great Spirit. The Christian boy fell upon his knees, feeling that the only help was in the Father Who saw and heard them even in the wilderness. Both were comforted, and when they turned to Eunice there was a faint tinge of color on the pale cheeks, as if the evening red kissed her, the look of pain was gone, and she slept quietly without the moans that had made their hearts ache before.

"He hears! He hears!" cried Onawandah, and for the first time Reuben saw tears in his keen eyes, as the Indian boy turned his face to the sky full of a gratitude that no words were sweet enough to tell.

All night, Eunice lay peacefully sleeping, and the moon lighted Onawandah's lonely watch, for the boy Reuben was worn out with suspense, and slept beside his sister.

In the morning she was safe, and great was the rejoicing; but for two days the little invalid was not allowed to continue the journey, much as they longed to hurry on. It was a pretty sight, the bed of hemlock boughs spread under a green tent of woven branches, and on the pillow of moss the pale child watching the flicker of sunshine through the leaves, listening to the babble of a brook close by or sleeping tranquilly, lulled by the murmur of the pines. Patient, loving, and grateful, it was a pleasure to serve her, and both the lads were faithful nurses. Onawandah cooked birds for her to eat, and made a pleasant drink of the wild raspberry leaves to quench her thirst. Reuben snared rabbits, that she might have nourishing food, and longed to shoot a deer for provision, that she might not suffer hunger again on their journey. This boyish desire led him deeper in the wood than it was wise for him to go alone, for it was near nightfall, and wild creatures haunted the forest in those days. The fire, which Onawandah kept constantly burning, guarded their little camp where Eunice lay; but Reuben, with no weapon but his bow and hunting knife, was beyond this protection when he at last gave up his vain hunt and turned homeward. Suddenly, the sound of stealthy steps startled him, but he could see nothing through the dusk at first, and hurried on, fearing that some treacherous Indian was following him. Then he remembered his sister, and resolved not to betray her resting place if he could help it, for he had learned courage of Onawandah, and longed to be as brave and generous as his dusky hero.

So he paused to watch and wait, and soon saw the gleam of two fiery eyes, not behind, but above him, in a tree. Then he knew that it was an "Indian devil," as they called a species of fierce wildcat that lurked in the thickets and sprang on its prey like a small tiger.

"If I could only kill it alone, how proud Onawandah would be of me," thought Reuben, burning for the good opinion of his friend.

It would have been wiser to hurry on and give the beast no time to spring; but the boy was overbold, and, fitting an arrow to the string, aimed at the bright eyeball and let fly. A sharp snarl showed that some harm was done, and, rather daunted by the savage sound, Reuben raced away, meaning to come back next day for the prize he hoped he had secured.

But soon he heard the creature bounding after him, and he uttered one ringing shout for help, feeling too late that he had been foolhardy. Fortunately he was nearer camp than he thought. Onawandah heard him and was there in time to receive the wildcat, as, mad with the pain of the wound, it sprang at Reuben. There was no time for words, and the boy could only watch in breathless interest and anxiety the fight which went on between the brute and the Indian.

It was sharp but short, for Onawandah had his knife, and as soon as he could get the snarling, struggling beast down, he killed it with a skillful stroke. But not before it had torn and bitten him more dangerously than he knew; for the dusk hid the wounds, and excitement kept him from feeling them at first. Reuben thanked him heartily, and accepted his few words of warning with grateful docility;[11] then both hurried back to Eunice, who till next day knew nothing of her brother's danger.

11 **docility** (dŏ sĭl′ə tĭ): obedience.

CHARACTERIZATION

Onawandah made light of his scratches, as he called them, got their supper, and sent Reuben early to bed, for tomorrow they were to start again.

Excited by his adventure, the boy slept lightly, and waking in the night saw by the flicker of the fire Onawandah binding up a deep wound in his breast with wet moss and his own belt. A stifled groan betrayed how much he suffered; but when Reuben went to him, he would accept no help, said it was nothing, and sent him back to bed, preferring to endure the pain in stern silence, with true Indian pride and courage.

Next morning, they set out and pushed on as fast as Eunice's strength allowed. But it was evident that Onawandah suffered much, though he would not rest, forbade the children to speak of his wounds, and pressed on with feverish haste, as if he feared that his strength might not hold out. Reuben watched him anxiously, for there was a look in his face that troubled the boy and filled him with alarm, as well as with remorse and love. Eunice would not let him carry her as before, but trudged bravely behind him, though her feet ached and her breath often failed as she tried to keep up; and both children did all they could to comfort and sustain their friend, who seemed glad to give his life for them.

In three days they reached the river, and, as if Heaven helped them in their greatest need, found a canoe, left by some hunter, near the shore. In they sprang, and let the swift current bear them along, Eunice kneeling in the bow like a little figurehead of Hope, Reuben steering with his paddle, and Onawandah sitting with arms tightly folded over his breast, as if to control the sharp anguish of the neglected wound. He knew that it was past help now, and only cared to see the children safe; then, worn out but happy, he was proud to die, having paid his debt to the good parson, and proved that he was not a liar nor a traitor.

Hour after hour they floated down the great river, looking eagerly for signs of home, and when at last they entered the familiar valley, while the little girl cried for joy, and the boy paddled as he had never done before, Onawandah sat erect with his haggard eyes fixed on the dim distance, and sang his death-song in a clear, strong voice—though every breath was pain—bent on dying like a brave, without complaint or fear.

At last they saw the smoke from the cabins on the hillside and, hastily mooring the canoe, all sprang out, eager to be at home after their long and perilous wandering. But as his foot touched the land, Onawandah felt that he could do no more, and stretching his arms toward the parsonage, the windows of which glimmered as hospitably as they had done when he first saw them, he said, with a pathetic sort of triumph in his broken voice: "Go. I cannot. Tell the good father, Onawandah not lie, not forget. He keep his promise."

Then he dropped upon the grass and lay as if dead, while Reuben, bidding Eunice keep watch, ran as fast as his tired legs could carry him to tell the tale and bring help.

The little girl did her part tenderly, carrying water in her hands to wet the white lips, tearing up her ragged skirt to lay fresh bandages on the wound that had been bleeding the brave boy's life away, and, sitting by him, gathered his head into her arms, begging him to wait till Father came.

But poor Onawandah had waited too long; now he could only look up into the dear, loving, little face bent over him, and whisper wistfully: "Wild Rose will remember Onawandah?" as the light went out of his eyes, and his last breath was a smile for her.

When the parson and his people came hurrying up full of wonder, joy, and good will, they found Eunice weeping bitterly, and the Indian boy lying like a young warrior smiling at death.

"Ah, my neighbors, the savage has taught us a lesson we never can forget. Let us imitate his virtues, and do honor to his memory," said the pastor, as he held his little daughter close and looked down at the pathetic figure at his feet, whose silence was more eloquent than any words.

All felt it, and even old Becky had a remorseful sigh for the boy who had kept his word so well and given back her darlings safe.

They buried him where he lay; and for years the lonely mound under the great oak was kept green by loving hands. Wild roses bloomed there, and the murmur of the Long River of Pines was a fit lullaby for faithful Onawandah.

Understanding Literature

1. Since this is both an adventure story and one of character, the author presents conflict after conflict in a series of episodes. What is the main conflict in the story?

2. In the Bain household Becky is the only person who does not get along with Onawandah. Explain how both Becky and the Indian contribute to this unhappy relationship.

3. Parson Bain says of Onawandah, "We cannot tame an eagle as we can a barnyard fowl." What does he mean by this remark, and why does he say it? How did he "turn a foe into a friend"?

4. Becky's continued mistrust of the Indian is revealed in her unkind remarks about him. What does she mean when she says to Parson Bain, "I hope you mayn't find you've warmed a viper in your bosom, Master"?

5. In what ways are the characters of the children similar? In what ways are they dissimilar?

6. Do you find this an "old-fashioned" story? Why? Can you compare it to stories written today on similar subjects?

CHARACTERIZATION

Focusing on Words

Often you can understand a new or strange word by studying it in its *context*, that is, by the way it is used in a certain sentence. For example, the word *sentinel* may be unfamiliar to you, but if you saw it in the following sentence you could probably guess what it means by the way it is used: "While the pastor preached, a sentinel mounted guard at the door." You could probably tell that *sentinel* refers to a person, usually a soldier, who guards his fellow men from danger. In other cases, however, a word may have so many meanings that it would still be best to use a dictionary for those you are unsure of.

Try to define each of the following words by its use in the context of the sentence. If you still do not understand a word, look it up in the glossary.

1. ". . . yielding to a pitiful *impulse,* she brought her own basin of new milk. . . ."
2. "Two days later, it seemed as if . . . the confiding minister had been terribly *deceived.*"
3. ". . . though she was *neglected,* because they knew no better."
4. "Then he was off again . . . searching everywhere for the precious little herb that would *counteract* the poison."

Lincoln Steffens wanted only one thing for Christmas—a pony. He would not ask his parents for anything else. That Christmas morning when he waited to see if a pony would come was a morning never to be forgotten by the author.

A Miserable, Merry Christmas[*]

Lincoln Steffens

IMPROVING YOUR READING: A writer will frequently begin a story by introducing a character who wants something. The problem of whether or not he will get it becomes the basis of the tale. The reader's excitement, then, grows largely from this *suspense:* What will happen next?

MY FATHER's business seems to have been one of slow but steady growth. He and his local partner, Llewelen Tozer, had no vices. They were devoted to their families and to "the store," which grew with the town, which, in turn, grew and changed with the State from a gambling, mining, and ranching community to one of farming, fruit raising, and building. Immigration poured in, not gold-seekers now, but farmers, businessmen and home builders, who settled, planted, reaped, and traded in the natural riches of the State, which prospered greatly, "making" the people who will tell you that they "made the State."

As the store made money and I was getting through the primary school, my father bought a lot uptown, at Sixteenth and K Streets, and built us a "big" house. It was off the line of the city's growth, but it was near a new grammar school for me and my sisters, who were coming along fast after me. This interested the family, not me. They were always talking about school; they had not had much of it themselves, and they thought they had missed something. My father used to write speeches, my mother verses, and their theory seems to have been that they had talents which a school would have brought to flower. They agreed, therefore, that their children's gifts should have all the schooling there was. My view, then, was that I had had a good deal of it already, and I was not interested at all. It interfered with my own business, with my own education.

And indeed I remember very little

* From THE AUTOBIOGRAPHY OF LINCOLN STEFFENS, copyright, 1931, by Harcourt, Brace & World, Inc.; renewed © 1959, by Peter Steffens. Reprinted by permission of Harcourt, Brace & World, Inc.

CHARACTERIZATION

of the primary school. I learned to read, write, spell, and count, and reading was all right. I had a practical use for books, which I searched for ideas and parts to play with, characters to be, lives to live. The primary school was probably a good one, but I cannot remember learning anything except to read aloud "perfectly" from a teacher whom I adored and who was fond of me. She used to embrace me before the whole class and she favored me openly to the scandal of the other pupils, who called me "teacher's pet." Their scorn did not trouble me; I saw and I said that they envied me. I paid for her favor, however. When she married I had queer, unhappy feelings of resentment; I didn't want to meet her husband, and when I had to I wouldn't speak to him. He laughed, and she kissed me—happily for her, to me offensively. I never would see her again. Through with her, I fell in love immediately with Miss Kay, another grown young woman who wore glasses and had a fine, clear skin. I did not know her, I only saw her in the street, but once I followed her, found out where she lived, and used to pass her house, hoping to see her, and yet choking with embarrassment if I did. This fascination lasted for years; it was still a sort of super-romance to me when later I was "going with" another girl nearer my own age.

What interested me in our new neighborhood was not the school, nor the room I was to have in the house all to myself, but the stable which was built back of the house. My father let me direct the making of a stall, a little smaller than the other stalls, for my pony, and I prayed and hoped my sister Lou believed that that meant that I would get the pony, perhaps for Christmas. I pointed out to her that there were three other stalls and no horses at all. This I said in order that she should answer it. She could not. My father, sounded, said that someday we might have horses and a cow; meanwhile a stable added to the value of a house. "Someday" is a pain to a boy who lives in and knows only "now." My good little sisters, to comfort me, remarked that Christmas was coming, but Christmas was always coming and grownups were always talking about it, asking you what you wanted and then giving you what they wanted you to have. Though everybody knew what I wanted, I told them all again. My mother knew that I told God, too, every night. I wanted a pony, and to make sure that they understood, I declared that I wanted nothing else.

"Nothing but a pony?" my father asked.

"Nothing," I said.

"Not even a pair of high boots?"

That was hard. I did want boots, but I stuck to the pony. "No, not even boots."

"Nor candy? There ought to be something to fill your stocking with, and Santa Claus can't put a pony into a stocking."

That was true, and he couldn't lead a pony down the chimney either. But no. "All I want is a pony," I said. "If I can't have

a pony, give me nothing, nothing."

Now I had been looking myself for the pony I wanted, going to sales stables, inquiring of horsemen, and I had seen several that would do. My father let me "try" them. I tried so many ponies that I was learning fast to sit a horse. I chose several, but my father always found some fault with them. I was in despair. When Christmas was at hand I had given up all hope of a pony, and on Christmas Eve I hung up my stocking along with my sisters', of whom, by the way, I now had three. I haven't mentioned them or their coming because, you understand, they were girls, and girls, young girls, counted for nothing in my manly life. They did not mind me either; they were so happy that Christmas Eve that I caught some of their merriment. I speculated on[1] what I'd get; I hung up the biggest stocking I had, and we all went reluctantly to bed to wait till morning. Not to sleep; not right away. We were told that we must not only sleep promptly, we must not wake up till seven-thirty the next morning—or if we did, we must not go to the fireplace for our Christmas. Impossible.

We did sleep that night, but we woke up at six A.M. We lay in our beds and debated through the open doors whether to obey till, say, half-past six. Then we bolted. I don't know who started it, but there was a rush. We all disobeyed; we raced to disobey and get first to the fireplace in the front room downstairs. And

1 **speculated on:** thought about.

CHARACTERIZATION

there they were, the gifts, all sorts of wonderful things, mixed-up piles of presents; only, as I disentangled the mess, I saw that my stocking was empty; it hung limp; not a thing in it; and under and around it—nothing. My sisters had knelt down, each by her pile of gifts; they were squealing with delight, till they looked up and saw me standing there in my night-gown with nothing. They left their piles to come to me and look with me at my empty place. Nothing. They felt my stocking: nothing.

I don't remember whether I cried at that moment, but my sisters did. They ran with me back to my bed, and there we all cried till I became indignant. That helped some. I got up, dressed, and driving my sisters away, I went alone out into the yard, down to the stable, and there, all by myself, I wept. My mother came out to me by and by; she found me in my pony stall, sobbing on the floor, and she tried to comfort me. But I heard my father outside; he had come part way with her, and she was having some sort of angry quarrel with him. She tried to comfort me; besought me to come to breakfast. I could not; I wanted no comfort and no breakfast. She left me and went on into the house with sharp words for my father.

I don't know what kind of a breakfast the family had. My sisters said it was "awful." They were ashamed to enjoy their own toys. They came to me, and I was rude. I ran away from them. I went around to the front of the house, sat down on the steps, and, the crying over, I ached.

I was wronged, I was hurt—I can feel now what I felt then, and I am sure that if one could see the wounds upon our hearts, there would be found still upon mine a scar from that terrible Christmas morning. And my father, the practical joker, he must have been hurt, too, a little. I saw him looking out of the window. He was watching me or something for an hour or two, drawing back the curtain ever so little lest I catch him, but I saw his face, and I think I can see now the anxiety upon it, the worried impatience.

After—I don't know how long— surely an hour or two—I was brought to the climax of my agony by the sight of a man riding a pony down the street, a pony and a brand-new saddle; the most beautiful saddle I ever saw, and it was a boy's saddle; the man's feet were not in the stirrups; his legs were too long. The outfit was perfect; it was the realization of all my dreams, the answer to all my prayers. A fine new bridle, with a light curb bit. And the pony! As he drew near, I saw that the pony was really a small horse, what we called an Indian pony, a bay, with black mane and tail, and one white foot and a white star on his forehead. For such a horse as that I would have given, I could have forgiven, anything.

But the man, a disheveled[2] fellow with a blackened eye and a fresh-cut face, came along, reading the numbers on the houses, and, as my hopes —my impossible hopes—rose, he

2 disheveled: untidy.

looked at our door and passed by, he and the pony, and the saddle and the bridle. Too much. I fell upon the steps, and having wept before, I broke now into such a flood of tears that I was a floating wreck when I heard a voice.

"Say, kid," it said, "do you know a boy named Lennie Steffens?"

I looked up. It was the man on the pony, back again, at our horse block.

"Yes," I spluttered through my tears. "That's me."

"Well," he said, "then this is your horse. I've been looking all over for you and your house. Why don't you put your number where it can be seen?"

"Get down," I said, running out to him.

He went on saying something about "ought to have got here at seven o'clock; told me to bring the nag here and tie him to your post and leave him for you. But I got into a drunk —and a fight—and a hospital, and—"

"Get down," I said.

He got down, and he boosted me up to the saddle. He offered to fit the stirrups to me, but I didn't want him to. I wanted to ride.

"What's the matter with you?" he said, angrily. "What you crying for? Don't you like the horse? He's a dandy, this horse. I know him of old. He's fine at cattle; he'll drive 'em alone."

I hardly heard, I could scarcely wait, but he persisted. He adjusted the stirrups, and then, finally, off I rode, slowly, at a walk, so happy, so thrilled, that I did not know what I was doing. I did not look back at

the house or the man, I rode off up the street, taking note of everything —of the reins, of the pony's long mane, of the carved leather saddle. I had never seen anything so beautiful. And mine! I was going to ride up past Miss Kay's house. But I noticed on the horn of the saddle some stains like raindrops, so I turned and trotted home, not to the house but to the stable. There was the family, father, mother, sisters, all working for me, all happy. They had been putting in place the tools of my new business: blankets, currycomb, brush, pitchfork—everything, and there was hay in the loft.

"What did you come back so soon for?" somebody asked. "Why didn't you go on riding?"

I pointed to the stains. "I wasn't going to get my new saddle rained on," I said. And my father laughed. "It isn't raining," he said. "Those are not raindrops."

"They are tears," my mother gasped, and she gave my father a look which sent him off to the house. Worse still, my mother offered to wipe away the tears still running out of my eyes. I gave her such a look as she had given him, and she went off after my father, drying her own tears. My sisters remained and we all unsaddled the pony, put on his halter, led him to his stall, tied and fed him. It began really to rain; so all the rest of that memorable day we curried[3] and combed that pony. The girls plaited[4] his mane, forelock, and

3 **curried:** cleaned the hair with a metal-toothed comb.
4 **plaited:** braided.

tail, while I pitchforked hay to him and curried and brushed, curried and brushed. For a change we brought him out to drink; we led him up and down, blanketed like a race horse; we took turns at that. But the best, the most inexhaustible fun, was to clean him. When we went reluctantly to our midday Christmas dinner, we all smelt of horse, and my sisters had to wash their faces and hands. I was asked to, but I wouldn't, till my mother bade[5] me look in the mirror. Then I washed up—quick. My face was caked with the muddy lines of tears that had coursed over my cheeks to my mouth. Having washed away that shame, I ate my dinner, and as I ate I grew hungrier and hungrier. It was my first meal that day, and as I filled up on the tur-key and the stuffing, the cranberries and the pies, the fruit and the nuts—as I swelled, I could laugh. My mother said I still choked and sobbed now and then, but I laughed, too; I saw and enjoyed my sisters' presents till—I had to go out and attend to my pony, who was there, really and truly there, the promise, the beginning, of a happy double life. And—I went and looked to make sure—there was the saddle, too, and the bridle.

But that Christmas, which my father had planned so carefully, was it the best or the worst I ever knew? He often asked me that; I never could answer as a boy. I think now that it was both. It covered the whole distance from broken-hearted misery to bursting happiness—too fast. A grownup could hardly have stood it.

5 **bade** (băd): ordered.

Understanding Literature

1. Why is "A Miserable, Merry Christmas" a good title for the story?
2. The story of the pony begins with the fourth paragraph. What is the purpose of the first three paragraphs?
3. Because of the author's writing skill, you feel that you almost know Lennie personally. What kind of person is he? Find places in the story which help you describe him. What does he mean by saying that schooling interfered "with my own education"?
4. Explain what is meant in the next-to-the-last paragraph by "the promise, the beginning, of a happy double life."
5. Lennie's mother, father, and sisters are all secondary, or less important, characters in the story. In what ways do they add to the interest of "A Miserable, Merry Christmas"?

6. What is the climax of the story? At what point do you foresee the ending?
7. Reread the last paragraph. Why does the author conclude with the statement that "A grownup could hardly have stood it"?

Further Activity

Prepare a paper (or a talk) on some event in your life which you will always remember. In order to capture and keep the interest of your audience, try to build up suspense. You might do this by making the outcome of your story very uncertain, as Lincoln Steffens did in his story, or by making the outcome of the story very clear but making your audience wonder *when* the final event will occur. Avoid the often-used means of causing suspense: squeaking doors, groans in the distance, and the like. Try instead to write or talk about things that really happened to you in which suspense played an important part.

In this chapter from *Dandelion Wine,* the author presents a sketch of a woman: he tells you what she did with her life and how she influenced the lives of others.

Good-by, Grandma

Ray Bradbury

IMPROVING YOUR READING: An author must make it clear whose story he is telling. Here Ray Bradbury keeps the focus on Great-grandma. The other people are represented only by what they say; you do not see them. This story is filled with *images,* pictures of things you can sense. This is another way of characterizing a person. When you finish reading and adding up the images, you have a clear picture of Great-grandma. It is as though you were scanning the snapshots in an album. They tell you much about the person who kept them.

SHE WAS A woman with a broom or a dustpan or a washrag or a mixing spoon in her hand. You saw her cutting piecrust in the morning, humming to it, or you saw her setting out the baked pies at noon or taking them in, cool, at dusk. She rang porcelain cups like a Swiss bell ringer, to their place. She glided through the halls as steadily as a vacuum machine, seeking, finding, and setting to rights. She made mirrors of every window, to catch the sun. She strolled but twice through any garden, trowel[1] in hand, and the flowers raised their quivering fires upon the warm air in her wake. She slept quietly and turned no more than three times in a night, as relaxed as a white glove to which, at dawn, a brisk hand will return. Waking, she touched people like pictures, to set their frames straight.

1 **trowel:** a tool for digging up small plants.

But, now . . . ?

"Grandma," said everyone. "Great-grandma."

Now it was as if a huge sum in arithmetic were finally drawing to an end. She had stuffed turkeys, chickens, squabs, gentlemen, and boys. She had washed ceilings, walls, invalids, and children. She had laid linoleum, repaired bicycles, wound clocks, stoked furnaces, swabbed iodine on ten thousand grievous wounds. Her hands had flown all around about and down, gentling this, holding that, throwing baseballs, swinging bright croquet mallets, seeding black earth, or fixing covers over dumplings, ragouts, and children wildly strewn by slumber. She had pulled down shades, pinched out candles, turned switches, and—grown old. Looking back on thirty billions of things started, carried, finished and done, it all summed up, totaled out; the last decimal was placed, the final zero swung slowly into line. Now, chalk in hand, she stood back from life a silent hour before reaching for the eraser.

"Let me see now," said Great-grandma. "Let me see . . ."

With no fuss or further ado, she traveled the house in an ever-circling inventory, reached the stairs at last, and, making no special announcement, she took herself up three flights to her room where, silently, she laid herself out like a fossil imprint under the snowing cool sheets of her bed and began to die.

Again the voices:

"Grandma! Great-grandma!"

The rumor of what she was doing dropped down the stair well, hit, and spread ripples through the rooms, out doors and windows and along the street of elms to the edge of the green ravine.

"Here now, here!"

The family surrounded her bed.

"Just let me lie," she whispered.

Her ailment could not be seen in any microscope; it was a mild but ever-deepening tiredness, a dim weighting of her sparrow body; sleepy, sleepier, sleepiest.

As for her children and her children's children—it seemed impossible that with such a simple act, the most leisurely act in the world, she could cause such apprehension.[2]

"Great-grandma, now listen—what you're doing is no better than breaking a lease. This house will fall down without you. You must give us at least a year's notice!"

Great-grandma opened one eye. Ninety years gazed calmly out at her physicians like a dust-ghost from a high cupola[3] window in a fast-emptying house. "Tom . . . ?"

The boy was sent, alone, to her whispering bed.

"Tom," she said, faintly, far away, "in the Southern Seas there's a day in each man's life when he knows it's time to shake hands with all his friends and say good-by and sail away, and he does, and it's natural—it's just his time. That's how it is today. I'm so like you sometimes, sitting through Saturday matinees until nine at night when we send your dad to bring you home. Tom, when the time comes that the same cowboys are shooting the same Indians on the same mountaintop, then it's best to fold back the seat and head for the door, with no regrets and no walking backward up the aisle. So, I'm leaving while I'm still happy and still entertained."

Douglas was summoned next to her side.

"Grandma, who'll shingle the roof next spring?"

Every April for as far back as there were calendars, you thought you heard woodpeckers tapping the housetop. But no, it was Great-grandma somehow transported, singing, pounding nails, replacing shingles, high in the sky!

"Douglas," she whispered, "don't ever let anyone do the shingles unless it's fun for them."

"Yes'm."

---

2 **apprehension:** fear.

3 **cupola:** small structure built on the top of a building.

CHARACTERIZATION

"Look around come April, and say, 'Who'd like to fix the roof?' And whichever face lights up is the face you want, Douglas. Because up there on that roof you can see the whole town going toward the country and the country going toward the edge of the earth and the river shining, and the morning lake, and birds on the trees down under you, and the best of the wind all around above. Any one of those should be enough to make a person climb a weather vane some spring sunrise. It's a powerful hour, if you give it half a chance. . . ."

Her voice sank to a soft flutter.

Douglas was crying.

She roused herself again. "Now, why are you doing that?"

"Because," he said, "you won't be here tomorrow."

She turned a small hand mirror from herself to the boy. He looked at her face and himself in the mirror and then at her face again as she said, "Tomorrow morning I'll get up at seven and wash behind my ears; I'll run to church with Charlie Woodman; I'll picnic at Electric Park; I'll swim, run barefoot, fall out of trees, chew spearmint gum . . . Douglas, Douglas, for shame! You cut your fingernails, don't you?"

"Yes'm."

"And you don't yell when your body makes itself over every seven years or so, old cells dead and new ones added to your fingers and your heart. You don't mind that, do you?"

"No'm."

"Well, consider then, boy. Any man saves fingernail clippings is a fool. You ever see a snake bother to keep his peeled skin? That's about all you got here today in this bed is fingernails and snake skin. One good breath would send me up in flakes. Important thing is not the me that's lying here, but the me that's sitting on the edge of the bed looking back at me, and the me that's downstairs cooking supper, or out in the garage under the car, or in the library reading. All the new parts, they count. I'm not really dying today. No person ever died that had a family. I'll be around a long time. A thousand years from now a whole township of my offspring will be biting sour apples in the gumwood shade. That's my answer to anyone asks big questions! Quick now, send in the rest!"

At last the entire family stood, like people seeing someone off at the rail station, waiting in the room.

"Well," said Great-grandma, "there I am. I'm not humble, so it's nice seeing you standing around my bed. Now next week there's late gardening and closet-cleaning and clothes-buying for the children to do. And since that part of me which is called, for convenience, Great-grandma, won't be here to step it along, those other parts of me called Uncle Bert and Leo and Tom and Douglas, and all the other names, will have to take over, each to his own."

"Yes, Grandma."

"I don't want any Halloween parties here tomorrow. Don't want anyone saying anything sweet about me; I said it all in my time and my pride. I've tasted every victual and danced every dance; now there's one last tart I haven't bit on, one tune I haven't whistled. But I'm not afraid. I'm truly curious. Death won't get a crumb by my mouth I won't keep and savor.[4] So don't you worry over me. Now, all of you go, and let me find my sleep. . . ."

Somewhere a door closed quietly.

"That's better." Alone, she snuggled luxuriously down through the warm snowbank of linen and wool, sheet and cover, and the colors of the patchwork quilt were bright as the circus banners of old time. Lying there, she felt as small and secret as on those mornings eighty-some-odd years ago when, wakening, she comforted her tender bones in bed.

A long time back, she thought, I dreamed a dream, and was enjoying it so much when someone wakened me, and that was the day when I was born. And now? Now, let me see . . . She cast her mind back. Where was I? she thought. Ninety years

4 savor: taste with pleasure.

. . . how to take up the thread and the pattern of that lost dream again? She put out a small hand. *There* . . . Yes, that was it. She smiled. Deeper in the warm snow hill she turned her head upon her pillow. That was better. Now, yes, now she saw it shaping in her mind quietly, and with a serenity like a sea moving along an endless and self-refreshing shore. Now she let the old dream touch and lift her from the snow and drift her above the scarce-remembered bed.

Downstairs, she thought, they are polishing the silver, and rummaging the cellar, and dusting in the halls. She could hear them living all through the house.

"It's all right," whispered Great-grandma, as the dream floated her. "Like everything else in this life, it's fitting."

And the sea moved her back down the shore.

Understanding Literature

1. The author tells much of the story through a series of images, quick pictures which suggest whole scenes. In how much detail can you describe Great-grandma's house?
2. What kind of person is Great-grandma? How does she spend her time? Find phrases in the story which prove your ideas.
3. The author uses many comparisons which make the images more vivid. Instead of telling you that the window is clean, he says, "She made mirrors of every window." Explain the following comparisons which appear in the first paragraph:
   (a) glided . . . as steadily as a vacuum machine.
   (b) flowers raised their quivering fires.
   (c) as relaxed as a white glove.
   (d) she touched people like pictures, to set their frames straight.

CHARACTERIZATION

Find and explain other comparisons in the story.

4. How does Great-grandma compare her "leaving" with Tom's seeing a movie?

5. Why does Great-grandma tell Douglas not to "let anyone do the shingles unless it's fun for them"?

6. What is Great-grandma's response to Douglas's statement, "you won't be here tomorrow"?

7. Great-grandma says, "I'm not really dying today. No person ever died that had a family." Explain what is meant by her statement.

8. What does Great-grandma mean when she says, "Like everything else in this life, it's fitting"?

9. Explain the comparison made in the last line of the story, "And the sea moved her back down the shore."

10. Does it seem realistic for a person to feel the way Great-grandma does about dying? Give reasons for your answer.

Further Activity

Write a paragraph describing Great-grandma's living room as you would imagine it. Select only details which would fit her character as you have seen it in this story. You would not, for example, expect Great-grandma to have expensive-looking, showy decorations in her room nor would you expect the room to be dusty and untidy. Think about Great-grandma's character and then describe a room which you think she would be comfortable in and which she would want in her own home.

In each family a person who is ill becomes special, someone to be given extra attention and love. In this chapter from her book, *A New England Girlhood*, Nancy Hale recalls an illness and unhappiness at school during a period in her girlhood.

You Never Know

Nancy Hale

IMPROVING YOUR READING: The *flashback* technique which Nancy Hale uses is one you have probably seen on television or in movies. The author begins the story in the present, "flashes back" to the past, and concludes the story in the present. This device allows you to see the character at different times in her life: as she *is* in the present, and as she *was* in the past.

As I LIE here, trying to get over this idiotic cold before the Hansons' party, my mind becomes restless and inattentive if I try to read; I set up a game of patience[1] on a tray and even then it is as though my mind's eye were focused on some other scene; until sometimes I give up altogether trying to distract myself and simply lie here, resting, and letting my thoughts wander about as they will in my childhood, in the time when I was kept out of school so much by colds. I suppose there is a connection: I haven't had a cold in years, and I suppose this one reminds me, now, of those days when I had so many.

My mother was always very particular about taking me out of school at the first hint of a cough or a sniffle. So inconsiderate to spread a cold around, she used to say; but also my mother was a great one for prevention; she had some terrible inner picture of complications ensuing on the common cold: the house suddenly lighted up at night, temperature's gone to 104, run for the doctor, where's the croup kettle?[2] I don't think I ever, during the period of which I speak, at least, had anything but the simplest sequence of sore throat, head cold, and the usual cough afterward.

I have no doubt but what I enjoyed staying at home, reading, and eating nice things, and not having to do anything. Any child jumps at the chance not to go to school; but my relief was a little deeper than that. This was the period when Geraldine Ames was riding high as a leader in our class, and she was the president of a club against me.

A child never knows quite why it

---

1 **game of patience:** form of the card game solitaire.

2 **croup kettle:** vaporizer for easing the breathing process during colds.

CHARACTERIZATION

is singled out as the one who is all wrong. There appear to be different reasons—in my case that my parents were painters instead of my father's being a stockbroker or banker, and that my dresses, which my mother made, had their waistlines up under my arms instead of around the hips—but the child knows inside that these are not enough. The real reason is cosmic:[3] the child is *wrong*, that's all, the herd have named her so and there is nothing, there never, never will be anything, to do about it. I would come into the varnished-oak gymnasium for prayers at the beginning of school in the morning, and Geraldine, tall and pretty with long black braids, would catch the cloth of my dress as I passed her on my way to my place and give it a tweak and whisper "Crazy . . ." with that scornful and yet abysmally beautiful smile.

I remember walking down to school in the morning, that winter, and coming to the patch in the road where it crossed the County Meadows, where the wind literally whistled across the flats and through the row of willows, and where, if the weather was zero, it was the coldest of all. It must have been January; I had on my brushed-wool cap-and-mittens set which I had been given for Christmas and which I had adored then and paraded before the mirror in, admiring its orange-and-green stripes, but which I took no further pleasure in since, one noontime after school, as I was coming down the stairs from the

classrooms to the cloakroom, I had found Geraldine and one of her devotees kicking my cap around. I stood rooted to the bottom stair, watching, my heart sick. "This yours?" Geraldine asked, picking it up and tossing it at me disdainfully. "Crazy kind of a cap." I wept when I got home that day, for the beauty that had gone out of my cap-and-mittens set, and for being in the wrong. When my father got home that night, my mother told him about it. "Buck up," he said to me. "You let them see that you're as good and better than they are. Stand up for good old you." But that was impossible; he did not understand. Geraldine was beautiful and in the right, and I was in the wrong.

That morning as I crossed the bitter windy County Meadows, school seemed to loom ahead of me like a heavy woe. The January gale went through my heather-mixture coat. Suddenly I felt a tickle in the roof of my mouth. I'm getting a cold, I thought. I hesitated for a moment, and then turned around to walk home again, obedient to my mother's dictum:[4] "Always tell me at the first suggestion of a cold." I walked back up the icy street, up the hill to my warm snug home and my bed and the books that stood arrayed on my white-painted bookshelves. I don't think there is any question but that I was running away.

My mother believed in light, nourishing food for colds: poached eggs, warm and consoling on a bed of soggy

---

3 **cosmic:** vast; enormous.   4 **dictum:** command.

toast; chicken broth; baked potatoes, like hot little stoves one could hold in both hands before opening them and spreading them with butter and sprinkling them with salt; milk toast —toasted white bread laid in a soup plate, salted, with hot milk poured over it; the butter from the toast rose and floated, yellow puddles, on the white surface; cream of wheat—and as I put the cream and sugar on I would remember the game my father used to play with me when I was tiny: Once upon a time there was an island; and then white rain came, and rained and rained until it covered the island almost all up; and then it snowed, and snowed and snowed. . . .

When I stopped sneezing, and my mother could persuade herself that I was not going to develop pneumonia this time, I would sometimes leave my bed, with its white-painted arms for putting books on, and go and lie on the chaise longue[5] in her room.

Her room was papered with a white paper that had a trellis; at the top was a frieze[6] of green ivy leaves. The bureau, one of the Victorian sort decorated with carved fruit, had been painted white, by my mother, and the grapes that formed the handles painted green, with brown stems; it was very beautiful. The chaise longue upon which I lay was covered in bright green satin, and had white woodwork, traced with a line of green. I had a brown comfortable,[7] brought with me from my room,

tucked around me, and wore my old brown wool dressing gown with a pattern of Indians on it: it was two Christmases old, and I had loved it once, but I doubted all my own possessions now; perhaps that was why I so particularly enjoyed lying on the green satin chaise longue in my mother's bedroom. I stared up at the ceiling, where some long cracks and a stain made a shepherdess with sheep and an old man with a long beard, like God. It was so beautifully clear and uncluttered up there on the ceiling, with no furniture; it was easy to imagine oneself walking about upside down, with free, skating motions.

Sometimes my mother would read to me. I remember Miss Edgeworth, Mrs. Ewing, and especially the historical novels of Charlotte M. Yonge. One afternoon she was reading to me from *The Chaplet of Pearls,* which was very exciting. The setting sun of midafternoon cast a red glow on the snowdrifts outside, which reflected back through the bedroom windows, pink all over the white trellised walls. That hour, of sunset in the middle of a snowy winter afternoon, always seemed majestic, frozen, almost final. . . . My mother was reading the part where Charles IX,[8] from the staircase to his apartments in the Louvre,[9] witnesses the murder of Admiral Coligny in the Massacre of St. Bartholomew. At least that is the way I remember it. It seemed

---

5 **chaise longue** (shāz′lông′): long couch with a support for the back at one end.
6 **frieze**: ornamented border.
7 **comfortable**: quilted cover.

8 **Charles IX**: King of France from 1560 to 1574.
9 **Louvre** (lōō′vr): palace in Paris now used for a museum of art and for public offices.

CHARACTERIZATION

terribly real to me; I could see the carnage,[10] hear the shrieking in that frightful midnight. I stood on the staircase, I was the King, I stared down at the murder and the blood-stained Guises . . . only the stair-case was the staircase at school and the murder was being committed in the cloakroom below.

After a while my mother stopped reading and I began to play with cards, on a wooden board intended for cutting out dresses; but it was not pleasant, the kings and queens looked nasty and ferretlike;[11] I thought of the jeering stoats[12] and weasels in the Wild Wood, in *The Wind in the Willows*. My mother came and laid her hand on my forehead. "You've got a temperature again," she said, and hustled me back to my own bed. I think I was feverish all that night. My father came and stood in the door to my room when he got home. "Poor old girl," he said. "Got a tem-perament." He never called it "tem-perature."

Sometimes, when I was getting well from one of those colds, I, too, used to draw pictures, only they were not very good. What seemed to turn out best was copying colored pictures out of art books of my mother's and father's; the color was what I liked to put in. I had two water-color paintboxes, one rather limited, left from my infancy, the other large and with handsome pans for mixing the colors. My father tried to encourage me to copy Ingres

10 **carnage:** slaughter; bloodshed.
11 **ferretlike:** like weasels.
12 **stoats:** ermines, small furry animals.

and Watteau[13] in red chalk. But what I liked best to do was to copy the pictures of saints out of an old art calendar.

The reason for this was that I had been given some gold paint, and I particularly enjoyed painting the haloes round the saints' heads in thick, solid gold. I would sit at the upright black desk in my room, dressed in a great many sweaters for fear I would catch more cold, and prop the calendar, which was long and narrow, up against the pigeon-holes, to copy from. First I made a drawing on my water-color pad of the saint in pencil, long and narrow and fitting into a pointed arch as in the picture I was copying; then I opened my paintboxes and began to fill in the colors, dipping my paint-brush in the jelly glass of water beside me. Most of the saints were men, with long gray or brown beards, blue or rich purple mantles, and white garments edged with the Greek key, which also gave me an opportunity to use gold paint. I always left the halo for last, and filled it in with the grainy, sparkly gold paint very carefully, so as not to smear, or run into the hair color. Sometimes, painting a halo and taking my time over it, I would wonder what haloes were, what they were supposed to be made of: whether they were hard and thin like gold plates, or just light radiating from the saint. They seemed to be a sort of label saints wore. I imagined that the label must represent the way saints were inside; they must have something inside that was round and shining and complete. One afternoon as I was painting a halo, with the electric light, which hung from the ceiling inside a Japanese lantern, turned on because it was snowing hard outside, I began to wonder how it would feel to have a halo on, round and gold and enveloping my whole head. But all I could think of was how a cold in the head felt—round, too, as a matter of fact, and enveloping; but thick and like cotton wool.

My mother came to the door of my room and said, "Bettina Nash is downstairs and wants to see you. I told her she could, I don't think you have any germs now, but be sure to sit beside the fire out of the draft—" I didn't wait to hear her finish. I was out of that room as fast as I could dash. I slowed down to enter the living room, though, of course. Bettina was dressed in thick sweaters instead of a coat; there was still snow on her shoulders and on the top of her red skating cap. "C'mon out why don't you? It's good coasting this after," she said.

"I can't. I'm getting over a cold," I said, dismally, and she actually seemed to sympathize with me, for she said, "Gee, that's awful. Can't you get over it quick or something?" She went away, after a while, but something had changed, a chink had opened, for she was one of Geraldine's cohorts and she had come to see me. I can't remember even going back to that boring old saint, that afternoon or ever. I was never any real good at painting, anyway.

13 Ingres (ăN′gr) and Watteau (wŏ tō′): French painters of the 19th and 18th centuries.

CHARACTERIZATION

That afternoon a tide had turned, for me, for the next thing I remember is being one of Geraldine's cohorts myself. I don't know why she decided to accept me, but I remember basking in the precious peace of her approval, which we all sought avidly by agreeing with everything she said. "Dja see that new kid in fourth class?" she would say, as we stood about under the sighing pines in the schoolyard at recess. "She's *crazy*." "Crazy-looking thing," we would chime in; crazy meant anything wrong, anything different from the norm, which was, of course, Geraldine herself: pigtailed, gingham-dressed, belted at the hipline, scornful, *right*. I would chime in as loud as any of them, for now all was well, somebody else was crazy, not me.

These scenes, like the pictures from an old-fashioned magic lantern, are what have been running incessantly through the back of my mind as I lie here, trying to get over this stupid cold in time for Louise Hanson's party. It's too absurd; I *never* have colds. I suppose you could figure out that by having the cold I'm trying to escape from going to the party, since I know Louise hates me.

I've been told the kind of malicious thing she says behind my back.

But I'm not a child any longer, to run away. My husband says, "What do you care? If she hates you, just give her the go-by." He doesn't understand. Louise Hanson gives the best parties in town, the most important parties, and I'm not going to let hurt feelings keep me from going to this one. Besides, if there's one thing all those memories prove, it's that you never can tell. For all I know now, by this time next year I may be Louise Hanson's most intimate friend—just the way I used to get asked to stay to supper at Geraldine Ames's, long, long ago.

I wish I could throw off this cold. It's boring to stay in bed, when you're grown-up; nobody brings you trays of good things to eat, not these days. I've read all the magazines, and I can't bear games of patience, really—those horrid little faces on the cards. There isn't anything to do, just lie here with my cold filling my whole head and feeling like some kind of cotton-wool halo. I suppose I could get up, cold and all; but then, it pays to be cautious. You never know what a cold may turn into.

Understanding Literature

1. Explain the connection between the first paragraph of the story and the last three paragraphs. How is the care of this illness contrasted with the care given to the author as a child? What similarities do you notice between the person as an adult and the person as a child, seen in flashback? How do these similarities aid in weaving the threads of the story together?

2. How is the girl's cold related to the problem of her lack of acceptance by her classmates?
3. Why does the girl's brushed-wool cap-and-mittens set lose its beauty for her? In what other way could she have reacted to Geraldine's insults?
4. How is the girl's behavior, after she becomes Geraldine's friend, similar to the behavior of many people in this type of situation?

Further Activities

1. In the story Geraldine is the leader in her group. This group has power to make people comfortable or uncomfortable, accepted or rejected, happy or sad. How can such a person make others feel like "outsiders"? What qualities does such a leader have to have? Are these qualities always good ones? In what way do you think an "outsider" could become accepted by the group? Is the effort always worth the reward? Prepare to discuss these ideas.
2. The passage in which the mother's room is described is an especially vivid one. Examine this passage carefully until you are able to point out the details which make this passage so sharp and clear. Examine in the same way the passage describing the food eaten by the sick child.

In this well-known Christmas story, two young people have no money to buy Christmas gifts for each other. The spirit of giving at its best is illustrated by the sacrifice each makes to bring happiness to the other.

The Gift of the Magi

O. Henry

IMPROVING YOUR READING: An author reveals the characteristics of the people in his stories by showing them in a series of episodes or under conditions of strain and stress. Observe Della's reactions to her immediate problem and Della's and Jim's reactions to their general situation at the end of the story. What do their reactions reveal about them?

ONE DOLLAR AND eighty-seven cents. That was all. And sixty cents of it was in pennies. Pennies saved one and two at a time by bulldozing[1] the grocer and the vegetable man and the butcher until one's cheeks burned with the silent imputation of parsimony[2] that such close dealing implied. Three times Della counted it. One dollar and eighty-seven cents. And the next day would be Christmas.

There was clearly nothing to do but flop down on the shabby little couch and howl. So Della did it. Which instigates the moral reflection[3] that life is made up of sobs, sniffles, and smiles, with sniffles predominating.

While the mistress of the home is gradually subsiding from the first stage to the second, take a look at the home. A furnished flat at $8 per week. It did not exactly beggar description, but it certainly had that word[4] on the lookout for the mendicancy squad.[5]

In the vestibule below was a letter box into which no letter would go, and an electric button from which no mortal finger could coax a ring. Also appertaining thereunto[6] was a card bearing the name "Mr. James Dillingham Young."

The "Dillingham" had been flung to the breeze during a former period of prosperity when its possessor was being paid $30 per week. Now, when the income was shrunk to $20, the letters of "Dillingham" looked blurred, as though they were thinking seriously of contracting to a

---

1 **bulldozing:** bullying.
2 **imputation of parsimony:** charge of stinginess.
3 **instigates the moral reflection:** prompts the careful conclusion.

4 **that word:** beggar.
5 **mendicancy squad:** group that searches for those engaged in illegal begging.
6 **appertaining thereunto:** referring to that.

modest and unassuming D. But whenever Mr. James Dillingham Young came home and reached his flat above he was called "Jim" and greatly hugged by Mrs. James Dillingham Young, already introduced to you as Della. Which is all very good.

Della finished her cry and attended to her cheeks with the powder rag. She stood by the window and looked out dully at a gray cat walking a gray fence in a gray back yard. Tomorrow would be Christmas Day, and she had only $1.87 with which to buy Jim a present. She had been saving every penny she could for months, with this result. Twenty dollars a week doesn't go far. Expenses had been greater than she had calculated. They always are. Only $1.87 to buy a present for Jim. Her Jim. Many a happy hour she had spent planning for something nice for him. Something fine and rare and sterling—something just a little bit near to being worthy of the honor of being owned by Jim.

There was a pier glass[7] between the windows of the room. Perhaps you have seen a pier glass in an $8 flat. A very thin and very agile person may, by observing his reflection in a rapid sequence of longitudinal[8] strips, obtain a fairly accurate conception of his looks. Della, being slender, had mastered the art.

Suddenly she whirled from the window and stood before the glass. Her eyes were shining brilliantly, but her face had lost its color within twenty seconds. Rapidly she pulled down her hair and let it fall to its full length.

Now, there were two possessions of the James Dillingham Youngs in which they both took a mighty pride. One was Jim's gold watch that had been his father's and his grandfather's. The other was Della's hair. Had the Queen of Sheba lived in the flat across the airshaft, Della would have let her hair hang out the window some day to dry just to depreciate[9] Her Majesty's jewels and gifts. Had King Solomon been the janitor, with all his treasures piled up in the basement, Jim would have pulled out his watch every time he passed, just to see him pluck at his beard from envy.

So now Della's beautiful hair fell about her, rippling and shining like a cascade of brown waters. It reached below her knee and made itself almost a garment for her. And then she did it up again nervously and quickly. Once she faltered for a minute and stood still while a tear or two splashed on the worn red carpet.

On went her old brown jacket; on went her old brown hat. With a whirl of skirts and with the brilliant sparkle still in her eyes, she fluttered out the door and down the stairs to the street.

Where she stopped the sign read: "Mme. Sofronie. Hair Goods of All Kinds." One flight up Della ran, and collected herself, panting. Madame,

7 **pier glass:** narrow mirror designed to fit the wall space between two windows.
8 **longitudinal:** lengthwise.

9 **depreciate** (dǐ prē′shǐ āt′): belittle; detract from.

large, too white, chilly, hardly looked the "Sofronie."

"Will you buy my hair?" asked Della.

"I buy hair," said Madame. "Take yer hat off and let's have a sight at the looks of it."

Down rippled the brown cascade.

"Twenty dollars," said Madame, lifting the mass with a practiced hand.

"Give it to me quick," said Della.

Oh, and the next two hours tripped by on rosy wings. Forget the hashed metaphor. She was ransacking the stores for Jim's present.

She found it at last. It surely had been made for Jim and no one else. There was no other like it in any of the stores, and she had turned all of them inside out. It was a platinum fob chain[10] simple and chaste in design, properly proclaiming its value by substance alone and not by meretricious[11] ornamentation—as all good things should do. It was even worthy of The Watch. As soon as she saw it she knew that it must be Jim's. It was like him. Quietness and value—the description applied to both. Twenty-one dollars they took from her for it, and she hurried home with the 87 cents. With that chain on his watch Jim might be properly anxious about the time in any company. Grand as the watch was, he sometimes looked at it on the sly on account of the old leather strap that he used in place of a chain.

When Della reached home her intoxication[12] gave way a little to prudence and reason. She got out her curling irons and lighted the gas and went to work repairing the ravages[13] made by generosity added to love. Which is always a tremendous task, dear friends—a mammoth task.

Within forty minutes her head was covered with tiny, close-lying curls that made her look wonderfully like a truant schoolboy. She looked at her reflection in the mirror long, carefully, and critically.

"If Jim doesn't kill me," she said to herself, "before he takes a second look at me, he'll say I look like a Coney Island chorus girl. But what could I do—oh! what could I do with a dollar and eighty-seven cents?"

At seven o'clock the coffee was made and the frying pan was on the back of the stove hot and ready to cook the chops.

Jim was never late. Della doubled the fob chain in her hand and sat on the corner of the table near the door that he always entered. Then she heard his step on the stair away down on the first flight, and she turned white for just a moment. She had a habit of saying little silent prayers about the simplest everyday things, and now she whispered: "Please God, make him think I am still pretty."

The door opened and Jim stepped in and closed it. He looked thin and very serious. Poor fellow, he was only twenty-two—and to be burdened with a family! He needed a

---

10 **fob chain:** short chain for watches.
11 **meretricious:** gaudy; showy.

12 **intoxication:** excitement.
13 **ravages:** damages.

new overcoat and he was without gloves.

Jim stopped inside the door, as immovable as a setter at the scent of quail. His eyes were fixed upon Della, and there was an expression in them that she could not read, and it terrified her. It was not anger, nor surprise, nor disapproval, nor horror, nor any of the sentiments that she had been prepared for. He simply stared at her fixedly with that peculiar expression on his face.

Della wriggled off the table and went for him.

"Jim, darling," she cried, "don't look at me that way. I had my hair cut off and sold it because I couldn't have lived through Christmas without giving you a present. It'll grow out again—you won't mind, will you? I just had to do it. My hair grows awfully fast. Say 'Merry Christmas!' Jim, and let's be happy. You don't know what a nice—what a beautiful, nice gift I've got for you."

"You've cut off your hair?" asked Jim, laboriously, as if he had not arrived at that patent fact yet even after the hardest mental labor.

"Cut it off and sold it," said Della. "Don't you like me just as well, anyhow? I'm me without my hair, ain't I?"

Jim looked about the room curiously.

"You say your hair is gone?" he said, with an air almost of idiocy.

"You needn't look for it," said Della. "It's sold, I tell you—sold and gone, too. It's Christmas Eve, boy. Be good to me, for it went for you. Maybe the hairs of my head were numbered," she went on with a sudden serious sweetness, "but nobody could ever count my love for you. Shall I put the chops on, Jim?"

Out of his trance Jim seemed quickly to wake. He enfolded his Della. For ten seconds let us regard with discreet scrutiny[14] some inconsequential[15] object in the other direction. Eight dollars a week or a million a year—what is the difference? A mathematician or a wit would give you the wrong answer. The magi brought valuable gifts, but that was not among them. This dark assertion[16] will be illuminated later on.

Jim drew a package from his overcoat pocket and threw it upon the table.

"Don't make any mistake, Dell," he said, "about me. I don't think there's anything in the way of a haircut or a shave or a shampoo that could make me like my girl any less. But if you'll unwrap that package you may see why you had me going a while at first."

White fingers and nimble tore at the string and paper. And then an ecstatic scream of joy; and then, alas! a quick feminine change to hysterical tears and wails, necessitating the immediate employment of all the comforting powers of the lord of the flat.

For there lay The Combs—the set of combs, side and back, that Della had worshiped for long in a Broadway window. Beautiful combs, pure

14 **discreet scrutiny:** tactful inspection.
15 **inconsequential:** unimportant.
16 **assertion:** declaration.

CHARACTERIZATION

tortoise shell, with jeweled rims—just the shade to wear in the beautiful vanished hair. They were expensive combs, she knew, and her heart had simply craved and yearned over them without the least hope of possession. And now, they were hers, but the tresses that should have adorned the coveted[17] adornments were gone.

But she hugged them to her bosom, and at length she was able to look up with dim eyes and a smile and say: "My hair grows so fast, Jim!"

And then Della leaped up like a little singed cat and cried, "Oh, oh!"

Jim had not yet seen his beautiful present. She held it out to him eagerly upon her open palm. The dull precious metal seemed to flash with a reflection of her bright and ardent spirit.

"Isn't it a dandy, Jim? I hunted all over town to find it. You'll have to look at the time a hundred times a day now. Give me your watch. I want to see how it looks on it."

17 **coveted:** desired.

Instead of obeying, Jim tumbled down on the couch and put his hands under the back of his head and smiled.

"Dell," said he, "let's put our Christmas presents away and keep 'em a while. They're too nice to use just at present. I sold the watch to get the money to buy your combs. And now suppose you put the chops on."

The magi, as you know, were wise men—wonderfully wise men—who brought gifts to the Babe in the manger. They invented the art of giving Christmas presents. Being wise, their gifts were no doubt wise ones, possibly bearing the privilege of exchange in case of duplication. And here I have lamely related to you the uneventful chronicle of two foolish children in a flat who most unwisely sacrificed for each other the greatest treasures of their house. But in a last word to the wise of these days let it be said that of all who give gifts these two were the wisest. Of all who give and receive gifts, such as they are wisest. Everywhere they are wisest. They are the magi.

Understanding Literature

1. Select conversation from the story that helps you understand Della and Jim. What actions are shown that characterize them? What actual description of these two people is given?
2. What evidence do you have that the events in this story took place a number of years ago?
3. A metaphor is an implied comparison of two different objects which are alike in at least one way. O. Henry says "the next

two hours tripped by on rosy wings" and then calls this a "hashed metaphor." What objects are being compared? Why is the metaphor "hashed"?

4. Although the story is of a serious nature, O. Henry shows a little lightness and humor in his treatment of Della. Where and how does he do this?

5. At what point do you feel you know what the outcome of the story will be? Why?

6. Reread the last three sentences of the story. Explain what these sentences mean. Why does O. Henry, in referring to Della and Jim, say, "They are the magi"?

7. When done well, a surprise ending, though unexpected, is closely related to the characters and the events in the story. It is not an ending that is attached to the story simply to startle the reader; it satisfies him. Why is the ending of this story a particularly good one?

8. What does the title mean?

In this poem the main character represents an idea. Notice the similarity between "Abou Ben Adhem" and the previous story, "The Gift of the Magi."

Abou Ben Adhem

Leigh Hunt

Abou Ben Adhem (may his tribe increase!)
Awoke one night from a deep dream of peace,
And saw, within the moonlight in his room,
Making it rich, and like a lily in bloom,
An angel writing in a book of gold:—   5
Exceeding[1] peace had made Ben Adhem bold,
And to the presence in the room he said,
"What writest thou?" —The vision raised its head,
And with a look made of all sweet accord,[2]
Answered, "The names of those who love the Lord."   10
"And is mine one?" said Abou. "Nay, not so,"
Replied the angel. Abou spoke more low,
But cheerly still; and said, "I pray thee then,
Write me as one that loves his fellow men."

    The angel wrote, and vanished. The next night   15
It came again with a great wakening light,
And showed the names whom love of God had blessed,
And lo! Ben Adhem's name led all the rest.

1 **Exceeding:** unlimited.   2 **accord:** agreement; harmony.

Understanding Literature

1. Why does Ben Adhem's name appear at the head of the list "of those who love the Lord"?
2. What idea does Abou Ben Adhem represent?

Further Activity

Write a two-paragraph theme in which you compare Abou Ben Adhem with Della and Jim in "The Gift of the Magi." You might begin the first paragraph by describing the character of Abou Ben Adhem. In the rest of the paragraph explain how the characters of Della and Jim are like or unlike Abou Ben Adhem's.

In the second paragraph explain what idea Abou Ben Adhem represents and discuss whether this idea is similar or dissimilar to the idea dramatized in "The Gift of the Magi."

The Art of Storytelling

You HAVE READ so far largely about plot and characterization. Action and people are important parts of a story, but an author is also concerned with the manner in which he tells his story, with the effect his story has on the reader, and with the meaning he wishes to convey, among many other things. If he wishes to have his characters seem like real people instead of fairy-tale heroes and heroines, he must make it clear why they act as they do and must make their reasons and actions believable. If an author wishes his readers to feel a certain way about the characters or events in his story, he must describe them in a way that will be sure to arouse that feeling. Or, on the other hand, if a writer has something important to say which he feels his readers should know about and if he chooses to say it through a story, the characters, the plot, the dialogue, and many other elements will need to contribute to his purpose. Since the author is so concerned with the way in which he tells his story and with the devices he uses, the reader will make a far better audience if he is aware of and understands these devices. In each of the following selections you will find some of the most important of these techniques explained and illustrated.

Reading can help you to understand other people; and if you understand others, you will be better prepared to live in the world around you. In this story from *The Friendly Persuasion*, Jess Birdwell misunderstands his wife's persistence. He hates geese; his wife loves them. A conflict is bound to develop. Jess's weakness is that he does not understand people very well. Eliza, his wife, is in no such predicament; she can twist anyone around her little finger.

The Pacing Goose*

Jessamyn West

IMPROVING YOUR READING: Watch for the many *conflicts* which develop in this story. Jess wants one thing and his wife wants another. Enoch, the hired man, is told to do something he does not want to do. Eliza has to win her case in court. As you wonder how each conflict will come out, you have a sense of suspense. But most of all the author is concerned with *motivation,* why people act as they do. Does the author of this story make it clear why the characters act as they do? In other words, has she motivated them?

In this story Jess and Eliza Birdwell are Quakers; that is, they belong to the Society of Friends, a religious group whose members frequently use "thee" and "thy" to all men as a mark of equality. Many Friends also refuse to take oaths and, being opposed to war, refuse to bear arms. Note how these characteristics are used in the story.

JESS SAT IN the kitchen at the long table by the west window where in winter he kept his grafting tools: the thin-bladed knife, the paper sweet with the smell of beeswax and the resin, the boxes of roots and scions.[1] Jess was a nurseryman[2] and spring meant for him not only spirits flowering—but the earth's. A week more of moderating weather and he'd be out, still in gum boots, but touching an earth that had thawed, whose riches were once again fluid enough to be sucked upward, toward those burgeonings[3] which by summer would have swelled into Early Harvests, Permains and Sweet Bows.

Spring's a various season, Jess thought, no two years the same: comes in with rains, mud deep enough to swallow horse and rider; comes in cold, snow falling so fast it weaves a web; comes in with a warm wind blowing about thy ears and bringing a smell of something flower-

1 **scions** (sī′ənz)**:** shoots ready for planting.
2 **nurseryman:** owner of a plant nursery, where plants and trees are raised for sale.

3 **burgeonings:** new growths.

* Copyright 1945 by Jessamyn West. Reprinted from her volume THE FRIENDLY PERSUASION by permission of Harcourt, Brace & World, Inc.

ing, not here, but southaways, across the Ohio, maybe, in Kentucky. Nothing here now but a smell of melting snow—which is no smell at all, but a kind of prickle in the nose, like a bygone sneeze. Comes in so various, winter put by and always so welcome.

"And us each spring so much the same."

"Thee speaking to me, Jess?"

"Nothing thee'd understand, Eliza."

Spring made Jess discontented with the human race—and with women, if anything more than men. It looked as if spring put them all in the shade: the season so resourceful and they each year meeting it with nothing changed from last year; digging up roots from the same sassafras thicket, licking sulphur and molasses from the same big-bowled spoon.

Behind him the table was set for supper, plates neatly turned to cover the bone-handled knives and forks, spoon vase aglitter with steel well burnished by brick dust, dishes of jam with more light to them than the sun, which was dwindling away, peaked and overcast outside his window.

"Spring opening up," he said, "and nobody in this house so much as putting down a line of poetry."

Eliza, who was lifting dried-peach pies from a hot oven, said nothing. She set the four of them in a neat row on the edge of her kitchen cabinet to cool, and slid her pans of cornbread into the oven. Then she turned to Jess, her cheeks red with heat, and her black eyes warm with what she had to say. "Thee'd maybe relish a nice little rhyme for thy supper, Jess Birdwell."

Jess sighed, then sniffed the pies, so rich with ripe peach flavor that the kitchen smelled like a summer orchard, nothing lacking but the sound of bees. "Now, Eliza," he said, "thee knows I wouldn't have thee anyways altered. Thee . . ."

"Thee," Eliza interrupted him, "is like all men. Thee wants to have thy poetry and eat it too."

Jess wondered how what he'd felt about spring, a season with the Lord's thumbprint fresh on it, could've led to anything so unspringlike as an argument about a batch of dried-peach pies.

"Eliza," he said firmly, "I didn't mean thee. Though it's crossed my mind sometimes as strange that none of the boys have ever turned, this time of year, to rhyming."

"Josh writes poems," Eliza said.

"Thee ever read what Josh writes, Eliza?"

Eliza nodded.

Ah, well, Jess thought, no use at this date to tell her what's the difference.

Eliza looked her husband over carefully. "Jess Birdwell," she said, "thee's full of humors.[4] Thy blood needs thinning. I'll boil thee up a good cup of sassafras tea."

Jess turned away from the green and gold sunset and the patches of snow it was gilding and fairly faced the dried-peach pies and Eliza, who

4 **full of humors:** moody.

was dropping dumplings into a pot of beans.

"That's just it, Eliza," he said. "That's just the rub."

Eliza gave him no encouragement, but he went on anyway. "Earth alters, season to season, spring comes in never two times the same, only us pounding on steady as pump bolts and not freshened by so much as a grass blade."

"Jess, thee's got spring fever."

"I could reckon time and temperature, each spring, by the way thee starts honing for geese. 'Jess, don't thee think we might have a few geese?' It's a tardy spring," Jess said. "Snow still on the ground and not a word yet from thee about geese."

Eliza pulled a chair out from the table and sat. "Jess, why's thee always been so set against geese?"

"I'm not set against geese. It's geese that's set against farming. They can mow down a half acre of sprouting corn while thee's trying to head them off—and in two minutes they'll level a row of pie plant it's taken two years to get started. No, Eliza, it's the geese that's against me."

"If thee had tight fences . . ." Eliza said.

"Eliza, I got tight fences, but the goose's never been hatched that'll admit fences exist. And an old gander'd just as soon go through a fence as hiss—and if he can't find a hole or crack in a fence he'll lift the latch."

"Jess," said Eliza flatly, "thee don't like geese."

"Well," said Jess, "I wouldn't go so far's to say I didn't like them, but I will say that if there's any meaner, dirtier animal, or one that glories in it more, I don't know it. And a thing I've never been able to understand about thee, Eliza, is what thee sees in the shifty-eyed birds."

"Geese," said Eliza, with a dreaminess unusual to her, "march along so lordly like . . . they're pretty as swans floating down a branch . . . in fall they stretch out their necks and honk to geese passing overhead as if they's wild. My father never had any trouble raising geese and I've heard him say many a time that there's no better food for a brisk morning than a fried goose egg."

Jess knew, with spring his topic, he'd ought to pass over Eliza's father and his fried goose egg but he couldn't help saying, "A fried goose egg always had a kind of bloated look to me, Eliza"—but then he went on fast. "The season's shaping up," he said. "I can see thee's all primed[5] to say, 'Jess, let's get a setting of goose eggs.'"

Eliza went over to the bean kettle and began to lift out dumplings. "It's a forwarder season than thee thinks, Jess," she said. "I got a setting under a hen now."

Jess looked at his wife. He didn't know what had made him want spring's variety in a human being— nor Eliza's substituting doing for asking. And speaking of it just now, as he had, made opposition kind of ticklish.

5 **primed:** prepared.

THE ART OF STORYTELLING

"When'd thee set them?" he asked finally.

"Yesterday," said Eliza.

"Where'd thee get the eggs?"

"Overbys'," said Eliza. The Overbys were their neighbors to the south.

"Well, they got enough for a surety," Jess said, "to give a few away."

"The Overbys don't give anything away, as thee knows. I paid for them. With my own money," Eliza added.

"How many?" Jess asked.

"Eight," Eliza said.

Jess turned back to his window. The sun had set, leaving a sad green sky and desolate black and white earth. "Five acres of corn gone," he calculated.

"Thee said," Eliza reminded him, "that what thee wanted was a little variety in me. 'Steady as a pump bolt,' were thy words."

"I know I did," Jess admitted glumly. "I talk too much."

"Draw up thy chair," Eliza said placidly, not contradicting him; "here's Enoch and the boys."

Next morning after breakfast Jess and Enoch left the kitchen together. The sun was the warmest the year had yet produced and the farm roofs were steaming; south branch, swollen by melting snow, was running so full the soft lap of its eddies[6] could be heard in the barnyard; a rooster tossed his voice into the bright air, loud and clear as if aiming to be heard by every fowl in Jennings County.

"Enoch," said Jess to his hired man, "what's thy feeling about geese?"

Enoch was instantly equipped, for the most part, with feelings on every subject. Geese was a homelier topic than he'd choose himself to enlarge upon, not one that could be much embellished[7] nor one on which Mr. Emerson,[8] so far's he could recall, had ever expressed an opinion. "In the fall of the year," he said, "long about November or December, there's nothing tastier on the table than roast goose."

"Goose on the table's not what I mean," Jess said. "I was speaking of goose on the hoof. Goose nipping off a stand of corn, Enoch, goose roistering round, honking and hissing so's thee can't hear thyself think, goose eyeing thee like a snake on stilts."

Enoch gazed at his employer for a few seconds. "Mr. Birdwell," he said, "I think that if they's an ornery bird, it's a goose. Ornery and undependable."

"I'm glad we's so like minded about them," Jess said. "Otherwise, I'd not like to ask thee to do this little job." He pulled a long darning needle from beneath the lapel of his coat.

Enoch eyed it with some mistrust. "I can't say's I've ever been handy with a needle, Mr. Birdwell."

"Thee'll be handy enough for this," Jess said with hearty conviction. "To

---

6 **eddies:** currents of water.

7 **embellished:** made more interesting.
8 **Mr. Emerson:** Ralph Waldo Emerson, 19th-century American essayist and poet.

come to it, Enoch, Eliza's set eight goose eggs. Next year with any luck she'd have two dozen. And so on. More and more. Feeling the way thee does, Enoch, about geese it's no more'n fair to give thee a chance to put a stop to this before it goes too far. One little puncture in each egg with this and the goose project's nipped in the bud and Eliza none the wiser."

"I'm mighty awkward with my hands," said Enoch, "doing fine work. Ticklish job like this I might drop an egg and break it."

"Enoch," said Jess, "thee's not developing a weakness for geese, is thee?"

"It ain't the geese," said Enoch frankly, "it's your wife. She's been mighty clever[9] to me and if she's got her heart set on geese, it'd go against the grain to disappoint her. Whyn't you do it, Mr. Birdwell?"

"Same reason," said Jess, "only more of them—and if Eliza ever asks if I tampered with that setting of eggs I figure on being able to say No." Jess held the needle nearer Enoch, who looked at it but still made no motion to take it.

"Likely no need to do a thing," Enoch said. "Two to one those eggs'll never hatch anyways. Overbys' such a fox-eared tribe they more'n likely sold her bad eggs to begin with."

"Thee's knowed about this," Jess asked, "all along?"

"Yes," Enoch said.

"Here's the needle," Jess said.

9 **clever:** good-natured.

"You look at this," Enoch inquired, "not so much as a favor asked as a part of the day's work with orders from you?"

"Yes," Jess said, "that's about the way I look at it."

Enoch took the needle, held it somewhat gingerly, and with the sun glinting across its length, walked slowly toward the chickenhouse.

It takes thirty days for a goose egg to hatch, and the time, with spring work to be done, went fast. The hen Eliza had picked was a good one and kept her mind strictly on her setting. Eliza kept her mind on the hen, and Jess and Enoch found their minds oftener than they liked on Eliza and her hoped-for geese.

At breakfast on the day the geese were due to break their shells Jess said, "If I's thee, Eliza, I wouldn't bank too much on them geese. I heard Enoch say a while back he wouldn't be surprised if not an egg hatched. Thought the eggs were likely no good."

Enoch was busy pouring coffee into a saucer, then busy cooling it, but Eliza waited until he was through. "Did thee say that, Enoch?"

Enoch looked at Jess. "Yes," he said, "I kind of recollect something of the sort."

"What made thee think so, Enoch?"

"Why," said Jess, for Enoch was busy with his coffee again, "it was the Overbys. Enoch's got a feeling they's kind of unreliable. Fox-eared, I think thee said, Enoch, didn't thee?"

Enoch's work took him outside almost at once and Jess himself said, "If thee'll just give me a little packet of food, Eliza, I won't trouble thee for anything at noon. I'm going to be over'n the south forty and it'll save time coming and going."

Eliza was surprised for Jess'd usually come twice as far for a hot dinner at midday, but she made him fried ham sandwiches and put them and some cold apple-turnovers in a bag.

"It's a pity thee has to miss thy dinner," she told him, but Jess only said, "Press of work, press of work," and hurriedly departed.

Jess came home that evening through the spring twilight, somewhat late, and found a number of things to do at the barn before he went up to the house. When he entered the kitchen nothing seemed amiss—lamps ruddy, table set, stove humming, and beside the stove a small box over which Eliza was bending. Jess stopped to look—and listen; from inside the box was coming a kind of birdlike peeping, soft and not unpleasant. Reluctantly he walked to Eliza's side. There, eating minced boiled egg, and between bites lifting its beak to Eliza, it seemed, and making those chirping sounds he'd heard was a gray-gold gosling.

Eliza looked up pleasantly. "Enoch was right," she said. "The eggs were bad. Only one hatched. I plan to call it Samantha," she told Jess. "It's a name I've always been partial to."

"Samantha," said Jess without any enthusiasm whatever for either name

or gosling. "How's thee know it's a she?"

"I don't," said Eliza, "but if it's a gander it's a name easily changed to Sam."

Enoch came in just then with a load of wood for the kitchen woodbox. "Enoch," asked Jess, "has thee seen Samantha—or Sam?"

Enoch mumbled but Jess understood him to say he had.

"It was my understanding, Enoch, that thy opinion was that all those eggs were bad."

"Well, Mr. Birdwell," said Enoch, "a man could make a mistake. He could count wrong."

"A man ought to be able to count to eight without going astray," Jess said.

Eliza was paying no attention to either of them; she was making little tweeting sounds herself, bending over the chirping gosling. "Does thee know," she asked Jess, "that this is the first pet I ever had in my life?"

"Thee's got Ebony," Jess said.

"I don't mean a caged pet," Eliza said, "but one to walk beside thee. I'm reconciled the others didn't hatch. With eight I'd've had to raise geese for the table. With one only I can make Samantha a pure pet."

A pure pet was what she made of her: Samantha ate what the family ate, with the exception of articles which Eliza thought might be indigestible and would risk on humans but not on her goose. Cake, pie, corn-on-the-cob, there was nothing too good for Samantha. From

a big-footed, gold-downed gosling she swelled, almost at once, like a slack sail which gets a sudden breeze, into a full-rounded convexity.[10]

"Emphasis on the vexity," Jess said when he thought of this. Samantha was everything he'd disliked in the general run of geese, with added traits peculiar to herself, which vexed[11] him. Because she was fed at the doorstep, she was always underfoot. No shout, however loud, would move her before she's ready to move. If she's talked to too strong she'd flail you with her wings and pinch the calf of your leg until for some days it would look to be mortifying.[12] She'd take food out of children's hands and the pansies Jess had planted in a circle at the base of the Juneberry tree she sheared so close that there was not a naked stem left to show for all his work. And when not being crossed in any way, Jess simply looking at her and meditating, trying to fathom[13] Samantha's fascination for Eliza, the goose would suddenly extend her snakelike neck, and almost touching Jess, hiss with such a hint of icy disapprobation[14] that Jess would involuntarily recoil.

But she was Eliza's pure pet, no two ways about that, and would lift her head for Eliza to scratch, and walk beside her with the lordly roll of the known elect.

"There was some goddess," Enoch remembered, "who always had a big

10 **convexity:** curve.
11 **vexed:** annoyed.
12 **mortifying:** affected with gangrene.

13 **fathom:** understand.
14 **disapprobation:** disapproval; dislike.

bird with her." Jess supposed Enoch was thinking of Juno and her peacock, but the reference didn't convince him that a goose was a suitable companion for any goddess—let alone Eliza, and he couldn't honestly feel much regret when one evening toward the end of November Eliza told him Samantha was missing. "She'll turn up," Jess said. "That bird's too ornery to die young."

Eliza said nothing, but next evening she proved Jess was right. "Samantha's over at Overbys'," she said.

"Well, did thee fetch her home?" Jess asked.

"No," said Eliza with righteous indignation, "they wouldn't let me. They said they had forty geese—and forty's what they got now, and they don't think Samantha's there. They provoked me so, Jess, I told them they'd sold me seven bad eggs and now they try to take the eighth away from me."

Jess felt a little abashed[15] at this, but he asked, "How can thee be so sure Samantha's there? She might've been carried off by a varmint."

Eliza was scornful. "Thee forgets I hand-raised Samantha from a gosling. I'd know her among four hundred—let alone forty."

"Whyn't thee buy her back then," Jess asked, "if that's the only way?"

"After what I said about their eggs," Eliza answered sadly, "the Overbys say they don't want any more dealings with me."

Eliza mourned so for the lost Samantha that first Enoch and then Jess went over to the Overbys' but no one there would admit the presence of a visiting goose—forty they had, and forty you could see by counting was what they had now. Short of force there didn't seem any way of getting Samantha home again.

When Eliza heard the Overbys were going to sell geese for Christmas eating she was frantic. "Jess," she said, "I just can't bear to think of Samantha, plucked naked and resting on a table waiting to be carved. She used to sing as sweet as any bird when she was little, and she'd walk by my side taking the air. She's the only goose I ever heard of," Eliza remembered mournfully, "who'd drink tea."

In Jess's opinion a goose'd eat anything at either end of the scale, but he didn't suppose this was a suitable time to mention it to Eliza. "Eliza," he said, "short of me and Enoch's going over there and using force on old man Overby—or sneaking over at night and breaking into their chicken pen, I don't know how in the world we're going to get Samantha back for thee."

"We could sue," said Eliza.

"Thee mean go to law?" Jess asked, astounded. Quakers stayed out of courts, believing in amicable[16] settlements without recourse to law.

"Yes," said Eliza. "I'd do it for Samantha. I'd think it my duty. Going to law'd be a misery for us . . . but not so lasting a misery as being roasted would be for Samantha."

Jess couldn't deny this, but he said, "I'd have to think it over. I've

---

15 abashed: embarrassed.

16 amicable (ăm′ə kə bəl): friendly; peaceable.

never been to law yet in my life and suing for a gone goose don't seem to me a very likely place to start."

Next morning Eliza served a good but silent breakfast, not sitting herself to eat with the rest of her family.

"Thee feeling dauncy,[17] Eliza?" Jess asked.

"I just can't eat," she said, "for thinking of Samantha."

Labe and Mattie had tears in their eyes. Little Jess was mournfully bellowing. Enoch looked mighty glum. Jess felt ashamed to be swallowing victuals in the midst of so much sorrow. Eliza stood at the end of the stove where the gosling's box had rested for the first few weeks of its life, looking down, as if remembering how it had sung and lifted its beak to her.

Jess couldn't stand it. "Eliza," he said, "if thee wants to go through with it I'll go to Vernon and fee a lawyer for thee. Thee'll have to go to court, be on the witness stand— and even then I misdoubt thee'll ever get thy goose back. Does thee still want me to do it?"

Eliza came to the table and stood with her hand on Jess' shoulder. "Yes, Jess," she said, "I want thee to do it."

Jess went to Vernon, fee'd a lawyer, had a restraining order put on the Overbys so they couldn't sell or kill the goose Eliza said was Samantha, and awaited with misgivings the day of the trial. It came in mid-December.

Eliza, Jess and Enoch rode to the trial through a fall of light, fresh snow. Brilliant sunlight, crisp air, glittering snow, and Rome's spirited stepping made the occasion, in spite of its purpose, seem festive. Eliza made it seem festive. Jess, who did not forget its purpose, regarded her with some wonder. He couldn't say what it was about her—dress and bonnet appeared to be simply her First Day[18] best—but she had a holiday air.

He considered it his duty to warn her. "Eliza," he said, "thee understands thee's not going to Meeting?[19] They're not going to sit silent while thee tells them how much thee loves Samantha and how she sang when young and drank tea. Old man Overby'll have his say and he's got a lawyer hired for no other purpose than to trip thee up."

Eliza was unimpressed. "What's our lawyer fee'd for, Jess?" she asked.

Jess took another tack. "Eliza," he told her, "I don't figger thee's got a chance in a thousand to get Samantha back."

"This is a court of justice, isn't it?" Eliza asked.

"Yes," Jess said.

"Then there's no need for thee to fash[20] thyself, Jess Birdwell. I'll get Samantha back."

Not getting Samantha back wasn't what fashed Jess—he reckoned he could bear up under that mighty well. What fashed him was the whole shooting match. . . . In some

---

17 **dauncy:** sickly.

18 **First Day:** Sunday.
19 **Meeting:** Quaker religious service.
20 **fash:** trouble.

130

THE ART OF STORYTELLING

few cases, matters of life and death, going to court might be necessary, and he could imagine such. But a suit over a goose named Samantha wasn't one of them. And poor Eliza. Law to her was all Greek and turkey tracks . . . and here she was bound for court as chipper as if she was Chief Justice Taney[21] himself. Jess sighed and shook his head. Getting shut of Samantha would be no hardship for him, but he was downcast for Eliza's sake and the way she'd have to turn homeward empty-handed.

In the courtroom hard, clear light reflected upward from the snow fell onto what Jess thought were hard faces: courthouse hangers on; farmers whose slackening work made the diversion[22] of a trial an inviting possibility; lovers of oddity who figured a tilt between a Quaker female, preacher, to boot, and an old sinner like Milt Overby over the ownership of a goose ought to produce some enlivening quirks. They stared at Eliza, exchanged salutes with Milt Overby and inspected Samantha who in her crate awaited the court's decision.

The two lawyers, Jess considered to be on a par. Nothing fancy, either one . . . old roadsters both, gone gray in service and with a knowledge of their business. The circuit judge was something else, unaccountably young, jug-eared and dressed more sprightly than a groom for his own wedding. A city whippersnapper, born and trained north of the Mississinewa, and now, in Jess's opinion, setting a squeamish foot in backwoods provinces, and irked to find himself trying so trifling a case. Didn't know a goose from a guinea hen, like as not, and would consider tossing a coin a more suitable manner of settling such a matter—just as near right in the end—and his valuable time saved.

Eliza, Jess saw, was of no such opinion. She, too, was scanning the young judge, and Jess, who knew her, saw from the look on her face that she was taken by him. A neat, thin, pious boy—far from home—he looked, no doubt to her; a young man who could do with better cooking and more regular eating.

The young man rapped the court to order. Spitting and shuffling slackened and in a high, precise voice he read, "Birdwell versus Overby. Charge, petty larceny. Appropriation and willful withholding of goose named Samantha." The name Samantha seemed to somewhat choke him, but he got it out.

"Ready for Birdwell," said Mr. Abel Samp, Eliza's lawyer.

"Ready for Overby," said the defendant's lawyer.

Eliza was the first witness on the stand. Jess sometimes forgot what a good-looking woman Eliza was, but the interest shown on lifted faces all about him refreshed his memory.

"Swear the plaintiff in," the judge said.

Eliza, in her sweet voice, spoke directly to the judge. "I don't swear," she said.

21 **Chief Justice Taney:** Chief Justice of U.S. Supreme Court (1836-1864).
22 **diversion:** pleasant change.

The judge explained that profanity was not asked for. "I understood," said Eliza, "that thee wasn't asking for profanity. No one would think that of thee. But we Quakers do not take oaths in court. We affirm."[23]

"Permit Mrs. Birdwell to affirm," said the judge. Eliza affirmed.

Mr. Samp then proceeded to question Eliza as to Samantha's birth and habits.

"Judge," Eliza began.

"Address the judge," Mr. Samp said, "as Your Honor."

"We Quakers," Eliza told the judge, gently, "do not make use of such titles. What is thy name? I think thee'll go far in our state and thy name's one I'd like to know."

The judge appeared somewhat distraught, undecided as to whether to make the tone of the court brisk and legal (if possible) or to follow Eliza's lead of urbane[24] sociability.

"Pomeroy," he said and made a slight bow in Eliza's direction.

Eliza returned the bow, deeper and with more grace. "Friend Pomeroy," she said, "it is indeed a pleasure to know thee."

Samantha's story as Eliza told it to Friend Pomeroy was surprisingly terse.[25] Affecting, and losing nothing by Eliza's telling, but to the point.

"Mrs. Birdwell," said Samp, "how long have you had an acquaintanceship with geese and their habits?"

"Since I was a child," Eliza said.

23 **affirm:** declare something to be true.

24 **urbane:** well-mannered; polished.
25 **terse:** brief; concise.

132 THE ART OF STORYTELLING

"My father was a great fancier of geese."

"And you think you could identify this goose Samantha, which you admit in looks was similar to the defendant's?"

"I could," Eliza said with much authority.

Mr. Samp, to Jess's surprise, left the matter there. "Take the witness," he said to Overby's lawyer— but the counsel for the defendant was in no hurry to cross-examine Eliza. Instead he put his client on the stand.

"Farewell, Samantha," Jess said to Enoch.

"You relieved?" Enoch asked.

"Putting Eliza first," Jess said, "as I do, no."

Milt Overby, whose natural truculence[26] was somewhat stimulated by a nip he'd had to offset snappy weather, bellowed his way through his testimony. At one juncture he set the judge aright when he asked some elementary questions concerning the habits and configurations of geese. "Where in tarnation you from?" he snorted. "What they mean sending us judges down here who don't know Toulouse from Wyandotte,[27] or goose from gander?"

The young judge used voice and gavel to quiet the guffawing which filled the courtroom and the trial proceeded. A number of witnesses for both sides were brought to the stand and while it was shown that Overbys had maybe eaten a goose or two and neglected out of pure fondness for the creatures to count them as among the departed, still nobody had been able to positively identify Samantha.

Mr. Overby's lawyer seemed somewhat loath to cross-examine Eliza, but he put her on the stand. She'd said she knew geese and her testimony had been direct and positive. "Mrs. Birdwell," he said, "how can you be so sure your goose was with my client's geese?"

Eliza's black eyes rested confidingly upon the judge. "Friend Pomeroy," she said, "I raised Samantha from a gosling."

Jess sighed. "Here it comes," he said, "how that goose could sing and drink tea."

Eliza continued, "And there's one thing about her that always set her apart from every other goose."

"Yes, Mrs. Birdwell," said Judge Pomeroy, who was inclined to forget, with Eliza on the stand, that he was in a courtroom.

"Samantha," said Eliza, with much earnestness, "from the day she was born had a gait unlike any other goose I ever saw and one that set her apart from all her Overby connections. I picked her out at once when I went over there, because of it. Thee couldn't've missed it, Friend Pomeroy."

"Yes, Mrs. Birdwell," said the judge with interest in his voice.

"Samantha," said Eliza, "was a born pacer.[28] Thee knows what a pacer is?"

---

26 **truculence:** fierceness.
27 **Toulouse . . . Wyandotte:** Toulouse is a French breed of fowl; Wyandotte, American.

28 **pacer:** that is, she moved with slow, regular steps.

"Certainly," said Judge Pomeroy. "A pacer," he repeated with no surprise—and with obvious pleasure that Eliza'd hit upon so clear and differentiating an aspect of her goose and one that made identification possible.

A titter was mounting through the courtroom—Judge Pomeroy lifted his head. He had no desire to be further instructed as to the history, habits and breeds of geese, and he liked to see a trial settled by some such little and too often overlooked subtlety.[29] Judge Pomeroy brought down his gavel. "The court awards decision in favor of the plaintiff.[30] Case dismissed." While the silence that followed on his words still prevailed Judge Pomeroy stepped briskly and with obvious pleasure out through the rear door.

Jess was also brisk-about departure. No use lingering until friend Pomeroy had been more thoroughly informed as to gaits in general and geese in particular. Mid-afternoon's a quiet time in any season. In winter with snow on the ground, no leaves to rustle and bare limbs rigid as rock against a cloudless sky, the hush is deepest of all. Nothing broke that hush in the surrey, except the squeak of leather and snow, the muffled footfalls of Rome Beauty. Jess and Eliza, on the front seat, rode without speaking. Enoch, in the back, seemed to meditate. Even Samantha in her crate at Enoch's feet was silent.

29 **subtlety:** delicate distinction.
30 **plaintiff:** one who made the complaint in the lawsuit.

Maple Grove Nursery was in sight before Jess spoke. "Eliza," he said, "would thee mind telling me—did thee ever see a trotting goose?"

Enoch ceased to meditate and listened. He had been wondering about this himself.

"Certainly not," said Eliza. "Thee knows as well as I, Jess Birdwell, an animal can't trot without hind feet and forefeet."

"So far, Eliza," Jess said, "we see eye to eye. Now maybe thee'd tell me—did thee ever see a goose that didn't pace?"

Eliza was truly amazed, it seemed. "Why, Jess," she said, "an ordinary goose just walks—but Samantha paces."

Jess was silent for a spell. "What'd thee say the difference is?"

"It's the swing, Jess Birdwell," said Eliza, "same as in a horse that nature's formed for a pacer . . . it's the natural bent, the way the spirit leads the beast to set his feet down. Samantha's a natural pacer."

That seemed as far as they'd likely get on the subject and Jess joined Enoch in meditation. In the barnyard, before she went up to the house, Eliza said, like an old hand at the business, "Attending court whettens the appetite. It's a little early but I thought if thee'd relish it"—and she looked at Jess and Enoch, never sparing a glance for Samantha, as if her menfolk's welfare was her sole concern—"I'd stir us up a bite to eat. Hot tea and fresh sweetcakes, say. Might fry a little sausage and open some cherry preserves. If thee'd relish it," she repeated.

THE ART OF STORYTELLING

Jess wasn't taken in, but he'd relish it, and so would Enoch, and they both said so. They hustled with the unhitching so they could uncrate Samantha and note her progress with eyes newly instructed as to what made a pacer. Jess dumped her in the snow, and Enoch tapped her with his hat. Samantha made for the back door.

"By sugar," said Jess, "Eliza's right. She paces." Samantha had the smooth roll of a racker[31]—there were no two ways about it. At heart she was a pacer, and what two legs could do in that line, Samantha accomplished.

"With four legs," Enoch said, "you could enter her in any county fair—rack[32] on," he cried with enthusiasm. As they followed Samantha to the house, Enoch, for whom any event existed chiefly in its after aspects as a cud for rumination, asked, "How you feel in respect of court trials, now, Mr. Birdwell?"

"I'm still against them," Jess said, "though they's three things this trial's taught me I might never otherwise have learned. Two's about women."

Enoch revered[33] all knowledge and he had a notion that information on this subject might have a more than transcendental[34] value. "What's the two things you learned about women, Mr. Birdwell?"

"Well, Enoch, I learned first, dependability's woman's greatest vir-

31 **racker:** that is, she moved with the regular gait of a horse.

32 **rack:** a framework to which animals are fastened for feeding.
33 **revered:** respected.
34 **transcendental:** abstract; remote; isolated.

tue. Steady as a pump bolt, day in, day out. When thee finds a woman like that, Enoch, don't try to change her. Not even in spring."

"No, sir," said Enoch, "I won't."

"Second, when it's a case of woman and the law—thee don't need to waste any worry on the woman."

"No, sir," said Enoch again.

When they reached the back steps, Enoch asked, "I understood you to say you'd learned three things, Mr. Birdwell. What's the third about?"

"Hired men," said Jess.

Enoch was taken aback, but he'd asked for it. "Yes, Mr. Birdwell," he said.

"Never hire one," Jess told him, "till thee finds out first if he can count to eight. Save thyself a lot of trouble that way, Enoch."

"How's I to know the eighth'd turn out to be Samantha?" Enoch asked.

Samantha herself, who was waiting at the doorstep for an expected tidbit, reached out and unhampered by either boots or work pants nipped Enoch firmly through his thin Sunday best.

"Thee say something, Enoch?" Jess asked.

Enoch had but he didn't repeat it. Instead he said, "Pacer or no pacer, that's Samantha," and the two of them stepped out of the snow into the warm kitchen, scented with baking sweetcakes and frying sausage.

Understanding Literature

1. Why does spring make Jess "discontented with the human race," and with women in particular? What change takes place in his life? Who is for that change? Who is against it?

2. Where and why does Jess introduce geese into the conversation? What is Jess's attitude toward geese? What does Eliza mean by "I got a setting under a hen now"?

3. The second scene is between Jess and Enoch. Jess asks, "Enoch, what's thy feeling toward geese?" What is the purpose of the question? What is Enoch's real feeling as it is developed in this scene?

4. Why does the author skip thirty days before the beginning of the third scene? Why does the author have Jess go off for the day?

5. When Jess comes home that evening (fourth scene), what does he find? Why does he say, "A man ought to be able to count to eight without going astray"?

6. The fifth scene ends with Jess's agreeing to hire a lawyer to get Samantha back. How has the author made this act believable? In other words, how has she motivated it?

7. In the trial scene how is the judge described? How does Jess describe him? How does Eliza describe him?
8. How does Eliza treat the judge? How does Overby treat him? What is the judge's attitude toward Eliza? Point out in the text lines which prove your answers to these questions.
9. Why does the judge award the goose to Eliza?
10. What are the three things which Jess learns from the trial? What is the purpose of his comment to Enoch, "Never hire one [a man] till thee finds out first if he can count to eight"? What is the meaning of Enoch's response to this comment?
11. Do the characters in the story seem well motivated; that is, does the author make it clear why the characters act as they do? Explain.
12. One phrase which is repeated in the story is "steady as a pump bolt." What does Jess mean by the phrase when he uses it in the first scene? What does he mean when he uses it in the last scene?

Further Activity

Choose *one* of the following topic sentences for a paragraph. Copy it onto your paper; then develop this topic sentence into a paragraph by citing evidence in the story to prove the truth of the statement.

1. Jess does not understand Eliza.
2. Eliza understands how to deal with the judge.

Even if you have never studied a musical instrument, you will understand the humor—and suffering—involved when Clarence Day's father attempted to make his son a violinist. This selection is from *Life with Father and Mother,* a well-known American story which describes family life in New York City in the late 19th century.

The Noblest Instrument

Clarence Day

IMPROVING YOUR READING: In this selection the author describes a particular group of events that played an important part in his childhood. Much of what probably happened would not interest the reader. One of the main problems for Clarence Day, therefore, as it is for any author, was *selection of detail,* for it is as important to leave things out, in this or any type of writing, as it is to put things in. Note that the author here does not give a detailed description of each day's practice, but describes only those aspects of his bout with the violin which contribute to the final impression he wants to create.

FATHER HAD BEEN away, reorganizing some old upstate railroad. He returned in an executive mood and proceeded to shake up our home. In spite of my failure as a singer, he was still bound to have us taught music. We boys were summoned before him and informed that we must at once learn to play on something. We might not appreciate it now, he said, but we should later on. "You, Clarence, will learn the violin. George, you the piano. Julian—well, Julian is too young yet. But you older boys must have lessons."

I was appalled[1] at this order. At the age of ten it seemed a disaster to lose any more of my freedom. The days were already too short for our games after school; and now here

was a chunk to come out of playtime three days every week. A chunk every day, we found afterward, because we had to practice.

George sat at the piano in the parlor, and faithfully learned to pound out his exercises. He had all the luck. He was not an inspired player, but at least he had some ear for music. He also had the advantage of playing on a good robust[2] instrument, which he didn't have to be careful not to drop, and was in no danger of breaking. Furthermore, he did not have to tune it. A piano had some good points.

But I had to go through a blacker and more gruesome experience. It was bad enough to have to come in from the street and the sunlight and

1 appalled: shocked.

2 robust: strong.

THE ART OF STORYTELLING

go down into our dark little basement where I took my lessons. But that was only the opening chill of the struggle that followed.

The whole thing was uncanny. The violin itself was a queer, fragile, cigar-boxy thing, that had to be handled most gingerly. Nothing sturdy about it. Why, a fellow was liable to crack it putting it into its case. And then my teacher, he was queer too. He had a queer pickled smell.

I dare say he wasn't queer at all really, but he seemed so to me, because he was different from the people I generally met. He was probably worth a dozen of some of them, but I didn't know it. He was one of the violins in the Philharmonic, and an excellent player; a grave, middle-aged little man—who was obliged to give lessons.

He wore a black, wrinkled frock coat, and a discolored gold watch chain. He had small, black-rimmed glasses; not tortoise shell, but thin rims of metal. His violin was dark, rich, and polished, and would do anything for him.

Mine was balky and awkward, brand-new, and of a light, common color.

The violin is intended for persons with a passion for music. I wasn't that kind of person. I liked to hear a band play a tune that we could march up and down to, but try as I would, I could seldom whistle such a tune afterward. My teacher didn't know this. He greeted me as a possible genius.

He taught me how to hold the contraption, tucked under my chin.

I learned how to move my fingers here and there on its handle or stem. I learned how to draw the bow across the strings, and thus produce sounds. . . .

Does a mother recall the first cry of her baby, I wonder? I still remember the strange cry at birth of that new violin.

My teacher, Herr M., looked as though he had suddenly taken a large glass of vinegar. He sucked in his breath. His lips were drawn back from his teeth, and his eyes tightly shut. Of course, he hadn't expected my notes to be sweet at the start; but still, there was something unearthly about that first cry. He snatched the violin from me, examined it, readjusted its pegs, and comforted it gently, by drawing his own bow across it. It was only a new and not especially fine violin, but the sounds it made for him were more natural— they were classifiable sounds. They were not richly musical, but at least they had been heard before on this earth.

He handed the instrument back to me with careful directions. I tucked it up under my chin again and grasped the end tight. I held my bow exactly as ordered. I looked up at him, waiting.

"Now," he said, nervously.

I slowly raised the bow, drew it downward. . . .

This time there were *two* dreadful cries in our little front basement. One came from my new violin and one from the heart of Herr M.

Herr M. presently came to, and smiled bravely at me, and said if I

wanted to rest a moment he would permit it. He seemed to think I might wish to lie down awhile and recover. I didn't feel any need of lying down. All I wanted was to get through the lesson. But Herr M. was shaken. He was by no means ready to let me proceed. He looked around desperately, saw the music book, and said he would now show me that. We sat down side by side on the window seat, with the book in his lap, while he pointed out the notes to me with his finger, and told me their names.

After a bit, when he felt better, he took up his own violin, and instructed me to watch him and note how he handled the strings. And then at last, he nerved himself to let me take my violin up again. "Softly, my child, softly," he begged me, and stood facing the wall. . . .

We got through the afternoon somehow, but it was a ghastly experience. Part of the time he was maddened by the mistakes I kept making, and part of the time he was plain wretched. He covered his eyes. He seemed ill. He looked often at his watch, even shook it as though it had stopped; but he stayed the full hour.

That was Wednesday. What struggles he had with himself before Friday, when my second lesson was due, I can only dimly imagine, and of course I never even gave them a thought at the time. He came back to recommence teaching me, but he had changed—he had hardened. Instead of being cross, he was stern; and instead of sad, bitter. He wasn't unkind to me, but we were no longer companions. He talked to himself, under his breath; and sometimes he took bits of paper, and did little sums on them, gloomily, and then tore them up.

During my third lesson I saw the tears come to his eyes. He went up to Father and said he was sorry but he honestly felt sure I'd never be able to play.

Father didn't like this at all. He said he felt sure I would. He dismissed Herr M. briefly—the poor man came stumbling back down in two minutes. In that short space of time he had gallantly gone upstairs in a glow, resolved upon sacrificing his earnings for the sake of telling the truth. He returned with his earnings still running, but with the look of a lost soul about him, as though he felt that his nerves and his sanity were doomed to destruction. He was low in his mind, and he talked to himself more than ever. Sometimes he spoke harshly of America, sometimes of fate.

But he no longer struggled. He accepted this thing as his destiny. He regarded me as an unfortunate something, outside the human species, whom he must simply try to labor with as well as he could. It was a grotesque experience, but he felt he must bear it.

He wasn't the only one—he was at least not alone in his sufferings. Mother, though expecting the worst, had tried to be hopeful about it, but at the end of a week or two I heard her and Margaret talking it over. I was slaughtering a scale in the front basement, when Mother came down and stood outside the door in the kitchen hall

and whispered, "Oh, Margaret!"

I watched them. Margaret was baking a cake. She screwed up her face, raised her arms, and brought them down with hands clenched.

"I don't know what we shall do, Margaret."

"The poor little feller," Margaret whispered. "He can't make the thing go."

This made me indignant. They were making me look like a lubber.[3] I wished to feel always that I could make anything go. . . .

I now began to feel a determination to master this thing. History shows us many examples of the misplaced determinations of men—they are one of the darkest aspects of human life, they spread so much needless pain: but I knew little history. And I viewed what little I did know romantically—I should have seen in such episodes their heroism, not their futility.[4] Any role that seemed heroic attracted me, no matter how senseless.

Not that I saw any chance for heroism in our front basement, of course. You had to have a battlefield or something. I saw only that I was appearing ridiculous. But that stung my pride. I hadn't wanted to learn anything whatever about fiddles or music, but since I was in for it, I'd do it, and show them I could. A boy will often put in enormous amounts of his time trying to prove he isn't as ridiculous as he thinks people think him.

Meanwhile Herr M. and I had dis-

3 **lubber:** big, clumsy person; fool.
4 **futility:** uselessness.

covered that I was nearsighted. On account of the violin's being an instrument that sticks out in front of one, I couldn't stand close enough to the music book to see the notes clearly. He didn't at first realize that I often made mistakes from that cause. When he and I finally comprehended that I had this defect, he had a sudden new hope that this might have been the whole trouble, and that when it was corrected I might play like a human being at last.

Neither of us ventured to take up this matter with Father. We knew that it would have been hard to convince him that my eyes were not perfect, I being a son of his and presumably made in his image; and we knew that he immediately would have felt we were trying to make

trouble for him, and would have shown an amount of resentment which it was best to avoid. So Herr M. instead lent me his glasses. These did fairly well. They turned the dim grayness of the notes into a queer bright distortion, but the main thing was they did make them brighter, so that I now saw more of them. How well I remember those little glasses. Poor, dingy old things. Herr M. was nervous about lending them to me; he feared that I'd drop them. It would have been safer if they had been spectacles: but no, they were pince-nez;[5] and I had to learn to balance them across my nose as well as I could. I couldn't wear them up near my eyes because my nose was

5 pince-nez (păns'nā'): eyeglasses which are clipped onto the nose.

too thin there; I had to put them about half-way down where there was enough flesh to hold them. I also had to tilt my head back, for the music stand was a little too tall for me. Herr M. sometimes mounted me on a stool, warning me not to step off. Then when I was all set, and when he without his glasses was blind, I would smash my way into the scales again.

All during the long winter months I worked away at this job. I gave no thought, of course, to the family. But they did to me. Our house was heated by a furnace, which had big warm air pipes; these ran up through the walls with wide outlets into each room, and sound traveled easily and ringingly through their roomy, tin passages. My violin could be heard in every part of the house. No one could settle down to anything while I was practicing. If visitors came they soon left. Mother couldn't even sing to the baby. She would wait, watching the clock, until my long hour of scalework was over, and then come downstairs and shriek at me that my time was up. She would find me sawing away with my forehead wet, and my hair wet and stringy, and even my clothes slowly getting damp from my exertions. She would feel my collar, which was done for, and say I must change it. "Oh, Mother! Please!"—for I was in a hurry now to run out and play. But she wasn't being fussy about my collar, I can see, looking back; she was using it merely as a barometer or gauge of my pores. She thought I had better dry my-

self before going out in the snow.

It was a hard winter for Mother. I believe she also had fears for the baby. She sometimes pleaded with Father; but no one could ever tell Father anything. He continued to stand like a rock against stopping my lessons.

Schopenhauer,[6] in his rules for debating, shows how to win a weak case by insidiously[7] transferring an argument from its right field, and discussing it instead from some irrelevant but impregnable[8] angle. Father knew nothing of Schopenhauer, and was never insidious, but, nevertheless, he had certain natural gifts for debate. In the first place his voice was powerful and stormy, and he let it out at full strength, and kept on letting it out with a vigor that stunned his opponents. As a second gift, he was convinced at all times that his opponents were wrong. Hence, even if they did win a point or two, it did them no good, for he dragged the issue to some other ground then, where he and Truth could prevail. When Mother said it surely was plain enough that I had no ear, what was his reply? Why, he said that the violin was the noblest instrument invented by man. Having silenced her with this solid premise he declared that it followed that any boy was lucky to be given the privilege of learning to play it. No boy should expect to learn it immediately. It

---

6 **Schopenhauer:** a 19th-century German philosopher.
7 **insidiously:** slyly; shrewdly.
8 **irrelevant but impregnable:** remote but able to resist attack.

required persistence. Everything, he had found, required persistence. The motto was, Never give up.

All his life, he declared, he had persevered[9] in spite of discouragement, and he meant to keep on persevering, and he meant me to, too. He said that none of us realized what he had had to go through. If he had been the kind that gave up at the very first obstacle, where would he have been now—where would any of the family have been? The answer was, apparently, that we'd either have been in a very bad way, poking round for crusts in the gutter, or else nonexistent. We might have never even been born if Father had not persevered.

Placed beside this record of Father's vast trials overcome, the little difficulty of my learning to play the violin seemed a trifle. I faithfully spurred myself on again, to work at the puzzle. Even my teacher seemed impressed with these views on persistence. Though older than Father, he had certainly not made as much money, and he bowed to the experience of a practical man who was a success. If he, Herr M., had been a success he would not have had to teach boys; and sitting in this black pit in which his need of money had placed him, he saw more than ever that he must learn the ways of this world. He listened with all his heart, as to a god, when Father shook his forefinger, and told him how to climb to the heights where financial rewards were achieved. The idea he got was

that perseverance was sure to lead to great wealth.

Consequently our front basement continued to be the home of lost causes.

Of course, I kept begging Herr M. to let me learn just one tune. Even though I seldom could whistle them, still I liked tunes; and I knew that, in my hours of practicing, a tune would be a comfort. That is, for myself. Here again I never gave a thought to the effect upon others.

Herr M., after many misgivings, to which I respectfully listened—though they were not spoken to me, they were muttered to himself, pessimistically[10]—hunted through a worn old book of selections, and after much doubtful fumbling chose as simple a thing as he could find for me—for me and the neighbors.

It was spring now, and windows were open. That tune became famous.

What would the musician who had tenderly composed this air, years before, have felt if he had foreseen what an end it would have, on Madison Avenue; and how, before death, it would be execrated[11] by that once peaceful neighborhood. I engraved it on their hearts; not in its true form but in my own eerie versions. It was the only tune I knew. Consequently I played and replayed it.

Even horrors when repeated grow old and lose part of their sting. But those I produced were, unluckily, never the same. To be sure, this tune kept its general structure the

---

9 **persevered:** persisted; carried on.

10 **pessimistically:** hopelessly.
11 **execrated:** detested; cursed.

same, even in my sweating hands. There was always the place where I climbed unsteadily up to its peak, and that difficult spot where it wavered, or staggered, and stuck; and then a sudden jerk of resumption[12]— I came out strong on that. Every afternoon when I got to that difficult spot, the neighbors dropped whatever they were doing to wait for that jerk, shrinking from the moment, and yet feverishly impatient for it to come.

But what made the tune and their anguish so different each day? I'll explain. The strings of a violin are wound at the end around pegs, and each peg must be screwed in and tightened till the string sounds just right. Herr M. left my violin properly tuned when he went. But suppose a string broke, or that somehow I jarred a peg loose. Its string then became slack and soundless. I had to retighten it. Not having an ear, I was highly uncertain about this.

Our neighbors never knew at what degree of tautness[13] I'd put such a string. I didn't myself. I just screwed her up tight enough to make a strong reliable sound. Neither they nor I could tell which string would thus appear in a new role each day, nor foresee the profound transformations this would produce in that tune.

All that spring this unhappy and ill-destined melody floated out through my window, and writhed in the air for one hour daily, in sunshine or storm. All that spring our neighbors and I daily toiled to its peak, and staggered over its hump, so to speak, and fell wailing through space.

12 resumption: beginning again.
13 tautness: tightness.

Things now began to be said to Mother which drove her to act. She explained to Father that the end had come at last. Absolutely. "This awful nightmare cannot go on," she said.

Father pooh-poohed her.

She cried. She told him what it was doing to her. He said that she was excited, and that her descriptions of the sounds I made were exaggerated and hysterical—must be. She was always too vehement, he shouted. She must learn to be calm.

"But you're downtown, *you* don't have to hear it!"

Father remained wholly skeptical.

She endeavored to shame him. She told him what awful things the neighbors were saying about him, because of the noise I was making, for which he was responsible.

He couldn't be made to look at it that way. If there really were any unpleasantness then I was responsible. He had provided me with a good teacher and a good violin—so he reasoned. In short, he had done his best, and no father could have done more. If I made hideous sounds after all that, the fault must be mine. He said that Mother should be stricter with me, if necessary, and make me try harder.

This was the last straw. I couldn't try harder. When Mother told me his verdict I said nothing, but my body rebelled. Self-discipline had its limits—and I wanted to be out: it was spring. I skimped my hours of practice when I heard the fellows playing outside. I came home late for lessons—even forgot them. Little by little they stopped.

Father was outraged. His final argument, I remember, was that my violin had cost twenty-five dollars; if I didn't learn it the money would be wasted, and he couldn't afford it. But it was put to him that my younger brother, Julian, could learn it instead, later on. Then summer came, anyhow, and we went for three months to the seashore; and in the confusion of this Father was defeated and I was set free.

In the autumn little Julian was led away one afternoon, and imprisoned in the front basement in my place. I don't remember how long they kept him down there, but it was several years. He had an ear, however, and I believe he learned to play fairly well. This would have made a happy ending for Herr M. after all; but it was some other teacher, a younger man, who was engaged to teach Julian. Father said Herr M. was a failure.

Understanding Literature

1. In this selection Clarence Day's father is characterized in particular detail. What were some of his father's characteristics? In what way was the author similar to his father?
2. In what respects was the violin teacher, Herr M., very different from the author's father?
3. Why did the author feel, at one point, that he had to master the violin? What finally made him give up?
4. Although the violin lessons lasted for several months, Day includes only a few main incidents during this time. Why does he include these particular events?

Further Activity

Write a short essay in which you describe an incident that you think will interest a reader. You might choose your early experiences with an instrument, as Clarence Day did, a trip which you took with an older person, or an event which to you seems typical of your family. After you plan your essay, look back at the way Day wrote about his experience. He did not describe everything that happened; he chose only those details that he thought would be most interesting. Try to achieve the same goal in your essay.

In this story Frank O'Connor, a famous Irish writer, describes a school he attended in Ireland. The boy in the story does the right thing, but he still gets in trouble. He just cannot win.

The Idealist

Frank O'Connor

IMPROVING YOUR READING: *Satire* is a technique used to expose human folly to ridicule or scorn, for the purpose of improving humanity. Here the author is satirizing, or making fun of, a teacher who drove his students into wrong actions because of the way he punished them. Observe, too, the use of *irony*, a type of contrast. The leading character expects things to turn out one way but actually they turn out in a way just the opposite.

I DON'T know how it is about education, but it never seemed to do anything for me but get me into trouble.

Adventure stories weren't so bad, but as a kid I was very serious and preferred realism to romance. School stories were what I liked best, and, judged by our standards, these were romantic enough for anyone. The schools were English, so I suppose you couldn't expect anything else. They were always called "the venerable[1] pile," and there was usually a ghost in them; they were built in a square that was called "the quad," and, according to the pictures, they were all clock towers, spires, and pinnacles, like the lunatic asylum with us. The fellows in the stories were all good climbers, and got in and out of school at night on ropes made of knotted sheets. They dressed queerly; they wore long trousers, short, black jackets, and top hats. Whenever they did anything wrong they were given "lines" in Latin. When it was a bad case, they were flogged and never showed any sign of pain; only the bad fellows, and they always said: "Ow! Ow!"

Most of them were grand chaps who always stuck together and were great at football and cricket. They never told lies and wouldn't talk to anyone who did. If they were caught out and asked a point-blank question, they always told the truth, unless someone else was with them, and then even if they were to be expelled for it they wouldn't give his name, even if he was a thief, which, as a matter of fact, he frequently was. It was surprising in such good schools, with fathers who never gave less than five quid,[2] the number of thieves there were. The fellows in our

1 venerable: honorable; sacred.

2 quid: slang term for a British pound.

school hardly ever stole, though they only got a penny a week, and sometimes not even that, as when their fathers were on the booze and their mothers had to go to the pawn.

I worked hard at the football and cricket, though of course we never had a proper football and the cricket we played was with a hurley[3] stick against a wicket chalked on some wall. The officers in the barrack played proper cricket, and on summer evenings I used to go and watch them, like one of the souls in Purgatory[4] watching the joys of Paradise.

Even so, I couldn't help being disgusted at the bad way things were run in our school. Our "venerable pile" was a red-brick building without tower or pinnacle a fellow could climb, and no ghost at all: we had no team, so a fellow, no matter how hard he worked, could never play for the school, and, instead of giving you "lines," Latin or any other sort, Murderer Moloney either lifted you by the ears or bashed you with a cane. When he got tired of bashing you on the hands he bashed you on the legs.

But these were only superficial things. What was really wrong was ourselves. The fellows sucked up to the masters and told them all that went on. If they were caught out in anything they tried to put the blame on someone else, even if it meant telling lies. When they were caned they sniveled and said it wasn't fair; drew back their hands as if they were terrified, so that the cane caught only the tips of their fingers, and then screamed and stood on one leg, shaking out their fingers in the hope of getting it counted as one. Finally they roared that their wrist was broken and crawled back to their desks with their hands squeezed under their armpits, howling. I mean you couldn't help feeling ashamed, imagining what chaps from a decent school would think if they saw it.

My own way to school led me past the barrack gate. In those peaceful days sentries never minded you going past the guardroom to have a look at the chaps drilling in the barrack square; if you came at dinnertime they even called you in and gave you plumduff and tea. Naturally, with such temptations I was often late. The only excuse, short of a letter from your mother, was to say you were at early Mass. The Murderer would never know whether you were or not, and if he did anything to you you could easily get him into trouble with the parish priest. Even as kids we knew who the real boss of the school was.

But after I started reading those confounded school stories I was never happy about saying I had been to Mass. It was a lie, and I knew that the chaps in the stories would have died sooner than tell it. They were all round me like invisible presences, and I hated to do anything which I felt they might disapprove of.

One morning I came in very late and rather frightened.

"What kept you till this hour,

3 **hurley:** Irish version of hockey.
4 **Purgatory:** according to some Christian teachings, the place of temporary punishment after death.

THE ART OF STORYTELLING

Delaney?" Murderer Moloney asked, looking at the clock.

I wanted to say I had been at Mass, but I couldn't. The invisible presences were all about me.

"I was delayed at the barrack, sir," I replied in panic.

There was a faint titter from the class, and Moloney raised his brows in mild surprise. He was a big powerful man with fair hair and blue eyes and a manner that at times was deceptively mild.

"Oh, indeed," he said, politely enough. "And what delayed you?"

"I was watching the soldiers drilling, sir," I said.

The class tittered again. This was a new line entirely for them.

"Oh," Moloney said casually, "I never knew you were such a military man. Hold out your hand!"

Compared with the laughter the slaps were nothing, and besides, I had the example of the invisible presences to sustain me. I did not flinch. I returned to my desk slowly and quietly without sniveling or squeezing my hands, and the Murderer looked after me, raising his brows again as though to indicate that this was a new line for him, too. But the others gaped and whispered as if I were some strange animal. At playtime they gathered about me, full of curiosity and excitement.

"Delaney, why did you say that about the barrack?"

"Because 'twas true," I replied firmly. "I wasn't going to tell him a lie."

"What lie?"

"That I was at Mass."

"Then couldn't you say you had to go on a message?"

"That would be a lie too."

"Cripes, Delaney," they said, "you'd better mind yourself. The Murderer is in an awful wax.[5] He'll massacre you."

I knew that. I knew only too well that the Murderer's professional pride had been deeply wounded, and for the rest of the day I was on my best behavior. But my best wasn't enough, for I underrated the Murderer's guile. Though he pretended to be reading, he was watching me the whole time.

"Delaney," he said at last without raising his head from the book, "was that you talking?"

" 'Twas, sir," I replied in consternation.

The whole class laughed. They couldn't believe but that I was deliberately trailing my coat,[6] and, of course, the laugh must have convinced him that I was. I suppose if people do tell you lies all day and every day, it soon becomes a sort of perquisite[7] which you resent being deprived of.

"Oh," he said, throwing down his book, "we'll soon stop that."

This time it was a tougher job, because he was really on his mettle.[8] But so was I. I knew this was the testing point for me, and if only I could keep my head I should provide a model for the whole class. When I had got through the ordeal with-

5 **wax:** fit of bad temper.
6 **trailing my coat:** offering a challenge; defying him.
7 **perquisite** (pûr′kwə zĭt): an expected profit.
8 **on his mettle:** inspired to do his best.

out moving a muscle, and returned to my desk with my hands by my sides, the invisible presences gave me a great clap. But the visible ones were nearly as annoyed as the Murderer himself. After school half a dozen of them followed me down the school yard.

"Go on!" they shouted truculently.[9] "Shaping as usual!"

"I was not shaping."

"You were shaping. You're always showing off. Trying to pretend he didn't hurt you—a blooming crybaby like you!"

"I wasn't trying to pretend," I shouted, even then resisting the temptation to nurse my bruised hands. "Only decent fellows don't cry over every little pain like kids."

"Go on!" they bawled after me. "You ould idiot!" And, as I went down the school lane, still trying to keep what the stories called "a stiff upper lip," and consoling myself with the thought that my torment was over until next morning, I heard their mocking voices after me.

"Loony Larry! Yah, Loony Larry!"

I realized that if I was to keep on terms with the invisible presences I should have to watch my step at school.

So I did, all through that year. But one day an awful thing happened. I was coming in from the yard, and in the porch outside our schoolroom I saw a fellow called Gorman taking something from a coat on the rack. I always described Gorman to myself as "the black sheep

9 **truculently:** threateningly; savagely.

of the school." He was a fellow I disliked and feared; a handsome, sulky, spoiled, and sneering lout. I paid no attention to him because I had escaped for a few moments into my dreamworld in which fathers never gave less than fivers and the honor of the school was always saved by some quiet, unassuming fellow like myself—"a dark horse," as the stories called him.

"Who are you looking at?" Gorman asked threateningly.

"I wasn't looking at anyone," I replied with an indignant start.

"I was only getting a pencil out of my coat," he added, clenching his fists.

"Nobody said you weren't," I replied, thinking that this was a very queer subject to start a row about.

"You'd better not, either," he snarled. "You can mind your own business."

"You mind yours!" I retorted, purely for the purpose of saving face. "I never spoke to you at all."

And that, so far as I was concerned, was the end of it.

But after playtime the Murderer, looking exceptionally serious, stood before the class, balancing a pencil in both hands.

"Everyone who left the classroom this morning, stand out!" he called. Then he lowered his head and looked at us from under his brows. "Mind now, I said everyone!"

I stood out with the others, including Gorman. We were all very puzzled.

"Did you take anything from a coat on the rack this morning?" the

Murderer asked, laying a heavy, hairy paw on Gorman's shoulder and staring menacingly into his eyes.

"Me, sir?" Gorman exclaimed innocently. "No, sir."

"Did you see anyone else doing it?"

"No, sir."

"You?" he asked another lad, but even before he reached me at all I realized why Gorman had told the lie and wondered frantically what I should do.

"You?" he asked me, and his big red face was close to mine, his blue eyes were only a few inches away, and the smell of his toilet soap was in my nostrils. My panic made me say the wrong thing as though I had planned it.

"I didn't take anything, sir," I said in a low voice.

"Did you see someone else do it?" he asked, raising his brows and showing quite plainly that he had noticed my evasion. "Have you a tongue in your head?" he shouted suddenly, and the whole class, electrified, stared at me. "You?" he added curtly to the next boy as though he had lost interest in me.

"No, sir."

"Back to your desks, the rest of you!" he ordered. "Delaney, you stay here."

He waited till everyone was seated again before going on.

"Turn out your pockets."

I did, and a half-stifled giggle rose, which the Murderer quelled[10] with a thunderous glance. Even for a small boy I had pockets that were

10 **quelled:** stopped; hushed.

museums in themselves: the purpose of half the things I brought to light I couldn't have explained myself. They were antiques, prehistoric and unlabelled. Among them was a school story borrowed the previous evening from a queer fellow who chewed paper as if it were gum. The Murderer reached out for it, and holding it at arm's length, shook it out with an expression of deepening disgust as he noticed the nibbled corners and margins.

"Oh," he said disdainfully, "so this is how you waste your time! What do you do with this rubbish—eat it?"

"'Tisn't mine, sir," I said against the laugh that sprang up. "I borrowed it."

"Is that what you did with the money?" he asked quickly, his fat head on one side.

"Money?" I repeated in confusion. "What money?"

"The shilling that was stolen from Flanagan's overcoat this morning."

(Flanagan was a little hunchback whose people coddled him; no one else in the school would have possessed that much money.)

"I never took Flanagan's shilling," I said, beginning to cry, "and you have no right to say I did."

"I have the right to say you're the most impudent and defiant puppy in the school," he replied, his voice hoarse with rage, "and I wouldn't put it past you. What else can anyone expect and you reading this dirty, rotten, filthy rubbish?" And he tore my school story in halves and flung them to the furthest corner of the classroom. "Dirty, filthy, English

rubbish! Now, hold out your hand."

This time the invisible presences deserted me. Hearing themselves described in these contemptuous[11] terms, they fled. The Murderer went mad in the way people do whenever they're up against something they don't understand. Even the other fellows were shocked, and, heaven knows, they had little sympathy with me.

"You should put the police on him," they advised me later in the playground. "He lifted the cane over his shoulder. He could get the gaol[12] for that."

"But why didn't you say you didn't see anyone?" asked the eldest, a fellow called Spillane.

"Because I did," I said, beginning to sob all over again at the memory of my wrongs. "I saw Gorman."

"Gorman?" Spillane echoed incredulously.[13] "Was it Gorman took Flanagan's money? And why didn't you say so?"

"Because it wouldn't be right," I sobbed.

"Why wouldn't it be right?"

"Because Gorman should have told the truth himself," I said. "And if this was a proper school he'd be sent to Coventry."

"He'd be sent where?"

"Coventry. No one would ever speak to him again."

"But why would Gorman tell the truth if he took the money?" Spillane asked as you'd speak to a baby. "Jay, Delaney," he added pityingly,

11 **contemptuous:** scornful; disrespectful.
12 **gaol:** British spelling of *jail.*
13 **incredulously:** not willing to believe.

"you're getting madder and madder. Now, look at what you're after bringing on yourself!"

Suddenly Gorman came lumbering up, red and angry.

"Delaney," he shouted threateningly, "did you say I took Flanagan's money?"

Gorman, though I of course didn't realize it, was as much at sea as Moloney and the rest. Seeing me take all that punishment rather than give him away, he concluded that I must be more afraid of him than of Moloney, and that the proper thing to do was to make me more so. He couldn't have come at a time when I cared less for him. I didn't even bother to reply but lashed out with all my strength at his brutal face. This was the last thing he expected. He screamed, and his hand came away from his face, all blood. Then he threw off his satchel and came at me, but at the same moment a door opened behind us and a lame teacher called Murphy emerged. We all ran like mad and the fight was forgotten.

It didn't remain forgotten, though. Next morning after prayers the Murderer scowled at me.

"Delaney, were you fighting in the yard after school yesterday?"

For a second or two I didn't reply. I couldn't help feeling that it wasn't worth it. But before the invisible presences fled forever, I made another effort.

"I was, sir," I said, and this time there wasn't even a titter. I was out of my mind. The whole class knew it and was awe-stricken.

"Who were you fighting?"

"I'd sooner not say, sir," I replied, hysteria beginning to well up in me. It was all very well for the invisible presences, but they hadn't to deal with the Murderer.

"Who was he fighting with?" he asked lightly, resting his hands on the desk and studying the ceiling.

"Gorman, sir," replied three or four voices—as easy as that!

"Did Gorman hit him first?"

"No, sir. He hit Gorman first."

"Stand out," he said, taking up the cane. "Now," he added, going up to Gorman, "you take this and hit him. And make sure you hit him hard," he went on, giving Gorman's arm an encouraging squeeze. "He thinks he's a great fellow. You show him now what we think of him."

Gorman came towards me with a broad grin. He thought it a great joke. The class thought it a great joke. They began to roar with laughter. Even the Murderer permitted himself a modest grin at his own cleverness.

"Hold out your hand," he said to me.

I didn't. I began to feel trapped and a little crazy.

"Hold out your hand, I say," he shouted, beginning to lose his temper.

"I will not," I shouted back, losing all control of myself.

"You what?" he cried incredulously, dashing at me round the classroom with his hand raised as though to strike me. "What's that you said, you dirty little thief?"

"I'm not a thief, I'm not a thief," I screamed. "And if he comes near me I'll kick the shins off him. You have no right to give him that cane, and you have no right to call me a thief either. If you do it again, I'll go down to the police and then we'll see who the thief is."

"You refused to answer my questions," he roared, and if I had been in my right mind I should have known he had suddenly taken fright; probably the word *police* had frightened him.

"No," I said through my sobs, "and I won't answer them now either. I'm not a spy."

"Oh," he retorted with a sarcastic sniff, "so that's what you call a spy, Mr. Delaney?"

"Yes, and that's what they all are, all the fellows here—dirty spies!—but I'm not going to be a spy for you. You can do your own spying."

"That's enough now, that's enough!" he said, raising his fat hand almost beseechingly. "There's no need to lose control of yourself, my dear young fellow, and there's no need whatever to screech like that. 'Tis most unmanly. Go back to your seat now and I'll talk to you another time."

I obeyed, but I did no work. No one else did much either. The hysteria had spread to the class. I alternated between fits of exultation at my own successful defiance of the Murderer, and panic at the prospect of his revenge; and at each change of mood I put my face in my hands and sobbed again. The Murderer didn't even order me to stop. He didn't so much as look at me.

After that I was the hero of the school for the whole afternoon. Gorman tried to resume the fight, but Spillane ordered him away contemptuously—a fellow who had taken the master's cane to another had no status. But that wasn't the sort of hero I wanted to be. I preferred something less sensational.

Next morning I was in such a state of panic that I didn't know how I should face school at all. I dawdled, between two minds as to whether or not I should mitch.[14] The silence of the school lane and yard awed me. I had made myself late as well.

"What kept you, Delaney?" the Murderer asked quietly.

I knew it was no good.

"I was at Mass, sir."

"All right. Take your seat."

He seemed a bit surprised. What I had not realized was the incidental advantage of our system over the English one. By this time half a dozen of his pets had brought the Murderer the true story of Flanagan's shilling, and if he didn't feel a monster he probably felt a fool.

But by that time I didn't care. In my school sack I had another story. Not a school story this time, though. School stories were a washout. "Bang! Bang!"—that was the only way to deal with men like the Murderer. "The only good teacher is a dead teacher."

14 **mitch:** play truant; skip school.

THE ART OF STORYTELLING

Understanding Literature

1. How does reading cause trouble for the narrator, Delaney, in this story?
2. What are the major differences between the English schools Delaney reads about and his own school?
3. Why does the boy begin telling the truth? The author describes several scenes in which Delaney tells the truth. How do the scenes differ?
4. Why does the teacher suddenly become frightened?
5. When Gorman tries to resume the fight, he has "no status" at all. Why has he lost his standing with the boys? Why does he not lose this standing when he steals the money?
6. Why, at the end of the story, does Delaney again use the old excuse of being at Mass when he is late? What else might he have said or done at this point?
7. The last line of the story is obviously a typical quotation from what kind of a story? What does his taste in reading show about Delaney? What is the significance of the title, "The Idealist"?
8. In this story the author is certainly not making fun of people who tell the truth. Whom *is* he satirizing?
9. Since the type of teacher presented in this story is rarely seen today, the author is certainly not describing all teachers. What is the author's attitude toward this particular teacher? What is his attitude toward Delaney? Remember that the "I"—the narrator—of the story and the author are not necessarily the same person.

Further Activities

1. Write a short paragraph that begins with the following sentence: In "The Idealist" the narrator says, "I don't know how it is about education, but it never seemed to do anything for me but get me into trouble." In the rest of the paragraph summarize the main idea of the story, showing how the boy gets into trouble. Do not go into detail.
2. At one point in the story the narrator says: "The Murderer went mad in the way people do whenever they're up against something they don't understand." In one or two paragraphs try to explain why lack of understanding can have this effect. To illustrate your explanation you might describe a situation in which you have seen someone behave in this way.

Colette, a 20th-century French writer, here presents an essay on her childhood—as she remembers it.

Where Are the Children?

Colette

IMPROVING YOUR READING: The author's *selection of detail*, the images and scenes which she chooses to recall, should give you a sense of how she feels about the memories of her house.

THE HOUSE WAS large, topped by a lofty garret. The steep gradient[1] of the street compelled the coach houses, stables, and poultry house, the laundry and the dairy, to huddle on a lower level all round a closed courtyard.

By leaning over the garden wall, I could scratch with my finger the poultry-house roof. The Upper Garden overlooked the Lower Garden—a warm, confined enclosure reserved for the cultivation of aubergines[2] and pimentos—where the smell of tomato leaves mingled in July with that of the apricots ripening on the walls. In the Upper Garden were two twin firs, a walnut tree whose intolerant shade killed any flowers beneath it, some rosebushes, a neglected lawn and a dilapidated arbor. At the bottom, along the Rue des Vignes, a boundary wall reinforced with a strong iron railing ought to have ensured the privacy of the two gardens, but I never knew those railings other than twisted and torn from their cement foundations, and grappling in mid-air with the invincible[3] arms of a hundred-year-old wistaria.[4]

In the Rue de l'Hospice, a two-way flight of steps led up to the front door in the gloomy façade[5] with its large bare windows. It was the typical burgher's house in an old village, but its dignity was upset a little by the steep gradient of the street, the stone steps being lopsided, ten on one side and six on the other.

A large solemn house, rather forbidding, with its shrill bell and its carriage entrance with a huge bolt like an ancient dungeon, a house that smiled only on its garden side. The back, invisible to passers-by, was a sun-trap, swathed[6] in a mantle of wistaria and bignonia too heavy for the trellis of worn ironwork, which sagged in the middle like a hammock and provided shade for the

---

1 **gradient:** slope.
2 **aubergines** (ō′bĕr zhēnz): eggplants.
3 **invincible:** unconquerable.
4 **wistaria:** flowered vine.
5 **façade** (fə säd′): front or face of a building.
6 **swathed:** wrapped; enveloped.

THE ART OF STORYTELLING

little flagged terrace and the threshold of the sitting room.

Is it worth while, I wonder, seeking for adequate words to describe the rest? I shall never be able to conjure up[7] the splendor that adorns, in my memory, the ruddy festoons[8] of an autumn vine borne down by its own weight and clinging despairingly to some branch of the fir trees. And the massive lilacs, whose compact flowers—blue in the shade and purple in the sunshine—withered so soon, stifled by their own exuberance.[9] The lilacs long since dead will not be revived at my bidding, any more than the terrifying moonlight—silver, quicksilver, leaden-gray, with facets[10] of dazzling amethyst or scintillating[11] points of sapphire—all depending on a certain pane in the blue glass window of the summer house at the bottom of the garden.

Both house and garden are living still, I know; but what of that, if the magic has deserted them? If the secret is lost that opened to me a whole world—light, scents, birds and trees in perfect harmony, the murmur of human voices now silent forever—a world of which I have ceased to be worthy?

It would happen sometimes long ago, when this house and garden harbored a family, that a book lying open on the flagstones of the terrace or on the grass, a skipping rope twisted like a snake across the path, or perhaps a miniature garden, pebble-edged and planted with decapitated flowers, revealed both the presence of children and their varying ages. But such evidence was hardly ever accompanied by childish shouts or laughter, and my home, though warm and full, bore an odd resemblance to those houses which, once the holidays have come to an end, are suddenly emptied of joy. The silence, the muted[12] breeze of the enclosed garden, the pages of the book stirred only by invisible fingers, all seemed to be asking, "Where are the children?"

It was then, from beneath the ancient iron trellis sagging to the left under the wistaria, that my mother would make her appearance, small and plump in those days when age had not yet wasted her. She would scan the thick green clumps and, raising her head, fling her call into the air: "Children! Where are the children?"

Where indeed? Nowhere. My mother's cry would ring through the garden, striking the great wall of the barn and returning to her as a faint exhausted echo. "Where . . . ? Children . . . ?"

Nowhere. My mother would throw back her head and gaze heavenwards, as though waiting for a flock of winged children to alight from the skies. After a moment she would repeat her call; then, grown tired of questioning the heavens, she would crack a dry poppyhead with her fingernail, rub the greenfly from

7 **conjure up:** that is, make it clear to the reader.
8 **festoons:** wreaths; garlands.
9 **exuberance:** great abundance.
10 **facets:** surfaces.
11 **scintillating:** sparkling.

12 **muted:** faint; gentle.

a rose shoot, fill her pockets with un-ripe walnuts, and return to the house shaking her head over the vanished children.

And all the while, from among the leaves of the walnut tree above her, gleamed the pale, pointed face of a child who lay stretched like a tom-cat along a big branch, and never uttered a word. A less shortsighted mother might well have suspected that the spasmodic salutations[13] ex-changed by the twin tops of the two firs were due to some influence other than that of the sudden October squalls! And in the square dormer, above the pulley for hauling up fodder, would she not have per-ceived, if she had screwed up her eyes, two pale patches among the hay—the face of a young boy and the pages of his book?

But she had given up looking for us, had despaired of trying to reach us. Our uncanny turbulence[14] was never accompanied by any sound. I do not believe there can ever have been children so active and so mute. Looking back at what we were, I am amazed. No one had imposed upon us either our cheerful silence or our limited sociability. My nineteen-year-old brother, engrossed in con-structing some hydrotherapeutic ap-paratus[15] out of linen bladders, strands of wire and glass tubes, never prevented the younger, aged four-teen, from disemboweling[16] a watch

or from transposing on the piano, with never a false note, a melody or an air from a symphony heard at a concert in the county town. He did not even interfere with his junior's incomprehensible[17] passion for dec-orating the garden with little tomb-stones cut out of cardboard, and each inscribed, beneath the sign of the cross, with the names, epitaph, and genealogy[18] of the imaginary person deceased.

My sister with the too long hair might read forever with never a pause; the two boys would brush past her as though they did not see the young girl sitting abstracted[19] and entranced, and never bother her. When I was small, I was at liberty to keep up as best I could with my long-legged brothers as they ranged the woods in pursuit of swallowtails, White Admirals, Purple Emperors, or hunted for grass snakes, or gathered armfuls of the tall July foxgloves which grew in the clearings already aglow with patches of purple heather. But I followed them in silence, pick-ing blackberries, bird cherries, a chance wild flower, or roving the hedgerows and waterlogged mead-ows like an independent dog out hunting on its own.

"Where are the children?" She would suddenly appear like an over-solicitous[20] mother-dog breathlessly pursuing her constant quest, head lifted and scenting the breeze. Some-times her white linen sleeves bore

---

13 spasmodic salutations: irregular gestures of greeting.
14 uncanny turbulence: mysterious unrest.
15 hydrotherapeutic apparatus: system for treat-ing diseases by means of baths.
16 disemboweling: taking apart.

17 incomprehensible: impossible to understand.
18 genealogy: line of ancestors; bloodline.
19 abstracted: lost in thought.
20 oversolicitous: too-fearful.

THE ART OF STORYTELLING

witness that she had come from kneading dough for cakes or making the pudding that had a velvety hot sauce of rum and jam. If she had been washing the Havanese dog, she would be enveloped in a long blue apron, and sometimes she would be waving a banner of rustling yellow paper, the paper used round the butcher's meat, which meant that she hoped to reassemble, at the same time as her elusive[21] children, her carnivorous[22] family of vagabond cats.

To her traditional cry she would add, in the same anxious and appealing key, a reminder of the time of day. "Four o'clock, and they haven't come in to tea! Where are the children? . . ." "Half-past six! Will they come home to dinner? Where are the children? . . ." That lovely voice; how I should weep for joy if I could hear it now! Our only sin, our single misdeed, was silence, and a kind of miraculous vanishing. For perfectly innocent reasons, for the sake of a liberty that no one denied us, we clambered over the railing, leaving behind our shoes, and returned by way of an unnecessary ladder or a neighbor's low wall.

Our anxious mother's keen sense of smell would discover on us traces of wild garlic from a distant ravine or of marsh mint from a treacherous bog. The dripping pocket of one of the boys would disgorge the bathing slip worn in malarial ponds, and the "little one," cut about the knees and skinned at the elbows, would be bleeding complacently[23] under plasters of cobweb and wild pepper bound on with rushes.

"Tomorrow I shall keep you locked up! All of you, do you hear, every single one of you!"

Tomorrow! Next day the eldest, slipping on the slated roof where he was fitting a tank, broke his collarbone and remained at the foot of the wall waiting, politely silent and half unconscious, until someone came to pick him up. Next day an eighteen-rung ladder crashed plumb on the forehead of the younger son, who never uttered a cry, but brought home with becoming modesty a lump like a purple egg between his eyes.

"Where are the children?"

Two are at rest. The others grow older day by day. If there be a place of waiting after this life, then surely she who so often waited for us has not ceased to tremble for those two who are yet alive.

For the eldest of us all, at any rate, she has done with looking at the dark windowpane every evening and saying, "I feel that child is not happy. I feel she is suffering." And for the elder of the boys she no longer listens, breathlessly, to the wheels of a doctor's trap[24] coming over the snow at night, or to the hoofbeats of the gray mare.

But I know that for the two who remain she seeks and wanders still, invisible, tormented by her inability to watch over them enough.

"Where, oh where are the children? . . ."

---

21 **elusive:** runaway; fugitive.
22 **carnivorous:** meat-eating.
23 **complacently:** in a satisfied way; contentedly.
24 **trap:** one-horse carriage.

Understanding Literature

1. Describe in your own words Colette's house and its grounds.
2. Colette shortens her descriptions by using comparisons. What do you see in your imagination when you read the following phrases?
    (a) ". . . a house that smiled only on its garden side."
    (b) ". . . a mantle of wistaria and bignonia too heavy for the trellis of worn ironwork, which sagged in the middle like a hammock. . . ."
    (c) ". . . the ruddy festoons of an autumn vine borne down by its own weight and clinging despairingly to some branch of the fir trees."
    (d) ". . . a miniature garden, pebble-edged and planted with decapitated flowers. . . ."
3. In the paragraph beginning "And all the while. . . ," where are the children?
4. Colette is offering to her readers a series of pictures, as though they were paintings of scenes. Where does each scene begin and end? Can you find the words that indicate that the scenes are taken from the past?
5. Where is she not painting pictures, but, rather, commenting directly on her life as a child?
6. What is Colette's feeling about her childhood? What evidence can you find for your answer?

Further Activity

A person is in contact with the world through his senses: sight, smell, touch, taste, and hearing. The more he uses these senses the more he is aware of what is around him in the world. A good reader should be able to follow in his mind a writer's appeals to these senses. When Colette's mother cracks a dry poppyhead, the reader should hear it; when she rubs the greenfly from a rose shoot, he should see it; when she fills her pockets with unripe walnuts, he should feel them.

List the five senses on your paper, and under each put three expressions from this essay which are appeals to that particular sense experience. When you have completed your lists, you should be able to answer this question: At what points in the essay does Colette let you see, smell, touch, taste, or hear what she does?

In this story Hamlin Garland describes the difficulties of loneliness. He places a lonely woman in a town where people try to be nice; they offer chairs and apples. But finally another woman offers something of herself to this lonely woman, and a day's pleasure is begun.

A Day's Pleasure

Hamlin Garland

IMPROVING YOUR READING: Watch for the many *contrasts* developed in this story. The leading character, Delia Markham, is contrasted to other people in the story, and she is placed in several settings which contrast with the one in which you first find her.

Observe, too, the role of the *minor characters*. Although a story is usually centered on one person, the minor characters have various functions in directing the action of the story. When you meet a minor character, you should ask, Why is he here? How does he influence the action?

WHEN MARKHAM came in from shoveling his last wagonload of corn into the crib he found that his wife had put the children to bed, and was kneading a batch of dough with the dogged action of a tired and sullen woman.

He slipped his soggy boots off his feet, and having laid a piece of wood on top of the stove, put his heels on it comfortably. His chair squeaked as he leaned back on its hinder legs, but he paid no attention; he was used to it, exactly as he was used to his wife's lameness and ceaseless toil.

"That closes up my corn," he said after a silence. "I guess I'll go to town tomorrow to git my horses shod."

"I guess I'll git ready and go along," said his wife, in a sorry[1] at-

tempt to be firm and confident of tone.

"What do you want to go to town fer?" he grumbled.

"What does anybody want to go to town fer?" she burst out, facing him. "I ain't been out o' this house fer six months, while you go an' go!"

"Oh, it ain't six months. You went down that day I got the mower."

"When was that? The tenth of July, and you know it."

"Well, mebbe 'twas. I didn't think it was so long ago. I ain't no objection to your goin', only I'm goin' to take a load of wheat."

"Well, jest leave off a sack, an' that'll balance me an' the baby," she said spiritedly.

"All right," he replied good-naturedly, seeing she was roused. "Only that wheat ought to be put up tonight if you're goin'. You won't have any time to hold sacks for me

1 **sorry:** here, pitiful.

in the morning with them young ones to get off to school."

"Well, let's go do it then," she said, sullenly resolute.

"I hate to go out agin; but I s'pose we'd better."

He yawned dismally and began pulling his boots on again, stamping his swollen feet into them with grunts of pain. She put on his coat and one of the boy's caps, and they went out to the granary. The night was cold and clear.

"Don't look so much like snow as it did last night," said Sam. "It may turn warm."

Laying out the sacks in the light of the lantern, they sorted out those which were whole, and Sam climbed into the bin with a tin pail in his hand, and the work began.

He was a sturdy fellow, and he worked desperately fast; the shining tin pail dived deep into the cold wheat and dragged heavily on the woman's tired hands as it came to the mouth of the sack, and she trembled with fatigue, but held on and dragged the sacks away when filled, and brought others, till at last Sam climbed out, puffing and wheezing, to tie them up.

"I guess I'll load 'em in the morning," he said. "You needn't wait fer me. I'll tie 'em up alone."

"Oh, I don't mind," she replied, feeling a little touched by his unexpectedly easy acquiescence to[2] her request. When they went back to the house the moon had risen.

It had scarcely set when they were wakened by the crowing roosters. The man rolled stiffly out of bed and began rattling at the stove in the dark, cold kitchen.

His wife arose lamer and stiffer than usual, and began twisting her thin hair into a knot.

Sam did not stop to wash, but went out to the barn. The woman, however, hastily soused her face into the hard limestone water at the sink, and put the kettle on. Then she called the children. She knew it was early, and they would need several callings. She pushed breakfast forward, running over in her mind the things she must have: two spools of thread, six yards of cotton flannel, a can of coffee, and mittens for Kitty. These she must have—there were oceans of things she needed.

The children soon came scudding down out of the darkness of the upstairs to dress tumultuously[3] at the kitchen stove. They humped and shivered, holding up their bare feet from the cold floor, like chickens in new-fallen snow. They were irritable, and snarled and snapped and struck like cats and dogs. Mrs. Markham stood it for a while with mere commands to "hush up," but at last her patience gave out, and she charged down on the struggling mob and cuffed them right and left.

They ate their breakfast by lamplight, and when Sam went back to his work around the barnyard it was scarcely dawn. The children, left alone with their mother, began to tease her to let them go to town also.

---

2 **acquiescence to:** acceptance of.

3 **tumultuously:** frantically; riotously.

THE ART OF STORYTELLING

"No, sir—nobody goes but baby. Your father's goin' to take a load of wheat."

She was weak with the worry of it all when she had sent the older children away to school and the kitchen work was finished. She went into the cold bedroom off the little sitting room and put on her best dress. It had never been a good fit, and now she was getting so thin it hung in wrinkled folds everywhere about the shoulders and waist. She lay down on the bed a moment to ease that dull pain in her back. She had a moment's distaste for going out at all. The thought of sleep was more alluring. Then the thought of the long, long day, and the sickening sameness of her life, swept over her again, and she rose and prepared the baby for the journey.

It was but little after sunrise when Sam drove out into the road and started for Belleplain. His wife sat perched upon the wheat sacks behind him, holding the baby in her lap, a cotton quilt under her, and a cotton horse-blanket over her knees.

Sam was disposed to be very good-natured, and he talked back at her occasionally, though she could only understand him when he turned his face toward her. The baby stared out at the passing fence posts, and wiggled his hands out of his mittens at every opportunity. He was merry at least.

It grew warmer as they went on, and a strong south wind arose. The dust settled upon the woman's shawl and hat. Her hair loosened and blew unkemptly[4] about her face. The road which led across the high, level prairie was quite smooth and dry, but still it jolted her, and the pain in her back increased. She had nothing to lean against, and the weight of the child grew greater, till she was forced to place him on the sacks beside her, though she could not loose her hold for a moment.

The town drew in sight—a cluster of small frame houses and stores on the dry prairie beside a railway station. There were no trees yet which could be called shade trees. The pitilessly severe light of the sun flooded everything. A few teams were hitched about, and in the lee[5] of the stores a few men could be seen seated comfortably, their broad hat-rims flopping up and down, their faces brown as leather.

Markham put his wife out at one of the grocery stores, and drove off down toward the elevators to sell his wheat.

The grocer greeted Mrs. Markham in a perfunctorily[6] kind manner, and offered her a chair, which she took gratefully. She sat for a quarter of an hour almost without moving, leaning against the back of the high chair. At last the child began to get restless and troublesome, and she spent half an hour helping him amuse himself around the nail-kegs.

At length she rose and went out on the walk, carrying the baby. She went into the dry-goods store and took a seat on one of the little re-

4 **unkemptly:** carelessly.
5 **lee:** sheltered side.
6 **perfunctorily:** mechanically; routinely.

volving stools. A woman was buying some woolen goods for a dress. It was worth twenty-seven cents a yard, the clerk said, but he would knock off two cents if she took ten yards. It looked warm, and Mrs. Markham wished she could afford it for Mary.

A pretty young girl came in and laughed and chatted with the clerk, and bought a pair of gloves. She was the daughter of the grocer. Her happiness made the wife and mother sad. When Sam came back she asked him for some money.

"What you want to do with it?" he asked.

"I want to spend it," she said.

She was not to be trifled with, so he gave her a dollar.

"I need a dollar more."

"Well, I've got to go take up that note at the bank."

"Well, the children's got to have some new underclo'es," she said.

He handed her a two-dollar bill and then went out to pay his note.

She bought her cotton flannel and mittens and thread, and then sat leaning against the counter. It was noon, and she was hungry. She went out to the wagon, got the lunch she had brought, and took it into the grocery to eat it—where she could get a drink of water.

The grocer gave the baby a stick of candy and handed the mother an apple.

"It'll kind o' go down with your doughnuts," he said.

After eating her lunch she got up and went out. She felt ashamed to sit there any longer. She entered another dry-goods store, but when the clerk came toward her saying, "Anything to-day, Mrs. ——?" she answered, "No, I guess not," and turned away with foolish face.

She walked up and down the street, desolately homeless. She did not know what to do with herself. She knew no one except the grocer. She grew bitter as she saw a couple of ladies pass, holding their demi-trains[7] in the latest city fashion. Another woman went by pushing a baby carriage, in which sat a child just about as big as her own. It was bouncing itself up and down on the long slender springs, and laughing and shouting. Its clean round face glowed from its pretty fringed hood. She looked down at the dusty clothes and grimy face of her own little one, and walked on savagely.

She went into the drugstore where the soda fountain was, but it made her thirsty to sit there and she went out on the street again. She heard Sam laugh, and saw him in a group of men over by the blacksmith shop. He was having a good time and had forgotten her.

Her back ached so intolerably that she concluded to go in and rest once more in the grocer's chair. The baby was growing cross and fretful. She bought five cents' worth of candy to take home to the children, and gave baby a little piece to keep him quiet. She wished Sam would come. It must be getting late. The grocer said it was not much after one. Time seemed terribly long. She felt that she ought to do something while she was in town. She ran over her purchases—yes, that was all she had

7 **demi-trains:** short pieces of ladies' dresses which ordinarily trail behind them.

planned to buy. She fell to figuring on the things she needed. It was terrible. It ran away up into twenty or thirty dollars at the least. Sam, as well as she, needed underwear for the cold winter, but they would have to wear the old ones, even if they were thin and ragged. She would not need a dress, she thought bitterly, because she never went anywhere. She rose and went out on the street once more, and wandered up and down, looking at everything in the hope of enjoying something.

A man from Boon Creek backed a load of apples up to the sidewalk, and as he stood waiting for the grocer he noticed Mrs. Markham and the baby, and gave the baby an apple. This was a pleasure. He had such a hearty way about him. He on his part saw an ordinary farmer's wife with dusty dress, unkempt hair, and tired face. He did not know exactly why she appealed to him, but he tried to cheer her up.

The grocer was familiar with these bedraggled and weary wives. He was accustomed to see them sit for hours in his big wooden chair, and nurse tired and fretful children. Their forlorn, aimless, pathetic wandering up and down the street was a daily occurrence, and had never possessed any special meaning to him.

II

In a cottage around the corner from the grocery store two men and a woman were finishing a dainty luncheon. The woman was dressed in cool, white garments, and she seemed to make the day one of perfect comfort.

The home of the Honorable Mr. Hall was by no means the costliest in town, but his wife made it the most attractive. He was one of the leading lawyers of the county, and a man of culture and progressive views. He was entertaining a friend who had lectured the night before in the Congregational church.

They were by no means in serious discussion. The talk was rather frivolous.[8] Hall had the ability to caricature[9] men with a few gestures and attitudes, and was giving to his Eastern friend some descriptions of the old-fashioned Western lawyers he had met in his practice. He was very amusing, and his guest laughed heartily for a time.

But suddenly Hall became aware that Otis was not listening. Then he perceived that he was peering out of the window at someone, and that on his face a look of bitter sadness was falling.

Hall stopped. "What do you see, Otis?"

Otis replied, "I see a forlorn, weary woman."

Mrs. Hall rose and went to the window. Mrs. Markham was walking by the house, her baby in her arms. Savage anger and weeping were in her eyes and on her lips, and there was hopeless tragedy in her shambling walk and weak back.

In the silence Otis went on: "I saw the poor, dejected creature twice this morning. I couldn't forget her."

"Who is she?" asked Mrs. Hall, very softly.

"Her name is Markham; she's Sam Markham's wife," said Hall.

The young wife led the way into the sitting room, and the men took seats and lit their cigars. Hall was meditating a diversion[10] when Otis resumed suddenly:

"That woman came to town today to get a change, to have a little play-spell, and she's wandering around like a starved and weary cat. I wonder if there is a woman in this town with sympathy enough and courage enough to go out and help that woman? The saloonkeepers, the politicians, and the grocers make it pleasant for the man—so pleasant that he forgets his wife. But the wife is left without a word."

Mrs. Hall's work dropped, and on her pretty face was a look of pain. The man's harsh words had wounded her—and wakened her. She took up her hat and hurried out on the walk. The men looked at each other, and then the husband said:

"It's going to be a little sultry[11] for the men around these diggings. Suppose we go out for a walk."

Delia felt a hand on her arm as she stood at the corner.

"You look tired, Mrs. Markham; won't you come in a little while? I'm Mrs. Hall."

Mrs. Markham turned with a scowl on her face and a biting word on her tongue, but something in the sweet, round little face of the other woman

8 **frivolous:** unimportant.
9 **caricature:** give an exaggerated imitation of.

10 **meditating a diversion:** that is, wondering how he would entertain his guest.
11 **sultry:** stuffy; stifling.

silenced her, and her brow smoothed out.

"Thank you kindly, but it's most time to go home. I'm looking fer Mr. Markham now."

"Oh, come in a little while; the baby is cross and tired out; please do."

Mrs. Markham yielded to the friendly voice, and together the two women reached the gate just as two men hurriedly turned the other corner.

"Let me relieve you," said Mrs. Hall.

The mother hesitated: "He's so dusty."

"Oh, that won't matter. Oh, what a big fellow he is! I haven't any of my own," said Mrs. Hall, and a look passed like an electric spark between the two women, and Delia was her willing guest from that moment.

They went into the little sitting room, so dainty and lovely to the farmer's wife, and as she sank into an easy chair she was faint and drowsy with the pleasure of it. She submitted to being brushed. She gave the baby into the hands of the Swedish girl, who washed its face and hands and sang it to sleep, while its mother sipped some tea. Through it all she lay back in her easy chair, not speaking a word, while the ache passed out of her back, and her hot, swollen head ceased to throb.

But she saw everything—the piano, the pictures, the curtains, the wallpaper, the little tea stand. They were almost as grateful to her as the food and fragrant tea. Such housekeeping as this she had never seen. Her mother had worn her kitchen floor thin as brown paper in keeping a speckless house, and she had been in houses that were larger and costlier, but something of the charm of her hostess was in the arrangement of vases, chairs, or pictures. It was tasteful.

Mrs. Hall did not ask about her affairs. She talked to her about the sturdy little baby, and about the things upon which Delia's eyes dwelt. If she seemed interested in a vase she was told what it was and where it was made. She was shown all the pictures and books. Mrs. Hall seemed to read her visitor's mind. She kept as far from the farm and her guest's affairs as possible, and at last she opened the piano and sang to her—not slow-moving hymns, but catchy love songs full of sentiment, and then played some simple melodies, knowing that Mrs. Markham's eyes were studying her hands, her rings, and the flash of her fingers on the keys—seeing more than she heard—and through it all Mrs. Hall conveyed the impression that she, too, was having a good time.

The rattle of the wagon outside roused them both. Sam was at the gate for her. Mrs. Markham rose hastily. "Oh, it's almost sundown!" she gasped in astonishment as she looked out of the window.

"Oh, that won't kill anybody," replied her hostess. "Don't hurry.

Carrie, take the baby out to the wagon for Mrs. Markham while I help her with her things."

"Oh, I've had such a good time," Mrs. Markham said as they went down the little walk.

"So have I," replied Mrs. Hall. She took the baby a moment as her guest climbed in. "Oh, you big, fat fellow!" she cried as she gave him a squeeze. "You must bring your wife in oftener, Mr. Markham," she said, as she handed the baby up.

Sam was staring with amazement.

"Thank you, I will," he finally managed to say.

"Good night," said Mrs. Markham.

"Good night, dear," called Mrs. Hall, and the wagon began to rattle off.

The tenderness and sympathy in her voice brought the tears to Delia's eyes—not hot or bitter tears, but tears that cooled her eyes and cleared her mind.

The wind had gone down, and the red sunlight fell mistily over the world of corn and stubble. The crickets were still chirping and the feeding cattle were drifting toward the farmyards. The day had been made beautiful by human sympathy.

Understanding Literature

1. Judging by the beginning of the story, how do you think Markham and his wife ordinarily live? What kind of a relationship exists between them?
2. In what ways is Mrs. Markham different from other people in the town?
3. What is the function of Mr. Otis in the story?
4. Why does Mrs. Markham "turn with a scowl" when Mrs. Hall invites her inside?
5. How is the Halls' house contrasted with the Markhams'? How is the appearance of Mrs. Hall contrasted with that of Mrs. Markham?
6. By the end of this story what has Mrs. Hall learned about herself and about others? What has Mrs. Markham learned about other people?

Further Activities

1. Prepare a short talk on how either Mrs. Hall or Mrs. Markham might spend a typical day. Be sure to prove whatever you say by some hint which you get in the story.
2. In one paragraph define what Hamlin Garland means in his story by "human sympathy." Begin your paragraph with the statement: "In 'A Day's Pleasure' human sympathy means. . . ." Go on to explain what you take the phrase to mean. In the rest of the paragraph summarize the scene in the story in which human sympathy is acted out. Be sure to include specific details which are evidence of genuine human sympathy.

Focusing on Words

You will miss much of the characterization in the story unless you know the meaning of the following italicized words. Try to define each by the way it is used in the sentence. Consult the glossary about those you are unsure of.

1. "the *dogged* action of a tired and *sullen* woman" (p. 161, col. 1)
2. "she said *spiritedly*" (p. 161, col. 2)
3. "she said, sullenly *resolute*" (p. 162, col. 1)
4. "she trembled with *fatigue*" (p. 162, col. 1)
5. "the *sickening sameness* of her life" (p. 163, col. 1)

6. "She walked up and down the street, *desolately homeless.*" (p. 165, col. 1)
7. "The grocer was familiar with these *bedraggled* and weary wives." (p. 165, col. 2)
8. "Their forlorn, *aimless, pathetic* wandering" (p. 165, col. 2)
9. "I see a *forlorn*, weary woman." (p. 166, col. 1)
10. "there was hopeless tragedy in her *shambling* walk" (p. 166, col. 1)
11. "the poor, *dejected* creature" (p. 166, col. 1)

This story by Anatole France, a French novelist and satirist, is based on an old legend that has been retold many times.

Our Lady's Juggler

Anatole France

Improving Your Reading: *Theme* refers to the central idea in a piece of literature. This story illustrates a theme. As you read, observe what the author is trying to say about the relationship between man and God.

In the days of King Louis there was a poor juggler in France, a native of Compiègne,[1] Barnaby by name, who went about from town to town performing feats of skill and strength.

On fair days he would unfold an old worn-out carpet in the public square, and when by means of a jovial address, which he had learned of a very ancient juggler, and which he never varied in the least, he had drawn together the children and loafers, he assumed extraordinary attitudes, and balanced a tin plate on the tip of his nose. At first the crowd would feign[2] indifference.

But when, supporting himself on his hands face downwards, he threw into the air six copper balls, which glittered in the sunshine, and caught them again with his feet; or when throwing himself backwards until his heels and the nape of the neck met, giving his body the form of a perfect wheel, he would juggle in this posture with a dozen knives, a murmur of admiration would escape the spectators, and pieces of money rain down upon the carpet.

Nevertheless, like the majority of those who live by their wits, Barnaby of Compiègne had a great struggle to make a living.

Earning his bread in the sweat of his brow, he bore rather more than his share of the penalties consequent upon the misdoings of our father Adam.[3]

Again, he was unable to work as constantly as he would have been willing to do. The warmth of the sun and the broad daylight were as necessary to enable him to display his brilliant parts as to the trees if flower and fruit should be expected of them. In wintertime he was nothing more than a tree stripped of its leaves, and as it were dead. The frozen ground was hard to the juggler, and, like the grasshopper of

---

1 **Compiègne** (kôN pyĕn′y): city in northern France.
2 **feign** (fān): pretend.

3 **consequent . . . Adam:** because of Adam's sin of disobedience.

which Marie de France[4] tells us, the inclement[5] season caused him to suffer both cold and hunger. But as he was simple-natured he bore his ills patiently.

He had never meditated on the origin of wealth, nor upon the inequality of human conditions. He believed firmly that if this life should prove hard, the life to come could not fail to redress the balance,[6] and this hope upheld him. He did not resemble those thievish and miscreant Merry Andrews[7] who sell their souls to the devil. He never blasphemed God's name; he lived uprightly, and although he had no wife of his own, he did not covet[8] his neighbor's, since woman is ever the enemy of the strong man, as it appears by the history of Samson recorded in the Scriptures.

In truth, his was not a nature much disposed to carnal[9] delights, and it was a greater deprivation to him to forsake the tankard than the Hebe[10] who bore it. For whilst not wanting in[11] sobriety, he was fond of a drink when the weather waxed[12] hot. He was a worthy man who feared God, and was very devoted to the Blessed Virgin.

Never did he fail on entering a church to fall upon his knees before the image of the Mother of God, and offer up this prayer to her:

"Blessed Lady, keep watch over my life until it shall please God that I die, and when I am dead, ensure to me the possession of the joys of paradise."

II

Now on a certain evening after a dreary wet day, as Barnaby pursued his road, sad and bent, carrying under his arm his balls and knives wrapped up in his old carpet, on the watch for some barn where, though he might not sup, he might sleep, he perceived on the road, going in the same direction as himself, a monk, whom he saluted courteously. And as they walked at the same rate they fell into conversation with one another.

"Fellow traveler," said the monk, "how comes it about that you are clothed all in green? Is it perhaps in order to take the part of a jester in some mystery play?"[13]

"Not at all, good father," replied Barnaby. "Such as you see me, I am called Barnaby, and for my calling I am a juggler. There would be no pleasanter calling in the world if it would always provide one with daily bread."

"Friend Barnaby," returned the monk, "be careful what you say. There is no calling more pleasant than the monastic life. Those who lead it are occupied with the praises of God, the Blessed Virgin, and the saints; and, indeed, the religious life

---

4 **Marie de France:** a French poet of the 12th century who revised some English fables.
5 **inclement** (ĭn klĕm′ənt): stormy; harsh.
6 **redress the balance:** that is, could not fail to be better.
7 **thievish . . . Andrews:** here, types of clowns who were dishonest and irreligious.
8 **covet:** wish for.
9 **carnal:** unspiritual; physical.
10 **Hebe:** cupbearer of Greek mythology.
11 **not . . . in:** not without.
12 **waxed:** grew.

13 **mystery play:** a type of medieval drama based on Biblical incidents.

is one ceaseless hymn to the Lord."

Barnaby replied—

"Good father, I own that I spoke like an ignorant man. Your calling cannot be in any respect compared to mine, and although there may be some merit in dancing with a penny balanced on a stick on the tip of one's nose, it is not a merit which comes within hail of your own. Gladly would I, like you, good father, sing my office day by day, and especially, the office of the most Holy Virgin, to whom I have vowed a singular[14] devotion. In order to embrace the monastic life I would willingly abandon the art by which from Soissons to Beauvais I am well known in upwards of six hundred towns and villages."

The monk was touched by the juggler's simplicity, and as he was not lacking in discernment,[15] he at once recognized in Barnaby one of those men of whom it is said in the Scriptures: "Peace on earth to men of good will." And for this reason he replied—

"Friend Barnaby, come with me, and I will have you admitted into the monastery of which I am prior.[16] He who guided St. Mary of Egypt in the desert set me upon your path to lead you into the way of salvation."

It was in this manner, then, that Barnaby became a monk. In the monastery into which he was received the religious vied[17] with one another in the worship of the Blessed Virgin, and in her honor each employed all the knowledge and all the skill which God had given him.

The prior on his part wrote books dealing according to the rules of scholarship with the virtues of the Mother of God.

Brother Maurice, with a deft[18] hand copied out these treatises upon sheets of vellum.[19]

Brother Alexander adorned the leaves with delicate miniature paintings. Here were displayed the Queen of Heaven seated upon Solomon's throne, and while four lions were on guard at her feet, around the nimbus[20] which encircled her head hovered seven doves, which are the seven gifts of the Holy Spirit, the gifts, namely, of Fear, Piety, Knowledge, Strength, Counsel, Understanding, and Wisdom. For her companions she had six virgins with hair of gold, namely, Humility, Prudence, Seclusion, Submission, Virginity, and Obedience.

At her feet were two little naked figures, perfectly white, in an attitude of supplication.[21] These were souls imploring her all-powerful intercession for their soul's health, and we may be sure not imploring in vain.

Upon another page facing this, Brother Alexander represented Eve, so that the Fall and the Redemption could be perceived at one and the same time—Eve the Wife abased,[22] and Mary the Virgin exalted.

14 **singular:** exceptional; especially pious.
15 **discernment** (dĭ sûrn′mənt): insight; accurate judgment.
16 **prior:** the head of the house of a religious order.
17 **vied:** competed.

18 **deft:** skillful.
19 **vellum:** paper similar to parchment.
20 **nimbus:** halo.
21 **in . . . supplication:** praying.
22 **abased:** humbled.

Furthermore, to the marvel of the beholder, this book contained presentments[23] of the Well of Living Waters, the Fountain, the Lily, the Moon, the Sun, and the Garden enclosed of which the Song of Songs tells us, the Gate of Heaven and the City of God, and all these things were symbols of the Blessed Virgin.

Brother Marbode was likewise one of the most loving children of Mary.

He spent all his days carving images in stone, so that his beard, his eyebrows, and his hair were white with dust, and his eyes continually swollen and weeping; but his strength and cheerfulness were not diminished, although he was now well gone in years, and it was clear that the Queen of Paradise still cherished her servant in his old age. Marbode represented her seated upon a throne, her brow encircled with an orb-shaped nimbus set with pearls. And he took care that the folds of her dress should cover the feet of her, concerning whom the prophet declared: "My beloved is as a garden enclosed."

Sometimes, too, he depicted her in the semblance[24] of a child full of grace, and appearing to say, "Thou art my God, even from my mother's womb."

In the priory, moreover, were poets who composed hymns in Latin, both in prose and verse, in honor of the Blessed Virgin Mary, and amongst the company was even a brother from Picardy who sang the miracles of Our Lady in rhymed verse and in the vulgar tongue.[25]

III

Being a witness of this emulation[26] in praise and the glorious harvest of their labors, Barnaby mourned his own ignorance and simplicity.

"Alas!" he sighed, as he took his solitary walk in the little shelterless garden of the monastery, "wretched wight[27] that I am, to be unable, like my brothers, worthily to praise the Holy Mother of God, to whom I have vowed my whole heart's affection. Alas! alas! I am but a rough man and unskilled in the arts, and I can render you in service, blessed Lady, neither edifying[28] sermons, nor treatises set out in order according to rule, nor ingenious paintings, nor statues truthfully sculptured, nor verses whose march is measured to the beat of feet.[29] No gift have I, alas!"

After this fashion he groaned and gave himself up to sorrow. But one evening, when the monks were spending their hour of liberty in conversation, he heard one of them tell the tale of a religious man who could repeat nothing other than the Ave Maria. This poor man was despised for his ignorance; but after his death there issued forth from his mouth five roses in honor of the five letters of the name Mary (Marie), and thus his sanctity was made manifest.[30]

---

23 **presentments:** representations; suggestions.
24 **semblance:** form.

25 **vulgar tongue:** language spoken by the general public.
26 **emulation:** rivalry; competition.
27 **wight:** creature; man.
28 **edifying:** instructive; beneficial.
29 **whose . . . feet:** which have a definite rhythm.
30 **made manifest:** shown; displayed.

Whilst he listened to this narrative Barnaby marveled yet once again at the loving kindness of the Virgin; but the lesson of that blessed death did not avail to console him, for his heart overflowed with zeal, and he longed to advance the glory of his Lady, who is in heaven.

How to compass[31] this he sought but could find no way, and day by day he became the more cast down, when one morning he awakened filled full with joy, hastened to the chapel, and remained there alone for more than an hour. After dinner he returned to the chapel once more.

And, starting from that moment, he repaired[32] daily to the chapel at such hours as it was deserted, and spent within it a good part of the time which the other monks devoted to the liberal and mechanical arts. His sadness vanished, nor did he any longer groan.

A demeanor[33] so strange awakened the curiosity of the monks.

These began to ask one another for what purpose Brother Barnaby could be indulging so persistently in retreat.

The prior, whose duty it is to let nothing escape him in the behavior of his children in religion, resolved to keep a watch over Barnaby during his withdrawals to the chapel. One day, then, when he was shut up there after his custom, the prior, accompanied by two of the older monks, went to discover through the chinks in the door what was going on within the chapel.

They saw Barnaby before the altar of the Blessed Virgin, head downwards, with his feet in the air, and he was juggling with six balls of copper and a dozen knives. In honor of the Holy Mother of God he was performing those feats, which aforetime had won him most renown. Not recognizing that the simple fellow was thus placing at the service of the Blessed Virgin his knowledge and skill, the two old monks exclaimed against the sacrilege.[34]

The prior was aware how stainless was Barnaby's soul, but he concluded that he had been seized with madness. They were all three preparing to lead him swiftly from the chapel, when they saw the Blessed Virgin descend the steps of the altar and advance to wipe away with a fold of her azure robe the sweat which was dropping from her juggler's forehead.

Then the prior, falling upon his face upon the pavement, uttered these words—

"Blessed are the simplehearted, for they shall see God."

"Amen!" responded the old brethren, and kissed the ground.

---

31 **to compass:** to accomplish.
32 **repaired:** here, returned.
33 **demeanor:** behavior.

34 **sacrilege:** disrespect for something sacred.

Understanding Literature

1. In the first part of the story, what do you learn about Barnaby?
2. Why does the monk apply to Barnaby the phrase "Peace on earth to men of good will"?
3. How do the different monks show their devotion to the Virgin?
4. How does the story of "a religious man who could repeat nothing other than the Ave Maria" affect Barnaby?
5. What is the main idea, the theme, illustrated by this story?

Further Activities

1. Write a single sentence in which you tell what you think is Barnaby's main character trait; that is, the most distinctive feature in his character, such as evilness or silliness. Then, in a few more sentences prove what you have said by referring to incidents in the story.
2. Write a short paragraph beginning: "In some ways Barnaby is a simple man; in other ways he is not." Prove each main idea (that he is simple and that he is not) by referring to specific incidents or ideas in the story. Organize your paper by proving, in the first part of the paragraph, that he is a simple man and by proving, in the second part, that he is *not* a simple man.

Building America

You HAVE LEARNED about America through her history; here you will see America in literature. Through poetry, biography, essay, and story you get closer to your subject; you watch the characters act out important parts of their lives. But even more than that, the selections which follow characterize a country; they tell you much about America's traditions, beliefs, and heroes.

You will read about the courage required by Columbus to cross an unknown ocean; about some of the people who helped America win her independence; about those who explored and developed America's West; and, finally, about the major event in 19th-century American history—the Civil War. This unit is only a glimpse at the early stages of America's history, but it is a glimpse that reveals the tremendous courage and spirit that helped to make this country great.

One of the greatest acts in American history was performed by Genoa-born Christopher Columbus, discoverer of the New World. Circumstances had fortunately brought him to Portugal at a time when that country was carrying on a thriving ocean trade throughout the known world. Columbus spent his time there as a maker of maps and talking with the old seamen, and it was in Portugal that he decided that he could reach the Indies—Eastern Asia—by sailing west. Because an unknown continent lay in his way, Columbus never reached the Indies; but Americans now honor Columbus for his accidental discovery, even though he never knew the full extent of what he had done.

To understand the persistence, the knowledge, and the courage which led Columbus to make the greatest voyage of discovery ever recorded in human history, you must know something about the situation of the time. Portugal, when Columbus lived there, was a vast seafaring empire. Its ships moved out into the Atlantic to the Azores and down the coast of Africa, trading everywhere they went and returning with rich cargoes. Its people were courageous mariners and explorers as well as expert mapmakers and navigators.

The dream of many men of the time, as it was for Columbus, was to find an ocean route to the East. The lure of Eastern Asia was great. From India, China, and other countries came small caravans over land, carrying gold and precious stones, silk and cotton, spices and perfumes across Asia to Constantinople or Levantine ports, where the cargo was then loaded on ships for distribution throughout Europe. An ocean route would make many more of these rich goods available to western markets. But while the Portuguese sought to reach India by a southern route around Africa, Columbus thought he could reach the East by sailing due west of the Azores—out into the dark, turbulent North Atlantic.

Although he correctly believed that the earth was round, Columbus made several miscalculations in his planning. The Greeks had long before divided the earth's circle into 360 degrees, but how long was a degree? The answer would depend on the size of the world. Columbus calculated a degree to be far shorter than it is, and thus he greatly underestimated the size of the world. He also miscalculated how far eastward Asia stretched. He finally estimated that 2400 nautical miles would take him from the Canary Islands to Japan. Actually the distance is 10,600 miles. If America had not lain between him and his destination, he probably would never have been heard from again.

It was in April, 1492, more than ten years after he first had his idea, that Columbus persuaded Isabella, Queen of Spain, to support his voyage of discovery. He sailed in August.

This version of the voyage is by Samuel Eliot Morison, a teacher, biographer, and sailor, who in 1939-40 organized an expedition of two sailing ships to follow the route of Columbus. The selection which follows is from Mr. Morison's book *Christopher Columbus, Mariner*.

First Crossing of the Atlantic

Samuel Eliot Morison

By THE SECOND day of August, 1492, everything at last was ready. That night every man and boy of the fleet confessed his sins, received absolution and made his communion at the church of Palos, which by happy coincidence was dedicated to Saint George, patron saint of Genoa. Columbus went on board his flagship in the small hours of Friday the third and gave the signal to get under way. Before the sun rose, all three vessels had anchors aweigh, and with sails hanging limp from their yards were floating down the Rio Tinto on the morning ebb, using their long sweeps to maintain steerageway.[1] As they swung into the Saltés and passed La Rábida close aboard, they could hear the friars chanting the ancient hymn *Iam lucis orto sidere* with its haunting refrain *Et nunc et in perpetuum*, which we render "Evermore and evermore. . . ."

Columbus's plan for the voyage was simple, and its simplicity insured his success. Not for him the boisterous head winds, the monstrous seas and the dark, unbridled waters of the North Atlantic, which had already baffled so many Portuguese. He would run south before the prevailing northerlies[2] to the Canary Islands, and there make, as it were, a right-angle turn; for he had observed on his African voyages that the winter winds in the latitude of the Canaries blew from the east, and that the ocean around them, more often than not, was calm as a millpond. An even better reason to take his departure from the Canaries was their position astride latitude 28 degrees North, which, he believed, cut Japan, passing en route the mythical Isle of Antilia,[3] which would make a good break in the westward passage. Until about a hundred years ago when chronom-

2 **northerlies**: winds blowing from the north.
3 **mythical . . . Antilia**: fabled land that Europeans once believed was located in the unknown west.

1 **steerageway**: sufficient speed to steer the boat.

eters became generally available to find longitude, sailors always tried to find the latitude of their destination and then would "run their westing" (or easting) down until they hit it. That is what Columbus proposed to do with respect to Japan, which he had figured out to be only 2400 nautical miles due west of the Canaries.

The first leg of the voyage was made in less than a week. Then, within sight of the Grand Canary, the fleet ran into a calm that lasted two or three days. Columbus decided to send *Pinta* into Las Palmas for some needed repairs while *Santa María* and *Niña* went to Gomera, westernmost of the Canaries that the Spaniards had wrested from their native inhabitants. At Gomera the Captain General (as we should call Columbus on this voyage before he made Admiral) sent men ashore to fill extra water casks, buy breadstuffs and cheese, and put a supply of native beef in pickle. He then sailed to Las Palmas to superintend *Pinta's* repairs and returned with her to Gomera.

On September 2 all three ships were anchored off San Sebastián, the port of that island. Columbus then met for the first time Doña Beatriz de Bobadilla, widow of the former captain of the island. Beatriz was a beautiful lady still under thirty, and Columbus is said to have fallen in love with her; but if that is true, he did not love her warmly enough to tarry to the next full moon. Additional ship's stores were quickly hoisted on board and struck below, and on September 6, 1492, the fleet

weighed anchor for the last time in the Old World. They had still another island to pass, the lofty Ferro or Hierro. Owing to calms and variables[4] Ferro and the 12,000-foot peak of Tenerife were in sight until the ninth, but by nightfall that day, every trace of land had sunk below the eastern horizon, and the three vessels were alone on an uncharted ocean. Columbus himself gave out the course: "West; nothing to the north, nothing to the south."

Before going into the details of the voyage, let us see how those vessels were navigated, and how a day was passed at sea. Celestial navigation[5] was then in its infancy, but rough estimates of latitude could be made from the height of the North Star above the horizon and its relation to the two outer stars (the "Guards") of the Little Dipper. A meridian altitude[6] of the sun, applied to available tables of the sun's declination, also gave latitude, by a simple formula. But the instruments of observation—a solid wood or brass quadrant and the seaman's astrolabe—were so crude, and the movement of a ship threw them off to such an extent, that most navigators took their latitude sights ashore. Columbus relied almost completely on "dead reckoning," which means plotting your course and position on a chart from the three elements of direction, time and distance.

The direction he had from one or more compasses which were similar

4 **variables:** shifting winds.
5 **Celestial navigation:** controlling the course of a ship by watching the heavens.
6 **meridian altitude:** highest point.

to those used in small craft until recently—a circular card graduated to the 32 points (N, N by E, NNE, NE by N, NE, and so on), with a lodestone[7] under the north point, mounted on a pin and enclosed in a binnacle with gimbals[8] so it could swing freely with the motion of the ship. Columbus's standard compass was mounted on the poop deck where the officer of the watch could see it. The helmsman, who steered with a heavy tiller attached directly to the rudder head, was below decks and could see very little. He may have had another compass to steer by, but in the smaller vessels, at least, he was conned[9] by the officer of the deck and kept a steady course by the feel of the helm. On a sailing vessel you can do that; it would be impossible in any power craft.

Time on the vessels of that day was measured by a half-hour glass which hung from a beam so the sand could flow freely from the upper to the lower half. As soon as the sand was all down, a ship's boy turned the glass and the officer of the deck recorded it by making a stroke on a slate. Eight glasses made a watch; the modern ship's bells were originally a means of marking the glasses. This half-hour-glass time could be corrected daily in fair weather by noting the moment when the sun lay due south, which was local noon.

Distance was the most variable of these three elements. Columbus had no chip log or other method of measuring the speed of his vessels. He and the watch officers merely estimated it and noted it down. By carefully checking Columbus's Journal of his First Voyage, Captain J. W. McElroy ascertained[10] that he made an average 9 per cent overestimate of his distance. This did not prevent his finding the way home, because the mistake was constant, and time and course were correct. It only resulted in Columbus placing the islands of his discovery farther west than they really were.

Even after making the proper reduction for this overestimate, the speed of his vessels is surprising. Ships of that day were expected to make 3 to 5 knots[11] in a light breeze, up to 9½ in a strong, fair gale, and at times to be capable of 12 knots. In October 1492, on the outward passage, the Columbus fleet made an average of 142 miles per day for five consecutive days, and the best day's run, 182 miles, averaged 8 knots. On the homeward passage, in February 1493, *Niña* and *Pinta* covered 198 miles one day, and at times hit it up to 11 knots. Any yachtsman today would be proud to make the records that the great Admiral did on some of his transatlantic crossings in the 15th century. Improvements in sailing vessels since 1492 have been more in seaworthiness and comfort than in speed.

One reason Columbus always

---

7 **lodestone:** magnet.
8 **binnacle with gimbals:** case with a device for suspending the compass so that it will always remain level.
9 **conned:** directed.

10 **ascertained:** discovered.
11 **knots:** A knot is a measure of speed, equal to one nautical mile per hour.

wanted two or more vessels was to have someone to rescue survivors in case of sinking. But he made an unusual record for that era by never losing a ship at sea, unless we count the *Santa María*, grounded without loss of life. Comforts and conveniences were almost totally lacking. Cooking was done on deck over a bed of sand in a wooden firebox protected from the wind by a hood. The diet was a monotonous one of salt meat, hardtack and dried peas. For drink they had wine, while it lasted, and water in casks, which often went bad. Only the Captain General and the ships' captains had cabins with bunks; the others slept where they could, in their clothes. . . .

On September 9, the day he dropped the last land below the horizon, Columbus decided to keep a true reckoning of his course for his own use and a false one to give out to the people, so that they would not be frightened at sailing so far from land. But, owing to his overestimate of speed, the "false" reckoning was more nearly correct than the "true"!

During the first ten days (September 9 to 18), the easterly trade wind blew steadily, and the fleet made 1163 nautical miles westing. This was the honeymoon of the voyage. *Que era plazer grande el gusto de las mañanas* —"What a delight was the savor of the mornings!" wrote Columbus in his Journal. That entry speaks to the heart of anyone who has sailed in the trades; it recalls the beauty of the dawn, kindling clouds and sails rose color, the smell of dew drying on a wooden deck, and, something Co-

lumbus didn't have, the first cup of coffee. Since his ships were at the northern edge of the northeast trades, where the wind first strikes the water, the sea was smooth, and the air, remarked the Captain General in his Journal, was "like April in Andalusia; the only thing wanting was to hear the song of the nightingale." But there were plenty of other birds following the ships: the little Mother Carey's chickens, dabbling for plankton in the bow waves and wakes; the boatswain bird, so called (as old seamen used to say) because it carries a marlinspike in its tail; the man-of-war or frigate bird, "thou ship of the air that never furl'st thy sails," as Walt Whitman[12] wrote; and when the fleet passed beyond the range of these birds, the big Jaeger gulls gave it a call. During this period the fleet encountered its first field of sargassum or gulfweed and found that it was no hindrance to navigation. "Saw plenty weed" was an almost daily notation in the Captain General's log. The gulfweed bothered him much less than observing a westerly variation[13] of the compass, for in European waters the variation is always easterly.

On September 19, only ten days out from Ferro, the fleet temporarily ran into an area of variable winds and rain. It was near the point on Columbus's chart where the fabled island of Antilia should have been, and all hands expected to sight land.

12 **Walt Whitman**: 19th-century American poet.
13 **variation**: a reference to the compass error due to the difference between the magnetic North Pole and the true North Pole.

The Captain General even had the deep-sea lead hove,[14] and found no bottom at 200 fathoms; no wonder, since the ocean is about 2300 fathoms deep at the point he had reached. But the seamen who, on the tenth day of the northeast trades, were beginning to wonder whether they could ever beat back home were cheered by the change of wind.

During the next five days only 234 miles were made good. During this spell of moderate weather it was easy to converse from ship to ship and to talk about this or that island, St. Brendan's or Antilia, which they might pick up. In the middle of one of these colloquies,[15] a seaman of *Pinta* gave the "Land Ho!" and everyone thought he saw an island against the setting sun. Columbus fell on his knees to thank God, ordered *Gloria in excelsis Deo* to be sung by all hands, and set a course for the island. But at dawn no island was visible; there was none. It was simply a cloud bank above the western horizon resembling land, a common phenomenon at sea. Martín Alonso Pinzón apparently wished to beat about and search for this island, but Columbus refused, because, he said, "his object was to reach the Indies, and if he delayed, it would not have made sense."

The trade wind now returned, but moderately, and during the six days September 26 to October 1, the fleet made only 382 miles. Under these circumstances the people began to mutter and grumble. Three weeks was probably more than they had ever been outside sight of land before. They were all getting on each other's nerves, as happens even nowadays on a long voyage to a known destination. There was nothing for the men to do in the light wind except to follow the ship's routine, and troll for fish. Grievances, real or imaginary, were blown up; cliques[16] were formed; Spain was farther away every minute, and what lay ahead? Probably nothing, except in the eye of that cursed Genoese. Let's make him turn back, or throw him overboard!

On the first day of October the wind increased, and in five days (October 2 to 6) the fleet made 710 miles. On the sixth, when they had passed longitude 65 degrees West and actually lay directly north of Puerto Rico, Martín Alonso Pinzón shot his agile *Pinta* under the flagship's stern and shouted, "Alter course, sir, to southwest by west . . . Japan!" Columbus did not understand whether Martín Alonso meant that he thought they had missed Japan and should steer southwest by west for China, or that Japan lay in that direction; but he knew and Pinzón knew that the fleet had sailed more than 2400 miles which, according to their calculations, lay between the Canaries and Japan. Naturally Columbus was uneasy, but he held to the west course magnetic, which, owing to the variation for which he

---

14 **deep-sea . . . hove:** deep-sea weight thrown overboard.
15 **colloquies** (kŏl'ə kwĭz): conversations.

16 **cliques** (klēks): small exclusive groups of people.

did not allow, was about west by south, true.

On October 7, when there was another false landfall, great flocks of birds passed over the ships, flying westsouthwest; this was the autumn migration from eastern North America to the West Indies. Columbus decided that he had better follow the birds rather than his chart, and changed course accordingly that evening. That was "good joss";[17] it was his shortest course to the nearest land. Now, every night, the men were heartened by seeing against the moon (full on October 5) flocks of birds flying their way. But by the tenth, mutiny flared up again. No land for thirty-one days. Even by the phony reckoning which Columbus gave out they had sailed much farther west than anyone had expected. Enough of this nonsense, sailing west to nowhere; let the Captain General turn back or else! Columbus, says the record, "cheered them as best he could, holding out good hope of the advantages they might gain; and, he added, it was useless to complain, *since he had come to go to the Indies, and so had to continue until he found them, with Our Lord's help.*"

That was typical of Columbus's determination. Yet even he, conscious[18] of divine guidance, could not have kept on indefinitely without the support of his captains and officers. According to one account, it was Martín Alonzo Pinzón who cheered him by shouting, *Adelante! Adelante!* which

17 **good joss:** slang for *good luck.*

18 **conscious:** aware.

an American poet has translated, "Sail on! Sail on!" But, according to Oviedo, one of the earliest historians who talked with the participants, it was Columbus alone who persuaded the Pinzóns and La Cosa to sail on, with the promise that if land were not found within three days, he would turn back. If this version is correct, as I believe it is, the Captain General's promise to his captains was made on October 9. Next day the trade wind blew fresher, sending the fleet along at 7 knots; it so continued on the eleventh, with a heavy following sea. But signs of land, such as branches of trees with green leaves and flowers, became so frequent that the people were content with their Captain General's decision, and the mutinous mutterings died out in the keen anticipation of making a landfall in the Indies.

As the sun set under a clear horizon October 11, the northeast trade breezed up to gale force, and the three ships tore along at 9 knots. But Columbus refused to shorten sail, since his promised time was running out. He signaled everyone to keep a particularly sharp watch, and offered extra rewards for first landfall in addition to the year's pay promised by the Sovereigns. That night of destiny was clear and beautiful with a late rising moon, but the sea was the roughest of the entire passage. The men were tense and expectant, the officers testy[19] and anxious, the Captain General serene in the confidence

that presently God would reveal to him the promised Indies.

At 10 P.M., an hour before moonrise, Columbus and a seaman, almost simultaneously, thought they saw a light "like a little wax candle rising and falling." Others said they saw it too, but most did not; and after a few minutes it disappeared. Volumes have been written to explain what this light was or might have been. To a seaman it requires no explanation. It was an illusion, created by overtense watchfulness. When uncertain of your exact position, and straining to make a night landfall, you are apt to see imaginary lights and flashes and to hear nonexistent bells and breakers.

On rush the ships, pitching, rolling, throwing spray—white waves at their bows and white wakes reflecting the moon. *Pinta* is perhaps half a mile in the lead, *Santa María* on her port quarter, *Niña* on the other side. Now one, now another forges ahead, but they are all making the greatest speed of which they are capable. With the sixth glass of the night watch, the last sands are running out of an era that began with the dawn of history. A few minutes now and destiny will turn up a glass the flow of whose sands we are still watching. Not since the birth of Christ has there been a night so full of meaning for the human race.

At 2 A.M., October 12, Rodrigo de Triana, lookout on *Pinta*, sees something like a white cliff shining in the moonlight, and sings out, *Tierra! tierra!* "Land! land!" Captain Pinzón verifies the landfall, fires a gun as

---

19 testy: impatient; easily annoyed.

agreed, and shortens sail to allow the flagship to catch up. As *Santa María* approaches, the Captain General shouts across the rushing waters, "Señor Martín Alonso, you *did* find land! Five thousand maravedis for you as a bonus!"

Yes, land it was this time, a little island of the Bahamas group. The fleet was headed for the sand cliffs on its windward side and would have been wrecked had it held course. But these seamen were too expert to allow that to happen. The Captain General ordered sail to be shortened and the fleet to jog off and on until daylight, which was equivalent to a southwesterly drift clear of the island. At dawn they made full sail, passed the southern point of the island and sought an opening on the west coast, through the barrier reef.

Before noon they found it, sailed into the shallow bay now called Long or Fernandez, and anchored in the lee of the land, in five fathoms.

Here on a gleaming beach of white coral occurred the famous first landing of Columbus. The Captain General (now by general consent called Admiral) went ashore in the flagship's boat with the royal standard of Castile displayed, the two Captains Pinzón in their boats, flying the banner of the Expedition—the green crowned cross on a white field. "And, all having rendered thanks to Our Lord, kneeling on the ground, embracing it with tears of joy for the immeasurable mercy of having reached it, the Admiral rose and gave this island the name *San Salvador*"—Holy Saviour.

Understanding Literature

1. What evidence is there in this selection which shows that the author was a sailor? What specific details does Morison use to give you a sense of a real voyage?
2. What means did Columbus use to keep his ship on course?
3. How much of Columbus's success was due to knowledge, how much to courage, how much to luck?

The name Ben Franklin is one you have heard many times and in connection with many things—government, lightning rods, diplomacy, science, the Declaration of Independence, inventions. Here you will see what Ben Franklin was like as a boy.

from That Lively Man, Ben Franklin*

Jeanette Eaton

IMPROVING YOUR READING: The following selection is biographical; it is based on the facts of Franklin's life. But the author presents these facts in fictional form; that is, much of her presentation contains details that the 20th-century biographer could not possibly know. When you read any biography, you should ask: How much of it seems to be based on fact and how much of it is certainly fiction?

"Now, BEN, my boy, we'll see how well our latest *Gazette* looks in print."

Winking at the apprentice who stood ready beside the big press, the workman lifted a lever at the side. Slowly the heavy weight rose from the inked form. Snatching up the damp paper, the man gave it a glance, nodded, and handed it to the boy.

In an absent-minded way, while his quick eye roved down the page, Ben read aloud: "The *Boston Gazette,* April twenty-second, Seventeen Hundred and Nineteen."

"The print is clear enough," said the workman. "I suppose, Ben, you'll be going over the proof before your brother does, but I'll let him take a glance at it." Striding across the long room toward a desk in the corner, he called out, "Mr. Franklin, here is a first printing of the *Gazette.*"

A tall young fellow in maroon coat and knickerbockers was at that moment rising from his seat to reach from its peg his three-cornered hat. He turned and said, "Give the sheet to Ben while I'm at dinner. It's two o'clock, you know."

As he crossed the room, the door opened. On the threshold stood a young man. "Mr. James Franklin," he sang out gaily, "printer for all and sundry,[1] printer of the *Boston Gazette,* 'tis time to think of broiled cod and apple cake!"

"Aye, I'm coming, my friend," replied James.

"And you, Ben Franklin!" shouted the visitor. "Are you not faring forth also?"

From his corner Ben flashed a smile full of mischief and merriment. "Nay, sir, I spread a feast right here!"

1 all and sundry: everyone.

* From THAT LIVELY MAN, BEN FRANKLIN by Jeanette Eaton, copyright 1948 by William Morrow and Company, Inc., by permission of William Morrow and Company, Inc.

James turned to say in a harsh tone, "Don't forget, young jackanapes, I'll feast on you if you make mistakes in this proof!"

As the door closed on the two men, the chief workman, slipping off his leather apron and into his jacket, stared curiously at the apprentice. Ben had seated himself at a table by the rear window. Before him was a pitcher of milk and a cup and he was unwrapping a small package.

"Ben," said the workman, "you tell me you save part of the board money your brother pays out by dining on milk and a penny bun. What I'd like to know is what you do with your savings."

With a proud grin the boy answered, "I buy books."

"Books!" exclaimed the other. "Why, hardly a day goes by but what some bookseller's apprentice loans you by stealth one of his master's new books from London. And one of your brother's customers lets you read books from his library. What more do you want?"

"I like to have books I need not give back so fast. Look at this one!" Eagerly Ben spread out on the table a big brown volume. "Here is bound together a full year of that London newspaper, the *Spectator*. And a wittier paper was never printed. I should like to set type for such pieces as those London wits wrote, instead of this dull *Boston Gazette*."

"Hmm!" said the workman, going to the door. "Your brother is lucky to get the contract to print the *Gazette*. It brings him in a pretty penny."

Left alone, Ben munched his roll and reflected. He had been apprenticed to his brother for almost two years. Already he could set type better and faster than the journeyman printer. Moreover, he was learning to read proof, although he still made mistakes for which James cuffed him soundly. Certainly he liked this trade better than any of the others his father had urged upon him. As for the time he was apprenticed in his father's soap and candle shop—ugh, how he had hated it! The smell of boiling fat in which Josiah Franklin lived all day, to earn a good living for his large family, was revolting to his youngest son. What Ben had wanted was to go to sea. His father would not consent to that, but had agreed to let the boy change his trade and learn to be a printer.

"If only it didn't take so long to become a journeyman and earn wages!" thought Ben, as he drained his last sip of milk. "Nine years in all! Not till I'm twenty-one. That's seven long years from now."

He got up, crossed the room, and stared out through the small panes of thick glass in the front window. Passers-by on the roughly paved street were bending almost double to make headway against the cold April wind from Boston Harbor. Capes and neck scarves blew out like sails. Ben's eyes widened as he caught sight of Dr. Cotton Mather, famous preacher and member of the Assembly's Council which ruled Boston and the Massachusetts Colony. Even this stern man, who held himself so high, was buffeted[2] by the disrespectful wind.

Just then a clock on the wall of the shop chimed the quarter hour. With a start Ben strode back to his table. "I mustn't be late for school!" he thought, smiling to himself.

In another moment his quill was busily scratching away. He was trying to write an article which would be as gay and witty as those he read in the *Spectator*.

The single pupil in the Benjamin Franklin school had to work hard to please his master. Although Ben had read books ever since he could remember, he had had only a few years in the free schools and but one in the Grammar School, where he had failed in arithmetic. Now he was writing, reading, and studying with might and main to make up for lost time. Often he read far into the night.

Luckily he was strong and healthy enough to stand long hours of work. Somehow he always found time for fun. With special friends he took long walks, exploring the country for miles around the small town of Boston. What he loved best was swimming.

That year in May there was a holiday. Ben spent almost the whole afternoon in the water. When he reached home, it was nearly suppertime. He found his father and his favorite sister, little Jane, in the front bedroom, which also served as a kind of parlor.

"Mercy, Ben!" cried Jane, springing up with a swirl of the long skirts which even small girls wore in those days. "I feared you might be drowned!"

"Not I!" He laughed and looked quickly for the affectionate smile his father always turned upon his favorite son.

"Father," he said eagerly, "I tried a pretty experiment today. I made the wind draw me across the pond."

Encouraged by his listeners, the boy went on to describe his game. First he flew high in the air a big kite he had made and tied to a stout stick. Then he flung himself into the water on his back, holding the stick in both hands behind his head. Slowly the kite had pulled him across the pond to the other shore. "It was very agreeable indeed!" he wound up.

Laughing, Josiah said, "It is good to try new things, my son. Keep on using your head to judge what your eyes see. That is the way to learn."

Ben's father sometimes gave him useful criticism on writing. But Josiah had no idea of the boy's other efforts at self-education. He was trying to gain self-control in every way. He gave up eating meat to prove that he was not a slave to any sort of diet. He stopped arguing with his friends, as he so loved to do, and learned to listen to their opinions in silence, whether or not he agreed with them. His most difficult tests of self-control were caused by his brother's impatience and hot temper in the printing shop.

Late in the year 1720 an exciting change took place in the Franklin

2 **buffeted:** struck.

JEANETTE EATON

189

printing business. James lost his contract to print the *Boston Gazette*. After he had raged and worried for a bit, he decided to publish a paper of his own to be called the *Courant*. Its purpose was to discuss news and local events in a lively way. Several of his friends promised to write for the paper under assumed names.

No one was more thrilled about this venture than Ben. But when he brought his father the first issue of the *Courant*, he did so with a long face. After supper Josiah spread out the paper on the kitchen table, trimmed the candles, and began to read. Jane knelt on the wooden settle to look over his shoulder.

" 'Tis a noble-looking newspaper," she exclaimed. But when she turned to her brother, she cried out, "What ails you, Ben, that you look displeased? I thought you were happy over the *Courant!*"

"I do not hold with James in attacking those brave men who try inoculation against smallpox," he explained. "Too many people are dying of it. Why cast ridicule upon[3] an experiment which may succeed?"

Josiah put down the paper and stared at him. "Why, my son, all Boston cries out against this folly! I can hardly believe that a learned man like Dr. Mather should undertake inoculation. James pokes rare fun at him in this first issue."

"And in doing so," replied Ben with heat, "James joins the ignorant folk who fear a new idea. I believe

inoculation will prove to be a good defense against this dread disease."

Opinion in Boston, however, was strongly against vaccination. The *Courant* was sold from one end of the town to the other. James was triumphant. When Ben protested against his publishing another attack in the next issue, James whacked him soundly and called him a saucy fellow. The brothers hardly spoke to one another until the *Courant* dropped the subject and turned to lighter themes.

From then on Ben delighted in the newspaper. For a year he studied carefully the gay little pieces written by James and his friends. He compared them with the *Spectator* and often thought the *Courant* might improve in wit.

Alone in the shop one afternoon, Benjamin sat reading a fresh proof of the paper. He was nibbling a large red apple as he slowly went over the contributions. Every now and then he gave a sniff which meant, "I could have put this matter better myself!" Suddenly his eyes with their heavy lids opened wide. In the silence of the empty room he whispered, "Why don't I try?"

That night and the next the candle in Ben's tiny room under the roof burned late. He was scribbling, tearing up what he had written, and beginning again. A few days later the apprentice was setting copy for the next issue of the newspaper. It was nine o'clock on a March morning. Now and then the boy turned an intent glance toward the far corner of the shop.

---

3 **cast ridicule upon:** laugh at.

At the editor's desk, James and one of the men who wrote for the *Courant* were poring over a number of closely written pages. Both men were nodding and smiling. It was plain that they were pleased with what they read. At last James strode across the room and tossed the papers to the typesetter.

"Here, Ben, set up this letter. Someone thrust it under our door last night. We want to use it in the paper at once."

Benjamin nodded and bent over the type form. Not for worlds would he have shown his delight and excitement. The letter, signed by the name Silence Dogood, was the very one he had sat up two nights to compose. It was he who had dashed down the street after supper to slip his carefully copied letter under the door of the shop. All night he had tossed and turned, wondering what James would think of it. And now his brother liked it, accepted it! The boy could hardly wait to set it up. In the issue of April 2nd, 1722, Benjamin Franklin, aged sixteen, first saw his own writing in print.

According to her maker, Silence was a respectable widow with three children. She had "a natural inclination to observe and reprove the faults of others," and intended to make good use of this talent. Describing her life in detail, the widow declared that every fortnight she was going to contribute to the readers of the *Courant* a letter which she hoped would "add somewhat to their entertainment."

Since James had accepted the first letter, thought Ben, he must be willing for the writer to keep the promise to contribute regularly. His heart thumped with the wonder of it. Now he could use his study of the *Spectator* and his practice in composition. Now all the odd and funny things he had noted so often in his walks about the town could be set down in print.

In no time at all Silence Dogood became for him almost as real as himself. She was, like the grandsons and granddaughters of the Puritans in Boston, ready to judge the wrong-doer. But she also possessed Ben Franklin's mischievous humor. Since she admitted to being a great reader, Mrs. Dogood felt free to use words and expressions worthy of a scholar.

Ben enjoyed devoting one letter to the behavior of the students at Harvard College. Silence thought too many of them, after causing their parents much trouble and expense, returned home "as great blockheads as ever, only more proud and self-conceited."

Benjamin himself tried writing ballads. Now he had Mrs. Dogood write a piece making fun of New England poetry, and his remarks were quoted by all the bookish young men of Boston. In another letter he joked gently about the bold young women who walked on Boston Common late in the evening. Men who drank too much and pretended they were sober gave Ben another chance for delightful humor. With every letter his wit and his writing improved. James looked eagerly for the contributions and published every one. The Dogood

letters, indeed, became the talk of the town.

One Sunday, coming out of North Church where he had heard Cotton Mather preach, Ben was caught up in a group of gentlemen and ladies who had paused to exchange greetings. He listened with amazement to their conversation.

"Do you imagine," one fashionable lady said laughingly, "that Dr. Mather read Silence Dogood's letter about the people who only pretend to be religious? That was a pretty bit of humor."

"Who might Mrs. Dogood be, think you?" asked one of the men.

"Who indeed!" sniffed another lady, in a voice matching her prim gray woolen gown. "She writes with too bold a pen for me!"

Slowly moving on his way, Ben shook with silent glee. What would those people have said had they known that Mrs. Dogood was right there in their midst, disguised as a youth in his best Sunday suit and buckled shoes?

There were plenty of blithe spirits in Boston to enjoy the fun which Ben created. But the men in power were a sober lot. Once the Colony had been governed by leaders of the Puritan Church. But under a new charter granted in 1692, voting depended not on religion but on property. The Massachusetts legislature was elected by people who owned a certain amount of money or land. The Governor was appointed by the English King and the Council was also chosen by the English Government. The Councilors were men of education and wealth. In the early part of the 18th century they still carried on the narrow tradition of the old Puritans. They scorned and feared any effort on the part of the people to question their authority.

No wonder, therefore, that the Council kept watching this upstart newspaper called the *Courant*. Had it not held up to public laughter one of the most famous Councilors, Dr. Mather? One day an officer of the law came to the printing shop and commanded James Franklin, on order of the Council, to come at once to the Town House for questioning.

Ink-stained Benjamin rushed anxiously to the door to watch them go. He heard his brother ask in a haughty tone, "What might this inquiry be about?" Some words from the constable floated back. Ben guessed that a recent article in the newspaper showed contempt for the government. Before the day was over, news came to the shop that James had been clapped into jail.

Naturally the Franklin family was horrified. But Benjamin at once began to have a glorious time. For a whole week he was in sole charge of the paper. He hardly took time to eat or sleep. Of course Silence Dogood kept him company and composed a long article for the next issue.

"Without freedom of thought," wrote Silence, "there can be no such thing as wisdom; and no such thing as public liberty without freedom of speech."

When James came out of jail, he spoke highly of the article. "Mrs.

Dogood could not have written anything that better fitted my case," said he. His friends were pleased to find the printer in such a lighthearted mood. He sat down and wrote an amusing account of his stay in jail. For once, he was even amiable[4] to his apprentice.

Then came a morning when James reached the shop half an hour earlier than usual. He found Benjamin at a table scribbling away like fury. In two strides the printer was beside his brother.

"Why aren't you setting type?" he shouted. "What are you scrivening here?" Ben's guilty look of being caught red-handed made James snatch the paper from him. For a moment James read in silence. Then his jaw dropped. He swayed back on his heels.

"No!" he cried. "It isn't possible! What? *You!* You are Silence Dogood! You are the shrewd widow with three children!"

Benjamin looked up without speaking. His brother's face wore an expression stranger than mere anger. Jealousy was written large upon it. That a seventeen-year-old could write well enough to fool him, fool the whole town, well, it was too much to bear! James glared and slapped the paper down.

"But you have always liked these letters!" shouted Ben furiously.

A bitter argument followed. Ben was called a saucy deceiver. In turn, he called his brother a stupid tyrant. The quarrel ended in the

4 amiable: friendly; kindhearted.

usual way. James snatched up a ruler, took the apprentice by the collar, and gave him blow after blow.

Nevertheless, only a few months passed before James desperately needed his young brother's help. Again James wrote something offensive to the Council. This time he was forbidden to print the *Courant* or any other newspaper. To get around the grim sentence, James and his supporters decided to publish the paper under the name of Benjamin Franklin.

At first, the boy was pleased. But soon he found that it was only his name that was wanted. James scolded, commanded, and boxed the ears of the so-called publisher as if he were a stupid drudge. Day by day Ben's rebellion seethed more fiercely.

One afternoon his resentment boiled over. Flinging off his apron, he faced his brother. "James, I can no longer do with your ways. You are neither amiable nor just. I'll not stay another day to be kicked and cuffed for small reason."

"What?" James sprang from his chair in furious surprise. "You dare not break your contract! You're bound to me for four more years!"

"It matters not. I'll find work as journeyman printer at some shop. I'm skilled enough. I can bear it here no longer."

Through clenched teeth James said, "The greater fool you! You will not get one day of printing work in Boston."

It was no empty threat. James told every other master printer in the town about his faithless apprentice. No one would employ a boy who had dared break his contract. Even Josiah Franklin shook his head and told his son he had made a grave mistake. Slowly it grew clear to the rebel that there really was no chance for him in any Boston printing shop.

After many anxious days and sleepless nights, Benjamin made up his mind to run away. It seemed the only thing to do. With the help of a friend he got passage on a ship bound for New York. By selling most of his precious books, bought with such difficulty, he gathered together a little money. One evening he managed to take on board the ship his chest packed with his Sunday suit, clean shirts, stockings, and underwear. Early next morning, before anyone was awake, he tiptoed down the stairs. In the big empty kitchen he silently said good-by to his home.

Two hours later he was standing on deck as the vessel edged away from Woodman's Wharf. He could see the church spires of Boston rising above the clustered houses, the green of the Common, the sober bulk of Town House and the jail. Resentfully the youth stared at the scene.

Narrow-minded Councilmen, jealous James, skimpy living, faces that frowned on dancing and other simple joys—how glad he was to escape them all! He was not afraid to make his way by himself. Hadn't he a trade? Of course, he would miss his kind and loving parents and his sister Jane. But excitement was crowding out every other feeling. He was off to see the world! Clutching his hat as the salt breeze swept the ship, young Franklin turned his face to the sea.

Understanding Literature

1. Reread the note at the beginning of the story. What information does the author give which she could not really know about Franklin?
2. What is the conflict or problem in this selection?
3. Cite lines which help the reader to understand what kind of person Ben was. You will notice that many of the lines which tell you something of Ben's character are not purely description. What Ben said himself, what others said about him, and the way he reacted to certain problems are all sources of information about Ben's character.

Focusing on Words

Probably there are no words in the selection from *That Lively Man, Ben Franklin* which were so new to you or so difficult that they hindered your understanding of the story. The author uses several words, however, that you will want to know more about. These are also words that aid the reader in realizing the time in which the story takes place. Define the italicized words in the following sentences:

1. "A tall young fellow in maroon coat and *knickerbockers* was at that moment rising from his seat. . . ."
2. The chief workman "stared curiously at the *apprentice*."
3. "Already he could set type better and faster than the *journeyman* printer."
4. "Jane knelt on the wooden *settle* to look over his shoulder."
5. " 'Why aren't you setting type?' he shouted. 'What are you *scrivening* here?' "

Further Activities

1. Using the histories, biographies, and magazine articles in your school and town libraries, prepare a written report on Franklin and his many inventions. In the first paragraph describe briefly all his different inventions. In the second and third paragraphs describe his work on one particular invention and the use now made of this invention.
2. Use the resources of your libraries to prepare a report on Franklin's important work in the formation of the United States government.

JEANETTE EATON

195

Like most people, you probably think of George Washington as "the Father of his Country." In this poem you will see him as a hunter and messenger on his way to deliver a message to the French.

Young Washington

The Embassy to the French Forts, 1753
Arthur Guiterman

Tie the moccasin, bind the pack,
  Sling your rifle across your back,
Up! and follow the mountain track,
  Tread the Indian Trail.
North and west is the road we fare   5
Toward the forts of the Frenchmen, where
"Peace or War!" is the word we bear,
  Life and Death in the scale.

The leaves of October are dry on the ground,
The sheaves of Virginia are gathered and bound,   10
Her fallows are glad with the cry of the hound,
  The partridges whirr in the fern;
But deep are the forests and keen are the foes
Where Monongahela in wilderness flows;
We've labors and perils and torrents and snows   15
  To conquer before we return.

Hall and council room, farm and chase,
Coat of scarlet and frill of lace
All are excellent things in place;
  Joy in these if ye can.   20
Mine be hunting shirt, knife and gun,
Camp aglow on the sheltered run,
Friend and foe in the checkered sun;
  That's the life for a man!

Understanding Literature

1. Where is Washington going? When, why, and how is he
traveling?

2. What does the second stanza add to the setting? What are the possible dangers of the trip?
3. Arthur Guiterman uses comparison and contrast in the last stanza to give his readers a better understanding of the life Washington really enjoyed as a young man. What is the comparison that is made?
4. What is the main idea within each of the three stanzas?

In the period of history in which America was fighting to win her independence from England, Paul Revere was a leading citizen of Boston. Although well-known for his skill as a silversmith, he is probably remembered far more because of his exciting midnight ride described by Longfellow.

Paul Revere's Ride

Henry Wadsworth Longfellow

IMPROVING YOUR READING: "Paul Revere's Ride" is different from many other poems in that each verse does not have the same number of lines. Some of the verses are very short, and others are quite long. The rhyme scheme, too, does not follow a set pattern, although many of the lines do rhyme with each other. The rhythm, or beat, of the poem makes it very enjoyable to hear read aloud.

Listen, my children, and you shall hear
Of the midnight ride of Paul Revere,
On the eighteenth of April, in Seventy-five;
Hardly a man is now alive
Who remembers that famous day and year.   5

He said to his friend, "If the British march
By land or sea from the town tonight,
Hang a lantern aloft in the belfry arch
Of the North Church tower as a signal light—
One, if by land, and two, if by sea;   10
And I on the opposite shore will be,
Ready to ride and spread the alarm
Through every Middlesex village and farm,
For the country folk to be up and to arm."

Then he said, "Good night!" and with muffled oar 15
Silently rowed to the Charlestown shore,
Just as the moon rose over the bay,
Where swinging wide at her moorings lay
The *Somerset*, British man-of-war;
A phantom[1] ship, with each mast and spar 20
Across the moon like a prison bar,
And a huge black hulk, that was magnified
By its own reflection in the tide.

Meanwhile, his friend, through alley and street,
Wanders and watches with eager ears, 25
Till in the silence around him he hears
The muster of men at the barrack door,
The sound of arms, and the tramp of feet,
And the measured tread of the grenadiers,
Marching down to their boats on the shore. 30

Then he climbed the tower of the Old North Church,
By the wooden stairs, with stealthy tread,
To the belfry chamber overhead,
And startled the pigeons from their perch
On the somber rafters, that round him made 35
Masses and moving shapes of shade—
By the trembling ladder, steep and tall,
To the highest window in the wall,
Where he paused to listen and look down
A moment on the roofs of the town, 40
And the moonlight flowing over all.

Beneath, in the churchyard, lay the dead,
In their night encampment on the hill,
Wrapped in silence so deep and still
That he could hear, like a sentinel's tread, 45
The watchful night wind, as it went
Creeping along from tent to tent,
And seeming to whisper, "All is well!"
A moment only he feels the spell
Of the place and the hour, and the secret dread 50

1 **phantom:** ghostlike.

Of the lonely belfry and the dead;
For suddenly all his thoughts are bent
On a shadowy something far away,
Where the river widens to meet the bay—
A line of black that bends and floats   55
On the rising tide, like a bridge of boats.

Meanwhile, impatient to mount and ride,
Booted and spurred, with a heavy stride
On the opposite shore walked Paul Revere.
Now he patted his horse's side,   60
Now gazed at the landscape far and near,
Then, impetuous, stamped the earth,
And turned and tightened his saddle girth;
But mostly he watched with eager search
The belfry tower of the Old North Church,   65
As it rose above the graves on the hill,
Lonely and spectral² and somber and still.
And lo! as he looks, on the belfry's height
A glimmer, and then a gleam of light!
He springs to the saddle, the bridle he turns,   70
But lingers and gazes, till full on his sight
A second lamp in the belfry burns!

A hurry of hoofs in a village street,
A shape in the moonlight, a bulk in the dark,
And beneath, from the pebbles, in passing, a spark   75
Struck out by a steed flying fearless and fleet:
That was all!   And yet, through the gloom and the light,
The fate of a nation was riding that night;
And the spark struck out by that steed, in his flight,
Kindled the land into flame with its heat.   80
He has left the village and mounted the steep,
And beneath him, tranquil and broad and deep,
Is the Mystic, meeting the ocean tides;
And under the alders that skirt its edge,
Now soft on the sand, now loud on the ledge,   85
Is heard the tramp of his steed as he rides.

2 **spectral:** ghostly.

HENRY WADSWORTH LONGFELLOW   **199**

It was twelve by the village clock,
When he crossed the bridge into Medford town.
He heard the crowing of the cock,
And the barking of the farmer's dog, 90
And felt the damp of the river fog,
That rises after the sun goes down.

It was one by the village clock,
When he galloped into Lexington.
He saw the gilded weathercock 95
Swim in the moonlight as he passed,
And the meetinghouse windows, blank and bare,
Gaze at him with a spectral glare,
As if they already stood aghast
At the bloody work they would look upon. 100

It was two by the village clock,
When he came to the bridge in Concord town.
He heard the bleating of the flock,
And the twitter of birds among the trees,
And felt the breath of the morning breeze 105
Blowing over the meadows brown.
And one was safe and asleep in his bed
Who at the bridge would be first to fall,
Who that day would be lying dead,
Pierced by a British musket ball. 110

You know the rest. In the books you have read,
How the British Regulars fired and fled—
How the farmers gave them ball for ball,
From behind each fence and farmyard wall,
Chasing the redcoats down the lane, 115
Then crossing the fields to emerge again
Under the trees at the turn of the road,
And only pausing to fire and load.

So through the night rode Paul Revere;
And so through the night went his cry of alarm 120
To every Middlesex village and farm—
A cry of defiance and not of fear,
A voice in the darkness, a knock at the door,
And a word that shall echo forevermore!
For, borne on the nightwind of the Past, 125

Through all our history, to the last,
In the hour of darkness and peril and need,
The people will waken and listen to hear
The hurrying hoofbeats of that steed,
And the midnight message of Paul Revere.   130

Understanding Literature

1. Read the lines which give the setting (time and place) for the action of this poem.
2. What was the purpose of the signal Paul Revere was awaiting?
3. Point out the lines in the poem which tell the reader of action that was set in motion by Paul Revere's ride.
4. Observe the rhythm of the poem, especially in lines 73-80. What effect is the poet trying to create with these lines?
5. Notice the construction of this poem. What part of the poem serves as the introduction? At what point does the climax occur? How is the suspense built up? How much of the poem would you think of as the conclusion?

Others have deserted from General Washington's army at Valley Forge. Neil is cold, hungry, and weary, and his home is but two miles away from the location of his assigned mission. Christopher, Neil's companion, is afraid Neil will not be able to resist the temptation to desert.

Patrol at Valley Forge

Russell Gordon Carter

IMPROVING YOUR READING: This story has a double plot; it has two *conflicts*, or problems, to be resolved. Identify these problems as you read, and be ready to discuss how the two plots are interwoven.

SILHOUETTED AGAINST the twilight of a winter morning early in the year 1778—bleak and bitterly cold like so many other mornings at Valley Forge during that tragic period of the Revolution—the tall sergeant filled the small doorway of the log hut as he shouted, "Private Williams an' Private Fenwood, report at once for patrol duty to Corporal Purvis at the Star Redoubt!"

As the door banged shut and his footsteps squeaked in the dry snow, Christopher Williams blinked and yawned and, still clutching his tattered blanket round him, pushed himself slowly erect, teeth chattering, slim body shivering. To his surprise, Neil Fenwood, his close companion of the past month, was already on his feet and asking for shoes. "Shoes," Neil called in a disgruntled sleep-heavy voice, "I can't go on patrol 'thout shoes!"

One of the men huddled close to the nine others on the bare ground mumbled, "Ye can wear mine." And another, lifting his head, added, "An' Christ'pher can wear mine."

"Also a jacket," Neil said. "Who'll let me borry his jacket?"

"Here, take this thing o' mine," someone grunted, and Neil bent forward.

"Christ'pher's welcome to this ragged greatcoat I have on," another voice added, but Christopher said, "Nay, I'll wear my blanket." And squeezing his head through a hole near the middle, he let the folds fall about him.

As the two Continentals,[1] both Pennsylvanians under General Wayne's command, picked up their muskets and left the hut, Christopher wondered if ever a morning had been colder or more forlorn—even at Valley Forge. The stars in the graying sky were still blue-bright and glittering,

1 **Continentals:** members of the Continental army during the American Revolution.

dancing beyond the wisps of wood smoke rising from the wooden chimneys of the crudely built huts that housed Washington's half-starved and depleted[2] army—one-third the number of the British under Lord Howe living in luxury at Philadelphia, a score of miles to the southeast, and supported by British ships-of-war lying in the Delaware.

While ice particles cracked and tinkled under the feet of the two soldiers, and silent sentries wrapped in old rugs and blankets, and with legs encased in straw, stared at them with tired eyes, it seemed to Christopher that never again would he feel the warmth of summer. . . . But there was something that troubled him even more than the terrific cold, and he didn't know what to do about it.

At the Star Redoubt, to the east of Fort Washington, which crowned the summit of Mount Joy, Corporal Jacob Purvis was waiting with musket hugged against his gaunt body. He was much older than the two others and had seen service at Bunker Hill and also at Saratoga where, in October of the preceding year, the British general, Burgoyne, had surrendered with his whole army in a rare American victory.

"We have a hazardous mission," Purvis explained. " 'Tis reported there's a hogshead[3] o' shoes lying somewhere off the Old Lime Road—shoes for this army, abandoned by teamsters, 'tis said, who lacked the courage to make the full trip from York State. Mebbe the report is false like so many others, but General Washington feels 'tis worth a scouting party, as ye might say. So we three are to enter enemy territory and have a look."

"Old Lime is close to the Old York Road, eh, is it not?" Neil asked quickly—a little too quickly, Christopher thought, and glancing sidewise, he was almost certain what was in his companion's mind. More than once during recent weeks, when reports of increasing desertions had reached the hut, Neil had listened with a strange look in his eyes—so strange that several of the others had remarked upon it.

"Aye," Purvis agreed, "Old Lime lies close to Old York, an' Old York leads direct to Coryell's Ferry."

Neil cleared his throat and then was silent—and again the look was in his eyes.

As the patrol set off toward Matson's Ford across the Schuylkill, which bounded the encampment on the north, through the mind of Christopher ran the thought: "Neil has at last decided to desert! It wasn't like him to respond so readily to the sergeant's call. For some time he has been thinking of deserting, of that I am certain! And now—Coryell's Ferry and Neil's home only two miles distant on the near shore! 'Twill be easy for him to slip away from us. I wonder, ought I to speak to the corporal about it? Maybe somebody could help him."

It was a hard question. Even when the three were across the Schuylkill and beyond the Ridge Road running

2 **depleted:** reduced; decreased in number.
3 **hogshead:** large cask.

northwest from Philadelphia to Potts Grove, Christopher was not sure what he ought to do. He liked Neil, and he knew his companion liked him, but Neil was younger by a year and a half—not yet eighteen—and at Valley Forge he had evidently seen more than was good for him. Burials, for example, day after day; three of them yesterday and five the day before. Also men ill and dying of disease and malnutrition. And then, only last week, Neil's own cousin, Private Denis Jepson, going to the hospital and having a foot amputated because of frostbite. In addition, there were the daily hardships everyone suffered: the lack of warm clothing and the scarcity and monotony of the food: no vegetables and almost no. meat, but in their place "fire cake and water"—dough paste baked in the embers and water to wash it down—along with other inadequate fare. All this because of an inefficient Quartermaster Department[4] and a Congress that had listened to men jealous of the Commander-in-Chief and felt it knew better than Washington and his generals how to wage war against the British professional soldiers.

A low word of warning from Purvis broke in upon Christopher's thoughts as the patrol was emerging from a patch of woods above Wissahickon Creek. The next instant a spurt of gold leaped against the snow across the stream, and while the valley re-echoed to the crash of a musket, the corporal spun sidewise and crumpled to the ground, a hand clutching his shoulder where crimson formed a widening stain.

"A foul plague upon it!" Purvis muttered while Christopher and Neil dragged him to a sheltered spot. "I spied the lobsterback[5] e'en whilst he was aiming his piece!" And he closed his eyes and gritted his teeth.

Kneeling beside him after they had stopped the flow of blood and bound the wound, Christopher said, "You will have to go back. Think you, you can walk?"

The corporal struggled to his feet, protesting that he didn't want to go back. Again and again he called down a foul plague upon his misfortune. Then at last, with a hand clutching a sapling, he said to Christopher, "Ah, you are right, I shall have to go back!"

"One of us will go with you," Christopher said, and looked straight at Neil.

"Nay, I can walk alone!" Purvis protested. "You two must fulfill the mission. Aye, those are my orders to you: fulfill the mission! You, Christopher Williams, are in command. And now harken and I will tell you more about the spot where 'tis said the treacherous teamsters jettisoned[6] the hogshead. Just off Old Lime, somewhere not far north o' Whitemarsh, there is a ravine with twin pines marking the opening and tow-

---

4 **Quartermaster Department:** department which provides clothing, shelter, and food for troops.

5 **lobsterback:** British soldier, so-called because of his red uniform.
6 **jettisoned:** abandoned; left behind.

ering above all other trees—" And on the palm of a trembling hand he traced an imaginary map while he gave further details.

Screened by heavy low growth, the two younger scouts stood silent as the corporal, still berating[7] his ill fortune, made his way slowly westward. When at last he was out of sight, Christopher said quietly, "We shall carry out orders and return with our report, whether favorable or unfavorable. Are you ready?"

Neil lifted somber blue eyes and glanced at the low gray sky, then with a shudder stared at the dark blood splotches in the snow where the corporal had lain. That was his only answer, and again Christopher wondered what he ought to do. Supposing he were to speak bluntly; he asked himself, could he convince his companion that desertion—even though many had already deserted from Valley Forge—was an ignoble act? He was not sure, so once more he kept the words back.

Turning, he led the way northward, taking advantage of all possible cover.

Snow was falling in slow lazy flakes when they crossed the ice-bound Wissahickon and set off up the wooded eastern slope. The Old Lime Road now was only a short distance ahead, and thanks to the corporal's directions and description, Christopher was confident of finding the ravine. It was the other thing that continued to trouble him. Somehow, even though he might have to use force, he said to himself that Neil must remain loyal!

They were deep in enemy country now, but thus far they had encountered no one except the British picket who had wounded the corporal. Halting at last on the shoulder of a low hill and taking a bite from a hard mass of dough he had tied in a corner of the blanket, Christopher motioned with his musket and said: "There below us, Neil, is the Old Lime Road, albeit 'tis hidden by thick growth—and yonder to the north I see twin pines!"

Neil nodded. "Aye," he agreed in a dull voice, "and maybe there's a ravine there, and maybe there's none—and if there be a ravine, perhaps it holds a hogshead o' shoes and perhaps it holds naught. So far as it concerns me, I can say with truth it matters little!"

Christopher's fingers tightened on his musket, but when he spoke, it was in a tone that gave no hint of his deep emotion. "At any rate, we shall do our duty," he said and, with musket quartered across his chest, set off obliquely[8] down the hillside.

A high tangle of snow-bent alders and berry bushes bordered a sharp turn almost a quarter of a mile below the twin pines, and it was there that the two scouts emerged upon the road. Christopher had snarled his blanket on a bush and was in the act

---

7 **berating:** scolding.

8 **obliquely** (ə blēk′lĭ): indirectly.

of freeing it when, to his surprise, he heard the nearby creak of wheels. As he whirled sidewise, a heavy voice boomed upon the winter air: "Stand firm, both o' ye, and drop yer pieces!"

Then with dark eyes wide and mouth open, he was looking at a startling sight. Just at the turn stood a white horse harnessed to a light carriage with two low wheels, and beneath the folding top sat two British officers, one of them holding the reins and the other, with arm extended, aiming a pistol!

"Quick, drop yer pieces an' raise yer hands!"

Neil had already dropped his musket; now Christopher let his own slide reluctantly to the snow and slowly lifted his hands.

Slipping out of the carriage, the officer with the pistol advanced and, gathering up the weapons, tossed them into the bushes. Then with a glance toward his companion, who also had climbed out and was now at the horse's head, he suddenly laughed in a way that deepened the color in his round red mottled[9] face.

"Egad, Lieutenant!" he exclaimed. "This be comic! Remember what we talked of at mess this morning? The Third Rule o' War! Aye, the Third Rule as listed amongst the six the rebel Washington has seen fit to draw up for the benefit of better soldiers than himself. Well, here now before us is a apt picture to illustrate it: two ragged wretches who will accompany us back to Philadelphia after a very pleasant afternoon ride in our calash!"[10]

While Christopher stood with teeth clenched, and Neil motionless behind him, the British officers laughed heartily, as if never had there been greater cause for merriment. Finally the one at the horse's head said to the prisoners, "Knew ye, your rebel general had drawn up six rules o' war?"

"We have heard talk of General Washington's views on warfare," Christopher replied curtly while his gaze roved this way and that, hopefully seeking a possible means of escape.

"And know ye the Third Rule?" the florid-faced officer inquired.

Christopher shook his head. "Nay," he replied and gauged the distance between himself and the man . . . a dozen feet . . . perhaps only ten. . . . Cautiously he lowered his hands a little . . .

The officer flourished his pistol and laughed again. Then he said with mock solemnity, "Give ear now and I will quote it, the Third Rule o' War: 'The first qualification of a soldier is fortitude under fatigue and privation: courage is only the second. Hardship, poverty and actual want are the soldier's best school.' There, egad! And the two of you, one in a tattered blanket and t'other in a ragged jacket, and broken shoes upon your feet—aye, the two o' ye are pupils right out of Washington's best school—Valley Forge!" And he and

---

9 **mottled:** spotted.

10 **calash:** carriage.

his companion roared with laughter, their heads thrown back, their well-nourished bodies shaking.

But this time the laughter ended with harsh abruptness as Christopher hurled himself forward. It was a desperate chance, and he knew it—but the unexpected lunge in the midst of British hilarity caught the florid-faced officer off guard, and the pistol exploded harmlessly. Then Christopher and the man went down together, grunting, gasping, fists pounding, hands seeking a firm hold upon throats . . . while the wind caught the fluffed-up snow from their struggle and sent it flying.

Other sounds of struggle, along with the creak and clatter of wheels, trembled upon the quiet air, but for Christopher they were remote and meaningless as, with head smothered beneath the broad chest of his adver-

sary,[11] he gasped for breath and clutched desperately at the collar of the officer's greatcoat. Long weeks of living mainly on fire cake and water had taken their toll of his strength. Nevertheless, somehow he managed at last to struggle out from under and then to jolt his enemy's chin with a short upward blow of his fist.

He was about to deliver another blow when a lean hand seized the Britisher and jerked him sidewise while a familiar voice shouted, "Surrender, or you'll get a ball from your brother officer's own pistol!" And there, snow-dusted and with a splotch of blood on his face, stood Neil!

"Surrender!" he repeated, and as he thrust the cold pistol against the

11 **adversary** (ăd′vər sĕr′ĭ): enemy.

other's temple, the officer relaxed and fell backward. Then pushing himself slowly to a sitting posture, he blinked and stared at the two Americans—just as his brother officer sprawled in the snow a few paces distant was blinking and staring at them.

Christopher rose to his feet, but before he could utter a word, Neil thrust the pistol into his hand and said hoarsely, "You can manage now!" Then he turned and went running up the road.

"Neil!" Christopher shouted after him. "Neil! Neil!"

But the only response was a few unintelligible words. Then Neil was lost to sight.

For several long seconds Christopher stood with feet apart and forehead wrinkled, his thoughts whirling like the flakes of snow in the increasing northwest wind. With a sickening sense of loss and of hurt, the explanation of Neil's conduct came to him suddenly and in a way that left no room for doubt.

"He has always had a strong liking for me," Christopher said to himself, "and that is why he attacked and disarmed the other officer and then came to my rescue—because he could not see me taken prisoner. But now, having left me able to manage, he has carried out his plan to desert!" Then he noticed that the calash was gone and, addressing the officer still sprawled on the ground, demanded, "Where is the horse?"

"Whirled and bolted in fright," was the response. "And I don't wonder! Never in all my years was I attacked so furiously or so savagely!" And scooping up a double handful of snow, he held it first against a great discolored lump above one eye and then against the side of his jaw.

Without taking his gaze from the prisoners, Christopher strode toward the bushes and recovered the muskets. Then standing once more before the two men, he asked himself, "Now what shall I do?" And at once came the answer: "Fulfill the mission!"

To the prisoners then he said, "Get to your feet and march—aye, up the road!" And as they quietly obeyed, it seemed to him incredible that these same two officers serving a King three thousand miles across the ocean could ever have laughed so scornfully over Washington's Third Rule of War.

Round the turn they made their way while their captor, holding the pistol in one hand and the muskets in the hollow of his arm, marched alertly half a dozen paces behind them. Along a bare stretch of straight road they marched, and then toward another turn, beyond which the twin pines rose dark and snow-mottled.

As they were rounding the second turn, Christopher suddenly caught his breath—for there near the opening of a small ravine stood the horse and calash, and in the snow alongside, where it had obviously been rolled, lay—a hogshead!

While he continued to stare, wide-eyed, Neil came striding forth from the ravine. "There's six others in there!" he announced—and something in his voice and manner made him seem altogether different from the Neil Fenwood whom Christopher had known at Valley Forge. "All six of the others also hold shoes!" Neil went on eagerly. "Seven hogsheads altogether! But a pox upon it, Christopher, we can take only the one! They'll have to send a special party after the other—"

Christopher moistened his lips, speechless. It had been a day of surprising happenings, but this, the latest, was the most surprising of all. Neil had not deserted and had no intention of deserting! Instead, leaving his companion to guard the prisoners, he had raced up the road to halt and recover the runaway horse and calash—and then had explored the ravine and found, not just one hogshead, but seven! It occurred to Christopher now that if he had caught the words Neil had flung over his shoulder, they might have explained his purpose.

Bending forward, he noted the markings on the hogshead. "Shoes," he thought. "Save for food, there is naught the army needs more!" Aloud he said to the prisoners, "Lift the hogshead into the calash."

The prisoners didn't want to lift it. They were officers, they pointed out, and should not be asked to do such menial[12] labor as lifting hogsheads. "Ne'rtheless, you will lift this one!" Christopher insisted—and noting the determined look in his eyes, they decided to obey.

Then with the hogshead filling almost the whole of the vehicle, the party set forth back along the Old Lime Road and thence westward across a bare meadow—the prisoners marching ahead, Christopher following with musket held at the alert and a loaded pistol in his waistband, then Neil with shouldered musket several paces in the rear, leading the horse and calash with its strange cargo. Onward they moved across the meadow under a darkening sky and in the teeth of the increasing storm . . . thence onward along old abandoned back roads and through stretches of woodland and across the Wissahickon . . . onward, onward, halting at times to rest or to bite off a few mouthfuls of dough paste or to make sure of direction . . . onward until the day had faded . . . then onward again through the night toward the junction of Valley Creek and the Schuylkill River.

It was mid-morning and the snow was still blowing when at last the party crossed the river at Swede's Ford and presently, to the astonishment of sentries and officers on duty, entered camp. There the two scouts yielded prisoners and calash to a detachment under one of Wayne's lieutenants and, on inquiry, learned that Corporal Purvis was secure in a hut that served as a hospital. General Wayne himself came striding down the hill a few moments later and in crisp tones asked for the story behind the capture.

Almost too weary to stand erect, Christopher managed nevertheless to give a summary account.

"Seven!" Wayne exclaimed. "Seven, you said? Seven full hogs-

12 menial: low; humble.

heads! This is something for the Commander-in-Chief to hear from your own lips! Come, both of you." And he strode toward the stone house —the former home of Isaac Potts, who had operated a forge—that General Washington now used for his headquarters.

When the three entered the doorway, Washington with the young Marquis de Lafayette beside him was seated at a long table, studying a map. Others at the table whom Christopher recognized were General Knox, chief of artillery, and the elderly Baron de Kalb, who had come from France on the same ship with Lafayette. As the Commander-in-Chief glanced up, Wayne greeted him and then told of the reason for the visit.

Washington rose to his feet—tall, easy in his movements, his face grave but serene. "You are right, General," he said to Wayne, "I wish to hear the story from the lips of the patrol leader himself."

Then once again—and in full detail this time—Christopher explained what had happened, giving enthusiastic credit to Neil for the part he had played and also mentioning how the two officers had laughed and what they had said about the Third Rule of War.

When he had finished, Washington smiled after the manner of a father to a son and stretched forth a hand first to Christopher and then to Neil.

"Both of you are a credit to the army!" he said with deep feeling. "Fortitude under fatigue and priva-tion—you nobly exemplify the maxim in your persons and in your deeds! Our enemies are correct: the two of you in a sense portray the whole army at Valley Forge! But those men were wrong to laugh. That they will discover with the passage of time."

Then turning to Wayne, he added, "See to it, General, that the six other hogsheads are soon within our possession. And see to it also that these two gallant soldiers of yours are among the first to benefit from the hogshead we already possess—and also of course that they are fed and rested." Then seating himself, he bent over the map again.

As Christopher and Neil went down the hill together a few minutes later, Neil seized his companion's hand and pressed it hard. In a voice that quivered he said, "You may never know the whole of it, Christopher, but this day—nay, yesterday—I passed a milestone in my life and am the better for it—thanks to you!"

Christopher regarded him inquiringly.

"Aye, thanks to you!" Neil repeated. "When you refused to be taken prisoner and lunged to attack, you set an example that seemed suddenly to kindle a bright fire within me! Save for you, I never could have done what I did. In truth, I—I—in truth, Christopher, I had thought of—"

"Say no more!" Christopher added quickly and put an arm across his friend's shoulders. Then he smiled. "Think of it, Neil—shoes! We are to have shoes!"

210

"Aye, and new ones!" Neil exclaimed.

Then for the first time in weeks, and despite hunger and fatigue, the two friends found themselves laughing while they made their way through the storm toward their log hut.

Reading Skills

1. Why is the corporal unable to complete the mission?
2. Which names of people and places do you recognize as being authentic, or real, ones?
3. Why do the two British soldiers ridicule Neil and Christopher?
4. Why does Christopher attack the British officers at the precise moment he does?
5. When does Christopher discover he is right in thinking Neil planned to desert?
6. Explain what General Washington means when he says to Neil and Christopher, "Fortitude under fatigue and privation—you nobly exemplify the maxim in your persons and in your deeds!"

Understanding Literature

1. There are really two main problems to be solved in this story. What are these two conflicts? Why would the story be weaker in plot if both problems were not presented?
2. The author has the two boys tell their story to General Washington personally instead of having someone else report the find of the seven hogsheads. Why does this give the story a more satisfactory ending?
3. What problem causes the tension and suspense in the story? Which details help to increase the suspense? What would happen to the story if Christopher simply asked Neil if he planned to desert?

RUSSELL GORDON CARTER

Thomas Jefferson was a great man of many talents. Not only was he the author of the Declaration of Independence and one of America's greatest Presidents, but he was also a musician, scientist, mathematician, and educator. He served his country in many ways for nearly forty years. Through this poem, Rosemary and Stephen Vincent Benét tell much about the character and many achievements of Thomas Jefferson.

Thomas Jefferson

1743-1826

Rosemary and Stephen Vincent Benét

Thomas Jefferson,
What do you say
Under the gravestone
Hidden away?

"I was a giver,   5
I was a molder,
I was a builder
With a strong shoulder."

Six feet and over,
Large-boned and ruddy,   10
The eyes gray-hazel
But bright with study.

The big hands clever
With pen and fiddle
And ready, ever,   15
For any riddle.

From buying empires
To planting 'taters,
From Declarations
To trick dumb-waiters.   20

"I liked the people,
The sweat and crowd of them,
Trusted them always
And spoke aloud of them.

"I liked all learning   25
And wished to share it
Abroad like pollen
For all who merit.

"I liked fine houses
With Greek pilasters,[1]   30
And built them surely,
My touch a master's.

"I liked queer gadgets
And secret shelves,
And helping nations   35
To rule themselves.

"Jealous of others?
Not always candid?
But huge of vision
And open-handed.   40

"A wild-goose chaser?
Now and again,
Build Monticello,
You little men!

"Design my plow, sirs,   45
They use it still,
Or found my college
At Charlottesville.

1 pilasters: columns.

"And still go questing
New things and thinkers,   50
And keep as busy
As twenty tinkers.

"While always guarding
The people's freedom—
You need more hands, sir? 55
I didn't need 'em.

"They call you rascal?
They called me worse.
You'd do grand things, sir,
But lack the purse?   60

"I got no riches.
I died a debtor.
I died free-hearted
And that was better.

"For life was freakish   65
But life was fervent,
And I was always
Life's willing servant.

"Life, life's too weighty?
Too long a haul, sir?   70
I lived past eighty.
I liked it all, sir."

Understanding Literature

1. Why is part of the poem enclosed in quotation marks?
2. What were some of Thomas Jefferson's many accomplishments?
3. What do the last two verses tell you about Thomas Jefferson's character?

After the American Revolution, many Americans began to move westward. Two very famous people who explored the new, untamed country in 1803 were Meriwether Lewis and William Clark. These two leaders and their men suffered many hardships, but the following poem presents their expedition in lighthearted verse.

Lewis and Clark

1774-1809   1770-1838

Rosemary and Stephen Vincent Benét

Lewis and Clark
Said, "Come on, let's embark
For a boating trip up the Missouri!
It's the President's wish
And we might catch some fish,   5
Though the river is muddy as fury."

So they started away
On a breezy May day,
Full of courage and lore scientific,
And, before they came back,   10
They had blazed out a track
From St. Louis straight to the Pacific.

Now, if *you* want to go
From St. Louis (in Mo.)
To Portland (the Ore. not the Me. one),   15
You can fly there in planes
Or board limited trains
Or the family car, if there be one.

It may take you two weeks,
If your car's full of squeaks   20
And you stop for the sights and the strangers,
But it took them (don't laugh!)
Just one year and a half,
Full of Buffalo, Indians and dangers.

They ate prairie-dog soup   25
When they suffered from croup,
For the weather was often quite drizzly.

They learned "How do you do?"
In Shoshone and Sioux,
And how to be chased by a grizzly.   30

They crossed mountain and river
With never a quiver,
And the Rockies themselves weren't too big for them,
For they scrambled across
With their teeth full of moss,   35
But their fiddler still playing a jig for them.

Missouri's Great Falls,
And the Yellowstone's walls
And the mighty Columbia's billows,
They viewed or traversed,   40
Of all white men the first
To make the whole Northwest their pillows.

And, when they returned,
It was glory well-earned
That they gave to the national chorus.   45
They were ragged and lean
But they'd seen what they'd seen,
And it spread out an Empire before us.

Understanding Literature

1. What were some of the experiences Lewis and Clark had on
   their expedition?
2. Although this band of explorers endured many hardships, this
   poem describes the expedition in a lighthearted manner. What
   is the effect of this technique?

Further Activity

The Lewis and Clark expedition is one of the most interesting
feats of exploration in America's history. In a brief paper of two
or three paragraphs, describe one aspect of the expedition. You
might choose one of the following topics to emphasize:

1. The backgrounds of the men who accompanied Lewis and
   Clark on the expedition.
2. A major event in the course of the expedition.
3. The character and career of either Lewis or Clark.
4. The importance of the Lewis and Clark expedition to the
   history of the United States.

ROSEMARY AND STEPHEN VINCENT BENÉT   **215**

People other than those associated with the founding of our country, with war, and with the struggle for freedom are important to the history of America. The vastness of the West, the towering mountains, and the endlessly waving prairies lured men who were looking for adventure and wealth. Among these men were the fur trappers—and the animal they were after was the beaver.

A Wild Strain

Paul Horgan

IMPROVING YOUR READING: Different materials require different methods of reading. The stories so far in this unit are ones which you could read quickly, because there was little factual material that you would need to retain. In "A Wild Strain," however, there are more descriptions and explanations. Observe how this kind of writing differs from the other pieces in the unit. This selection is from Horgan's book *Great River: The Rio Grande in North American History.*

THE MOUNTAIN SYSTEM of the northern Rio Grande was a vast, secret world. Wandering Indians there made shrines of twig and feather and bone, and went their ways. Close to the high clouds that made their rivers, the inhuman peaks doubled the roar of thunder, or hissed with sheets of rain, or abided[1] in massive silence. Below them lay every variation of park and meadow and lost lake; gashed canyon and rocky roomlike penetralia in the stupendous temples of the high wilderness. Along hidden watercourses and in little cupped lakes lived and worked the family of a small creature destined to be the first cause of great change in the human life of the river during the early 19th century. It was the beaver.

In still pool or mild current the beaver made his house of mud and twig. Its doorway was under water. The occupants dived to enter it and came up beyond into the dry shelter of their lodge that they had built of sticks and mud, where their food was stored and where they were safe from animal predators.[2] The backwater before the den had to be three feet deep, and if this did not exist naturally, the beavers built dams to collect it. They chose a tree by the edge. Sitting upright, they chewed away bark in a belt, eating of it now and then from their paws. Down to bare wood, they gnawed away until the tree was ready to fall. Often it fell into water where it would make a stout beginning for a dam. Working in concert[3] they brought from

2 **predators** (prĕd'ə tərz): plunderers.
3 **in concert:** together.

1 **abided:** existed.

near-by woods bundles of stick and bush and starting out from the bank began to shore up their barrier. They dived to the bottom of the water and brought up loads of mud. This was plaster. With their broad tails they troweled mud over the laid timbers, layer upon layer, always extending the reach of the dam until it touched the opposite limit of the course or cove where they worked. At times they paused to play, racing each other in the water, diving, and loudly slapping the water with their tails.

When house and dam were finished, it was time to lay up provisions within against winter when there would be no green sprouts of willow and cottonwood and fresh grass to eat in season. The beaver clan went foraging, often far inland from their water, in search of bark. The best bark was on the smaller branches high out of reach. The beavers brought down the tree, and then stripped the tender young bark off the branches laid low. They cut the bark into three-foot strips, pulled them to their water, and there floated them to the lodge. They made little signs to guide them as they went—mounds of twig and earth which they impregnated[4] with castorum, a musk secreted[5] by the animal itself, that attracted their sense of smell and reassuringly meant *beaver* and told them where the road lay. Once in the lodge and eating, they were neat and fastidious.[6] They took out through the water doorway all the refuse of a meal and threw it into the current. Drifting away, it lodged down-current out of their way—bits of gnawed stick and knotty branch and hard root.

In the spring came the young. Leaving the mother during gestation, the male went traveling, often far away to other water, where he swam and frolicked, ate tender greens at the bank, and did not return home until the offspring were born. Then he took them in charge, trained them in work, and in the late summer led them out to forage before the sharp frosts and the thickening of their fur against the cold. Everywhere in the secret lakes and along the tributaries and in the quieter passages of the main river this lively cycle was continued by beavers in incalculable thousands, and wherever mountain and water met, evidences of it were scattered and lodged undisturbed—until the last Spanish and the first Mexican years of the Rio Grande.

For by then the beaver's fur was in great demand for the making of men's hats. The hatters of London and Paris, New York, Boston and Philadelphia consumed great cargoes of beaver pelt, and the fur trade moved westward out of St. Louis over the American continent to Astoria and the northern Rockies. While Stephen Austin[7] was completing his organized arrangements with the new government of Mexico to bring new settlers from the east nearer to the lower Rio Grande, the

---

4 **impregnated:** soaked.
5 **musk secreted:** perfumed substance given out.
6 **fastidious** (făs tǐd'ĭ əs): dainty.

7 **Stephen Austin:** a 19th-century American colonizer in Texas.

river's upper reaches knew another sort of growing infiltration by men who whether they came alone, or with a few companions, or many, still came without formal approval by the Mexican government, and with no resounding program of colonial loyalty or pious hope.

They came to take beaver in the mountain waters, in spring and autumn up north, or all through the winter in New Mexico if the season was mild. Many of them were French Canadians; the rest were from anywhere in the United States, though mostly from the frontier settlements. They outfitted themselves at St. Louis, and remembering what was commonly known out of Pike's[8] reports, crossed the plains and entered the mountains by the hundreds in the 1820's. Among their number were men who made the first trails beyond the prairies, that led overland so early as 1826, to the Pacific. Jedediah Smith, Charles Beaubien, the Roubidoux brothers, Céran St. Vrain, Bill Williams, the youthful runaway Kit Carson for whose return a reward of one cent was posted by the employer to whom he was apprenticed—such men went to the mountains after beaver skins to sell for a few dollars a pound, and all unwitting showed the way across the continent.

The movement had already had its pioneer in James Pursley, the Kentuckian, who had been detained at Santa Fe in 1805 under the Spanish governor. Others entering New Mexico from the plains were arrested, to be marched down the Rio Grande to El Paso and the prisons of Chihuahua in 1812, after confiscation of their goods, and were not released until the freeing of Mexico in 1821. Another party of trappers were taken by the provincial Spanish government in 1817, jailed in irons for forty-eight days at Santa Fe, and were finally released after being stripped of thirty thousand dollars' worth of furs and supplies. Such actions by the government were meant to protect the trapping industry already worked on a small scale by the Mexicans of the valley. Regulations declared that only permanent residents might hunt beaver. They were required to buy a hunting license, their number in any party was carefully fixed and recorded, and so were the length of time to be spent in the hunt and the weapons to be used—traps, firearms, or snares. If the early American trappers could not buy official licenses, they soon found a way to get around the law. "The North Americans began to corrupt the New Mexicans," noted a Santa Fe lawyer, "by purchasing their licenses from them," and so risked arrest.

But still the trappers came, and against other hazards. The greatest of these were the roving Indians on the prairies and the eastern upsweeps of the Rocky Mountains. For an Indian hunter could read the menace[9] that came with the white hunter; and he moved with every savagery

---

8 Pike's: a reference to Z. M. Pike (1779-1813), American general and explorer.

9 menace: threat.

to defend his hunting grounds. The trapper retaliated.[10] He fought the Indian with Indian ways, and took scalps, and burned tepee villages, and abducted women, and pressed westward. He fought distance, hunger, and thirst, and if he was unwary enough to oe bitten by a rattlesnake, he cauterized[11] the wound by burning a thick pinch of gunpowder in it. Once in the mountains he met his second greatest adversary[12] in great numbers. This was the great grizzly bear, who was curious, fearless and gifted with a massive ursine[13] intelligence. With lumbering speed the grizzlies could travel forty miles between dawn and dark through mountains. It was not unusual for trappers to kill five or six in a day, or to see fifty or sixty, and one hunter declared that one day he saw two hundred and twenty of them. The grizzly towered above a man. His forepaws were eight or nine inches wide, and his claws six inches long. He weighed from fifteen-to-eighteen hundred pounds. His embrace was certain death. So steadily did he smell and find the trappers that in a few decades by their guns his kind was made almost extinct.

The earthen village of Ranchos de Taos near the Rio Grande was the northern town nearest the beaver waters of the mountains, and there came the mountain men to organize their supplies for the trapping seasons. They found that some men of the Ranchos de Taos already, though to a limited degree, followed the trapper's life. Seeing how swarthy they were, the newcomers thought they must be of mixed Negro and Indian blood. It was astonishing how primitive were the ways of life in Taos—the farmers used only oxen in cultivating their fields, and a miserable plow made of a Y-shaped branch from a tree, with an iron head to its end that turned the earth. Hoes, axes and other tools were all old-fashioned. There were no sawmills; no mechanical ingenuities to speed up work; and—what was oddest to the squinting and raring trappers from the East—the people seemed to have no desire for such means to change their slow, simple ways.

The mountain men encountered at Taos their first experience of the Mexican government. Taos was the seat of the northernmost customs house of Mexico. As the trappers brought little to declare in goods for sale, they were evidently allowed to go about their preparations for departure into the mountains. They bought what flour and produce they could, and recruited an occasional Taoseño to join their parties, and made ready their equipment. In the far northern Rockies the trapping parties were often large, numbering from fifty to a hundred men. Most of these were camp personnel who maintained a base for the trappers and hunters who went forward into the wilderness. The "Frenchmen" from Canada sometimes kept Indian wives, and established in the moun-

10 **retaliated:** returned like for like.
11 **cauterized** (kô′tə rīzd′): burned as a cure.
12 **adversary:** enemy.
13 **ursine** (ûr′sīn): bearlike.

tains a semipermanent household with rude domestic amenities.[14] Other parties were smaller, and instead of working for the great fur companies as contract employees, went their ways alone, as "free" trappers. Those who descended to the Rio Grande's northern reaches were more often than not in small units of a dozen, or three or four, or even a single man, who meant to take their furs and sell them to the highest bidder at the season's end. But all the trappers shared aspects of costume, equipment and even character, many of which grew from the tradition of the forest frontiersman of the late 18th century.

The mountain man was almost Indian-colored from exposure to the weather. His hair hung upon his shoulders. He was bearded. Next to his skin he wore a red flannel loincloth. His outer clothes were of buckskin, fringed at all the seams. The jacket sometimes reached to the knee over tight, wrinkled leggings. His feet were covered by moccasins made of deer or buffalo leather. Around his waist was a leather belt into which he thrust his flintlock pistols, his knife for skinning or scalping, and his shingling hatchet. Over one shoulder hung his bullet pouch, and over the other his powder horn. To their baldrics[15] were attached his bullet mold, ball screw, wiper and an awl for working leather. When he moved he shimmered with fringe and rang and clacked with accouterments[16] of metal and wood. The most important of these were his traps, of which he carried five or six, and his firearm with its slender separate crutch of hardwood. It was always a rifle—never a shotgun, which he scorned as an effete[17] fowling piece. Made in the gun works of the brothers Jacob and Samuel Hawken, of St. Louis, the rifle had two locks for which he kept about him a hundred flints, twenty-five pounds of powder and several pounds of lead. The barrel, thirty-six inches long, was made by hand of soft iron. The recoil of its blast shocked into a hardwood stock beautifully turned and slender. Peering vividly out from under his low-crowned hat of rough wool, he was an American original, as hard as the hardest thing that could happen to him.

Alone, or with a companion or a small party, he packed his supplies on two horses and, riding a third, left Taos for the mountains in the autumn. He was wary of roaming Indians, dangerous animals—and other trapper parties. For nobody could stake a claim on hunting country, and every trapper party competed against every other. He did his best to keep his movement and direction secret, to throw others off the trail, and find the wildest country where he would be most free from rivalry. Following the groins of the foothills, the mountain men came among high slopes and rocky screens. If two worked as a pair, they sought for a

---

14 amenities (ə mĕn′ə tĭz): agreeable features.
15 baldrics: belts.
16 accouterments: equipment.
17 effete (ĭ fēt′): worn out.

concealed place where they could make camp and tether[18] their horses, near beaver water. There they built a shelter, and if their goal was a mountain lake, or a slow passage of stream, they set to work hacking out a cottonwood canoe. In natural forest paths they looked for the little musky mounds that marked beaver trails. They searched currents for the drift of gnawed beaver sticks. Every such sign took them closer to their prey. When they were sure they had found its little world, at evening under the pure suspended light of mountain skies they silently coasted along the shores of quiet water to set their traps.

They laid each trap two or three inches underwater on the slope of

the shore, and, a little removed, they fixed a pole in deep mud and chained the trap to it. They stripped a twig of its bark and dipped one end into a supply of castorum, the beaver's own secretion that would be his bait. They fastened the twig between the open jaws of the trap leaving the musky end four inches above water. The beaver in the nighttime was drawn to it by scent. He raised his muzzle to inhale, his hind quarters went lower in the water, and the trap seized him. He threw himself into deeper water; but the trap held him, and the pole held the trap, and presently he sank to drown. In the high, still daybreak, the trappers coasted by their traps again in the canoe, and took up their catch.

Working a rocky stream from the bank the trappers lodged the trap

18 tether: tie; fasten.

PAUL HORGAN

and its chained pole in the current, where the beaver found the scent. In his struggles he might drag the trap and pole to the shore, where his burden became entangled in "thickets of brook willows," and held him till found. Sometimes he struggled to deeper midstream water, where the pole floated as a marker; and then the trappers putting off their buckskins that if saturated would dry slowly and then be hard as wood, went naked and shivering into the cold mountain stream to swim for their take. And some parties rafted down the whole length of the river in New Mexico, all the way to El Paso. Their method astonished the New Mexicans, to whom it seemed suspect because it was new. Was it proper to use a new kind of trap, and float noiselessly to a beaver site taking their catch by surprise, and spend the night in midstream with the raft moored to trees on each bank to be out of the reach of wild animals? And at the end of the journey, to sell the timbers of the raft for a good price at El Paso where wood was so scarce, take up the catch and vanish overland eastward without reporting to the government? The New Mexicans frowned at such ingenuity, energy and novelty.

When in the mountains they had exhausted a beaver site the trappers moved on to another. With their traps over their shoulders they forded streams amidst floating ice; or with their traps hanging down their backs, they scaled and descended the hard ridges between watercourses where the harder the country the better

the chance that no others had come there before them. The trap weighed about five pounds, and its chain was about five feet long. A full-grown beaver weighed between thirty and forty pounds. The catch was an awkward burden to carry back to camp for skinning. Removing the pelt from the animal, the trappers stretched it on a frame of sprung willow withes to dry. The flesh they cooked by hanging it before a fire from a thong. The carcass turned by its own weight, roasting evenly. The broad, flat tail they liked best of all. They cut it off, skinned it, toasted it at the end of a stick, and ate it with relish, as a relief from the usual hunter's diet of deer, elk, antelope, bear, lynx, or buffalo meat, or buffalo marrowbones, or buffalo blood drunk spurting and warm from the throat of a newly killed specimen.

All through the winter-fast months the mountain men worked, obedient to animal laws and themselves almost animal in their isolation, freedom and harmony with the wilderness. Their peltries were cached[19] and the piles grew, in the end to be baled with rawhide thongs. A trapper took in a good season about four hundred pounds of beaver skins. Somtimes his cache was invaded and destroyed by prowling animals, or stolen by mountain Indians; and then his months of hardship went for nothing. But if he kept his pile, he was ready to come out of the boxed mountains whose cool winds brush-

19 peltries . . . cached: skins were hidden.

ing all day over high-tilted meadows carried the scent of wild flowers down the open slopes where he descended with his haul. At five dollars a pound it would bring him two thousand dollars in the market.

But once again in Taos, he might then meet trouble with the Mexican authorities. Now that he had his cargo, they showed an interest in him. If he was unlucky, they questioned him, examined his bales, and invoking[20] regulations that nobody mentioned when he started out months before, confiscated[21] his whole catch. If he resisted he was taken to Santa Fe and jailed, with official talk about the Mexican decree of 1824 that prohibited trapping by foreigners in Mexican territory. Since there were no public warehouses hunters could only store their catches in towns by making deals with local citizens for storage space on private premises. If a Mexican citizen gave protection to a foreign trapper he was in danger from his own government. At Peña Blanca on the Río Grande in 1827 one Luís María Cabeza de Vaca hid in his house the "contraband" of beaver skins left there for safe keeping by a trapper named Young. From Santa Fe a corporal and eight soldiers of the presidial company came to seize it. Cabeza de Vaca resisted them, firing upon them in protection of his home. The soldiers returned the fire and killed him. The official report of the affair stated that "the deceased died

while defending a violation of the ... rights of the Nation," and asked exoneration[22] for the corporal and his squad.

But local officials might be bribed, and a license trumped up, and the catch restored to the trapper. In any case, after his mountain months, he was ready to burst his bonds of solitude, and he did so with raw delight. All his general passion and violence that his mountain work required him to suppress while moving lithe and crafty after watchful creatures he now broke free in the clay village where he returned among men and women. He had a frosty look of filth over him. His hair was knotted and his beard was a catch-all for the refuse of months. His clothes reeked like his body. His mouth was dry with one kind of thirst. If the one tavern in the town was full, he went to a house and asked for a corner of the packed mud floor where he could throw his gear, and was granted it. The family knew what he came to seek with his comrades. The women took kettles out of doors and built fires around them to heat water. When it was hot they brought it in, and found him waiting in his crusted skin sitting in a wooden tub. The women poured the water over him. He thrashed. He was as hairy as an animal. The water hit him and he gave the recognized cry of the mountain man—"Wagh!"—a grunt, a warning, and a boast. Bathing as violently as he did all other acts, he

20 **invoking:** appealing to.
21 **confiscated:** seized.

22 **exoneration:** release from blame.

began again to know forgotten satisfactions. As he emerged with wet light running on his skin, white everywhere but on face and hands whose weather would not wash off, he was a new man. . . .

Presently he traveled to a trading post on the prairies, or to St. Louis, to sell his catch. In the frontier cities of the United States he was a prodigal[23] spender, uneasy in their relatively ordered society, loose as it was compared to life in older and more easterly places. When the season rolled around again, he was off again to his lost lakes and rivers where obscurely content he felt most like the self he imagined until it came true.

For over three decades the trapping trade flourished. At its height the annual shipment of beaver skins from Abiquiu on the Chama and Taos on the Rio Grande was worth two hundred thousand dollars. But in the 1830's the market for beaver began to break, for the China trade out of England and New England was growing, and the clipper ships were bringing silk in great quantities to the manufacturing cities of the world. Fashion changed. Silk was offered for hats instead of fur; and the change brought the decline and finally the almost virtual abolishment of the Rocky Mountain fur trade. The trapper was cast adrift to find new work. He could abide it only in the land of his hardy prowess, and there he found it, whether he joined the overland commercial caravans as a wagon hand, or the American Army's later surveying expeditions as a guide, or amazingly settled on river land as a farmer. He knew the craft of the wilderness and he made its first trails for the westering white man. Some of the earliest venturers in the Mexico trade were trappers; and as the trade continued to grow and establish its bases ever farther west, the trappers met it with their wares; and what had been a memorized path became a visible road; and along it moved another of the unofficial invasions of the Mexican Rio Grande that could only end by changing nations. The first sustained effort toward that end was made by the individual trapper. His greatest power to achieve it lay in his individualism. Where the Mexican was hedged by governmental authority, the trapper made his own. Where the Mexican was formal, he was wild. Where the one was indolent,[24] the other was consumed[25] by a fanatical driving impulse. The invasion, unorganized as it was, commercial in purpose, wild and free in its individuals, seemed to express some secret personal motive beyond the material. The trappers forecast a new, a wild, strain of human society to come to the northern river.

---

24 **indolent** (ĭn′də lənt): lazy.
25 **consumed:** possessed.

23 **prodigal** (prŏd′ə gəl): wasteful.

Reading Skills

1. What kind of men, in appearance and character, were the trappers of the northern Rio Grande? Why, and from where, did they come to trap the beaver?
2. Describe some of the hardships and hazards which the trappers had to face and overcome.
3. Paul Horgan calls the trapper "an American original." What does this phrase mean?
4. Describe the method used to trap the beaver. Why were the New Mexicans astonished and somewhat upset by this method?
5. What caused beaver trapping to decline? What then became of the trappers?
6. Although the trappers were basically interested only in returning with many furs, they unknowingly did America a service. Explain.

The name Crazy Horse sounds as if it could not be real, but it is. History books will tell you that Crazy Horse and Sitting Bull, both famous Sioux Indian chieftains, fought against the prospectors who were seeking gold. In 1877 Crazy Horse was arrested by American soldiers and was killed while trying to escape.

Crazy Horse
?-1877

Rosemary and Stephen Vincent Benét

The Indians of the Wild West
We found were hard to tame,
For they seemed really quite possessed
To keep their ways the same.

They liked to hunt, they liked to fight,   5
And (this I grieve to say)
They could not see the white man's right
To take their land away.

So there was fire upon the Plains,
And deeds of derring-do,   10
Where Sioux were bashing soldier's brains
And soldiers bashing Sioux'.

And here is bold Chief Crazy Horse,
A warrior, keen and tried,
Who fought with fortitude and force   15
—But on the losing side.

Where Custer fell, where Miles pursued,
He led his native sons,
And did his best, though it was crude
And lacked the Gatling guns.   20

It was his land. They were his men.
He cheered and led them on.
—The hunting ground is pasture, now.
The buffalo are gone.

Understanding Literature

1. Do the poets seem to be on the side of the Indians or of the white men? How do you know?
2. Point out specific lines in which the poets are ironical, that is, lines in which they say the opposite of what they mean.
3. What is the authors' opinion of what the white man did to the Wild West? How do you know?

Further Activities

1. Identify the following allusions, or references, which were made in this poem. Consult history books in your libraries for those references unfamiliar to you.
   (*a*) "where Custer fell" (stanza 5).
   (*b*) "where Miles pursued" (stanza 5).
   (*c*) "And lacked the Gatling guns" (stanza 5).
2. Using the history books in your libraries, prepare a brief written report on the life of Crazy Horse and his part in the death of General Custer. Include details of Crazy Horse's early life which help to explain his character, his motives, and his ambitions.

Abraham Lincoln hardly needs an introduction. He did many great things in his lifetime: he was the sixteenth President of the United States; he led his country through the years of the Civil War; he issued the Emancipation Proclamation; and he died in the service of his country. Such a man should be able to rest in peace. Why, then, does the poet, forty-nine years after Lincoln's death, say that "Abraham Lincoln walks at midnight"?

Abraham Lincoln Walks at Midnight

(In Springfield, Illinois)

Vachel Lindsay

IMPROVING YOUR READING: The *connotation* of a word is the implication, or suggestion, a word carries with it in addition to its literal meaning. The word *friend*, for example, literally means "one who is not an enemy." But *friend* usually suggests, or *connotes*, many other things: companionship, someone to confide in, someone to depend upon, someone who likes and trusts you. The word *friend*, therefore, has pleasant connotations; *enemy*, on the other hand, has unpleasant connotations. In "Abraham Lincoln Walks at Midnight" which words suggest, or *connote*, more than they mean literally?

It is portentous,[1] and a thing of state
That here at midnight, in our little town
A mourning figure walks, and will not rest,
Near the old courthouse pacing up and down,

Or by his homestead, or in shadowed yards   5
He lingers where his children used to play,
Or through the market, on the well-worn stones
He stalks until the dawn-stars burn away.

A bronzed, lank[2] man! His suit of ancient black,
A famous high top hat and plain worn shawl   10
Make him the quaint great figure that men love,
The prairie lawyer, master of us all.

He cannot sleep upon his hillside now.
He is among us:—as in times before!

1 **portentous:** significant; a sign of something about to happen.
2 **lank:** lean; thin.

And we who toss and lie awake for long   15
Breathe deep, and start, to see him pass the door.

His head is bowed.   He thinks on men and kings.
Yea, when the sick world cries, how can he sleep?
Too many peasants fight, they know not why,
Too many homesteads in black terror weep.   20

The sins of all the war lords burn his heart.
He sees the dreadnaughts[3] scouring every main.[4]
He carries on his shawl-wrapped shoulders now
The bitterness, the folly and the pain.

He cannot rest until a spirit-dawn   25
Shall come;—the shining hope of Europe free:
The league of sober folk, the Workers' Earth,
Bringing long peace to Cornland, Alp and Sea.

It breaks his heart that kings must murder still,
That all his hours of travail[5] here for men   30
Seem yet in vain.   And who will bring white peace
That he may sleep upon his hill again?

3 **dreadnaughts:** battleships.
4 **main:** ocean.
5 **travail:** mental and physical labor.

Understanding Literature

1. Why is Abraham Lincoln especially suitable as the main character in this poem?
2. Why is Lincoln walking at midnight?   What particular things
   keep him from sleeping?   What historical event probably moved
   Vachel Lindsay to write this poem?
3. What is meant by "the bitterness, the folly and the pain" which
   Lincoln carries on his shoulders?
4. What must happen before Lincoln will be able to "sleep upon
   his hill again"?   What does the poet mean by "a spirit-dawn"
   (l. 25) and by "white peace" (l. 31)?
5. Observe the words which the poet uses in describing Lincoln.
   What are the connotations of these words; that is, what ideas is
   the poet trying to suggest about Lincoln by using these particular words: *mourning, pacing, lingers, stalks, quaint, master,
   bowed?*   First consider the literal meaning of each word; then
   consider all the implications, or suggestions, of the word.

Most people are aware of the great tragedies of war. The thousands of people crippled or killed and the battles won at the cost of too many lives are the things that make newspaper headlines. But the headlines rarely tell of the other tragedies: the little skirmishes in which just two or three are killed, or the relationships between people which war twists or leaves unfulfilled. Although this story takes place during the Civil War, similar events could happen during any war.

A Gray Sleeve

Stephen Crane

IMPROVING YOUR READING: As you read "A Gray Sleeve," you will find that the author makes you feel the mystery surrounding the house. He establishes a *mood* by describing the stillness of the woods, the feeling of the unknown about the house, and the way the characters in the story react in this situation. Be ready to discuss these and other details which contribute to the mood of the story.

I

"IT LOOKS AS if it might rain this afternoon," remarked the lieutenant of artillery.

"So it does," the infantry captain assented. He glanced casually at the sky. When his eyes had lowered to the green-shadowed landscape before him, he said fretfully: "I wish those fellows out yonder would quit pelting at us. They've been at it since noon."

At the edge of a grove of maples, across wide fields, there occasionally appeared little puffs of smoke of a dull hue in this gloom of sky which expressed an impending[1] rain. The long wave of blue and steel in the field moved uneasily at the eternal barking of the far-away sharpshooters, and the men, leaning upon their rifles, stared at the grove of maples. Once a private turned to borrow some tobacco from a comrade in the rear rank, but, with his hand still stretched out, he continued to twist his head and glance at the distant trees. He was afraid the enemy would shoot him at a time when he was not looking.

Suddenly the artillery officer said: "See what's coming!"

Along the rear of the brigade of infantry a column of cavalry was sweeping at a hard gallop. A lieutenant, riding some yards to the right of the column, bawled furiously at the four troopers just at the rear of the colors. They had lost distance and made a little gap, but at the shouts of the lieutenant they urged their horses forward. The bugler,

1 impending: approaching.

careering along behind the captain of the troop, fought and tugged like a wrestler to keep his frantic animal from bolting far ahead of the column.

On the springy turf the innumerable hoofs thundered in a swift storm of sound. In the brown faces of the troopers their eyes were set like bits of flashing steel.

The long line of the infantry regiments standing at ease underwent a sudden movement at the rush of the passing squadron. The foot soldiers turned their heads to gaze at the torrent of horses and men.

The yellow folds of the flag fluttered back in silken, shuddering waves, as if it were a reluctant thing. Occasionally a giant spring of a charger would rear the firm and sturdy figure of a soldier suddenly head and shoulders above his comrades. Over the noise of the scudding hoofs could be heard the creaking of leather trappings, the jingle and clank of steel, and the tense, low-toned commands or appeals of the men to their horses; and the horses were mad with the headlong sweep of this movement. Powerful underjaws bent back and straightened, so that the bits were clamped as rigidly as vices upon the teeth, and glistening necks arched in desperate resistance to the hands at the bridles. Swinging their heads in rage at the granite[2] laws of their lives, which compelled even their angers and their ardors to chosen directions and chosen faces, their flight was as a flight of harnessed demons.

The captain's bay kept its pace at the head of the squadron with the lithe[3] bounds of a thoroughbred, and this horse was proud as a chief at the roaring trample of his fellows behind him. The captain's glance was calmly upon the grove of maples whence the sharpshooters of the enemy had been picking at the blue line. He seemed to be reflecting.[4] He stolidly[5] rose and fell with the plunges of his horse in all the indifference of a deacon's figure seated plumply in church. And it occurred to many of the watching infantry to wonder why this officer could remain imperturbable and reflective when his squadron was thundering and swarming behind him like the rushing of a flood.

The column swung in a saber-curve toward a break in a fence, and dashed into a roadway. Once a little plank bridge was encountered, and the sound of the hoofs upon it was like the long roll of many drums. An old captain in the infantry turned to his first lieutenant and made a remark, which was a compound of bitter disparagement[6] of cavalry in general and soldierly admiration of this particular troop.

Suddenly the bugle sounded, and the column halted with a jolting upheaval amid sharp, brief cries. A moment later the men had tumbled from their horses, and, carbines in hand,

---

2 **granite:** unchangeable.

3 **lithe** (līth)**:** limber; flexible.
4 **reflecting:** thinking.
5 **stolidly:** inattentively; mechanically.
6 **disparagement:** criticism; condemnation.

STEPHEN CRANE

were running in a swarm toward the grove of maples. In the road one of every four of the troopers was standing with braced legs, and pulling and hauling at the bridles of four frenzied horses.

The captain was running awkwardly in his boots. He held his saber low, so that the point often threatened to catch in the turf. His yellow hair ruffled out from under his faded cap. "Go in hard now!" he roared, in a voice of hoarse fury. His face was violently red.

The troopers threw themselves upon the grove like wolves upon a great animal. Along the whole front of woods there was the dry crackling of musketry, with bitter, swift flashes and smoke that writhed like stung phantoms. The troopers yelled shrilly and spanged bullets low into the foliage.

For a moment, when near the woods, the line almost halted. The men struggled and fought for a time like swimmers encountering a powerful current. Then with a supreme effort they went on again. They dashed madly at the grove, whose foliage from the high light of the field was as inscrutable[7] as a wall.

Then suddenly each detail of the calm trees became apparent, and with a few more frantic leaps the men were in the cool gloom of the woods. There was a heavy odor as from burned paper. Wisps of gray smoke wound upward. The men halted and, grimy, perspiring, and puffing, they searched the recesses of the woods with eager, fierce glances. Figures could be seen flitting afar off. A

7 **inscrutable:** here, hard to pass through.

232   BUILDING AMERICA

dozen carbines rattled at them in an angry volley.

During this pause the captain strode along the line, his face lit with a broad smile of contentment. "When he sends this crowd to do anything, I guess he'll find we do it pretty sharp," he said to the grinning lieutenant.

"Say, they didn't stand that rush a minute, did they?" said the subaltern.[8] Both officers were profoundly dusty in their uniforms, and their faces were soiled like those of two urchins.

Out in the grass behind them were three tumbled and silent forms.

Presently the line moved forward again. The men went from tree to tree like hunters stalking game. Some at the left of the line fired occasionally, and those at the right gazed curiously in that direction. The men still breathed heavily from their scramble across the field.

Of a sudden a trooper halted and said: "Hello! there's a house!" Everyone paused. The men turned to look at their leader.

The captain stretched his neck and swung his head from side to side. "By George, it is a house!" he said.

Through the wealth of leaves there vaguely loomed the form of a large white house. These troopers, brown-faced from many days of campaigning, each feature of them telling of their placid confidence and courage, were stopped abruptly by the appearance of this house. There was some subtle suggestion—some tale of an unknown thing—which watched them from they knew not what part of it.

A rail fence girded a wide lawn of tangled grass. Seven pines stood along a driveway which led from two distant posts of a vanished gate. The blue-clothed troopers moved forward until they stood at the fence peering over it.

The captain put one hand on the top rail and seemed to be about to climb the fence, when suddenly he hesitated, and said in a low voice: "Watson, what do you think of it?"

The lieutenant stared at the house. "Derned if I know!" he replied.

The captain pondered. It happened that the whole company had turned a gaze of profound awe and doubt upon this edifice[9] which confronted them. The men were very silent.

At last the captain swore and said: "We are certainly a pack of fools. Derned old deserted house halting a company of Union cavalry, and making us gape like babies!"

"Yes, but there's something—something——" insisted the subaltern in a half stammer.

"Well, if there's 'something—something' in there, I'll get it out," said the captain. "Send Sharpe clean around to the other side with about twelve men, so we will sure bag your 'something—something,' and I'll take a few of the boys and find out what's in the derned old thing!"

He chose the nearest eight men for his "storming party," as the lieutenant called it. After he had waited

---

8 **subaltern:** officer of lower rank than captain.

9 **edifice:** building.

some minutes for the others to get into position, he said "Come ahead" to his eight men, and climbed the fence.

The brighter light of the tangled lawn made him suddenly feel tremendously apparent, and he wondered if there could be some mystic[10] thing in the house which was regarding this approach. His men trudged silently at his back. They stared at the windows and lost themselves in deep speculations as to the probability of there being, perhaps, eyes behind the blinds—malignant[11] eyes, piercing eyes.

Suddenly a corporal in the party gave vent to a startled exclamation, and half threw his carbine into position. The captain turned quickly, and the corporal said: "I saw an arm move the blinds—an arm with a gray sleeve!"

"Don't be a fool, Jones, now," said the captain sharply.

"I swear t'——" began the corporal, but the captain silenced him.

When they arrived at the front of the house, the troopers paused, while the captain went softly up the front steps. He stood before the large front door and studied it. Some crickets chirped in the long grass, and the nearest pine could be heard in its endless sighs. One of the privates moved uneasily, and his foot crunched the gravel. Suddenly the captain swore angrily and kicked the door with a loud crash. It flew open.

II

THE BRIGHT LIGHTS of the day flashed into the old house when the captain angrily kicked open the door. He was aware of a wide hallway, carpeted with matting and extending deep into the dwelling. There was also an old walnut hat-rack and a little marble-topped table with a vase and two books upon it. Farther back was a great, venerable[12] fireplace containing dreary ashes.

But directly in front of the captain was a young girl. The flying open of the door had obviously been an utter astonishment to her, and she remained transfixed there in the middle of the floor, staring at the captain with wide eyes.

She was like a child caught at the time of a raid upon the cake. She wavered to and fro upon her feet, and held her hands behind her. There were two little points of terror in her eyes, as she gazed up at the young captain in dusty blue, with his reddish, bronze complexion, his yellow hair, his bright saber held threateningly.

These two remained motionless and silent, simply staring at each other for some moments.

The captain felt his rage fade out of him and leave his mind limp. He had been violently angry, because this house had made him feel hesitant, wary.[13] He did not like to be wary. He liked to feel confident,

---

10 **mystic:** mysterious; hidden.
11 **malignant:** evil.

12 **venerable:** old.
13 **wary:** cautious; suspicious.

sure. So he had kicked the door open, and had been prepared to march in like a soldier of wrath.

But now he began, for one thing, to wonder if his uniform was so dusty and old in appearance. Moreover, he had a feeling that his face was covered with a compound of dust, grime, and perspiration. He took a step forward and said: "I didn't mean to frighten you." But his voice was coarse from his battle-howling. It seemed to him to have hempen fibers in it.

The girl's breath came in little, quick gasps, and she looked at him as she would have looked at a serpent.

"I didn't mean to frighten you," he said again.

The girl, still with her hands behind her, began to back away.

"Is there anyone else in the house?" he went on, while slowly following her. "I don't wish to disturb you, but we had a fight with some rebel skirmishers in the woods, and I thought maybe some of them might have come in here. In fact, I was pretty sure of it. Are there any of them here?"

The girl looked at him and said, "No!" He wondered why extreme agitation[14] made the eyes of some women so limpid[15] and bright.

"Who is here besides yourself?"

By this time his pursuit had driven her to the end of the hall, and she remained there with her back to the wall and her hands still behind her.

When she answered this question, she did not look at him but down at the floor. She cleared her voice and then said: "There is no one here."

"No one?"

She lifted her eyes to him in that appeal that the human being must make even to falling trees, crashing boulders, the sea in a storm, and said, "No, no, there is no one here." He could plainly see her tremble.

Of a sudden he bethought him that she continually kept her hands behind her. As he recalled her air when first discovered, he remembered she appeared precisely as a child detected at one of the crimes of childhood. Moreover, she had always backed away from him. He thought now that she was concealing something which was an evidence of the presence of the enemy in the house.

"What are you holding behind you?" he said suddenly.

She gave a little quick moan, as if some grim hand had throttled her.

"What are you holding behind you?"

"Oh, nothing—please. I am not holding anything behind me; indeed I'm not."

"Very well. Hold your hands out in front of you, then."

"Oh, indeed, I'm not holding anything behind me. Indeed I'm not."

"Well," he began. Then he paused and remained for a moment dubious.[16] Finally, he laughed. "Well,

---

14 **agitation:** nervousness; distress.
15 **limpid:** clear.

16 **dubious:** doubtful.

I shall have my men search the house, anyhow. I'm sorry to trouble you, but I feel sure that there is someone here whom we want." He turned to the corporal, who with the other men was gaping quietly in at the door, and said: "Jones, go through the house."

As for himself, he remained planted in front of the girl, for she evidently did not dare to move and allow him to see what she held so carefully behind her back. So she was his prisoner.

The men rummaged around on the ground floor of the house. Sometimes the captain called to them, "Try that closet," "Is there any cellar?" But they found no one, and at last they went trooping toward the stairs which led to the second floor.

But at this movement on the part of the men the girl uttered a cry—a cry of such fright and appeal that the men paused. "Oh, don't go up there! Please don't go up there!—ple—ease! There is no one there! Indeed—indeed there is not! Oh, ple—ease!"

"Go on, Jones," said the captain calmly.

The obedient corporal made a preliminary step, and the girl bounded toward the stairs with another cry.

As she passed him, the captain caught sight of that which she had concealed behind her back, and which she had forgotten in this supreme moment. It was a pistol.

She ran to the first step, and standing there, faced the men, one hand extended with perpendicular palm, and the other holding the pistol at her side. "Oh, please, don't go up

236

there! Nobody is there—indeed, there is not! P-l-e-a-s-e!" Then suddenly she sank swiftly down upon the step, and, huddling forlornly, began to weep in the agony and with the convulsive tremors[17] of an infant. The pistol fell from her fingers and rattled down to the floor.

The astonished troopers looked at their astonished captain. There was a short silence.

Finally, the captain stooped and picked up the pistol. It was a heavy weapon of the army pattern. He ascertained[18] that it was empty.

He leaned toward the shaking girl, and said gently: "Will you tell me what you were going to do with this pistol?"

He had to repeat the question a number of times, but at last a muffled voice said, "Nothing."

"Nothing!" He insisted quietly upon a further answer. At the tender tones of the captain's voice, the phlegmatic[19] corporal turned and winked gravely at the man next to him.

"Won't you tell me?"

The girl shook her head.

"Please tell me!"

The silent privates were moving their feet uneasily and wondering how long they were to wait.

The captain said: "Please, won't you tell me?"

Then this girl's voice began in stricken tones half coherent, and amid violent sobbing: "It was grandpa's. He—he—he said he was going to shoot anybody who came in here—he didn't care if there were thousands of 'em. And—and I know he would, and I was afraid they'd kill him. And so—and—so I stole away his pistol—and I was going to hide it when you—you—you kicked open the door."

The men straightened up and looked at each other. The girl began to weep again.

The captain mopped his brow. He peered down at the girl. He mopped his brow again. Suddenly he said: "Ah, don't cry like that."

He moved restlessly and looked down at his boots. He mopped his brow again.

Then he gripped the corporal by the arm and dragged him some yards back from the others. "Jones," he said, in an intensely earnest voice, "will you tell me what in the devil I am going to do?"

The corporal's countenance[20] became illuminated with satisfaction at being thus requested to advise his superior officer. He adopted an air of great thought, and finally said: "Well, of course, the feller with the gray sleeve must be upstairs, and we must get past the girl and up there somehow. Suppose I take her by the arm and lead her——"

"What!" interrupted the captain from between his clinched teeth. As he turned away from the corporal, he said fiercely over his shoulder: "You touch that girl and I'll split your skull!"

---

17 tremors: shivering; trembling.
18 ascertained: made certain.
19 phlegmatic: weary; indifferent.

20 countenance: face.

III

THE CORPORAL looked after his captain with an expression of mingled amazement, grief, and philosophy. He seemed to be saying to himself that there unfortunately were times, after all, when one could not rely upon the most reliable of men. When he returned to the group he found the captain bending over the girl and saying: "Why is it that you don't want us to search upstairs?"

The girl's head was buried in her crossed arms. Locks of her hair had escaped from their fastenings, and these fell upon her shoulder.

"Won't you tell me?"

The corporal here winked again at the man next to him.

"Because," the girl moaned—"because—there isn't anybody up there."

The captain at last said timidly: "Well, I'm afraid—I'm afraid we'll have to——"

The girl sprang to her feet again, and implored him with her hands. She looked deep into his eyes with her glance, which was at this time like that of the fawn when it says to the hunter, "Have mercy upon me!"

These two stood regarding each other. The captain's foot was on the bottom step, but he seemed to be shrinking. He wore an air of being deeply wretched and ashamed. There was a silence.

Suddenly the corporal said in a quick, low tone: "Look out, captain!"

All turned their eyes swiftly toward the head of the stairs. There had appeared there a youth in a gray uniform. He stood looking coolly down at them. No word was said by the troopers. The girl gave vent to a little wail of desolation, "O Harry!"

He began slowly to descend the stairs. His right arm was in a white sling, and there were some fresh bloodstains upon the cloth. His face was rigid and deathly pale, but his eyes flashed like lights. The girl was again moaning in an utterly dreary fashion, as the youth came slowly down toward the silent men in blue.

Six steps from the bottom of the flight he halted and said: "I reckon it's me you're looking for."

The troopers had crowded forward a trifle and, posed in lithe, nervous attitudes, were watching him like cats. The captain remained unmoved. At the youth's question he merely nodded his head and said, "Yes."

The young man in gray looked down at the girl, and then, in the same even tone which now, however, seemed to vibrate with suppressed fury, he said: "And is that any reason why you should insult my sister?"

At this sentence, the girl intervened, desperately, between the young man in gray and the officer in blue. "Oh, don't, Harry, don't! He was good to me! He was good to me, Harry—indeed he was!"

The youth came on in his quiet, erect fashion, until the girl could have touched either of the men with her hand, for the captain still remained with his foot upon the first step. She continually repeated: "O Harry! O Harry!"

The youth in gray maneuvered to glare into the captain's face, first over

238

one shoulder of the girl and then over the other. In a voice that rang like metal, he said: "You are armed and unwounded, while I have no weapons and am wounded; but——"

The captain had stepped back and sheathed his saber. The eyes of these two men were gleaming fire, but otherwise the captain's countenance was imperturbable. He said: "You are mistaken. You have no reason to——"

"You lie!"

All save the captain and the youth in gray started in an electric movement. These two words crackled in the air like shattered glass. There was a breathless silence.

The captain cleared his throat. His look at the youth contained a quality of singular and terrible ferocity, but he said in his stolid tone: "I

don't suppose you mean what you say now."

Upon his arm he had felt the pressure of some unconscious little fingers. The girl was leaning against the wall as if she no longer knew how to keep her balance, but those fingers—he held his arm very still. She murmured: "O Harry, don't! He was good to me—indeed he was!"

The corporal had come forward until he in a measure confronted the youth in gray, for he saw those fingers upon the captain's arm, and he knew that sometimes very strong men were not able to move hand nor foot under such conditions.

The youth had suddenly seemed to become weak. He breathed heavily and clung to the rail. He was glaring at the captain, and apparently summoning all his will power to combat his weakness. The corporal addressed him with profound straightforwardness: "Don't you be a derned fool!" The youth turned toward him so fiercely that the corporal threw up a knee and an elbow like a boy who expects to be cuffed.

The girl pleaded with the captain. "You won't hurt him, will you? He don't know what he's saying. He's wounded, you know. Please don't mind him!"

"I won't touch him," said the captain, with rather extraordinary earnestness; "don't you worry about him at all. I won't touch him!"

Then he looked at her, and the girl suddenly withdrew her fingers from his arm.

The corporal contemplated the top of the stairs, and remarked without surprise: "There's another of 'em coming!"

An old man was clambering down the stairs with much speed. He waved a cane wildly. "Get out of my house, you thieves! Get out! I won't have you cross my threshold! Get out!" He mumbled and wagged his head in an old man's fury. It was plainly his intention to assault them.

And so it occurred that a young girl became engaged in protecting a stalwart captain, fully armed, and with eight grim troopers at his back, from the attack of an old man with a walking stick!

A blush passed over the temples and brow of the captain, and he looked particularly savage and weary. Despite the girl's efforts, he suddenly faced the old man.

"Look here," he said distinctly,

"we came in because we had been fighting in the woods yonder, and we concluded that some of the enemy were in this house, especially when we saw a gray sleeve at the window. But this young man is wounded, and I have nothing to say to him. I will even take it for granted that there are no others like him upstairs. We will go away, leaving your old house just as we found it! And we are no more thieves and rascals than you are!"

The old man simply roared: "I haven't got a cow nor a pig nor a chicken on the place! Your soldiers have stolen everything they could carry away. They have torn down half my fences for firewood. This afternoon some of your accursed bullets even broke my window-panes!"

The girl had been faltering: "Grandpa! O grandpa!"

The captain looked at the girl. She returned his glance from the shadow of the old man's shoulder. After studying her face a moment, he said: "Well, we will go now." He strode toward the door, and his men clanked docilely[21] after him.

At this time there was the sound of harsh cries and rushing footsteps from without. The door flew open, and a whirlwind composed of blue-coated troopers came in with a swoop. It was headed by the lieutenant. "Oh, here you are!" he cried, catching his breath. "We thought ——Oh, look at the girl!"

21 docilely (dŏs'əl lĭ): obediently.

The captain said intensely: "Shut up, you fool!"

The men settled to a halt with a clash and a bang. There could be heard the dulled sound of many hoofs outside of the house.

"Did you order up the horses?" inquired the captain.

"Yes. We thought——"

"Well, then, let's get out of here," interrupted the captain morosely.[22]

The men began to filter out into the open air. The youth in gray had been hanging dismally to the railing of the stairway. He now was climbing slowly up to the second floor. The old man was addressing himself directly to the serene corporal.

"Not a chicken on the place!" he cried.

"Well, I didn't take your chickens, did I?"

"No, maybe you didn't, but——"

The captain crossed the hall and stood before the girl in rather a culprit's fashion. "You are not angry at me, are you?" he asked timidly.

"No," she said. She hesitated a moment, and then suddenly held out her hand. "You were good to me— and I'm—much obliged."

The captain took her hand, and then he blushed, for he found himself unable to formulate a sentence that applied in any way to the situation.

She did not seem to heed that hand for a time.

He loosened his grasp presently, for he was ashamed to hold it so long without saying anything clever. At last, with an air of charging an intrenched brigade, he contrived to say: "I would rather do anything than frighten or trouble you."

His brow was warmly perspiring. He had a sense of being hideous in his dusty uniform and with his grimy face.

She said, "Oh, I'm so glad it was you instead of somebody who might have—might have hurt brother Harry and grandpa!"

He told her, "I wouldn't have hurt 'em for anything!"

There was a little silence.

"Well, good-by!" he said at last.

"Good-by!"

He walked toward the door past the old man, who was scolding at the vanishing figure of the corporal. The captain looked back. She had remained there watching him.

At the bugle's order, the troopers standing beside their horses swung briskly into the saddle. The lieutenant said to the first sergeant:

"Williams, did they ever meet before?"

"Hanged if I know!"

"Well, say——"

The captain saw a curtain move at one of the windows. He cantered from his position at the head of the column and steered his horse between two flower beds.

"Well, good-by!"

The squadron trampled slowly past.

"Good-by!"

They shook hands.

He evidently had something enormously important to say to her, but it seems that he could not manage it.

---

22 **morosely**: disagreeably; glumly.

He struggled heroically. The bay charger, with his great mystically solemn eyes, looked around the corner of his shoulder at the girl.

The captain studied a pine tree. The girl inspected the grass beneath the window. The captain said hoarsely: "I don't suppose—I don't suppose—I'll ever see you again!"

She looked at him affrightedly and shrank back from the window. He seemed to have woefully expected a reception of this kind for his question. He gave her instantly a glance of appeal.

She said: "Why, no, I don't suppose you will."

"Never?"

"Why, no, 'tain't possible. You—you are a —Yankee!"

"Oh, I know it, but——" Eventually he continued: "Well, some day, you know, when there's no more fighting, we might——" He observed that she had again withdrawn suddenly into the shadow, so he said: "Well, good-by!"

When he held her fingers she bowed her head, and he saw a pink blush steal over the curves of her cheek and neck.

"Am I never going to see you again?"

She made no reply.

"Never?" he repeated.

After a long time, he bent over to hear a faint reply: "Sometimes—when there are no troops in the neighborhood—grandpa don't mind if I—walk over as far as that old oak tree yonder—in the afternoons."

It appeared that the captain's grip was very strong, for she uttered an exclamation and looked at her fingers as if she expected to find them mere fragments. He rode away.

The bay horse leaped a flower bed. They were almost to the drive, when the girl uttered a panic-stricken cry.

The captain wheeled his horse violently, and upon his return journey went straight through a flower bed.

The girl had clasped her hands. She beseeched him wildly with her eyes. "Oh, please, don't believe it! I never walk to the old oak tree. Indeed I don't! I never—never—never walk there."

The bridle drooped on the bay charger's neck. The captain's figure seemed limp. With an expression of profound dejection and gloom he stared off at where the leaden sky met the dark green line of the woods. The long-impending rain began to fall with a mournful patter, drop and drop. There was a silence.

At last a low voice said, "Well—I might—sometimes I might—perhaps —but only once in a great while—I might walk to the old tree—in the afternoons."

Understanding Literature

1. Describe the scene as the cavalry arrives. What is the mood at the beginning of the story?
2. How do the troopers act upon noticing the house? Describe the captain's actions.
3. Why do the brother and the grandfather appear?
4. Why does the captain have as much patience with the rebel soldier as he does?
5. What contrasts are built up between the way the captain approaches the house and the way he acts inside? between the brother and the sister? between the captain and the grandfather?
6. What effect does the girl have on the captain?
7. What is the significance of her walking "to the old tree—in the afternoons"?
8. In the opening sentence the lieutenant says that it may rain. How does the rain that begins at the end of the story fit in with the mood of the story?
9. What is the story saying about the effect of war on people?

Watch, America

Robert Nathan

Where the northern ocean darkens,
Where the rolling rivers run,
Past the cold and empty headlands,
Toward the slow and westering sun,
There our fathers, long before us,   5
Armed with freedom, faced the deep;
What they won with love and labor,
Let their children watch and keep.

By our dark and dreaming forests,
By our free and shining skies,   10
By our green and ripening prairies,
Where the western mountains rise;
God who gave our fathers freedom,
God who made our fathers brave,
What they built with love and anguish,   15
Let their children watch and save.

Myths, Fables, and Legends

THROUGHOUT HISTORY questions concerning life, the world, and the universe have puzzled man. What causes the seasons? What causes storms and lightning? What happens to people after they die? Why are the deserts dry and scorched? Some of our earliest and most fascinating literature comes from a period before Christ (B.C.) in which the ancient Greeks and Romans were attempting to answer questions like these in order to understand their world better. These ancient people did not believe in one God; they attempted to answer puzzling questions by inventing many gods. These gods lived in the middle of the earth, on a high mountain named Mount Olympus, which was surrounded by a gate of clouds guarded by the goddesses named the Seasons. Ruling over the gods of Olympus as well as over the people of the earth were Jupiter and his wife Juno. These gods and goddesses of the Greek people had very exciting superhuman powers, but they also had many very human weaknesses and quarreled among themselves and played tricks not only on each other but also on the people of earth.

We know about these gods and goddesses through *myths,* many of which are ancient explanations of occurrences in nature; other myths do not explain anything in nature, but they can teach us a great deal about human nature. These myths, the origins of which are unknown, have come down to us after having been told and retold by many different people until, probably after many changes, they were written down by various poets whose works are available to us. In the pages that follow, you will read about the Greek myths as well as the myths of the Scandinavian countries.

You will also read some *fables,* which, like the myths, are not true but which have a different purpose. Instead of trying to explain life and the world as the myths do, fables usually attempt to teach or enforce some useful truth or moral, and frequently, unlike the myths, contain animals which speak and act like human beings.

The selections at the end of this unit are *legends.* Legends differ from either myths or fables. Although they are also stories which have come down from the past, many people believe them to be true, even though the facts in the legends cannot be proved.

When you have finished this unit, you will be familiar with some of the literature of several different regions—Greece, ancient Rome, England, the Scandinavian countries, India, and France. You will also be able to understand the *allusions,* or references, to many mythological and legendary figures which you will meet throughout your study of literature, and you will understand the qualities which these figures represent. As you look around you, too, you will recognize many mythological and legendary references used today—such as the Venus pencil, Atlas tires, the pictures of Mercury on advertisements, the space projects with mythological names, such as Project Mercury and Project Apollo, and many more.

The versions of the myths, fables, and legends which you are about to read were written by authors well-known for their studies of mythology. Their versions of the tales are not the only ones, but they are among the best-known. When you are finished with this unit, you might be interested in reading other versions of the same stories to see how they differ.

Chart
of
The Greek Gods

The following chart is a brief summary of the major gods and goddesses in Greek mythology. You will want to refer back to it as you read the myths.

The Titans

Cronus (Saturn)*	Ruler of the Titans until Zeus dethroned him
Ocean	River encircling the earth
Tethys (tē'thĭs)	Wife of Ocean
Hyperion	Father of the sun, the moon, and the dawn
Mnemosyne (nē mŏs'ə nē')	Memory
Themis (thē'mĭs)	Justice
Iapetus (ī ăp'ə təs)	Father of Atlas
Atlas	Bore the world on his shoulder
Prometheus (prə mē'thē əs)	Savior of mankind

The Twelve Great
Olympians

(lived on Mount Olympus in Thessaly, in the northeast of Greece).

Zeus (zōōs) (Jupiter)	King of the gods
Hera (Juno)	Queen of the gods
Poseidon (pō sī'dən) (Neptune)	God of the sea
Hades (Pluto)	God of the underworld
Hestia (Vesta)	Goddess of the hearth and its fire
Ares (âr'ēz) (Mars)	God of war
Pallas Athene (păl'əs ə thē'nĭ) (Minerva)	Goddess of wisdom
Apollo (Phoebus Apollo)	God of the sun
Aphrodite (ăf'rə dī'tĭ) (Venus)	Goddess of love and beauty
Hermes (hûr'mēz) (Mercury)	Messenger of the gods; presided over any event which required skill and dexterity
Artemis (är'tə mĭs) (Diana)	Goddess of the moon
Hephaestus (hē fĕs'təs) (Vulcan)	Artist; made weapons for the gods

*Names in parentheses are Latin names given to the gods by the Romans.

Explanations for the creation of the earth and the creation of man have puzzled man throughout the ages. How does the Biblical story of creation compare with the one that follows?

This selection was written by Thomas Bulfinch, an American who died in 1867. Since his use of the English language may seem a little stiff and formal to you, you will be interested in comparing his style of telling a story with the styles of the other authors in this unit.

Prometheus and Pandora

Thomas Bulfinch

THE CREATION of the world is a problem naturally fitted to excite the liveliest interest of man, its inhabitant. The ancient pagans[1] had their own way of telling the story, which is as follows:

Before earth and sea and heaven were created, all things wore one aspect, to which we give the name of Chaos—a confused and shapeless mass, nothing but dead weight, in which, however, slumbered the seeds of things. Earth, sea, and air were all mixed up together; so the earth was not solid, the sea was not fluid, and the air was not transparent. God and Nature at last interposed, and put an end to this discord, separating earth from sea, and heaven from both. The fiery part, being the lightest, sprang up, and formed the skies; the air was next in weight and place. The earth, being heavier, sank below; and the water took the lowest place, and buoyed up the earth.

Here some god—it is not known

1 **pagans:** people who are not Christians, Jews, or Mohammedans.

which—gave his good offices in arranging and disposing the earth. He appointed rivers and bays their places, raised mountains, scooped out valleys, distributed woods, fountains, fertile fields, and stony plains. The air being cleared, the stars began to appear, fishes took possession of the sea, birds of the air, and four-footed beasts of the land.

But a nobler animal was wanted, and Man was made. It is not known whether the creator made him of divine materials, or whether in the earth, so lately separated from heaven, there lurked still some heavenly seeds.

Prometheus took some of this earth, and kneading it up with water, made man in the image of the gods. He gave him an upright stature, so that while all other animals turn their faces downward, and look to the earth, he raises his to heaven, and gazes on the stars.

Prometheus was one of the Titans, a gigantic race, who inhabited the earth before the creation of man. To him and his brother Epimetheus was committed the office of making man, and providing him and all other animals with the faculties necessary for their preservation. Epimetheus undertook to do this, and Prometheus was to overlook his work, when it was done. Epimetheus accordingly proceeded to bestow upon the different animals the various gifts of courage, strength, swiftness, sagacity;[2] wings to one, claws to another, a shelly covering to a third, etc.

But when man came to be provided for, who was to be superior to all other animals, Epimetheus had been so prodigal[3] of his resources that he had nothing left to bestow upon him. In his perplexity he resorted to his brother Prometheus, who, with the aid of Minerva, went up to heaven, and lighted his torch at the chariot of the sun, and brought down fire to man. With this gift man was more than a match for all other animals. It enabled him to make weapons wherewith to subdue them; tools with which to cultivate the earth; to warm his dwelling, so as to be comparatively independent of climate; and to introduce the arts and to coin money, the means of trade and commerce.

Woman was not yet made. The story (absurd enough!) is that Jupiter made her, and sent her to Prometheus and his brother, to punish them for their presumption[4] in stealing fire from heaven; and man, for accepting the gift. The first woman was named Pandora. She was made in heaven, every god contributing something to perfect her. Venus gave her beauty, Mercury persuasion, Apollo music, etc. Thus equipped, she was conveyed to earth, and presented to Epimetheus, who gladly accepted her, though cautioned by his brother to beware of Jupiter and his gifts. Epimetheus had in his house a jar, in which were kept certain noxious[5] articles for which, in fitting man for his new abode, he had had no occasion.

Pandora was seized with an eager curiosity to know what this jar contained; and one day she slipped off the cover and looked in. Forthwith there escaped a multitude of plagues for hapless[6] man—such as gout, rheumatism, and colic for his body, and envy, spite, and revenge for his mind—and scattered themselves far and wide. Pandora hastened to replace the lid; but, alas! the whole contents of the jar had escaped, one thing only excepted, which lay at the bottom, and that was *hope*. So we see at this day, whatever evils are abroad, hope never entirely leaves us; and while we have *that*, no amount of other ills can make us completely wretched.

Prometheus has been a favorite subject with the poets. He is represented as the friend of mankind, who taught them civilization and the arts. But as, in so doing, he transgressed[7] the will of Jupiter, he drew down on himself the anger of the ruler of gods

---

2 **sagacity:** wisdom.
3 **prodigal:** wasteful.
4 **presumption:** bold venture going beyond limits imposed by the gods.

5 **noxious:** harmful.
6 **hapless:** unlucky.
7 **transgressed:** violated.

and men. Jupiter had him chained to a rock on Mount Caucasus. This state of torment might have been brought to an end at any time by Prometheus, if he had been willing to submit to his oppressor; for he possessed a secret which involved the stability[8] of Jove's throne, and if he would have revealed it, he might have been at once taken into favor. But that he disdained[9] to do. He has therefore become the symbol of magnanimous[10] endurance of unmerited suffering, and strength of will resisting oppression.

"I would not quit
This bleak ravine, these unrepentant[11] pains. . . .
Pity the self-despising slaves of Jove,
Not me, within whose mind sits peace serene."

Shelley

8 **stability:** firmness.
9 **disdained:** proudly refused.

10 **magnanimous:** honorable; noble.
11 **unrepentant:** lacking in sorrow or remorse for wrongdoing.

Understanding Literature

1. A myth may be an explanation of something about nature or the universe. What does the Prometheus myth explain? In what ways is this explanation similar to that found in the Book of Genesis in the Old Testament?
2. The word *chaos* is often used to describe confusion. What does the proper noun *Chaos* represent in this myth?
3. According to this myth, in what ways does man differ from the other animals of the earth?
4. In what ways does Prometheus's gift of fire benefit mankind? Why might this gift have violated the will of Jupiter?
5. In Greek mythology Pandora is the first woman on earth. What characteristic does she have which proves to be disastrous? Explain. In what ways is she similar to Eve in the Old Testament?
6. Why is it significant that *hope* is the only thing left in the jar? What is another quality that might be as important to man?
7. The lines quoted at the end of the selection you have just read are from a long poem, *Prometheus Unbound,* by Percy Bysshe Shelley, a 19th-century English poet. Who do you think is speaking these lines? What do they mean?
8. What do you think this myth is saying about the dangers that might be faced by people who try to do more than is expected of them? Why is Prometheus considered a hero?

Did you ever wonder why some of the months of the year are cold and bleak, whereas others are warm and good for planting? While modern science gives a different answer, the following myth gives the early Greek explanation of the origin of the seasons.

Demeter (Ceres)

Edith Hamilton

DEMETER[1] HAD an only daughter, Persephone[2] (in Latin Proserpine), the maiden of the spring. She lost her and in her terrible grief she withheld her gifts from the earth, which turned into a frozen desert. The green and flowering land was icebound and lifeless because Persephone had disappeared.

The lord of the dark underworld, the king of the multitudinous[3] dead, carried her off when, enticed[4] by the wondrous bloom of the narcissus, she strayed too far from her companions. In his chariot drawn by coal-black steeds he rose up through a chasm in the earth, and grasping the maiden by the wrist set her beside him. He bore her away, weeping, down to the underworld. The high hills echoed her cry and the depths of the sea, and her mother heard it. She sped like a bird over sea and land seeking her daughter. But no one would tell her the truth, "no man nor god, nor any sure messenger from the birds." Nine days Demeter wandered, and all that time she would not taste of ambrosia or put sweet nectar to her lips. At last she came to the Sun and he told her all the story: Persephone was down in the world beneath the earth, among the shadowy dead.

Then a still greater grief entered Demeter's heart. She left Olympus; she dwelt on earth, but so disguised that none knew her, and, indeed, the gods are not easily discerned by mortal men. In her desolate[5] wanderings she came to Eleusis and sat by the wayside near a wall. She seemed an aged woman, such as in great houses care for the children or guard the storerooms. Four lovely maidens, sisters, coming to draw water from the well, saw her and asked her pityingly what she did there. She answered that she had fled from pirates who had meant to sell her as a slave, and that she knew no one in this strange land to go to for help. They told her that any house in the town would welcome her, but that they would like best to bring her to their own if she would wait there while they went to ask their mother. The goddess bent her head in assent,[6] and the girls, filling

1 **Demeter** (dǐ mē′tər).
2 **Persephone** (pər sĕf′ə nǐ).
3 **multitudinous:** great numbers.
4 **enticed:** attracted.

5 **desolate:** lonely.
6 **assent:** approval.

their shining pitchers with water, hurried home. Their mother, Metaneira, bade them return at once and invite the stranger to come, and speeding back they found the glorious goddess still sitting there, deeply veiled and covered to her slender feet by her dark robe. She followed them, and as she crossed the threshold to the hall where the mother sat holding her young son, a divine radiance filled the doorway and awe fell upon Metaneira.

She bade Demeter be seated and herself offered her honeysweet wine, but the goddess would not taste it. She asked instead for barley-water flavored with mint, the cooling draught of the reaper at harvest time and also the sacred cup given the worshipers at Eleusis. Thus refreshed she took the child and held him to her fragrant bosom and his mother's heart was glad. So Demeter nursed Demophoön,[7] the son that Metaneira had borne to wise Celeus. And the child grew like a young god, for daily Demeter anointed him with ambrosia and at night she would place him in the red heart of the fire. Her purpose was to give him immortal youth.

Something, however, made the mother uneasy, so that one night she kept watch and screamed in terror when she saw the child laid in the fire. The goddess was angered; she seized the boy and cast him on the ground. She had meant to set him free from old age and from death, but that was not to be. Still, he had lain upon her knees and slept in her arms and therefore he should have honor throughout his life.

Then she showed herself the goddess manifest.[8] Beauty breathed about her and a lovely fragrance; light shone from her so that the great house was filled with brightness. She was Demeter, she told the awestruck women. They must build her a great temple near the town and so win back the favor of her heart.

Thus she left them, and Metaneira fell speechless to the earth and all there trembled with fear. In the morning they told Celeus what had happened and he called the people together and revealed to them the command of the goddess. They worked willingly to build her a temple, and when it was finished Demeter came to it and sat there—apart from the gods in Olympus, alone, wasting away with longing for her daughter.

That year was most dreadful and cruel for mankind over all the earth. Nothing grew; no seed sprang up; in vain the oxen drew the plowshare through the furrows. It seemed the whole race of men would die of famine. At last Zeus saw that he must take the matter in hand. He sent the gods to Demeter, one after another, to try to turn her from her anger, but she listened to none of them. Never would she let the earth bear fruit until she had seen her daughter. Then Zeus realized that his brother must give way. He told Hermes to go down to the under-

7 Demophoön (dĭ mŏf'ō ŏn).

8 manifest: unconcealed.

world and to bid the lord of it let his bride go back to Demeter.

Hermes found the two sitting side by side, Persephone shrinking away, reluctant because she longed for her mother. At Hermes's words she sprang up joyfully, eager to go. Her husband knew that he must obey the word of Zeus and send her up to earth away from him, but he prayed her as she left him to have kind thoughts of him and not be so sorrowful that she was the wife of one who was great among the immortals. And he made her eat a pomegranate[9] seed, knowing in his heart that if she did so she must return to him.

He got ready his golden car and Hermes took the reins and drove the black horses straight to the temple where Demeter was. She ran out to meet her daughter as swiftly as a Maenad runs down the mountainside. Persephone sprang into her arms and was held fast there. All day they talked of what had happened to them both, and Demeter grieved when she heard of the pomegranate seed, fearing that she could not keep her daughter with her.

Then Zeus sent another messenger to her, a great personage, none other than his revered mother Rhea, the oldest of the gods. Swiftly she hastened down from the heights of Olympus to the barren, leafless earth, and standing at the door of the temple she spoke to Demeter.

Come, my daughter, for Zeus, far-seeing, loud-thundering, bids you.
Come once again to the halls of the gods where you shall have honor.

Where you will have your desire, your daughter, to comfort your sorrow
As each year is accomplished and bitter winter is ended.
For a third part only the kingdom of darkness shall hold her.
For the rest you will keep her, you and the happy immortals.
Peace now. Give men life which comes alone from your giving.

Demeter did not refuse, poor comfort though it was that she must lose Persephone for four months every year and see her young loveliness go down to the world of the dead. But she was kind; the "Good Goddess," men always called her. She was sorry for the desolation she had brought about. She made the fields once more rich with abundant fruit and the whole world bright with flowers and green leaves. Also she went to the princes of Eleusis who had built her temple and she chose one, Triptolemus, to be her ambassador to men, instructing them how to sow the corn. She taught him and Celeus and the others her sacred rites, "mysteries which no one may utter, for deep awe checks the tongue. Blessed is he who has seen them; his lot will be good in the world to come."

In the stories of both goddesses, Demeter and Persephone, the idea of sorrow was foremost. Demeter, goddess of the harvest wealth, was still more the divine sorrowing mother who saw her daughter die each year. Persephone was the radiant maiden of the spring and the summertime, whose light step upon the dry, brown hillside was enough to make it fresh

9 pomegranate: thick-skinned reddish fruit.

and blooming, as Sappho[10] writes,

I heard the footfall of the flower spring . . .

—Persephone's footfall. But all the while Persephone knew how brief that beauty was; fruits, flowers, leaves, all the fair growth of earth, must end with the coming of the cold and pass like herself into the power of death. After the lord of the dark world below carried her away she was never again the gay young creature who had played in the flowery meadow without a thought of care or trouble. She did indeed rise from the dead every spring, but she brought with her the memory of where she had come from; with all her bright beauty there was something strange and awesome about her. She was often said to be "the maiden whose name may not be spoken."

The Olympians were "the happy gods," "the deathless gods," far removed from suffering mortals destined to die. But in their grief and at the hour of death, men could turn for compassion to the goddess who sorrowed and the goddess who died.

10 **Sappho:** ancient Greek poet.

Understanding Literature

1. Summarize the story of the origin of the seasons.
2. Demeter's care of and plans for Demophoön make a story within a story. What is the probable purpose for including this secondary story? What phenomenon of nature is explained by Demeter's absence from her duties as the harvest queen?
3. Why did men call Demeter the "Good Goddess"?
4. Why are Demeter and Persephone associated with the idea of sorrow?
5. The tone of a piece of writing depends to a great extent on the author's careful selection of words. In "Demeter" a feeling of beauty, power, and royalty is associated with the gods. For example, Persephone is described as "the maiden of the spring," and Demeter is described as the "glorious goddess." What other words or phrases do you find in this myth which seem unusually descriptive?

Why are some parts of the earth dry desert land, whereas others are moist and fertile? This myth gives one answer.

Phaethon, Son of Apollo

Olivia E. Coolidge

THOUGH APOLLO always honored the memory of Daphne, she was not his only love. Another was a mortal, Clymene,[1] by whom he had a son named Phaethon.[2] Phaethon grew up with his mother, who, since she was mortal, could not dwell in the halls of Olympus or in the palace of the sun. She lived not far from the East in the land of Ethiopia, and as her son grew up, she would point to the place where Eos, goddess of the dawn, lighted up the sky and tell him that there his father dwelt. Phaethon loved to boast of his divine father as he saw the golden chariot riding high through the air. He would remind his comrades of other sons of gods and mortal women who, by virtue of their great deeds, had themselves become gods at last. He must always be first in everything, and in most things this was easy, since he was in truth stronger, swifter, and more daring than the others. Even if he were not victorious, Phaethon always claimed to be first in honor. He could never bear to be beaten, even if he must risk his life in some rash way to win.

Most of the princes of Ethiopia willingly paid Phaethon honor, since they admired him greatly for his fire and beauty. There was one boy, however, Epaphos,[3] who was rumored to be a child of Zeus himself. Since this was not certainly proved, Phaethon chose to disbelieve it and to demand from Epaphos the deference[4] that he obtained from all others. Epaphos was proud too, and one day he lost his temper with Phaethon and turned on him, saying, "You are a fool to believe all that your mother tells you. You are all swelled up with false ideas about your father."

Crimson with rage, the lad rushed home to his mother and demanded that she prove to him the truth of the story that she had often told. "Give me some proof," he implored her, "with which I can answer this insult of Epaphos. It is a matter of life and death to me, for if I cannot, I shall die of shame."

"I swear to you," replied his mother solemnly, "by the bright orb of the sun itself that you are his son. If I swear falsely, may I never look on the sun again, but die before the

1 Clymene (klĭm′ə nē).
2 Phaethon (fā′ə thən).

3 Epaphos (ĕp′ə fəs).
4 deference: respect.

MYTHS, FABLES, AND LEGENDS

next time he mounts the heavens. More than this I cannot do, but you, my child, can go to the eastern palace of Phoebus Apollo—it lies not far away—and there speak with the god himself."

The son of Clymene leaped up with joy at his mother's words. The palace of Apollo was indeed not far. It stood just below the eastern horizon, its tall pillars glistening with bronze and gold. Above these it was white with gleaming ivory, and the great doors were flashing silver, embossed with pictures of earth, sky, and sea, and the gods that dwelt therein. Up the steep hill and the bright steps climbed Phaethon, passing unafraid through the silver doors, and stood in the presence of the sun. Here at last he was forced to turn away his face, for Phoebus sat in state on his golden throne. It gleamed with emeralds and precious stones, while on the head of the god was a brilliant diamond crown upon which no eye could look undazzled.

Phaethon hid his face, but the god had recognized his son, and he spoke kindly, asking him why he had come. Then Phaethon plucked up courage and said, "I come to ask you if you are indeed my father. If you are so, I beg you to give me some proof of it so that all may recognize me as Phoebus's son."

The god smiled, being well pleased with his son's beauty and daring. He took off his crown so that Phaethon could look at him, and coming down from his throne, he put his arms around the boy, and said, "You are indeed my son and Clymene's, and worthy to be called so. Ask of me whatever thing you wish to prove your origin to men, and you shall have it."

Phaethon swayed for a moment and was dizzy with excitement at the touch of the god. His heart leaped; the blood rushed into his face. Now he felt that he was truly divine, unlike other men, and he did not wish to be counted with men any more. He looked up for a moment at his radiant father. "Let me drive the chariot of the sun across the heavens for one day," he said.

Apollo frowned and shook his head. "I cannot break my promise, but I will dissuade you if I can," he answered. "How can you drive my chariot, whose horses need a strong hand on the reins? The climb is too steep for you. The immense height will make you dizzy. The swift streams of air in the upper heaven will sweep you off your course. Even the immortal gods could not drive my chariot. How then can you? Be wise and make some other choice."

The pride of Phaethon was stubborn, for he thought the god was merely trying to frighten him. Besides, if he could guide the sun's chariot, would he not have proved his right to be divine rather than mortal? For that he would risk his life. Indeed, once he had seen Apollo's splendor, he did not wish to go back and live among men. Therefore, he insisted on his right until Apollo had to give way.

When the father saw that nothing else would satisfy the boy, he bade the Hours bring forth his chariot and yoke the horses. The chariot was of gold and had two gold-rimmed wheels with spokes of silver. In it there was room for one man to stand and hold the reins. Around the front and sides of it ran a rail, but the back was open. At the end of a long pole there were yokes for the four horses. The pole was of gold and shone with precious jewels: the golden topaz, the bright diamond, the green emerald, and the flashing ruby. While the Hours were yoking the swift, pawing horses, rosy-fingered Dawn hastened to the gates of heaven to draw them open. Meanwhile Apollo anointed his son's face with a magic ointment, that he might be able to bear the heat of the fire-breathing horses and the golden chariot. At last Phaethon mounted the chariot and grasped the reins, the barriers were let down, and the horses shot up into the air.

At first the fiery horses sped forward up the accustomed trail, but behind them the chariot was too light without the weight of the immortal god. It bounded from side to side and was dashed up and down. Phaethon was too frightened and too dizzy to pull the reins, nor would he have known anyway whether he was on the usual path. As soon as the horses felt that there was no hand controlling them, they soared up, up with fiery speed into the heavens till the earth grew pale and cold beneath them. Phaethon shut his eyes, trembling at the dizzy, precipitous[5] height. Then the horses dropped down, more swiftly than a falling

stone, flinging themselves madly from side to side in panic because they were masterless. Phaethon dropped the reins entirely and clung with all his might to the chariot rail. Meanwhile as they came near the earth, it dried up and cracked apart. Meadows were reduced to white ashes, cornfields smoked and shriveled, cities perished in flame. Far and wide on the wooded mountains the forests were ablaze, and even the snow-clad Alps were bare and dry. Rivers steamed and dried to dust. The great North African plain was scorched until it became the desert that it is today. Even the sea shrank back to pools and caves, until dried fishes were left baking upon the white-hot sands. At last the great earth mother called upon Zeus to save her from utter destruction, and Zeus hurled a mighty thunderbolt at the unhappy Phaethon, who was still crouched in the chariot, clinging desperately to the rail. The dart cast him out, and he fell flaming in a long trail through the air. The chariot broke in pieces at the mighty blow, and the maddened horses rushed snorting back to the stable of their master, Apollo.

Unhappy Clymene and her daughters wandered over the whole earth seeking the body of the boy they loved so well. When they found him, they took him and buried him. Over his grave they wept and could not be comforted. At last the gods in pity for their grief changed them into poplar trees, which weep with tears of amber in memory of Phaethon.

5 precipitous: steep.

MYTHS, FABLES, AND LEGENDS

Understanding Literature

1. Describe the scene that prompts Phaethon to ask his mother for proof that Apollo is his father.
2. Why does Phaethon insist that Apollo carry through his promise in spite of Apollo's attempt to dissuade him?
3. In what ways does the earth suffer because of Phaethon's driving the chariot?
4. What happens to Phaethon's mother, Clymene?
5. What qualities in human nature does this myth illustrate?
6. In this myth many of the words and phrases of description are particularly fitting for the sun-god. For example, the myth states that Phaethon is admired "greatly for his *fire* and *beauty*." Another time, Phaethon is described as being "crimson with rage." Find other examples of description that are particularly appropriate in a myth about the sun-god and his son.

Further Activity

Apollo is a very important god in Greek and Roman mythology, just as the sun is a very important part of our universe. The myth that you have just read is one of many which concern this powerful god. There is a myth about how Apollo's cattle are stolen by his brother Mercury. Another myth explains the reason why Apollo always wears a wreath of laurel and relates how a laurel crown becomes the prize for athletes and musicians. Still another myth about Apollo tells of Clytie's love for him and why Clytie is changed to a sunflower. Use your library facilities to prepare a report on as many myths about Apollo as you can.

Man has always wanted to fly freely through the air. Today he can do it in airplanes and even rockets, but here is a story of one boy and his father who tried it another way.

Daedalus

Olivia E. Coolidge

IN THE VERY early days it was not the mainland of Greece that was the most important, but the island of Crete, which lies below the Aegean sea, south of most of the other islands. In it there are still ruins of a great palace, almost more a city than a palace, with so many rooms and passages that it must have had many people dwelling in it. These people were evidently traders and powerful on the sea. They must have been skilled shipbuilders, and from the remains we have found, we know they were also great architects, craftsmen, and artists. In later times the island sank into unimportance, and its former prominence was forgotten. Nevertheless the story of its greatness lingers on and is associated with the skills for which we know it was famous.

In legend the king of the island of Crete was called Minos. He had a great fleet and power that extended far and wide, dominating, among other places, the city of Athens. He seems to have been a fierce tyrant, for he forced the Athenians to send him a yearly tribute of seven youths and seven maidens, whom he fed to a horrible monster that he owned.

This animal was called the Minotaur and was a creature with the head of a bull and the body of a man. To keep him safe and to prevent his victims from escaping, it was necessary to build him some special dwelling. For this purpose Minos hired a famous architect whose name was Daedalus.[1]

Daedalus, the Greeks used to say, was the first great artist, craftsman, and engineer. It was he who invented many of the tools of carpentry: the saw, the gimlet, and an efficient glue. He also was the first to make statues more lifelike than a roughly carved pillar. Before this time statues had held their legs stiffly together and their arms down by their sides. Daedalus made them stepping forward and holding something in front of them. He is said to have built a great reservoir, fortified a city, and done many other engineering works. But the most famous of all the things he made was the house he built for Minos to keep the Minotaur in. This house was a labyrinth or maze, with countless winding passages, so that it was hard to find the

1 **Daedalus** (dĕd′ə ləs).

way in or out. Perhaps the idea got into the story from a vague memory of the countless confusing passages in the Cretan palace. In any case Daedalus is supposed to have built a maze for Minos, so elaborate in its windings that no man without a clue could possibly escape from it.

Minos was delighted with his labyrinth and held the architect in great honor. Unfortunately, when the wandering artist wished to take his fee and go, the King had other ideas. There were many things that could well be made for him by the greatest craftsman in the world, and he saw no reason why he should let the man build things for someone else. Being king over an island, Minos found it easy to keep Daedalus where he was. He simply forbade all ships to give the artist passage, provided him with an elaborate workshop, and suggested that he might as well settle down and be happy.

Thus Minos gained the services of Daedalus, but the great craftsman was not content. Beyond anything else he loved freedom to wander as he pleased, seeing the world and picking up new ideas. He was not the kind of man who could easily settle down. Therefore when he saw that he could not possibly get away by ship, he turned his talents to working out something else. Minos did not visit the fine workshop he had given his artist, but if he had, he would have seen a curious sight. The whole place was deep in feathers. There were feathers of all shapes and sizes, some just thrown down anyhow as they had been brought in, and some neatly sorted into heaps. A young boy, Icarus, Daedalus's only son and companion, was doing the sorting, while Daedalus himself was busy with twine, wax, and glue, fixing the feathers together in orderly rows on a wooden framework.

Daedalus was making wings. He had seen that it would be impossible to cross the sea by boat because of Minos's order, so he had determined to fly across it. After studying the wings of birds for a long time, he designed some which he thought would support a man, and now he was working on them. Icarus was terribly excited and was helping eagerly. He did not so much dislike living in Crete, but he wanted to fly as the gods do. Think of being the first man to have wings!

The wings took a long time to finish, but at last they were done, a mighty pair for Daedalus, and a smaller one for his son. The workshop being in the top of a lofty tower, Daedalus planned that they should simply launch themselves into the air from it. As they stood there, fastening the wings onto their shoulders, Daedalus gave his excited son some last instructions.

"I shall go first," he said, "to show the way. We must go straight across the sea by the shortest route, lest we become tired and drown before we can reach land. Follow me, and remember the wings on your shoulders are not natural wings, like those of Cupid. We are men and must use tools to do what the gods can do for themselves. Even with our tools we

262

must always fall short of them. If you fly too near the sea, the feathers will become wet and heavy, and you will drown; if you fly up into the air as the gods do, the wax will melt in the sun long before you reach Olympus. Then your wings will fall off and you will perish. Follow me as I go through the middle of the air, neither too high nor too low. So you will be safe."

He spoke and jumped, falling like a stone till the wind caught him and he steadied. Then he began to rise again as the wings beat steadily from his shoulders. He turned and beckoned Icarus to come on. Icarus jumped. The fall was terrible; so was the sudden stop as his spread wings caught the air. Still, he had the presence of mind to work his arms as he had seen his father do, and pretty soon he was sailing ahead in long swoops over the sea.

Presently the boy began to play tricks in the air. His father flew steadily on, but it would be easy, Icarus thought, to catch up with him. Father was too old to enjoy this properly. The swoops were rather sickening, but climbing was wonderful. Up, up he went, like the lark, like the eagle, like the gods. His father called something, but the wind whistled the sound away.

Icarus realized he ought to come down, but nobody had ever been up there before, except the gods. Perhaps the real difference between gods and men was that gods could fly. If he wanted to reach Olympus, he would have to take some risk.

Up, up Icarus went, soaring into the bright sun. In vain Daedalus called to him. He was only a black speck by now. At last he was coming down. He was coming very fast, much too fast. In another second Daedalus caught sight of the boy, whirling headlong. The framework was still on his shoulders, but the feathers had all fallen off, as the hot sun had melted the wax. One moment he saw him; then with a mighty splash Icarus hit the water and was gone. Daedalus circled round over the sea, not daring to go too low lest his own wings become soaked. There was no point in both being drowned. But not even a clutching hand broke surface. The white foam hung on the water for a space; then it too disappeared.

Daedalus flew on. He reached the land at last, white-faced and exhausted, but he would neither use his wings nor teach others how to make them. He had learned man's limitations. It is not right for him to soar like the gods.

Understanding Literature

1. Describe the Minotaur. How is he fed? Where is he kept?
2. Why is Daedalus considered the first great artist?
3. Describe the method Daedalus and Icarus use to escape from Crete. What is the fate of Icarus?
4. What quality in human nature does the story of Icarus illustrate?
5. At the end of this myth we learn that Daedalus would never again use his wings nor would he teach others how to make them. "He had learned man's limitations. It is not right for him to soar like the gods." What modern examples can you think of, in addition to airplane travel, which show that this idea is not generally accepted today? Do you think that Daedalus is right to any extent? Explain.

Further Activity

In the second and third paragraphs of "Daedalus" you read about the Minotaur. To find out what happens to this horrible monster—and whether anyone ever *does* find his way out of the maze—you will want to read another famous Greek myth: the story of Theseus. *Bulfinch's Mythology* and *Mythology* by Edith Hamilton are two sources which will help you prepare a report to the class.

In literature you will find frequent references to the Gorgons, of whom Medusa is the most famous. These three female monsters have huge teeth and claws, and snakes in place of hair. They turn to stone any animal or person who looks at them.

Perseus

Thomas Bulfinch

PERSEUS[1] was the son of Jupiter and Danaë. His grandfather Acrisius, alarmed by an oracle which had told him that his daughter's child would be the instrument of his death, caused the mother and child to be shut up in a chest and set adrift on the sea. The chest floated towards Seriphus, where it was found by a fisherman who conveyed the mother and infant to Polydectes, the king of the country, by whom they were treated with kindness. When Perseus was grown up Polydectes sent him to attempt the conquest of Medusa,[2] a terrible monster who had laid waste the country. She was once a beautiful maiden whose hair was her chief glory, but as she dared to vie in beauty with Minerva, the goddess deprived her of her charms and changed her beautiful ringlets into hissing serpents. She became a cruel monster of so frightful an aspect that no living thing could behold her without being turned into stone. All around the cavern where she dwelt might be seen the stony figures of men and animals which had chanced to catch a glimpse of her and had been petrified with the sight. Perseus, favored by Minerva and Mer-

cury, the former of whom lent him her shield and the latter his winged shoes, approached Medusa while she slept and taking care not to look directly at her, but guided by her image reflected in the bright shield which he bore, he cut off her head and gave it to Minerva, who fixed it in the middle of her Aegis.[3]

[The following is a *flashback*. It takes place before Perseus gives Medusa's head to Minerva.]

After the slaughter of Medusa, Perseus, bearing with him the head of the Gorgon, flew far and wide, over land and sea. As night came on, he reached the western limit of the earth, where the sun goes down. Here he would gladly have rested till morning. It was the realm of King Atlas, whose bulk surpassed that of all other men. He was rich in flocks and herds and had no neighbor or rival to dispute his state. But his chief pride was in his gardens, whose fruit was of gold, hanging from golden branches, half hid with golden leaves. Perseus said to him, "I come as a guest. If you honor illustrious[4] descent, I claim Jupiter for my father; if mighty deeds, I

1 **Perseus** (pûr′sūs).
2 **Medusa** (mə dū′sə).

3 **Aegis** (ē′jĭs): shield.
4 **illustrious**: famous.

MYTHS, FABLES, AND LEGENDS

plead the conquest of the Gorgon. I seek rest and food." But Atlas remembered that an ancient prophecy had warned him that a son of Jove should one day rob him of his golden apples. So he answered, "Begone! or neither your false claims of glory nor parentage shall protect you;" and he attempted to thrust him out. Perseus, finding the giant too strong for him, said, "Since you value my friendship so little, deign to accept a present;" and turning his face away, he held up the Gorgon's head. Atlas, with all his bulk, was changed into stone. His beard and hair became forests, his arms and shoulders cliffs, his head a summit, and his bones rocks. Each part increased in bulk till he became a mountain, and (such was the pleasure of the gods) heaven with all its stars rests upon his shoulders.

Perseus, continuing his flight, arrived at the country of the Ethiopians, of which Cepheus[5] was king. Cassiopeia[6] his queen, proud of her beauty, had dared to compare herself to the sea-nymphs, which roused their indignation to such a degree that they sent a prodigious[7] sea-monster to ravage the coast. To appease[8] the deities, Cepheus was directed by the oracle to expose his daughter Andromeda to be devoured by the monster. As Perseus looked down from his aerial height he beheld the virgin chained to a rock, and waiting the approach of the serpent. She was so pale and motionless that if it had not been for her flowing tears and her hair that moved in the breeze, he would have taken her for a marble statue. He was so startled at the sight that he almost forgot to wave his wings. As he hovered over her he said, "O virgin, undeserving of those chains, but rather of such as bind fond lovers together, tell me, I beseech you, your name, and the name of your country, and why you are thus bound." At first she was silent from modesty, and, if she could, would have hid her face with her hands; but when he repeated his questions, for fear she might be thought guilty of some fault which she dared not tell, she disclosed her name and that of her country, and her mother's pride of beauty. Before she had done speaking, a sound was heard off upon the water, and the sea-monster appeared, with his head raised above the surface, cleaving the waves with his broad breast. The virgin shrieked, the father and mother who had now arrived at the scene, wretched both, but the mother more justly so, stood by, not able to afford protection, but only to pour forth lamentations and to embrace the victim. Then spoke Perseus: "There will be time enough for tears; this hour is all we have for rescue. My rank as the son of Jove and my renown as the slayer of the Gorgon might make me acceptable as a suitor; but I will try to win her by services rendered, if the gods will only be propitious.[9] If she be

---

5 **Cepheus** (sē′fūs).
6 **Cassiopeia** (kăs′ĭ ə pē′ə).
7 **prodigious** (prə dĭj′əs): marvelous; extraordinary.
8 **appease**: calm; soothe.

9 **propitious** (prə pĭsh′əs): favorably inclined.

rescued by my valor, I demand that she be my reward." The parents consent (how could they hesitate?) and promise a royal dowry with her.

And now the monster was within the range of a stone thrown by a skillful slinger, when with a sudden bound the youth soared into the air. As an eagle, when from his lofty flight he sees a serpent basking in the sun, pounces upon him and seizes him by the neck to prevent him from turning his head round and using his fangs, so the youth darted down upon the back of the monster and plunged his sword into its shoulder. Irritated by the wound, the monster raised himself into the air, then plunged into the depth; then, like a wild boar surrounded by a pack of barking dogs, turned swiftly from side to side, while the youth eluded its attacks

by means of his wings. Wherever he can find a passage for his sword between the scales he makes a wound, piercing now the side, now the flank, as it slopes towards the tail. The brute spouts from his nostrils water mixed with blood. The wings of the hero are wet with it, and he dares no longer trust to them. Alighting on a rock which rose above the waves, and holding on by a projecting fragment, as the monster floated near he gave him a death stroke. The people who had gathered on the shore shouted so that the hills re-echoed with the sound. The parents, transported with joy, embraced their future son-in-law, calling him their deliverer and the savior of their house, and the virgin, both cause and reward of the contest, descended from the rock.

The joyful parents, with Perseus and Andromeda, repaired[10] to the palace, where a banquet was spread for them, and all was joy and festivity. But suddenly a noise was heard of warlike clamor, and Phineus,[11] the betrothed of the virgin, with a party of his adherents, burst in, demanding the maiden as his own. It was in vain that Cepheus remonstrated—"You should have claimed her when she lay bound to the rock, the monster's victim. The sentence of the gods dooming her to such a fate dissolved all engagements, as death itself would have done." Phineus made no reply, but hurled his javelin at Perseus, but it missed its mark and fell harmless. Perseus would have thrown his in turn, but the cowardly assailant ran and took shelter behind the altar. But his act was a signal for an onset by his band upon the guests of Cepheus. They defended themselves and a general conflict ensued,[12] the old king retreating from the scene after fruitless expostulations, calling the gods to witness that he was guiltless of this outrage on the rights of hospitality.

Perseus and his friends maintained for some time the unequal contest; but the numbers of the assailants were too great for them, and destruction seemed inevitable, when a sudden thought struck Perseus—"I will make my enemy defend me." Then with a loud voice he exclaimed, "If I have any friend here let him turn away his eyes!" and held aloft the Gorgon's head. "Seek not to frighten us with your jugglery," said Thescelus, and raised his javelin in the act to throw, and became stone in the very attitude. Ampyx was about to plunge his sword into the body of a prostrate foe, but his arm stiffened and he could neither thrust forward nor withdraw it. Another, in the midst of a vociferous[13] challenge, stopped, his mouth open, but no sound issuing. One of Perseus's friends, Aconteus, caught sight of the Gorgon and stiffened like the rest. Astyages struck him with his sword, but instead of wounding, it recoiled with a ringing noise.

Phineus beheld this dreadful result of his unjust aggression, and felt confounded. He called aloud to his friends, but got no answer; he touched them and found them stone. Falling on his knees and stretching out his hands to Perseus, but turning his head away, he begged for mercy. "Take all," said he, "give me but my life." "Base coward," said Perseus, "thus much I will grant you; no weapon shall touch you; moreover, you shall be preserved in my house as a memorial of these events." So saying, he held the Gorgon's head to the side where Phineus was looking, and in the very form in which he knelt, with his hands outstretched and face averted, he became fixed immovably, a mass of stone!

---

10 **repaired:** here, returned.
11 **Phineus** (fĭ′nūs).
12 **ensued:** followed.

13 **vociferous** (vō sĭf′ər əs): noisy.

Understanding Literature

1. Why does Minerva change Medusa from a beautiful maiden to a hideous monster?
2. How does Perseus avoid being turned into stone?
3. In what ways does King Atlas change after looking at Medusa's head?
4. Why is Andromeda being sacrificed?
5. According to King Cepheus, why is Phineus's engagement to Andromeda no longer binding?
6. In what way does Perseus use Medusa's head in the battle between his friends and the followers of Phineus?
7. Describe what happens to Phineus in the final scene of this battle.
8. What human frailty or weakness is illustrated by the story of the sacrifice of Andromeda?
9. What is the purpose of the several secondary stories contained within the myth of Perseus?

Further Activities

1. In many ways the myth describing Perseus and his rescue of Andromeda is not too different from modern-day hero stories. Write a brief story in which a 20th-century Perseus rescues a 20th-century Andromeda. Use a modern setting and a present-day problem.
2. According to the myths, a winged horse arises from the blood which drops to the ground when Perseus cuts off Medusa's head. This horse, named Pegasus, is later captured by Bellerophon. Using your library resources, prepare a report on the myth which describes what finally happens to Pegasus and Bellerophon.

Hercules, the great hero of Greece, has to do twelve labors, often referred to in ordinary conversation as well as in literature. The following myth explains why he has to do them and what they are.

Hercules

Edith Hamilton

THE GREATEST HERO of Greece was Hercules. He was a personage of quite another order from the great hero of Athens, Theseus.[1] He was what all Greece except Athens most admired. The Athenians were different from the other Greeks and their hero therefore was different. Theseus was, of course, bravest of the brave as all heroes are, but unlike other heroes he was as compassionate[2] as he was brave and a man of great intellect as well as great bodily strength. It was natural that the Athenians should have such a hero because they valued thought and ideas as no other part of the country did. In Theseus their ideal was embodied. But Hercules embodied what the rest of Greece most valued. His qualities were those the Greeks in general honored and admired. Except for unflinching courage, they were not those that distinguished Theseus.

Hercules was the strongest man on earth and he had the supreme self-confidence magnificent physical strength gives. He considered himself on an equality with the gods— and with some reason. They needed his help to conquer the giants. In the final victory of the Olympians over the brutish sons of Earth, Hercules's arrows played an important part. He treated the gods accordingly. Once when the priestess at Delphi gave no response to the question he asked, he seized the tripod she sat on and declared that he would carry it off and have an oracle of his own. Apollo, of course, would not put up with this, but Hercules was perfectly willing to fight him and Zeus had to intervene. The quarrel was easily settled, however. Hercules was quite good-natured about it. He did not want to quarrel with Apollo, he only wanted an answer from his oracle. If Apollo would give it the matter was settled as far as he was concerned. Apollo on his side, facing this undaunted person, felt an admiration for his boldness and made his priestess deliver the response.

Throughout his life Hercules had this perfect confidence that no matter who was against him he could never be defeated, and facts bore

1 Theseus (thē′sōōs).
2 compassionate: sympathetic.

him out. Whenever he fought with anyone the issue was certain beforehand. He could be overcome only by a supernatural force. Hera used hers against him with terrible effect and in the end he was killed by magic, but nothing that lived in the air, sea, or on land ever defeated him.

Intelligence did not figure largely in anything he did and was often conspicuously absent. Once when he was too hot he pointed an arrow at the sun and threatened to shoot him. Another time when the boat he was in was tossed about by the waves he told the waters that he would punish them if they did not grow calm. His intellect was not strong. His emotions were. They were quickly aroused and apt to get out of control, as when he deserted the *Argo* and forgot all about his comrades and the Quest of the Golden Fleece in his despairing grief at losing his young armor-bearer, Hylas. This power of deep feeling in a man of his tremendous strength was oddly endearing, but it worked immense harm, too. He had sudden outbursts of furious anger which were always fatal to the often innocent objects. When the rage had passed and he had come to himself he would show a most disarming penitence[3] and agree humbly to any punishment it was proposed to inflict on him. Without his consent he could not have been punished by anyone—yet nobody ever endured so many punishments. He spent a large part of his life expiating[4] one

unfortunate deed after another and never rebelling against the almost impossible demands made upon him. Sometimes he punished himself when others were inclined to exonerate[5] him.

It would have been ludicrous[6] to put him in command of a kingdom as Theseus was put; he had more than enough to do to command himself. He could never have thought out any new or great idea as the Athenian hero was held to have done. His thinking was limited to devising a way to kill a monster which was threatening to kill him. Nevertheless he had true greatness. Not because he had complete courage based upon overwhelming strength, which is merely a matter of course, but because, by his sorrow for wrongdoing and his willingness to do anything to expiate it, he showed greatness of soul. If only he had had some greatness of mind as well, at least enough to lead him along the ways of reason, he would have been the perfect hero.

He was born in Thebes and for a long time was held to be the son of Amphitryon, a distinguished general. In those earlier years he was called Alcides, or descendant of Alcaeus who was Amphitryon's father. But in reality he was the son of Zeus. His mother, Alcmena,[7] bore two children, Hercules to Zeus and Iphicles to Amphitryon. The difference in the boys' descent was clearly shown in the way each acted in face of a

---

3 **disarming penitence:** touching regret for his sin.
4 **expiating:** atoning for; making up for.

5 **exonerate:** pardon.
6 **ludicrous:** ridiculous.
7 **Alcmena** (ălk mē′nə).

great danger which came to them before they were a year old. Hera, as always, was furiously jealous and she determined to kill Hercules.

One evening Alcmena gave both the children their bath and their fill of milk and laid them in their crib, caressing them and saying, "Sleep, my little ones, soul of my soul. Happy be your slumber and happy your awakening." She rocked the cradle and in a moment the babies were asleep. But at darkest midnight when all was silent in the house two great snakes came crawling into the nursery. There was a light in the room and as the two reared up above the crib, with weaving heads and flickering tongues, the children woke. Iphicles screamed and tried to get out of bed, but Hercules sat up and grasped the deadly creatures by the throat. They turned and twisted and wound their coils around his body, but he held them fast. The mother heard Iphicles's screams and, calling to her husband, rushed to the nursery. There sat Hercules laughing, in each hand a long limp body. He gave them gleefully to Amphitryon. They were dead. All knew then that the child was destined to great things. Teiresias, the blind prophet of Thebes, told Alcmena: "I swear that many a Greek woman as she cards the wool at eventide shall sing of this your son and you who bore him. He shall be the hero of all mankind."

Great care was taken with his education, but teaching him what he did not wish to learn was a dangerous business. He seems not to have liked music, which was a most important part of a Greek boy's training, or else he disliked his music master. He flew into a rage with him and brained him with his lute.[8] This was the first time he dealt a fatal blow without intending it. He did not mean to kill the poor musician; he just struck out on the impulse of the moment without thinking, hardly aware of his strength. He was sorry, very sorry, but that did not keep him from doing the same thing again and again. The other subjects he was taught, fencing, wrestling and driving, he took to more kindly, and his teachers in these branches all survived. By the time he was eighteen he was full-grown and he killed, alone by himself, a great lion which lived in the woods of Cithaeron, the Thespian lion. Ever after he wore its skin as a cloak with the head forming a kind of hood over his own head.

His next exploit was to fight and conquer the Minyans, who had been exacting a burdensome tribute from the Thebans. The grateful citizens gave him as a reward the hand of the Princess Megara. He was devoted to her and to their children and yet this marriage brought upon him the greatest sorrow of his life as well as trials and dangers such as no one ever went through, before or after. When Megara had borne him three sons he went mad. Hera, who never forgot a wrong, sent the madness upon him. He killed his children and Megara, too, as she tried to protect the youngest. Then his sanity returned. He found himself in his bloodstained hall, the dead bodies of his sons and his wife beside him. He had no idea what had happened, how they had been killed. Only a moment since, as it seemed to him, they had all been talking together. As he stood there in utter bewilderment the terrified people who were watching him from a distance saw that the mad fit was over, and Amphitryon dared to approach him. There was no keeping the truth from Hercules. He had to know how this horror had come to pass and Amphitryon told him. Hercules heard him out; then he said, "And I myself am the murderer of my dearest."

"Yes," Amphitryon answered trembling. "But you were out of your mind."

Hercules paid no attention to the implied excuse.

"Shall I spare my own life then?" he said. "I will avenge upon myself these deaths."

But before he could rush out and kill himself, even as he started to do so, his desperate purpose was changed and his life was spared. This miracle—it was nothing less—of recalling Hercules, from frenzied feeling and violent action to sober reason and sorrowful acceptance, was not wrought by a god descending from the sky. It was a miracle caused by human friendship. His friend Theseus stood before him and stretched out his hands to clasp those bloodstained hands. Thus according to the common Greek idea he would himself become defiled and have a part in Hercules's guilt.

8 lute: ancient stringed instrument.

"Do not start back," he told Hercules. "Do not keep me from sharing all with you. Evil I share with you is not evil to me. And hear me. Men great of soul can bear the blows of heaven and not flinch."

Hercules said, "Do you know what I have done?"

"I know this," Theseus answered. "Your sorrows reach from earth to heaven."

"So I will die," said Hercules.

"No hero spoke those words," Theseus said.

"What can I do but die?" Hercules cried. "Live? A branded man, for all to say, 'Look. There is he who killed his wife and sons!' Everywhere my jailers, the sharp scorpions of the tongue!"

"Even so, suffer and be strong," Theseus answered. "You shall come to Athens with me, share my home and all things with me. And you will give to me and to the city a great return, the glory of having helped you."

A long silence followed. At last Hercules spoke, slow, heavy words. "So let it be," he said. "I will be strong and wait for death."

The two went to Athens, but Hercules did not stay there long. Theseus, the thinker, rejected the idea that a man could be guilty of murder when he had not known what he was doing and that those who helped such a one could be reckoned defiled. The Athenians agreed and welcomed the poor hero. But he himself could not understand such ideas. He could not think the thing out at all; he could only feel. He

had killed his family. Therefore he was defiled and a defiler of others. He deserved that all should turn from him with loathing. At Delphi where he went to consult the oracle, the priestess looked at the matter just as he did. He needed to be purified, she told him, and only a terrible penance[9] could do that. She bade him go to his cousin Eurystheus, King of Mycenae (of Tiryns in some stories) and submit to whatever he demanded of him. He went willingly, ready to do anything that could make him clean again. It is plain from the rest of the story that the priestess knew what Eurystheus was like and that he would beyond question purge[10] Hercules thoroughly.

Eurystheus was by no means stupid, but of a very ingenious turn of mind, and when the strongest man on earth came to him humbly prepared to be his slave, he devised a series of penances which from the point of view of difficulty and danger could not have been improved upon. It must be said, however, that he was helped and urged on by Hera. To the end of Hercules's life she never forgave him for being Zeus's son. The tasks Eurystheus gave him to do are called "the Labors of Hercules." There were twelve of them and each one was all but impossible.

The first was to kill the lion of Nemea, a beast no weapons could wound. That difficulty Hercules solved by choking the life out of him. Then he heaved the huge carcass up

9 penance: atonement; punishment.
10 purge: cleanse; purify.

on his back and carried it into Mycenae. After that, Eurystheus, a cautious man, would not let him inside the city. He gave him his orders from afar.

The second labor was to go to Lerna and kill a creature with nine heads called the Hydra which lived in a swamp there. This was exceedingly hard to do, because one of the heads was immortal and the others almost as bad, inasmuch as when Hercules chopped off one, two grew up instead. However, he was helped by his nephew Iolaus who brought him a burning brand with which he seared[11] the neck as he cut each head off so that it could not sprout again. When all had been chopped off he disposed of the one that was immortal by burying it securely under a great rock.

The third labor was to bring back alive a stag with horns of gold, sacred to Artemis, which live in the forests of Cerynitia. He could have killed it easily, but to take it alive was another matter and he hunted it a whole year before he succeeded.

The fourth labor was to capture a great boar which had its lair on Mount Erymanthus. He chased the beast from one place to another until it was exhausted; then he drove it into deep snow and trapped it.

The fifth labor was to clean the Augean stables in a single day. Augeas had thousands of cattle and their stalls had not been cleared out for years. Hercules diverted the courses of two rivers and made them flow through the stables in a great flood that washed out the filth in no time at all.

The sixth labor was to drive away the Stymphalian birds, which were a plague to the people of Stymphalus because of their enormous numbers. He was helped by Athena to drive them out of their coverts,[12] and as they flew up he shot them.

The seventh labor was to go to Crete and fetch from there the beautiful savage bull that Poseidon had given Minos. Hercules mastered him, put him in a boat and brought him to Eurystheus.

The eighth labor was to get the man-eating mares of King Diomedes of Thrace. Hercules slew Diomedes first and then drove off the mares unopposed.

The ninth labor was to bring back the girdle[13] of Hippolyta, the Queen of the Amazons. When Hercules arrived she met him kindly and told him she would give him the girdle, but Hera stirred up trouble. She made the Amazons think that Hercules was going to carry off their queen, and they charged down on his ship. Hercules, without a thought of how kind Hippolyta had been, without any thought at all, instantly killed her, taking it for granted that she was responsible for the attack. He was able to fight off the others and get away with the girdle.

The tenth labor was to bring back the cattle of Geryon, who was a monster with three bodies living on Erythia, a western island. On his way

11 **seared:** burned.

12 **coverts:** shelters.
13 **girdle:** belt; sash.

MYTHS, FABLES, AND LEGENDS

there Hercules reached the land at the end of the Mediterranean and he set up as a memorial of his journey two great rocks, called the Pillars of Hercules (now Gibraltar and Ceuta). Then he got the oxen and took them to Mycenae.

The eleventh labor was the most difficult of all so far. It was to bring back the Golden Apples of the Hesperides, and he did not know where they were to be found. Atlas, who bore the vault of heaven upon his shoulders, was the father of the Hesperides, so Hercules went to him and asked him to get the apples for him. He offered to take upon himself the burden of the sky while Atlas was away. Atlas, seeing a chance of being relieved forever from his heavy task, gladly agreed. He came back with the apples, but he did not give them to Hercules. He told Hercules he could keep on holding up the sky, for Atlas himself would take the apples to Eurystheus. On this occasion Hercules had only his wits to trust to; he had to give all his strength to supporting that mighty load. He was successful, but because of Atlas's stupidity rather than his own cleverness. He agreed to Atlas's plan, but asked him to take the sky back for just a moment so that Hercules could put a pad on his shoulders to ease the pressure. Atlas did so, and Hercules picked up the apples and went off.

The twelfth labor was the worst of all. It took him down to the lower world, and it was then that he freed Theseus from the Chair of Forgetfulness. His task was to bring Cerberus, the three-headed dog, up from Hades. Pluto gave his permission provided Hercules used no weapons to overcome him. He could use his hands only. Even so, he forced the terrible monster to submit to him. He lifted him and carried him all the way up to the earth and on to Mycenae. Eurystheus very sensibly did not want to keep him and made Hercules carry him back. This was his last labor.

Understanding Literature

1. What incident in Hercules' childhood indicates that he is destined to do great things?
2. How is Hercules saved from killing himself after he murders his wife and children?
3. Hercules is assigned the twelve labors as atonement for his sin. Describe each labor briefly.
4. The qualities of Hercules are those the Greeks generally honored and admired. What are the qualities which make him a great hero?
5. Why is he not the perfect hero? Which of his actions are due to the flaws in his character?

6. The selection you have just read is only part of the story of Hercules. Do you think that Hercules becomes a more thoughtful and better man when his labors are done, or do you think he probably commits more rash actions? Explain. To what extent do you think people learn by their mistakes and experiences?

Further Activities

1. Using the resources in your library, prepare a brief report on the "choice of Hercules," which is not described here, and on the life of Hercules after his labors. Edith Hamilton's *Mythology,* from which this selection is taken, would be one good source for part of your report.
2. The story of Hercules's great strength is similar to that of Samson in the Bible. Read about Samson in the Book of Judges, Chapters 13-16, in the Old Testament. In one or two paragraphs describe the similarities and dissimilarities in the characters and actions of Hercules and Samson.
3. When Hercules wants to kill himself, Theseus says to him, "Men great of soul can bear the blows of heaven and not flinch." In your personal experiences you have probably met or heard of someone who endured a tragic event but was not overcome by it. Write a brief theme in which you describe who this person was, what tragic experience he had, and how he did not flinch in spite of "the blows of heaven."

   If you do not know someone whose experiences you can describe, choose an historical figure or one from a story or novel you have read.

"Was this the face that launched a thousand ships?" After hearing this famous quotation, you have probably wondered which woman was so beautiful that she could have been the cause of a war. The following myth tells of the origin of the Trojan War. This war is described in a Greek epic poem by Homer, the *Iliad*, which you will read more about later in this book.

The Judgment of Paris

Edith Hamilton

THE EVIL GODDESS of Discord, Eris, was naturally not popular in Olympus, and when the gods gave a banquet they were apt to leave her out. Resenting this deeply, she determined to make trouble—and she succeeded very well indeed. At an important marriage, that of King Peleus and the sea nymph Thetis, to which she alone of all the divinities was not invited, she threw into the banqueting hall a golden apple marked *For the Fairest*. Of course all the goddesses wanted it, but in the end the choice was narrowed down to three: Aphrodite,[1] Hera, and Pallas Athena. They asked Zeus to judge between them, but very wisely he refused to have anything to do with the matter. He told them to go to Mount Ida, near Troy, where the young prince Paris, also called Alexander, was keeping his father's sheep. He was an excellent judge of beauty, Zeus told them. Paris, though a royal prince, was doing shepherd's work because his father Priam, the King of Troy, had been warned that this prince would some day be the ruin of his country, and so had sent him away. At the moment Paris was living with a lovely nymph named Oenone.[2]

His amazement can be imagined when there appeared before him the wondrous forms of the three great goddesses. He was not asked, however, to gaze at the radiant divinities and choose which of them seemed to him the fairest, but only to consider the bribes each offered and choose which seemed to him best worth taking. Nevertheless, the choice was not easy. What men care for most was set before him. Hera promised to make him Lord of Europe and Asia; Athena, that he would lead the Trojans to victory against the Greeks and lay Greece in ruins; Aphrodite, that the fairest woman in all the world should be his. Paris, a weakling and something of a coward, too, as later events showed, chose the last. He gave Aphrodite the golden apple.

That was the Judgment of Paris,

1 Aphrodite (ăf′rə dī′tĭ).

2 Oenone (ē nō′nĭ).

famed everywhere as the real reason why the Trojan War was fought.

The fairest woman in the world was Helen, the daughter of Zeus and Leda and the sister of Castor and Pollux. Such was the report of her beauty that not a young prince in Greece but wanted to marry her. When her suitors assembled in her home to make a formal proposal for her hand they were so many and from such powerful families that her father, King Tyndareus, was afraid to select one among them, fearing that the others would unite against him. He therefore exacted first a solemn oath from all that they would champion the cause of Helen's husband, whoever he might be, if any wrong was done to him through his marriage. It was, after all, to each man's advantage to take the oath, since each was hoping he would be the person chosen, so they all bound themselves to punish to the uttermost anyone who carried or tried to carry Helen away. Then Tyndareus chose Menelaus,[3] the brother of Agamemnon,[4] and made him King of Sparta as well.

So matters stood when Paris gave the golden apple to Aphrodite. The Goddess of Love and Beauty knew very well where the most beautiful woman on earth was to be found. She led the young shepherd, with never a thought of Oenone left forlorn, straight to Sparta, where Menelaus and Helen received him graciously as their guest. The ties between guest and host were strong. Each was bound to help and never harm the other. But Paris broke that sacred bond. Menelaus trusting completely to it left Paris in his home and went off to Crete. Then,

Paris who coming
Entered a friend's kind dwelling,
Shamed the hand there that gave him food,
Stealing away a woman.

Menelaus got back to find Helen gone, and he called upon all Greece to help him. The chieftains responded, as they were bound to do. They came eager for the great enterprise, to cross the sea and lay mighty Troy in ashes.

3 **Menelaus** (měn′ə lā′əs).
4 **Agamemnon** (ăg′ə měm′nŏn).

Understanding Literature

1. How does the evil goddess of Discord, Eris, take revenge on Peleus and Thetis?
2. Who are the three beautiful goddesses whom Paris has to choose among?
3. What bribe does each offer to him? Which does Paris choose? What does Paris' choice show about his character?
4. Who is the fairest woman in the world? What oath has her father made all her suitors take? To whom is she married? In what city do they live?

Focusing on Words

1. Many of the mythological characters you have been reading about have contributed their names to form various English words. The word *cereal*, for example, comes from the name of the goddess Ceres. Can you explain why?
2. Another word that comes from a character about whom you read is *Promethean*, which means "life-giving; daringly original or creative." Why does it have these meanings?
3. Each of the following sentences contains a reference to Greek mythology. Explain what each sentence means and what it refers to.
   (*a*) He was exhausted after his Herculean labors.
   (*b*) They might have caught a glimpse of a Gorgon's head, judging from their reaction to the horrible spectacle.
   (*c*) Like the course of Phaethon, his career was brilliant but wild; it ended in disaster both for himself and those it affected.
   (*d*) Whatever he said sounded as though it were delivered from the heights of Olympus.
   (*e*) In his splendid flights of fancy, he showed as little self-restraint as Icarus.
   (*f*) She had the beauty of Helen and caused almost as much trouble.

Myths of the North

According to the poets of the Norse mythology, the Norse gods were interested mainly in heroism, especially in the essential heroic qualities of courage and bravery. These rough and powerful gods and the myths which grew about them became, for the people of the frozen North, the basis of a religion; in this religion a heroic death was a triumph, even though the hero had no heaven of eternal peace and beauty to look forward to. But with the arrival of Christianity in the Scandinavian countries, this religion built around the Norse gods was soon discarded. Although it is not definitely known where Norse myths began, it is thought that they originated in Norway, Greenland, Ireland, England, or Iceland. It *is* known, however, that they were first written down in Iceland, a cold, northern land. This fact helps to explain why Giantland is a cold, misty place.

You will more fully enjoy and understand the next two selections if you study the following names:

Asgard: Home of the gods in the center of the earth.
Giants: Spirits of frost or mountains. Giantland was a cold, misty country which lay beyond the ocean that surrounded the earth.
Odin: Allfather and sky-god who could see all the world from his throne in Asgard.
Freya or Freyja: Goddess of love and beauty.
Loki: God of fire who often used trickery to get his wishes.

Now that you have read some of the Greek and Roman myths, you will be interested in comparing them with the myths of the Scandinavian countries.

The Building of the Wall

Padraic Colum

ALWAYS THERE had been war between the giants and the gods—between the giants who would have destroyed the world and the race of men, and the gods who would have protected the race of men and would have made the world more beautiful.

There are many stories to be told about the gods, but the first one that shall be told to you is the one about the building of their city.

The gods had made their way up to the top of a high mountain and there they decided to build a great city for themselves that the giants could never overthrow. The city they would call Asgard, which means "the place of the gods." They would build it on a beautiful plain that was on the top of that high mountain. And they wanted to raise round their city the highest and strongest wall that had ever been built.

Now one day when they were be-ginning to build their halls and their palaces a strange being came to them. Odin, the father of the gods, went and spoke to him. "What dost thou want on the mountain of the gods?" he asked the Stranger.

"I know what is in the mind of the gods," the Stranger said. "They would build a city here. I cannot build palaces, but I can build great walls that can never be overthrown. Let me build the wall round your city."

"How long will it take you to build a wall that will go round our city?" said the father of the gods.

"A year, O Odin," said the Stranger.

Now Odin knew that if a great wall could be built around it the gods would not have to spend all their time defending their city, Asgard, from the giants, and he knew that if As-gard were protected, he himself could go amongst men and teach them and help them. He thought that no payment the Stranger could ask would be too much for the building of that wall.

That day the Stranger came to the council of the gods, and he swore that in a year he would have the great wall built. Then Odin made oath that the gods would give him what he asked in payment if the wall was finished to the last stone in a year from that day.

The Stranger went away and came back on the morrow. It was the first day of summer when he started work. He brought no one to help him except a great horse.

Now the gods thought that this horse would do no more than drag blocks of stone for the building of the wall. But the horse did more than this. He set the stones in their places and mortared them together. And day and night and by light and dark the horse worked, and soon a great wall was rising round the palaces that the gods themselves were building.

"What reward will the Stranger ask for the work he is doing for us?" the gods asked one another.

Odin went to the Stranger. "We marvel at the work you and your horse are doing for us," he said. "No one can doubt that the great wall of Asgard will be built up by the first day of summer. What reward do you claim? We would have it ready for you."

The Stranger turned from the work he was doing, leaving the great horse to pile up the blocks of stone. "O father of the gods," he said, "O Odin, the reward I shall ask for my work is the Sun and the Moon, and Freya, who watches over the flowers and grasses, for my wife."

Now when Odin heard this he was terribly angered, for the price the Stranger asked for his work was beyond all prices. He went amongst the other gods who were then building their shining palaces within the great wall and he told them what reward the Stranger had asked. The gods said, "Without the Sun and the Moon the world will wither away." And the goddesses said, "Without Freya all will be gloom in Asgard."

They would have let the wall remain unbuilt rather than let the Stranger have the reward he claimed for building it. But one who was in the company of the gods spoke. He was Loki, a being who only half belonged to the gods; his father was the Wind Giant. "Let the Stranger build the wall round Asgard," Loki said, "and I will find a way to make him give up the hard bargain he has made with the gods. Go to him and tell him that the wall must be finished by the first day of summer, and that if it is not finished to the last stone on that day the price he asks will not be given to him."

The gods went to the Stranger and they told him that if the last stone was not laid on the wall on the first day of the summer not Sol or Mani, the Sun and the Moon, nor Freya would be given him. And now they knew that the Stranger was one of the giants.

The giant and his great horse piled

up the wall more quickly than before. At night, while the giant slept, the horse worked on and on, hauling up stones and laying them on the wall with his great forefeet. And day by day the wall around Asgard grew higher and higher.

But the gods had no joy in seeing that great wall rising higher and higher around their palaces. The giant and his horse would finish the work by the first day of summer, and then he would take the Sun and the Moon, Sol and Mani, and Freya away with him.

But Loki was not disturbed. He kept telling the gods that he would find a way to prevent him from finishing his work, and thus he would make the giant forfeit the terrible price he had led Odin to promise him.

It was three days to summertime. All the wall was finished except the gateway. Over the gateway a stone was still to be placed. And the giant, before he went to sleep, bade his horse haul up a great block of stone so that they might put it above the gateway in the morning, and so finish the work two full days before summer.

It happened to be a beautiful moonlit night. Svadilfare, the giant's great horse, was hauling the largest stone he ever hauled when he saw a little mare come galloping towards him. The great horse had never seen so pretty a little mare and he looked at her with surprise.

"Svadilfare, slave," said the little mare to him and went frisking past. Svadilfare put down the stone he was hauling and called to the little mare. She came back to him. "Why do you call me 'Svadilfare, slave'?" said the great horse.

"Because you have to work night and day for your master," said the little mare. "He keeps you working, working, working, and never lets you enjoy yourself. You dare not leave that stone down and come and play with me."

"Who told you I dare not do it?" said Svadilfare.

"I know you daren't do it," said the little mare, and she kicked up her heels and ran across the moonlit meadow.

Now the truth is that Svadilfare was tired of working day and night. When he saw the little mare go galloping off he became suddenly discontented. He left the stone he was hauling on the ground. He looked round and he saw the little mare looking back at him. He galloped after her.

He did not catch up on the little mare. She went on swiftly before him. On she went over the moonlit meadow, turning and looking back now and again at the great Svadilfare, who came heavily after her. Down the mountainside the mare went, and Svadilfare, who now rejoiced in his liberty and in the freshness of the wind and in the smell of the flowers, still followed her. With the morning's light they came near a cave and the little mare went into it. They went through the cave. Then Svadilfare caught up on the little mare and the two went wandering together, the little mare telling Svad-

MYTHS, FABLES, AND LEGENDS

ilfare stories of the Dwarfs and the Elves.

They came to a grove and they stayed together in it, the little mare playing so nicely with him that the great horse forgot all about time passing. And while they were in the grove the giant was going up and down, searching for his great horse.

He had come to the wall in the morning, expecting to put the stone over the gateway and so finish his work. But the stone that was to be lifted up was not near him. He called for Svadilfare, but his great horse did not come. He went to search for him, and he searched all down the mountainside and he searched as far across the earth as the realm of the giants. But he did not find Svadilfare.

The gods saw the first day of summer come and the gateway of the wall stand unfinished. They said to each other that if it were not finished by the evening they need not give Sol and Mani to the giant, nor the maiden Freya to be his wife. The hours of the summer day went past and the giant did not raise the stone over the gateway. In the evening he came before them.

"Your work is not finished," Odin said. "You forced us to a hard bargain and now we need not keep it with you. You shall not be given Sol and Mani nor the maiden Freya."

"Only the wall I have built is so strong I would tear it down," said the giant. He tried to throw down one of the palaces, but the gods laid hands on him and thrust him outside the wall he had built. "Go, and trouble Asgard no more," Odin commanded.

Then Loki returned to Asgard. He told the gods how he had transformed himself into a little mare and had led away Svadilfare, the giant's great horse. And the gods sat in their golden palaces behind the great wall and rejoiced that their city was now secure, and that no enemy could ever enter it or overthrow it. But Odin, the father of the gods, as he sat upon his throne was sad in his heart, sad that the gods had got their wall built by a trick; that oaths had been broken, and that a blow had been struck in injustice in Asgard.

Understanding Literature

1. Why are the giants and the gods constantly fighting one another?
2. Odin, the father of the gods, wants a wall built around Asgard for what two reasons?
3. Describe the trick that Loki plays on the Stranger and Svadilfare to keep them from finishing the wall.
4. Why is Odin the only god who is unhappy about the way the Stranger has been tricked?
5. With what in Greek mythology does Asgard compare? With whom does Odin compare?
6. Which common human qualities are portrayed in this myth?

As you read, note the difference between the climate and country in which the gods live and the climate and country of the giants.

The Apples of Idun

Olivia E. Coolidge

ALLFATHER ODIN was traveling with Loki and Honer in desolate wastes where they could discover nothing to eat. "Let us go down into this valley ahead," said Loki. "The pasture looks green by the river, and we may find deer."

"I see oxen in the shade of those oaks," replied Odin. "By all means let us go down."

The gods turned their steps to the valley, but the way was long, and the midsummer sun was at its height. Bees buzzed in the heath flowers, rabbits kicked up their heels as they fled to a safer patch of grass. Skylarks overhead filled the air with loud music. "They all feed while we stay hungry," grumbled Loki. "In Asgard we live like true gods. Here I am empty and hot, and my feet are sore. What is the use of such journeys?"

Odin smiled. "We should learn to know the earth because it is ours," he replied. "Sometimes we ride the clouds or fly on wings like the birds, but often we must travel as men do, yard by yard over stone after stone. We shall always remember these hills,

their sandy soil, their sparse yellow flowers, their little dried pines, and the green valley below."

"We shall indeed," muttered Loki. "It is a memory I well could have spared."

Dusty and hot, the travelers entered the valley as the long summer evening was drawing on. They paused to drink at the river, but they did not linger, for they were faint with hunger, and the grass was now softer under their feet. Beneath three spreading oaks they killed an ox and busied themselves preparing their meal. A pile of dry branches was collected, the ox was cut up, water fetched and thrown in the pot. At last the three gods could sit down, their feet out before them, and their backs to the trunk of a tree. On the fire rested their cooking pot, its great lid already quivering as little spurts of water escaped to fall hissing into the flames. A savory smell arose.

"I can wait no longer!" exclaimed Loki. Odin smiled as he closed his keen blue eye. Loki jumped up and, running to the fire, took a look at the stew. He seized a pointed stick to lift out one of the shoulders. "Raw!" he said in disgust. "Still perfectly raw!" He banged down the lid.

Odin smiled again. Silence fell. The skylark was weary, but the melodious thrush began her evening song. The grass was golden with buttercups. A kingfisher flashed over the stream. The smell of cooking became very pleasant and caused Odin to open his eye. "You might try the stew now," he said to Loki. "I should think we had given it time."

"I do all the work," grumbled Loki, but he got up and went to the fire. "Raw!" he said again in a fury.

This time Odin was interested and sat straight up. "Surely not," he remarked.

"Look at it!" cried Loki brandishing a piece on his stick. "Still as red as it was when we put it in. It's not reasonable!"

"It is certainly strange," replied Odin. "Well, put it back and pile up the fire."

"I am faint with hunger," complained Loki, "and everything falls on me." He piled on some more wood, still grumbling, before he came back and flung himself down on the grass.

A long time passed. The sun was behind the hills by now, and Odin drew his blue cloak about him. The three gods dozed no more, but sat with their hungry eyes fixed on the iron pot. "If it is not done by now, it never will be," said Odin at last. He got up himself, but he fared no better than Loki. The meat smelled appetizing, and the water was boiling and bubbling around it. Never-

theless when Odin lifted a piece from the pot, he found it raw and cold. "There is some magic spell at work here," he declared.

"I can cook your meat," cried a hoarse voice from above them. The three gods looked up. High in the oak tree was sitting an eagle so huge that the great branch bent beneath his weight like a tiny twig. "Give me a portion of your supper," he said. "Let me take my choice before you begin, and the meal shall be done in an instant."

"Willingly," answered Odin, uncovering the pot once more.

The creature leaped into the air with a whirring of wings and came sailing down to the fire, claws and beak outstretched. Quickly he snatched up half of the ox and was back in the tree with his dripping burden before the gods could utter a sound. He laid his prey in a crotch and swooped again to seize the other half, leaving the gods nothing but water.

Loki was beside himself with passion. "You thief!" he screamed, and snatching up one of the branches he had laid by to replenish the fire, he struck at the eagle as it turned to make for the oak. The branch hit full on the bird's back and stuck there as if glued, while Loki's hands adhered to the other end. The creature gave a sharp screech of laughter and flew off, dragging Loki after him. He skimmed over the ground so that the unfortunate god was pulled over stones and through briars, yelling that his arms were being torn from their sockets.

In a second or two his shrieks were already coming faintly, and in another moment the pair were over the hills out of hearing. "Let him go," said Odin, "and we will slaughter another ox. I can do nothing for Loki, who is in the power of a giant. He is cunning enough to get free from a dozen enchantments and will certainly join us again before we come to our journey's end."

Sure enough, on the next day Loki met them. He was covered with scratches, and the knees of his leggings were in holes, but he was well enough, though sulky.

"How did you get away?" asked his companions.

"He dropped me after a while," said Loki sullenly. "I suppose he had enough of it. My arms were almost pulled off."

"It is strange that he let you go without ransom," said Odin.

"Well he did," lied Loki, "though he might have dragged me forever for all the help I got from you." He strode on ahead, looking around furiously from time to time to see that the two gods were not laughing together behind his back.

The next day Idun,[1] the youth goddess, was sitting in her attic chamber in Asgard, looking out from her window at the flowering cherry trees. It was always spring in Idun's garden, where the scent of white mayflower lay heavy on the air. A cuckoo called in the distance, and on the window ledge perched a robin close by the goddess's hand. She looked around to see Loki entering, and her

1 **Idun** (ē′dōͦn).

MYTHS, FABLES, AND LEGENDS

fair blue eyes lighted up with a smile. Even Loki, the faithless one, was welcome to Idun, who loved and trusted all.

"You have been on a long journey, Loki," she said gaily, "and I think you have come back for an apple from me." With that she picked up a little gold casket which sat on the bench by her side. She put her hand in and took out an apple for him, all rosy and golden. From it came a savor so sweet that with a flutter of wings the birds in the orchard came flocking to her window. Blackbirds, starlings, and doves jostled one another for space on the ledges, yet dared not come in, for fair Idun raised her arm and gently barred their path.

As Loki bit into the apple, his bruises felt no longer sore. The fruits of Idun, which were the apples of youth, sent new strength through his limbs. A wild desire seized him to go out in the sunlight, to wrestle, to swim, or even to start another of these toilsome journeys which Odin loved to make through the world.

Idun turned to the casket and shut it. As she did so, there was a faint, musical sound. "You hear," she smiled. "There is already another apple within."

"Idun," said Loki earnestly, "these are wonderful fruits, but out in the forest is a tree with apples of silver and gold. Music plays through its branches, which bear blossoms sweet as the wild rose together with the marvelous fruit. You know we eat your apples daily to keep us young, but they say that one of these others

will bring immortal youth which needs no renewal."

"It is not true," cried Idun, blushing indignantly. "There are no apples better than mine."

"Come out into the woods and look, then," begged Loki. "Bring your casket with you that we may compare the fruits."

"We must go secretly," said she. "I cannot believe you, and I would not have it said that I doubted my apples at all."

Loki and Idun stole out of Asgard into the wild, dark woods. "Come this way, Idun," said Loki, smiling down at her as he put his hand on her arm.

"The sun is sinking," said Idun. "Is the tree very far away?"

"Not so far, and the moon is rising. Besides, the golden fruit will light our path." He guided her up a steep hill. "From the top where it is rocky and bare," said he, "you can look down into the next valley and see the tree gleam. From there our road will be easy." He hurried her up the slope.

The sun had quite disappeared when Idun stood on the rock gazing out over the valley, which was half hidden in the gathering dark. "Why, there is no light to be seen!" said she in a disappointed tone. Loki made no answer, but stood looking up at the faint stars.

"Thjasse! Great Thjasse!" cried he.

"Loki," said she anxiously, pulling at his arm. "Loki, there is no light in the valley, and a cloud is covering the moon!"

"Thjasse! Great Thjasse!" cried

Loki again. "Here is Idun, the ransom I promised when you released me from the stick. Take her and let me go home."

There was no cloud over the moon, only the wings of an enormous eagle. Idun could see his red eyes and the great claws outstretched. She screamed and covered her face as the monster clutched her. Loki heard cry after cry as the two vanished into the dark.

Next morning the gods who came to the garden of Idun found it deserted, but at first they were in no wise alarmed. "She is visiting Gerd or Freyja," they said to one another. "Tomorrow she will surely be here."

The next day Idun was still absent, and in seven days more she had not returned. The blossoms on her trees had turned brown, the birds were all fled, and a chill had crept into the air. Without the magic apples of youth, Odin's hair became straggling and thin. Thor's bushy beard was streaked with gray. Fair Freyja stayed within doors, or veiled her face if she needed to walk abroad.

At last the gods met in council. All denied knowledge of Idun, Loki among the rest. "Well, then," said Odin, "where did each one of you see her last?"

Nearly all the gods had seen her last in her chamber or her garden. One, however, replied, "Idun stole out of Asgard with Loki as though they wished to escape unseen."

All turned on Loki. Thor clutched him tightly by the shoulder until he cried out in pain.

"Let me go," he cried. "I will con- fess that I gave her to Thjasse, the giant. It was he who, disguised as an eagle, dragged me on the end of a stick. Odin left me to ransom my life as best I could, so I promised him Idun. What else could I do?"

"Let me crush him," shouted Thor.

"By no means," answered Allfather Odin. "Release him. I think he has spoken well. Loki freed himself from the giant, but the price he paid was too high. It remains for him to rescue sweet Idun or else perish at the hands of Thor."

"Freyja," cried Loki, "lend me your garment of feathers. I will fly as a falcon to Giantland and return with fair Idun or die."

Loki flew as a falcon from Asgard, soared over the hills and the valleys, and skimmed over the bottomless sea. At last the gray cliffs of Giantland towered above him, shrouded in mist. He turned and flew to his left hand, seeking some inlet, for the cliffs went up into the clouds where he had not strength to soar. At last he found a place where a great gray river tumbled into the ocean through a gap in the dripping rocks. It seemed a forbidding inlet, but it was welcome to him, for his wings were icy and numb. He entered the gorge of the river and saw where the hall of the giant, Thjasse, towered on the hillside, a fortress of ice and rock.

The little falcon flew by the base of Thjasse's wall and alighted in a small crevice at its foot where a great bird had once built a nest. He huddled deep in the straw, while the wet mist swirled outside, and the damp icicles dripped slowly from the crags. It was dry in the little hollow, so that presently he found himself rested and warm. Now for it! he thought as he crawled out of his hole, launched himself into the air, and began the steep climb towards the upper windows where he hoped to find Idun's bower.

The falcon went spiraling upwards past the sheer face of the rocky wall which towered into the sky. Long before he came to the windows, his heart was beating fast, and his wings were failing. Here, however, the stones were smooth, and he could find no perch. Therefore, though he circled ever more slowly, he had to fly on.

At last it seemed to him he could go no higher. Every time his circle brought him close to the rock, the same worn stones met his gaze. He glanced despairingly downward. Nothing was to be seen there but mist. I dare not fall, he said to himself as with a mighty effort he rose another foot or two. This time as he approached the wall, he saw a break in the rock. It was the window of Idun's chamber above the end of the giant's great hall. Hope gave him renewed strength, and with a fierce beating of wings he circled once more, reached the ledge, and dropped half dead upon it, close beside Idun's hand.

Idun was sitting huddled up in the corner of a vast chair, her feet yards from the stone floor of the chamber, looking out into the mist. Tears ran down her cheeks as she gazed out towards Asgard, thinking of the beautiful earth, of her garden, and of the

gods who loved her as though she were daughter to them all. She stretched out her hands to the bird with a cry of delight, dried it softly with her robe, set it on her shoulder, and warmed it against her cheek.

"Idun," said Loki at last in gentle tones, "I will take you to Asgard. Do not be afraid to trust me, for I come at the risk of my life."

Idun started at Loki's voice, but she answered eagerly, "I will do anything you wish if you will only carry me away."

"Where is the giant?"

"Gone forth to fish. If the catch is good, he will not return till dark."

"Trust me, then," said Loki from the window ledge. He touched her with the tip of his wing, and in an instant she and her casket shrank to the size of a thumbnail. Loki laid her gently in a walnut shell, and gathering the nut in his claws, leaped into the air.

They were over the gray sea when they came out of the mist and saw the earth as a strip of green on the distant shore. Every moment the hills became clearer until soon they were over the land. Loki cast a long look behind him and saw a black speck far off on the edge of the sky. "It is the eagle!" he said to himself as he flew on like an arrow.

Over the mountains he looked back again. The bird was much nearer by now. He could see its great wings cleaving the air, and terror gave him strength to speed like the wind. When the ramparts of Asgard came into view, he did not need to look back, for he could hear

the air whistling through the wings of the eagle behind him. With the fury of despair he raced for home.

"It is Loki!" cried the gods as they crowded the ramparts. "It is Loki, and behind him the eagle."

"Set fire on the ramparts," cried Allfather Odin. "Whether Loki is slain or not, the giant shall never escape."

Swiftly the gods heaped shavings along the walls and stood by with torches. The birds were so close by now that they could see the great beak of the eagle touch the feathers on Loki's tail. Loki felt his enemy and knew at the same time that he was almost home. With a furious spurt he shot over the ramparts and tumbled like a stone in the courtyard on the other side.

Already the gods had set fire to their shavings, and flame leaped instantly up from the wall. The eagle, coming too fast to stop himself, lurched right through the fire, setting his wings ablaze. Suddenly he fell from the air and alighted in the courtyard in his own shape of a monstrous man with his garments smoking about him and his great beard singed with flame. He glared at them all, bellowing furiously, but before he could rise, Thor swung his hammer, Mjolnir, that never missed its mark.

That night the gods drank to the rescue of Idun, and the death of the giant, while Loki sat boasting among them as if the trouble had been none of his fault.

Understanding Literature

1. What reason does Odin give Loki for their traveling on the earth?
2. What problem do Loki and Odin have as they try to cook their food and how does each react to the problem?
3. How did Loki get Idun to leave the protective walls of Asgard?
4. What are the differences between the climate and country in which the gods live and the climate and country in which the giants live?

Further Activities

1. Very often the words an author chooses will be so sharp and clear that the reader will have a distinct mental picture of the scene described. In literature this is called *visual imagery*. There are also other kinds of imagery. For example, an author may handle a description so skillfully that you can almost feel heat rising from the sands of the desert. Or the description of a newly mown field may be written so accurately and sensitively that you can almost smell the fresh grass. In other words, it is often the imagery and its appeal to the senses of sight, touch, smell, sound, or taste that move you to share in the pain, sorrow, or happiness of a work of literature.

   In "The Apples of Idun" there is imagery in the section in which Loki as a falcon flies to rescue Idun. Find passages in which you can almost feel the intense cold and dampness, and where you can actually visualize the scene described, or share the sensation of height when Loki attempts to reach Idun's chamber. What words or group of words are particularly effective in making the imagery more vivid to you?

2. Myths attempt to explain things which man finds difficult to understand. Using your imagination and inventing your own gods and goddesses, create an original myth to explain how man came to have one or two of his many good qualities, such as bravery, kindness, love, or virtue.

3. You have now read about many different gods and goddesses with many different types of power. In one or two well-organized paragraphs, tell which god you would prefer to be if by magic you could become him. Explain why.

THE
FABLES
OF
ÆSOP

from The Fables of Aesop

edited by **Joseph Jacobs**

As you have seen, myths are about supernatural beings and events. They deal with religious rites and beliefs, and were used, in general, to explain the mysteries of nature.

The *fable*, another type of story, usually enforces some useful truth or moral and is frequently narrated or acted by animals; thus fables are sometimes called *beast fables*. Fables are usually connected with the name of Aesop, who is supposed to have lived between 620 and 560 B.C. While some authorities believe there was no such person, others think he is a legendary figure, that is, a man who probably lived although no one can actually prove that he did.

THE MILKMAID AND HER PAIL

PATTY, THE MILKMAID, was going to market carrying her milk in a pail on her head. As she went along she began calculating what she would do with the money she would get for the milk. "I'll buy some fowls from Farmer Brown," said she, "and they will lay eggs each morning, which I will sell to the parson's wife. With the money that I get from the sale of these eggs I'll buy myself a new dimity frock and a chip hat; and when I go to market, won't all the young men come up and speak to me! Polly Shaw will be that jealous; but I don't care. I shall just look at her and toss my head like this." As she spoke, she tossed her head back, the pail fell off it and all the milk was spilt. So she had to go home and tell her mother what had occurred.

"Ah, my child," said her mother,

"Do not count your chickens before they are hatched."

THE EAGLE AND THE ARROW

AN EAGLE WAS soaring through the air when suddenly it heard the whizz of an arrow, and felt itself wounded to death. Slowly it fluttered down to the earth, with its lifeblood pouring out of it. Looking down upon the arrow with which it had been pierced, it found that the haft[1] of the arrow had been feathered with one

1 haft: handle.

of its own plumes. "Alas!" it cried, as it died,

"We often give our enemies the means for our own destruction."

THE JAY AND THE PEACOCKS

A JAY venturing into a yard where peacocks used to walk, found there a number of feathers which had fallen from the peacocks when they were molting.[2] He tied them all to his tail and strutted down toward the peacocks. When he came near them they soon discovered the cheat, and striding up to him pecked at him and plucked away his borrowed plumes. So the jay could do no better than go back to the other jays, who had watched his behavior from a distance; but they were equally annoyed with him, and told him:

"It is not only fine feathers that make fine birds."

THE HARES AND THE FROGS

THE HARES WERE so persecuted by the other beasts, they did not know where to go. As soon as they saw a single animal approach them, off they used to run. One day they saw a troop of wild horses stampeding about, and in quite a panic all the hares scuttled off to a lake hard by, determined to drown themselves rather than live in such a continual state of fear. But just as they got near the bank of the lake, a troop of frogs, frightened in their turn by the approach of the hares, scuttled off, and jumped into the water. "Truly," said one of the hares, "things are not so bad as they seem:

"There is always someone worse off than yourself."

THE LION AND THE MOUSE

ONCE WHEN A lion was asleep a little mouse began running up and down upon him; this soon wakened the lion, who placed his huge paw upon him, and opened his big jaws to swallow him. "Pardon, O King," cried the little mouse; "forgive me this time, I shall never forget it: who knows but what I may be able to do you a turn some of these days?" The lion was so tickled at the idea of the mouse being able to help him, that he lifted up his paw and let him go. Some time after the lion was caught in a trap, and the hunters, who desired to carry him alive to the king, tied him to a tree while they went in search of a wagon to carry him on. Just then the little mouse happened to pass by, and seeing the sad plight[3] in which the lion was, went up to him and soon gnawed away the ropes that bound the king of the beasts. "Was I not right?" said the little mouse.

"Little friends may prove great friends."

THE TOWN MOUSE AND THE COUNTRY MOUSE

NOW YOU MUST know that a town mouse once upon a time went on a visit to his cousin in the country.

---

2 **molting:** shedding their feathers.

3 **plight:** situation; condition.

MYTHS, FABLES, AND LEGENDS

He was rough and ready, this cousin, but he loved his town friend and made him heartily welcome. Beans and bacon, cheese and bread, were all he had to offer, but he offered them freely. The town mouse rather turned up his long nose at this country fare, and said: "I cannot understand, Cousin, how you can put up with such poor food as this, but of course you cannot expect anything better in the country; come you with me and I will show you how to live. When you have been in town a week you will wonder how you could ever have stood a country life." No sooner said than done: the two mice set off for the town and arrived at the town mouse's residence late at night. "You will want some refreshment after our long journey," said the polite town mouse, and took his friend into the grand dining room. There they found the remains of a fine feast, and soon the two mice were eating up jellies and cakes and all that was nice. Suddenly they heard growling and barking. "What is that?" said the country mouse. "It is only the dogs of the house," answered the other. "Only!" said the country mouse. "I do not like that music at my dinner." Just at that moment the door flew open, in came two huge mastiffs, and the two mice had to scamper down and run off. "Good-by, Cousin," said the country mouse. "What! Going so soon?" said the other. "Yes," he replied;

"Better beans and bacon in peace than cakes and ale in fear."

THE FOX AND THE CROW

A FOX ONCE saw a crow fly off with a piece of cheese in its beak and settle on a branch of a tree. "That's for me, as I am a fox," said Master Reynard, and he walked up to the foot of the tree. "Good day, Mistress Crow," he cried. "How well you are looking today: how glossy your feathers; how bright your eye. I feel sure your voice must surpass that of other birds, just as your figure does; let me hear but one song from you that I may greet you as the queen of birds." The crow lifted up her head and began to caw her best, but the moment she opened her mouth the piece of cheese fell to the ground, only to be snapped up by Master Fox. "That will do," said he. "That was all I wanted. In exchange for your cheese I will give you a piece of advice for the future—

"Do not trust flatterers."

Understanding Literature

1. The italicized words at the end of each of these fables explain the moral or lesson being taught. Explain each moral in your own words.
2. To what extent is each of these morals a good lesson even for the present day? In what situations might these morals be applied?

3. Certain authorities think that some of the fables were written to be used for political purposes. Could any of these fables you have just read be used in some way as advice to politicians? as advice to a country about its relationship with another country?
4. What are the characteristics of the fable which make it enjoyable reading?

Further Activity

Try to write a fable, modeled on Aesop's, to illustrate one of the following sayings:

1. Self-conceit may lead to self-destruction.
2. It is easy to be brave from a safe distance.
3. Injuries may be forgiven, but not forgotten.
4. Familiarity breeds contempt.
5. It is best to prepare for the days of necessity.
6. Appearances are deceptive.
7. United we stand, divided we fall.

Fables of India

from The Fables of India

adapted by **Joseph Gaer**

Although Aesop is the name most of you immediately associate with fables, the Hindus of India were actually the first *fablers*. In India three main collections of fables exist. The ones which you are about to read are from *The Jataka*, a collection of stories about the many incarnations of the Buddha, the great religious teacher of India. These fables have been used to instruct the children of India.

The Monkey Gardeners

In the royal gardens of Benares,[1] a group of monkeys were allowed to roam and do as they pleased. These monkeys were great mimics. If the King came by, strolling along one of the paths, they would line up and walk behind him, just as straight and with as much dignity. If the young prince came along playing a game, they pretended they too were playing the same game. Most of all they liked to imitate the gardener. They followed him wherever he went, and whatever his task, they all imitated his motions.

A great festival was proclaimed throughout the city one day, and the gardener was eager to attend the ceremonies. But he had newly transplanted trees in the garden and did not know whom he could get to water them during the day. Then he remembered how well the monkeys imitated everything he did, and he went to their leader and said:

"His Majesty the King bestowed a great honor on you in permitting you to remain in the gardens, where you can feed on all the fruit."

"Oh, yes!" replied the monkey.

"Now there is a great festivity in the city to which I must go," the gardener went on. "To show your gratitude to His Majesty, do you think you can water the young trees while I am gone?"

"Oh, yes!" said the monkey, eagerly.

"But remember, do not waste any water," said the gardener.

"Oh, yes!" the monkey assured him.

The gardener went off to the festivities. The monkeys went happily to work and gathered together all the waterskins. They filled the containers with water and went right out to the newly planted young trees.

---

1 **Benares** (bə nä′rĭz): holy city of the Hindus in India.

"Remember," commanded the leader, "do not waste any water!"

"How shall we know how much is enough, how much is too little, and how much is too much?" asked the monkeys.

"That is very simple," said he. "First you pull up the tree and look at the size of the roots. Those with long roots need much water; those with short roots need only a little water."

"How wise you are!" said all the other monkeys.

They began industriously pulling up all the newly planted trees, and watered each according to the length of its roots, just as they had been instructed.

At this point a wise man came by and noticed what the monkeys were doing. He asked them why they pulled up the trees before they watered them.

"Because we must water them according to the length of their roots," they explained.

And the wise man (who was the Bodisat)[2] said:

"Like these monkeys turned gardeners, the ignorant and the foolish, even in their desire to do good, only succeed in doing harm."

THE FOX IN SAINT'S CLOTHING

ONE DAY a fox spied a flock of guinea hens and roosters. He stopped at a respectful distance, balancing himself with great skill on one foot. Then he turned his head up to the sky and opened his mouth as wide as he could.

The fowl noticed this curious pose and came closer to observe him. One cock finally asked:

"What is your name?"

"My name is Saintly," answered the fox without turning his head.

"Why do you stand on one leg?" asked a hen.

"Because my great weight would be too much for the earth to bear if I stood on it with all my four legs," answered the fox, without moving a hairsbreadth.

"Why do you keep your mouth open and swallow the wind?" asked another guinea hen.

"Because I live on air. It is my only food," the fox replied.

"Why do you keep your head turned up toward the sky?" asked a young cock.

"Because I worship the sun," answered the fox.

The guinea hens looked at the yellow skin of the scrawny fox and were convinced that he was wearing the yellow robe of a beggar monk.

"What saintliness!" they exclaimed in awe, and the entire flock paid homage[3] to him.

When they began to leave, the fox announced: "I shall be here again tomorrow to pray on this same spot, and I wish you would come and pray with me."

The next day the fox appeared in the same spot, and the flock of guinea hens came again to pay their respects and to pray with him. As they be-

2 the Bodisat: the Buddha.

3 homage (hŏm'ĭj): respect.

gan to leave, the fox watched them from the corners of his eyes. When the last of the hens was ready to follow the flock, he caught her with great dexterity,[4] quickly gobbled her up, swiftly wiped his mouth, and returned to his praying pose.

This went on for several days, until the guinea hens began to notice how their number was diminishing. One powerful cock had been suspicious of the fox from the start, and he decided to find out whether his suspicions were justified.

The next time they came to pay their respects to the pious fox, the young cock straggled behind and was the last to leave.

Whereupon the fox sprang at him. But the cock turned quickly. He flew at the fox and pecked at his eyes, crowing loud enough for all the guinea hens to hear him.

"Now we know the reason for your coming here and pretending to be a saint!"

Back trooped all the other hens and cocks and they pecked the fox to death. Then they thanked the young cock (who was the Bodisat in this form) for having saved the flock from the hypocritical[5] fox.

THE TALKATIVE TORTOISE

IN A POND in the Himalaya Mountains there once lived a handsomely marked young tortoise. He was not vicious like his cousin the snapping turtle, but he had the failing of liking to talk too much. Two wild ducks

4 **dexterity:** quickness; skill.
5 **hypocritical:** insincere; double-dealing.

came to the pond in search of food one day, and the tortoise started to talk to them almost as soon as they alighted on the water.

Nevertheless the ducks and the tortoise became great friends, and the ducks said one day:

"We have a fine home on Mount Beautiful in the Himalayas, next to the Cave of Gold. Why don't you come and live with us, friend Tortoise?"

"How can I, a tortoise, get up to your place?"

"We thought of that," said the wild ducks. "We can take you to our home, if only you can keep from talking and not say a single word until we get there. Do you think you can do that and keep your mouth closed all that time?"

"I certainly can do that!" the tortoise assured them.

The ducks took a sturdy stick and asked the tortoise to bite hard on the center. Then they each took hold of an end of the stick with their strong bills and rose into the air, swiftly flying toward the mountains.

As they flew over the palace of the King of Benares, a number of village children saw the wild ducks in flight, carrying a tortoise on a stick.

"Look! Look! Two wild ducks are carrying a tortoise on a stick!" they shouted excitedly to their parents.

Their outcries angered the tortoise, and he wanted to shout back at them:

"If my friends want to carry me like this, what affair is that of yours, you wretches!"

But when he opened his mouth to

MYTHS, FABLES, AND LEGENDS

speak, he let go of the stick and fell with great force into the open courtyard of the palace; and he split in two.

The king's attendants came running up in excitement, shouting: "A tortoise has fallen out of the sky into the courtyard!"

Everyone, including the king and his Brahman and all his courtiers, gathered around the spot where the dead tortoise lay.

The king turned and asked the Brahman: "Teacher! What made this creature fall here?"

Now, this king was very talkative and no one could ever get a word in edgewise. The Brahman gladly took this opportunity to admonish him. He answered:

"My King, his tongue killed him."

The king looked at him in amazement. And he asked: "How could his tongue bring him to his death?"

"O King, this tortoise held secure
A stick between his teeth;
But when he tried to chatter
He quickly met this fate.

Behold him, O excellent of strength,
And speak not out of season!
You see how this tortoise fell—
He talked too much and that's the reason!"

The king asked: "Are you referring to me, Teacher?"

And the teacher (who was the Bodisat born as a Brahman) replied: "O Great King! Be it you, or be it another. Whoever talks too much sooner or later meets with disaster."

Understanding Literature

1. What are the two morals taught in "The Monkey Gardeners"?
2. What is the moral of each of the other fables?
3. In a Jataka there is always one character who is the Bodisat in disguise. What three roles does the Bodisat assume in the three fables you have just read?
4. Each of the three fables which you have just studied is compactly and concisely written. In each of them the setting and characters are made clear. What is the setting for each fable? What is the problem? Who are the main characters?
5. The Jatakas have been used to teach or instruct the children of India. Why would teaching the children through the use of fables or beast fables be more effective than issuing commands or briefly stating what is right and what is wrong?
6. In what situations would the lessons given in the three fables prove helpful?

Further Activity

In the study of literature you may often be asked to *paraphrase* a passage from a selection. To paraphrase is to restate and give the meaning of a passage in your own words. To be able to paraphrase well indicates that you understand thoroughly what you have read. Paraphrase in writing the lesson taught in each of the three Jatakas or paraphrase one complete fable. Be brief, but do not omit anything of importance.

Focusing on Words

The meaning of a word is often made partly clear by the sentence in which it occurs. Write down what you think each of the italicized words in the following sentences means; then check your answers in the glossary or a dictionary.

1. ". . . the guinea hens began to notice how their number was *diminishing.*"
2. "He was not *vicious* like his cousin the snapping turtle. . . ."
3. "The Brahman gladly took this opportunity to *admonish* him."

The *Iliad* and the *Odyssey*, summarized here, are two famous epic poems believed to have been written by a Greek poet, Homer, who probably lived around 700 or 800 B.C. An *epic* is a long poem which tells a story about one hero—a human hero—and describes deeds of great or even superhuman courage. You will notice in these selections that the gods of Olympus are still powerful and influential, but the center of interest is now man on earth.

Homer, the Great Storyteller

Eva March Tappan

A LONG, LONG time ago—perhaps three thousands years or more—there was a man named Homer. No one knows much about him; but there are legends that he was born on the island of Chios and that he was blind. He wandered about the land, homeless, but welcome wherever he chose to go, because he was a poet. He once described how a blind poet was treated at a great banquet, and probably that is the way in which people treated him. He said that when the feast was ready, a page was sent to lead in the honored guest. A silver-studded chair was brought forward for him and set against a pillar. On the pillar the page hung his harp, so near him that he could touch it if he wished. A little table was placed before him, and on it was put a tray spread with food and wine. When the feasting was at an end, he sang a glorious song of the mighty deeds of men. The Greeks liked to hear stories just as well as the people of today, and they shouted with delight. Then they all went out to the racecourse, the page leading the blind singer carefully along the way. There were races and wrestling matches and boxing and throwing of the discus. After this, the poet took his harp and stepped to the center of the circle. The young men gathered around him eagerly, and he chanted a story of Ares, the war god, and Aphrodite, goddess of beauty and love.

Homer composed two great poems. One is the *Iliad*, which takes its name from Ilium, or Troy, a town in Asia Minor. For ten long years the Greeks tried to capture Ilium. They had good reason for waging war against the Trojans, for Paris, son of the King of Troy, had stolen away the Grecian Helen, the most beautiful woman in the world. She was the wife of a Greek prince named Menelaus; and the other princes of Greece joined him in attacking Troy. They took some smaller places round about and divided the booty, as the custom was. In the tenth year of the war,

Achilles and Agamemnon, two of the greatest of the princes, quarreled about one of these divisions, and here the *Iliad* begins. Achilles was so angry that he took his followers, the Myrmidons, left the camp, and declared that he would have nothing more to do with the war, he would return to Greece.

Now the Greeks were in trouble, indeed, for Achilles was their most valiant leader, and his men were exceedingly brave soldiers. They sent his friend Patroclus to beg him to come back. Achilles would not yield, even to him; but he finally agreed to allow his followers to return and also to lend his armor and equipment to Patroclus.

When the Trojans saw the chariot and armor of Achilles, they ran for their lives, as Patroclus had expected; but at length Hector, son of King Priam, ventured to face his enemy, and Patroclus fell. Achilles was heartbroken. It was all his own fault, he declared, and he groaned so heavily that his wailing was heard in the depths of the ocean. He vowed that, come what might, he would be revenged. He went back to the camp and made up the quarrel with Agamemnon; and then he rushed forth into battle. The Trojans were so terrified that they all ran back into the city save one, Hector. But when Achilles dashed forward upon him, his heart failed, and he, too, ran for his life. Three times Achilles chased him around the walls of Troy, then thrust him through with his spear. He tied cords to the feet of his fallen enemy and dragged his body back

and forth before the eyes of the Trojans; and when the following morning had come, he dragged it twice around the tomb of Patroclus.

The Greeks believed that if a person's body had not received funeral rites, he would be condemned to wander for one hundred years on the banks of the Styx, the gloomy river of the dead; but Achilles declared in his wrath that the body of Hector should be thrown to the dogs. Then King Priam loaded into his litter rolls of handsome cloth, rich garments, and golden dishes, and made his way to the tent of the fierce warrior. "Your father is an old man like me," he pleaded. "Think of him and show pity. I have brought a wealth of ransom. Take it and give me the body of my son." The fiery Achilles yielded and even agreed to a twelve-days' truce so that the funeral might be celebrated with all due honor. The tale ends with the building of an immense pyre and the burning of the body of Hector.

Homer's second poem is the *Odyssey*. Troy finally fell into the hands of the Greeks, but Ulysses, or Odysseus,[1] one of the leaders, was unfortunate enough to be hated by Poseidon, god of the sea. His home was on the island of Ithaca; but before Poseidon would allow him to return to it, he drove the homesick wanderer back and forth over the Mediterranean Sea for ten long years and made him undergo all sorts of danger. The *Odyssey* tells the story of his wanderings and his wonderful ad-

1 **Odysseus** (ō dĭs′ūs).

ventures. First, he was driven by a storm to the land of the Lotus-eaters. Whoever ate the lotus forgot his home and friends, and cared for nothing but to stay in the lotus country and idle his life away in vain and empty dreams. Some of Odysseus's men tasted this fruit; and he had to drag them on board the ship and even tie them to the benches to keep them from staying behind.

Odysseus's second adventure was in the country of the Cyclopes,[2] monstrous giants, each having one huge eye in the middle of his forehead. One of these giants, Polyphemus,[3] found the Greeks in his cave when he drove home his sheep and goats. He devoured two of the men at once, and others on the following day. But Odysseus was planning revenge. He offered the giant a great bowl of wine, which pleased him mightily. "What is your name?" the Cyclops asked. "No man," replied Odysseus. Then Polyphemus promised him as a great favor that he should be the last of the company to be eaten. But when the giant was sleeping stupidly, Odysseus and his men took a stick of green olive wood as big as the mast of a ship, heated one end in the fire until it was a burning coal, and plunged it into the eye of Polyphemus. He roared with pain, and the other giants ran from all sides to his aid. "What is it? Who is murdering you?" they cried. "No man," howled the giant, "No man is killing me." "If it is no man," they said, "then your ill-ness comes from Zeus, and you must bear it. We can do nothing," and they went their way.

The Greeks made their escape, but it was not long before they were in trouble again. They landed on the floating island which was the home of Aeolus, god of the winds. He was kind and friendly, and when they departed, he gave Odysseus a leathern sack tied up with a silver cord. All the stormwinds were safely shut up in this sack; but Odysseus's men supposed it was full of treasure. They were so afraid they would not get their share that while their leader slept, they tore it open. Aeolus had given them a favorable breeze, and they were so close to their own island that they could see men heaping wood on the fires, but now the stormwinds rushed out of the bag, and the vessel was driven back again over the waters.

They landed on the island of the enchantress Circe,[4] who had an unpleasant habit of changing people into the animals that they most resembled. They passed by the Sirens, beautiful, treacherous maidens who sang so sweetly from a soft green meadow near the shore that no seamen who heard them could help throwing themselves into the water to make their way nearer to the marvelous music. The wise Odysseus had himself bound to the mast and forbade his sailors to free him, whatever he might say or do. Therefore he was able to hear the magical songs in safety. Neither did he lose his

2 **Cyclopes** (sī′klō′ pēz).
3 **Polyphemus** (pŏl′ĭ fē′məs).

4 **Circe** (sûr′sĭ).

vessel, for he had stopped up the ears of the sailors with wax. They passed between the snaky monster Scylla and the horrible whirlpool Charybdis;[5] and after many long years of wandering and hardship Odysseus arrived on the shore of his beloved Ithaca.

Penelope, wife of Odysseus, had been tormented by a throng of suitors, who for years had been feasting upon her food and wasting her property. Her son Telemachus[6] was only a youth and not yet strong enough to drive them away. Penelope never gave up the hope that Odysseus would return, and to gain time she put the suitors off by every device in her power. When everything else had failed, she began to weave a web in her loom, and promised that when it was done, she would choose among them. She worked at this for three years, and the suitors waited; but in the fourth year her maids found out the secret, that she was pulling out by night what she wove by day. In the very nick of time Odysseus appeared. He and Telemachus slew the wicked suitors and punished all who had been unfaithful in his absence. Then Telemachus and Penelope and the aged father of Odysseus rejoiced, for at last their lord had come to his own again.

These are bits of the stories that Homer tells in the *Iliad* and the *Odyssey*; but their greatest charm is in his manner of telling them. He seems to know just how each one of his characters feels. He understands the anger of Achilles, and he sympa-

5 **Charybdis** (kə rĭb′dĭs).
6 **Telemachus** (tə lĕm′ə kəs).

MYTHS, FABLES, AND LEGENDS

thizes with the sorrow of Hector's wife when the hero is going forth to battle. He knows how to use words so marvelously well that he can make one line sound like the tramping of horses on a plain and another like the beating of waves against the rocks. He describes every event as if he himself had seen it, and he never forgets to mention the little things which so many people pass over. Best of all, the stories are told so simply and naturally that, even after the many centuries, we can hardly help feeling that Homer is alive and is telling them directly to us.

Understanding Literature

1. Why was Homer always welcome wherever he went?
2. Summarize the cause and main events of the Trojan War as described in the *Iliad*.
3. Describe the adventures Odysseus has in traveling home after the Trojan War as related in the *Odyssey*.
4. What characteristics does Odysseus have that show the kind of man the Greeks admired and respected?
5. Tell the story of Penelope and her suitors.
6. In what ways are the gods involved in the tale?
7. Epics are often called *hero tales*. Why would the *Iliad* and the *Odyssey* be considered hero tales? How do hero tales differ from myths?
8. According to the author of this selection, why are these two great poems by Homer still enjoyed today?

Arthur may have been a real British chieftain or general who lived during the early 6th century; however, he is best known as a legendary king of Britain, famed for his virtue and valor. According to the numerous legends which grew up about him, knights rode out from his court to find adventure and to perform brave and daring deeds. In the 15th century, Sir Thomas Malory wrote a book based upon these legends about King Arthur and his court. The following selections are adapted from three of the stories in Malory's book. In these selections you will meet Arthur, Merlin the magician, the mysterious Lady of the Lake, and the treacherous Morgan le Fay.

Stories of King Arthur

Mary Macleod

The Marvel of the Sword

WHEN UTHER PENDRAGON, King of England, died, the country for a long while stood in great danger, for every lord that was mighty gathered his forces, and many wished to be king. For King Uther's own son, Prince Arthur, who should have succeeded him, was but a child, and Merlin, the mighty magician, had hidden him away.

Now a strange thing had happened at Arthur's birth, and this was how it was.

Some time before, Merlin had done Uther a great service, on condition that the King should grant him whatever he wished for. This the King swore a solemn oath to do. Then Merlin made him promise that when his child was born it should be delivered to Merlin to bring up as he chose, for this would be to the child's own great advantage. The King had given his promise so he was obliged to agree. Then Merlin said he knew a very true and faithful man, one of

King Uther's lords, by name Sir Ector, who had large possessions in many parts of England and Wales, and that the child should be given to him to bring up.

On the night the baby was born, while it was still unchristened, King Uther commanded two knights and two ladies to take it, wrapped in a cloth of gold, and deliver it to a poor man whom they would find waiting at the postern gate of the castle. This poor man was Merlin in disguise, although they did not know it. So the child was delivered unto Merlin and he carried him to Sir Ector, and made a holy man christen him, and named him Arthur; and Sir Ector's wife cherished him as her own child.

Within two years King Uther fell sick of a great malady, and for three days and three nights he was speechless. All the barons were in much sorrow, and asked Merlin what was best to be done.

"There is no remedy," said Merlin,

312   MYTHS, FABLES, AND LEGENDS

"God will have His Will. But look ye all, barons, come before King Uther tomorrow, and God will make him speak."

So the next day Merlin and all the barons came before the King, and Merlin said aloud to King Uther:

"Sir, after your days shall your son Arthur be king of this realm and all that belongs to it?"

Then Uther Pendragon turned to him and said in hearing of them all:

"I give my son Arthur God's blessing and mine, and bid him pray for my soul, and righteously and honorably claim the Crown, on forfeiture of my blessing."

And with that, King Uther died.

But Arthur was still only a baby, not two years old, and Merlin knew it would be no use yet to proclaim him king. For there were many powerful nobles in England in those days, who were all trying to get the kingdom for themselves, and perhaps they would kill the little prince. So there was much strife and debate in the land for a long time.

When several years had passed, Merlin went to the Archbishop of Canterbury and counseled him to send for all the lords of the realm, and all the gentlemen of arms, that they should come to London at Christmas, and for this cause—that a miracle would show who should be rightly king of the realm. So all the lords and gentlemen made themselves ready, and came to London, and long before dawn on Christmas Day they were all gathered in the great church of Saint Paul's to pray.

When the first service was over, there was seen in the churchyard a large stone, foursquare, like marble, and in the midst of it was like an anvil of steel, a foot high. In this was stuck by the point a beautiful sword, with naked blade, and there were letters written in gold about the sword, which said thus:

WHOSO PULLETH THIS SWORD OUT
OF THIS STONE AND ANVIL IS RIGHTLY
KING OF ALL ENGLAND.

Then the people marveled, and told it to the archbishop.

"I command," said the archbishop, "that you keep within the church, and pray unto God still; and that no man touch the sword till the service is over."

So when the prayers in church were over, all the lords went to behold the stone and the sword; and when they read the writing some of them—such as wished to be king—tried to pull the sword out of the anvil. But not one could make it stir.

"The man is not here, that shall achieve the sword," said the archbishop, "but doubt not God will make him known. But let us provide ten knights, men of good fame, to keep guard over the sword."

So it was ordained, and proclamation was made that everyone who wished might try to win the sword. And upon New Year's Day the barons arranged to have a great tournament, in which all knights who would joust or tourney might take a part. This was ordained to keep together the lords and commons, for the archbishop trusted that it would be made known who should win the sword.

How Arthur Was Crowned King

On New Year's Day, after church, the barons rode to the field, some to joust, and some to tourney, and so it happened that Sir Ector, who had large estates near London, came also to the tournament; and with him rode Sir Kay, his son, with young Arthur, his foster brother.

As they rode, Sir Kay found he had lost his sword, for he had left it at his father's lodging, so he begged young Arthur to go and fetch it for him.

"That will I, gladly," said Arthur, and he rode fast away.

But when he came to the house, he found no one at home to give him the sword, for every one had gone to see the jousting. Then Arthur was angry and said to himself:

"I will ride to the churchyard, and take the sword with me that sticketh in the stone, for my brother, Sir Kay, shall not be without a sword this day."

When he came to the churchyard he alighted, and tied his horse to the stile, and went to the tent. But he found there no knights, who should have been guarding the sword, for they were all away at the joust. Seizing the sword by the handle he lightly and fiercely pulled it out of the stone, then took his horse and rode his way, till he came to Sir Kay his brother, to whom he delivered the sword.

As soon as Sir Kay saw it, he knew well it was the sword of the Stone, so he rode to his father Sir Ector, and said:

"Sir, lo, here is the sword of the Stone, wherefore I must be king of this land."

When Sir Ector saw the sword he turned back, and came to the church, and there they all three alighted and went into the church, and he made his son swear truly how he got the sword.

"By my brother Arthur," said Sir Kay, "for he brought it to me."

"How did you get this sword?" said Sir Ector to Arthur.

And the boy told him.

"Now," said Sir Ector, "I understand you must be king of this land."

"Wherefore I?" said Arthur; "and for what cause?"

"Sir," said Ector, "because God will have it so; for never man could draw out this sword but he that shall rightly be king. Now let me see whether you can put the sword there as it was, and pull it out again."

"There is no difficulty," said Arthur, and he put it back into the stone.

Then Sir Ector tried to pull out the sword, and failed; and Sir Kay also pulled with all his might, but it would not move.

"Now you shall try," said Sir Ector to Arthur.

"I will, well," said Arthur, and pulled the sword out easily.

At this Sir Ector and Sir Kay knelt down on the ground before him.

"Alas," said Arthur, "mine own dear father and brother, why do you kneel to me?"

"Nay, nay, my lord Arthur, it is

not so; I was never your father, nor of your blood; but I know well you are of higher blood than I thought you were."

Then Sir Ector told him all, how he had taken him to bring up, and by whose command; and how he had received him from Merlin. And when he understood that Ector was not his father, Arthur was deeply grieved.

"Will you be my good, gracious lord, when you are king?" asked the knight.

"If not, I should be to blame," said Arthur, "for you are the man in the world to whom I am the most beholden, and my good lady and mother your wife, who has fostered and kept me as well as her own children. And if ever it be God's will that I be king, as you say, you shall desire of me what I shall do, and I shall not fail you; God forbid I should fail you."

"Sir," said Sir Ector, "I will ask no more of you but that you will make my son, your foster brother Sir Kay, seneschal[1] of all your lands."

"That shall be done," said Arthur, "and by my faith, never man but he shall have that office while he and I live."

Then they went to the archbishop and told him how the sword was achieved, and by whom.

On Twelfth Day all the barons came to the Stone in the churchyard, so that any who wished might try to win the sword. But not one of them all could take it out, except Arthur.

Many of them therefore were very angry, and said it was a great shame to them and to the country to be governed by a boy not of high blood, for as yet none of them knew that he was the son of King Uther Pendragon. So they agreed to delay the decision till Candlemas,[2] which is the second day of February.

But when Candlemas came, and Arthur once more was the only one who could pull out the sword, they put it off till Easter; and when Easter came, and Arthur again prevailed in presence of them all, they put it off till the Feast of Pentecost.[3]

Then by Merlin's advice the archbishop summoned some of the best knights that were to be got—such knights as in his own day King Uther Pendragon had best loved, and trusted most—and these were appointed to attend young Arthur, and never to leave him night or day till the Feast of Pentecost.

When the great day came, all manner of men once more made the attempt, and once more not one of them all could prevail but Arthur. Before all the lords and commons there assembled he pulled out the sword, whereupon all the commons cried out at once:

"We will have Arthur for our king! We will put him no more in delay, for we all see that it is God's will that he shall be our king, and he who holdeth against it, we will slay him."

And therewith they knelt down all at once, both rich and poor, and be-

---

1 seneschal (sĕn′ə shəl): manager of the king's estate and property.
2 Candlemas: religious feast day on which all candles used on church altars are blessed.
3 Feast of Pentecost: seventh Sunday after Easter.

sought pardon of Arthur, because they had delayed him so long.

And Arthur forgave them, and took the sword in both his hands, and offered it on the altar where the archbishop was, and so he was made knight by the best man there.

After that, he was crowned at once, and there he swore to his lords and commons to be a true king, and to govern with true justice from thenceforth all the days of his life.

The Sword Excalibur

After throwing Pellinore into an enchanted sleep, Merlin took up King Arthur, and rode forth on Pellinore's horse.

"Alas!" said Arthur, "what hast thou done, Merlin? Hast thou slain this good knight by thy crafts? There lived not so worshipful a knight as he was; I would rather than a year's income that he were alive."

"Do not be troubled," said Merlin, "for he is less hurt than you. He is only asleep, and will awake within three hours. There liveth not a greater knight than he is, and he shall hereafter do you right good service. His name is Pellinore, and he shall have two sons, that shall be passing good men—Percival of Wales, and Lamerack of Wales."

Leaving Sir Pellinore, King Arthur and Merlin went to a hermit, who was a good man, and skilled in the art of healing. He attended so carefully to the King's wounds, that in three days they were quite well, and Arthur was able to go on his way

with Merlin. Then as they rode, Arthur said, "I have no sword."

"No matter," said Merlin, "nearby is a sword that shall be yours if I can get it."

So they rode till they came to a lake, which was a fair water and broad; and in the midst of the lake, Arthur saw an arm, clothed in white samite,[1] that held in its hand a beautiful sword.

"Lo," said Merlin, "yonder is the sword I spoke of."

With that they saw a damsel rowing across the lake.

"What damsel is that?" said Arthur.

"That is the Lady of the Lake," said Merlin, "and within that lake is a rock, and therein is as fair a place as any on earth, and richly adorned. This damsel will soon come to you; then speak you fair to her, so that she will give you that sword."

Presently the damsel came to Arthur, and saluted him, and he her again.

"Damsel," said Arthur, "what sword is that which yonder the arm holdeth above the water? I would it were mine, for I have no sword."

"Sir Arthur, King," said the damsel, "that sword is mine; the name of it is Excalibur, that is as much as to say *Cut-Steel*. If you will give me a gift when I ask you, ye shall have it."

"By my faith," said Arthur, "I will give you what gift ye shall ask."

"Well," said the damsel, "go you into yonder barge, and row yourself to the sword, and take it and the

---

1 **samite:** heavy white silk fabric, interwoven with gold and silver.

scabbard[2] with you, and I will ask my gift when I see my time."

So King Arthur and Merlin alighted, and tied their horses to two trees, and went into the barge, and when they came to the sword that the hand held, Arthur lifted it by the handle, and took it with him. And the arm and hand went under the water; and so they came to the land, and rode away.

Then King Arthur looked on the sword, and liked it passing well.

"Which like you the better, the sword or the scabbard?" asked Merlin.

"I like the sword better," replied Arthur.

"You are the more unwise," said Merlin, "for the scabbard is worth ten of the sword. While you have the scabbard upon you, ye shall never lose any blood, be ye never so sorely wounded. Therefore keep well the scabbard always with you."

So they returned to Carleon, where King Arthur's knights were passing glad to see him. When they heard of his adventures they marveled that he would so jeopardy[3]

himself alone. But all men of honor said it was merry to be under such a chieftain who would put his person in adventures as other poor knights did.

Some time after this, Merlin again warned King Arthur to keep the scabbard of the sword Excalibur very securely, for as long as he had it upon him he would never lose any blood, however sorely he might be wounded. For greater safety, Arthur entrusted the sword and scabbard to his sister, Morgan le Fay. But Morgan le Fay was a false and treacherous woman. She loved another knight better than her husband King Uriens, or her brother King Arthur, and she made up a wicked plot, by which they would both be slain. Then she meant to marry this other knight, Sir Accolon, and place him on King Arthur's throne, when she herself would become queen of the whole realm. Therefore she made by enchantment another scabbard exactly like Excalibur's, which she gave to Arthur when he was going to fight; but Excalibur and its scabbard she kept for Sir Accolon.

---

2 **scabbard:** case for a sword.
3 **jeopardy:** endanger.

Understanding Literature: "The Marvel of the Sword" and "How Arthur Was Crowned King"

1. What is the political condition of England after Uther's death?
2. Explain the inscription on the sword. When the ambitious lords cannot stir the sword, what does the archbishop advise?
3. What incident prompts Arthur to pull the sword from the stone? How do Sir Kay and Sir Ector react to Arthur's success with the sword?

4. Why do the barons and great lords delay recognizing Arthur as king? Who finally demands that Arthur be made king?

Understanding Literature: "The Sword Excalibur"

1. What evidence of Merlin's magic powers does the reader find?
2. Merlin warns King Arthur twice about the importance of the scabbard for the sword Excalibur. What is this warning?
3. King Arthur's sister, Morgan le Fay, is described as a "false and treacherous woman." What proof of this are you given?
4. What are some of the evidences of myth or fantasy connected with the Arthurian legends that you have read?

Further Activities

1. To become a knight a person had to have a strict and rigorous education which usually began for a boy at the age of twelve. As he matured and became more skilled in certain areas, he progressed from page to squire to knight. Prepare a report on the system of knighthood with material found in your library.
2. Jousts and tournaments were military contests in which the skill and courage of the knights were tested. Prepare a report on the weapons, the armor, and the pageantry involved in these contests.
3. In much of the legendary literature of different countries you find some mystery surrounding the status and birth of the hero. What reason or reasons can you give for this?
4. The code of chivalry was the set of rules by which the knights lived. What were the chief characteristics of this code?

On the following pages are selections adapted from a famous French epic, *The Song of Roland,* set in 8th-century France. This poem, probably written during the 12th century, is set during the life of King Charlemagne,[1] an actual historical figure who lived from 742 to 814. Roland, the hero of the epic, is, however, legendary and represents a kind of ideal hero, very similar to King Arthur.

Stories of Roland

Roland Sees the King

Emeline G. Crommelin

CHARLEMAGNE, OR the Great Charles, was a powerful king of France. He had in his vast kingdom many noble knights whose brave deeds have been told again and again, ever since they were first sung by the minstrel at the famous Battle of Hastings in England, a thousand years ago.

Roland was a little beggar lad. He lived with his mother near the forest of this king's country, where he gathered the nuts for food.

"When you first see King Charlemagne," Roland's mother had often said to him, "it will be the beginning of a new life for you. You will be a beggar boy no longer."

Roland was just twelve years old when he first saw the King—and this was the way it happened: It was known that Charlemagne and his army were to be entertained at a castle in Italy. Roland, hearing this, and remembering his mother's words,

was eager to catch a glimpse of the man who was to change his life. He hastened to a hillside that overlooked the road along which the King and his men were expected to pass. Roland's only companion was Oliver, the son of the governor of the town. The two boys climbed the hillside, and there watched anxiously for the approach of their hero. Poor Roland's head and limbs were bare. His patched, scanty clothing was a strange contrast to Oliver's rich dress of a court page.

"I am sure they are coming!" shouted Roland. "I see a light among the trees. I think it must be the flashing of the sun upon their bright armor. It grows brighter and brighter as they come near."

Very soon the noise of the tramping of many feet was heard, and the rustling of dry leaves in the wood— then a cloud of dust rose above the trees. The bright shields and glittering warcoats were seen in the dis-

1 **Charlemagne** (shär′lə män′).

tance. The beggar boy leaned forward to see the King and his army in battle array. First came the heralds of the King, who bore the banner of France. Then followed messengers, a body of guards, and a long line of bishops and priests.

"See, Roland!" cried Oliver, "that must be the King himself." Roland knew it was King Charlemagne, for who else could bear himself so proudly and so nobly?

The two lads were so filled with admiration, they could scarcely speak. When the last gay banner had disappeared, Roland told Oliver that some day they should both be knights and ride to battle with the King. Together, by the roadside, the boys knelt, and promised to be true to each other, and to the King, as long as they should live.

As the boys rose from their knees, they sealed their promise by exchanging gifts. Oliver took from his belt a richly carved dagger, while Roland drew forth from his ragged garment a rusty old sword blade.

Thus Roland and Oliver parted at the close of that eventful day when they first saw Charlemagne, whose faithful knights they afterward became.

Roland, filled with joy, hurried to his poor dwelling, and rushing into his mother's arms, exclaimed:

"Mother, I have seen the *King!*— his knights and his peers. Would I were a knight, that I, too, might go forth to war."

Roland begged to know the secret of his life—and this is what he learned: His mother was the Princess Bertha; his father was a gallant count; and King Charlemagne, whose fame was known in all lands, was his uncle. Roland wept for joy. He bade his mother good-by, and believing that the new life had already begun, he hastened to demand his rights of the King of France.

Charlemagne and the peers of the realm were dining at the governor's castle. The courts and halls were filled with knights and squires. They talked of war, of chivalry, and of heroism. Above the voices of the feasters were heard the strains of sweet music. Suddenly, in the midst of the feast, Roland, with proud step and flashing eye, entered the banquet hall.

The King, surprised to see a half-clad boy thus interrupt the royal feast, exclaimed:

"Is not the forest a better place for you, my boy, than this castle at a royal feast?"

"The slave eats the nuts in the forest," answered Roland, proudly; "and the peasant drinks the clear water from the brook; but the best things on your table belong to my mother."

Charlemagne smiled at the boy's reply, and said:

"Your mother must be a grand lady, indeed. Has she servants? Has she a carver and a cupbearer? Has she soldiers, watchmen, and minstrels?"

"She has, indeed," the lad replied: "my two arms are her soldiers; my eyes are her watchmen; my lips are her minstrels. I should like you to see my mother, who dwells in the forest."

The King was as much puzzled as he was delighted with the child's answers. After Roland left the dining hall, Charlemagne turned to Malagis, the dwarf, and asked:

"What think you of this strange boy, who has dared interrupt our feast? Has he not a kingly bearing, in spite of his tattered garments?"

"My lord," said the dwarf, "I think the lad belongs *not* in the forest, but in the palace; for I believe that kings are his ancestors, and that royal blood flows through his veins. He will perform great deeds in the years to come. Let no harm come to him. Have him brought before you again. I see by the stars that, somehow, his life and yours are strangely mingled."

Immediately the King sent his squires to bring the boy and his mother to the castle. When they appeared before the King, he saw that Roland's mother was the Lady Bertha, his own sister, who had married against his wishes and been banished with her husband from the kingdom.

Charlemagne's joy was great. He ordered a feast to be prepared in their honor, and Roland sat at the right hand of the King. The lad was made a page in the service of a duke. His ragged clothes were exchanged for a rich gown of velvet and gold. He was no longer Roland the beggar-lad, who gathered nuts in the forest, but Roland, the nephew of the great King of France.

Roland Becomes a Knight

Emeline G. Crommelin

Some of Roland's ancestors were the noblest heroes the world had ever seen. As the dwarf in the King's court had said, surely the blood of heroes flowed in the lad's veins.

Of all the knights and warriors in Charlemagne's kingdom, Roland was the bravest and most skillful. When he reached manhood, it was right he should have suitable armor as a knight of the King. His armor was so wondrously wrought that some said it was made for him by Vulcan, the blacksmith of the Golden Age. His helmet was made of steel, inlaid with pearls, and engraved on it were strange words and battle scenes. The metal had been taken from the earth by the dwarf-folk who lived in the North. When Roland first put on the helmet, his comrades said:

"What need has he of such wonderful armor? It would be better to give it to some one who has not a charmed life."

Roland's shield was made of steel, copper, and gold. His spurs had once belonged to King Arthur when he and his Knights of the Round Table dwelt on the earth. They were given to Roland by the fairy queen of Avalon, where King Arthur had gone to be healed of his grievous wound.

In the days when Roland lived, heroes had names for their swords. Roland called his sword Durandal, which surpassed his uncle's sword, and even the famous Excalibur, that King Arthur received from the Lady of the Lake. This sword had been carried by Hector in the battles with the Greeks. There were strange letters on one side of it, which no one but the dwarf could read:

LET HONOR BE TO HIM
WHO MOST DESERVETH IT.

On the other side of it were the words:

I AM DURANDAL, WHICH TROJAN
HECTOR WORE.

Some thought that an angel or a fairy had given the sword to Charlemagne, and told him to gird it on a young knight who had never known reproach or fear. However that may have been, Roland prized this sword beyond measure. Next to it, he cared most for his famous ivory horn, which hung from his neck by a gold chain. It was set with precious gems and inlaid with silver and gold. No one in the kingdom had ever been able to blow upon this horn. Knights had come from far and near to try; but no one had succeeded. When Roland became a knight Charlemagne was anxious to give the horn to him, and bade him try to blow a blast, saying:

"My dear nephew, you have never yet been conquered in a battle, nor have you failed in anything you have undertaken. Here is that which will test your strength. It is the horn of my grandfather. In his days, when men were stronger and seemingly more valiant than now, the most wondrous sounds were made to come forth from it. Men have grown wondrous weak of lungs—not a man in all France can blow the horn now."

When the King had finished speaking, Roland took the horn, looked at it, put it to his lips, and blew. There came forth a sound more wonderful than any one there had ever heard. It resounded through the halls of the great palace, out into the streets, over hills and mountains, and through the forest.

When the people heard it they were astonished. Some thought the end of the world had come. Others thought it was thunder filled with music.

"I give you this horn," said the King to Roland, "for you have won it fairly. No one can ever doubt your right to it. I give it to you on one condition, that you shall never blow it save in time of battle and in great distress."

When Roland had received the horn, he was fully armed as a knight for battle, with his shield and helmet, his trusty sword, and his wonderful horn.

Understanding Literature

1. Describe the ceremony Oliver and Roland perform after seeing King Charlemagne and his followers. In what ways are Oliver and Roland contrasted?
2. What does Roland's mother disclose about his relationship to King Charlemagne?
3. Describe the first meeting of Roland with King Charlemagne. What is it about this meeting which prompts Charlemagne to remark that Roland has a "kingly bearing"?
4. Which character in the story of Roland is similar to Merlin in the King Arthur stories? Explain.
5. What equipment does Roland have that corresponds with the wonderful sword Excalibur of King Arthur? What is the history of the sword of Roland?
6. Only Roland has the ability to blow the beautiful ivory horn. To what feat of King Arthur's is this similar?
7. In these selections are allusions to Vulcan and Hector, whom you read about earlier. Identify them.
8. Which parts of the story of Roland seem based on fact? Which parts are obviously fantasy? In what way does the fantasy add to the enjoyment of the story?

Further Activities

1. Prepare a report on the life and work of King Charlemagne.
2. The Battle of Hastings is mentioned in the first paragraph of "Roland Sees the King." Prepare a report on this topic, using the card catalog in your library to locate information.

A red-eyed, fearful monster demands a sacrifice of a beautiful maiden each day. As Roland journeys to Ireland at the request of King Charlemagne, he hears the story of the monster from an old Irish harper on board the ship. Roland asks the sea captain to steer straight for the Island of Ebuda, where these terrible sacrifices are taking place.

How Roland Slew a Sea Monster

James Baldwin

WHEN, AT LENGTH, the days of mourning for Duke Godfrey were passed, Ogier and the knights who were with him turned their faces southward, and rode back again to France. But Roland parted from their company, and went another way, for Charlemagne had entrusted him with a message to Oberto, the King of Ireland; and to that country he directed his course. At the nearest port on the coast a little ship awaited him; and in this he embarked, and sailed across the western sea.

For many days the vessel plowed the waters, and the sky was clear, and the wind was fair, and the voyage was a happy one. And those on board beguiled the hours with pleasant talk and with many wonderful tales of the sea. The captain was a browned and weather-beaten Norseman, who had sailed the waters for more than twoscore years, and who knew every strait and shallow and every point of land, from Gothland to the Pillars of Hercules. And he delighted to tell of the many scenes of danger through which he had passed, and of the feats of daring which he had seen on land and sea, and of the strange beings which people the deep. One day he talked about the mermaids and the men of the sea; and he told of the great Midgard snake whom the Northmen believe to lie hidden in the deepest ocean; and he related the story of Old Aegir the Ocean King, and of his nine daughters, the white-veiled Waves. And when he had finished, Roland said that what he had told reminded him of certain stories which he had heard in the South—stories of the old pagan times, when the gods were thought to live on earth, and to take some sort of interest in the doings of men. And he spoke of Poseidon, whom the Greeks called the ruler of the sea; and of old Nereus and his fifty daughters, the silver-footed sea nymphs. And this led him to relate the beautiful fable of Andromeda, and her rescue by Perseus from the sea monster whom Poseidon had sent to devour her.

"But the gods are all dead now," said he, "and neither Aegir nor Poseidon rules the sea."

Then an old Irish harper who happened to be on shipboard spoke, and said, "Sir knight, if all reports be true, some of the sea deities still live, and are known in regions where the Christian religion has not yet been preached. Indeed, I have heard that in the Island of Ebuda, a day's sail west of Ireland, old Proteus, the servant of Poseidon, is even now imitating the deeds of his ancient master."

Then the company insisted that the harper should tell them all that he knew about this matter, and he did as they desired him.

"In the golden age," said he, "it was the task of Proteus to keep the seals and sea calves for his master Poseidon, to lead them into the pleasantest waters and to the freshest pastures, and to see that no one wilfully harmed them. When the times changed, and his old master was dethroned and no longer needed his services, he still kept on herding and caring for the seals and sea calves; for the power of habit was so strong that he could not tear himself away from his old haunts, nor change his occupation. And as he was usually very peaceable, and thought to be quite harmless, very little attention was paid to him; and he was allowed to live on, and ply his vocation, long after all the other sea deities were deposed and forgotten. One day, as he was driving about in his swan chariot, and looking after his herds, he came

to this Island of Ebuda of which I have just spoken. It chanced, that, as he drove close by the shore, the golden-haired daughter of the King of Ebuda stood on the beach. She was more passing fair than ever were the sea nymphs of old, or the mermaids, or the white-veiled daughters of Aegir. And the heart of the ancient Proteus was moved with love for the maiden, and he forthwith besought the King that he would give her to him in marriage. But the father of the maiden scorned his suit. Should he, the King of Ebuda, wed his only daughter to the last of a dying race—to the last and the least worthy of the sea-gods? Let him go back to his seals and sea calves, and never again think of making himself the peer of human beings.

"Then the love of old Proteus was changed to hate, and he vowed that he would not rest nor slumber until he had avenged the slight that had thus been put upon him. And he sent great troops of sea calves to ravage the coasts of Ebuda; and after them he caused a huge and shapeless monster, called an orc, to come, and overrun the whole island. Never was there greater distress and terror. The frightened people fled from their farms and villages, and sought safety in the walled towns; and, between famine and the ravages of the sea monsters, it seemed as if the entire nation would be destroyed. Now, it appears that there was in Ebuda some kind of an oracle, in whose decisions the people placed great trust. And the King prayed the oracle that he might know how to appease the anger of old Proteus, and turn his fearful wrath away. And the oracle answered, and said that this could be done only by offering a daily sacrifice to Proteus to be devoured by the monster orc.

" 'What shall that sacrifice be?' asked the King.

" 'The fairest maiden that can be found either in Ebuda or in the neighboring isles,' was the answer.

" 'And how long shall this fearful payment of tribute continue?' asked the King.

"And the oracle answered, 'Until a hero shall come to Ebuda's shores brave enough and strong enough to slay the orc. Then, and not till then, will Proteus withdraw the curse which he has laid upon you, and leave your people in peace.'

"And it was done as the oracle had bidden. Each day a damsel, the fairest that could be found, was offered to the orc; and the creature ceased his ravages, and allowed the people to return to their homes and farms. And each day, as a new victim was led to the horrible sacrifice, the people prayed for the coming of the hero who should save their loved ones from this dreadful doom. But he came not.

"And it is said that still in the Island of Ebuda this cruel usage is continued, and that the pagan folk who live in that land no longer look upon this sacrifice with horror and aversion, but that, grown barbarous and unfeeling, they send their ships to the neighboring coasts, and bring home scores of fair captives to be offered to the bloodthirsty orc.

Many a noble Irish maiden, I know, has been stolen from our shores, and sacrificed thus horribly by the Ebudans."

"Where sayest thou this savage Island of Ebuda lies?" asked Roland.

"In the great western ocean," answered the harper. "It lies many leagues west of green Erin."

"Turn, then, thy course, good sea captain," said Roland to the master of the ship. "Steer straight for that island kingdom. If such barbarous custom still continues there, it shall not be much longer."

But the winds, as if in league with the wrathful Proteus, hesitated to hasten the vessel on its way; and as the eagerness of the knight waxed stronger, so was the progress of the ship delayed. Sometimes the breeze died away, and there was a calm; the sails hung loose and useless upon the masts, and, had not the seamen plied their oars, the vessel would have stood still. Sometimes a west wind sprang up, and blew strong against them, and they were forced to tack about, and veer far from their intended course. And so it befell that many days passed by, ere, at length, they came in sight of the wooded shores of Ebuda, and the captain pointed out the high rock where the fair victims were daily left as food for the ravenous orc.

When they drew near the place, Roland ordered the ship's boat to be lowered; and in it he placed the largest anchor and the strongest cable that could be found. Then he sat down in the boat; and alone and unarmed, save that he carried the trusty Durandal, he rowed toward the rock. It was about the hour of sunrise—the time when the monster, they said, was wont to come for his daily meal. As the hero rowed close to the shore, he fancied that he heard faint moans, and feeble cries of distress. He looked around, and saw a maiden chained to the rock with iron links, her feet wetted by the rising tide, and her face hidden beneath the long tresses of golden hair that fell about her neck and shoulders. His heart melted with pity, and the sight nerved his arm for the strange contest which was near. He was about to speak to the maiden, when a sudden sound was heard—a roaring like that of a strong wind among the forest trees, or of the waves rolling madly into some ocean cave. He heard the loud shouts of his companions on shipboard: the breakers began to rise around his little boat. The monster was at hand, huge as a rock-built castle, dark and terrible as a thundercloud, fearless as the waves themselves.

Quickly Roland went to meet the beast; he stood up in the boat with the anchor in his hand; quietly he awaited the onset. The orc saw him, and opened his jaws to swallow both him and the boat. The red eyes of the creature glared like baleful bonfires in the morning light; his huge tail lashed the waters into a foam. It was a fearful moment, but Roland faltered not. He raised the heavy anchor still higher; and then, with the strength of a knight well trained in the use of every weapon, he

hurled it into the monster's wide-open mouth. And there it remained, propping the huge jaws apart, and so firmly fixed that the orc could by no means remove it. At nearly the same moment Roland drew his sword, the mighty Durandal; and, calling up all his strength, he struck the monster a blow which almost severed his head from his body. Then guarding the rope to which the anchor was fastened, he seized the oars, and rowed swiftly to the shore. He leaped upon the beach; and, encouraged by the shouts and cheers of his friends on board the ship, he dragged the now dead monster to the land.

And now he bethought him of the captive maiden chained to the rock, and half fallen into a swoon, scarcely knowing that she had been saved from the terrible death that had threatened her. With a single stroke of Durandal, the hero severed the iron links; and then he took her gently by the hand, and led her away from that dreadful rock, and seated her in a pleasant, sunny place high on the shore. With kind and cheerful words he sought to arouse her drooping spirits; for she seemed dazed and bewildered, as if waking from a dream, and unable for a time to remember where she was. He asked her her name, and inquired how she, so unlike the dwellers in Ebuda, had been cast on this barbarous shore and offered in sacrifice to the bloodthirsty orc. She told him that her name was Olympia, and that, in her own home beyond the seas, she was a princess, loved and

honored by hosts of subjects. And then she related, how, one day while walking alone on the seashore, she had been seized by pirates from Ebuda, and, with other fair captives, had been brought to this savage shore, and reserved as a peace offering to the monster whom the Ebudans foolishly believed to have been sent by old Proteus.

Scarcely had the princess ended her story when a new and unexpected danger threatened our hero. The folk of Ebuda had heard of the strange combat between the knight and the orc, and now in great numbers they came trooping to the shore. They stood upon the cliffs above, and along the beach, and some came down even to the water's edge, to see the dead monster and the hero who had slain him. But, although they had been freed from the terror of their lives, they were not pleased; neither felt they in the least thankful to their deliverer.

"Alas!" cried they, "this man has slain the servant of old Proteus, and now it will go hard with us who were charged with his keeping. For will not the sea-god curse us again, and send his herds of sea calves to lay waste our shores? Better it is to endure a single evil than to risk the coming of a multitude of others. The poor orc was not as bad as he might have been; and, now he is dead, there is no telling what may befall us."

"That is true," answered others; "and the only safe way for us to do is to turn away the wrath of old Proteus by punishing the man who has lifted up his sacrilegious hand against the orc. Let us pitch this busy meddler, whoever he may be, into the sea, that he may give his own account to the outraged sea-god whom we serve."

Then a great clamor and shouting arose; and those who stood highest upon the cliffs began hurling stones and darts at Roland; and those who were nearest rushed toward him with drawn swords. There is no telling what would have been the end of this affray, had not a company of armed knights rushed unexpectedly upon the scene. They were men of Ireland, who with their king, Oberto, had come with a fleet of ships to punish the savage islanders for their piracies upon the Irish shores. So great was the surprise of the Ebudans that they turned at once, and fled in wild dismay from the shore; nor did they stop in their flight until they were safely shut up within their city walls.

The meeting between Roland and King Oberto was a happy one; for they had been pages together at the court of Charlemagne, and they recognized each other as old and tried friends. And when the Irish king saw the dead orc, and heard Roland's story of the combat which had taken place, he resolved that he would return at once to his own land and leave the Ebudans in peace. And when all had gone aboard their ships again, the sails were spread, and the fleet sped gayly back toward Ireland. And Roland and the Princess Olympia were guests on board the King's own vessel. And old stories tell us that Oberto afterwards wedded Olympia, making her the Queen of Ireland; and that for many years they lived most happily together, loved and honored by all their subjects. As for Roland, he tarried not long at the Irish court; but, having delivered the message which he bore from Charlemagne, he took ship again and hastened back to France.

Understanding Literature

1. What "fable" does Roland tell which reminds the old Irish harper of the orc and of the maidens who lived on the Island of Ebuda?
2. How does the story that the old harper tells add to the interest of Roland's actual contact with the monster and the rescue of the maiden?
3. What causes Proteus to vow revenge upon the people of Ebuda?
4. In what way does the oracle suggest that the anger of Proteus can be appeased?
5. Explain why the people of the Island of Ebuda have grown "barbarous and unfeeling" about the daily sacrifice of a maiden.
6. Describe the way in which Roland kills the fearful orc and rescues Olympia. Who is Olympia?
7. Explain why the people of Ebuda are not pleased about the death of the orc.
8. King Charlemagne is mentioned only at the very beginning of the story and at the very end. Why is it necessary to the story that he be mentioned at all?
9. What factual material may have been involved in the legend "How Roland Slew a Sea Monster"?
10. You have now read about two famous legendary heroes, King Arthur and Roland. What two great countries do they represent? In what respects are they alike and unlike? What have you learned about the people of the two periods of history represented by King Arthur and Roland?

Robin Hood, a legendary figure of 12th-century England and already well-known to you, is a different type of hero from Roland or Arthur. The tale, too, has a *mood* different from that of other legends. Filled with the roguish escapades and tricks of the gallant hero, these stories are light, humorous, and rarely serious. These selections by Howard Pyle, a noted writer and illustrator, have been retold from the old tales. Many words no longer common in modern English have been retained to add a feeling of authenticity or genuineness to the story.

Stories of Robin Hood

Robin Hood and Little John

from **The Merry Adventures of Robin Hood**

Howard Pyle

IN MERRY ENGLAND in the time of old, when good King Henry the Second ruled the land, there lived within the green glades of Sherwood Forest, near Nottingham Town, a famous outlaw whose name was Robin Hood. No archer ever lived that could speed a gray goose shaft with such skill and cunning as his, nor were there ever such yeomen as the sevenscore merry men that roamed with him through the greenwood shades. Right merrily they dwelt within the depths of Sherwood Forest, suffering neither care nor want, but passing the time in merry games of archery or bouts of cudgel play, living upon the King's venison, washed down with drafts of ale of October brewing.

Not only Robin himself but all the band were outlaws and dwelt apart from other men, yet they were beloved by the country people round about, for no one ever came to jolly Robin for help in time of need and went away again with an empty fist.

And now I will tell how it came about that Robin Hood fell afoul of the law.

When Robin was a youth of eighteen, stout of sinew and bold of heart, the Sheriff of Nottingham proclaimed a shooting match and offered a prize of a butt of ale to whomsoever should shoot the best shaft in Nottinghamshire. "Now," quoth Robin, "will I go too, for fain would I draw a string for the bright eyes of my lass, and a butt of good October brewing." So up he got and took his good stout yew bow and a score or more of broad clothyard arrows, and started off from Locksley Town through Sherwood Forest to Nottingham.

It was at the dawn of day in the merry Maytime, when hedgerows are green and flowers bedeck the meadows; daisies pied and yellow cuckoo buds and fair primroses all along the briery hedges; when apple buds blossom and sweet birds sing, the lark at dawn of day, the throstle cock and cuckoo; when lads and lasses look upon each other with sweet thoughts; when busy housewives spread their linen to bleach upon the bright green grass. Sweet was the greenwood as he walked along its paths, and bright the green and rustling leaves, amid which the little birds sang with might and main: and blithely Robin whistled as he trudged along, thinking of Maid Marian and her bright eyes, for at such times a youth's thoughts are wont to turn pleasantly upon the lass that he loves the best.

As thus he walked along with a brisk step and a merry whistle, he came suddenly upon some foresters seated beneath a great oak tree. Fifteen there were in all, making themselves merry with feasting and drinking as they sat around a huge pasty, to which each man helped himself, thrusting his hands into the pie, and washing down that which they ate with great horns of ale which they drew all foaming from a barrel that stood nigh. Each man was clad in Lincoln green, and a fine show they made, seated upon the sward[1] beneath that fair, spreading tree. Then one of them, with his mouth full, called out to Robin, "Hulloa, where goest thou, little lad, with thy one penny bow and thy farthing shafts?"

Then Robin grew angry, for no stripling[2] likes to be taunted with his green years.

"Now," quoth he, "my bow and eke mine arrows are as good as thine;

and moreover, I go to the shooting match at Nottingham Town, which same has been proclaimed by our good Sheriff of Nottinghamshire; there I will shoot with other stout yeomen, for a prize has been offered of a fine butt of ale."

Then one who held a horn of ale in his hand, said, "Ho! listen to the lad! Why, boy, thy mother's milk is yet scarce dry upon thy lips, and yet thou pratest[3] of standing up with good stout men at Nottingham butts, thou who art scarce able to draw one string of a two stone bow."

"I'll hold the best of you twenty marks," quoth bold Robin, "that I hit the clout at threescore rods,[4] by the good help of Our Lady fair."

At this all laughed aloud, and one said, "Well boasted, thou fair infant, well boasted! and well thou knowest that no target is nigh to make good thy wager."

And another cried, "He will be taking ale with his milk next."

At this Robin grew right mad. "Hark ye," said he; "yonder, at the glade's end, I see a herd of deer, even more than threescore rods distant. I'll hold you twenty marks that, by leave of Our Lady, I cause the best hart among them to die."

"Now done!" cried he who had spoken first. "And here are twenty marks. I wager that thou causest no beast to die, with or without the aid of Our Lady."

Then Robin took his good yew bow in his hand, and placing the tip

---

1 sward: grass.
2 stripling: young man.

3 pratest: chatter.
4 hit . . . rods: hit the mark at 60 rods or 330 yards.

MYTHS, FABLES, AND LEGENDS

at his instep, he strung it right deftly; then he nocked a broad clothyard arrow, and, raising the bow, drew the gray goose-feather to his ear; the next moment the bowstring rang and the arrow sped down the glade as a sparrowhawk skims in a northern wind. High leaped the noblest hart of all the herd, only to fall dead, reddening the green path with his heart's blood.

"Ha!" cried Robin, "how likest thou that shot, good fellow? I wot[5] the wager were mine, an it were three hundred pounds."

Then all the foresters were filled with rage, and he who had spoken the first and had lost the wager was more angry than all.

"Nay," cried he, "the wager is none of thine, and get thee gone, straightway, or, by all the saints of heaven, I'll baste thy sides until thou wilt ne'er be able to walk again."

"Knowest thou not," said another, "that thou hast killed the King's deer, and, by the laws of our gracious lord and sovereign, King Harry, thine ears should be shaven close to thy head?"

"Catch him!" cried a third.

"Nay," said a fourth, "let him e'en go because of his tender years."

Never a word said Robin Hood, but he looked at the foresters with a grim face; then, turning on his heel, strode away from them down the forest glade. But his heart was bitterly angry, for his blood was hot and youthful and prone to boil.

Now, well would it have been for him who had first spoken had he left Robin Hood alone; but his anger was hot, both because the youth had gotten the better of him and because of the deep draughts of ale that he had been quaffing. So, of a sudden, without any warning, he sprang to his feet, and seized upon his bow and fitted it to a shaft. "Ay," cried he, "and I'll hurry thee anon"; and he sent the arrow whistling after Robin.

It was well for Robin Hood that that same forester's head was spinning with ale, or else he would never have taken another step; as it was, the arrow whistled within three inches of his head. Then he turned around and quickly drew his own bow, and sent an arrow back in return.

"Ye said I was no archer," cried he aloud, "but say so now again!"

The shaft flew straight; the archer fell forward with a cry, and lay on his face upon the ground, his arrows rattling about him from out of his quiver, the gray goose shaft wet with his heart's blood. Then, before the others could gather their wits about them, Robin Hood was gone into the depths of the greenwood. Some started after him, but not with much heart, for each feared to suffer the death of his fellow; so presently they all came and lifted the dead man up and bore him away to Nottingham Town.

Meanwhile Robin Hood ran through the greenwood. Gone was all the joy and brightness from everything, for his heart was sick within him, and it was borne in upon his soul that he had slain a man.

5 **wot:** know.

"Alas!" cried he, "thou hast found me an archer that will make thy wife to wring! I would that thou hadst ne'er said one word to me, or that I had never passed thy way, or e'en that my right forefinger had been stricken off ere that this had happened! In haste I smote,[6] but grieve I sore at leisure!" And then, even in his trouble, he remembered the old saw that "What is done is done; and the egg cracked cannot be cured."

And so he came to dwell in the greenwood that was to be his home for many a year to come, never again to see the happy days with the lads and lasses of sweet Locksley Town; for he was outlawed, not only because he had killed a man, but also because he had poached upon the King's deer, and two hundred pounds were set upon his head, as a reward for whoever would bring him to the court of the King.

Now the Sheriff of Nottingham swore that he himself would bring this knave, Robin Hood, to justice, and for two reasons: first, because he wanted the two hundred pounds, and next, because the forester that Robin Hood had killed was of kin to him.

But Robin Hood lay hidden in Sherwood Forest for one year, and in that time there gathered around him many others like himself, cast out from other folk for this cause and for that. Some had shot deer in hungry wintertime, when they could get no other food, and had been seen in the act by the foresters, but had

6 smote: struck.

escaped, thus saving their ears; some had been turned out of their inheritance, that their farms might be added to the King's lands in Sherwood Forest; some had been despoiled by a great baron or a rich abbot or a powerful esquire—all, for one cause or another, had come to Sherwood to escape wrong and oppression.

So, in all that year, fivescore or more good stout yeomen gathered about Robin Hood, and chose him to be their leader and chief. Then they vowed that even as they themselves had been despoiled they would despoil their oppressors, whether baron, abbot, knight, or squire, and that from each they would take that which had been wrung from the poor by unjust taxes, or land rents, or in wrongful fines; but to the poor folk they would give a helping hand in need and trouble, and would return to them that which had been unjustly taken from them. Beside this, they swore never to harm a child nor to wrong a woman, be she maid, wife, or widow; so that, after a while, when the people began to find that no harm was meant to them, but that money or food came in time of want to many a poor family, they came to praise Robin and his merry men, and to tell many tales of him and of his doings in Sherwood Forest, for they felt him to be one of themselves.

Up rose Robin Hood one merry morn when all the birds were singing blithely among the leaves, and up rose all his merry men, each fellow washing his head and hands in the cold brown brook that leaped laughing from stone to stone. Then said Robin: "For fourteen days have we seen no sport, so now I will go abroad to seek adventures forthwith. But tarry ye, my merry men all, here in the greenwood; only see that ye mind well my call. Three blasts upon the bugle horn I will blow in my hour of need; then come quickly, for I shall want your aid."

So saying, he strode away through the leafy forest glades until he had come to the verge of Sherwood. There he wandered for a long time, through highway and byway, through dingly dell and forest skirts. Now he met a fair buxom lass in a shady lane, and each gave the other a merry word and passed their way; now he saw a fair lady upon an ambling pad,[7] to whom he doffed his cap, and who bowed sedately in return to the fair youth; now he saw a fat monk on a pannier-laden[8] ass; now a gallant knight, with spear and shield and armor that flashed brightly in the sunlight; now a page clad in crimson; and now a stout burgher from good Nottingham Town, pacing along with serious footsteps; all these sights he saw, but adventure found he none. At last he took a road by the forest skirts; a bypath that dipped toward a broad, pebbly stream spanned by a narrow bridge made of a log of wood. As he drew nigh this bridge he saw a tall stranger coming from the other side. Thereupon

Robin quickened his pace, as did the stranger likewise; each thinking to cross first.

"Now stand thou back," quoth Robin, "and let the better man cross first."

"Nay," answered the stranger, "then stand back thine own self, for the better man, I wot, am I."

"That will we presently see," quoth Robin; "and meanwhile stand thou where thou art, or else, by the bright brow of Saint Aelfrida, I will show thee right good Nottingham play with a clothyard shaft betwixt thy ribs."

"Now," quoth the stranger, "I will tan thy hide till it be as many colors as a beggar's cloak, if thou darest so much as touch a string of that same bow that thou holdest in thy hands."

"Thou pratest like an ass," said Robin, "for I could send this shaft clean through thy proud heart before a curtal friar[9] could say grace over a roast goose at Michaelmastide."[10]

"And thou pratest like a coward," answered the stranger, "for thou standest there with a good yew bow to shoot at my heart, while I have nought in my hand but a plain black-thorn staff wherewith to meet thee."

"Now," quoth Robin, "by the faith of my heart, never have I had a coward's name in all my life before. I will lay by my trusty bow and eke my arrows, and if thou darest abide my coming, I will go and cut a cudgel to test thy manhood withal."

9 **curtal friar:** member of a religious order which dresses in short frocks.
10 **Michaelmastide:** religious feast day on September 29.

7 **pad:** road horse.
8 **pannier-laden:** loaded with baskets.

"Ay, marry,[11] that will I abide thy coming, and joyously, too," quoth the stranger; whereupon he leaned sturdily upon his staff to await Robin.

Then Robin Hood stepped quickly to the coverside and cut a good staff of ground oak, straight, without flaw, and six feet in length, and came back trimming away the tender stems from it, while the stranger waited for him, leaning upon his staff, and whistling as he gazed round about. Robin observed him furtively as he trimmed his staff, measuring him from top to toe from out the corner of his eye, and thought that he had never seen a lustier or a stouter man. Tall was Robin, but taller was the stranger by a head and a neck, for he was seven feet in height. Broad was Robin across the shoulders, but broader was the stranger by twice the breadth of a palm, while he measured at least an ell around the waist.

"Nevertheless," said Robin to himself, "I will baste thy hide right merrily, my good fellow"; then, aloud, "Lo, here is my good staff, lusty and tough. Now wait my coming, an thou darest, and meet me, an thou fearest not; then we will fight until one or the other of us tumble into the stream by dint of blows."

"Marry, that meeteth[12] my whole heart!" cried the stranger, twirling his staff above his head, betwixt his fingers and thumb, until it whistled again.

Never did the Knights of Arthur's Round Table meet in a stouter fight than did these two. In a moment Robin stepped quickly upon the bridge where the stranger stood; first he made a feint,[13] and then delivered a blow at the stranger's head that, had it met its mark, would have tumbled him speedily into the water; but the stranger turned the blow right deftly, and in return gave one as stout, which Robin also turned as the stranger had done. So they stood, each in his place, neither moving a finger's breadth back, for one good hour, and many blows were given and received by each in that time, till here and there were sore bones and bumps, yet neither thought of crying "Enough," or seemed likely to fall from off the bridge. Now and then they stopped to rest, and each thought that he never had seen in all his life before such a hand at quarterstaff. At last Robin gave the stranger a blow upon the ribs that made his jacket smoke like a damp straw thatch in the sun. So shrewd was the stroke that the stranger came within a hair's breadth of falling off the bridge; but he regained himself right quickly, and, by a dexterous blow, gave Robin a crack on the crown that caused the blood to flow. Then Robin grew mad with anger, and smote with all his might at the other; but the stranger warded the blow, and once again thwacked Robin, and this time so fairly that he fell heels over head into the water, as the queen pin falls in a game of bowls.

---

11 **marry:** indeed.
12 **meeteth:** suits.

13 **feint:** fake blow, intended to throw an opponent off balance.

MYTHS, FABLES, AND LEGENDS

"And where art thou now, my good lad?" shouted the stranger, roaring with laughter.

"Oh, in the flood and floating adown with the tide," cried Robin; nor could he forbear laughing himself at his sorry plight. Then, gaining his feet, he waded to the bank, the little fish speeding hither and thither, all frightened at his splashing.

"Give me thy hand," cried he, when he had reached the bank. "I must needs own thou art a brave and a sturdy soul, and, withal, a good stout stroke with the cudgels. By this and by that, my head hummeth like to a hive of bees on a hot June day."

Then he clapped his horn to his lips, and winded a blast that went echoing sweetly down the forest paths. "Ay, marry," quoth he again, "thou art a tall lad, and eke a brave one, for ne'er, I trow, is there a man betwixt here and Canterbury Town could do the like to me that thou hast done."

"And thou," quoth the stranger, laughing, "takest thy cudgeling like a brave heart and a stout yeoman."

But now the distant twigs and branches rustled with the coming of men, and suddenly a score or two of good stout yeomen, all clad in Lincoln green, burst from out the covert, with merry Will Stutely at their head.

"Good master," cried Will, "how is this? Truly thou art all wet from head to foot, and that to the very skin."

"Why, marry," answered jolly Robin, "yon stout fellow hath tumbled me neck and crop into the water, and hath given me a drubbing beside."

"Then shall he not go without a ducking and eke a drubbing himself!" cried Will Stutely. "Have at him, lads!"

Then Will and a score of yeomen leaped upon the stranger, but though they sprang quickly they found him ready and felt him strike right and left with his stout staff, so that, though he went down with press of numbers, some of them rubbed cracked crowns before he was overcome.

"Nay, forbear!" cried Robin, laughing until his sore sides ached again; "he is a right good man and true, and no harm shall befall him. Now hark ye, good youth, wilt thou stay with me and be one of my band? Three suits of Lincoln green shalt thou have each year, beside forty marks in fee, and share with us whatsoever good shall befall us. Thou shalt eat sweet venison and quaff the stoutest ale, and mine own good right-hand man shalt thou be, for never did I see such a cudgel player in all my life before. Speak! wilt thou be one of my good merry men?"

"That know I not," quoth the stranger, surlily, for he was angry at being so tumbled about. "If ye handle yew bow and apple shaft no better than ye do oaken cudgel, I wot ye are not fit to be called yeomen in my country; but if there be any man here that can shoot a better shaft than I, then will I bethink me of joining with you."

"Now by my faith," said Robin, "thou art a right saucy varlet, sirrah; yet I will stoop to thee as I never stooped to man before. Good Stutely, cut thou a fair white piece of bark four fingers in breadth, and set it fourscore yards distant on yonder oak. Now, stranger, hit that fairly with a gray goose shaft and call thyself an archer."

"Ay, marry, that will I," answered he. "Give me a good stout bow and a fair broad arrow, and if I hit it not strip me and beat me blue with bowstrings."

Then he chose the stoutest bow amongst them all, next to Robin's own, and a straight gray goose shaft, well-feathered and smooth, and stepping to the mark—while all the band, sitting or lying upon the greensward, watched to see him shoot—he drew the arrow to his cheek and loosed the shaft right deftly, sending it so straight down the path that it clove the mark in the very center. "Aha!" cried he, "mend thou that if thou canst"; while even the yeomen clapped their hands at so fair a shot.

"That is a keen shot, indeed," quoth Robin, "mend it I cannot, but mar it I may, perhaps."

Then taking up his own good stout bow and nocking an arrow with care he shot with his very greatest skill. Straight flew the arrow, and so true that it lit fairly upon the stranger's shaft and split it into splinters. Then all the yeomen leaped to their feet and shouted for joy that their master had shot so well.

"Now by the lusty yew bow of good Saint Withold," cried the stranger, "that is a shot indeed, and never saw I the like in all my life before! Now truly will I be thy man henceforth and for aye. Good Adam Bell[14] was a fair shot, but never shot he so!"

"Then have I gained a right good man this day," quoth jolly Robin. "What name goest thou by, good fellow?"

"Men call me John Little whence I came," answered the stranger.

Then Will Stutely, who loved a good jest, spoke up. "Nay, fair little stranger," said he, "I like not thy name and fain would I have it otherwise. Little art thou indeed, and small of bone and sinew, therefore shalt thou be christened Little John, and I will be thy godfather."

Then Robin Hood and all his band laughed aloud until the stranger began to grow angry.

"An thou make a jest of me," quoth he to Will Stutely, "thou wilt have sore bones and little pay, and that in short season."

"Nay, good friend," said Robin Hood, "bottle thine anger, for the name fitteth thee well. Little John shall thou be called henceforth, and Little John shall it be. So come, my merry men, and we will go and prepare a christening feast for this fair infant."

So turning their backs upon the stream, they plunged into the forest once more, through which they traced their steps till they reached the spot where they dwelt in the depths of the woodland. There had they built huts of bark and branches of trees, and made couches of sweet

14 **Adam Bell:** famous bowman in many ballads.

rushes spread over with skins of fallow deer. Here stood a great oak tree with branches spreading broadly around, beneath which was a seat of green moss where Robin Hood was wont to sit at feast and at merrymaking with his stout men about him. Here they found the rest of the band, some of whom had come in with a brace of fat does. Then they all built great fires and after a time roasted the does and broached a barrel of humming ale. Then when the feast was ready they all sat down, but Robin placed Little John at his right hand, for he was henceforth to be the second in the band.

Then when the feast was done Will Stutely spoke up. "It is now time, I ween, to christen our bonny babe, is it not so, merry boys?" And "Aye! Aye!" cried all, laughing till the woods echoed with their mirth.

"Then seven sponsors shall we have," quoth Will Stutely; and hunting among all the band he chose the seven stoutest men of them all.

"Now by Saint Dunstan," cried Little John, springing to his feet, "more than one of you shall rue it an you lay finger upon me."

But without a word they all ran upon him at once, seizing him by his legs and arms and holding him tightly in spite of his struggles, and they bore him forth while all stood around to see the sport. Then one came forward who had been chosen to play the priest because he had a bald crown, and in his hands he carried a brimming pot of ale. "Now who bringeth this babe?" asked he right soberly.

"That do I," answered Will Stutely. "And what name callest thou him?"

"Little John call I him."

"Now Little John," quoth the mock priest, "thou hast not lived heretofore, but only got thee along through the world, but henceforth thou wilt live indeed. When thou livedst not thou wast called John Little, but now that thou dost live indeed, Little John shalt thou be called, so christen I thee." And at these last words he emptied the pot of ale upon Little John's head.

Then all shouted with laughter as they saw the good brown ale stream over Little John's beard and trickle from his nose and chin, while his eyes blinked with the smart of it. At first he was of a mind to' be angry, but found he could not because the others were so merry; so he, too, laughed with the rest. Then Robin took this sweet, pretty babe, clothed him all anew from top to toe in Lincoln green, and give him a good stout bow, and so made him a member of the merry band.

And thus it was that Robin Hood became outlawed; thus a band of merry companions gathered about him, and thus he gained his right-hand man, Little John.

Understanding Literature

1. Describe the incident which forces Robin Hood to become an outlaw.
2. What kinds of men does Robin Hood gather into his band?
3. Describe Robin Hood's adventure with Little John.
4. From his general treatment of Little John, what can we learn about Robin Hood's character?
5. Why do the common people so readily accept Robin Hood as their hero?
6. Explain how the situations, the setting, and the vocabulary create a light, gay mood for the story of Robin Hood.
7. What is the setting of the Robin Hood stories? What paragraph is most descriptive about the setting? Which groups of words are particularly clear in forming a picture (or an image)?

In this story Robin Hood, who so enjoys playing tricks himself, is tricked by another person, King Richard the Lion-Hearted, around whom many legends have grown. At the conclusion of this story, the problems of the outlawed Robin Hood and his outlaw band seemed to be solved for the moment.

King Richard Cometh to Sherwood Forest

from The Merry Adventures of Robin Hood

Howard Pyle

NOT MORE THAN two months had passed and gone since these stirring adventures that have just been told of befell Robin Hood and Little John, when all Nottinghamshire was in a mighty stir and tumult, for King Richard of the Lion's Heart was making a royal progress through merry England, and everyone expected him to come to Nottingham Town in his journeying. Messengers went riding back and forth between the Sheriff and the King, until at last the time was fixed upon when his majesty was to stop in Nottingham, as the guest of his worship.

And now came more bustle than ever; a great running hither and thither, a rapping of hammers and a babble of voices sounded everywhere through the place, for the folk were building great arches across the streets, beneath which the King was to pass, and were draping these arches with silken banners and streamers of many colors. Great hubbub was going on in the Guild

Hall of the town, also, for here a grand banquet was to be given to the King and the nobles of his train, and the best master carpenters were busy building a throne where the King and the Sheriff were to sit at the head of the table, side by side.

It seemed to many of the good folk of the place as if the day that should bring the King into the town would never come; but all the same it did come in its own season, and bright shone the sun down into the stony streets, which were all alive with a restless sea of people. On either side of the way great crowds of town and country folk stood packed as close together as dried herring in a box, so that the Sheriff's men, halberds[1] in hands, could hardly press them back to leave space for the King's riding.

"Take care whom thou pushest against!" cried a great, burly friar to one of these men. "Wouldst thou dig thine elbows into me, sirrah?

1 halberds: long-handled weapons.

By'r Lady of the Fountain, an thou dost not treat me with more deference[2] I will crack thy knave's pate[3] for thee, even though thou be one of the mighty Sheriff's men."

At this a great shout of laughter arose from a number of tall yeomen in Lincoln green that were scattered through the crowd thereabouts; but one that seemed of more authority than the others nudged the holy man with his elbow. "Peace, Tuck," said he, "didst thou not promise me, ere thou camest here, that thou wouldst put a check upon thy tongue?"

"Ay, marry," grumbled the other, "but 'a did not think to have a hard-footed knave trample all over my poor toes as though they were no more than so many acorns in the forest."

But of a sudden all this bickering ceased, for a clear sound of many bugle horns came winding down the street. Then all the people craned their necks and gazed in the direction whence the sound came, and the crowding and the pushing and the swaying grew greater than ever. And now a gallant array of men came gleaming into sight, and the cheering of the people ran down the crowd as the fire runs in dry grass.

Eight and twenty heralds in velvet and cloth of gold came riding forwards. Over their heads fluttered a cloud of snow-white feathers, and each herald bore in his hand a long silver trumpet, which he blew musically. From each trumpet hung a heavy banner of velvet and cloth of gold, with the royal arms of England emblazoned thereon. After these came riding fivescore noble knights, two by two, all fully armed, saving that their heads were uncovered. In their hands they bore tall lances, from the tops of which fluttered pennons of many colors and devices. By the side of each knight walked a page clad in rich clothes of silk and velvet, and each page bore in his hands his master's helmet, from which waved long, floating plumes of feathers. Never had Nottingham seen a fairer sight than those fivescore noble knights, from whose armor the sun blazed in dazzling light as they came riding on their great war horses, with clashing of arms and jingling of chains. Behind the knights came the barons and the nobles of the mid-country, in robes of silk and cloth of gold, with golden chains about their necks and jewels at their girdles. Behind these again came a great array of men-at-arms, with spears and halberds in their hands, and, in the midst of these, two riders side by side. One of the horsemen was the Sheriff of Nottingham in his robes of office. The other, who was a head taller than the Sheriff, was clad in a rich but simple garb, with a broad, heavy chain about his neck. His hair and beard were like threads of gold, and his eyes were as blue as the summer sky. As he rode along he bowed to the right hand and the left, and a mighty roar of voices followed him as he passed; for this was King Richard.

Then, above all the tumult and the shouting a great voice was heard

2 **deference:** respect.
3 **pate:** head.

roaring, "Heaven, its saints bless thee, our gracious King Richard! and likewise Our Lady of the Fountain, bless thee!" Then King Richard, looking toward the spot whence the sound came, saw a tall, burly, strapping priest standing in front of all the crowd with his legs wide apart as he backed against those behind.

"By my soul, Sheriff," said the King, laughing, "ye have the tallest priests in Nottinghamshire that e'er I saw in all my life. If Heaven never answered prayers because of deafness, methinks I would nevertheless have blessings bestowed upon me, for that man yonder would make the great stone image of Saint Peter rub its ears and hearken unto him. I would that I had an army of such as he."

To this the Sheriff answered never a word, but all the blood left his cheeks, and he caught at the pommel of his saddle to keep himself from falling; for he also saw the fellow that so shouted, and knew him to be Friar Tuck; and, moreover, behind Friar Tuck he saw the faces of Robin Hood and Little John and Will Scarlet and Will Stutely and Allan a Dale and others of the band.

"How now," said the King hastily, "art thou ill, Sheriff, that thou growest so white?"

"Nay, your majesty," said the Sheriff, "it was nought but a sudden pain that will soon pass by." Thus he spake, for he was ashamed that the King should know that Robin Hood feared him so little that he thus dared to come within the very gates of Nottingham Town.

Thus rode the King into Nottingham Town on that bright afternoon in the early fall season; and none rejoiced more than Robin Hood and his merry men to see him come so royally unto his own.

Eventide[4] had come; the great feast in the Guild Hall at Nottingham Town was done, and the wine passed freely. A thousand waxen lights gleamed along the board, at which sat lord and noble and knight and squire in goodly array. At the head of the table, upon a throne all hung with cloth of gold, sat King Richard with the Sheriff of Nottingham beside him.

Quoth the King to the Sheriff, laughing as he spoke, "I have heard much spoken concerning the doings of certain fellows hereabouts, one Robin Hood and his band, who are outlaws and abide in Sherwood Forest. Canst thou not tell me somewhat of them, Sir Sheriff? for I hear that thou hast had dealings with them more than once."

At these words the Sheriff of Nottingham looked down gloomily, and the Bishop of Hereford, who was present, gnawed his nether[5] lip. Quoth the Sheriff, "I can tell your majesty but little concerning the doings of those naughty fellows, saving that they are the boldest lawbreakers in all the land."

Then up spake young Sir Henry of the Lea, a great favorite with the King, under whom he had fought in Palestine. "May it please your maj-

4 **Eventide:** evening.
5 **nether:** lower.

esty," said he, "when I was away in Palestine I heard ofttimes from my father, and in most cases I heard of this very fellow, Robin Hood. If your majesty would like I will tell you a certain adventure of this outlaw."

Then the King laughingly bade him tell his tale, whereupon he told how Robin Hood had aided Sir Richard of the Lea with money that he had borrowed from the Bishop of Hereford. Again and again the King and those present roared with laughter, whilst the poor Bishop waxed cherry red in the face with vexation, for the matter was a sore thing with him. When Sir Henry of the Lea was done, others of those present, seeing how the King enjoyed this merry tale, told other tales concerning Robin and his merry men.

"By the hilt of my sword," said stout King Richard, "this is as bold and merry a knave as ever I heard tell of. Marry, I must take this matter in hand and do what thou couldst not do, Sheriff, to wit, clear the forest of him and his band."

That night the King sat in the place that was set apart for his lodging whilst in Nottingham Town. With him were young Sir Henry of the Lea and two other knights and three barons of Nottinghamshire; but the King's mind still dwelt upon Robin Hood. "Now," quoth he, "I would freely give a hundred pounds to meet this roguish fellow, Robin Hood, and to see somewhat of his doings in Sherwood Forest."

Then up spake Sir Hubert of Bingham, laughing: "If your majesty hath such a desire upon you it is not so hard to satisfy. If your majesty is willing to lose one hundred pounds, I will engage to cause you not only to meet this fellow, but to feast with him in Sherwood."

"Marry, Sir Hubert," quoth the King, "this pleaseth me well. But how wilt thou cause me to meet Robin Hood?"

"Why, thus," said Sir Hubert, "let your majesty and us here present put on the robes of seven of the Order of Black Friars, and let your majesty hang a purse of one hundred pounds beneath your gown; then let us undertake to ride from here to Mansfield Town tomorrow, and, without I am much mistaken, we will both meet with Robin Hood and dine with him before the day be passed."

"I like thy plan, Sir Hubert," quoth the King merrily, "and tomorrow we will try it and see whether there be virtue in it."

So it happened that when early the next morning the Sheriff came to where his liege lord was abiding, to pay his duty to him, the King told him what they had talked of the night before, and what merry adventure they were set upon undertaking that morning. But when the Sheriff heard this he smote his forehead with his fist. "Alas!" said he, "what evil counsel is this that hath been given thee! O my gracious lord and king, you know not what you do! This villain that you thus go to seek hath no reverence either for king or king's laws."

"But did I not hear aright when I was told that this Robin Hood hath shed no blood since he was outlawed, saving only that of that vile Guy of Gisbourne, for whose death all honest men should thank him?"

"Yea, your majesty," said the Sheriff, "you have heard aright. Nevertheless"—

"Then," quoth the King, breaking in on the Sheriff's speech, "what have I to fear in meeting him, having done him no harm? Truly, there is no danger in this. But mayhap thou wilt go with us, Sir Sheriff."

"Nay," quoth the Sheriff hastily, "Heaven forbid!"

But now seven habits such as black friars wear were brought, and the King and those about him having clad themselves therein, and his majesty having hung a purse with a hundred golden pounds in it beneath his robes, they all went forth and mounted the mules that had been brought to the door for them. Then the King bade the Sheriff be silent as to their doings, and so they set forth upon their way. Onward they traveled, laughing and jesting, until they passed through the open country; between bare harvest fields whence the harvest had been gathered home; through scattered glades that began to thicken as they went farther along, till they came within the heavy shade of the forest itself. They traveled in the forest for several miles without meeting any one such as they sought, until they had come to that part of the road that lay nearest to Newstead Abbey.

"By the holy Saint Martin," quoth the King, "I would that I had a better head for remembering things of great need. Here have we come away and brought never so much as a drop of anything to drink with us. Now I would give half a hundred pounds for somewhat to quench my thirst withal."

No sooner had the King so spoken, than out from the covert[6] at the roadside stepped a tall fellow with yellow beard and hair and a pair of merry blue eyes. "Truly, holy brother," said he, laying his hand upon the King's bridle rein, "it were an unchristian thing to not give fitting answer to so fair a bargain. We keep an inn hereabouts, and for fifty pounds we will not only give thee a good draught of wine, but will give thee as noble a feast as ever thou didst tickle thy gullet withal." So saying he put his fingers to his lips and blew a shrill whistle. Then straightway the bushes and branches on either side of the road swayed and crackled, and threescore broad-shouldered yeomen in Lincoln green burst out of the covert.

"How now, fellow," quoth the King, "who art thou, thou naughty rogue? Hast thou no regard for such holy men as we are?"

"Not a whit," quoth merry Robin Hood, for the fellow was he, "for in sooth all the holiness belonging to rich friars, such as ye are, one could drop into a thimble and the good wife would never feel it with the tip of her finger. As for my name, it is Robin Hood, and thou mayst have heard it before."

6 **covert:** secret place.

"Now out upon thee!" quoth King Richard. "Thou art a bold and naughty fellow and a lawless one withal, as I have often heard tell. Now, prythee, let me, and these brethren of mine, travel forward in peace and quietness."

"It may not be," said Robin, "for it would look but ill of us to let such holy men travel onward with empty stomachs. But I doubt not that thou hast a fat purse to pay thy score at our inn since thou offerest freely so much for a poor draught of wine. Show me thy purse, reverend brother, or I may perchance have to strip thy robes from thee to search for it myself."

"Nay, use no force," said the King sternly. "Here is my purse, but lay not thy lawless hands upon our person."

"Hut, tut," quoth merry Robin, "what proud words are these? Art thou the King of England, to talk so to me? Here, Will, take this purse and see what there is within."

Will Scarlet took the purse and counted out the money. Then Robin bade him keep fifty pounds for themselves, and put fifty back into the purse. This he handed to the King. "Here, brother," quoth he, "take this half of thy money, and thank Saint Martin, on whom thou didst call before, that thou hast fallen into the hands of such gentle rogues that they will not strip thee bare, as they might do. But wilt thou not put back thy cowl?[7] for I would fain see thy face."

"Nay," said the King, drawing back, "I may not put back my cowl, for we seven have vowed that we will not show our faces for four and twenty hours."

"Then keep them covered in peace," said Robin, "and far be it from me to make you break your vows."

So he called seven of his yeomen and bade them each one take a mule by the bridle; then, turning their faces toward the depths of the woodlands, they journeyed onward until they came to the open glade and the greenwood tree.

Little John, with threescore yeomen at his heels, had also gone forth that morning to wait along the roads and bring a rich guest to Sherwood glade, if such might be his luck, for many with fat purses must travel the roads at this time, when such great doings were going on in Nottinghamshire; but though Little John and so many others were gone, Friar Tuck and twoscore or more stout yeomen were seated or lying around beneath the great tree, and when Robin and the others came they leaped to their feet to meet him.

"By my soul," quoth merry King Richard, when he had gotten down from his mule and stood looking about him, "thou hast in very truth a fine lot of young men about thee, Robin. Methinks King Richard himself would be glad of such a bodyguard."

"These are not all of my fellows," said Robin, proudly, "for threescore more of them are away on business with my good right-hand man, Little

7 cowl: monk's hood.

John. But, as for King Richard, I tell thee, brother, there is not a man of us all but would pour out our blood like water for him. Ye churchmen cannot rightly understand our King; but we yeomen love him right loyally for the sake of his brave doings which are so like our own."

But now Friar Tuck came bustling up. "Gi' ye good den, brothers," said he. "I am right glad to welcome some of my cloth in this naughty place. Truly, methinks these rogues of outlaws would stand but an ill chance were it not for the prayers of Holy Tuck, who laboreth so hard for their well-being." Here he winked one eye slyly and stuck his tongue into his cheek.

"Who art thou, mad priest?" said the King in a serious voice, albeit he smiled beneath his cowl.

At this Friar Tuck looked all around with a slow gaze. "Look you now," quoth he, "never let me hear you say again that I am no patient man. Here is a knave of a friar calleth me a mad priest, and yet I smite him not. My name is Friar Tuck, fellow—the holy Friar Tuck."

"There, Tuck," said Robin, "thou hast said enow. Prythee, cease thy talk and bring some wine. These reverend men are athirst, and sin' they have paid so richly for their score they must e'en have the best."

Friar Tuck bridled[8] at being so checked in his speech, nevertheless he went straightway to do Robin's bidding; so presently a great crock

8 **bridled:** was annoyed.

was brought, and wine was poured out for all the guests and for Robin Hood. Then Robin held his cup aloft. "Stay!" cried he. "Tarry in your drinking till I give you a pledge. Here is to good King Richard of great renown, and may all enemies to him be confounded."

Then all drank the King's health, even the King himself. "Methinks, good fellow," said he, "thou hast drunk to thine own confusion."

"Never a whit," quoth merry Robin, "for I tell thee that we of Sherwood are more loyal to our lord the King than those of thine order. We would give up our lives for his benefiting, whilst ye are content to lie snug in your abbeys and priories let reign who will."

At this the King laughed. Quoth he, "Perhaps King Richard's welfare is more to me than thou wottest of, fellow. But enough of that matter. We have paid well for our fare, so canst thou not show us some merry entertainment? I have oft heard that ye are wondrous archers; wilt thou not show us somewhat of your skill?"

"With all my heart," said Robin, "we are always pleased to show our guests all the sport that is to be seen. As Gaffer Swanthold sayeth, ' 'Tis a hard heart that will not give a caged starling of the best'; and caged starlings ye are with us. Ho, lads! set up a garland at the end of the glade."

Then, as the yeomen ran to do their master's bidding, Tuck turned to one of the mock friars. "Hearest thou our master?" quoth he, with a sly wink. "Whenever he cometh across some poor piece of wit he straightway layeth it on the shoulders of this Gaffer Swanthold—whoever he may be—so that the poor goodman goeth traveling about with all the odds and ends and tags and rags of our master's brain packed on his back." Thus spake Friar Tuck, but in a low voice so that Robin could not hear him, for he felt somewhat nettled at Robin's cutting his talk so short.

In the meantime the mark at which they were to shoot was set up at sixscore paces distance. It was a garland of leaves and flowers two spans in width, which same was hung upon a stake in front of a broad tree trunk. "There," quoth Robin, "yon is a fair mark, lads. Each of you shoot three arrows thereat; and if any fellow misseth by so much as one arrow, he shall have a buffet of Will Scarlet's fist."

"Hearken to him!" quoth Friar Tuck. "Why, master, thou dost bestow buffets from thy strapping nephew as though they were lovetaps from some bouncing lass. I warrant thou art safe to hit the garland thyself, or thou wouldst not be so free of his cuffing."

First David of Doncaster shot, and lodged all three of his arrows within the garland. "Well done, David!" cried Robin, "thou hast saved thine ears from a warming this day." Next Midge, the Miller, shot, and he, also, lodged his arrows in the garland. Then followed Wat, the Tinker, but alas for him! for one of his shafts missed the mark by the breadth of two fingers.

"Come hither, fellow," said Will Scarlet, in his soft, gentle voice, "I owe thee somewhat that I would pay forthwith." Then Wat, the Tinker, came forward and stood in front of Will Scarlet, screwing up his face and shutting his eyes tightly, as though he already felt his ears ringing with the buffet. Will Scarlet rolled up his sleeve, and, standing on tiptoe to give the greater swing to his arm, he struck with might and main. *"Whoof!"* came his palm against the Tinker's head, and down went stout Wat to the grass, heels over head, as the wooden image at the fair goes down when the skillful player throws a cudgel at it. Then, as the Tinker sat up upon the grass, rubbing his ear and winking and blinking at the bright stars that danced before his eyes, the yeomen roared with mirth till the forest rang. As for King Richard, he laughed till the tears ran down his cheeks. Thus the band shot, each in turn, some getting off scot free, and some winning a buffet that always sent them to the grass. And now, last of all, Robin took his place, and all was hushed as he shot. The first shaft he shot split a piece from the stake on which the garland was hung; the second lodged within an inch of the other. "By my halidom,"[9] said King Richard to himself, "I would give a thousand pounds for this fellow to be one of my guard!" And now, for the third time Robin shot; but, alas for him! the arrow was ill-feathered,

9 By my halidom: a mild oath.

and, wavering to one side, it smote an inch outside the garland.

At this a great roar went up, those of the yeomen who sat upon the grass rolling over and over and shouting with laughter, for never before had they seen their master so miss his mark; but Robin flung his bow upon the ground with vexation. "Now, out upon it!" cried he. "That shaft had an ill feather to it, for I felt it as it left my fingers. Give me a clean arrow, and I will engage to split the wand with it."

At these words the yeomen laughed louder than ever. "Nay, good uncle," said Will Scarlet, in his soft, sweet voice, "thou hast had thy fair chance and hast missed thine aim out and out. I swear the arrow was as good as any that hath been loosed this day. Come hither; I owe thee somewhat, and would fain pay it."

"Go, good master," roared Friar Tuck, "and may my blessing go with thee. Thou hast bestowed these love-taps of Will Scarlet's with great freedom. It were pity an thou gottest not thine own share."

"It may not be," said merry Robin. "I am King here, and no subject may raise hand against the King. But even our great King Richard may yield to the holy Pope without shame, and even take a tap from him by way of penance; therefore I will yield myself to this holy friar, who seemeth to be one in authority, and will take my punishment from him." Thus saying, he turned to the King, "I prythee, brother, wilt thou take my punishing into thy holy hands?"

"With all my heart," quoth merry King Richard, rising from where he was sitting. "I owe thee somewhat for having lifted a heavy weight of fifty pounds from my purse. So make room for him on the green, lads."

"An thou makest me tumble," quoth Robin, "I will freely give thee back thy fifty pounds; but I tell thee, brother, if thou makest me not feel grass all along my back, I will take every farthing thou hast for thy boastful speech."

"So be it," said the King, "I am willing to venture it." Thereupon he rolled up his sleeve and showed an arm that made the yeomen stare. But Robin, with his feet wide apart, stood firmly planted, waiting the other, smiling. Then the King swung back his arm, and balancing himself a moment, he delivered a buffet at Robin that fell like a thunderbolt. Down went Robin headlong upon the grass, for the stroke would have felled a stone wall. Then how the yeomen shouted with laughter till their sides ached, for never had they seen such a buffet given in all their lives. As for Robin, he presently sat up and looked all around him, as though he had dropped from a cloud and had lit in a place he had never seen before. After a while, still gazing about him at his laughing yeomen, he put his finger tips softly to his ear and felt all around it tenderly. "Will Scarlet," said he, "count this fellow out his fifty pounds; I want nothing more either of his money or of him. A murrain[10] seize him and his buffeting! I would that I had taken my dues from thee, for I verily believe he hath

deafened mine ear from ever hearing again."

Then, while gusts of laughter still broke from the band, Will Scarlet counted out the fifty pounds, and the King dropped it back into his purse again. "I give thee thanks, fellow," said he, "and if ever thou shouldst wish for another box of the ear to match the one thou hast, come to me and I will fit thee with it for nought."

So spake the merry King; but, even as he ended, there came suddenly the sound of many voices, and out from the covert burst Little John and threescore men, with Sir Richard of the Lea in the midst. Across the glade they came running, and, as they came, Sir Richard shouted to Robin: "Make haste, dear friend, gather thy band together and come with me! King Richard left Nottingham Town this very morning, and cometh to seek thee in the woodlands. I know not how he cometh, for it was but a rumor of this that reached me; nevertheless, I know that it is the truth. Therefore hasten with all thy men, and come to Castle Lea, for there thou mayst lie hidden till thy present danger passeth. Who are these strangers that thou hast with thee?"

"Why," quoth merry Robin, rising from the grass, "these are certain gentle guests that came with us from the highroad over by Newstead Abbey. I know not their names, but I have become right well acquaint with this lusty rogue's palm this morning. Marry, the pleasure of this acquaintance hath cost me a deaf ear and fifty pounds to boot!"

10 murrain: plague.

352

Sir Richard looked keenly at the tall friar, who, drawing himself up to his full height, looked fixedly back at the knight. Then of a sudden Sir Richard's cheeks grew pale, for he knew who it was that he looked upon. Quickly he leaped from off his horse's back and flung himself upon his knees before the other. At this, the King, seeing that Sir Richard knew him, threw back his cowl, and all the yeomen saw his face and knew him also, for there was not one of them but had been in the crowd in the good town of Nottingham, and had seen him riding side by side with the Sheriff. Down they fell upon their knees, nor could they say a word. Then the King looked all around right grimly, and, last of all, his glance came back and rested again upon Sir Richard of the Lea.

"How is this, Sir Richard?" said he, sternly. "How darest thou step between me and these fellows? and how darest thou offer thy knightly Castle of the Lea for a refuge to them? Wilt thou make it a hiding place for the most renowned outlaws in England?"

Then Sir Richard of the Lea raised his eyes to the King's face. "Far be it from me," said he, "to do aught that could bring your majesty's anger upon me. Yet, sooner would I face your majesty's wrath than suffer aught of harm that I could stay to fall upon Robin Hood and his band; for to them I owe life, honor, everything. Should I, then, desert him in his hour of need?"

Ere the Knight had done speaking, one of the mock friars that stood near the King came forward and knelt beside Sir Richard, and throwing back his cowl showed the face of young Sir Henry of the Lea. Then Sir Henry grasped his father's hand and said, "Here kneels one who hath served thee well, King Richard, and, as thou knowest, hath stepped between thee and death in Palestine; yet do I abide by my dear father, and here I say also, that I would freely give shelter to this noble outlaw, Robin Hood, even though it brought thy wrath upon me, for my father's honor and my father's welfare are as dear to me as mine own."

King Richard looked from one to the other of the kneeling knights, and at last the frown faded from his brow and a smile twitched at the corners of his lips. "Marry, Sir Richard," quoth the King, "thou art a bold-spoken knight, and thy freedom of speech weigheth not heavily against thee with me. This young son of thine taketh after his sire both in boldness of speech and of deed, for, as he sayeth, he stepped one time betwixt me and death; wherefore I would pardon thee for his sake even if thou hadst done more than thou hast. Rise all of you, for ye shall suffer no harm through me this day, for it were pity that a merry time should end in such a manner as to mar its joyousness."

Then all arose and the King beckoned Robin Hood to come to him. "How now," quoth he, "is thine ear still too deaf to hear me speak?"

"Mine ears would be deafened in death ere they would cease to hear your majesty's voice," said Robin.

"As for the blow that your majesty struck me, I would say that though my sins are haply many, methinks they have been paid up in full thereby."

"Thinkest thou so?" said the King with somewhat of sternness in his voice. "Now I tell thee that but for three things, to wit, my mercifulness, my love for a stout woodsman, and the loyalty thou hast avowed for me, thine ears, mayhap, might have been more tightly closed than ever a buffet from me could have shut them. Talk not lightly of thy sins, good Robin. But come, look up. Thy danger is past, for hereby I give thee and all thy band free pardon. But, in sooth, I cannot let you roam the forest as ye have done in the past; therefore I will take thee at thy word, when thou didst say thou wouldst give thy service to me, and thou shalt go back to London with me. We will take that bold knave Little John also, and likewise thy cousin, Will Scarlet, and thy minstrel, Allan a Dale. As for the rest of thy band, we will take their names and have them duly recorded as royal rangers; for methinks it were wiser to have them changed to law-abiding caretakers of our deer in Sherwood than to leave them to run at large as outlawed slayers thereof. But now get a feast ready; I would fain see how ye live in the leafy woodlands."

So Robin bade his men make ready a grand feast. Straightway great fires were kindled and burned brightly, at which savory things roasted sweetly. While this was go-

ing forward, the King bade Robin call Allan a Dale for he would hear him sing. So word was passed for Allan, and presently he came, bringing his harp.

"Marry," said King Richard, "if thy singing match thy looks it is fair enough. Prythee, strike up a ditty and let us have a taste of thy skill."

Then Allan touched his harp lightly, and all words were hushed while he sang thus:

" 'Oh where hast thou been, my daughter?
    Oh where hast thou been this day,
      Daughter, my daughter?'
  'Oh, I have been to the river's side,
  Where the waters lie all gray and wide,
  And the gray sky broods o'er the leaden
      tide,
    And the shrill wind sighs a straining.'

" 'What sawest thou there, my daughter?
    What sawest thou there this day,
      Daughter, my daughter?'
  'Oh, I saw a boat come drifting nigh,
  Where the quivering rushes hiss and sigh,
  And the water soughs as it gurgles by,
    And the shrill wind sighs a straining.'

" 'What sailed in the boat, my daughter?
    What sailed in the boat this day,
      Daughter, my daughter?'
  'Oh, there was one all clad in white,
  And about his face hung a pallid light,
  And his eyes gleamed sharp like the
      stars at night
    And the shrill wind sighed a straining.'

" 'And what said he, my daughter?
    What said he to thee this day,
      Daughter, my daughter?'
  'Oh, said he nought, but did he this:
  Thrice on my lips did he press a kiss,
  And my heartstrings shrunk with an
      awful bliss,
    And the shrill wind sighed a straining.'

354

" 'Why growest thou so cold, my daughter?
  Why growest thou so cold and white,
    Daughter, my daughter?'
Oh never a word the daughter said,
But she sat all straight with a drooping
      head,
For her heart was stilled and her face
    was dead:
And the shrill wind sighed a straining."

All listened in silence; and when Allan a Dale had done King Richard heaved a sigh. "By the breath of my body, Allan," quoth he, "thou hast such a wondrous sweet voice that it strangely moves my heart. But what doleful ditty is this for the lips of a stout yeoman? I would rather hear thee sing a song of love and battle than a sad thing like that. Moreover, I understand it not; what meanest thou by the words?"

"I know not, your majesty," said Allan, shaking his head, "for ofttimes I sing that which I do not clearly understand mine own self."

"Well, well," quoth the King, "let it pass; only I tell thee this, Allan, thou shouldst turn thy songs to such matters as I spoke of, to wit, love or war; for in sooth thou hast a sweeter voice than Blondell, and methought he was the best minstrel that ever I heard."

But now one came forward and said that the feast was ready; so Robin Hood brought King Richard and those with him to where it lay all spread out on fair white linen cloths which lay upon the soft green grass. Then King Richard sat him down and feasted and drank, and when he was done he swore roundly that he had never sat at such a lusty repast in all his life before.

That night he lay in Sherwood Forest upon a bed of sweet green leaves, and early the next morning he set forth from the woodlands for Nottingham Town, Robin Hood and all of his band going with him. You may guess what a stir there was in the good town when all these famous outlaws came marching into the streets. As for the Sheriff, he knew not what to say nor where to look when he saw Robin Hood in such high favor with the King, whilst all his heart was filled with gall because of the vexation[11] that lay upon him.

The next day the King took leave of Nottingham Town; so Robin Hood and Little John and Will Scarlet and Allan a Dale shook hands with all the rest of the band, kissing the cheeks of each man, and swearing that they would often come to Sherwood and see them. Then each mounted his horse and rode away in the train of the King.

11 **vexation:** irritation.

Understanding Literature

1. When Robin Hood proposes a toast to King Richard, the King replies, "Methinks, good fellow, . . . thou hast drunk to thine own confusion." What does the King mean by this?
2. In all legends the hero must be skillful and adept with weapons. Robin Hood is particularly skillful with what weapon? Give proof of his skill.
3. What do you know about Will Scarlet, Allan a Dale, and Friar Tuck from their appearances in this story?
4. What is King Richard's solution to the problem of Robin Hood's escapades? What does this solution show about King Richard's character?
5. King Richard says that he does not understand Allan a Dale's song. What do you think the song is about?
6. Very often the reader will know something or be told something that the characters within a story know nothing about. This technique, used in several places in "King Richard Cometh to Sherwood Forest," makes the reader feel more involved in the story. In which situations in this selection is the reader taken into the author's confidence whereas an actual character in the story is left in ignorance?
7. Compare Robin Hood as a hero to the other legendary heroes you have read about in this unit. In what ways are they similar? In what ways are they dissimilar?

The One-Act Play

THE ONE-ACT PLAY is another way of telling a story. It differs from the short story mainly in that the play is intended to be acted out on the stage; the author is therefore limited to writing what his characters say and do. The author cannot break in to tell you what he wants you to know; he must have his characters dramatize the information, act it out. Because a play is intended to be performed on a stage, when you are reading a play you have to imagine what the actors are doing and how they would say their lines. Otherwise you are like a person who reads notes of music, but does not create any sounds or "hear" them in his imagination.

Now, what is a one-act play? First, it is a play that is brief and to the point. It takes place at one time, in one setting, and deals with one crucial situation. It supplies only enough other detail so that you understand the crucial situation. It tries to produce one impression, such as horror or humor.

The play must begin quickly. The first three or four speeches form the introduction or *exposition:* You learn when and where the action is taking place, who the characters are and how they are related to one another, and what has taken place before the curtain went up.

After the exposition is developed, the play usually moves into the complication, or *conflict*, which must be resolved in the play. The need for a solution creates the *suspense*. The action then proceeds to the *climax*, the point of greatest emotional impact. This is followed by the *resolution*, in which the problem of the play is solved and the outcome of the situation is made clear.

As the play begins, the characters talk and reveal the situation. But they are also acting in a particular *setting*, usually described by the author in italics at the beginning of the written version of the play. The setting may be a friendly country inn or a lonely one far from other people; it may be an extravagantly furnished room or a poor shack. Whatever the scene, it may tell you something about the people. It may create a happy or a mysterious atmosphere for the play. It will suggest the time of day and probably the season of the year, and these facts may have some bearing on the meaning of the play. And the setting may help to advance the plot; perhaps the story could not have happened in another setting.

In addition to a description of the setting, the author generally includes *stage directions*, the directions to the reader or actor. Do not skip over them. Sometimes the author extends these comments to tell you something about what the characters look like. He may use further stage directions at key points in the play to explain how the characters should say certain lines, or how they should react to certain situations.

As the play proceeds, the *dialogue*, the conversation of the characters, can explain things to the audience even though the characters speak only to each other. They may say something which moves the plot along; they may express ideas which the author wants to convey; and, what is most important, the characters can and often will reveal the kind of people they are by what they say.

The major element of the play is the *characterization*, the author's revelation of what his characters are like. There are several methods the playwright can use to present or characterize the people in his drama: through what they say, through what they do, and through what others say about them. Sometimes you will even find the author making direct comments about the characters in the stage directions.

Since dramas are intended to be acted for an audience, perhaps you will be able to perform or read a part in one of the plays that follows. Do not try it without rehearsing. No play is so simple that you can get up and read it adequately without asking yourself: What kind of person am I portraying? How would he say this line? What key words would he emphasize? At what point in the play would he speak happily, angrily, sadly, quickly, slowly? Study your part first and then act it. Only by thinking and practice can you become another person, and the chance to become another person, even for a short while, is one of the great attractions of the world of the theater.

After stealing a large ruby in India, the characters in this play are being pursued by three Indian priests. The thieves have settled down temporarily and safely, so they think, in a remote inn. Can they get away with the robbery?

A Night at an Inn *

Lord Dunsany

IMPROVING YOUR READING: This play is a *melodrama*. Its plot is romantic; it does not deal with everyday occurrences. In this type of play you are more concerned with the plot, what happens, than with the motivation of the characters, why something happens. The people are merely types; their good acts are rewarded and their bad acts are punished. In any melodrama the playwright attempts to awaken feelings of sympathy, horror, or joy. The appeal of this play is that it makes you feel a sense of horror.

CHARACTERS

A. E. SCOTT-FORTESCUE (THE TOFF), *a dilapidated gentleman*

WILLIAM JONES (BILL)
ALBERT THOMAS
JACOB SMITH (SNIGGERS) } *merchant sailors*

FIRST PRIEST OF KLESH
SECOND PRIEST OF KLESH
THIRD PRIEST OF KLESH
KLESH

(*The curtain rises on a room in an inn.* SNIGGERS *and* BILL *are talking,* THE TOFF[1] *is reading a paper.* ALBERT *sits a little apart.*)

SNIGGERS. What's his idea, I wonder?

BILL. I don't know.

SNIGGERS. And how much longer will he keep us here?

BILL. We've been here three days.

SNIGGERS. And 'aven't seen a soul.

BILL. And a pretty penny it cost us when he rented the pub.

SNIGGERS. 'Ow long did 'e rent the pub for?

BILL. You never know with him.

SNIGGERS. It's lonely enough.

BILL. 'Ow long did you rent the pub for, Toffy?

1 **Toff:** English slang term for a fine gentleman; a man about town.

* Copyright, 1916, by Sunwise Turn, Inc.
Copyright, 1944 (In Renewal), by Edward John Moreton Drax Plunkett.
All Rights Reserved.

CAUTION: Professionals and amateurs are hereby warned that "A NIGHT AT AN INN," being fully protected under the copyright laws of the United States of America, the British Empire, including the Dominion of Canada, and all other countries of the Copyright Union, is subject to a royalty. All rights, including professional, amateur, motion pictures, recitation, public reading, radio and television broadcasting and the rights of translation into foreign languages are strictly reserved. Amateurs may give stage production of this play upon payment of a royalty of Ten Dollars for each performance one week before the play is to be given to Samuel French, Inc., at 25 West 45th Street, New York 36, N.Y., or 7623 Sunset Blvd., Hollywood 46, Calif., or if in Canada to Samuel French (Canada) Ltd., at 27 Grenville St., Toronto, Ont.

(THE TOFF *continues to read a* *sporting paper; he takes no* *notice of what is said.*)

SNIGGERS. 'E's *such* a toff.

BILL. Yet 'e's clever, no mistake.

SNIGGERS. Those clever ones are the beggars to make a muddle. Their plans are clever enough, but they don't work, and then they make a mess of things much worse than you or me.

BILL. Ah!

SNIGGERS. I don't like this place.

BILL. Why not?

SNIGGERS. I don't like the looks of it.

BILL. He's keeping us here because here those men can't find us. The three heathen priests what was looking for us so. But we want to go, and sell our ruby soon.

ALBERT. There's no sense in it.

BILL. Why not, Albert?

ALBERT. Because I gave those devils the slip in Hull.

BILL. You give 'em the slip, Albert?

ALBERT. The slip, all three of them. The fellows with the gold spots on their foreheads. I had the ruby then and I give them the slip in Hull.

BILL. How did you do it, Albert?

ALBERT. I had the ruby and they were following me. . . .

BILL. Who told them you had the ruby? You didn't show it.

ALBERT. No. . . . But they kind of know.

SNIGGERS. They kind of know, Albert?

ALBERT. Yes, they know if you've got it. Well, they sort of mouched[2] after me, and I tells a policeman and he says, Oh, they were only three poor heathens and they wouldn't hurt me. Ugh! When I thought of what they did in Malta to poor old Jim.

BILL. Yes, and to George in Bombay before we started.

SNIGGERS. Ugh!

BILL. Why didn't you give 'em in charge?

ALBERT. What about the ruby, Bill?

BILL. Ah!

ALBERT. Well, I did better than that. I walks up and down through Hull. I walks slow enough. And then I turns a corner and I runs. I never sees a corner but I turns it. But sometimes I let a corner pass just to fool them. I twists about like a hare. Then I sits down and waits. No priests.

SNIGGERS. What?

BILL. Well done, Albert!

SNIGGERS (*after a sigh of content*). Why didn't you tell us?

ALBERT. 'Cause 'e won't let you speak. 'E's got 'is plans and 'e thinks we're silly folk. Things must be done 'is way. And all the time I've give 'em the slip. Might 'ave 'ad one o' them crooked knives in him before now but for me who give 'em the slip in Hull.

BILL. Well done, Albert! Do you hear that, Toffy? Albert has give 'em the slip.

THE TOFF. Yes, I hear.

SNIGGERS. Well, what do you say to that?

2 **mouched:** sneaked; crept.

THE TOFF. O . . . Well done, Albert!

ALBERT. And what a' you going to do?

THE TOFF. Going to wait.

ALBERT. Don't seem to know what 'e's waiting for.

SNIGGERS. It's a nasty place.

ALBERT. It's getting silly, Bill. Our money's gone and we want to sell the ruby. Let's get on to a town.

BILL. But 'e won't come.

ALBERT. Then we'll leave him.

SNIGGERS. We'll be all right if we keep away from Hull.

ALBERT. We'll go to London.

BILL. But 'e must 'ave 'is share.

SNIGGERS. All right. Only let's go. (to THE TOFF.) We're going, do you hear? Give us the ruby.

THE TOFF. Certainly.

> (He gives them a ruby from his waistcoat pocket; it is the size of a small hen's egg. He goes on reading his paper.)

ALBERT. Come on, Sniggers.

> (Exeunt ALBERT and SNIGGERS.)

BILL. Good-by, old man. We'll give you your fair share, but there's nothing to do here—no girls, no halls, and we must sell the ruby.

THE TOFF. I'm not a fool, Bill.

BILL. No, no, of course not. Of course you ain't, and you've helped us a lot. Good-by. You'll say good-by?

THE TOFF. Oh, yes, good-by.

> (Still reads his paper. Exit BILL. THE TOFF puts his revolver on the table beside him and goes on with his papers. After a moment the three men come rushing in again, frightened.)

SNIGGERS (out of breath). We've come back, Toffy.

THE TOFF. So you have.

ALBERT. Toffy. . . . How did they get here?

THE TOFF. They walked, of course.

ALBERT. But it's eighty miles.

SNIGGERS. Did you know they were here, Toffy?

THE TOFF. Expected them about now.

ALBERT. Eighty miles!

BILL. Toffy, old man . . . what are we to do?

THE TOFF. Ask Albert.

BILL. If they can do things like this, there's no one can save us but you, Toffy. . . . I always knew you were a clever one. We won't be fools any more. We'll obey you, Toffy.

THE TOFF. You're brave enough and strong enough. There isn't many that would steal a ruby eye out of an idol's head, and such an idol as that was to look at, and on such a night. You're brave enough, Bill. But you're all three of you fools. Jim would have none of my plans, and where's Jim? And George. What did they do to him?

SNIGGERS. Don't, Toffy!

THE TOFF. Well, then, your strength is no use to you. You want cleverness; or they'll have you the way they had George and Jim.

ALL. Ugh!

THE TOFF. Those priests would follow you round the world in circles. Year after year, till they got the idol's eye. And if we died with it, they'd follow our grandchildren. That fool thinks he can escape from men like that by running round three streets in the town of Hull.

ALBERT. God's truth, *you* 'aven't escaped them, because they're '*ere*.

THE TOFF. So I supposed.

ALBERT. You *supposed*.

THE TOFF. Yes, I believe there's no announcement in the Society papers. But I took this country seat especially to receive them. There's plenty of room if you dig, it is pleasantly situated, and, what is more important, it is in a very quiet neighborhood. So I am at home to them this afternoon.

BILL. Well, *you're* a deep one.

THE TOFF. And remember, you've only my wits between you and death, and don't put your futile[3] plans against those of an educated gentleman.

ALBERT. If you're a gentleman, why don't you go about among gentlemen instead of the likes of us?

THE TOFF. Because I was too clever for them as I am too clever for you.

ALBERT. Too clever for them?

THE TOFF. I never lost a game of cards in my life.

BILL. You never lost a game?

THE TOFF. Not when there was money in it.

BILL. Well, well!

THE TOFF. Have a game of poker?

ALL. No, thanks.

THE TOFF. Then do as you're told.

BILL. All right, Toffy.

SNIGGERS. I saw something just then. Hadn't we better draw the curtains?

3 **futile:** useless.

THE TOFF. No.

SNIGGERS. What?

THE TOFF. Don't draw the curtains.

SNIGGERS. Oh, all right.

BILL. But, Toffy, they can see us. One doesn't let the enemy do that. I don't see why. . . .

THE TOFF. No, of course you don't.

BILL. Oh, all right, Toffy.

(*All begin to pull out revolvers.*)

THE TOFF (*putting his own away*). No revolvers, please.

ALBERT. Why not?

THE TOFF. Because I don't want any noise at my party. We might get guests that hadn't been invited. *Knives* are a different matter.

(*All draw knives.* **THE TOFF** *signs to them not to draw them yet.* **TOFFY** *has already taken back his ruby.*)

BILL. I think they're coming, Toffy.

THE TOFF. Not yet.

ALBERT. When will they come?

THE TOFF. When I am quite ready to receive them. Not before.

SNIGGERS. I should like to get this over.

THE TOFF. Should you? Then we'll have them now.

SNIGGERS. Now?

THE TOFF. Yes. Listen to me. You shall do as you see me do. You will all pretend to go out. I'll show you how. I've got the ruby. When they see me alone they will come for their idol's eye.

BILL. How can they tell like this which of us has it?

THE TOFF. I confess I don't know, but they seem to.

SNIGGERS. What will you do when
they come in?

THE TOFF. I shall do nothing.

SNIGGERS. What?

THE TOFF. They will creep up behind me. Then, my friends, Sniggers
and Bill and Albert, who gave them
the slip, will do what they can.

BILL. All right, Toffy. Trust us.

THE TOFF. If you're a little slow,
you will see enacted the cheerful
spectacle that accompanied the demise[4] of Jim.

SNIGGERS. Don't, Toffy. We'll be
there, all right.

THE TOFF. Very well. Now watch
me.

(*He goes past the windows to
the inner door R. He opens
it inwards, then under cover*

*of the open door, he slips
down on his knee and closes
it, remaining on the inside, appearing to have gone out. He
signs to the others, who understand. Then he appears to
re-enter in the same manner.*)

THE TOFF. Now, I shall sit with
my back to the door. You go out
one by one, so far as our friends can
make out. Crouch very low to be
on the safe side. They mustn't see
you through the window.

(BILL *makes his sham[5] exit.*)

THE TOFF. Remember, no revolvers. The police are, I believe, proverbially inquisitive.[6]

(*The other two follow* BILL.
*All three are now crouching
inside the door R.* THE TOFF

5 **sham:** false.
6 **proverbially inquisitive:** commonly spoken of as
curious.

4 **demise** (dǐ mīz′): death.

puts the ruby beside him on the table. He lights a cigarette. The door at the back opens so slowly that you can hardly say at what moment it began. THE TOFF *picks up his paper. A native of India wriggles along the floor ever so slowly, seeking cover from chairs. He moves L. where* THE TOFF *is. The three sailors are R.* SNIGGERS *and* ALBERT *lean forward.* BILL'S *arm keeps them back. An armchair had better conceal them from the Indian. The* PRIEST *nears* THE TOFF. BILL *watches to see if any more are coming. Then he leaps forward alone—he has taken his boots off—and knifes the* PRIEST. *The* PRIEST *tries to shout but* BILL'S *left hand is over his mouth.* THE TOFF *continues to read his sporting paper. He never looks around.*)

BILL (*sotto voce*).[7] There's only one, Toffy. What shall we do?

THE TOFF (*without turning his head*). Only one?

BILL. Yes.

THE TOFF. Wait a moment. Let me think. (*Still apparently absorbed in his paper.*) Ah, yes. You go back, Bill. We must attract another guest. . . . Now, are you ready?

BILL. Yes.

THE TOFF. All right. You shall now see my demise at my Yorkshire residence. You must receive guests for me. (*He leaps up in full view of*

the window, flings up both arms and falls to the floor near the dead PRIEST.) Now, be ready.

(*His eyes close. There is a long pause. Again the door opens, very, very slowly. Another* PRIEST *creeps in. He has three golden spots upon his forehead. He looks round, then he creeps up to his companion and turns him over and looks inside of his clenched hands. Then he looks at the recumbent*[8] TOFF. *Then he creeps toward him.* BILL *slips after him and knifes him like the other with his left hand over his mouth.*)

BILL (*sotto voce*). We've only got two, Toffy.

THE TOFF. Still another.

BILL. What'll we do?

THE TOFF (*sitting up*). Hum.

BILL. This is the best way, much.

THE TOFF. Out of the question. Never play the same game twice.

BILL. Why not, Toffy?

THE TOFF. Doesn't work if you do.

BILL. Well?

THE TOFF. I have it, Albert. You will now walk into the room. I showed you how to do it.

ALBERT. Yes.

THE TOFF. Just run over here and have a fight at this window with these two men.

ALBERT. But they're. . . .

THE TOFF. Yes, they're dead, my perspicuous[9] Albert. But Bill and I

8 **recumbent:** inactive; lying down.
9 **perspicuous:** probably confused with *perspicacious:* shrewd; quick-witted.

7 *sotto voce* (sŏt′ō vō′chĭ): in a whisper.

are going to resuscitate[10] them. . . . Come on.

(BILL *picks up a body under the arms.*)

THE TOFF. That's right, Bill. (*Does the same.*) Come and help us, Sniggers. (SNIGGERS *comes.*) Keep low, keep low. Wave their arms about, Sniggers. Don't show yourself. Now, Albert, over you go. Our Albert is slain. Back you get, Bill. Back, Sniggers. Still, Albert. Mustn't move when he comes. Not a muscle.

(*A face appears at the window and stays for some time. Then the door opens and, looking craftily round, the third* PRIEST *enters. He looks at his companions' bodies and turns round. He suspects something. He takes up one of the knives and with a knife in each hand he puts his back to the wall. He looks to the left and right.*)

THE TOFF. Come on, Bill.

(*The* PRIEST *rushes to the door.* THE TOFF *knifes the last* PRIEST *from behind.*)

BILL. Well done, Toffy. Oh, you are a deep one!

ALBERT. A deep one if ever there was one.

SNIGGERS. There ain't any more, Bill, are there?

THE TOFF. No more in the world, my friend.

BILL. Aye, that's all there are. There were only three in the temple.

10 **resuscitate:** revive; recall to life.

Three priests and their beastly idol.

ALBERT. What is it worth, Toffy? Is it worth a thousand pounds?

THE TOFF. It's worth all they've got in the shop. Worth just whatever we like to ask for it.

ALBERT. Then we're millionaires now.

THE TOFF. Yes, and, what is more important, we no longer have any heirs.

BILL. We'll have to sell it now.

ALBERT. That won't be easy. It's a pity it isn't small and we had half a dozen. Hadn't the idol any other on him?

BILL. No, he was green jade all over and only had this one eye. He had it in the middle of his forehead and was a long sight uglier than anything else in the world.

SNIGGERS. I'm sure we ought all to be very grateful to Toffy.

BILL. And, indeed, we ought.

ALBERT. If it hadn't been for him.

BILL. Yes, if it hadn't been for old Toffy. . . .

SNIGGERS. He's a deep one.

THE TOFF. Well, you see I just have a knack of foreseeing things.

SNIGGERS. I should think you did.

BILL. Why, I don't suppose anything happens that our Toff doesn't foresee. Does it, Toffy?

THE TOFF. Well, I don't think it does, Bill. I don't think it often does.

BILL. Life is no more than just a game of cards to our old Toff.

THE TOFF. Well, we've taken these fellows' trick.

SNIGGERS (*going to window*). It wouldn't do for anyone to see them.

THE TOFF. Oh, nobody will come

this way. We're all alone on a moor.

BILL. Where will we put them?

THE TOFF. Bury them in the cellar, but there's no hurry.

BILL. And what then, Toffy?

THE TOFF. Why, then we'll go to London and upset the ruby business. We have really come through this job very nicely.

BILL. I think the first thing that we ought to do is to give a little supper to old Toffy. We'll bury these fellows tonight.

ALBERT. Yes, let's.

SNIGGERS. The very thing!

BILL. And we'll all drink his health.

ALBERT. Good old Toffy!

SNIGGERS. He ought to have been a general or a premier.

(*They get bottles from cupboard, etc.*)

THE TOFF. Well, we've earned our bit of a supper. (*They sit down.*)

BILL (*glass in hand*). Here's to old Toffy, who guessed everything!

ALBERT AND SNIGGERS. Good old Toffy!

BILL. Toffy, who saved our lives and made our fortunes.

ALBERT AND SNIGGERS. Hear! Hear!

THE TOFF. And here's to Bill, who saved me twice tonight.

SNIGGERS. Hear, hear! Hear! He·r!

ALBERT. He foresees everything.

BILL. A speech, Toffy. A speech from our general.

ALL. Yes, a speech.

SNIGGERS. A speech.

THE TOFF. Well, get me some water. This whisky's too much for my head, and I must keep it clear

till our friends are safe in the cellar.

BILL. Water? Yes, of course. Get him some water, Sniggers.

SNIGGERS. We don't use water here. Where shall I get it?

BILL. Outside in the garden.

(*Exit* SNIGGERS.)

ALBERT. Here's to the future!

BILL. Here's to Albert Thomas, Esquire.

ALBERT. And William Jones, Esquire.

(*Re-enter* SNIGGERS, *terrified.*)

THE TOFF. Hullo, here's Jacob Smith, Esquire, J. P., alias Sniggers, back again.

SNIGGERS. Toffy, I've been thinking about my share in that ruby. I don't want it, Toffy; I don't want it.

THE TOFF. Nonsense, Sniggers. Nonsense.

SNIGGERS. You shall have it, Toffy, you shall have it yourself, only say Sniggers has no share in this 'ere ruby. Say it, Toffy, say it!

BILL. Want to turn informer, Sniggers?

SNIGGERS. No, no. Only I don't want the ruby, Toffy. . . .

THE TOFF. No more nonsense, Sniggers. We're all in together in this. If one hangs, we all hang; but they won't outwit me. Besides, it's not a hanging affair, they had their knives.

SNIGGERS. Toffy, Toffy, I always treated you fair, Toffy. I was always one to say, "Give Toffy a chance." Take back my share, Toffy.

THE TOFF. What's the matter? What are you driving at?

SNIGGERS. Take it back, Toffy.

THE TOFF. Answer me, what are you up to?

SNIGGERS. I don't want my share any more.

BILL. Have you seen the police?

(ALBERT *pulls out his knife.*)

SNIGGERS. There's no police.

THE TOFF. Well, then, what's the matter?

BILL. Out with it.

SNIGGERS. I swear to God. . . .

ALBERT. Well?

THE TOFF. Don't interrupt.

SNIGGERS. I swear I saw something *what I didn't like.*

THE TOFF. What you didn't like?

SNIGGERS (*in tears*). O Toffy, Toffy, take it back. Take my share. Say you take it.

THE TOFF. What has he seen?

(*Dead silence, only broken by SNIGGERS' sobs. Then steps are heard. Enter a hideous idol. It is blind and gropes its way to the ruby and picks it up and screws it into a socket in the forehead. SNIGGERS still weeps softly; the rest stare in horror. The idol steps out, not groping. Its steps move off, then stop.*)

THE TOFF. O great heavens!

ALBERT (*in a childish, plaintive[11] voice*). What is it, Toffy?

BILL. Albert, it is that obscene idol (*in a whisper*) come from India.

ALBERT. It is gone.

BILL. It has taken its eye.

SNIGGERS. We are saved.

A VOICE OFF (*with outlandish ac-*cent). Meestaire William Jones, Able Seaman.

(THE TOFF *has never spoken, never moved. He only gazes stupidly in horror.*)

BILL. Albert, Albert, what is this?

(*He rises and walks out. One moan is heard. SNIGGERS goes to the window. He falls back sickly.*)

ALBERT (*in a whisper*). What has happened?

SNIGGERS. I have seen it. I have seen it. Oh, I have seen it!

(*He returns to table.*)

THE TOFF (*laying his hand very gently on SNIGGERS' arm, speaking softly and winningly*). What was it, Sniggers?

SNIGGERS. I have seen it.

ALBERT. What?

SNIGGERS. Oh!

VOICE. Meestaire Albert Thomas, Able Seaman.

ALBERT. Must I go, Toffy, Toffy, must I go?

SNIGGERS (*clutching him*). Don't move.

ALBERT (*going*). Toffy, Toffy.

(*Exit.*)

VOICE. Meestaire Jacob Smith, Able Seaman.

SNIGGERS. I can't go, Toffy. I can't go. I can't do it. (*He goes.*)

VOICE. Meestaire Arnold Everett Scott-Fortescue, late Esquire, Able Seaman.

THE TOFF. I did not foresee it.

(*Exit.*)

CURTAIN

---

11 plaintive: sorrowful.

Understanding Literature

1. The play opens with a conversation between Sniggers, Bill, and Albert. Up to the time that The Toff gives them the ruby, what do you learn about the situation? Who are these people? What problem causes the suspense?

2. After The Toff gives up the ruby, why do the men come back so frightened? Why do they decide to obey The Toff? How is he different from the other three? What is his plan? How does he lure the first priest into the Inn? What are the priests after?

3. How does The Toff lure the next two priests? What happens as each enters?

4. After the priests have been done away with and all seems well, Bill says, "Why, I don't suppose anything happens that our Toff doesn't foresee." This speech becomes ironic as the action that actually occurs is the opposite of what they expected to happen. Explain the irony in terms of what they expect and what they get.

5. Why does the author have Sniggers go outside for water? How does this action affect the play?

6. How would the last scene (after Sniggers's return from outside) be acted? Why is it more effective to keep the Voice off stage? How is the last line ironic?

7. At the point when the thieves seem safe, they compare their actions to a game of cards. How is the action of the play like a game of cards?

8. Point out the qualities of this play which are characteristic of a melodrama.

This is a play about a ghost and a practical joke. The problem can be expressed in a question: Will the ghost of Jerry Bundler appear on this lonely winter night?

The Ghost of Jerry Bundler°

W. W. Jacobs and Charles Rock

IMPROVING YOUR READING: The presentation of a play, whether by amateurs or by professional actors, involves a great deal of planning and work. In addition to learning their lines and "becoming" the characters in the play, the actors must, under the guidance of a director, learn their positions on the stage. The director *blocks* the action; that is, he tells the actors where to stand or sit and when to move from one part of the stage to another. Unless these details are carefully planned, the staging of a play is awkward and confusing.

The version of "The Ghost of Jerry Bundler" printed here is an *acting edition;* it contains much more detail concerning the scene and the properties than does a reading edition, which is the version in which the other plays in this unit are printed. As you read the play you will notice stage directions such as up *C*, *RC*, and *L*. These are abbreviations for upstage center, right center, and left, which are divisions of the stage. This simplified diagram should make these stage positions clear.

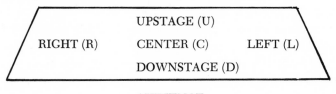

UPSTAGE (U)

RIGHT (R)   CENTER (C)   LEFT (L)

DOWNSTAGE (D)

AUDIENCE

As you read this play, try to visualize in your mind where each character is. You should also keep track of the entrances and exits of the actors. The skillful playwright makes the entrances and exits believable; if a man enters or leaves the stage, he must have a reason. Watch the skill with which Jacobs and Rock move their characters around. They want some characters to know certain things, yet they must keep the information from others. Then, too, the audience must know the whole story.

° Copyright, 1908, by W. W. Jacobs and Charles Rock.
Copyright, 1935 (In renewal), by William Wymark Jacobs.
All Rights Reserved.

CAUTION: Professionals and amateurs are hereby warned that "THE GHOST OF JERRY BUNDLER," being fully protected under the copyright laws of the United States of America, the British Empire, including the Dominion of Canada, and all other countries of the Copyright Union, is subject to a royalty. All rights, including professional, amateur, motion pictures, recitation, public reading, radio and television broadcasting and the rights of translation into foreign languages are strictly reserved. Amateurs may give stage production of this play upon payment of a royalty of Five Dollars for each performance one week before the play is to be given to Samuel French, Inc., at 25 West 45th St., New York 36, N.Y., or 7623 Sunset Blvd., Hollywood 46, Calif., or if in Canada to Samuel French (Canada) Ltd., at 27 Grenville St., Toronto, Ont.

HIRST	SOMERS
PENFOLD	BELDON
MALCOLM	DR. LEEK

GEORGE (a waiter)

SCENE: *The Commercial Room in an old-fashioned hotel in a small country town. An air of old-fashioned comfort is in evidence everywhere. Old sporting prints on the walls.*

On the table up c[1] *are half a dozen candlesticks, old-fashioned shape with snuffer attached. Two pairs of carpet slippers are set up within fender.[2] Red curtains to window recess. Shutters or blinds to windows. Armchair and about six other chairs in the room. One old-fashioned settle.[3] One small table. Clock. Decanter of water, half a dozen toddy tumblers. Matches, etc. The only light is a ruddy glow from the fire. Kettle on hob.[4] Moonlight from* R *of window when shutter is opened. Practical chandelier from ceiling or lights at side of mantelpiece. DOCTOR'S coat and muffler on chair up* L,[5] *his cap on mantelpiece.*

All lights out, dark stage. Opening music. Curtain rise—ticking of clock heard. Wind, then church clock chimes, the Lights come very slowly up, when the red glow is seen in the fireplace the low murmurs of the characters heard, and gradually get louder as lights come up to when SOMERS'S voice tops all.

(The stage occupied by all characters except GEORGE *the waiter. Discovered,* PENFOLD, *sitting in armchair* L *of fire, above it.* DOCTOR LEEK *standing above fire and leaning on mantelshelf.* HIRST *sitting on settle below fire and nearest to audience.* SOMERS *seated on settle with him but above him.* MALCOLM *and* BELDON *on chairs* RC, *facing fire.* ALL *are smoking, and drink from their respective glasses from time to time.* SOMERS *has just finished a story as Curtain rises.)*

OMNES.[6] Oh, I say, that sounds impossible, etc.

SOMERS. Haunted or not haunted, the fact remains that no one stays in the house long. It's been let to several tenants since the time of the murder, but they never completed their tenancy. The last tenant held out for a month, but at last he gave up like the rest, and cleared out, although he had done the place up thoroughly, and must have been

1 **up C:** upstage, or at the rear of the stage, in the center.
2 **fender:** fireplace screen.
3 **settle:** long wooden bench with arms, a high solid back, and a compartment below it frequently used as a chest.
4 **hob:** shelf at the back or side of a fireplace where things may be kept warm.
5 **up L:** upstage left.

6 **Omnes:** all; all characters speaking together.

pounds out of pocket[7] by the transaction.

MALCOLM. Well, it's a capital ghost story, I admit, that is, as a story, but I for one can't swallow it.

HIRST. I don't know, it is not nearly so improbable as some I have heard. Of course it's an old idea that spirits like to get into the company of human beings. A man told me once, that he traveled down by the Great Western, with a ghost as fellow passenger, and hadn't the slightest suspicion of it, until the inspector came for tickets. My friend said, the way that ghost tried to keep up appearances, by feeling in all its pockets, and even looking on the floor for its ticket, was quite touching. Ultimately it gave it up, and with a loud groan vanished through the ventilator.

(SOMERS, MALCOLM *and* LEEK *laugh heartily.*)

BELDON. Oh, I say come now, that'll do.

PENFOLD (*seriously*). Personally I don't think it's a subject for jesting. I have never seen an apparition myself, but I have known people who have, and I consider that they form a very interesting link between us and the afterlife. There's a ghost story connected with this house, you know.

OMNES. Eh! Oh? Really!

MALCOLM (*rising and going to mantelpiece, takes up his glass of toddy*). Well, I have used this house for some years now. I travel for Blennet and Burgess—wool—and

come here regularly three times a year, and I've never heard of it. (*Sits down again on his chair, holding glass in his hand.*)

LEEK. And I've been here pretty often too, though I have only been in practice here for a couple of years, and I have never heard it mentioned, and I must say I don't believe in anything of the sort. In my opinion ghosts are the invention of weak-minded idiots.

PENFOLD. Weak-minded idiots or not, there is a ghost story connected with this house, but it dates a long time back. (GEORGE, *the waiter, enters* DL, *with tray and serviette.*[8]) Oh, here's George, he'll bear me out. You've heard of Jerry Bundler, George?

GEORGE (C). Well, I've just 'eard odds and ends, sir, but I never put much count to 'em. There was one chap 'ere, who was under me when fust I come, he said he seed it, and the Guv'nor sacked him there and then. (*Goes to table by window, puts tray down, takes up glass and wipes it slowly.*)

(MEN *laugh.*)

PENFOLD. Well, my father was a native of this town, and he knew the story well. He was a truthful man and a steady churchgoer. But I have heard him declare that once in his life he saw the ghost of Jerry Bundler in this house; let me see, George, you don't remember my old dad, do you?

(GEORGE *puts down glasses over table.*)

7 **pounds out of pocket:** minus a considerable amount of money.

8 **serviette:** table napkin.

GEORGE. No, sir. I come here forty years ago next Easter, but I fancy he was before my time.

PENFOLD. Yes, though not by long. He died when I was twenty, and I shall be sixty-two next month, but that's neither here nor there.

(GEORGE *goes up to table* C *tidying up and listening.*)

LEEK. Who was this Jerry Bundler?

PENFOLD. A London thief, pickpocket, highwayman—anything he could turn his dishonest hand to, and he was run to earth in this house some eighty years ago. (GEORGE *puts glass down and stands listening.*) He took his last supper in this room. (PENFOLD *leans forward.* BELDON *looks round to* L *nervously.*) That night soon after he had gone to bed, a couple of Bow Street runners, the predecessors of our present detective force, turned up here. They had followed him from London, but had lost scent a bit, so didn't arrive till late. A word to the landlord, whose description of the stranger who had retired to rest, pointed to the fact that he was the man they were after, of course enlisted his aid and that of the male servants and stable hands. The officers crept quietly up to Jerry's bedroom and tried the door, it wouldn't budge. It was of heavy oak and bolted from within. (OMNES *lean forward, showing interest.*) Leaving his comrade and a couple of grooms to guard the bedroom door, the other officer went into the yard, and, procuring a short ladder, by this means reached the window of the room in which Jerry was sleeping. The Inn servants and stable hands

372

saw him get on to the sill and try to open the window. Suddenly there was a crash of glass, and with a cry, he fell in a heap on to the stones at their feet. Then in the moonlight, they saw the face of the highwayman peering over the sill. (OMNES *move uneasily.*) They sent for the blacksmith, and with his sledge-hammer he battered in the strong oak panels, and the first thing that met their eyes was the body of Jerry Bundler dangling from the top of the four-post bed by his own handkerchief.

(OMNES *sit back, draw their breath, and are generally uneasy. Slight pause.*)

SOMERS. I say, which bedroom was it? (*Earnestly*).

PENFOLD. That I can't tell you, but the story goes that Jerry still haunts this house, and my father used to declare positively that the last time he slept here, the ghost of Jerry Bundler lowered itself from the top of his four-post bed and tried to strangle him.

BELDON (*jumps up, gets behind his chair, twists chair round; nervously*). O, I say, that'll do. I wish you'd thought to ask your father which bedroom it was.

PENFOLD. What for?

BELDON. Well, I should take jolly good care not to sleep in it, that's all. (*Goes to back.*)

(PENFOLD *rising, goes to fire, and knocks out his pipe;* LEEK *gets by armchair.*)

PENFOLD. There's nothing to fear. I don't believe for a moment that ghosts could really hurt one.

(GEORGE *lights candle at table.*) In fact, my father used to say that it was only the unpleasantness of the thing that upset him, and that, for all practical purposes, Jerry's fingers might have been made of cotton wool for all the harm they could do.

(GEORGE *hands candle, gets to door and holds it open.*)

BELDON. That's all very fine, a ghost story is a ghost story, but when a gentleman tells a tale of a ghost that haunts the house in which one is going to sleep, I call it most ungentlemanly.

(BELDON *places his chair to* L *of table* R. PENFOLD *goes up to* C. LEEK *sits in armchair.* BELDON *goes to fireplace.*)

PENFOLD. Pooh! Nonsense. (*At table up* C.) (*During his speech* GEORGE *lights one of the candles.*) Ghosts can't hurt you. For my own part, I should rather like to see one.

OMNES. Oh, come now——(*etc.*)

PENFOLD. Well, I'll bid you good night, gentlemen.

(*He goes toward door* L. GEORGE *opens it for him; he passes out as they all say:*)

OMNES. Good night.

(HIRST *rises, crosses to* LC.)

BELDON (*up* R, *calling after him*). And I hope Jerry'll pay you a visit.

MALCOLM (*rises, goes to fire*). Well, I'm going to have another drink if you gentlemen will join me. I think it'll do us all good after that tale. George, take the orders.

(GEORGE *comes down with sal-*

ver[9] to table R, *gathers up glasses.*)

SOMERS. Not quite so much hot water in mine.

MALCOLM. I'll have the same again, George.

BELDON. A leetle bit of lemon in mine, George.

LEEK. Soda for me, please.

HIRST. Same.

(GEORGE *goes to table* R, *collects glasses, crosses to door* L, *speaks:*)

GEORGE (*to* MALCOLM). Shall I light the gas, Mr. Malcolm? (*At door.*)

MALCOLM. No, the fire's very comfortable, unless any of you gentlemen prefer the gas.

OMNES. No, not at all—(*etc.*)

MALCOLM. Never mind, George. (*This to* GEORGE *as no one wants the gas.*) The firelight is pleasanter. (*Exit* GEORGE *for orders* L.) (BELDON *gets* C.)

MALCOLM (*at fire*). Does any gentleman know another——?

SOMERS (*seated* R). Well, I remember hearing——

BELDON (*up* C). Oh, I say—that'll do. (OMNES *laugh.*)

LEEK. Yes, I think you all look as if you'd heard enough ghost stories to do you the rest of your lives. And you're not all as anxious to see the real article as the old gentleman who's just gone.

HIRST (*looking to* L). Old humbug! I should like to put him to the test.

(C) (*Bus.*)[10] I say, suppose I dress up as Jerry Bundler and go and give him a chance of displaying his courage? I bet I'd make the old party sit up.

MALCOLM. Capital!

BELDON. A good idea.

LEEK. I shouldn't, if I were you.

HIRST. Just for the joke, gentlemen (C).

SOMERS. No, no—drop it, Hirst.

HIRST. Only for the joke. Look here, I've got some things that'll do very well. We're going to have some amateur theatricals at my house. We're doing a couple of scenes from THE RIVALS,[11] Somers (*pointing to* SOMERS), and I have been up to town to get the costumes, wigs, etc., today. I've got them upstairs—knee breeches, stockings, buckled shoes, and all that sort of thing. It's a rare chance. If you wait a bit, I'll give you a full dress rehearsal, entitled "Jerry Bundler, or the Nocturnal Stranger." (*At door* L.)

LEEK (*sneeringly*). You won't frighten us, will you?

HIRST. I don't know so much about that—it's a question of acting, that's all.

MALCOLM. I'll bet you a level sov,[12] you don't frighten me.

HIRST (*quietly*). A level sov. (*Pauses.*) Done. I'll take the bet to frighten you first, and the old boy afterwards. These gentlemen shall be the judges. (*Points to* LEEK *and* BELDON.)

10 Bus.: an abbreviation for *business*, a stage direction which indicates that the actor should engage in some sort of action; in this case the action is not specified. The term is sometimes written as *biz.*
11 The Rivals: a play by Richard Sheridan (1751-1816), an Irish dramatist.
12 sov: sovereign, a gold coin of Great Britain.

9 salver: a tray.

BELDON (*up* C). You won't frighten us because we're prepared for you, but you'd better leave the old man alone. It's dangerous play. (*Appeals to* LEEK.)

HIRST. Well, I'll try you first. (*Moves to door and pauses.*) No gas, mind.

OMNES. No! no!

HIRST (*laughs*). I'll give you a run for your money.

(GEORGE *enters, holds door open.*)

(*Exit* HIRST.)

(GEORGE *passes drinks round. Five drinks.* SOMERS *takes the one ordered for* HIRST *and puts it on the table* R. BELDON *sits* RC. GEORGE *crosses to table, puts two drinks down, goes to fire and gives drinks, then up to table, puts tray down, takes up glass and begins to wipe it, gets down* L *for lines.*)

LEEK (*to* MALCOLM). I think you'll win your bet, sir, but I vote we give him a chance. Suppose we have cigars round, and if he's not back by the time we've finished them I must be off, as I have a quarter of an hour's walk before me. (*Looks at watch.*) He's a friend of yours, isn't he?

SOMERS. Yes, I have known him a good many years now, and I must say he's a rum chap;[13] just crazy about acting and practical joking, though I've often told him he carries the latter too far at times. In this case it doesn't matter, but I won't let him try it on the *old gentleman*. You see we know what he's going to do, and are prepared, but he doesn't, and it might lead to illness or worse; the old chap's sixty-two and such a shock might have serious consequences. But Hirst won't mind giving up that part of it, so long as he gets an opportunity of acting to us.

LEEK (*knocks pipe on grate*). Well, I hope he'll hurry up. It's getting pretty late. (*To* SOMERS.)

MALCOLM. Well, gentlemen, your health!

SOMERS. Good luck.

LEEK. Hurrah!

BELDON. Chin-chin!

LEEK. By the way, how is it you happen to be here tonight?

SOMERS. Oh, we missed the connection at Tolleston Junction and as the accommodation at the Railway Arms there was rather meager, the Station Master advised us to drive on here, put up for the night, and catch the Great Northern express from Exton in the morning. (*Rises, crosses to* L.) Oh, George, that reminds me —you might see that "Boots" calls us at seven sharp.

(BELDON *rises, goes up to them to fire.*)

GEORGE. Certainly, sir. What are your numbers?

SOMERS. 13 and 14.

GEORGE. I'll put it on the slate, special, sir. (*Goes to door* L.)

LEEK. I beg pardon, gentlemen, I forgot the cigars; George, bring some cigars back with you.

BELDON. A very mild one for me.

GEORGE. Very well, sir. (*Takes up tray from sideboard.*)   (*Exit* L.)

---

13 a rum chap: an odd fellow.

(SOMERS *sits* RC.)

MALCOLM. I think you were very wise coming on here. (*Sits on settle* R.) I stayed at the Railway Arms, Tolleston, once—never again though. Is your friend clever at acting?

SOMERS. I don't think he's clever enough to frighten you. I'm to spend Christmas at his place, and he's asked me to assist at the theatricals he spoke of. Nothing would satisfy him till I consented, and I must honestly say I am very sorry I ever did, for I expect I shall be pretty bad. I know I have scarcely slept a wink these last few nights, trying to get the words into my head.

(GEORGE *enters backwards, pale and trembling.*)

MALCOLM. Why! Look—what the devil's the matter with George? (*Crosses to* GEORGE.)

GEORGE. I've seen it, gentlemen. (*Downstage* LC.)

OMNES. Seen who?

(BELDON *down* R *edge of table* R. LEEK *up* RC. SOMERS *up* R.)

GEORGE. The ghost. Jer—Bun—

MALCOLM. Why, you're frightened, George.

GEORGE. Yes, sir. It was the suddenness of it, and besides I didn't look for seeing it in the bar. There was only a glimmer of light there, and it was sitting on the floor. I nearly touched it.

MALCOLM (*goes to door, looks off, then returns—to others*). It must be Hirst up to his tricks. George was out of the room when he suggested it. (*To* GEORGE.) Pull yourself together, man.

GEORGE. Yes, sir—but it took me unawares. I'd never have gone to the bar myself if I'd known it was there, and I don't believe you would, either, sir.

MALCOLM. Nonsense, I'll go and fetch him in. (*Crosses to* L.)

GEORGE (*clutching him by the sleeve*). You don't know what it's like, sir. It ain't fit to look at by yourself, it ain't indeed. It's got the awfullest deathlike face, and short cropped red hair—it's—(*Smothered cry is heard.*) What's that? (*Backs to* C *and leans on chair.*)

(ALL *start, and a quick pattering of footsteps is heard rapidly approaching the room. The door flies open and* HIRST *flings himself gasping and shivering into* MALCOLM'S *arms. The door remains open. He has only his trousers and shirt on, his face very white with fear and his own hair all standing on end.* LEEK *lights the gas, then goes to* R *of* HIRST.)

OMNES. What's the matter?

MALCOLM. Why, it's Hirst. (*Shakes him roughly by the shoulder.*) What's up?

HIRST. I've seen—oh! I'll never play the fool again. (*Goes* C.)

OTHERS. Seen what?

HIRST. Him—it—the ghost—anything.

MALCOLM (*uneasily*). Rot!

HIRST. I was coming down the stairs to get something I'd forgotten, when I felt a tap—(*He breaks off suddenly gazing through open door.*) I thought I saw it again—Look—at the

foot of the stairs, can't you see any-thing? (*Shaking* LEEK.)

LEEK (*crosses to door peering down passage*). No, there's nothing there. (*Stays up* L.)

(HIRST *gives a sigh of relief.*)

MALCOLM (LC). Go on—you felt a tap——

HIRST (C). I turned and saw it—a little wicked head with short red hair —and a white dead face—horrible.

(*Clock chimes three-quarters.*)

(*They assist him into chair* L *of table* R.)

GEORGE (*up* C). That's what I saw in the bar—'orrid—it was devilish. (*Coming* C.)

(MALCOLM *crosses to* L. HIRST *shudders.*)

MALCOLM. Well, it's a most unac-countable thing. It's the last time I come to this house. (*Goes to* R *of* LEEK.)

GEORGE. I leave tomorrow. I wouldn't go down to that bar alone— no, not for fifty pounds. (*Goes up* R *to armchair.*)

SOMERS (*crosses to door* R *then re-turns to* RC). It's talking about the thing that's caused it, I expect. We've had it in our minds, and we've been practically forming a spiritu-alistic circle without knowing it. (*Goes to back of table* R.)

BELDON (*crosses to* RC). Hang the old gentleman. Upon my soul I'm half afraid to go to bed.

MALCOLM. Doctor, it's odd they should both think they saw some-thing.

(*They both drop down* LC.)

GEORGE (*up* C). I saw it as plainly

as I see you, sir. P'raps if you keep your eyes turned up the passage you'll see it for yourself. (*Points.*)

(*They all look.* BELDON *goes to* SOMERS.)

BELDON. There—what was that?

MALCOLM. Who'll go with me to the bar?

LEEK. I will. (*Goes to door.*)

BELDON (*gulps*). So—will I. (*Crosses to door* L. *They go to the door. To* MALCOLM.) After you.

(*They slowly pass into the passage.* GEORGE *watching them. All exit except* HIRST *and* SOMERS.)

SOMERS. How do you feel now, old man?

HIRST (*changing his frightened manner to one of assurance*). Splendid!

SOMERS. But—(*a step back*).

HIRST. I tell you I feel splendid.

SOMERS. But the ghost—(*Steps back to* C.)

HIRST. Well, upon my word, Somers—you're not as sharp as I thought you.

SOMERS. What do you mean?

HIRST. Why, that I was the ghost George saw. (*Crosses to* LC.) By Jove, he *was* in a funk![14] I followed him to the door and overheard his description of what he'd seen, then I burst in myself and pretended I'd seen it too. I'm going to win that, bet—(VOICES *heard. Crosses to* R.) Look out, they're coming back. (*Sits.*)

SOMERS. Yes, but——

HIRST. Don't give me away—hush!

14 in a funk: frightened.

(*Re-enter* MALCOLM, LEEK, BELDON *and* GEORGE L.)

(BELDON *and* GEORGE *go up to back* C.)

HIRST. Did you see it? (*In his frightened manner.*)

MALCOLM (C). I don't know—I thought I saw something, but it might have been fancy. I'm in the mood to see anything just now. (*To* HIRST.) How are you feeling now, sir?

HIRST. Oh, I feel a bit better now. I daresay you think I'm easily scared —but you didn't see it.

MALCOLM. Well, I'm not quite sure. (*Goes to fire.*)

LEEK. You've had a bit of a shock. Best thing you can do is to go to bed.

HIRST (*finishing his drink*). Very well. Will you (*rises*) share my room with me, Somers?

(GEORGE *lights two candles.*)

SOMERS (*crosses to* LC). I will with pleasure. (*Gets up to table* C *and gets a candle.*) Provided you don't mind sleeping with the gas full on all night. (*Goes to door* L.)

LEEK (*to* HIRST). You'll be all right in the morning.

HIRST. Good night, all. (*As he crosses to door.*)

OMNES. Good night.

(ALL *talking at fire, not looking to* L *as* HIRST *and* SOMERS *exeunt;* HIRST *chuckles and gives* SOMERS *a sly dig.*)

SOMERS. Good night.

MALCOLM (*at fireplace*). Well, I suppose the bet's off, though as far as I can see I won it. I never saw a man so scared in all my life. Sort of poetic justice about it. (LEEK with revolver in his hand, is just putting it into his pocket. Seeing him.) Why, what's that you've got there?

LEEK. A revolver. (At fire.) You see I do a lot of night driving, visiting patients in outlying districts—they're a tough lot round here, and one never knows what might happen, so I have been accustomed to carry it. I just pulled it out so as to have it handy. I meant to have a pot at that ghost if I had seen him. There's no law against it, is there? I never heard of a close time for ghosts.

BELDON.—Oh, I say, never mind ghosts. Will *you* share my room? (*To* MALCOLM.)

(GEORGE *comes down a little, holding candle.*)

MALCOLM. With pleasure. I'm not exactly frightened, but I'd sooner have company, and I daresay George here would be glad to be allowed to make up a bed on the floor.

BELDON. Certainly.

MALCOLM. Well, that's settled. A majority of three to one ought to stop any ghost. Will that arrangement suit you, George?

GEORGE. Thank you, sir. And if you gentlemen would kindly come down to the bar with me while I put out the gas, I could never be sufficiently grateful, and when (*at door*) we come back we can let the Doctor out at the front door. Will that do, sir?

LEEK. All right; I'll be getting my coat on (GEORGE *gets to door. They exit at door* L. LEEK *picks up his coat off chair up* L, *puts it on and then turns up trousers. Footsteps heard in flies,*[15] *then goes to the window* R, *pulls curtain aside and opens the shutters of the window nearest the fire. A flood of moonlight streams in from* R. *Clock strikes twelve.*) By Jove, what a lovely night. That poor devil did get a fright and no mistake. (*Crossing down to fireplace for his cap which is on the mantelpiece.* MALCOLM, BELDON *and* GEORGE *return—the door closes after them.*) Well, no sign of it, eh?

MALCOLM. No, we've seen nothing this time. Here, give me the candle, George, while you turn out the gas.

LEEK. All right, George, I'll put this one out. (*Turns out gas below fire.*)

(MALCOLM *and* BELDON *are up at sideboard;* GEORGE, *having put the other gas out, goes up to them and is just lighting the candles for them. The* DOCTOR *is filling his pipe at mantelshelf, and stooping to get a light with a paper spill.*[16] LEEK *whistles and lights spill. The handle of the door is heard moving.* OMNES *stand motionless—*MALCOLM *and* BELDON *very frightened. They all watch. The room is lit only by the firelight which is very much fainter than it was at the beginning of the play, by the candle which* GEORGE *holds, and by the flood of moonlight from the window.*)

15 flies: space over the stage.
16 spill: a roll of paper used to light lamps or pipes.

(*The door slowly opens, a hand is seen, then a figure appears in dark breeches, white stockings, buckled shoes, white shirt, very neat in every detail with a long white or spotted handkerchief tied round the neck, the long end hanging down in front. The face cadaverous,[17] with sunken eyes and a leering smile, and close cropped red hair. The figure blinks at the candle, then slowly raises its hands and unties the handkerchief, its head falls on to one shoulder, it holds handkerchief out at arm's length and advances toward* **MALCOLM**.)

(*Just as the figure reaches the place where the moonbeams touch the floor,* **LEEK** *fires—he has very quietly and unobtrusively drawn his revolver.* **GEORGE** *drops the candle and the figure, writhing, drops to the floor. It coughs once a choking cough.* **MALCOLM** *goes slowly forward, touches it with his foot, and kneels by figure, lifts figure up, gazes at it, and pulls the red wig off, discovering* **HIRST**. **MALCOLM** *gasps out "*DOCTOR.*"* **LEEK** *places the revolver on chair, kneels behind* **HIRST**. **MALCOLM** *is* LC, *kneeling. At this moment* **SOMERS** *enters very brightly with lighted candle*).

SOMERS. Well, did Hirst win his bet? (*Seeing* **HIRST** *on floor, he realizes the matter*.) You didn't—I told him not to! I told him not to! I told him—(*falls fainting into arms of* **GEORGE**).

17 **cadaverous** (kə dăv′ər əs)**:** like that of a corpse; ghastly.

CURTAIN.

Understanding Literature

1. As the play opens, what attitudes are the characters taking toward ghost stories? How does Penfold's story of Jerry Bundler affect Beldon?
2. After Penfold leaves, Hirst decides to test Penfold's courage. What is his plan?
3. What bet is made between Malcolm and Hirst? Notice which people know about Hirst's plan.
4. After Hirst leaves, what do you learn about him from the talk of the others?
5. George re-enters; then Hirst. What information do they bring? How does their information affect each of the other characters?
6. While Hirst and Somers are alone, what information are you given? How would the play be different in its effect on the

audience if you did not get this information? Even when you know about the ghost, why is there still suspense in the play?

7. After Hirst and Somers leave, how does the author make it believable that Leek should be carrying a gun?

8. One version of this play has a very different ending. After Somers re-enters the room and asks if Hirst has won his bet, there is a slight pause. Then Hirst suddenly sits up and says that the doctor is a very poor shot; furthermore, Hirst wants to be paid for winning the bet. Which do you think is the better ending? Why?

In this play two average people who think that nothing exciting will ever happen to them get involved in some extraordinary events.

The Man in the Bowler Hat[*]

A. A. *Milne*

IMPROVING YOUR READING: This play makes fun of a melodramatic play. It is a *farce*, a type of comedy that contains improbable characters in improbable situations. You will see that many details quite common in melodrama are greatly exaggerated for the sake of increasing the humorous effect.

The scene is MARY's *sitting room. It is the most ordinary sitting room in the world.* JOHN *and* MARY, *two of the most ordinary people, he in the early forties, she in the late thirties, are sitting in front of the fire after dinner. He, as usual, is reading the paper; she, as usual, is knitting. They talk in a desultory[1] way.*

MARY. Did I tell you that Mrs. Patchett had just had another baby?

JOHN (*not looking up from his paper*). Yes, dear, you told me.

MARY. Did I? Are you sure?

JOHN. Last week.

1 **desultory** (dĕs′əl tôr′ĭ): aimless.

MARY. But she only had it yesterday. Mr. Patchett told me this morning when I was ordering the cauliflower.

JOHN. Ah! Then perhaps you told me she was going to have one.

MARY. Yes, I think that must have been it.

JOHN. This is the one that she was going to have?

MARY. It weighed seven pounds exactly.

JOHN. Of course, being a grocer he would have the scales ready. Boy or girl?

MARY. Boy.

JOHN. The first boy, isn't it?

MARY. The second.

·* Copyright, 1923, by Samuel French, Ltd.
Copyright, 1951, (In Renewal) by Alan Alexander Milne.
All Rights Reserved.
CAUTION: Professionals and amateurs are hereby warned that "THE MAN IN THE BOWLER HAT," being fully protected under the copyright laws of the United States of America, the British Empire, including the Dominion of Canada, and all other countries of the Copyright Union, is subject to a royalty. All rights, including professional, amateur, motion pictures, recitation, public reading, radio and television broadcasting and the rights of translation into foreign languages are strictly reserved. Amateurs may give stage production of this play upon payment of a royalty of Ten Dollars for each performance one week before the play is given to Samuel French, Inc., at 25 West 45th Street, New York, N.Y. or 7623 Sunset Blvd., Hollywood, Calif., or if in Canada, Samuel French (Canada) Ltd., 27 Grenville Street, Toronto, Ont., Canada.

THE ONE-ACT PLAY

JOHN. The first one that weighed seven pounds—exactly.

(*They are silent again, he reading, she knitting.*)

MARY. Anything in the paper tonight?

JOHN. A threatened strike of boiler makers.

MARY. Does that matter very much?

JOHN. It says here that the situation is extremely serious.

MARY. Tell me about it.

JOHN (*not very good at it*). Well, the—er—boiler makers are threatening to strike. (*Weightily.*) They are threatening not to make any more—er—boilers.

MARY. Kitchen boilers?

JOHN (*with an explanatory gesture*). Boilers. They are threatening not to make any more of them. And —well—that's how it is. (*Returning to his paper.*) The situation is extremely serious. Exciting scenes have been witnessed.

MARY. What sort of scenes?

JOHN. Well, naturally, when you have a lot of men threatening not to make any more boilers—and er—a lot of other men threatening that if they *don't* make any—well, exciting scenes are witnessed. *Have* been witnessed by this man, this special correspondent.

MARY (*after a pause*). It's a funny thing that nothing exciting ever happens to *us*.

JOHN. It depends what you mean by exciting. I went round in ninety-five[2] last Saturday, as I think I told you.

MARY. But I mean something really thrilling—and dangerous. Like in a novel or on a stage.

JOHN. My dear Mary, nothing like that ever happens in real life. I mean, it wouldn't happen to *us*.

MARY. Would you like it if it did?

(*He says nothing for a moment. Then he puts down his paper and sits there thinking. At last he turns to her.*)

JOHN (*almost shyly*). I used to imagine things like that happening. Years ago. Rescuing a beautiful maiden, and—and all that sort of thing. And being wrecked on a desert island with her . . . (*He turns away from her, staring into his dreams.*) Or pushing open a little green door in a long high wall and finding myself in a wonderful garden under the bluest of blue skies, and waiting, waiting—for something.

MARY. I used to imagine things too. People fighting duels because of me. Silly, isn't it? Nothing ever really happens like that.

JOHN (*still with his thoughts*). No.

(*At this moment a STRANGE MAN comes in. Contrary to all etiquette, he is wearing a bowler hat[3] and an overcoat, and has a half-smoked cigar in his mouth. He walks quickly across the room and sits down in a chair, with his back to the audience. JOHN and MARY, deep in their thoughts, do not notice him.*)

MARY (*looking into the fire*). I suppose we're too old for it now.

---

2 **went round in ninety-five:** golf score.

3 **bowler hat:** stiff felt hat rounded at the top.

John. I suppose so.

Mary. If it had only happened once—just for the memories.

John. So that we could say to each other—— Good heavens, what's that?

> (*It was the crack of a revolver. No mistaking it, even by* **John**, *who has never been much of a hand with revolvers.*)

Mary (*frightened*). John!

> (*There is a scuffling noise outside the door. They look eagerly toward it. Then suddenly there is dead silence. The* **Man in the Bowler Hat** *flicks some of his cigar ash onto the carpet—Mary's carpet.*)

John. Look!

> (*Very slowly the door begins to open. Through the crack comes a long, sinuous[4] hand. The door opens farther, and the hand is followed by a long, sinuous body. Still the* **Man in the Bowler Hat** *says nothing. Then the door is closed, and leaning up against it, breathing rather quickly, is the* **Hero**, *in his hand a revolver.* **John** *and* **Mary** *look at each other wonderingly.*)

John (*with a preliminary cough*). I—I beg your pardon.

Hero (*turning quickly, finger to his lips*). H'sh!

John (*apologetically*). I beg your pardon!

> (*The* **Hero** *listens anxiously at the door. Then, evidently re-*

assured for the moment, he comes toward them.)

Hero (*to* **John**). Quick, take this! (*He presses his revolver into* **John's** *hand.*)

John. I—er—what do I——

Hero (*to* **Mary**). And you! This! (*He takes another revolver from his hip pocket and presses it into* **Mary's** *hand.*)

Mary. Thank you. Do we——

Hero (*sternly*). H'sh!

Mary. Oh, I beg your pardon.

Hero. Listen!

> (*They all listen.* **John** *and* **Mary** *have never listened so intently before, but to no purpose. They hear nothing.*)

John (*in a whisper*). What is it?

Hero. Nothing.

John. Yes, that's what *I* heard.

Hero. Have you got a—— (*He breaks off and broods.[5]*)

Mary. A what?

Hero (*shaking his head*). No, it's too late now.

John (*to* **Mary**). Haven't we got one?

Hero. You wait here; that will be best. I shall be back in a moment.

John. What do we do?

Hero. Listen; that's all. Listen.

John (*eagerly*). Yes, yes.

Hero. I shall be back directly.

> (*Just as he is making for the window the door opens and the* **Heroine**—*obviously*—*comes in. For a moment they stand gazing at each other.*)

Heroine. Oh! (*but with a world of expression in it*).

---

4 **sinuous** (sĭn′yŏŏ əs)**:** winding; like a serpent.

5 **broods:** thinks seriously.

HERO. Oh! (*with even more expression*).

HEROINE. My love!

HERO. My beautiful!

(*They meet and are locked in an embrace.*)

JOHN (*to* MARY). I suppose they're engaged to be married.

MARY. Oh, I think they must be.

JOHN. They've evidently met before.

HERO (*lifting his head for a moment*). My Dolores!

JOHN (*to* MARY). I think this must be both "How do you do?" and "Good-by."

MARY (*wistfully*).[6] He is very good-looking.

JOHN (*casually*). Oh, do you think so? Now *she* is pretty, if you like.

MARY (*doubtfully*). Ye-es. Very bad style, of course.

JOHN (*indignantly*). My dear Mary——

HEROINE (*to* HERO). Quick, quick, you must go!

HERO. Never—now that I have found you again.

HEROINE. Yes, yes! My father is hot upon your tracks. He will be here at any moment in his two-seater.

HERO (*turning pale*). Your father!

HEROINE. I walked on ahead to warn you. He has come for—*It!*

JOHN (*to* MARY). What on earth's It?

HERO (*sinking back into a chair*). It!

HEROINE. Yes.

JOHN (*behind his hand to* MARY).

Income-tax collector.

HERO. The Rajah's ruby!

MARY. Oh, how exciting!

HEROINE. Yes; he knows you have it. He is determined to wrest[7] it from you.

HERO. Never!

JOHN. Well done!

HEROINE. There is no mischief he might not do if once it were in his possession. Three prominent members of society would be ruined, there would be another war in Mexico, and the exchange value of the ruble[8] would be seriously impaired.[9] Promise me you will never give it up.

HERO. I promise.

HEROINE. I must go. I am betraying my father by coming here; but I love you.

JOHN (*to* MARY). She does love him. I thought she did.

MARY. How could she help it?

HERO. I adore you!

JOHN. You see, he adores her too. It certainly looked like it.

MARY. I still don't think she's very good style.

HEROINE. Then—good-by!

(*They embrace again.*)

JOHN (*after a decent interval*). Excuse me, sir, but if you have a train to catch—I mean if your future father-in-law's two-seater is any good at all, oughtn't you to be—er——

HERO (*releasing* HEROINE). Good-by!

(*He conducts her to the door, gives her a last long, lingering look, and lets her go.*)

---

6 **wistfully:** desirously; yearningly.

7 **wrest:** snatch.
8 **ruble:** Soviet coin.
9 **impaired:** decreased.

MARY (*to herself*). Pretty, of course, in a kind of way, but I must say I don't *like* that style.

(*The* HERO *comes out of his reverie*[10] *and proceeds to business.*)

HERO (*briskly, to* JOHN). You have those revolvers?

JOHN. Yes.

HERO. Then wait here and listen. More than one life depends upon it.

JOHN. How many more?

HERO. If you hear the slightest noise——

JOHN (*eagerly*). Yes?

HERO. H'sh!

(*He goes to the window, waits there listening for a moment, and then slips out.* JOHN *and* MARY *remain, their ears turned attentively.*)

JOHN (*with a start*). H'sh! What's that?

MARY. What was it, dear?

JOHN. I don't know.

MARY. It's so awkward when you don't quite know what you're listening *for*.

JOHN. H'sh! We were told to listen, and we must listen. More than one life depends on it.

MARY. All right, dear.

(*They continue to listen. A little weary of it,* MARY *looks down the barrel of the revolver to see if she can see anything interesting.*)

JOHN (*observing her*). Don't do that! It's very dangerous to point a loaded revolver at yourself. If anything happened it would be too late to say afterwards that you didn't mean it.

MARY. Very well, John. Oh, look!

(*Again the door opens quickly, and a sinister gentleman in a mask inserts himself into the room. We recognize him at once as the* CHIEF VILLAIN. *Very noiselessly, his back to* JOHN *and* MARY, *he creeps along the wall toward the window.*)

JOHN (*in a whisper*). Father-in-law.

MARY. Do we—— (*indicates the revolver*).

JOHN (*doubtfully*). I—I suppose—— (*He raises his gun hesitatingly.*)

MARY. Oughtn't you say something first?

JOHN. Yes—er—— (*He clears his throat warningly.*) Ahem! (*The* CHIEF VILLAIN *continues to creep toward the window.*) You, sir!

MARY (*politely*). Do you want anything, or—or anything?

(*The* CHIEF VILLAIN *is now at the window.*)

JOHN. Just a moment, sir.

(*The* CHIEF VILLAIN *opens the window and steps out between the curtains.*)

MARY. Oh, he's gone!

JOHN. I call that very bad manners.

MARY. Do you think he'll—he'll come back?

JOHN (*with determination*). I shall shoot him like a dog if he does (*waving aside all protests*).

MARY. Yes, dear, perhaps that *would* be best.

JOHN. Look out! He's coming back.

---

10 reverie: daydream.

(*He raises his revolver as the door opens. Again the* CHIEF VILLAIN *enters cautiously and creeps toward the window.*)

MARY (*in a whisper*). Shoot!

JOHN (*awkwardly*). Er—I suppose it *is* the same man?

MARY. Yes, yes!

JOHN. I mean—it wouldn't be quite fair if—— (*He coughs warningly.*) Excuse me, sir!

MARY. Quick, before he goes!

JOHN (*raising his revolver nervously*). I ought to tell you, sir—— (*To* MARY.) You know, I still think this is a different one.

(*The* CHIEF VILLAIN *again disappears through the window.*)

MARY (*in great disappointment*). Oh, he's gone!

JOHN (*firmly*). It was a different one. The other one hadn't got a mustache.

MARY. He had, John. It was the same man; of course it was.

JOHN. Oh! Well, if I had known that—if I had only been certain of it, I should have shot him like a dog.

A VOICE (*which sounds like the* HERO's). Help, help!

MARY. John, listen!

JOHN. I *am* listening.

A VOICE. He-e-elp!

MARY. Oughtn't we to do something?

JOHN. We *are* doing something. We're listening. That's what he told us to do.

A VOICE. Help!

JOHN (*listening*). That's the other man; the one who came in first.

MARY. The nice-looking one. Oh, John, we *must* do something.

JOHN. If he calls out again I shall—I shall—do something. I shall take steps. I may even have to shoot somebody. But I will *not* have——

A VOICE. Quick, quick!

MARY. There!

JOHN. Er—was that the same voice?

MARY (*moving to the door*). Yes, of course it was. It sounded as if it were in the hall. Come along.

JOHN. Wait a moment. (*She turns round.*) We must keep cool, Mary. We mustn't be impetuous.[11] Just hold this a moment. (*He hands her his revolver.*)

MARY (*surprised*). Why, what——

JOHN. I shall take my coat off. (*He takes off his coat very slowly.*) I'm going through with this. I'm not easily roused, but when once——

A VOICE. Help! Quick!

JOHN (*reassuringly*). All right, my man, all right. (*Very leisurely he rolls up his sleeves.*) I'm not going to have this sort of thing going on in *my* house. I'm not going to have it. (*Doubtfully.*) I don't think I need take my waistcoat off too. What do *you* think, Mary?

MARY (*impatiently*). No, dear, of course not; you look very nice.

JOHN (*very determined*). Now, then, let's have that revolver. (*She gives it to him.*) I shall say, "Hands up!"—very sharply, like that—"*Hands up!*"—and then if he doesn't put his hands up I shall—I shall say, "Hands up!" again. That will show him that I'm not to be trifled with.[12] Now, then, dear, are you ready?

MARY (*eagerly*). Yes!

11 **impetuous:** hasty; reckless.
12 **trifled with:** made light of.

JOHN. Then——

    (*But at that moment the lights
go out.*)

MARY. Oh!

JOHN (*annoyed*). Now, why did you
do that, Mary?

MARY. I didn't do it, dear.

JOHN. Then who did?

MARY. I don't know. They just
went out.

JOHN. Then I shall write to the
company tomorrow and complain. I
shall complain to the company about
the lights, and I shall complain to
the landlord about the way people
go in and out of this house, and
shriek and——

MARY (*in alarm*). Oh!

JOHN. *Don't* do that! What is it?

MARY. I can feel somebody quite
close to me.

JOHN. Well, that's me.

MARY. Not you, somebody else.
Oh! He touched me! John!

JOHN (*addressing the darkness*).
Really, sir, I must ask you not to——

MARY. Listen! I can hear breath-
ings all round me!

JOHN. Excuse me, sir, but do you
mind *not* breathing all round my
wife?

MARY. There! Now I can't hear
anything.

JOHN (*complacently*).[13] There you
are, my dear. You see what firmness
does. I wasn't going to have *that*
sort of thing going on in my house.

    (*The lights go up and reveal the*
    HERO *gagged so that only his*
    eyes are visible, and bound to
    a chair.)

---

13 **complacently:** contentedly; with satisfaction.

THE ONE-ACT PLAY

MARY (*clinging to her husband*). Oh, John!

JOHN (*with sudden desperate bravery*). Hands up! (*He levels his revolver.*)

MARY. Don't be silly; how can he?

JOHN. All right, dear, I was only practicing. (*He blows a speck of dust off his revolver and holds it up to the light again.*) Yes; it's quite a handy little fellow. I think I shall be able to do some business with this all right.

MARY. Poor fellow! I wonder who it is.

(*The HERO tries to speak with his eyes and movements of the head.*)

JOHN. He wants something. Perhaps it's the evening paper. (*He makes a movement toward it.*)

MARY. Listen!

(*The HERO begins to tap with his feet.*)

JOHN. He's signaling something.

MARY. Dots and dashes!

JOHN. That's the Morse code; that's what that is. Where's my dictionary? (*He fetches it hastily and begins to turn over the pages.*)

MARY. Quick, dear!

JOHN (*reading*). Here we are. "1. Morse—The walrus." (*Looking at the HERO:*) No, that must be wrong. Ah, this is better! "2. Morse code signaling of telegraph operators—as 'He sends a good Morse.'"

MARY. Well? What does it say?

JOHN. Nothing. That's all. Then we come to "*Morsel*—a small piece of food, a mouthful, a bite. Also a small meal."

MARY (*brilliantly*). A mouthful! That's what he meant. He wants the gag taken out of his mouth. (*She goes to him.*)

JOHN. That's very clever of you, Mary. I should never have thought of that.

MARY (*untying the gag*). Then! . . . Why, it's the man who came in first, the nice-looking one!

JOHN. Yes, he said he was coming back.

(*Before the HERO can express his thanks—if that is what he wants to express—the CHIEF VILLAIN, accompanied by a BAD MAN, comes in. JOHN and MARY instinctively retreat.*)

CHIEF VILLAIN (*sardonically*).[14] Ha!

JOHN (*politely*). Ha to you, sir.

(*The CHIEF VILLAIN fixes JOHN with a terrible eye.*)

JOHN (*nervously to MARY*). Say "Ha!" to the gentleman, dear.

MARY (*faintly*). Ha!

CHIEF VILLAIN. And what the Mephistopheles[15] are *you* doing here?

JOHN (*to MARY*). What are we doing here?

MARY (*bravely*). This is our house.

JOHN. Yes, this is our house.

CHIEF VILLAIN. Then siddown! (*JOHN sits down meekly.*) Is this your wife?

JOHN. Yes. (*Introducing them.*) Er—my wife—er—Mr. Er——

CHIEF VILLAIN. Then tell her to siddown too.

JOHN (*to MARY*). He wants you to siddown. (*She does so.*)

---

14 **sardonically**: scornfully; mockingly.
15 **Mephistopheles** (mĕf'ə stŏf'ə lēz'): another name for the Devil.

CHIEF VILLAIN. That's better. (*To* BAD MAN.) Just take their guns off 'em.

BAD MAN (*taking the guns*). Do you want them tied up or gagged or anything?

CHIEF VILLAIN. No; they're not worth it.

JOHN (*humbly*). Thank you.

CHIEF VILLAIN. Now, then, to business. (*To* HERO.) Where's the Rajah's ruby?

HERO (*firmly*). I shan't tell you.

CHIEF VILLAIN. You won't?

HERO. I won't.

CHIEF VILLAIN. That's awkward. (*After much thought.*) You absolutely refuse to?

HERO. I absolutely refuse to.

CHIEF VILLAIN. Ha! (*To* BAD MAN.) Torture the prisoner.

BAD MAN (*cheerfully*). Right you are, governor. (*He feels on the lapel of his coat and then says to* MARY.) Could you oblige me with the loan of a pin, mum?

MARY. I don't think—— (*Finding one.*) Here you are.

BAD MAN. Thanks. (*He advances threateningly upon the prisoner.*)

CHIEF VILLAIN. Wait! (*To* HERO.) Before proceeding to extremities I will give you one more chance. Where is the Rajah's Raby?

BAD MAN. You mean the Rabah's Rujy, don't you, governor?

CHIEF VILLAIN. That's what I said.

JOHN (*wishing to help*). You *said* the Rubah's Rajy, but I think you meant the Rujy's——

CHIEF VILLAIN. Silence! (*To* HERO.) I ask you again—where is the Ruj—I mean where is the Rab—well, anyhow, where *is* it?

HERO. I won't tell you.

CHIEF VILLAIN. Proceed, Mr. Smithers.

BAD MAN. Well, you've asked for it, mate. (*He pushes the pin gently into the* HERO's *arm.*)

HERO. Ow!

MARY. Oh, poor fellow!

CHIEF VILLAIN. Silence! Where is—— (*The* HERO *shakes his head.*) Torture him again, Mr. Smithers.

HERO. No, no! Mercy! I'll tell you.

JOHN (*indignantly*). Oh, I say!

BAD MAN. Shall I just give him another one for luck, governor?

HERO. Certainly not!

JOHN (*to* MARY). Personally, I think he should have held out much longer.

CHIEF VILLAIN. Very well, then. Where is the Rajah's Ruby?

HERO. In the cloakroom of Waterloo Station—in a hatbox.

CHIEF VILLAIN (*doubtfully*). In the cloakroom at Waterloo Station, you say?

HERO. Yes. In a hatbox. Now release me.

CHIEF VILLAIN. How do I know it's there?

HERO. Well, how do *I* know?

CHIEF VILLAIN. True. (*Holding out his hand.*) Well, give me the ticket for it.

HERO. I haven't got it.

BAD MAN. Now, then, none of that.

HERO. I haven't, really.

JOHN. I don't think he'd say he hadn't got it if he had got it. Do you, Mary?

MARY. Oh, I'm sure he wouldn't.

CHIEF VILLAIN. Silence! (*To* HERO.) Where is the ticket?

HERO. In the cloakroom of Paddington Station. In a hatbox.

CHIEF VILLAIN. The same hatbox?

HERO. Of course not. The other one was at Waterloo Station.

CHIEF VILLAIN. Well, then, where's the ticket for the hatbox in the Paddington cloakroom?

HERO. In the cloakroom at Charing Cross. In a hatbox.

CHIEF VILLAIN (*annoyed*). Look here, how many hatboxes have you got?

HERO. Lots.

CHIEF VILLAIN. Oh! Now let's get this straight. You say that the Rajah's Ruby is in a hatbox in the cloakroom at Paddington——

HERO. Waterloo.

CHIEF VILLAIN. Waterloo; and that the ticket for that hatbox is in a hatbox in the cloakroom at Euston——

HERO. Paddington.

CHIEF VILLAIN. Paddington; and that the ticket for the ticket, which is in a hatbox at Paddington, for the Ruby which is in a hatbox at King's Cross——

BAD MAN. Euston.

JOHN. St. Pancras.

CHIEF VILLAIN (*angrily*). Oh, shut up! The ticket for the ticket, which is in a hatbox at Paddington, for the Ruby which is in a hatbox at—at——

JOHN. St. Panc——

HERO. Waterloo.

CHIEF VILLAIN. Waterloo, thank you. This ticket is in a hatbox at—er——

JOHN. St. Pancras.

CHIEF VILLAIN. Shut up! In a hatbox at——

HERO. Charing Cross.

CHIEF VILLAIN. Exactly. (*Triumphantly.*) Then give me the ticket.

HERO. Which one?

CHIEF VILLAIN (*uneasily*). The one we're talking about.

JOHN (*helpfully*). The St. Pancras one.

CHIEF VILLAIN (*in a fury*). Will you shut up? (*To* HERO.) Now listen. (*Very slowly and with an enormous effort of concentration:*) I want the ticket for the hatbox at Charing Cross, which contains the ticket for the hatbox at (JOHN'S *lips, which are forming the words "St. Pancras," are hastily smothered by the* BAD MAN'S *hand.*)—at Paddington, which contains the ticket for the hatbox at Waterloo, which contains the Rajah's Ruby. (*Proudly.*) There!

HERO. I beg your pardon?

CHIEF VILLAIN (*violently*). I will *not* say it again! Give me the ticket.

HERO (*sadly*). I haven't got it.

CHIEF VILLAIN (*in an awestruck whisper*). You haven't got it?

HERO. No.

CHIEF VILLAIN (*after several vain attempts to speak*). Where is it?

HERO. In the cloakroom at Victoria Station.

CHIEF VILLAIN (*moistening his lips and speaking very faintly*). Not—not in a hatbox?

HERO. Yes.

CHIEF VILLAIN (*without much hope*). And the ticket for that?

HERO. In the cloakroom at Euston.

CHIEF VILLAIN (*quite broken up*). Also in a hatbox?

Hero. Yes.

Chief Villain. How much longer do we go on?

Hero (*cheerfully*). Oh, a long time yet.

Chief Villain (*to* **Bad Man**). How many London stations are there?

John. Well, there's St. Pancras, and——

Mary. Liverpool Street.

Bad Man. About twenty big ones, governor.

Chief Villain. Twenty! And do we go round them all?

Hero. Yes.

Chief Villain. And what do we do when we've worked through the lot?

Hero. Then we go all round them again.

Chief Villain (*anxiously*). And—and so on?

Hero. And so on.

Chief Villain (*his hand to his head*). This is terrible. I must think. (*To* **Bad Man**.) Just torture him again while I think.

Bad Man (*cheerily*). Right you are, governor. (*He approaches his victim.*)

Hero (*uneasily*). I say, look here——

John. I don't think it's quite fair, you know——

Mary (*suddenly*). Give me back my pin!

Bad Man. Must obey orders, gentlemen. (*Coaxingly to* **Hero**.) Just a little way in (*indicating with his finger*)—that much.

John (*to* **Mary**). I think perhaps "that much" wouldn't matter. What do——

Chief Villain (*triumphantly*). I've

392

got it! (*He rises with an air, the problem solved. They all look at him.*)

JOHN. What?

CHIEF VILLAIN (*impressively to* HERO). There is somewhere—logically, there must be somewhere—a final, an ultimate hatbox!

JOHN. By Jove! That's true!

HERO. Yes.

CHIEF VILLAIN. Where *is* that hatbox?

JOHN. St. Pancras.

CHIEF VILLAIN. Shut up! (*To* HERO.) Where is that hatbox?

HERO. In the cloakroom at Charing Cross.

CHIEF VILLAIN. Ah! (*He holds out his hand.*) Then give me the ticket for it.

BAD MAN (*threateningly*). Come on, now! The ticket!

HERO (*shaking his head sadly*). I can't.

CHIEF VILLAIN (*almost inarticulate with emotion*). You don't mean to say as you've—lost—it?

HERO (*in a whisper, with bowed head*). I've lost it.

(*With a terrible shriek the* CHIEF VILLAIN *falls back fainting into the arms of the* BAD MAN. *Instinctively* JOHN *and* MARY *embrace, sobbing to each other,* "He's lost it!" *And at that moment the* HEROINE *rushes in, crying,* "My love, you've lost it!" *and puts her arms around the* HERO. *Only the* MAN IN THE BOWLER HAT *remains unmoved. Slowly he removes the cigar from his mouth and speaks.*)

BOWLER HAT. Yes. . . . That's all right. Just a bit ragged still. . . . We'll take it again at eleven tomorrow. Second Act, please.

(*And so the rehearsal goes on.*)

CURTAIN

Understanding Literature

1. What does the conversation between John and Mary in the early part of the play (up to the entrance of the Hero) tell you about them?

2. In the section of the play dealing with the rehearsal, you see John and Mary in what they think is the real world and the actors in a stage world. What contrasts do you see in the behavior of the two groups? How does Mary react to the excitement? How does John react?

3. Much of the humor of the play arises because John keeps saying things that are the opposite of what you would expect him to say. Where do you find instances of this? Read his lines and then suggest the lines that you might have expected him to say.

4. How would the play be different if the Man in the Bowler Hat were left out? Why is the play named after him?
5. Which characteristics of the melodrama does this play exaggerate? In what ways are the situation and the characters improbable?
6. What similarities do you see between this play and "A Night at an Inn"? What differences?

Observing Caution Notices
in the Performance of Plays

As you started reading each of the previous three plays, you probably noticed a caution notice printed at the bottom of the title page. Should your class or your school decide to perform one of these plays for a school assembly program, or, in fact, for any audience, it is necessary for you to obtain permission to do so. All of these plays have been copyrighted. The caution notice is printed for the protection of the author, who deserves to receive compensation for performances of his play.

Read the following caution notice carefully. This play, unlike the others in the unit, is out of copyright in the United States. However, it is still fully protected under copyright laws in Canada, and this protection covers many types of performances.

Caution notice for SPREADING THE NEWS by Lady Gregory

CAUTION: Professionals and amateurs are hereby warned that "Spreading the News," being fully protected under the copyright laws of the British Empire, including the Dominion of Canada, and all other countries of the Copyright Union, is subject to a royalty. All rights, including professional, amateur, motion pictures, recitation, public reading, radio and television broadcasting and the rights of translation into foreign languages are strictly reserved. Amateurs may give stage production of this play in Canada upon payment of a royalty of Five Dollars for each performance one week before the play is to be given to Samuel French (Canada) Ltd., at 27 Grenville St., Toronto, Ont.

One of the greatest of all one-act plays, "Spreading the News" was first produced in Ireland in 1904. If you read it carefully and see the mad mixture of fact and opinion, you will enjoy the spreading rumor.

Spreading the News

Lady Gregory

IMPROVING YOUR READING: This play illustrates a major characteristic of a good *plot*, that every speech or action is related to another speech or action. Each word or deed here leads to the next. The result of the tight plot construction is a fantastic piling up of comical misunderstandings.

CHARACTERS

BARTLEY FALLON	JAMES RYAN
MRS. FALLON	MRS. TARPEY
JACK SMITH	MRS. TULLY
SHAWN EARLY	A POLICEMAN (*Jo Muldoon*)
TIM CASEY	A REMOVABLE MAGISTRATE

(SCENE: *The outskirts of a Fair. An Apple Stall.* MRS. TARPEY *sitting at it.* MAGISTRATE *and* POLICEMAN *enter.*)

MAGISTRATE.[1] So that is the Fair Green. Cattle and sheep and mud. No system. What a repulsive sight!

POLICEMAN. That is so, indeed.

MAGISTRATE. I suppose there is a good deal of disorder in this place?

POLICEMAN. There is.

MAGISTRATE. Common assault?

POLICEMAN. It's common enough.

MAGISTRATE. Agrarian[2] crime, no doubt?

POLICEMAN. That is so.

MAGISTRATE. Boycotting?[3] Maiming of cattle? Firing into houses?

POLICEMAN. There was one time, and there might be again.

MAGISTRATE. That is bad. Does it go any farther than that?

POLICEMAN. Far enough, indeed.

MAGISTRATE. Homicide, then! This district has been shamefully neglected! I will change all that. When I was in the Andaman Islands,[4] my system never failed. Yes, yes, I will change all that. What has that woman on her stall?

POLICEMAN. Apples mostly—— and sweets.

MAGISTRATE. Just see if there are

3 **Boycotting:** refusing to do business with a company.
4 **Andaman Islands:** islands in that part of the Indian Ocean called the Bay of Bengal.

1 **Magistrate:** chief government officer.
2 **Agrarian:** agricultural.

any unlicensed goods underneath ——spirits or the like. We had evasions of the salt tax in the Andaman Islands.

POLICEMAN (*sniffing cautiously and upsetting a heap of apples*). I see no spirits here——or salt.

MAGISTRATE (*to* MRS. TARPEY). Do you know this town well, my good woman?

MRS. TARPEY (*holding out some apples*). A penny the half-dozen, your honor?

POLICEMAN (*shouting*). The gentleman is asking do you know the town! He's the new magistrate!

MRS. TARPEY (*rising and ducking*).[5] Do I know the town? I do, to be sure.

MAGISTRATE (*shouting*). What is its chief business?

MRS. TARPEY. Business, is it? What business would the people here have but to be minding one another's business?

MAGISTRATE. I mean what trade have they?

MRS. TARPEY. Not a trade. No trade at all but to be talking.

MAGISTRATE. I shall learn nothing here.

> (JAMES RYAN *comes in, pipe in mouth. Seeing* MAGISTRATE *he retreats quickly, taking pipe from mouth.*)

MAGISTRATE. The smoke from that man's pipe had a greenish look; he may be growing unlicensed tobacco at home. I wish I had brought my telescope to this district. Come to the post office, I will telegraph for it.

5 ducking: bowing.

I found it very useful in the Andaman Islands.

> (MAGISTRATE *and* POLICEMAN *go out left.*)

MRS. TARPEY. Bad luck to Jo Muldoon, knocking my apples this way and that way. (*Begins arranging them.*) Showing off he was to the new magistrate.

> (*Enter* BARTLEY FALLON *and* MRS. FALLON.)

BARTLEY. Indeed it's a poor country and a scarce country to be living in. But I'm thinking if I went to America it's long ago the day I'd be dead!

MRS. FALLON. So you might, indeed.

> (*She puts her basket on a barrel and begins putting parcels in it, taking them from under her cloak.*)

BARTLEY. And it's a great expense for a poor man to be buried in America.

MRS. FALLON. Never fear, Bartley Fallon, but I'll give you a good burying the day you'll die.

BARTLEY. Maybe it's yourself will be buried in the graveyard of Cloonmara before me, Mary Fallon, and I myself that will be dying unbeknownst some night, and no one a-near me. And the cat itself may be gone straying through the country, and the mice squealing over the quilt.

MRS. FALLON. Leave off talking of dying. It might be twenty years you'll be living yet.

BARTLEY (*with a deep sigh*). I'm thinking if I'll be living at the end of twenty years, it's a very old man I'll be then!

396

MRS. TARPEY (*turns and sees them*). Good morrow, Bartley Fallon; good morrow, Mrs. Fallon. Well, Bartley, you'll find no cause for complaining today; they are all saying it was a good fair.

BARTLEY (*raising his voice*). It was not a good fair, Mrs. Tarpey. It was a scattered sort of a fair. If we didn't expect more, we got less. That's the way with me always; whatever I have to sell goes down and whatever I have to buy goes up. If there's ever any misfortune coming to this world, it's on myself it pitches, like a flock of crows on seed potatoes.

MRS. FALLON. Leave off talking of misfortunes and listen to Jack Smith that is coming the way, and he singing.

(*Voice of* JACK SMITH *heard singing:*)

I thought, my first love,
   There'd be but one house between you and me,
And I thought I would find
   Yourself coaxing my child on your knee.
Over the tide
   I would leap with the leap of a swan,
Till I came to the side
   Of the wife of the Red-haired man!

(JACK SMITH *comes in; he is a red-haired man, and is carrying a hayfork.*)

MRS. TARPEY. That should be a good song if I had my hearing.

MRS. FALLON (*shouting*). It's "The Red-haired Man's Wife."

MRS. TARPEY. I know it well. That's the song that has a skin on it!
(*She turns her back to them and goes on arranging her apples.*)

MRS. FALLON. Where's herself, Jack Smith?

JACK SMITH. She was delayed with her washing; bleaching the clothes on the hedge she is, and she daren't leave them, with all the tinkers that do be passing to the fair. It isn't to the fair I came myself, but up to the Five Acre Meadow I'm going, where I have a contract for the hay. We'll get a share of it into tramps[6] today. (*He lays down hayfork and lights his pipe.*)

BARTLEY. You will not get it into tramps today. The rain will be down on it by evening, and on myself too. It's seldom I ever started on a journey but the rain would come down on me before I'd find any place of shelter.

JACK SMITH. If it didn't itself, Bartley, it is my belief you would carry a leaky pail on your head in place of a hat, the way you'd not be without some cause of complaining.
(*A voice heard "Go on, now, go on out o' that. Go on I say."*)

JACK SMITH. Look at that young mare of Pat Ryan's that is backing into Shaughnessy's bullocks with the dint of the crowd! Don't be daunted, Pat, I'll give you a hand with her.
(*He goes out, leaving his hayfork.*)

MRS. FALLON. It's time for ourselves to be going home. I have all I bought put in the basket. Look at there, Jack Smith's hayfork he left after him! He'll be wanting it. (*Calls.*) Jack Smith! Jack Smith! ——He's gone through the crowd

6 tramps: stacks.

——hurry after him, Bartley, he'll be wanting it.

Bartley. I'll do that. This is no safe place to be leaving it. (*He takes up fork awkwardly and upsets the basket.*) Look at that now! If there is any basket in the fair upset, it must be our own basket!

(*He goes out to right.*)

Mrs. Fallon. Get out of that! It is your own fault, it is. Talk of misfortunes and misfortunes will come. Glory be! Look at my new eggcups rolling in every part—— and my two pound of sugar with the paper broke——

Mrs. Tarpey (*turning from stall*). God help us, Mrs. Fallon, what happened your basket?

Mrs. Fallon. It's himself that knocked it down, bad manners to him. (*Putting things up.*) My grand sugar that's destroyed, and he'll not drink his tea without it. I had best go back to the shop for more, much good may it do him!

(*Enter* **Tim Casey.**)

Tim Casey. Where is Bartley Fallon, Mrs. Fallon? I want a word with him before he'll leave the fair. I was afraid he might have gone home by this, for he's a temperate[7] man.

Mrs. Fallon. I wish he did go home! It'd be best for me if he went home straight from the fair green, or if he never came with me at all! Where is he, is it? He's gone up the road (*jerks elbow*) following Jack Smith with a hayfork.

(*She goes out to left.*)

Tim Casey. Following Jack Smith

7 **temperate:** moderate; self-controlled.

with a hayfork! Did ever any one hear the like of that. (*Shouts.*) Did you hear that news, Mrs. Tarpey?

MRS. TARPEY. I heard no news at all.

TIM CASEY. Some dispute I suppose it was that rose between Jack Smith and Bartley Fallon, and it seems Jack made off, and Bartley is following him with a hayfork!

MRS. TARPEY. Is he now? Well, that was quick work! It's not ten minutes since the two of them were here, Bartley going home and Jack going to the Five Acre Meadow; and I had my apples to settle up, that Jo Muldoon of the police had scattered, and when I looked round again Jack Smith was gone, and Bartley Fallon was gone, and Mrs. Fallon's basket upset, and all in it strewed upon the ground——the tea here——the two pound of sugar there——the eggcups there——Look, now, what a great hardship the deafness puts upon me, that I didn't hear the commincement of the fight! Wait till I tell James Ryan that I see below, he is a neighbor of Bartley's, it would be a pity if he wouldn't hear the news!

(*She goes out. Enter* SHAWN EARLY *and* MRS. TULLY.)

TIM CASEY. Listen, Shawn Early! Listen, Mrs. Tully, to the news! Jack Smith and Bartley Fallon had a falling out, and Jack knocked Mrs. Fallon's basket into the road, and Bartley made an attack on him with a hayfork, and away with Jack, and Bartley after him. Look at the sugar here yet on the road!

SHAWN EARLY. Do you tell me so?

Well, that's a queer thing, and Bartley Fallon so quiet a man!

MRS. TULLY. I wouldn't wonder at all. I would never think well of a man that would have that sort of a moldering[8] look. It's likely he has overtaken Jack by this.

(*Enter* JAMES RYAN *and* MRS. TARPEY.)

JAMES RYAN. That is great news Mrs. Tarpey was telling me! I suppose that's what brought the police and the magistrate up this way. I was wondering to see them in it a while ago.

SHAWN EARLY. The police after them? Bartley Fallon must have injured Jack so. They wouldn't meddle in a fight that was only for show!

MRS. TULLY. Why wouldn't he injure him? There was many a man killed with no more of a weapon than a hayfork.

JAMES RYAN. Wait till I run north as far as Kelly's bar to spread the news! (*He goes out.*)

TIM CASEY. I'll go tell Jack Smith's first cousin that is standing there south of the church after selling his lambs. (*Goes out.*)

MRS. TULLY. I'll go telling a few of the neighbors I see beyond to the west. (*Goes out.*)

SHAWN EARLY. I'll give word of it beyond at the east of the green.

(*Is going out when* MRS. TARPEY *seizes hold of him.*)

MRS. TARPEY. Stop a minute, Shawn Early, and tell me did you see red Jack Smith's wife, Kitty Keary, in any place?

8 **moldering:** crumbling; decaying.

SHAWN EARLY. I did. At her own house she was, drying clothes on the hedge as I passed.

MRS. TARPEY. What did you say she was doing?

SHAWN EARLY (breaking away). Laying out a sheet on the hedge.

(He goes.)

MRS. TARPEY. Laying out a sheet for the dead! The Lord have mercy on us! Jack Smith dead, and his wife laying out a sheet for his burying! (Calls out.) Why didn't you tell me that before, Shawn Early? Isn't the deafness the great hardship? Half the world might be dead without me knowing of it or getting word of it at all! (She sits down and rocks herself.) O my poor Jack Smith! To be going to his work so nice and so hearty, and to be left stretched on the ground in the full light of the day!

(Enter TIM CASEY.)

TIM CASEY. What is it, Mrs. Tarpey? What happened since?

MRS. TARPEY. O my poor Jack Smith!

TIM CASEY. Did Bartley overtake him?

MRS. TARPEY. O the poor man!

TIM CASEY. Is it killed he is?

MRS. TARPEY. Stretched in the Five Acre Meadow!

TIM CASEY. The Lord have mercy on us! Is that a fact?

MRS. TARPEY. Without the rites of the Church or a ha' porth!

TIM CASEY. Who was telling you?

MRS. TARPEY. And the wife laying out a sheet for his corpse. (Sits up and wipes her eyes.) I suppose

they'll wake him[9] the same as another?

(Enter MRS. TULLY, SHAWN EARLY, and JAMES RYAN.)

MRS. TULLY. There is great talk about this work in every quarter of the fair.

MRS. TARPEY. Ochone![10] cold and dead. And myself maybe the last he was speaking to!

JAMES RYAN. The Lord save us! Is it dead he is?

TIM CASEY. Dead surely, and the wife getting provision for the wake.

SHAWN EARLY. Well, now, hadn't Bartley Fallon great venom in him?

MRS. TULLY. You may be sure he had some cause. Why would he have made an end of him if he had not? (To MRS. TARPEY, raising her voice.) What was it rose the dispute at all, Mrs. Tarpey?

MRS. TARPEY. Not a one of me knows. The last I saw of them, Jack Smith was standing there, and Bartley Fallon was standing there, quiet and easy, and he listening to "The Red-haired Man's Wife."

MRS. TULLY. Do you hear that, Tim Casey? Do you hear that, Shawn Early and James Ryan? Bartley Fallon was here this morning listening to red Jack Smith's wife, Kitty Keary that was! Listening to her and whispering with her! It was she started the fight so!

SHAWN EARLY. She must have followed him from her own house. It is likely some person roused him.

TIM CASEY. I never knew, before,

9 wake him: watch over his body at night.
10 Ochone (əKH ōn′): Alas.

Bartley Fallon was great with Jack Smith's wife.

MRS. TULLY. How would you know it? Sure it's not in the streets they would be calling it. If Mrs. Fallon didn't know of it, and if I that have the next house to them didn't know of it, and if Jack Smith himself didn't know of it, it is not likely you would know of it, Tim Casey.

SHAWN EARLY. Let Bartley Fallon take charge of her from this out so, and let him provide for her. It is little pity she will get from any person in this parish.

TIM CASEY. How can he take charge of her? Sure he has a wife of his own. Sure you don't think he'd turn souper and marry her?

JAMES RYAN. It would be easy for him to marry her if he brought her to America.

SHAWN EARLY. With or without Kitty Keary, believe me it is for America he's making at this minute. I saw the new magistrate and Jo Muldoon of the police going to the post office as I came up—there was hurry on them—you may be sure it was to telegraph they went, the way he'll be stopped in the docks at Queenstown!

MRS. TULLY. It's likely Kitty Keary is gone with him, and not minding a sheet or a wake at all. The poor man, to be deserted by his own wife, and the breath hardly gone out yet from his body that is lying bloody in the field!

(*Enter* MRS. FALLON.)

MRS. FALLON. What is it the whole of the town is talking about? And what is it you yourselves are talking about? Is it about my man Bartley Fallon you are talking? Is it lies about him you are telling, saying that he went killing Jack Smith? My grief that ever he came into this place at all!

JAMES RYAN. Be easy now, Mrs. Fallon. Sure there is no one at all in the whole fair but is sorry for you!

MRS. FALLON. Sorry for me, is it? Why would anyone be sorry for me? Let you be sorry for yourselves, and that there may be shame on you forever and at the day of judgment, for the words you are saying and the lies you are telling to take away the character of my poor man, and to take the good name off of him, and to drive him to destruction! That is what you are doing!

SHAWN EARLY. Take comfort now, Mrs. Fallon. The police are not so smart as they think. Sure he might give them the slip yet, the same as Lynchehaun.

MRS. TULLY. If they do get him, and if they do put a rope around his neck, there is no one can say he does not deserve it!

MRS. FALLON. Is that what you are saying, Bridget Tully, and is that what you think? I tell you it's too much talk you have, making yourself out to be such a great one, and to be running down every respectable person! A rope, is it? It isn't much of a rope was needed to tie up your own furniture the day you came into Martin Tully's house, and you never bringing as much as a blanket, or a penny, or a suit of clothes with you, and I myself bringing seventy pounds

and two feather beds. And now you are stiffer than a woman would have a hundred pounds! It is too much talk the whole of you have. A rope, is it? I tell you the whole of this town is full of liars and schemers that would hang you up for half a glass of whiskey. (*Turning to go.*) People they are you wouldn't believe as much as daylight from without you'd get up to have a look at it yourself. Killing Jack Smith indeed! Where are you at all, Bartley, till I bring you out of this? My nice, quiet little man! My decent comrade! He that is as kind and as harmless as an innocent beast of the field! He'll be doing no harm at all if he'll shed the blood of some of you after this day's work! That much would be no harm at all. (*Calls out.*) Bartley! Bartley Fallon! Where are you? (*Going out.*) Did anyone see Bartley Fallon?

(*All turn to look after her.*)

James Ryan. It is hard for her to believe any such a thing, God help her!

(*Enter* **Bartley Fallon** *from right, carrying hayfork.*)

Bartley. It is what I often said to myself, if there is ever any misfortune coming to this world, it is on myself it is sure to come!

(*All turn round and face him.*)

Bartley. To be going about with this fork, and to find no one to take it, and no place to leave it down, and I wanting to be gone out of this. ——Is that you, Shawn Early? (*Holds out fork.*) It's well I met you. You have no call to be leaving the fair for a while the way I have, and how can I go till I'm rid of this fork?

Will you take it and keep it until such time as Jack Smith——

SHAWN EARLY (*backing*). I will not take it, Bartley Fallon, I'm very thankful to you!

BARTLEY (*turning to apple stall*). Look at it now, Mrs. Tarpey, it was here I got it; let me thrust it in under the stall. It will lie there safe enough, and no one will take notice of it until such time as Jack Smith——

MRS. TARPEY. Take your fork out of that! Is it to put trouble on me and to destroy me you want? putting it there for the police to be rooting it out maybe.

(*Thrusts him back.*)

BARTLEY. That is a very unneighborly thing for you to do, Mrs. Tarpey. Hadn't I enough care on me with that fork before this, running up and down with it like the swinging of a clock, and afeard to lay it down in any place. I wish I never touched it or meddled with it at all!

JAMES RYAN. It is a pity, indeed, you ever did.

BARTLEY. Will you yourself take it, James Ryan? You were always a neighborly man.

JAMES RYAN (*backing*). There is many a thing I would do for you, Bartley Fallon, but I won't do that!

SHAWN EARLY. I tell you there is no man will give you any help or any encouragement for this day's work. If it was something agrarian now——

BARTLEY. If no one at all will take it, maybe it's best to give it up to the police.

TIM CASEY. There'd be a welcome for it with them, surely! (*Laughter.*)

MRS. TULLY. And it is to the police Kitty Keary herself will be brought.

MRS. TARPEY (*rocking to and fro*). I wonder now who will take the expense of the wake for poor Jack Smith?

BARTLEY. The wake for Jack Smith!

TIM CASEY. Why wouldn't he get a wake as well as another? Would you begrudge him that much?

BARTLEY. Red Jack Smith dead! Who was telling you?

SHAWN EARLY. The whole town knows of it by this.

BARTLEY. Do they say what way did he die?

JAMES RYAN. You don't know that yourself, I suppose, Bartley Fallon? You don't know he was followed and that he was laid dead with the stab of a hayfork?

BARTLEY. The stab of a hayfork!

SHAWN EARLY. You don't know, I suppose, that the body was found in the Five Acre Meadow?

BARTLEY. The Five Acre Meadow!

TIM CASEY. It is likely you don't know that the police are after the man that did it?

BARTLEY. The man that did it!

MRS. TULLY. You don't know, maybe, that he was made away with for the sake of Kitty Keary, his wife?

BARTLEY. Kitty Keary, his wife!

(*Sits down bewildered.*)

MRS. TULLY. And what have you to say now, Bartley Fallon?

BARTLEY (*crossing himself*). I to bring that fork here, and to find that news before me! It is much if I can ever stir from this place at all, or reach as far as the road!

TIM CASEY. Look, boys, at the new magistrate, and Jo Muldoon along with him! It's best for us to quit this.

SHAWN EARLY. That is so. It is best not to be mixed in this business at all.

JAMES RYAN. Bad as he is, I wouldn't like to be an informer against any man.

(*All hurry away except* **MRS. TARPEY,** *who remains behind her stall. Enter magistrate and policeman.*)

MAGISTRATE. I knew the district was in a bad state, but I did not expect to be confronted with a murder at the first fair I came to.

POLICEMAN. I am sure you did not, indeed.

MAGISTRATE. It was well I had not gone home. I caught a few words here and there that roused my suspicions.

POLICEMAN. So they would, too.

MAGISTRATE. You heard the same story from everyone you asked?

POLICEMAN. The same story—or if it was not altogether the same, anyway it was no less than the first story.

MAGISTRATE. What is that man doing? He is sitting alone with a hayfork. He has a guilty look. The murder was done with a hayfork!

POLICEMAN (*in a whisper*). That's the very man they say did the act; Bartley Fallon himself!

MAGISTRATE. He must have found escape difficult——he is trying to

brazen it out.[11] A convict in the Andaman Islands tried the same game, but he could not escape my system! Stand aside—— Don't go far——have the handcuffs ready. (*He walks up to* **BARTLEY,** *folds his arms, and stands before him.*) Here, my man, do you know anything of John Smith?

BARTLEY. Of John Smith! Who is he, now?

POLICEMAN. Jack Smith, sir—— Red Jack Smith!

MAGISTRATE (*coming a step nearer and tapping him on the shoulder*). Where is Jack Smith?

BARTLEY (*with a deep sigh, and shaking his head slowly*). Where is he, indeed?

MAGISTRATE. What have you to tell?

BARTLEY. It is where he was this morning, standing in this spot, singing his share of songs—no, but lighting his pipe—scraping a match on the sole of his shoe——

MAGISTRATE. I ask you, for the third time, where is he?

BARTLEY. I wouldn't like to say that. It is a great mystery, and it is hard to say of any man, did he earn hatred or love.

MAGISTRATE. Tell me all you know.

BARTLEY. All that I know—— Well, there are the three estates; there is Limbo,[12] and there is Purgatory,[13] and there is——

MAGISTRATE. Nonsense! This is trifling! Get to the point.

11 **brazen it out:** face it shamelessly.
12 **Limbo:** according to some Christian teachings, the dwelling place of those souls unable to enter Heaven.
13 **Purgatory:** in some Christian teachings, the place of temporary punishment after death.

THE ONE-ACT PLAY

BARTLEY. Maybe you don't hold with the clergy so? That is the teaching of the clergy. Maybe you hold with the old people. It is what they do be saying, that the shadow goes wandering, and the soul is tired, and the body is taking a rest —— The shadow! (*Starts up.*) I was nearly sure I saw Jack Smith not ten minutes ago at the corner of the forge, and I lost him again—— Was it his ghost I saw, do you think?

MAGISTRATE (*to* **POLICEMAN**). Conscience-struck! He will confess all now!

BARTLEY. His ghost to come before me! It is likely it was on account of that fork! I to have it and he to have no way to defend himself the time he met with his death!

MAGISTRATE (*to* **POLICEMAN**). I must note down his words. (*Takes out notebook.*) (*To* **BARTLEY**.) I warn you that your words are being noted.

BARTLEY. If I had ha' run faster in the beginning, this terror would not be on me at the latter end! Maybe he will cast it up against me at the day of judgment—— I wouldn't wonder at all at that.

MAGISTRATE (*writing*). At the day of judgment——

BARTLEY. It was soon for his ghost to appear to me——is it coming after me always by day it will be, and stripping the clothes off in the night-time?—— I wouldn't wonder at all at that, being as I am an unfortunate man!

MAGISTRATE (*sternly*). Tell me this truly. What was the motive of this crime?

BARTLEY. The motive, is it?

MAGISTRATE. Yes; the motive; the cause.

BARTLEY. I'd sooner not say that.

MAGISTRATE. You had better tell me truly. Was it money?

BARTLEY. Not at all! What did poor Jack Smith ever have in his pockets unless it might be his hands that would be in them?

MAGISTRATE. Any dispute about land?

BARTLEY (*indignantly*). Not at all! He never was a grabber or grabbed from anyone!

MAGISTRATE. You will find it better for you if you tell me at once.

BARTLEY. I tell you I wouldn't for the whole world wish to say what it was——it is a thing I would not like to be talking about.

MAGISTRATE. There is no use in hiding it. It will be discovered in the end.

BARTLEY. Well, I suppose it will, seeing that mostly everybody knows it before. Whisper here now. I will tell no lie; where would be the use? (*Puts his hand to his mouth, and* **MAGISTRATE** *stoops.*) Don't be putting the blame on the parish, for such a thing was never done in the parish before——it was done for the sake of Kitty Keary, Jack Smith's wife.

MAGISTRATE (*to* **POLICEMAN**). Put on the handcuffs. We have been saved some trouble. I knew he would confess if taken in the right way.

(**POLICEMAN** *puts on handcuffs.*)

BARTLEY. Handcuffs now! Glory be! I always said, if there was ever

any misfortune coming to this place it was on myself it would fall. I to be in handcuffs! There's no wonder at all in that.

(*Enter* Mrs. Fallon, *followed by the rest. She is looking back at them as she speaks.*)

Mrs. Fallon. Telling lies the whole of the people of this town are; telling lies, telling lies as fast as a dog will trot! Speaking against my poor respectable man! Saying he made an end of Jack Smith! My decent comrade! There is no better man and no kinder man in the whole of the five parishes! It's little annoyance he ever gave to anyone! (*Turns and sees him.*) What in the earthly world do I see before me? Bartley Fallon in charge of the police! Handcuffs on him! O Bartley, what did you do at all at all?

Bartley. O Mary, there has a great misfortune come upon me! It is what I always said, that if there is ever any misfortune——

Mrs. Fallon. What did he do at all, or is it bewitched I am?

Magistrate. This man has been arrested on a charge of murder.

Mrs. Fallon. Whose charge is that? Don't believe them! They are all liars in this place! Give me back my man!

Magistrate. It is natural you should take his part, but you have no cause of complaint against your neighbors. He has been arrested for the murder of John Smith, on his own confession.

Mrs. Fallon. The saints of heaven protect us! And what did he want killing Jack Smith?

Magistrate. It is best you should

know all. He did it on account of a love affair with the murdered man's wife.

MRS. FALLON. With Jack Smith's wife! With Kitty Keary!——Ochone, the traitor!

THE CROWD. A great shame, indeed. He is a traitor, indeed.

MRS. TULLY. To America he was bringing her, Mrs. Fallon.

BARTLEY. What are you saying, Mary? I tell you——

MRS. FALLON. Don't say a word! I won't listen to any word you'll say! (Stops her ears.) O, isn't he the treacherous villain? Ohone go deo!

BARTLEY. Be quiet till I speak! Listen to what I say!

MRS. FALLON. Sitting beside me on the ass car coming to the town, so quiet and so respectable, and treachery like that in his heart!

BARTLEY. Is it your wits you have lost or is it I myself that have lost my wits?

MRS. FALLON. And it's hard I earned you, slaving, slaving——and you grumbling, and sighing, and coughing, and discontented, and the priest wore out anointing you, with all the times you threatened to die!

BARTLEY. Let you be quiet till I tell you!

MRS. FALLON. You to bring such a disgrace into the parish! A thing that was never heard of before!

BARTLEY. Will you shut your mouth and hear me speaking?

MRS. FALLON. And if it was for any sort of a fine handsome woman, but for a little fistful of a woman like Kitty Keary, that's not four feet high hardly, and not three teeth in her

head unless she got new ones! May God reward you, Bartley Fallon, for the black treachery in your heart and the wickedness in your mind, and the red blood of poor Jack Smith that is wet upon your hand!

(Voice of JACK SMITH heard singing.)

The sea shall be dry,
  The earth under mourning and ban!
Then loud shall he cry
  For the wife of the red-haired man!

BARTLEY. It's Jack Smith's voice ——I never knew a ghost to sing before——. It is after myself and the fork he is coming! (Goes back. Enter JACK SMITH.) Let one of you give him the fork and I will be clear of him now and for eternity!

MRS. TARPEY. The Lord have mercy on us! Red Jack Smith! The man that was going to be waked!

JAMES RYAN. Is it back from the grave you are come?

SHAWN EARLY. Is it alive you are, or is it dead you are?

TIM CASEY. Is it yourself at all that's in it?

MRS. TULLY. Is it letting on you were to be dead?

MRS. FALLON. Dead or alive, let you stop Kitty Keary, your wife, from bringing my man away with her to America!

JACK SMITH. It is what I think, the wits are gone astray on the whole of you. What would my wife want bringing Bartley Fallon to America?

MRS. FALLON. To leave yourself, and to get quit of you she wants, Jack Smith, and to bring him away from myself. That's what the two of them had settled together.

JACK SMITH. I'll break the head of any man that says that! Who is it says it? (*To* **TIM CASEY.**) Was it you said it? (*To* **SHAWN EARLY.**) Was it you?

ALL TOGETHER (*backing and shaking their heads*). It wasn't I said it!

JACK SMITH. Tell me the name of any man that said it!

ALL TOGETHER (*pointing to* **BARTLEY**). It was *him* that said it!

JACK SMITH. Let me at him till I break his head!

> (**BARTLEY** *backs in terror. Neighbors hold* **JACK SMITH** *back.*)

JACK SMITH (*trying to free himself*). Let me at him! Isn't he the pleasant sort of a scarecrow for any woman to be crossing the ocean with! It's back from the docks of New York he'd be turned (*trying to rush at him again*), with a lie in his mouth and treachery in his heart, and another man's wife by his side, and he passing her off as his own! Let me at him, can't you.

(*Makes another rush, but is held back.*)

MAGISTRATE (*pointing to* **JACK SMITH**). Policeman, put the handcuffs on this man. I see it all now. A case of false impersonation, a conspiracy to defeat the ends of justice. There was a case in the Andaman Islands, a murderer of the Mopsa tribe, a religious enthusiast——

POLICEMAN. So he might be, too.

MAGISTRATE. We must take both these men to the scene of the murder. We must confront them with the body of the real Jack Smith.

JACK SMITH. I'll break the head of any man that will find my dead body!

MAGISTRATE. I'll call more help from the barracks. (*Blows* **POLICEMAN'S** *whistle.*)

BARTLEY. It is what I am thinking, if myself and Jack Smith are put together in the one cell for the night, the handcuffs will be taken off him, and his hands will be free, and murder will be done that time surely!

MAGISTRATE. Come on! (*They turn to the right.*)

CURTAIN

Understanding Literature

1. How does the magistrate behave as he talks with the policeman in the beginning of the play?
2. What information does partially deaf Mrs. Tarpey give them about the town? In the light of the whole play, how are her answers ironic?
3. What are Bartley and Mrs. Fallon talking about as they come on the stage?

4. As Jack Smith comes on, what is he singing about? Why does the author have him leave his hayfork behind? How does it help to tie the play together?
5. When does the play change from real action into false interpretations of the action? How do the rumors spread?
6. What does each character add to the spreading of the news? What real evidence is each character using? What false judgments does each make about the facts?
7. What does Mrs. Tarpey's partial deafness add to the play?
8. Summarize what "news" is spread. How much is fact? How much is opinion?
9. What is the situation as Bartley Fallon returns with the hayfork? How is he treated? As Bartley talks, how does the author make it seem to Bartley's listeners that he is the murderer?
10. By what steps do you arrive at the true situation?
11. How does the magistrate behave at the end of the play?

Poetry

This unit contains many different types of poems which, in turn, are concerned with many different subjects. After reading the following essay, you will know what one poet thinks poetry is all about. After reading the poems which follow it, you will be able to form your own ideas about what a poem is and what makes a good one.

Short Talk on Poetry[*]

*with different kinds of explanations for young people
as to how little anybody knows about poetry, how it is made,
what it is made of, how long men have been making it,
where it came from, when it began, who started it and why,
and who knows all about it.*

Carl Sandburg

WHAT IS POETRY? Is the answer hidden somewhere? Is it one of those answers locked in a box and nobody has the key? There are such questions and answers.

Once a man reading a newspaper clipped a poem written by a small boy in a school in New York City. The lines read:

There stands the elephant.
Bold and strong—
There he stands chewing his food.
We are strengthless against his strength.

And the man has kept this poem for many years. He has a feeling the boy did a good, honest piece of writing. The boy stood wondering and thinking before the biggest four-legged animal on earth today. And the boy put his wonder and thought, his personal human secret, a touch of

man's fear in the wilderness, into the nineteen words of the poem. He asked, "What does the elephant do to me when I look at him? What is my impression of the elephant?" Then he answered his own questions.

Once there was a boy went to school and learned that any two-legged animal is a biped. And he said, "Here I've been a biped all the time and I didn't know it." So there are people sometimes who talk poetry without writing it but they don't know they are talking poetry. And every child, every boy and girl, sometimes has poetry in his head and heart—even though it doesn't get written.

Once there was a wee, curly-headed boy tugged at a cornstalk, tugged till he pulled the cornstalk up all by himself and told about it to his father, who said, "I guess you're getting to be a pretty strong boy now." The little one answered, "I

[*] From EARLY MOON by Carl Sandburg, copyright, 1930, by Harcourt, Brace, & World, Inc., © 1958 by Carl Sandburg and reprinted by permission of the publishers.

guess I am. The whole earth had a hold of the other end of the cornstalk and was pulling against me." Should we say this boy had imagination and what he told his father was so keen and alive it could be called poetry? Perhaps he was a poet without knowing it just like the boy who was a biped without knowing it.

Poetry is old, ancient, goes far back. It is among the oldest of human things. So old is it that no man knows how and why the first poems came.

When it shall happen sometime that men gather their gifts and go to work and write a history of language, then it may be that we shall have at the same time a history of poetry. For the first poems of man probably came about the same time the first men, women and children spoke the first human words on the earth.

Is any one surprised to hear that we do not have a history of poetry? Shall we believe that the learned men have written histories of all the important things of mankind? Surely there are many big histories yet to be written on big subjects. We do not have, for instance, a history of Money that goes back to when money first began, telling how and why. We do not have a history of Language which goes far back, telling how and why men first began to talk.

Yes, poetry is old. The first men that walked the earth, before men had learned to write, must have talked poetry to each other sometimes. Among the oldest things we have today which tell us about the Indians, the Chinese, the Egyptians,

how they lived and talked, thousands of years ago, are writings we know to be poetry. These writings have words that go along with time beats, with rhythm, one-two, one-two, or one-two-three-four, one-two-three-four. They had drums among the Indians, the Chinese, the Egyptians, thousands of years ago. And the words of their poetry move along like drumbeats, keeping time, now fast, now slow, drumming easy and slow at the opening of a war dance, drumming faster and faster, wild and furious, till it is so swift only the best-trained warriors can stand the speed of the dance that is drummed.

We have old poems, some so old no man knows how far they go back in time. One beautiful ancient English poem has no author, whose name we know. Where it came from no history books tell us. It goes like this—

On a misty moisty morning, when
　　cloudy was the weather,
I chanced to meet an old man all
　　clothed in leather.
He began to compliment and I began
　　to grin,
"How do you do? and how do you
　　do? and how do you do again?"

This is only one of many fine and strange poems we have out of the long ago. Nobody knows who wrote them or whether they were first spoken centuries before they were written down to meet our eyes in books.

What is poetry? This question no man has ever answered in such a way that all men have said, "Yes, now we know what poetry is." Many men have tried to explain what poetry is. Some men have written thick books so the question might be settled and made clear for all time. But they have all failed. Several fine poets have written essays and papers on what they believe poetry to be. Yet these poets did not do what they started out to do. They meant to explain in prose what poetry is and they ended up with writing poetry to explain poetry. This is like a man inside of a strange house trying to tell people outside who have never been in the house exactly how it feels to be in that house, which is not scientific nor exact and which is like saying, "The way to write poems is to write poems." It is only clear and understandable to those who already understand and therefore need no explanations.

When Walt Whitman[1] says, "The poet is the answerer," we are interested. If we could know just what he means by "the answerer" we would know what he means by "the poet." One poet says poetry must be "cold, lonely and distant," not knowing that some readers of poetry are glad to have books which are warm, friendly and so near that they almost breathe with life. Another poet has said poetry is "emotion remembered in tranquillity." What does that mean? It is anybody's guess what that means. To know exactly what it means we would have to know exactly what is emotion, what is tranquillity, and what we do when we remember. Otherwise it is an escape

from words into words, "passing the buck," or winding like a weasel through language that ends about where it begins. "He came out of the same hole he went in at."

There is a science called esthetics. It is the science which tries to find the laws of beauty. If as a science it ever became perfect then the books dealing with that science would become very important. Then when a builder finished a house and wished to know whether it was a beautiful house he would only have to open the books on esthetics and the books would tell him.

What is beauty? And when shall we call a thing beautiful? These, too, are questions no man has ever answered in such a way that all men have said, "Yes, now we know what beauty is and now we know how to tell the beautiful when we find it." The nearest that men have come to answering the question, "What is the beautiful?" has been in their saying the beautiful is *the appropriate,* that which serves. No hat is a beautiful hat which does not fit you and which the wind can easily blow off your head. A five-gallon hat on a cowboy riding a horse on an Arizona ranch is beautiful—but the same hat on a crowded city streetcar would be out of place, inappropriate. No song is beautiful in a room where persons desire complete quiet. No polite behavior has beauty unless it has thought and consideration for others. The most beautiful room is the one which best serves those who live in it.

The most beautiful skyscrapers are those without extras stuck on after

1 Walt Whitman: 19th-century American poet.

the real structure is finished. Why should a good, honest skyscraper have a dome or a mosque or a cement wedding cake plastered on top of it? Nearly always, what serves, what is appropriate to human use, is beautiful enough—without extras. A farm silo, a concrete grain elevator, a steel barge hauling iron ore on the Great Lakes, or a series of tall coal chutes rising as silhouettes on a moonlight night, may any one of them have as complete a beauty as the Greek Parthenon or a Gothic cathedral. Steichen, the photographer, declares he occasionally meets newspaper photographs which in design and as works of art are superior to many of the proclaimed masterpieces of painting and etching.

Now, poetry is supposed to be the esthetic art which gathers the beautiful into words. The first stuff for making poetry is words. No poems, strictly speaking, have ever been made without words. To make poems without words would be like a painter painting without paint or a bricklayer bricklaying without bricks. Of course, a feeling or a thought, or both must come to a poet before he begins using the words that make a poem. But the right words, the special and particular words for the purpose in view, these must come. For out of them the poem is made.

The words for a poem sometimes come swiftly and easily so that at last when the poem is put down on paper, the writer of them says, "I do not know how these words came. What is here was not my own abso-

lute doing any more than a dream that should come to me in a night of sleep." Yet again the words may come slowly, out of years of toil and sometimes anguish of changing phrases and arrangements.

While we do not know very much in an absolute way about the questions, "What is poetry? How is a poem made?" we do know the one little fact that poems are made of words and without words there can be no poetry. Beyond this we do not know much. However, there is one other little scientific fact we know about poetry. That is, what is poetry for any given individual depends on the individual and what his personality requires as poetry. This links up with one of the few accepted propositions of the science of esthetics: Beauty depends on personal taste. What is beauty for one person is not for another. What is poetry for one person may be balderdash or hogwash for another.

Each of us has a personality different from all others. It has even been said that as no two leaves in a forest are the same no two human characters are precisely alike. This personality that each of us has is strangely woven of millions of little facts, events, impressions out of the past and present. Your personality and mine go back to many mysterious human connections before we were born—and since. And what any one of us loves today with depth of passion, and what each of us tries to shape his life by, goes back to strange things in personality, things so darkly mixed and baffling that it is not easy

414

for any of us at a given time to an-swer the question, "Why do you love this and not that? Why do you want those and not them?" The old song with its line, "I want what I want when I want it," is not entirely comic in its backgrounds.

We do not know the start of the old folk saying, "Everyone to his taste as the old woman said when she kissed the cow." We are sure a blunt Indiana philosopher knew his ground well when he wrote, "What is one man's lettuce is another man's poison ivy." These are humorous comments on the deeply serious and involved reality known as human personality. They connect directly with the fact that what is poetry for some is not poetry for others. They indicate that sometimes we cannot help it that we do not merely *dislike* some poetry; we go farther and *hate* it. And why we should hate any particular poem, thing or person is no more clear than why we love others, for hate is usu-ally expensive in many ways and is a waste of time that belongs else-where. Charles Lamb[2] said he be-lieved an old story he had heard about two men, who had never be-fore seen each other, meeting one day in a street in London—and the moment they saw each other's faces they leaped and began fighting.

Lamb said those two men who be-gan hitting at each other's faces the moment they saw those faces, had "imperfect sympathies." Something clicked in each one saying, "Hit him! Kill him!" They couldn't help it.

2 **Charles Lamb:** English essayist (1775-1834).

Though they met in a crowded street of a great city, and there was no war on, they attacked each other like two soldiers with bayonets in front-line trenches.

And exactly like those two men meeting in a London street, some of us register instantly—though not so violently—to faces we meet, build-ings, colors, neckties, gowns, designs, pictures, books, plays—and poems. Something clicks in us and we know like a flash whether we like this or that new thing we meet for the first time.

And then may happen afterward a slow change of our viewpoint. What we saw nothing in to begin with takes on a glint or two we had not noticed at first; then as time passes, we gather values, intentions, gleams, that interest us and lead us on till we know we were ignorant, possessed of "imperfect sympathies," in our first impression of hate or dis-like. This change of viewpoint from dislike to interest, from indifference to enthusiasm, often has happened with the finest of men and women in respect to great masterpieces of lit-erature. Sometimes we do not know what a writer is talking about in his books because in life we have not met the people, facts, impressions which he is trying to deliver his mind and heart about in his book. Said a great modern artist, "Going along a railroad one day I see a thing I have seen many times. But this day I suddenly *see*. 'Tisn't that you *see* new, but things have prepared you for *a new vision*."

As the years pass by and experience writes out new records in our mind life, we go back to some works of art that we rejected in the early days and find values we missed. Work, love, laughter, pain, death, put impressions on us as time passes, and as we brood over what has happened.

Out of songs and scars and the mystery of personal development, we get eyes that pick out intentions we had not seen before in people, in works of art, in books and poetry.

Naturally, too, the reverse happens. What we register to at one period of life, what we find gay and full of fine nourishment at one time, we find later has lost interest for us. A few masterpieces may last across the years but we usually discard some. A few masterpieces are enough. Why this is so we do not know. For each individual his new acquisitions and old discards are different.

The books and poems at hand ready for each of us are so many and so different that we use and throw away, acquire and discard, according to personal taste, and often merely guided by whim like the man in the song, "I want what I want when I want it." Too often both among young people and grownups, there is a careless drifting and they take the easiest way in books and poetry. Millions read without asking themselves why they read and whether in all their reading they have learned anything worth the spending of their time.

It was not for nothing Thoreau[3] said an old newspaper would do for him just as well as a new one. Each of us can sit alone with our conscience for a while on the proposition of Robert Louis Stevenson that the intelligent man can find an Iliad[4] of the human race in a newspaper. And any kindly philosopher could write a thick book on why the shrewd, tolerant reader enjoys even a stupid, vain, hypocritical[5] book because the writer of the book is etching his own portrait on every page, stepping forth and talking off lines like one of the fools, clowns or pretenders in a Russian play. Healthy questions for each of us: "Why do I read books? What do books do to me? Can I improve my form as a reader? What does poetry do to me? Why do I need this or that poetry?"

We have heard much in our time about free verse being modern, as though it is a new-found style for men to use in speaking and writing, rising out of the machine age, skyscrapers, high speed and jazz. Now, if free verse is a form of writing poetry without rime, without regular meters, without established and formal rules governing it, we can easily go back to the earliest styles of poetry known to the human family—and the style is strictly free verse. Before men invented the alphabet, so that poems could be put down in writing, they spoke their poems. When one man spoke to another in

---

3 **Thoreau:** Henry David Thoreau, 19th-century American writer.

4 **Iliad:** a reference to the Greek epic poem by Homer. Here it means a long account of woes and disasters.

5 **hypocritical:** one that pretends to be better than it is.

a certain time beat and rhythm, if it happened that his words conveyed certain impressions and moods to his listeners, he was delivering poetry to them, whether he knew it or they knew it, and whether he or they had a name for an art which the poet was practicing on himself and them.

We may go through thousands of pages of the reports of songs, poems, and spoken dreams of American Indians as recorded in the volumes of the Bureau of Ethnology[6] of the Smithsonian Institution at Washington, and we find it all to be in the free verse style. The poems of the ancient Chinese writers Li Po, Tu Fu and others, as read in translations, and as notated by the translators, show how strange and marvelous moments of life can be captured and compressed in the manner called free verse. The Bible is one of the sublime sources of free verse. The orations of Moses, the Book of Proverbs, Ecclesiastes, the Sermon on the Mount, the "love chapter" of the Apostle Paul, these are in the free verse style of writing poetry.

If those who write in the free verse style fail at getting onto paper any lines worth reading twice, they are in the same class with those who in regular, ordered, formal verse fail to get onto paper lines worth reading twice. The crimes of free verse have been many. The same goes for sonnets, ballads, ballades, triolets, rondeaus, villanelles,[7] and the forms of verse which are governed by hexameters, pentameters, iambics,[8] strophes, and by laws which dictate how many syllables shall be permitted to perch on each line of the poem.

Perhaps no wrong is done and no temple of human justice violated in pointing out here that each authentic poet makes a style of his own. Sometimes this style is so clearly the poet's own that when he is imitated it is known who is imitated. Shakespeare, Villon,[9] Li Po, Whitman— each sent forth his language and impress of thought and feeling from a different style of gargoyle spout. In the spacious highways of great books each poet is allowed the stride that will get him where he wants to go.

Should children write poetry? Yes, whenever they feel like it. If nothing else happens they will find it a training for writing and speaking in other fields of human work and play. No novelist has been a worse writer for having practiced at poetry. Many a playwright, historian, essayist, editorial writer, could have improved his form by experimenting with poetry.

At what age should a child begin writing poetry? Any age. Poems are made of words and when a child is learning to talk, to shape words on its tongue, is a proper time for it to speak poetry—if it can.

Does it help a child poet to have praise for his poems? The child

---

6 **Ethnology:** science which studies the races of mankind.
7 **sonnets . . . villanelles:** different forms of poetry.

8 **hexameters . . . iambics:** rhythmic divisions of poetry.
9 **Villon:** Francois Villon, 15th-century French poet.

should be told that poetry is first of all for the poet, that great poets usually die saying their best work is not written. Perhaps it is wise for every child to be told that it is a mistake for either a child or a grown-up accomplished artist to be satisfied with any past performance.

The foremost American woman poet, Emily Dickinson, had scarcely any of her poetry published in her lifetime. What she wrote had to be. And it is doubtful if her poems would have had the same complete glory they have if she had been taken up and praised. On the other hand there have been poets saved to live and write beautiful pages because they found friends, an audience, and enough money to keep the wolf from sniffing round their little doorways.

The father of a great Irish poet once remarked, "What can be explained is not poetry." There are people who want a book of verse to be like the arithmetic—you turn to the back of the book and find the answers. Ken Nakazawa notes, "The poems that are obvious are like the puzzles that are already solved. They deny us the joy of seeking and creating."

Once a little girl showed to a friend a poem she had written. "Why didn't you make it longer?" asked the friend. "I could have," she answered, "but then it wouldn't have been a poem." She meant she left something in the air for the reader of the poem to linger over, as any of us do over a rose or a sunset or a face. Roses, sunsets, faces, have mystery. If we could explain them, then after having delivered our explanations we could say, "Take it from me, that's all there is to it, and there's no use your going any further for I've told you all there is and there isn't any more."

If poems could be explained, then poets would have to leave out roses, sunsets, faces, from their poems. Yet it seems that for thousands of years poets have been writing about roses, sunsets, faces, because they have mystery, significance, and a heavy or a light beauty, an appeal, a lesson and a symbolism that stays with us long as we live. It was something like this in the heart of the philosopher who declared, "What can be explained is not poetry."

Understanding Literature

1. Why, in Sandburg's opinion, are definitions of poetry unsatisfactory?
2. What is the science of esthetics?
3. What is the best definition of *the beautiful,* according to Sandburg? What are some examples of beauty that fit this definition? What is your opinion of this definition of *the beautiful?*
4. What are the only things about poetry that are really known?
5. What does Charles Lamb mean by "imperfect sympathies"? What causes a change in our sympathies?

6. What is free verse? What are some examples that Sandburg uses to prove that free verse is not a modern invention?
7. What does the statement that "what can be explained is not poetry" mean? Do you agree with this statement? Why or why not?

The Ballad

ONE OF THE OLDEST forms of poetry is the ballad, a narrative poem intended for singing or reciting and written in short stanzas. The ballad is usually about an exciting episode told in dramatic form: you see and hear the incident. These songs were made up by anonymous, or unknown, poets who traveled from town to town singing for the entertainment of groups, who were invited to join in on the refrain (repeated lines); in some instances the groups danced to the music of the ballad.

The major characteristics of ballads are that they are often about common people (though sometimes about the nobles too), that physical courage or love are frequent subjects, that they contain little characterization or description, and that action is told through dialogue (people speaking). Much of the story is left out, and you have to fill it in from what is implied, or suggested.

The ballad stanza, another main characteristic, is four lines long. The fourth line usually rhymes with the second. The rhythm is most frequently based on an unaccented sound followed by an accented one, that is, on a sound that receives no emphasis followed by one that is very much emphasized. This pattern of sound is known as iambic meter and indicated as ˘ ´. These lines from "Robin Hood and Alan a Dale" are examples of iambic meter: "As Robin Hood next morning stood,/ Amongst the leaves so gay." As in this example, the first and third lines of a ballad stanza usually have four accented syllables, and the second and fourth lines have three each. To read the rhythm correctly you must sometimes slur over sounds and run syllables together to make two syllables sound as one. These are general characteristics for ballads, although you will find exceptions.

Because early ballads were passed on orally from one person to another, many variations of a single ballad can be found. The names used may differ, and some of the details may vary, but the general idea of the story usually stays the same.

CARL SANDBURG

419

This ballad tells a story which is still being used as a plot for adventure stories. In the first line the mother (the "she" of line 1) rouses her husband (Lord Douglas) to say that their eldest daughter has gone off with her lover (Lord William). Douglas and his sons must follow and bring her back. They fight with Lord William with tragic results.

IMPROVING YOUR READING. Differences in the spelling of some words can be troublesome in reading ballads; but if you read aloud, you can understand most of the words by their sounds.

To get rhythm into his lines, a poet sometimes changes the normal order of words. For example, ". . . she saw . . . her father hard fighting, who loved her so dear" would read "her father who loved her so dear was fighting hard"; and "But a father I can never get mair" would read "But I can never get another father." If you have trouble understanding some lines, try to put the words into a more usual order.

The Douglas Tragedy

"Rise up, rise up, now, Lord Douglas," she says,
    "And put on your armor so bright;
Let it never be said that a daughter of thine
    Was married to a lord under night.

"Rise up, rise up, my seven bold sons,   5
    And put on your armor so bright,
And take better care of your youngest sister,
    For your eldest's awa' the last night."—

He's mounted her on a milk-white steed,
    And himself on a dapple gray,   10
With a bugelet horn hung down by his side,
    And lightly they rode away.

Lord William lookit o'er his left shoulder,
    To see what he could see,
And there he spy'd her seven brethren bold,   15
    Come riding o'er the lee.

"Light down,[1] light down, Lady Marg'ret," he said,
    "And hold my steed in your hand,
Until that against your seven brethren bold,
    And your father, I make a stand."—   20

She held his steed in her milk-white hand,
    And never shed one tear,
Until that she saw her seven brethren fa',[2]
    And her father hard fighting, who loved her so dear.

"O hold your hand, Lord William!" she said,   25
    "For your strokes they are wondrous sair;[3]
True lovers I can get many a ane,[4]
    But a father I can never get mair."—[5]

O, she's ta'en out her hankerchief,
    It was o' the holland sae fine,   30
And aye she dighted[6] her father's bloody wounds,
    That were redder than the wine.

"O chuse, O chuse, Lady Marg'ret," he said,
    "O whether will ye gang or bide?"—[7]
"I'll gang, I'll gang, Lord William," she said,   35
    "For you have left me no other guide."—

He's lifted her on a milk-white steed,
    And himself on a dapple gray,
With a bugelet horn hung down by his side,
    And slowly they baith[8] rade away.   40

O they rade on, and on they rade,
    And a' by the light of the moon,
Until they came to yon wan water,
    And there they lighted down.

1 light down: get down.   5 mair: any more.
2 fa': fall.   6 dighted: wiped.
3 sair: sure.   7 gang or bide: go or stay.
4 ane: another.   8 baith: both.

They lighted down to tak a drink
    Of the spring that ran sae clear;
And down the stream ran his gude heart's blood,
    And sair she 'gan to fear.

"Hold up, hold up, Lord William," she says,
    "For I fear that you are slain!"—
" 'Tis naething but the shadow of my scarlet cloak
    That shines in the water sae plain."—

O they rade on, and on they rade,
    And a' by the light of the moon,
Until they cam to his mother's ha'[9] door,
    And there they lighted down.

"Get up, get up, lady mother," he says,
    "Get up, and let me in!—
Get up, get up, lady mother," he says,
    "For this night my fair lady I've win.

"O mak my bed, lady mother," he says,
    "O mak it braid[10] and deep!
And lay Lady Marg'ret close at my back,
    And the sounder I will sleep."—

Lord William was dead lang ere midnight,
    Lady Marg'ret lang ere day—[11]
And all true lovers that go thegither,
    May they have mair luck than they!

Lord William was buried in St Marie's kirk,[12]
    Lady Marg'ret in Marie's quire;
Out o' the lady's grave grew a bonny red rose,
    And out o' the knight's a brier.

And they twa met, and they twa plat,[13]
    And fain they wad be near;
And a' the warld might ken[14] right weel,
    They were twa lovers dear.

45

50

55

60

65

70

75

9 **ha':** hall.
10 **braid:** broad.
11 **lang ere day:** long before daybreak.

12 **kirk:** church.
13 **plat:** intertwined.
14 **ken:** know.

But bye and rade the Black Douglas,[15]
   And wow but he was rough!
For he pull'd up the bonny brier,
   And flang'd in St. Mary's Loch.[16]   80

15 Black Douglas: Either Lady Margaret's father has recovered, or this is one of his descendents.
16 Loch: a deep bay.

Understanding Literature

1. What reason does the mother give for sending her husband and sons after Lord William?
2. Describe the battle. How does it end? Why does Lady Margaret choose to go on with Lord William?
3. Why does Margaret "'gan to fear"?
4. What information does Lord William give to his mother?
5. Why, would you guess, does Lady Margaret die?
6. How do the rose and brier stand for their love? In the last stanza what attitude does Douglas take toward their love?

Another ballad on love, this one characterizes cruel Barbara
Allan. Can you explain her action toward the young man?

Bonny Barbara Allan

It was in and about the Martinmas¹ time,
   When the green leaves were a falling,
That Sir John Graeme, in the West Country,
   Fell in love with Barbara Allan.

He sent his men down through the town,   5
   To the place where she was dwelling:
"O haste and come to my master dear,
   Gin² ye be Barbara Allan."

O hooly, hooly³ rose she up,
   To the place where he was lying,   10
And when she drew the curtain by,⁴
   "Young man, I think you're dying."

"O it's I'm sick, and very, very sick,
   And 't is a' for Barbara Allan."
"O the better for me ye's never be,   15
   Tho your heart's blood were a spilling.

"O dinna ye mind, young man," said she,
   "When ye was in the tavern a drinking,
That ye made the healths⁵ gae⁶ round and round,
   And slighted Barbara Allan?"   20

1 **Martinmas:** November 11,
feast of Saint Martin.
2 **Gin:** if.
3 **hooly:** slowly; softly.

4 **by:** aside.
5 **healths:** drink to one's health.
6 **gae:** go.

He turned his face unto the wall,
  And death was with him dealing:
"Adieu, adieu, my dear friends all,
  And be kind to Barbara Allan."

And slowly, slowly raise she up,   25
  And slowly, slowly left him,
And sighing said, she could not stay,
  Since death of life had reft[7] him.

She had not gane a mile but twa,
  When she heard the dead-bell ringing,   30
And every jow[8] that the dead-bell geid,[9]
  It cry'd, Woe to Barbara Allan!

"O mother, mother, make my bed.
  O make it saft and narrow.
Since my love died for me today,   35
  I'll die for him tomorrow."

7 **reft:** robbed.   8 **jow:** stroke.   9 **geid:** gave.

Understanding Literature

1. What relation does the time of the year in which the ballad is set have to its meaning?
2. Who are the speakers in the poem? Read the complete statements made by each.
3. Why does Sir John Graeme send for Barbara Allan? Why does he die? Why does she say that she will die?
4. Why does Barbara not admit her love for Sir John?

Highwaymen were the subjects of many stories and poems written in England in days of long ago. The humorous ballad "The Crafty Farmer" tells how one highwayman was outwitted.

IMPROVING YOUR READING. Notice how much of the story here is told through *dialogue*, the speeches of the characters. The dialogue helps to advance the action of the story and to give the effect of naturalness, as if this were a report of an actual conversation.

The Crafty Farmer

The song that I'm going to sing,
   I hope it will give you content,
Concerning a silly[1] old man,
   That was going to pay his rent.

As he was riding along,   5
   Along all on the highway,
A gentleman-thief overtook him,
   And thus to him did say.

"Well overtaken!" said the thief,
   "Well overtaken!" said he;   10
And "Well overtaken!" said the old man,
   "If thou be good company."

"How far are you going this way?"
   Which made the old man for to smile;
"By my faith," said the old man,   15
   "I'm just going two mile.

1 **silly:** plain; humble.

"I'm a poor farmer," he said,
  "And I farm a piece of ground,
And my half-year's rent, kind sir,
  Just comes to forty pound.   20

"And my landlord has not been at home,
  I've not seen him this twelvemonth or more,
Which makes my rent be large;
  I've to pay him just fourscore."

"Thou shouldst not have told any body,   25
  For thieves there's ganging many;
If any should light on thee,
  They'll rob thee of thy money."

"O never mind," said the old man,
  "Thieves I fear on no side,   30
For the money is safe in my bags,
  On the saddle on which I ride."

As they were riding along,
  The old man was thinking no ill,
The thief he pulled out a pistol   35
  And bid the old man stand still.

But the old man provd crafty,
  As in the world there are many;
He threw his saddle oer the hedge,
  Saying, "Fetch it, if thou'lt have any."   40

The thief got off his horse,
  With courage stout and bold,
To search for the old man's bag,
  And gave him horse to hold.

The old man put's foot i the stirrup   45
  And he got on astride;
To its side he clapt his spur up,
  You need not bid the old man ride.

"O stay!" said the thief, "O stay!   50
    And half the share thou shalt have."
"Nay, by my faith," said the old man,
    "For once I have bitten a knave."

The thief he was not content,
    But he thought there must be bags;   55
He out with his rusty old sword
    And chopt the old saddle in rags.

When he came to the landlord's house,
    This old man he was almost spent;[2]
Saying, "Come, show me a private room   60
    And I'll pay you a whole year's rent.

"I've met a fond fool by the way,
    I swapt horses and gave him no boot;
But never mind," said the old man,
    "For I got the fond fool by the foot."

He opened this rogue's portmantle,[3]   65
    It was glorious to behold;
There were three hundred pounds in silver,
    And three hundred pounds in gold.

And as he was riding home,
    And down a narrow lane,   70
He espied his mare tied to a hedge,
    Saying, "Prithee, Tib, wilt thou gang hame?"

When he got home to his wife
    And told her what he had done,
Up she rose and put on her clothes,   75
    And about the house did run.

She sung, and she sung, and she sung,
    She sung with a merry devotion,
Saying, "If ever our daughter gets wed,
    It will help to enlarge her portion."   80

---

2 **spent:** exhausted.
3 **portmantle:** traveling bag originally used on horseback.

Reading Skills

1. What was the purpose of the trip the farmer was taking?
2. What warning did the thief give the old man? Why did he give such a warning?
3. The farmer proves he is "crafty" in the way he handled the thieving episode. Explain.
4. What did the old man mean when he said, "For once I have bitten a knave"?
5. Explain what the farmer's wife meant at the very end of the ballad when she gaily sang:

> "If ever our daughter gets wed,
>   It will help to enlarge her portion."

Understanding Literature

1. "The Crafty Farmer" has many of the qualities which you now know to be in most ballads. List and discuss the qualities which are characteristic of the ballad.
2. This ballad is fast-moving, with no superfluous or extra words. What does each stanza add to the story?
3. What are the qualities that make this ballad humorous?

Selections in the **Myths, Fables, and Legends** unit of this book show that Robin Hood has a delightful, roguish sense of humor. And as you know, Little John is always ready for any game.

IMPROVING YOUR READING. As you read, notice how a light, enjoyable *mood* is created by the poet's choice of adjectives and use of bright colors. You should see in your mind's eye the pictures suggested by the poet.

Robin Hood and Alan a Dale

Come listen to me, you gallants so free,
    All you that love mirth for to hear,
And I will you tell of a bold outlaw,
    That lived in Nottinghamshire.

As Robin Hood in the forest stood,   5
    All under the greenwood tree,
There was he ware of a brave young man,
    As fine as fine might be.

The youngster was clothed in scarlet red,
    In scarlet fine and gay,   10
And he did frisk it over the plain,
    And chanted a roundelay.[1]

As Robin Hood next morning stood,
    Amongst the leaves so gay,
There did he espy[2] the same young man   15
    Come drooping along the way.

1 **roundelay:** a song with a refrain.
2 **espy:** caught sight of.

The scarlet he wore the day before,
    It was clean cast away;
And every step he fetch a sigh,
    "Alack and a well a day!"   20

Then steppèd forth brave Little John,
    And Much the miller's son,
Which made the young man bend his bow,
    When as he saw them come.

"Stand off, stand off!" the young man said,   25
    "What is your will with me?"—
"You must come before our master straight,
    Under yon greenwood tree."

And when he came bold Robin before,
    Robin askt him courteously,   30
"O hast thou any money to spare,
    For my merry men and me?"

"I have no money," the young man said,
    "But five shillings and a ring;
And that I have kept this seven long years,   35
    To have it at my wedding.

"Yesterday I should have married a maid,
    But she is now from me tane,[3]
And chosen to be an old knight's delight,
    Whereby my poor heart is slain."   40

"What is thy name?" then said Robin Hood,
    "Come tell me, without any fail."—
"By the faith of my body," then said the young man,
    "My name it is Alan a Dale."

"What wilt thou give me," said Robin Hood,   45
    "In ready gold or fee,
To help thee to thy true-love again,
    And deliver her unto thee?"

---

3 tane: taken.

"I have no money," then quoth the young man,
   "No ready gold nor fee,
But I will swear upon a book
   Thy true servant for to be."—

                                       50

"But how many miles to thy true-love?
   Come tell me without any guile."—[4]
"By the faith of my body," then said the young man,
   "It is but five little mile."

                                       55

Then Robin he hasted over the plain,
   He did neither stint nor lin,[5]
Until he came unto the church
   Where Alan should keep his wedding.

                                       60

"What dost thou do here?" the Bishop he said,
   "I prithee now tell to me:"
"I am a bold harper," quoth Robin Hood,
   "And the best in the north countrey."

                                       65

"O welcome, O welcome!" the Bishop he said,
   "That musick best pleaseth me."—
"You shall have no musick," quoth Robin Hood,
   "Till the bride and the bridegroom I see."

With that came in a wealthy knight,
   Which was both grave and old,
And after him a finikin[6] lass,
   Did shine like glistering gold.

                                       70

"This is no fit match," quoth bold Robin Hood,
   "That you do seem to make here;
For since we are come unto the church,
   The bride she shall chuse her own dear."

                                       75

Then Robin Hood put his horn to his mouth,
   And blew blasts two or three;
When four and twenty bowmen bold
   Come leaping over the lee.[7]

                                       80

---

4 **guile:** deceit; falsehood.
5 **lin:** stop.

6 **finikin:** dainty.
7 **lee:** probably means "plain" here; also, a shelter.

And when they came into the churchyard,
    Marching all on a row,
The first man was Alan a Dale,
    To give bold Robin his bow.

"This is thy true-love," Robin he said,   85
    "Young Alan, as I hear say;
And you shall be married at this same time,
    Before we depart away."

"That shall not be," the Bishop he said,
    "For thy word it shall not stand;   90
They shall be three times askt[8] in the church,
    As the law is of our land."

Robin Hood pull'd off the Bishop's coat,
    And put it upon Little John;
"By the faith of my body," then Robin said,   95
    "This cloath doth make thee a man."

When Little John went into the quire,[9]
    The people began for to laugh;
He askt them seven times in the church,
    Least three should not be enough.   100

"Who gives me this maid?" then said Little John;
    Quoth Robin, "That do I!
And he that doth take her from Alan a Dale
    Full dearly he shall her buy."

And thus having ended this merry wedding,   105
    The bride lookt as fresh as a queen,
And so they return'd to the merry greenwood,
    Amongst the leaves so green.

---

8 **askt:** The marriage intentions of a couple had to be announced in the
church on three separate occasions.
9 **quire:** choir, part of the church set aside for the singers.

Reading Skills

1. What is the mood of the young man in the third stanza? in the fourth and fifth stanzas? What caused the change? Paraphrase (retell in your own words) the tenth stanza.
2. What agreement is made between Alan a Dale and Robin Hood? How does Robin help Alan?
3. How does Robin overcome the Bishop's objections?

Understanding Literature

1. In several lines in this ballad you can find examples of *internal rhyme*. This is rhyme within the line. "Come listen to *me*, you gallants so *free*" and "As Robin *Hood* in the forest *stood*" are examples of internal rhyme. Find other examples.
2. The author, through his choice of sounds and words, establishes the *mood* he wants the reader to feel. The mood may be a sad one; a thoughtful, pensive one; a gay one. What is the mood of "Robin Hood and Alan a Dale"? Find words which help establish the *mood*.

"Lord Randal" is one of the most famous of all ballads and has existed in different forms in all parts of Europe at various times.

IMPROVING YOUR READING. A major characteristic of ballads is the *refrain,* a verse or phrase that is usually repeated at the end of each stanza. Note here that the wording of the refrain changes near the middle of the ballad. Can you see why?

Lord Randal

"O where ha you been, Lord Randal, my son?
And where ha you been, my handsome young man?"
"I ha been at the greenwood, mother, mak my bed soon,
For I'm wearied wi hunting and fain wad[1] lie down."

"An wha met ye there, Lord Randal, my son?   5
And wha met you there my handsome young man?"
"O I met wi my true-love, mother, mak my bed soon,
For I'm wearied wi huntin an fain wad lie down."

"And what did she give you, Lord Randal, my son?
And what did she give you, my handsome young man?"   10
"Eels fried in a pan, mother, mak my bed soon,
For I'm wearied wi huntin, and fain wad lie down."

"And wha gat your leavins, Lord Randal, my son?
And wha gat your leavins, my handsome young man?"
"My hawks and my hounds, mother, mak my bed soon,   15
For I'm wearied wi hunting and fain wad lie down."

"And what becam of them, Lord Randal, my son?
And what becam of them, my handsome young man?"
"They stretched their legs out an died, mother, mak my bed
　　soon,
For I'm wearied wi huntin and fain wad lie down."   20

1 **fain wad:** would gladly.

"O I fear you are poisoned, Lord Randal, my son.
I fear you are poisoned, my handsome young man."
"O yes, I am poisoned, mother, mak my bed soon,
For I'm sick at the heart and I fain wad lie down."

"What d' ye leave to your mother, Lord Randal, my son?   25
What d' ye leave to your mother, my handsome young man?"
"Four and twenty milk kye,[2] mother, mak my bed soon,
For I'm sick at the heart and I fain wad lie down."

"What d' ye leave to your sister, Lord Randal, my son?
What d' ye leave to your sister, my handsome young man?"   30
"My gold and my silver, mother, mak my bed soon,
For I'm sick at the heart, an I fain wad lie down."

"What d' ye leave to your brother, Lord Randal, my son?
What d' ye leave to your brother, my handsome young man?"
"My houses and my lands, mother, mak my bed soon,   35
For I'm sick at the heart, and I fain wad lie down."

"What d' ye leave to your true-love, Lord Randal, my son?
What d' ye leave to your true-love, my handsome young man?"
"I leave her hell and fire, mother, mak my bed soon,
For I'm sick at the heart and I fain wad lie down."   40

2 kye: cattle.

Understanding Literature

1. What is the situation at the opening of the poem?
2. What questions are asked by the mother? How is each answered?
3. The refrain for about half the poem is "For I'm wearied wi huntin an fain wad lie down." At what point does it shift to "For I'm sick at the heart"? Why is this shift made?
4. How much of the story is told directly by the dialogue? How much is implied, or hinted at? Tell the whole story of the ballad in your own words.

Reading "Red Iron Ore"

As people came to America, they brought many of their ballads with them; and many new ones were composed to fit the situations people met in a new country. There were ballads of sailing, of railroading, of industry, of the Great Lakes, of the southern mountains, and many cowboy ballads and songs.

As in most ballads, some of the background for "Red Iron Ore" is authentic and factual. The setting for this story is the Great Lakes. The *E. C. Roberts* and the *Minch* were real ships, and this ballad tells of an actual contest between the ships and their crews to see who would reach Cleveland first. Observe, also, that "Red Iron Ore," like many early ballads, has a line which is repeated at the end of each stanza: "Derry down, down, down derry down." The performer of the ballad would sing the stanza, and his listeners would join in on the repeated line or *refrain*. In the following version the refrain is not printed after every stanza, but it could be sung after each.

Red Iron Ore*

Come all you bold sailors that follow the Lakes
On an iron ore vessel your living to make.
I shipped in Chicago, bid adieu to the shore,
Bound away to Escanaba¹ for red iron ore.
   Derry down, down, down derry down.   5

In the month of September, the seventeenth day,
Two dollars and a quarter is all they would pay,
And on Monday morning the *Bridgeport* did take
The *E. C. Roberts* out in the Lake.
   Derry down, down, down derry down.   10

The wind from the south'ard sprang up a fresh breeze,
And away through Lake Michigan the *Roberts* did sneeze.
Down through Lake Michigan the *Roberts* did roar,
And on Friday morning we passed through death's door.²

---

1 **Escanaba:** city in Michigan.   2 **passed . . . door:** almost died.

* From THE AMERICAN SONGBAG, compiled by Carl Sandburg, by permission of Harcourt, Brace & World, Inc.

This packet she howled across the mouth of Green Bay,   15
And before her cutwater she dashed the white spray.
We rounded the sand point, our anchor let go,
We furled in our canvas and the watch went below.

Next morning we hove alongside the *Exile*,
And soon was made fast to an iron ore pile,   20
They lowered their chutes and like thunder did roar,
They spouted into us that red iron ore.

Some sailors took shovels while others got spades,
And some took wheelbarrows, each man to his trade.
We looked like red devils, our fingers got sore,   25
We cursed Escanaba and that damned iron ore.

The tug *Escanaba* she towed out the *Minch*,
The *Roberts* she thought she had left in a pinch,
And as she passed by us she bid us good-by,
Saying, "We'll meet you in Cleveland next Fourth of July!"   30

Through Louse Island it blew a fresh breeze;
We made the Foxes, the Beavers, the Skillageles;
We flew by the *Minch* for to show her the way,
And she ne'er hove in sight till we were off Thunder Bay.

Across Saginaw Bay the *Roberts* did ride   35
With the dark and deep water rolling over her side.
And now for Port Huron the *Roberts* must go,
Where the tug *Kate Williams* she took us in tow.

We went through North Passage—O Lord, how it blew!
And all 'round the Dummy a large fleet there came too.   40
The night being dark, Old Nick it would scare.
We hove up next morning and for Cleveland did steer.

Now the *Roberts* is in Cleveland, made fast stem and stern,
And over the bottle we'll spin a big yarn.
But Captain Harvey Shannon had ought to stand treat   45
For getting into Cleveland ahead of the fleet.

Now my song is ended, I hope you won't laugh.
Our dunnage³ is packed and all hands are paid off.
Here's health to the *Roberts*, she's staunch, strong and true;
Not forgotten the bold boys that comprise her crew.   50
   Derry down, down, down derry down.

3 **dunnage:** baggage.

Understanding Literature

1. Who is the speaker, the "I," in the poem?
2. What characteristics of the trip out are compressed in the verbs *sneeze, roar,* and *dashed?*
3. How is the iron ore loaded into the *Roberts?* Describe the return trip.
4. What words particularly make you feel the strength of the men and the power and drive of the *E. C. Roberts?*

Cowboy ballads are very popular in the United States. The cowboys' role of watching over the cattle on the vast prairies was an important one—and a very lonesome one. The cattle recognized the voices of the cowboys, and often if a storm was brewing, the cowboy would sing to soothe the restless cattle—and to keep himself company.

IMPROVING YOUR READING. In his poetry a writer will often examine his own ideas concerning a vast question. Using poetry is a sensitive, thoughtful way of probing something difficult to understand. In the ballad "The Cowboy's Dream," the unknown author considers the question of what happens after death. Observe that, like the composers of other ballads, he seeks this answer in the language he knows best—in this case, that of the cowboy.

The Cowboy's Dream*

Tune: "Bring Back My Bonnie to Me"

When I think of the last great roundup
On the eve of eternity's dawn,
I think of the host of cowboys
That have been with us here and have gone.

Chorus:
    Roll on, roll on,   5
  Roll on, little dogies, roll on, roll on,
    Roll on, roll on,
  Roll on, little dogies, roll on.

I think of those big-hearted fellows,
Who'll divide with you blanket and bread,   10

* Collected, adapted & arranged by John A. & Alan Lomax. Copyright 1934 and renewed 1962. Ludlow Music, Inc., New York, N.Y. Used by permission..

With a piece of stray beef well roasted,
And charge for it never a red.[1]

I wonder if any will greet me,
On the sands of that evergreen shore,
With a hearty "God bless you, old fellow,"   15
That I've met so often before.

And I often look upward and wonder
If the green fields will seem half so fair,
If any the wrong trail have taken
And will fail to be over there.   20

The trail that leads down to perdition[2]
Is paved all the way with good deeds;
But in the great roundup of ages,
Dear boys, this won't answer your needs.

The trail to green pastures, though narrow,   25
Leads straight to the home in the sky,
To the headquarters ranch of the Father
In the land of the sweet by and by.

The Inspector will stand at the gateway,
Where the herd, one and all, must go by,   30
And the roundup by the angels in judgment
Must pass 'neath His all-searching eye.

No maverick or slick[3] will be tallied
In that great book of life in His home,
For he knows all the brands and the earmarks   35
That down through all ages have come.

But, along with the strays and the sleepers,
The tailings[4] must turn from the gate;
No road brand to give them admission.
But that awful sad cry: "Too late!"   40

---

1 **red:** red cent.
2 **perdition:** utter loss of the soul; loss of final happiness.

3 **maverick or slick:** unbranded range animals.
4 **tailings:** inferior ones.

But I trust in that last great roundup
When the Rider shall cut the big herd,
That the cowboy will be represented
In the earmark and brand of the Lord.

To be shipped to that bright, mystic region,   45
Over there in green pastures to lie,
And be led by the crystal still waters
To the home in the sweet by and by.

Reading Skills

1. What is a roundup? What is meant here by "the last great roundup/On the eve of eternity's dawn"?
2. What is meant here by "that evergreen shore"? by "the wrong trail"?
3. A synonym is a word that is similar in meaning to another word. List the various synonyms for God in this poem.
4. What does the line "When the Rider shall cut the big herd" mean?
5. What other title might you give the poem that would make its meaning clear?

Understanding Literature

1. What is the feeling or mood that predominates in this poem? In what way does the mood fit the subject of the poem?
2. In what ways is "The Cowboy's Dream" like the ballads you studied earlier?
3. Find examples of thought expressed in the language of the cowboy. Restate these thoughts in your own words. In this poem why is it effective to use language that is characteristic of the cowboy?

Further Activity

There are a number of people who have made a study of the ballad and its history. John A. Lomax, Alan Lomax, Carl Sandburg, Louise Pound, and Burl Ives are but a few. Prepare a report on some of the collections by these people, including information about the ballads and about the people who have collected them.

Narrative Poems

The ballads which you just studied told a story, and so do narrative poems. Narratives differ, however, in that they do not use the ballad stanza of four lines; their stanzas are usually longer. In ballads the writer usually gives the basic facts about the action of the poem without letting the reader know how he feels about it. In narratives, however, which are often about national heroes, the writer takes a stand of approval or disapproval of the actions in the poem. With one exception the narrative poems which follow are similar in that they are all about great deeds.

Reading "The Fight at the Bridge"

The first narrative is a section from a long poem about Horatius, a legendary Roman hero who supposedly defended Rome against an invading army from the ancient country of Etruria, now Tuscany, a region of modern Italy. The invaders had to cross a narrow bridge to get to the city. Horatius and two followers, Lartius and Herminius, volunteered to cross the bridge and hold it against the Tuscans (Etruscans) while the bridge was being destroyed behind them. After it was cut away, Horatius, though wounded, dived into the river and escaped.

The Fight at the Bridge
(from "Horatius")

Thomas Babington Macaulay

Meanwhile the Tuscan army,
  Right glorious to behold,
Came flashing back the noonday light,
Rank behind rank, like surges bright
  Of a broad sea of gold.   5
Four hundred trumpets sounded
  A peal of warlike glee,
As that great host, with measured tread,

And spears advanced, and ensigns[1] spread,
Rolled slowly toward the bridge's head,   10
   Where stood the dauntless Three.

The Three stood calm and silent
   And looked upon the foes,
And a great shout of laughter
   From all the vanguard[2] rose: 15
And forth three chiefs came spurring
   Before that deep array;[3]
To earth they sprang, their swords they drew,
And lifted high their shields, and flew
   To win the narrow way: 20

Aunus from green Tifernum,
   Lord of the Hill of Vines;
And Seius, whose eight hundred slaves
   Sicken in Ilva's mines;
And Picus, long to Clusium   25
   Vassal[4] in peace and war,
Who led to fight his Umbrian[5] powers
From that gray crag where, girt[6] with towers,
The fortress of Nequinum lowers
   O'er the pale waves of Nar.   30

Stout Lartius hurled down Aunus
   Into the stream beneath:
Herminius struck at Seius,
   And clove[7] him to the teeth:
At Picus brave Horatius   35
   Darted one fiery thrust,
And the proud Umbrian's gilded arms
   Clashed in the bloody dust.

But now no sound of laughter
   Was heard among the foes.   40
A wild and wrathful clamor
   From all the vanguard rose.

1 **ensigns:** banners; flags.
2 **vanguard:** army troops in the front line.
3 **array:** here, group of soldiers.
4 **Vassal:** servant.

5 **Umbrian:** native of Umbria, a region in central Italy.
6 **girt:** surrounded.
7 **clove:** cut.

Six spears' length from the entrance
  Halted that deep array,
And for a space no man came forth   45
  To win the narrow way.

But hark! the cry is "Astur!"
  And lo! the ranks divide;
And the great Lord of Luna
  Comes with his stately stride.   50
  Upon his ample shoulders
  Clangs loud the fourfold shield,
And in his hand he shakes the brand[8]
  Which none but he can wield.

He smiled on those bold Romans   55
  A smile serene and high;
He eyed the flinching Tuscans,
  And scorn was in his eye.
Quoth he, "The she-wolf's litter
  Stand savagely at bay: 60
But will ye dare to follow,
  If Astur clears the way?"

Then, whirling up his broadsword
  With both hands to the height,
He rushed against Horatius,   65
  And smote with all his might.
With shield and blade Horatius
  Right deftly turned the blow.
The blow, though turned, came yet too nigh;
It missed his helm, but gashed his thigh: 70
The Tuscans raised a joyful cry
  To see the red blood flow.

He reeled, and on Herminius
  He leaned one breathing space;
Then, like a wildcat mad with wounds,   75
  Sprang right at Astur's face:

---

8 **brand:** sword.

Through teeth and skull and helmet
  So fierce a thrust he sped,
The good sword stood a handbreadth out
  Behind the Tuscan's head.   80

And the great Lord of Luna
  Fell at that deadly stroke,
As falls on Mount Alvernus
  A thunder-smitten oak.
Far o'er the crashing forest   85
  The giant arms lie spread;
And the pale augurs,[9] muttering low,
  Gaze on the blasted head.

On Astur's throat Horatius
  Right firmly pressed his heel,   90
And thrice and four times tugged amain[10]
  Ere he wrenched out the steel.
"And see," he cried, "the welcome,
  Fair guests, that waits you here!
What noble Lucumo[11] comes next   95
  To taste our Roman cheer?"

But at his haughty challenge
  A sullen murmur ran,
Mingled of wrath and shame and dread,
  Along that glittering van.   100
There lacked not men of prowess,
  Nor men of lordly race;
For all Etruria's noblest
  Were round the fatal place.

But all Etruria's noblest   105
  Felt their hearts sink to see
On the earth the bloody corpses,
  In the path the dauntless Three:
And, from the ghastly entrance
  Where those bold Romans stood,   110

---

9 **augurs:** Roman prophets.
10 **amain:** with great power.
11 **Lucumo:** Etruscan prince.

All shrank, like boys who, unaware,
Ranging the woods to start a hare,
Come to the mouth of the dark lair
Where, growling low, a fierce old bear
   Lies amidst bones and blood.   115

Was none who would be foremost
   To lead such dire attack:
But those behind cried "Forward!"
   And those before cried "Back!"
And backward now and forward   120
   Wavers the deep array;
And on the tossing sea of steel
   To and fro the standards reel;
And the victorious trumpet-peal
   Dies fitfully away.   125

Understanding Literature

1. In the first stanza how do you see the Tuscan army? Who are "the dauntless Three"?
2. Why, in the second stanza, is there a shout of laughter? What is "the narrow way"? What do the three chiefs, Aunus, Seius, and Picus, propose to do? What happens to them?
3. Who is Astur (l. 47)? Describe his battle with Horatius.
4. What is "our Roman cheer" (l. 96)? What comparison is made in lines 111-115?
5. After the death of Astur there is great confusion among the Tuscans. Find the lines which indicate this confusion.

Reading "Columbus"

This poem uses several different techniques: it tells much of its story with dialogue, its setting is suggested with very few lines, and it uses a refrain, which is common in old ballads, as well as other forms of repetition. How many forms of repetition can you find?

Columbus

Joaquin Miller

Behind him lay the gray Azores,[1]
   Behind the Gates of Hercules;[2]
Before him not the ghost of shores,
   Before him only shoreless seas.
The good mate said: "Now must we pray,   5
   For lo! the very stars are gone.
Brave Adm'r'l, speak; what shall I say?"
   "Why, say: 'Sail on! sail on! and on!' "

"My men grow mutinous day by day;
   My men grow ghastly wan and weak."   10
The stout mate thought of home; a spray
   Of salt wave washed his swarthy cheek.
"What shall I say, brave Adm'r'l, say,
   If we sight naught but seas at dawn?"
"Why, you shall say at break of day: 15
   'Sail on! sail on! sail on! and on!' "

1 **Azores:** a group of nine islands belonging to Portugal in the Atlantic Ocean.
2 **Gates of Hercules:** Also called the Pillars of Hercules, these two projecting rocks are at the eastern end of the Strait of Gibraltar, a passage which lies between Spain and Africa and connects the Mediterranean Sea and the Atlantic Ocean. The Rock of Gibraltar is the more famous of the two Pillars.

POETRY

They sailed and sailed, as winds might blow,
    Until at last the blanched[3] mate said:
"Why, now not even God would know
    Should I and all my men fall dead.   20
These very winds forget their way,
    For God from these dread seas is gone.
Now speak, brave Adm'r'l; speak and say——"
    He said: "Sail on! sail on! and on!"

They sailed. They sailed. Then spake the mate: 25
    "This mad sea shows its teeth tonight.
He curls his lip, he lies in wait,
    With lifted teeth, as if to bite!
Brave Adm'r'l, say but one good word;
    What shall we do when hope is gone?"   30
The words leapt as a leaping sword:
    "Sail on! sail on! sail on! and on!"

Then, pale and worn, he kept his deck,
    And peered through darkness. Ah, that night
Of all dark nights! And then a speck—   35
    A light! A light! A light! A light!
It grew, a starlit flag unfurled!
    It grew to be Time's burst of dawn.
He gained a world; he gave that world
    Its grandest lesson: "On! sail on!"   40

---

3 blanched: whitened; paled.

Understanding Literature

1. Who are the speakers in the poem?
2. What are "shoreless seas," as the phrase is used here?
3. Why is the mate "blanched"?
4. How is the sea described? How are dark and light used in the poem?
5. Put the last four lines in your own words.
6. As in some of the old ballads, a refrain is used in "Columbus." Point out examples. What is the "grandest lesson" that part of the repetitive phrases emphasize?
7. Explain the author's use of contrast to show the perseverance and faith of Columbus.

In August of 1782 the *Royal George,* an English man-of-war, was undergoing repairs in Portsmouth Harbor, England. Suddenly the ship leaned to one side, filled with water, and sank with everyone aboard. The *Royal George,* the main vessel of Lord Howe's fleet, was commanded by Admiral Kempenfelt, who also lost his life in this tragic event. This poem by William Cowper (kōō′ pər) is a tribute to the men, the ship, and England. The carefully chosen words make one feel the tragedy of the ship's sinking.

IMPROVING YOUR READING. Observe the *comparisons* made in this poem: How can a tempest give a shock? How can England have thunder? How can a ship plow?

On the Loss of the *Royal George*

William Cowper

Toll for the brave!
   The brave that are no more!
All sunk beneath the wave,
   Fast by their native shore!

Eight hundred of the brave,   5
   Whose courage well was tried,
Had made the vessel heel,
   And laid her on her side;

A land breeze shook the shrouds,[1]
   And she was overset;   10
Down went the *Royal George,*
   With all her crew complete.

---

1 shrouds: here, ropes leading from a ship's mastheads to give support to the masts. What else does this word suggest?

Toll for the brave!
    Brave Kempenfelt is gone;
His last sea fight is fought;   15
    His work of glory done.

It was not in the battle;
    No tempest gave the shock;
She sprang no fatal leak;
    She ran upon no rock;   20

His sword was in its sheath;
    His fingers held the pen,
When Kempenfelt went down,
    With twice four hundred men.

Weigh² the vessel up,   25
    Once dreaded by our foes!
And mingle with our cup
    The tear that England owes.

Her timbers yet are sound,
    And she may float again   30
Full-charged with England's thunder,
    And plow the distant main.

But Kempenfelt is gone;
    His victories are o'er;
And he and his eight hundred   35
    Shall plow the wave no more.

2 **Weigh:** raise; lift.

Understanding Literature

1. Explain the first line, "Toll for the brave!"
2. What caused the *Royal George* to sink?
3. The poem tells of four ways in which the ship was *not* sunk. What are they?
4. Explain the following lines:
    (*a*) "No tempest gave the shock."
    (*b*) "And mingle with our cup
        The tear that England owes."
    (*c*) "Full-charged with England's thunder,
        And plow the distant main."

Reading "The Revenge"

England won her reputation as a powerful nation through her achievements at sea. The ballad which you are about to read tells the story of the English ship *Revenge* and the Spanish fleet. The incident described took place in 1591. "The Revenge, a Ballad of the Fleet" was written by Alfred, Lord Tennyson while he was poet laureate[1] of England. Although this is called a ballad, you will note that it does not use the usual four-line stanza form of the "popular ballads" that you found in the group of ballads at the beginning of this unit. Tennyson calls it a ballad, however, because he is presenting, as most ballads do, one highly dramatic episode.

IMPROVING YOUR READING. *Rhyme* is produced by the repetition of sounds. In this poem there is *end rhyme*, the rhyming of words which are at the end of the line, and there is *internal rhyme*, the rhyming of words which are within a line.

A method of comparison which poets use extensively is known as *simile* (sĭm′ ə lē′). A simile is a comparison of two different objects which are alike in at least one way. In the comparison the words *like* or *as* are used. The second line of this poem, "And a pinnace, like a fluttered bird, came flying from far away," contains a simile. A pinnace, a light sailing vessel, is compared to a bird. The two objects are alike, according to the poet, in that they both have wings which flutter in the wind. If you can see in your imagination the sails of a boat flapping rapidly as the wings of a bird do, you will have fully appreciated the simile. Look for others as you read this poem.

---

1 **poet laureate:** the royal title given to the most distinguished poet in England.

The Revenge

A BALLAD OF THE FLEET

Alfred, Lord Tennyson

At Flores in the Azores Sir Richard Grenville lay,
And a pinnace, like a fluttered bird, came flying from far away:
"Spanish ships of war at sea! we have sighted fifty-three!"
Then sware Lord Thomas Howard: "Fore God I am no coward;
But I cannot meet them here, for my ships are out of gear,[1]   5
And the half my men are sick. I must fly, but follow quick.
We are six ships of the line; can we fight with fifty-three?"

Then spake Sir Richard Grenville: "I know you are no coward;
You fly them for a moment to fight with them again.
But I've ninety men and more that are lying sick ashore.   10
I should count myself the coward if I left them, my Lord Howard,
To these Inquisition dogs and the devildoms of Spain."

So Lord Howard passed away with five ships of war that day,
Till he melted like a cloud in the silent summer heaven;
But Sir Richard bore in hand all his sick men from the land   15
Very carefully and slow,
Men of Bideford in Devon,
And we laid them on the ballast[2] down below;
For we brought them all aboard,
And they blest him in their pain, that they were not left to Spain,   20
To the thumbscrew and the stake, for the glory of the Lord.

---

1 out of gear: not properly rigged.
2 ballast: heavy material, such as sand or gravel, used to weight a ship to improve its steadiness.

He had only a hundred seamen to work the ship and to fight,
And he sailed away from Flores till the Spaniard came in sight,
With his huge sea-castles heaving upon the weather bow.
"Shall we fight or shall we fly?   25
Good Sir Richard, tell us now,
For to fight is but to die!
There 'll be little of us left by the time this sun be set."
And Sir Richard said again: "We be all good English men.
Let us bang these dogs of Seville, the children of the devil,   30
For I never turned my back upon Don[3] or devil yet."

Sir Richard spoke and he laughed, and we roared a hurrah, and so
The little *Revenge* ran on sheer into the heart of the foe,
With her hundred fighters on deck, and her ninety sick below;
For half of their fleet to the right and half to the left were seen,   35
And the little *Revenge* ran on thro' the long sea-lane between.

Thousands of their soldiers looked down from their decks and laughed,
Thousands of their seamen made mock at the mad little craft
Running on and on, till delayed
By their mountain-like *San Philip* that, of fifteen hundred tons,   40
And up-shadowing high above us with her yawning tiers of guns,
Took the breath from our sails, and we stayed.

And while now the great *San Philip* hung above us like a cloud
Whence the thunderbolt will fall
Long and loud,   45
Four galleons drew away
From the Spanish fleet that day,
And two upon the larboard and two upon the starboard lay,
And the battle-thunder broke from them all.

But anon the great *San Philip*, she bethought herself and went,   50
Having that within her womb that had left her ill content;
And the rest they came aboard us, and they fought us hand to hand,
For a dozen times they came with their pikes and musketeers,
And a dozen times we shook 'em off as a dog that shakes his ears
When he leaps from the water to the land.   55

And the sun went down, and the stars came out far over the summer sea,
But never a moment ceased the fight of the one and the fifty-three.
Ship after ship, the whole night long, their high-built galleons came,

3 **Don:** a Spanish gentleman.

Ship after ship, the whole night long, with her battle-thunder and flame;
Ship after ship, the whole night long, drew back with her dead and her shame. 60
For some were sunk and many were shattered, and so could fight us no more—
God of battles, was ever a battle like this in the world before?

For he said, "Fight on! fight on!"
Tho' his vessel was all but a wreck;
And it chanced that, when half of the short summer night was gone, 65
With a grisly wound to be dressed he had left the deck,
But a bullet struck him that was dressing it suddenly dead,
And himself he was wounded again in the side and the head,
And he said, "Fight on! fight on!"

And the night went down, and the sun smiled out far over the summer sea, 70
And the Spanish fleet with broken sides lay round us all in a ring;
But they dared not touch us again, for they feared that we still could sting,
So they watched what the end would be.
And we had not fought them in vain,
But in perilous plight were we, 75
Seeing forty of our poor hundred were slain,
And half of the rest of us maimed for life
In the crash of the cannonades and the desperate strife;
And the sick men down in the hold were most of them stark and cold,
And the pikes were all broken or bent, and the powder was all of it spent; 80
And the masts and the rigging were lying over the side;
But Sir Richard cried in his English pride:
"We have fought such a fight for a day and a night
As may never be fought again!
We have won great glory, my men! 85
And a day less or more
At sea or ashore,
We die—does it matter when?
Sink me the ship, Master Gunner—sink her, split her in twain!
Fall into the hands of God, not into the hands of Spain!" 90

And the gunner said, "Ay, ay," but the seamen made reply:
"We have children, we have wives,
And the Lord hath spared our lives.
We will make the Spaniard promise, if we yield, to let us go;
We shall live to fight again and to strike another blow." 95
And the lion there lay dying, and they yielded to the foe.

And the stately Spanish men to their flagship bore him then,
Where they laid him by the mast, old Sir Richard caught at last,
And they praised him to his face with their courtly foreign grace;
But he rose upon their decks, and he cried: 100
"I have fought for Queen and Faith like a valiant man and true;

I have only done my duty as a man is bound to do.
With a joyful spirit I Sir Richard Grenville die!"
And he fell upon their decks, and he died.

And they stared at the dead that had been so valiant and true,   105
And had holden the power and glory of Spain so cheap
That he dared her with one little ship and his English few;
Was he devil or man? He was devil for aught they knew,
But they sank his body with honor down into the deep,
And they manned the *Revenge* with a swarthier alien crew,   110
And away she sailed with her loss and longed for her own;
When a wind from the lands they had ruined awoke from sleep,
And the water began to heave and the weather to moan,
And or ever that evening ended a great gale blew,

And a wave like the wave that is raised by an earthquake grew,   115
Till it smote on their hulls and their sails and their masts and their flags,
And the whole sea plunged and fell on the shot-shattered navy of Spain,
And the little *Revenge* herself went down by the island crags
To be lost evermore in the main.

Reading Skills

1. For what reason did Lord Thomas Howard flee the Spanish ships? Do you agree with his decision?
2. Why did Sir Richard Grenville stay to fight?
3. What was Grenville's plan of attack? Describe the battle.
4. What was the reaction of the Spanish soldiers and sailors when they saw the small *Revenge?*
5. How did Sir Richard want to end the battle? What did happen to the *Revenge?* What happened to Sir Richard?
6. What comment is the poem making on bravery and patriotism?

Understanding Literature

1. Point out examples of *end rhyme* and *internal rhyme*.
2. What examples of simile can you find in "The Revenge"? Be sure to find examples that compare different objects and use *like* or *as* in the comparison.
3. What is the effect of the repetition used in the ninth stanza?
4. "The Revenge" is called a ballad. In what ways does it differ from the common ballad form? In what ways is it like the ballads you studied earlier?

This poem once again emphasizes the importance of the ocean to the English nation.

IMPROVING YOUR READING. One of the questions you should ask of any poem is: To whom is the poem addressed? The poet here is obviously speaking to mariners of England, but which ones?

Ye Mariners of England

Thomas Campbell

Ye Mariners of England!
That guard our native seas;
Whose flag has braved, a thousand years,
The battle and the breeze!
Your glorious standard launch again   5
To match another foe!
And sweep through the deep,
While the stormy winds do blow;
While the battle rages loud and long,
And the stormy winds do blow.   10

The spirits of your fathers
Shall start from every wave!—
For the deck it was their field of fame,
And Ocean was their grave:
Where Blake[1] and mighty Nelson[2] fell,   15
Your manly hearts shall glow,
As ye sweep through the deep,
While the stormy winds do blow;
While the battle rages loud and long,
And the stormy winds do blow.   20

Britannia[3] needs no bulwark,
No towers along the steep;

1 **Blake:** Robert Blake (1599-1657), an English admiral.
2 **Nelson:** Horatio, Viscount Nelson (1758-1805), an English admiral.
3 **Britannia:** Great Britain and the dominions.

Her march is o'er the mountain-waves,
Her home is on the deep.
With thunders from her native oak,[4]   25
She quells the floods below,—
As they roar on the shore,
When the stormy winds do blow;
When the battle rages loud and long,
And the stormy winds do blow.   30

The meteor flag of England
Shall yet terrific burn;
Till danger's troubled night depart,
And the star of peace return.
Then, then, ye ocean-warriors!   35
Our song and feast shall flow
To the fame of your name,
When the storm has ceased to blow;
When the fiery fight is heard no more,
And the storm has ceased to blow.   40

4 **native oak:** ships made of oak.

Understanding Literature

1. To which mariners is the poem addressed?
2. In the first stanza what is the speaker asking them to do?
3. In the second stanza what comment is made on "The spirits of your fathers"?
4. How is Britain (Britannia) described in the third stanza?
5. The refrain, the last three lines of the first three stanzas, is different from the last three lines of the last stanza. What change in the situation causes the change in the refrain?
6. The words *stormy* and *storm* are repeated in the refrain. Do they have any meaning beyond that of a literal storm?
7. Re-examine "Columbus," "On the Loss of the *Royal George*," "The Revenge," and "Ye Mariners of England." Compare them with each other in terms of: (*a*) the personal qualities of the naval leaders, (*b*) the relationships between the leaders and their crews, and (*c*) the importance of the situations to the mother country.
8. The literary devices which have been called to your attention in these four poems are personification, simile, and rhyme scheme. In rereading the four poems, what examples of these techniques do you find?

In the spring of 1940 thousands of British and French troops were trapped near Dunkirk, an important seaport on the coast of France. With the help of every type of small seacraft, an air cover by fighter planes, and the discipline of the soldiers, the British government was able to evacuate more than 330,000 men to England. This famous World War II rescue operation is celebrated in the following poem.

Dunkirk

Robert Nathan

Will came back from school that day,
And he had little to say.
But he stood a long time looking down
To where the gray-green Channel water
Slapped at the foot of the little town,   5
And to where his boat, the *Sarah P*,
Bobbed at the tide on an even keel,
With her one old sail, patched at the leech.[1]
Furled like a slattern down at heel.

He stood for a while above the beach,   10
He saw how the wind and current caught her;
He looked a long time out to sea.
There was steady wind, and the sky was pale,
And a haze in the east that looked like smoke.

Will went back to the house to dress.   15
He was halfway through, when his sister Bess
Who was near fourteen, and younger than he
By just two years, came home from play.
She asked him, "Where are you going, Will?"

1 **leech:** edge.

He said, "For a good long sail."   20
"Can I come along?"
                              "No, Bess," he spoke.
"I may be gone for a night and a day."
Bess looked at him.   She kept very still.
She had heard the news of the Flanders rout,
How the English were trapped above Dunkirk,   25
And the fleet had gone to get them out—
But everyone thought that it wouldn't work.
There was too much fear, there was too much doubt.

She looked at him, and he looked at her.
They were English children, born and bred.   30
He frowned her down, but she wouldn't stir.
She shook her proud young head.
"You'll need a crew," she said.

They raised the sail on the *Sarah P*,
Like a penoncel[2] on a young knight's lance,   35
And headed the *Sarah* out to sea,
To bring their soldiers home from France.
There was no command, there was no set plan,
But six hundred boats went out with them
On the gray-green waters, sailing fast,   40
River excursion and fisherman,
Tug and schooner and racing M,
And the little boats came following last.

From every harbor and town they went
Who had sailed their craft in the sun and rain,   45
From the South Downs, from the cliffs of Kent,
From the village street, from the country lane.
There are twenty miles of rolling sea
From coast to coast, by the seagull's flight,
But the tides were fair and the wind was free,   50
And they raised[3] Dunkirk by the fall of night.

They raised Dunkirk with its harbor torn
By the blasted stern and the sunken prow;
They had raced for fun on an English tide,

2 **penoncel** (pĕn'ən sĕl'): small flag; streamer.
3 **raised**: sighted.

They were English children bred and born, 55
And whether they lived, or whether they died,
They raced for England now.

Bess was as white as the *Sarah's* sail,
She set her teeth and smiled at Will.
He held his course for the smoky veil 60
Where the harbor narrowed thin and long.
The British ships were firing strong.

He took the *Sarah* into his hands,
He drove her in through fire and death
To the wet men waiting on the sands. 65
He got his load and he got his breath,
And she came about, and the wind fought her,

He shut his eyes and he tried to pray.
He saw his England where she lay,
The wind's green home, the sea's proud daughter, 70
Still in the moonlight, dreaming deep,
The English cliffs and the English loam—
He had fourteen men to get away.
And the moon was clear, and the night like day
For planes to see where the white sails creep 75
Over the black water.

He closed his eyes and he prayed for her,
For England's hope and for England's fate;
He prayed to the men who had made her great,
Who had built her land of forest and park, 80
Who had made the seas an English lake;
He prayed for a fog to bring the dark;
He prayed to get home for England's sake.
And the fog came down on the rolling sea,
And covered the ships with English mist. 85
And diving planes were baffled and blind.

For Nelson was there in the *Victory*,[4]
With his one good eye, and his sullen twist,
And guns were out on *The Golden Hind*,[5]

---

4 Nelson . . . *Victory*: an allusion to Lord Nelson and the ship which he commanded at Trafalgar in 1805 during the Napoleonic Wars.
5 *The Golden Hind*: ship commanded by Sir Francis Drake, famous 16th-century English navigator.

Their shot flashed over the *Sarah P*,   90
He could hear them cheer as he came about.

By burning wharves, by battered slips,
Galleon, frigate, and brigantine,
The old dead Captains fought their ships,
And the great dead Admirals led the line.   95
It was England's night, it was England's sea.

The fog rolled over the harbor key.
Bess held to the stays,[6] and conned[7] him out.

And all through the dark, while the *Sarah*'s wake
Hissed behind him, and vanished in foam,   100
There at his side sat Francis Drake,
And held him true, and steered him home.

---

6 stays: ropes supporting the mast.   **7 conned:** directed.

Understanding Literature

1. What is the mood of the poem? Which lines help to create this mood?
2. After he picks up his passengers, what does the boy pray for? To whom does he pray?
3. Why does the poet make allusions to Lord Nelson and Sir Francis Drake?
4. Why does Robert Nathan make a sixteen-year-old boy and his sister the main characters in his poem? How are pride of country and patriotism illustrated in this poem?

There is a city in Belgium named Ghent; in Germany about one hundred miles away is a city named Aix-la-Chapelle. But the ride described in "How They Brought the Good News from Ghent to Aix" never took place. Browning wrote the poem when he was at sea and thinking of the pleasure of riding his own horse.

IMPROVING YOUR READING. A poet works on your feelings not only through the imagery, but also through the *sound* of his lines. This poem sounds like a galloping horse. Notice, for example, the spacing of the hard, accented *g*'s in the second line. Where do you find other examples of hard sounds spaced through the lines?

How They Brought the Good News from Ghent to Aix

Robert Browning

I sprang to the stirrup, and Joris, and he;
I galloped, Dirck galloped, we galloped all three;
"Good speed!" cried the watch, as the gate bolts undrew;
"Speed!" echoed the wall to us galloping through;
Behind shut the postern,[1] the lights sank to rest,   5
And into the midnight we galloped abreast.

Not a word to each other; we kept the great pace
Neck by neck, stride by stride, never changing our place;
I turned in my saddle and made its girths tight,
Then shortened each stirrup, and set the pique[2] right,   10
Rebuckled the cheek strap, chained slacker the bit,
Nor galloped less steadily Roland a whit.

'T was moonset at starting; but while we drew near
Lokeren, the cocks crew and twilight dawned clear;
At Boom, a great yellow star came out to see;   15

1 **postern:** gate.
2 **pique** (pēk): apparently something peaked on the saddle, such as the pommel.

At Düffeld, 't was morning as plain as could be;
And from Mecheln church steeple we heard the half-chime,
So Joris broke silence with, "Yet there is time!"

At Aershot, up leaped of a sudden the sun,
And against him the cattle stood black every one,   20
To stare through the mist at us galloping past,
And I saw my stout galloper Roland at last,
With resolute shoulders, each butting away
The haze, as some bluff river headland its spray:

And his low head and crest, just one sharp ear bent back   25
For my voice, and the other pricked out on his track;
And one eye's black intelligence,—ever that glance
O'er its white edge at me, his own master, askance!
And the thick heavy spume-flakes which aye and anon
His fierce lips shook upwards in galloping on.   30

By Hasselt, Dirck groaned; and cried Joris, "Stay spur!
Your Roos galloped bravely, the fault 's not in her,
We 'll remember at Aix"—for one heard the quick wheeze
Of her chest, saw the stretched neck and staggering knees,
And sunk tail, and horrible heave of the flank,   35
As down on her haunches she shuddered and sank.

So, we were left galloping, Joris and I,
Past Looz and past Tongres, no cloud in the sky;
The broad sun above laughed a pitiless laugh,
'Neath our feet broke the brittle bright stubble like chaff;[3] 40
Till over by Dalhem a dome-spire sprang white,
And "Gallop," gasped Joris, "for Aix is in sight!"

"How they'll greet us!"—and all in a moment his roan
Rolled neck and croup over, lay dead as a stone;
And there was my Roland to bear the whole weight   45
Of the news which alone could save Aix from her fate,
With his nostrils like pits full of blood to the brim,
And with circles of red for his eye-sockets' rim.

3 **chaff:** husks of grains separated from seed by threshing.

Then I cast loose my buffcoat, each holster let fall,
Shook off both my jack boots, let go belt and all,   50
Stood up in the stirrup, leaned, patted his ear,
Called my Roland his pet name, my horse without peer;[4]
Clapped my hands, laughed and sang, any noise, bad or good,
Till at length into Aix Roland galloped and stood.

And all I remember is—friends flocking round   55
As I sat with his head 'twixt my knees on the ground;
And no voice but was praising this Roland of mine,
As I poured down his throat our last measure of wine,
Which (the burgesses voted by common consent)
Was no more than his due who brought good news from Ghent.   60

4 **peer:** equal.

Understanding Literature

1. How does Browning show the passing of time and the progress
   of the journey?
2. In what ways does the third rider help his horse, Roland, over
   the final part of the journey to Aix?
3. Compare the sound of the first stanza with that of the last.
   How does the sound fit the sense?
4. Paraphrase the following:

   (*a*) "At Aershot, up leaped of a sudden the sun,
       And against him the cattle stood black every one."

   (*b*) "And there was my Roland to bear the whole weight
       Of the news which alone could save Aix from her fate."

5. Why is it not important to your enjoyment of the poem to know
   what the "good news" is?

Lyric Poetry

The type of poetry used most frequently by poets is the lyric. The word itself comes from the same root word as lyre, a stringed musical instrument. Lyrics were originally a kind of song accompanied by the lyre. Today they are frequently brief, melodic poems in which the writer is expressing an emotion aroused by some scene or occasion. They are usually very personal poems about ideas which have always interested people: the beauty of nature, love and friendship, patriotism, the effects of the passing of time, and death. They enable the reader to look at well-known things in a new way.

Reading "I like to see it lap the Miles"

As you read "I like to see it lap the Miles," notice how quickly you know what "it" is even though "it" is never named.

"I like to see it lap the Miles"

Emily Dickinson

I like to see it lap the Miles—
And lick the Valleys up—
And stop to feed itself at Tanks—
And then—prodigious[1] step

Around a Pile of Mountains,   5
And, supercilious[2] peer
In Shanties—by the sides of Roads—
And then a Quarry pare

---

1 **prodigious** (prə dĭj′əs): marvelous; out of the course of nature.
2 **supercilious** (soō′pər sĭl′ĭ əs): haughty; proud.

To fit its Ribs
And crawl between   10
Complaining all the while
In horrid—hooting stanza—
Then chase itself down Hill—

And neigh like Boanerges[3]
Then—punctual as a Star,   15
Stop—docile and omnipotent
At its own stable door—

3 Boanerges (bō′ə nûr′jēz)**:** literally, sons of thunder; here, a term used for
any loud or noisy speaker or orator.

Understanding Literature

1. What is the "it" in this poem?
2. After consulting the glossary for the meanings of any words
   that you do not know, explain the following lines:

   (*a*) "And then a Quarry pare
       To fit its Ribs
       And crawl between
       Complaining all the while"

   (*b*) "Then—punctual as a Star,
       Stop—docile and omnipotent
       At its own stable door—"

3. What pictures or images should you see in your imagination as
   you read each line of this poem?
4. In this poem does Emily Dickinson feel fondness or repulsion
   for her subject? How do you know?

Allusion is used extensively in all literature. An allusion is a reference to a person or place which the author assumes the reader will recognize. By alluding to this person or place, the author enriches his writing without giving wordy explanations. If Juno were alluded to, you might recall from your study of Greek mythology that she was the queen of the gods, that she was the wife of Jupiter, and that she had a jealous nature. This knowledge would certainly enrich your reading.

In the following poem there is an allusion to Elysium which, according to Greek mythology, is the place where favored heroes are made immortal. The word now suggests a paradise. Understanding this word should make Emily Dickinson's poem much clearer to you.

"Elysium is as far as to"

Emily Dickinson

Elysium is as far as to
The very nearest Room
If in that Room a Friend await
Felicity[1] or Doom—

What fortitude the Soul contains,
That it can so endure
The accent of a coming Foot—
The opening of a Door—

1 **Felicity:** happiness.

Understanding Literature

1. Paraphrase the first stanza. Why is the "very nearest Room" Elysium, or a place of paradise? Why does Emily Dickinson use the word *Elysium* instead of the word *paradise?* What does her use of the word add to the poem?
2. Paraphrase the second stanza. What does *fortitude* mean? Why is fortitude needed to endure the "accent of a coming Foot"?
3. To whom do you think the poem is addressed? Under what circumstances might the poem have been written?

Reading "The Wind"

Robert Louis Stevenson is probably known to you through his books *Treasure Island* and *A Child's Garden of Verses*. "The Wind" is a short poem written in a light, easy style—but it does make one wonder and pause to think.

As noted before, a poet often uses *imagery* as a way of conveying his idea. An image is any appeal to the senses: seeing, touching, hearing, tasting, and smelling. Stevenson gives us several images in this poem which appeal to some of these senses.

The Wind

Robert Louis Stevenson

I saw you toss the kites high
And blow the birds about the sky;
And all around I heard you pass,
Like ladies' skirts across the grass—
    O wind, a-blowing all day long,   5
    O wind, that sings so loud a song!

I saw the different things you did,
But always you yourself you hid.
I felt you push, I heard you call,
I could not see yourself at all—   10
    O wind, a-blowing all day long,
    O wind, that sings so loud a song!

O you that are so strong and cold,
O blower, are you young or old?
Are you a beast of field and tree,   15
Or just a stronger child than me?
    O wind, a-blowing all day long,
    O wind, that sings so loud a song!

Understanding Literature

1. What evidence does the poet give to make the reader know that there is a wind even if it cannot be seen?
2. What questions about the wind go unanswered?
3. In what ways is wind personified in the poem?
4. To what senses do the images in this poem appeal?

The following poem is from *The Tempest*, a play by William Shakespeare. Ariel, a spirit, is describing a drowned man, but the sound of the lines is more important here than the subject.

IMPROVING YOUR READING. Other kinds of sound effects used by poets are *alliteration* and *assonance*. Alliteration is the repetition of the same sound at the beginning of several words in a line. In the first line of the following poem, "Full fathom five thy father lies," the repeated *f* sound is an example of alliteration.

In the second line of the poem, "Of his bones are coral made," the poet repeats the *o* sound. This repetition of vowel sounds is called *assonance*. The sounds are often not as exact a repetition as they would be in rhymed words, and they are repeated within a line. For example, the words *bones* and *thrones* (not in this poem) are exact repetitions of the *ones* sound—they rhyme. *Five, thy,* and *lies,* on the other hand, are connected only by the repetition of the sound of the vowel *i*—an example of assonance. Read the poem aloud and listen to the sound.

Ariel's Song

William Shakespeare

Full fathom five thy father lies;
　Of his bones are coral made;
Those are pearls that were his eyes;
　Nothing of him that doth fade
But doth suffer a sea change
Into something rich and strange.
Sea nymphs hourly ring his knell:
　　　　Burden.[1] Dingdong.
Hark! now I hear them—Dingdong bell.

1 **Burden:** refrain.

Most people take for granted much of the beauty of nature which is theirs to enjoy merely by recognizing it. Frequently it is the poet who brings the wonders of nature to man's attention.

IMPROVING YOUR READING. Often a poem is based largely on one major image—here, a field of daffodils. How many appeals to your five senses can you find in Wordsworth's imagery?

I Wandered Lonely as a Cloud

William Wordsworth

I wandered lonely as a cloud
That floats on high o'er vales and hills,
When all at once I saw a crowd,
A host, of golden daffodils;
Beside the lake, beneath the trees,   5
Fluttering and dancing in the breeze.

Continuous as the stars that shine
And twinkle on the milky way,
They stretched in never-ending line
Along the margin of a bay;   10
Ten thousand saw I at a glance,
Tossing their heads in sprightly dance.

The waves beside them danced; but they
Outdid the sparkling waves in glee;
A poet could not but be gay,   15
In such a jocund[1] company;
I gazed—and gazed—but little thought
What wealth the show to me had brought:

1 **jocund:** merry.

For oft, when on my couch I lie
In vacant or in pensive mood,   20
They flash upon that inward eye
Which is the bliss of solitude;
And then my heart with pleasure fills,
And dances with the daffodils.

Understanding Literature

1. What do you *see* as you read the poem? Describe the scene in your own words. Do you find appeals to other senses: touch, smell, or hearing?
2. To what things does Wordsworth compare the daffodils?
3. Which words seem to suggest how the poet feels about the scene?
4. How is the last stanza related to the first three? What is a vacant or pensive mood? What is the "inward eye"? Why is it the "bliss of solitude"?

Reading "Rural Dumpheap"

This poem also tries to bring the wonders of nature to man's attention and uses imagery to do so. But the tone is very different from that of "I Wandered Lonely as a Cloud."

Rural Dumpheap*

Melville Cane

This rusty mound of cans,
This scatter of tires and pans,
This litter of mattresses and twisted springs,
This rotting refuse, these abandoned things
Malodorously¹ flung,—this impudent pile   5
That dares to choke the current, to defile
The innocent season,—all are man's.

Man's inhumanity to sod
Makes countless snowdrops mourn,
And every gentle seed that's born   10
Gives battle for a dishonored god.

Within the heap and darkly, heaves
The growing mutiny of leaves,
While down the valley bird to bird
Relays the rallying word,   15
And courage calls on every breeze
To armies of anemones,²
And triumph scales the parapet,³
A host of violet.

O man, where is thy victory?   20
Despite this blight of tins,
The fern persists and cleaves and wins,
And, gladly, spring begins.

1 **Malodorously:** causing an offensive odor.   3 **parapet:** protective wall.
2 **anemones** (ə nĕm′ə nēz′)**:** types of flowers.

Understanding Literature

1. What is the setting of the first stanza? What is the "innocent season"?
2. Paraphrase the second stanza. What does "sod" mean?
3. In the third stanza how does the poet use the imagery of a battle? What is fighting what?
4. In the last stanza how does man lose the battle?
5. To whom is this poem addressed? Why?

* From AND PASTURES NEW, copyright, 1956, by Melville Cane. Reprinted by permission of Harcourt, Brace & World, Inc.

In this poem the author suggests some images and then makes a statement on what they mean.

IMPROVING YOUR READING. Your understanding of poetry will be enlarged if you determine as soon as possible the *mood* the poet wants you to feel. Does he want you to feel sad? Is the poem written in a light, gay vein? Is the subject being ridiculed? Is the poet serious in his attitude toward his topic? Although the following poem may seem to you to be very elementary, you will find it interesting to compare the mood of "Little Boy Blue" with that of the very different poem which follows it.

Little Boy Blue

Eugene Field

The little toy dog is covered with dust,
    But sturdy and stanch he stands;
And the little toy soldier is red with rust,
    And the musket molds in his hands.

Time was when the little toy dog was new,   5
    And the soldier was passing fair;
And that was the time when our Little Boy Blue
    Kissed them and put them there.

"Now, don't you go till I come," he said,
    "And don't you make any noise!"   10
So, toddling off to his trundle bed,
    He dreamt of the pretty toys;
And, as he was dreaming, an angel song
    Awakened our Little Boy Blue—
Oh! the years are many, the years are long,   15
    But the little toy friends are true!

Aye, faithful to Little Boy Blue they stand,
    Each in the same old place—
Awaiting the touch of a little hand,
    The smile of a little face;   20

And they wonder, as waiting the long years through
    In the dust of that little chair,
What has become of our Little Boy Blue,
    Since he kissed them and put them there.

Understanding Literature

1. What is the setting of the poem?
2. The toys "wonder" what has happened to Little Boy Blue.
   Point out the lines which tell the reader the answer to this.
3. What other human qualities are the toys given?
4. Point out the lines which show that time has passed.
5. What examples of alliteration do you find?
6. What is the mood of the poem?

Reading "Song"

Death is an everyday occurrence, but it is something no one truly understands. In "Little Boy Blue" by Eugene Field, death is presented in an unusual way; it is only suggested by the toys left in the boy's room. This is a sentimental presentation and one in which the word *death* is not even mentioned. In the next poem the author presents her thoughts on death in a very different way.

IMPROVING YOUR READING. In all types of literature the reader should determine the *point of view* from which the writing is done. The material may be presented by a character in the selection itself: this is the "I," or first person point of view. Or the material may be presented from the point of view of an outsider looking on and reporting events and thoughts. The material may also be presented from the author's point of view and may indicate his own thoughts and feelings. When the author tells the story and is free to expose the characters' ideas and opinions, to be in several different places at once, and to comment freely on the actions of his characters, the result, of course, is very different from that of a story which is written from the limited point of view of one of the characters in the story. Determining the point of view, being aware of the speaker in a poem or story, will aid you in a more complete understanding of the selection.

Song

Christina Rossetti

When I am dead, my dearest,
   Sing no sad songs for me;
Plant thou no roses at my head,
   Nor shady cypress tree:
Be the green grass above me   5
   With showers and dewdrops wet:
And if thou wilt, remember,
   And if thou wilt, forget.

I shall not see the shadows,
   I shall not feel the rain;   10
I shall not hear the nightingale
   Sing on as if in pain:
And dreaming through the twilight
   That doth not rise nor set,
Haply[1] I may remember,   15
   And haply may forget.

---

1 **Haply:** by chance.

Understanding Literature

1. What is the attitude of "I" in this poem toward death? Compare this attitude with that of the writer of "Little Boy Blue."
2. Who is speaking in this poem? To whom?
3. What is the meaning of line 2?
4. In lines 7 and 8 what should the person addressed "remember" and "forget"?
5. What is meant by "twilight" in the second stanza? Why does it "not rise nor set"?
6. What is the difference in mood between the first stanza and the second? How are the images in each different?

This poem uses *personification,* the poetic device of giving animals, objects, or qualities the characteristics of a human being.

City: San Francisco

Langston Hughes

In the morning the city
Spreads its wings
Making a song
In stone that sings.

In the evening the city
Goes to bed
Hanging lights
About its head.

Understanding Literature

1. In what ways is the city in the morning spreading its wings? How can a city make a song in stone?
2. What picture do you get of the city in the second stanza? What is meant here by the word "head"?
3. San Francisco is a city of many hills. Does this fact make any difference in your reading of the poem? From what point might the poet be looking at the scene, from the top or bottom of a hill?
4. Judging by his choice of words in this poem, what is the author's feeling toward the city?
5. In which of the two stanzas is there an example of personification? Why is the other stanza *not* personification?

Metaphors

THE THREE LYRICAL poems which follow do not have a common subject, but they are connected in another way. Each uses a figure of speech called a *metaphor*. You have already learned that *similes* are comparisons of unlike objects and always use the words *like* or *as*. In a simile the author states directly that one thing is like another, as "My luve is like a red, red rose." In a metaphor, however, the comparison is more subtle; it is *implied* rather than stated directly. You probably use many metaphors in your daily speech, but they are so worn with use that you hardly notice them. If you say, for example, that you are boiling with anger, you are comparing the agitation and nervousness you experience when angry to the rapid bubbling of boiling water. Or when you say that an idea dawned on you, you are implying that you were able to see and understand things more clearly in much the same way that the dawn of a new day enables you to see things clearly again.

The following lines from the play *As You Like It* by William Shakespeare contain an example of poetic metaphor. Can you see what metaphor Shakespeare has used?

> All the world's a stage,
> And all the men and women merely players.
> They have their exits and their entrances,
> And one man in his time plays many parts. . . .

Shakespeare has compared the world to a stage, and people to the actors in the play on this stage. These things are similar in that men and women come to the earth when they are born and leave it when they die—in the same way that actors enter and leave the stage when their parts begin and end. And, as an actor plays many different roles in his lifetime, so does a man play different roles in his lifetime, of infant, schoolboy, and adult. Why does the poet use a metaphor here at all? Because he wants you to look at life in a new way: as a play in which every man and woman has his special part.

As you read each of the three short poems which follow, ask yourself: How are the objects similar? What effect does the poet's comparison have on the poem?

Rain

Frank Marshall Davis

Today the rain
is an aged man
a gray old man
a curious old man
in a music store   5

Today houses
are strings of a harp
soprano harp strings
bass harp strings
in a music store   10

The ancient man
strums the harp
with thin long fingers
attentively picking
a weary jingle   15
a soft jazzy jangle
then dodders away
before the boss comes 'round. . . .

Understanding Literature

1. How is the rain like a man in a music store? How are the houses
   like the strings of a harp?
2. What is the mood of the poem? What words suggest the mood?
   What sounds are suggested in the poem?
3. When the man "dodders away," what idea is being stated about
   the rain?
4. What is meant by the last line?

Further Activity

   Try writing a similar poem about a very heavy rain with a high
wind. If you want to compare the storm to a man, what kind of
man will you choose? What else could you compare the storm to?
In writing keep fairly close to the same length lines and to the
three stanzas.

He Wishes for the Cloths of Heaven

William Butler Yeats

Had I the heavens' embroidered cloths,
Enwrought[1] with golden and silver light,
The blue and the dim and the dark cloths
Of night and light and the half light,
I would spread the cloths under your feet:
But I, being poor, have only my dreams;
I have spread my dreams under your feet;
Tread softly because you tread on my dreams.

1 Enwrought: ornamented; fashioned.

Understanding Literature

1. To whom might the poem be addressed?
2. What is the speaker offering to this person?
3. A metaphor is used in the first line. What things are being compared in the phrase "the heavens' embroidered cloths"? How can they be "Enwrought with golden and silver light"?
4. The speaker's dreams are used metaphorically in the last two lines. Explain the metaphor.

The Coin

Sara Teasdale

Into my heart's treasury
  I slipped a coin
That time cannot take
  Nor a thief purloin,[1]—
Oh, better than the minting
  Of a gold-crowned king
Is the safe-kept memory
  Of a lovely thing.

1 purloin: steal.

Understanding Literature

1. Paraphrase, or tell in your own words, what this short poem is about.
2. There is a metaphor in the first two lines. What objects are being compared? How are these objects alike?

"Oak and Lily," a more complicated poem than those you have read thus far, uses the techniques of simile and metaphor that you have seen in other poems. The metaphor in this poem, however, is an *extended metaphor*. This type of metaphor is not contained within one or two lines but extends for several lines or, as in this case, for the entire length of the poem.

Oak and Lily

Ben Jonson

It is not growing like a tree
In bulk, doth make men better be;
Or standing long an oak, three hundred year,
To fall a log at last, dry, bald, and sear[1]:
    A lily of a day,
    Is fairer far in May,
Although it fall and die that night;
It was the plant, and flower of light.
In small proportions we just beauties see;
And in short measures, life may perfect be.

1 **sear:** withered.

Understanding Literature

1. How can a man be like an oak? What human characteristics are given to the oak?
2. Explain the metaphor in this poem.
3. Paraphrase the last two lines. How do these two lines express the meaning of the earlier part of the poem?

As you can see by the lyric poems you have just read, a poet writes most often on the great themes that have always concerned men. The next group of poems deals with love and friendship, also common subjects for lyric poetry.

"Oh, when I was in love with you"

A. E. Housman

Oh, when I was in love with you,
    Then I was clean and brave,
And miles around the wonder grew
    How well did I behave.

And now the fancy passes by,
    And nothing will remain,
And miles around they'll say that I
    Am quite myself again.

Understanding Literature

1. Who is the speaker in the poem?
2. In the first stanza how does he behave? Why?
3. In the second stanza how does he behave? Why?

Reading "A Red, Red Rose"

In this poem the author uses one comparison after another to express his love (luve).

A Red, Red Rose

Robert Burns

O, my luve is like a red, red rose,
    That 's newly sprung in June.
O, my luve is like the melodie,
    That 's sweetly played in tune.

As fair art thou, my bonie lass,   5
    So deep in luve am I,
And I will luve thee still, my dear,
    Till a' the seas gang dry.

Till a' the seas gang dry, my dear,
    And the rocks melt wi' the sun!   10
And I will luve thee still, my dear,
    While the sands o' life shall run.

And fare thee weel, my only luve,
    And fare thee weel a while!
And I will come again, my luve,   15
    Tho' it were ten thousand mile!

Understanding Literature

1. What comparisons does the poet make to express his love? How does he exaggerate?
2. Paraphrase the last stanza.
3. Does the expression "my luve" refer to the person with whom the speaker is in love, or does it mean his love for that person?

Love's Secret

William Blake

Never seek to tell thy love,
    Love that never told can be;
For the gentle wind doth move
    Silently, invisibly.

I told my love, I told my love,   5
    I told her all my heart,
Trembling, cold, in ghastly fears.
    Ah! she did depart!

Soon after she was gone from me,
    A traveler came by,   10
Silently, invisibly:
    He took her with a sigh.

Understanding Literature

1. Why does the speaker say that love "never told can be"?
2. Why does his love depart?
3. Why is she attracted to the traveler?
4. What advice would the speaker in this poem give to the speaker in the last poem you read?

The next two poems describe another kind of love—love of the sea.

The Sea Gypsy

Richard Hovey

I am fevered with the sunset,
I am fretful with the bay,
For the wander-thirst is on me
And my soul is in Cathay.[1]

There 's a schooner in the offing,   5
With her topsails shot with fire,
And my heart has gone aboard her
For the Islands of Desire.

I must forth again tomorrow!
With the sunset I must be   10
Hull down on the trail of rapture
In the wonder of the sea.

1 **Cathay:** China.

Understanding Literature

1. Why is the speaker "fevered" and "fretful"?
2. Explain why his "soul is in Cathay."
3. How can the schooner's topsails be "shot with fire"?
4. What are the "Islands of Desire"?
5. How can the speaker be "Hull down on the trail of rapture"?

Before the Squall

Arthur Symons

The wind is rising on the sea,
   White flashes dance along the deep,
That moans as if uneasily
   It turned in an unquiet sleep.

Ridge after rocky ridge upheaves   5
   A toppling crest that falls in spray
Where the tormented beach receives
   The buffets of the sea's wild play.

On the horizon's nearing line,
   Where the sky rests, a visible wall,   10
Gray in the offing, I divine
   The sails that fly before the squall.

Understanding Literature

1. Describe the imagery in the first stanza.
2. Explain the metaphor in the second stanza.
3. What is the mood of the poem?

Another recurring theme of poetry is love of country. The two following poems express this idea.

My Native Land

Sir Walter Scott

Breathes there the man, with soul so dead,
Who never to himself hath said,
  This is my own, my native land?
Whose heart hath ne'er within him burned,
As home his footsteps he hath turned   5
  From wandering on a foreign strand?[1]
If such there breathe, go, mark him well;
For him no minstrel raptures swell;
High though his titles, proud his name,
Boundless his wealth as wish can claim,—   10
Despite those titles, power, and pelf,[2]
The wretch, concentered all in self,
Living, shall forfeit fair renown,
And, doubly dying, shall go down
To the vile dust from whence he sprung,   15
Unwept, unhonored, and unsung.

1 **strand:** shore.
2 **pelf:** riches.

Understanding Literature

1. Why would a traveler have a greater appreciation for his native land after being away?
2. What things cannot be a substitute for a native land?
3. What is meant by "doubly dying"?
4. Why would a man without a native land be "Unwept, unhonored, and unsung"?
5. Where in this poem do you find examples of alliteration and of inverted word order?

These lines are a short excerpt from *The Tragedy of King Richard the Second*, a play by William Shakespeare. John of Gaunt, an uncle to King Richard, shows his love of England in these words spoken shortly before his death.

IMPROVING YOUR READING. This passage consists of a series of metaphors. To what different objects is England compared?

"This royal throne of kings"

William Shakespeare

This royal throne of kings, this sceptered isle,
This earth of majesty, this seat of Mars,
This other Eden, demi-paradise,
This fortress built by Nature for herself
Against infection and the hand of war,   5
This happy breed of men, this little world,
This precious stone set in the silver sea,
Which serves it in the office of a wall,
Or as a moat defensive to a house,
Against the envy of less happier lands;   10
This blessed plot, this earth, this realm, this England. . . .

Understanding Literature

1. Explain the meaning of the phrase "this sceptered isle."
2. What is suggested in the comparison of England to an "earth of majesty"?
3. In line 2 there is an allusion to Mars. Explain the allusion. Why is England called the "seat of Mars"?
4. Explain lines 4 and 5.
5. These eleven lines convey an impression of great pride in England. Point out words which help to convey this impression.
6. The last line is an especially effective one. Why?

Reading "Tommy"

This poem protests the way that ordinary soldiers are treated in time of peace. The English call their regular army privates Tommy Atkins, as Americans in the two World Wars referred to theirs as doughboys and GI's. The English name was originally used as a model on forms which soldiers had to fill out.

IMPROVING YOUR READING. The basis of this poem is *irony*, the contrast between what one expects and what one gets.

Tommy

Rudyard Kipling

I went into a public-'ouse to get a pint o' beer,
The publican 'e up an' sez, "We serve no red-coats here."
The girls be'ind the bar they laughed an' giggled fit to die,
I outs into the street again an' to myself sez I:
    O it 's Tommy this, an' Tommy that, an' "Tommy, go away";   5
    But it 's "Thank you, Mister Atkins," when the band begins to play,
    The band begins to play, my boys, the band begins to play,
    O it 's "Thank you, Mister Atkins," when the band begins to play.

I went into a theater as sober as could be,
They gave a drunk civilian room, but 'ad n't none for me;   10
They sent me to the gallery or round the music-'alls,
But when it comes to fightin', Lord! they 'll shove me in the stalls!
    For it 's Tommy this, an' Tommy that, an' "Tommy, wait outside";
    But it 's "Special train for Atkins" when the trooper 's on the tide,
    The troopship 's on the tide, my boys, the troopship 's on the tide,   15
    O it 's "Special train for Atkins" when the trooper 's on the tide.

Yes, makin' mock o' uniforms that guard you while you sleep
Is cheaper than them uniforms, an' they 're starvation cheap;
An' hustlin' drunken soldiers when they 're goin' large a bit
Is five times better business than paradin' in full kit.   20
    Then it 's Tommy this, an' Tommy that, an' "Tommy, 'ow 's yer soul?"
    But it 's "Thin red line of 'eroes" when the drums begin to roll,
    The drums begin to roll, my boys, the drums begin to roll,
    O it 's "Thin red line of 'eroes" when the drums begin to roll.

We are n't no thin red 'eroes, nor we are n't no blackguards too,   25
But single men in barricks, most remarkable like you;
An' if sometimes our conduck is n't all your fancy paints,
Why, single men in barricks don't grow into plaster saints;
    While it 's Tommy this, an' Tommy that, an' "Tommy, fall be'ind,"
    But it 's "Please to walk in front, sir," when there 's trouble in the wind,   30
    There's trouble in the wind, my boys, there's trouble in the wind,
    O it 's "Please to walk in front, sir," when there 's trouble in the wind.

You talk o' better food for us, an' schools, an' fires, an' all:
We 'll wait for extry rations if you treat us rational.
Don't mess about the cook-room slops, but prove it to our face   35
The Widow's Uniform[1] is not the soldier-man's disgrace.
    For it 's Tommy this, an' Tommy that, an' "Chuck him out, the brute!"
    But it 's "Saviour of 'is country" when the guns begin to shoot;
    An' it 's Tommy this, an' Tommy that, an' anything you please;
    An' Tommy ain't a bloomin' fool—you bet that Tommy sees!   40

1 **Widow's Uniform:** an allusion to Queen Victoria, who was called widow by the soldiers.

Understanding Literature

1. Who is the speaker in this poem? What is his mood? What are his specific complaints?
2. The beginning of each stanza illustrates one treatment of Tommy, and the last three lines of each stanza illustrate a different treatment. What contrasts are used to show this difference? What causes the difference? How is the contrast ironic?
3. What use is made of repetition in this poem? of alliteration?
4. How does the writer feel about Tommy?

A poet is one who makes connections. Even an ordinary street scene may arouse in him memories and longing, sadness and joy. Claude McKay was born in the West Indies, but he spent many years in New York City. The sight of the tropical fruits makes him "hungry"—not for eating, but for "the old, familiar ways."

IMPROVING YOUR READING. The title of a poem is not just an addition to the poem but is usually an important part of it. Why do you think the author used this title, "The Tropics in New York"?

The Tropics in New York
Claude McKay

Bananas ripe and green, and gingerroot,
    Cocoa in pods and alligator pears,
And tangerines and mangoes and grapefruit,
    Fit for the highest prize at parish fairs,

Set in the window, bringing memories   5
    Of fruit trees laden by low-singing rills,[1]
And dewy dawns, and mystical blue skies
    In benediction over nunlike hills.

My eyes grew dim, and I could no more gaze;
    A wave of longing through my body swept,   10
And, hungry for the old, familiar ways,
    I turned aside and bowed my head and wept.

[1] **rills:** small streams.

Understanding Literature

1. The first three lines seem merely to be listing a number of tropical plants, but what *imagery* do they suggest?
2. The title of the poem places the speaker, the "I," in New York, but nowhere in the poem is the city specifically mentioned. What is the one phrase, however, that suggests a place other than the tropics?
3. In lines 7–8 the poet uses the words "mystical," "benediction," and "nunlike." What do these three words have in common? What, then, is the picture the poet presents in the phrase "mystical blue skies/In benediction over nunlike hills"?
4. Although the poem is written in three stanzas, there are only two main parts. Where does the division occur? How do you know? What is the poet doing in each part?

Although Symons uses "I," is he speaking only for himself? Or could he be speaking for all people who have this same idea of dreams?

IMPROVING YOUR READING. This poem is based on a metaphor. Note the two activities that are compared. How are they alike?

The Loom of Dreams

Arthur Symons

I broider the world upon a loom,[1]
I broider with dreams my tapestry;
Here in a little lonely room
I am master of earth and sea,
And the planets come to me,   5

I broider my life into the frame,
I broider my love, thread upon thread;
The world goes by with its glory and shame,
Crowns are bartered and blood is shed:
I sit and broider my dreams instead.   10

And the only world is the world of my dreams,
And my weaving the only happiness;
For what is the world but what it seems?
And who knows but that God, beyond our guess,
Sits weaving worlds out of loneliness?   15

[1] **loom:** frame for weaving yarn or thread into a fabric.

Understanding Literature

1. Explain the metaphors used in "The Loom of Dreams."
2. In what way is the person who dreams "master of earth and sea"?
3. What is meant by "The world goes by with its glory and shame"?
4. What does the poet mean by saying that "the only world is the world of my dreams"?
5. The poem ends with two questions which should prompt the reader to think further. What are they? What do they indicate about the poet's state of mind?

In this poem the speaker looks out on the snow which becomes, as the poem goes on, a *symbol* of his own suffering. The poem divides into two parts: one about the actual storm and one about what it stands for, or symbolizes.

The First Snowfall

James Russell Lowell

The snow had begun in the gloaming,
  And busily all the night
Had been heaping field and highway
  With a silence deep and white.

Every pine and fir and hemlock   5
  Wore ermine too dear for an earl,
And the poorest twig on the elm tree
  Was ridged inch deep with pearl.

From sheds new-roofed with Carrara[1]
  Came Chanticleer's[2] muffled crow,   10
The stiff rails softened to a swan's-down,
  And still fluttered down the snow.

I stood and watched by the window
  The noiseless work of the sky,
And the sudden flurries of snowbirds,   15
  Like brown leaves whirling by.

I thought of a mound in sweet Auburn[3]
  Where a little headstone stood;
How the flakes were folding it gently,
  As did robins the babes in the wood.   20

1 **Carrara:** white marble.
2 **Chanticleer's:** the rooster's.

3 **Auburn:** Mount Auburn cemetery, Cambridge, Massachusetts.

Up spoke our own little Mabel,
    Saying, "Father, who makes it snow?"
And I told of the good All-father
    Who cares for us here below.

Again I looked at the snowfall,   25
    And thought of the leaden sky
That arched o'er our first great sorrow,
    When that mound was heaped so high.

I remembered the gradual patience
    That fell from that cloud like snow,   30
Flake by flake, healing and hiding
    The scar that renewed our woe.

And again to the child I whispered,
    "The snow that husheth all,
Darling, the merciful Father   35
    Alone can make it fall!"

Then, with eyes that saw not, I kissed her,
    And she, kissing back, could not know
That *my* kiss was given to her sister,
    Folded close under deepening snow.   40

Understanding Literature

1. In the second, third, and fourth stanzas the poet uses a series of images to describe the snow. Explain these images.
2. As the poet looks, what is he thinking about?
3. In the seventh stanza what is "our first great sorrow"?
4. What is the poet saying in the last stanza?
5. How is the snowfall like his sorrow?
6. Why is the poem called "The First Snowfall"?

Reading "Curfew"

Curfew means literally "the covering of the fire." In England during the Middle Ages a bell was sounded in the evening as a signal for putting out fires. Longfellow, here, uses this idea as a *symbol* of the approaching end of life.

Curfew

Henry Wadsworth Longfellow

I

Solemnly, mournfully,
   Dealing its dole,
The Curfew Bell
   Is beginning to toll.

Cover the embers,   5
   And put out the light;
Toil comes with the morning,
   And rest with the night.

Dark grow the windows,
   And quenched is the fire;   10
Sound fades into silence—
   All footsteps retire.

No voice in the chambers,
   No sound in the hall!
Sleep and oblivion   15
   Reign over all!

II

The book is completed,
   And closed, like the day;
And the hand that has written it
   Lays it away.   20

Dim grow its fancies;
   Forgotten they lie;
Like coals in the ashes,
   They darken and die.

Song sinks into silence,   25
   The story is told,
The windows are darkened,
   The hearthstone is cold.

Darker and darker
   The black shadows fall;   30
Sleep and oblivion
   Reign over all.

Understanding Literature

1. In the first four stanzas the poet is describing the actual close of a day. What images does he use?
2. In what ways do the sounds of the words used in the first stanza reflect the sound of the bell?
3. In the second part of the poem, what is the end of life compared to? How are the two things alike?
4. What other metaphors repeat the same idea?
5. How does the last stanza differ from the fourth?

Poets are not always utterly serious. Like most human beings, they are frequently unable to resist poking fun at or laughing at many things that they see around them, as you will see in the two poems that follow. These short poems are examples of light verse, short lyric poems which are gay, clever, and written to entertain, although they sometimes have a serious purpose too.

Death at Suppertime

Phyllis McGinley

Between the dark and the daylight,
  When the night is beginning to lower,
Comes a pause in the day's occupation,
  That is known as the Children's Hour.[1]

Then endeth the skipping and skating,
  The giggles, the tantrums, and tears,
When, the innocent voices abating,
  Alert grow the innocent ears.

The little boys leap from the stairways,   5
  Girls lay down their dolls on the dot,
For promptly at five o'er the airways
  Comes violence geared to the tot.

Comes murder, comes arson, come G-men
  Pursuing unspeakable spies;   10
Come gangsters and tough-talking he-men
  With six-shooters strapped to their thighs;

Comes the corpse in the dust, comes the dictum
  "Ya' better start singin', ya' rat!"
While the torturer leers at his victim,   15
  The killer unleashes his gat.

---

1 See the poem "The Children's Hour" by Henry Wadsworth Longfellow.

With mayhem the twilight is reeling.
  Blood spatters; the tommy guns bark.
Hands reach for the sky or the ceiling
  As the dagger strikes home in the dark.   20

And lo! with what rapturous wonder
  The little ones hark to each tale
Of gambler shot down with his plunder
  Or outlaw abducting the mail.

Between the news and the tireless   25
  Commercials, while tempers turn sour,
Comes a season of horror by wireless
  That is known as the Children's Hour.

Song of the Open Road

Ogden Nash

I think that I shall never see
A billboard lovely as a tree.
Indeed, unless the billboards fall
I'll never see a tree at all.

Famous Characters in Literature

FROM THE brig *Hispaniola* to the city of London; from a Missouri town on a summer morning to New England on a winter afternoon; from a quiet seaport where cannon shots once awakened the inhabitants at midnight to the English countryside where animals live the lives of men—you can go to all these places by reading the selections in this chapter.

Even more interesting than the places you can visit are the people who inhabit them. Tom Sawyer sitting on a barrel in the shade watching friends do his work, Robinson Crusoe building his own solitary world, and Jo March fighting her worst enemy are the kinds of individuals you can come to know as you read.

All these people, as well as many others you will meet in this section, are characters in famous books that one day you will want to read if you have not already done so. In these selections the characters are introduced so that you can begin to know what is in store for you in many great books.

The authors of the stories lived at different times, in different places. Most of them wrote for adults, some for young people; but all the books in which these selections appear are still enjoyed by readers of all ages. Try to understand why, as you get to know the characters the authors created.

In *The Adventures of Tom Sawyer* Mark Twain wrote about a world he knew well, a small Mississippi River town. He grew up in Hannibal, Missouri, in the 1840's, and it is in such a town that Tom Sawyer lives with his Aunt Polly. The book tells the story of a summer in Tom's life, and several generations of its readers have relived a time in their own lives when "all the summer world was bright and fresh, and brimming with life."

from The Adventures of Tom Sawyer

Mark Twain

IMPROVING YOUR READING: You come to understand the characters and believe in the world that an author has created by noticing the way characters act and speak. Mark Twain *characterizes* Tom Sawyer by Tom's behavior and his words. As you read this chapter, note carefully how Mark Twain describes exactly the way Tom behaves, and decide for yourself just why he behaves as he does. Listen to the words that are spoken by Tom, Jim, and Ben, and consider how their words make the characters seem alive and real.

Mark Twain uses a great deal of *dialogue* in the middle section of this chapter. What is gained by his quoting the exact words of Tom, Jim, and Ben instead of explaining as an observer what happened and what was said?

THE GLORIOUS WHITEWASHER

SATURDAY MORNING was come, and all the summer world was bright and fresh, and brimming with life. There was a song in every heart; and if the heart was young the music issued at the lips. There was cheer in every face and a spring in every step. The locust trees were in bloom and the fragrance of the blossoms filled the air. Cardiff Hill, beyond the village and above it, was green with vegetation, and it lay just far enough away to seem a Delectable Land,[1] dreamy, reposeful, and inviting.

Tom appeared on the sidewalk with a bucket of whitewash and a long-handled brush. He surveyed the fence, and all gladness left him and a deep melancholy settled down upon his spirit. Thirty yards of board fence nine feet high. Life to him seemed hollow, and existence but a burden. Sighing he dipped his brush and passed it along the topmost plank; repeated the operation; did it again; compared the insignificant whitewashed streak with the far-reaching continent of unwhitewashed fence, and sat down on a

1 **Delectable Land:** In *Pilgrim's Progress,* a famous book written by John Bunyan in the 17th century, one could see the Celestial, or heavenly, City from the Delectable Mountains.

tree-box discouraged. Jim[2] came skipping out at the gate with a tin pail, and singing "Buffalo Gals." Bringing water from the town pump had always been hateful work in Tom's eyes, before, but now it did not strike him so. He remembered that there was company at the pump. White, mulatto, and Negro boys and girls were always there waiting their turns, resting, trading playthings, quarreling, fighting, skylarking. And he remembered that although the pump was only a hundred and fifty yards off, Jim never got back with a bucket of water under an hour—and even then somebody generally had to go after him. Tom said:

"Say, Jim, I'll fetch the water if you'll whitewash some."

Jim shook his head and said:

"Can't, Mars[3] Tom. Ole missis, she tole me I got to go an' git dis water an' not stop foolin' roun' wid anybody. She say she spec' Mars Tom gwine to ax me to whitewash, an' so she tole me go 'long an' 'tend to my own business—she 'lowed *she'd* 'tend to de whitewashin'."

"Oh, never you mind what she said, Jim. That's the way she always talks. Gimme the bucket—I won't be gone only a minute. *She* won't ever know."

"Oh, I dasn't, Mars Tom. Ole missis she'd take an' tar de head off'n me. 'Deed she would."

"*She!* She never licks anybody—whacks 'em over the head with her thimble—and who cares for that, I'd like to know. She talks awful, but talk don't hurt—anyways it don't if she don't cry. Jim, I'll give you a marvel.[4] I'll give you a white alley!"[5]

Jim began to waver.

"White alley, Jim! And it's a bully taw."[6]

"My! Dat's a mighty gay marvel, *I* tell you! But Mars Tom I's powerful 'fraid ole missis—"

"And besides, if you will I'll show you my sore toe."

Jim was only human—this attraction was too much for him. He put down his pail, took the white alley, and bent over the toe with absorbing interest while the bandage was being unwound. In another moment he was flying down the street with his pail and a tingling rear, Tom was whitewashing with vigor, and Aunt Polly was retiring from the field with a slipper in her hand and triumph in her eye.

But Tom's energy did not last. He began to think of the fun he had planned for this day, and his sorrows multiplied. Soon the free boys would come tripping along on all sorts of delicious expeditions, and they would make a world of fun of him for having to work—the very thought of it burnt him like fire. He got out his worldly wealth and examined it—bits of toys, marbles, and trash; enough to buy an exchange of *work*, maybe, but not half enough to buy so much as half an hour of pure

2 **Jim:** a slave of Tom's Aunt Polly.
3 **Mars:** dialect for *Master*. Notice that Mark Twain indicated how different characters speak by spelling words the way they would pronounce them.

4 **marvel:** dialect for *marble*.
5 **alley:** desirable playing marble.
6 **taw:** marble used as a shooter.

freedom. So he returned his straitened means to his pocket, and gave up the idea of trying to buy the boys. At this dark and hopeless moment an inspiration burst upon him! Nothing less than a great, magnificent inspiration.

He took up his brush and went tranquilly to work. Ben Rogers hove in sight presently—the very boy, of all boys, whose ridicule he had been dreading. Ben's gait was the hop-skip-and-jump—proof enough that his heart was light and his anticipations high. He was eating an apple, and giving a long, melodious whoop, at intervals, followed by a deep-toned ding-dong-dong, ding-dong-dong, for he was personating a steamboat. As he drew near, he slackened speed, took the middle of the street, leaned far over to starboard[7] and rounded to ponderously and with laborious pomp and circumstance—for he was personating the *Big Missouri*, and considered himself to be drawing nine feet of water. He was boat and captain and engine bells combined, so he had to imagine himself standing on his own hurricane deck[8] giving the orders and executing them:

"Stop her, sir! Ting-a-ling-ling!" The headway ran almost out and he drew up slowly toward the sidewalk.

"Ship up to back! Ting-a-ling-ling!" His arms straightened and stiffened down his sides.

"Set her back on the stabboard! Ting-a-ling-ling! Chow! ch-chow-wow! Chow!" His right hand, meantime, describing stately circles —for it was representing a forty-foot wheel.

"Let her go back on the labboard![9] Ting-a-ling-ling! Chow-ch-chow-chow!" The left hand began to describe circles.

"Stop the stabboard! Ting-a-ling-ling! Stop the labboard! Come ahead on the stabboard! Stop her! Let your outside turn over slow! Ting-a-ling-ling! Chow-ow-ow! Get out that head line! *Lively* now! Come—out with your spring line— what're you about there! Take a turn round that stump with the bight of it! Stand by that stage, now let her go! Done with the engines, sir! Ting-a-ling-ling! *Sh't! s'h't! sh't!*" (trying the gauge cocks).

Tom went on whitewashing—paid no attention to the steamboat. Ben stared a moment and then said:

"Hi-*yi! You're* up a stump, ain't you!"

No answer. Tom surveyed his last touch with the eye of an artist, then he gave his brush another gentle sweep and surveyed the result, as before. Ben ranged up alongside of him. Tom's mouth watered for the apple, but he stuck to his work. Ben said:

"Hello, old chap, you got to work, hey?"

Tom wheeled suddenly and said:

"Why, it's you, Ben! I warn't noticing."

---

7 **starboard:** To a person on board facing the bow, this is the right-hand side of a ship.
8 **hurricane deck:** upper deck on a river steamer.

9 **labboard:** larboard, the left-hand side of a ship to a person on board who faces the bow (the front). The word used now for this side of a ship is *port*.

FAMOUS CHARACTERS

"Say—*I'm* going in a-swimming, *I* am. Don't you wish you could? But of course you'd druther *work*— wouldn't you? Course you would!"

Tom contemplated the boy a bit, and said:

"What do you call work?"

"Why, ain't *that* work?"

Tom resumed his whitewashing, and answered carelessly:

"Well, maybe it is, and maybe it ain't. All I know, is, it suits Tom Sawyer."

"Oh come, now, you don't mean to let on that you *like* it?"

The brush continued to move.

"Like it? Well, I don't see why I oughtn't to like it. Does a boy get a chance to whitewash a fence every day?"

That put the thing in a new light. Ben stopped nibbling his apple. Tom swept his brush daintily back and forth—stepped back to note the effect—added a touch here and there —criticized the effect again—Ben watching every move and getting more and more interested, more and more absorbed. Presently he said:

"Say, Tom, let *me* whitewash a little."

Tom considered, was about to consent; but he altered his mind:

"No—no—I reckon it wouldn't hardly do, Ben. You see, Aunt Polly's awful particular about this fence—right here on the street, you know—but if it was the back fence I wouldn't mind and *she* wouldn't. Yes, she's awful particular about this fence; it's got to be done very careful; I reckon there ain't one boy in a thousand, maybe two thousand, that can do it the way it's got to be done."

"No—is that so? Oh come, now— lemme just try. Only just a little— I'd let *you*, if you was me, Tom."

"Ben, I'd like to, honest injun; but Aunt Polly—well, Jim wanted to do it, and she wouldn't let him; Sid wanted to do it, and she wouldn't let Sid. Now don't you see how I'm fixed? If you was to tackle this fence and anything was to happen to it—"

"Oh, shucks, I'll be just as careful. Now lemme try. Say—I'll give you the core of my apple."

"Well, here— No, Ben, now don't. I'm afeard—"

"I'll give you *all* of it!"

Tom gave up the brush with reluctance in his face, but alacrity[10] in his heart. And while the late steamer *Big Missouri* worked and sweated in the sun, the retired artist sat on a barrel in the shade close by, dangled his legs, munched his apple, and planned the slaughter of more innocents. There was no lack of material; boys happened along every little while; they came to jeer, but remained to whitewash. By the time Ben was fagged out, Tom had traded the next chance to Billy Fisher for a kite, in good repair; and when *he* played out, Johnny Miller bought in for a dead rat and a string to swing it with—and so on, and so on, hour after hour. And when the middle of the afternoon came, from being a poor poverty-stricken boy in the morning, Tom was literally rolling in wealth. He had beside the things before mentioned, twelve

10 **alacrity:** readiness; eagerness.

marbles, part of a jew's-harp, a piece of blue bottle glass to look through, a spool cannon, a key that wouldn't unlock anything, a fragment of chalk, a glass stopper of a decanter, a tin soldier, a couple of tadpoles, six fire-crackers, a kitten with only one eye, a brass doorknob, a dog collar—but no dog—the handle of a knife, four pieces of orange peel, and a dilapidated old window sash.

He had had a nice, good, idle time all the while—plenty of company— and the fence had three coats of whitewash on it! If he hadn't run out of whitewash, he would have bankrupted every boy in the village.

Tom said to himself that it was not such a hollow world, after all. He had discovered a great law of human action, without knowing it— namely, that in order to make a man or a boy covet[11] a thing, it is only necessary to make the thing difficult to attain. If he had been a great and wise philosopher, like the writer of this book, he would now have comprehended that Work consists of whatever a body is *obliged* to do, and that Play consists of whatever a body is not obliged to do. And this would help him to understand why constructing artificial flowers or performing on a treadmill is work, while rolling tenpins or climbing Mont Blanc[12] is only amusement. There are wealthy gentlemen in England who drive four-horse passenger coaches twenty or thirty miles on a daily line, in the summer, because the privilege costs them considerable money; but if they were offered wages for the service, that would turn it into work and then they would resign.

The boy mused awhile over the substantial change which had taken place in his worldly circumstances, and then wended toward headquarters to report.

11 **covet:** desire.

12 **Mont Blanc:** the highest peak in the Alps.

Understanding Literature

1. Describe in detail Tom's behavior as he first appears on the sidewalk on Saturday morning with his whitewash and brush. Mark Twain here describes Tom's actions to *characterize* Tom in what kind of mood?
2. Because Tom understands people, he knows that not only will he lose the freedom of a Saturday because he has to whitewash, but he will also have to endure something else. What is this "something else"? Does he prove to be right in expecting this?
3. As Tom is buying Jim's job of fetching water in exchange for a look at Tom's sore toe, there is an interruption. Find the sentence that refers to this interruption. What happens? How do you know what happens? Why is this a good way to describe the incident?

4. Change the *dialogue* in a few sentences to a simple explanation of what happened. (Example: Tom said that he would get the water if Jim would whitewash. Jim shook his head and said that he couldn't whitewash because his mistress told him not to stop on his way to get water.) Note the difference in effect. What effect does the dialogue have that the rewritten version does not have?
5. It is amusing to picture and hear for yourself Ben Rogers imitating a steamboat. This rather long scene also adds to the story in another way. Why is it more effective for Tom's purpose that the author should have Ben Rogers arrive on the scene as a steamboat, captain, and engine bell, with all the accompanying sound, rather than have him arrive simply and quietly?
6. Tom is *characterized* in this chapter as an intelligent boy who has learned a lesson in human behavior. Describe in detail some of Tom's behavior that shows he has discovered what Mark Twain calls "a great law of human action . . . that in order to make a man or a boy covet a thing, it is only necessary to make the thing difficult to attain."
7. What is Mark Twain's definition of *work?* According to this definition, who *works* to get the whitewashing done?

Further Activity

Reread the description of the conversation and actions of Tom and Ben. In imitation of this scene, write a scene which includes Tom's conversation with the second boy to arrive (give him any name you like).

Focusing on Words

1. As Ben Rogers appeared, Tom "took up his brush and went tranquilly to work." Why is it important that the author used the adverb *tranquilly* here, instead of writing, "He took up his brush and went to work"?
2. The word *hove* is the past tense of *heave*. You would not ordinarily say that a person heaves into sight; but if you look up the word *heave* in the glossary or a dictionary, you will find that one meaning of the word makes its use to describe Ben's approach particularly appropriate. Why is Mark Twain's use of the word appropriate here?
3. Explain what Mark Twain means when he writes: "Tom contemplated the boy a bit. . . ." What more does the word *contemplate* imply than the expression *looked at?*

Little Women is a story about the March sisters—Meg, Jo, Beth, and Amy—and their friends. The girls' mother, whom they call Marmee, is the head of the family while their father is away serving as a chaplain in the army during the Civil War. Laurie—Theodore Laurence—the boy who lives next door, is a friend of all the March girls.

from Little Women

Louisa May Alcott

IMPROVING YOUR READING: Each of the March girls has a distinct personality, and although they usually get along well together they sometimes have disagreements, or conflicts. In many short stories and plays the plot involves a *conflict*, either of people, things, or ideas. In the end of the story or play the conflict is usually *resolved*, or settled. Observe how the conflict in this selection is finally resolved.

JO MEETS APOLLYON[1]

"GIRLS, WHERE ARE you going?" asked Amy, coming into their room one Saturday afternoon, and finding them getting ready to go out, with an air of secrecy which excited her curiosity.

"Never mind; little girls shouldn't ask questions," returned Jo sharply.

Now if there *is* anything mortifying to our feelings, when we are young, it is to be told that; and to be bidden to "run away, dear," is still more trying to us. Amy bridled up at this insult, and determined to find out the secret, if she teased for an

hour. Turning to Meg, who never refused her anything very long, she said coaxingly, "Do tell me! I should think you might let me go, too; for Beth is fussing over her piano, and I haven't got anything to do, and am *so* lonely."

"I can't, dear, because you aren't invited," began Meg; but Jo broke in impatiently, "Now, Meg, be quiet, or you will spoil it all. You can't go, Amy; so don't be a baby, and whine about it."

"You are going somewhere with Laurie, I know you are; you were whispering and laughing together, on the sofa, last night, and you stopped when I came in. Aren't you going with him?"

"Yes, we are; now do be still, and stop bothering."

---

1 **Apollyon:** In the Bible (the Book of Revelations), Apollyon is the angel of the bottomless pit. His name means "The Destroyer." In *Pilgrim's Progress*, a famous 17th-century book by John Bunyan, Apollyon is a fiend armed with fiery darts. He is overcome by Christian, the hero of the book, in the Valley of Humiliation.

Amy held her tongue, but used her eyes, and saw Meg slip a fan into her pocket.

"I know! I know! you're going to the theatre to see the 'Seven Castles!'" she cried; adding resolutely, "and I *shall* go, for Mother said I might see it; and I've got my rag money, and it was mean not to tell me in time."

"Just listen to me a minute, and be a good child," said Meg soothingly. "Mother doesn't wish you to go this week, because your eyes are not well enough yet to bear the light of this fairy piece. Next week you can go with Beth and Hannah, and have a nice time."

"I don't like that half as well as going with you and Laurie. Please let me; I've been sick with this cold so long, and shut up, I'm dying for some fun. Do, Meg! I'll be ever so good," pleaded Amy, looking as pathetic as she could.

"Suppose we take her. I don't believe Mother would mind, if we bundle her up well," began Meg.

"If *she* goes *I* shan't; and if I don't, Laurie won't like it; and it will be very rude, after he invited only us, to go and drag in Amy. I should think she'd hate to poke herself where she isn't wanted," said Jo crossly, for she disliked the trouble of overseeing a fidgety child, when she wanted to enjoy herself.

Her tone and manner angered Amy, who began to put her boots on, saying, in her most aggravating way, "I *shall* go; Meg says I may; and if I pay for myself, Laurie hasn't anything to do with it."

"You can't sit with us, for our seats are reserved, and you mustn't sit alone; so Laurie will give you his place, and that will spoil our pleasure; or he'll get another seat for you, and that isn't proper, when you weren't asked. You shan't stir a step; so you may just stay where you are," scolded Jo, crosser than ever, having just pricked her finger in her hurry.

Sitting on the floor, with one boot on, Amy began to cry, and Meg to reason with her, when Laurie called from below, and the two girls hurried down, leaving their sister wailing; for now and then she forgot her grown-up ways, and acted like a spoiled child. Just as the party was setting out, Amy called over the banisters, in a threatening tone, "You'll be sorry for this, Jo March; see if you ain't."

"Fiddlesticks!" returned Jo, slamming the door.

They had a charming time, for "The Seven Castles of the Diamond Lake" were as brilliant and wonderful as heart could wish. But, in spite of the comical red imps, sparkling elves, and gorgeous princes and princesses, Jo's pleasure had a drop of bitterness in it; the fairy queen's yellow curls reminded her of Amy; and between the acts she amused herself with wondering what her sister would do to make her "sorry for it." She and Amy had had many lively skirmishes in the course of their lives, for both had quick tempers, and were apt to be violent when fairly roused. Amy teased Jo, and Jo irritated Amy, and semi-occasional explosions occurred, of which both were much

ashamed afterward. Although the oldest, Jo had the least self-control, and had hard times trying to curb the fiery spirit which was continually getting her into trouble; her anger never lasted long, and, having humbly confessed her fault, she sincerely repented, and tried to do better. Her sisters used to say that they rather liked to get Jo into a fury, because she was such an angel afterward. Poor Jo tried desperately to be good, but her bosom enemy was always ready to flame up and defeat her; and it took years of patient effort to subdue it.

When they got home, they found Amy reading in the parlor. She assumed an injured air as they came in; never lifted her eyes from her book, or asked a single question. Perhaps curiosity might have conquered re-sentment, if Beth had not been there to inquire, and receive a glowing description of the play. On going up to put away her best hat, Jo's first look was toward the bureau; for, in their last quarrel, Amy had soothed her feelings by turning Jo's top drawer upside down on the floor. Everything was in its place, however; and after a hasty glance into her various closets, bags, and boxes, Jo decided that Amy had forgiven and forgotten her wrongs.

There Jo was mistaken; for next day she made a discovery which produced a tempest. Meg, Beth, and Amy were sitting together, late in the afternoon, when Jo burst into the room, looking excited, and demanding breathlessly, "Has anyone taken my book?"

Meg and Beth said "No," at once

and looked surprised; Amy poked the fire, and said nothing. Jo saw her color rise, and was down upon her in a minute.

"Amy, you've got it!"

"No, I haven't."

"You know where it is, then!"

"No, I don't."

"That's a fib!" cried Jo, taking her by the shoulders, and looking fierce enough to frighten a much braver child than Amy.

"It isn't. I haven't got it, don't know where it is now, and don't care."

"You know something about it, and you'd better tell at once, or I'll make you," and Jo gave her a slight shake.

"Scold as much as you like, you'll never see your silly old book again," cried Amy, getting excited in her turn.

"Why not?"

"I burnt it up."

"What! my little book I was so fond of, and worked over, and meant to finish before Father got home? Have you really burnt it?" said Jo, turning very pale, while her eyes kindled and her hands clutched Amy nervously.

"Yes, I did! I told you I'd make you pay for being so cross yesterday, and I have, so—"

Amy got no farther, for Jo's hot temper mastered her, and she shook Amy till her teeth chattered in her head; crying, in a passion of grief and anger,—

"You wicked, wicked girl! I never can write it again, and I'll never forgive you as long as I live."

Meg flew to rescue Amy, and Beth to pacify Jo, but Jo was quite beside herself; and, with a parting box on her sister's ear, she rushed out of the room up to the old sofa in the garret, and finished her fight alone.

The storm cleared up below, for Mrs. March came home, and, having heard the story, soon brought Amy to a sense of the wrong she had done her sister. Jo's book was the pride of her heart, and was regarded by her family as a literary sprout of great promise. It was only half a dozen little fairy tales, but Jo had worked over them patiently, putting her whole heart into her work, hoping to make something good enough to print. She had just copied them with great care, and had destroyed the old manuscript, so that Amy's bonfire had consumed the loving work of several years. It seemed a small loss to others, but to Jo it was a dreadful calamity, and she felt that it never could be made up to her. Beth mourned as for a departed kitten, and Meg refused to defend her pet; Mrs. March looked grave and grieved, and Amy felt that no one would love her till she had asked pardon for the act which she now regretted more than any of them.

When the tea bell rung, Jo appeared, looking so grim and unapproachable that it took all Amy's courage to say meekly,—

"Please forgive me, Jo; I'm very, very sorry."

"I never shall forgive you," was Jo's stern answer; and, from that moment, she ignored Amy entirely.

No one spoke of the great trouble —not even Mrs. March—for all had learned by experience that when Jo was in that mood words were wasted; and the wisest course was to wait till some little accident, or her own generous nature, softened Jo's resentment, and healed the breach. It was not a happy evening; for, though they sewed as usual, while their mother read aloud from Bremer, Scott, or Edgeworth, something was wanting, and the sweet home peace was disturbed. They felt this most when singing time came; for Beth could only play, Jo stood dumb as a stone, and Amy broke down, so Meg and Mother sung alone. But, in spite of their efforts to be as cheery as larks, the flutelike voices did not seem to chord as well as usual, and all felt out of tune.

As Jo received her good-night kiss, Mrs. March whispered gently,—

"My dear, don't let the sun go down upon your anger; forgive each other, help each other, and begin again tomorrow."

Jo wanted to lay her head down on that motherly bosom, and cry her grief and anger all away; but tears were an unmanly weakness, and she felt so deeply injured that she really *couldn't* quite forgive yet. So she winked hard, shook her head, and said, gruffly because Amy was listening,—

"It was an abominable thing, and she don't deserve to be forgiven."

With that she marched off to bed, and there was no merry or confidential gossip that night.

Amy was much offended that her overtures of peace had been repulsed, and began to wish she had not humbled herself, to feel more injured than ever, and to plume herself on her superior virtue in a way which was particularly exasperating. Jo still looked like a thundercloud, and nothing went well all day. It was bitter cold in the morning; she dropped her precious turnover in the gutter, Aunt March had an attack of fidgets, Meg was pensive, Beth *would* look grieved and wistful when she got home, and Amy kept making remarks about people who were always talking about being good, and yet wouldn't try, when other people set them a virtuous example.

"Everybody is so hateful, I'll ask Laurie to go skating. He is always kind and jolly, and will put me to rights, I know," said Jo to herself, and off she went.

Amy heard the clash of skates, and looked out with an impatient exclamation,—

"There! she promised I should go next time, for this is the last ice we shall have. But it's no use to ask such a crosspatch to take me."

"Don't say that; you *were* very naughty, and it *is* hard to forgive the loss of her precious little book; but I think she might do it now, and I guess she will, if you try her at the right minute," said Meg. "Go after them; don't say anything till Jo has got good-natured with Laurie, then take a quiet minute, and just kiss her, or do some kind thing, and I'm sure she'll be friends again, with all her heart."

"I'll try," said Amy, for the advice suited her; and, after a flurry to get ready, she ran after the friends, who

512

were just disappearing over the hill.

It was not far to the river, but both were ready before Amy reached them. Jo saw her coming, and turned her back; Laurie did not see, for he was carefully skating along the shore, sounding the ice, for a warm spell had preceded the cold snap.

"I'll go on to the first bend, and see if it's all right, before we begin to race," Amy heard him say, as he shot away, looking like a young Russian, in his fur-trimmed coat and cap.

Jo heard Amy panting after her run, stamping her feet and blowing her fingers, as she tried to put her skates on; but Jo never turned, and went slowly zigzaging down the river, taking a bitter, unhappy sort of satisfaction in her sister's troubles. She had cherished her anger till it grew strong, and took possession of her, as evil thoughts and feelings always do, unless cast out at once. As Laurie turned the bend, he shouted back,—

"Keep near the shore; it isn't safe in the middle."

Jo heard, but Amy was just struggling to her feet, and did not catch a word. Jo glanced over her shoulder, and the little demon she was harboring said in her ear,—

"No matter whether she heard or not, let her take care of herself."

Laurie had vanished round the bend; Jo was just at the turn, and Amy, far behind, striking out toward the smoother ice in the middle of the river. For a minute Jo stood still, with a strange feeling at her heart; then she resolved to go on, but something held and turned her round, just in time to see Amy throw up her hands and go down, with the sudden crash of rotten ice, the splash of water, and a cry that made Jo's heart stand still with fear. She tried to call Laurie, but her voice was gone; she tried to rush forward, but her feet seemed to have no strength in them; and, for a second, she could only stand motionless, staring, with a terror-stricken face, at the little blue hood above the black water. Something rushed swiftly by her, and Laurie's voice cried out,—

"Bring a rail; quick, quick!"

How she did it, she never knew; but for the next few minutes she worked as if possessed, blindly obeying Laurie, who was quite self-possessed, and, lying flat, held Amy up by his arm and hockey till Jo dragged a rail from the fence, and together they got the child out, more frightened than hurt.

"Now then, we must walk her home as fast as we can; pile our things on her, while I get off these confounded skates," cried Laurie, wrapping his coat round Amy, and tugging away at the straps, which never seemed so intricate before.

Shivering, dripping, and crying, they got Amy home; and, after an exciting time of it, she fell asleep, rolled in blankets, before a hot fire. During the bustle Jo had scarcely spoken; but flown about, looking pale and wild, with her things half off, her dress torn, and her hands cut and bruised by ice and rails, and refractory[2] buckles. When Amy was com-

2 **refractory:** unmanageable.

fortably asleep, the house quiet, and Mrs. March sitting by the bed, she called Jo to her, and began to bind up the hurt hands.

"Are you sure she is safe?" whispered Jo, looking remorsefully at the golden head, which might have been swept away from her sight forever under the treacherous ice.

"Quite safe, dear; she is not hurt, and won't even take cold, I think, you were so sensible in covering and getting her home quickly," replied her mother cheerfully.

"Laurie did it all; I only let her go. Mother, if she *should* die, it would be my fault"; and Jo dropped down beside the bed, in a passion of penitent tears, telling all that had happened, bitterly condemning her hardness of heart, and sobbing out her gratitude for being spared the heavy punishment which might have come upon her.

"It's my dreadful temper! I try to cure it; I think I have, and then it breaks out worse than ever. O Mother, what shall I do? what shall I do?" cried poor Jo, in despair.

"Watch and pray, dear; never get tired of trying; and never think it is impossible to conquer your fault," said Mrs. March, drawing the blowzy head to her shoulder, and kissing the wet cheek so tenderly that Jo cried harder than ever.

"You don't know, you can't guess how bad it is! It seems as if I could do anything when I'm in a passion; I get so savage, I could hurt anyone, and enjoy it. I'm afraid I *shall* do something dreadful some day, and spoil my life, and make everybody

hate me. O mother, help me, do help me!"

"I will, my child, I will. Don't cry so bitterly, but remember this day, and resolve, with all your soul, that you will never know another like it. Jo, dear, we all have our temptations, some far greater than yours, and it often takes us all our lives to conquer them. You think your temper is the worst in the world; but mine used to be just like it."

"Yours, Mother? Why, you are never angry!" and, for the moment, Jo forgot remorse in surprise.

"I've been trying to cure it for forty years, and have only succeeded in controlling it. I am angry nearly every day of my life, Jo; but I have learned not to show it; and I still hope to learn not to feel it, though it may take me another forty years to do so."

The patience and the humility of the face she loved so well was a better lesson to Jo than the wisest lecture, the sharpest reproof. She felt comforted at once by the sympathy and confidence given her; the knowledge that her mother had a fault like hers, and tried to mend it, made her own easier to bear and strengthened her resolution to cure it; though forty years seemed rather a long time to watch and pray, to a girl of fifteen.

"Mother, are you angry when you fold your lips tight together, and go out of the room sometimes, when Aunt March scolds, or people worry you?" asked Jo, feeling nearer and dearer to her mother than ever before.

"Yes, I've learned to check the

514

hasty words that rise to my lips; and when I feel that they mean to break out against my will, I just go away a minute, and give myself a little shake, for being so weak and wicked," answered Mrs. March, with a sigh and a smile, as she smoothed and fastened up Jo's disheveled hair.

"How did you learn to keep still? That is what troubles me—for the sharp words fly out before I know what I'm about; and the more I say the worse I get, till it's a pleasure to hurt people's feelings, and say dreadful things. Tell me how you do it, Marmee dear."

"My good mother used to help me—"

"As you do us—" interrupted Jo, with a grateful kiss.

"But I lost her when I was a little older than you are, and for years had to struggle on alone, for I was too proud to confess my weakness to any one else. I had a hard time, Jo, and shed a good many bitter tears over my failures; for, in spite of my efforts, I never seemed to get on. Then your father came, and I was so happy that I found it easy to be good. But by and by, when I had four little daughters round me, and we were poor, then the old trouble began again; for I am not patient by nature, and it tried me very much to see my children wanting anything."

"Poor Mother! what helped you then?"

"Your father, Jo. He never loses patience—never doubts or complains—but always hopes, and works and waits so cheerfully, that one is ashamed to do otherwise before him.

He helped and comforted me, and showed me that I must try to practice all the virtues I would have my little girls possess, for I was their example. It was easier to try for your sakes than for my own; a startled or surprised look from one of you, when I spoke sharply, rebuked me more than any words could have done; and the love, respect, and confidence of my children was the sweetest reward I could receive for my efforts to be the woman I would have them copy."

"O Mother, if I'm ever half as good as you, I shall be satisfied," cried Jo, much touched.

"I hope you will be a great deal better, dear; but you must keep watch over your 'bosom enemy,' as Father calls it, or it may sadden, if not spoil your life. You have had a warning; remember it, and try with heart and soul to master this quick temper, before it brings you greater sorrow and regret than you have known today."

"I will try, Mother; I truly will. But you must help me, remind me, and keep me from flying out. I used to see Father sometimes put his finger on his lips, and look at you with a very kind, but sober face, and you always folded your lips tight or went away: was he reminding you then?" asked Jo softly.

"Yes; I asked him to help me so, and he never forgot it, but saved me from many a sharp word by that little gesture and kind look."

Jo saw that her mother's eyes filled and her lips trembled, as she spoke; and, fearing that she had said too much, she whispered anxiously, "Was it wrong to watch you, and to speak of it? I didn't mean to be rude, but it's so comfortable to say all I think to you, and feel so safe and happy here."

"My Jo, you may say anything to your mother, for it is my greatest happiness and pride to feel that my girls confide in me, and know how much I love them."

"I thought I'd grieved you."

"No, dear; but speaking of Father reminded me how much I miss him, how much I owe him, and how faithfully I should watch and work to keep his little daughters safe and good for him."

"Yet you told him to go, Mother, and didn't cry when he went, and never complain now, or seem as if you needed any help," said Jo, wondering. . . .

Amy stirred, and sighed in her sleep; and, as if eager to begin at once to mend her fault, Jo looked up with an expression on her face which it had never worn before.

"I let the sun go down on my anger; I wouldn't forgive her, and today, if it hadn't been for Laurie, it might have been too late! How could I be so wicked?" said Jo, half aloud, as she leaned over her sister, softly stroking the wet hair scattered on the pillow.

As if she heard, Amy opened her eyes, and held out her arms, with a smile that went straight to Jo's heart. Neither said a word, but they hugged one another close, in spite of the blankets, and everything was forgiven and forgotten in one hearty kiss.

Understanding Literature

1. What does the title of this chapter mean? Who or what is Apollyon in the story?
2. Why do the sisters like to tease Jo?
3. In what ways are Amy and Jo alike?
4. Both Amy and Jo feel they have been wronged, one by not being allowed to go to the theater, the other by having her book destroyed. With whom are you more in sympathy? Why?
5. Between what two people does the conflict occur here? How is it resolved (settled)? How might the conflict have been prevented?
6. Which person in this selection also experiences an inner conflict? What is this inner conflict?
7. Is the inner conflict of this story resolved? Explain.
8. Are Jo's and Amy's reactions and behavior believable? Explain.
9. In describing the scene at the river the author says of Jo, "she had cherished her anger till it grew strong, and took possession of her. . . ." How is this quotation related to the theme of this chapter?

"And I was going to sea myself; to sea in a schooner, with a piping boatswain, and pig-tailed singing seamen; to sea, bound for an unknown island, and to seek for buried treasures!" So young Jim Hawkins describes to himself the voyage of the *Hispaniola* just before the ship leaves Bristol, England, and shortly before you meet him and some of the crew in this chapter from *Treasure Island*.

During a series of adventures in the early part of the book, Jim comes into possession of a treasure map while his mother and he are running the Admiral Benbow Inn. Jim's friends, Dr. Livesey and Squire Trelawney, agree to fit out a ship and sail in search of the treasure, taking Jim as cabin boy. The crew has been chosen, the supplies are aboard, and the *Hispaniola* is ready to weigh anchor as you begin to read these two chapters from the middle of this famous adventure story.

from Treasure Island

Robert Louis Stevenson

IMPROVING YOUR READING: *Treasure Island* is first and foremost a good story. Stories of the sea, pirates, and lost treasure have long fascinated people, and here these ingredients are skillfully put together by Robert Louis Stevenson. There is *suspense* in the book, that quality of holding the reader almost breathless as he waits to discover the outcome of an incident. There are clear *transitions* from one scene to the next as Jim tells the story. (A transition is a way of transferring the reader's thoughts smoothly from one subject to another and showing the relationship of these two subjects to each other.) And, what is of utmost importance to any good book, the characters seem real.

THE VOYAGE

ALL THAT NIGHT we were in a great bustle getting things stowed in their place, and boatfuls of the squire's friends, Mr. Blandly and the like, coming off to wish him a good voyage and a safe return. We never had a night at the "Admiral Benbow" when I had half the work; and I was dog-tired when, a little before dawn, the boatswain[1] sounded his pipe, and the crew began to man the capstan bars.[2] I might have been twice as weary, yet I would not have left the deck; all was so new and interesting to me—the brief commands, the shrill note of the whistle, the men bustling to their places in the glimmer of the ship's lanterns.

"Now, Barbecue, tip us a stave," cried one voice.

1 **boatswain** (bō'sən): officer in charge of rigging, anchors, and cables.

2 **capstan bars:** revolving drums or cylinders, used on shipboard for raising the anchor by traction upon a rope or cable passing around the drum. Sailors walked around the capstan, pushing in front of them the heavy bars by which it was turned.

"The old one," cried another.

"Ay, ay, mates," said Long John, who was standing by, with his crutch under his arm, and at once broke out in the air and words I knew so well—

Fifteen men on the dead man's chest—

And then the whole crew bore chorus:

Yo-ho-ho, and a bottle of rum!

And at the third "ho!" drove the bars before them with a will.

Even at that exciting moment it carried me back to the old "Admiral Benbow" in a second; and I seemed to hear the voice of the captain piping in the chorus. But soon the anchor was short up; soon it was hanging dripping at the bows; soon the sails began to draw, and the land and shipping to flit by on either side; and before I could lie down to snatch an hour of slumber the *Hispaniola* had begun her voyage to the Isle of Treasure.

I am not going to relate that voyage in detail. It was fairly prosperous. The ship proved to be a good ship, the crew were capable seamen and the captain thoroughly understood his business. But before we came the length of Treasure Island, two or three things had happened which require to be known.

Mr. Arrow,[3] first of all, turned out even worse than the captain had feared. He had no command among the men, and people did what they pleased with him. But that was by no means the worst of it; for after a day or two at sea he began to appear on deck with hazy eye, red cheeks, stuttering tongue, and other marks of drunkenness. Time after time he was ordered below in disgrace. Sometimes he fell and cut himself; sometimes he lay all day long in his little bunk at one side of the companion; sometimes for a day or two he would be almost sober and attend to his work at least passably.

In the meantime, we could never make out where he got the drink. That was the ship's mystery. Watch him as we pleased, we could do nothing to solve it; and when we asked him to his face, he would only laugh, if he were drunk, and if he were sober, deny solemnly that he ever tasted anything but water.

He was not only useless as an officer, and a bad influence amongst the men, but it was plain that at this rate he must soon kill himself outright; so nobody was much surprised, nor very sorry, when one dark night, with a head sea, he disappeared entirely and was seen no more.

"Overboard!" said the captain. "Well, gentlemen, that saves the trouble of putting him in irons."

But there we were, without a mate; and it was necessary, of course, to advance one of the men. The boatswain, Job Anderson, was the likeliest man aboard, and, though he kept his old title, he served in a way as mate. Mr. Trelawney had followed the sea, and his knowledge made him very useful, for he often took a watch himself in easy weather. And the coxswain,[4] Israel Hands, was a care-

---

3 **Mr. Arrow:** first mate of the *Hispaniola.*

4 **coxswain** (kŏk′sən, kŏk′swān): man in charge of a ship's boat and its crew.

ful, wily, old, experienced seaman, who could be trusted at a pinch with almost anything.

He was a great confidant of Long John Silver, and so the mention of his name leads me on to speak of our ship's cook, Barbecue, as the men called him.

Aboard ship he carried his crutch by a lanyard round his neck, to have both hands as free as possible. It was something to see him wedge the foot of the crutch against a bulkhead, and, propped against it, yielding to every movement of the ship, get on with his cooking like some one safe ashore. Still more strange was it to see him in the heaviest of weather cross the deck. He had a line or two rigged up to help him across the widest spaces—Long John's earrings, they were called; and he would hand himself from one place to another, now using the crutch, now trailing it alongside by the lanyard, as quickly as another man could walk. Yet some of the men who had sailed with him before expressed their pity to see him so reduced.

"He's no common man, Barbecue," said the coxswain to me. "He had good schooling in his young days, and can speak like a book when so minded; and brave—a lion's nothing alongside of Long John! I seen him grapple four, and knock their heads together—him unarmed."

All the crew respected and even obeyed him. He had a way of talking to each, and doing everybody some particular service. To me he was unweariedly kind; and always glad to see me in the galley, which he kept as clean as a new pin; the

ROBERT LOUIS STEVENSON

519

dishes hanging up burnished, and his parrot in a cage in one corner.

"Come away, Hawkins," he would say; "come and have a yarn with John. Nobody more welcome than yourself, my son. Sit you down and hear the news. Here's Cap'n Flint— I calls my parrot Cap'n Flint, after the famous buccaneer—here's Cap'n Flint predicting success to our v'yage. Wasn't you, cap'n?"

And the parrot would say, with great rapidity, "Pieces of eight![5] pieces of eight! pieces of eight!" till John threw his handkerchief over the cage.

"Now, that bird," he would say, "is, may be, two hundred years old, Hawkins—they lives forever mostly; and if anybody's seen more wickedness, it must be the devil himself. She's sailed with England, the great Cap'n England, the pirate. She's been at Madagascar, and at Malabar, and Surinam, and Providence, and Portobello. She was at the fishing up of the wrecked plate ships.[6] It's there she learned 'Pieces of eight,' and little wonder; three hundred and fifty thousand of 'em, Hawkins! She was at the boarding of the Viceroy of the Indies out of Goa,[7] she was; and to look at her you would think she was a babby. But you smelt powder —didn't you, cap'n?"

"Stand by to go about,"[8] the parrot would scream.

5 **Pieces of eight:** large silver coins of Spain.
6 **wrecked plate ships:** refers to the theft by pirates of a vast amount of silver from wrecked Spanish ships.
7 **boarding . . . Goa:** reference to one of Captain England's exploits, the capturing of a Portuguese ship.
8 **go about:** change direction; change tack.

"Ah, she's a handsome craft, she is," the cook would say, and give her sugar from his pocket, and then the bird would peck at the bars and swear straight on, passing belief for wickedness. "There," John would add, "you can't touch pitch and not be mucked, lad. Here's this poor old innocent bird o' mine swearing blue fire, and none the wiser, you may lay to that. She would swear the same, in a manner of speaking, before chaplain." And John would touch his forelock with a solemn way he had, that made me think he was the best of men.

In the meantime, squire and Captain Smollett were still on pretty distant terms with one another. The squire made no bones about the matter; he despised the captain. The captain, on his part, never spoke but when he was spoken to, and then sharp and short and dry, and not a word wasted. He owned, when driven into a corner, that he seemed to have been wrong about the crew, that some of them were as brisk as he wanted to see, and all had behaved fairly well. As for the ship, he had taken a downright fancy to her. "She'll lie a point nearer the wind than a man has a right to expect of his own married wife, sir. But," he would add, "all I say is we're not home again, and I don't like the cruise."

The squire, at this, would turn away and march up and down the deck, chin in air.

"A trifle more of that man," he would say, "and I should explode."

We had some heavy weather,

which only proved the qualities of the *Hispaniola*. Every man on board seemed well content, and they must have been hard to please if they had been otherwise; for it is my belief there was never a ship's company so spoiled since Noah put to sea. Double grog[9] was going on the least excuse; there was duff[10] on odd days, as, for instance, if the squire heard it was any man's birthday; and always a barrel of apples standing broached[11] in the waist, for any one to help himself that had a fancy.

"Never knew good come of it yet," the captain said to Dr. Livesey. "Spoil foc's'le[12] hands, make devils. That's my belief."

But good did come of the apple barrel, as you shall hear; for if it had not been for that, we should have had no note of warning, and might all have perished by the hand of treachery.

This was how it came about.

We had run up the trades[13] to get the wind of the island[14] we were after—I am not allowed to be more plain—and now we were running down for it with a bright lookout day and night. It was about the last day of our outward voyage, by the largest computation; some time that night, or, at latest, before noon of the morrow, we should sight the Treasure Island. We were heading S.S.W.,

and had a steady breeze abeam and a quiet sea. The *Hispaniola* rolled steadily, dipping her bowsprit now and then with a whiff of spray. All was drawing alow and aloft; everyone was in the bravest spirits, because we were now so near an end of the first part of our adventure.

Now, just after sundown, when all my work was over, and I was on my way to my berth, it occurred to me that I should like an apple. I ran on deck. The watch was all forward looking out for the island. The man at the helm was watching the luff[15] of the sail, and whistling away gently to himself; and that was the only sound excepting the swish of the sea against the bows and around the sides of the ship.

In I got bodily into the apple barrel, and found there was scarce an apple left; but, sitting down there in the dark, what with the sound of the waters and rocking movement of the ship, I had either fallen asleep, or was on the point of doing so, when a heavy man sat down with rather a clash close by. The barrel shook as he leaned his shoulders against it, and I was just about to jump up when the man began to speak. It was Silver's voice, and, before I had heard a dozen words, I would not have shown myself for all the world, but lay there, trembling and listening, in the extreme of fear and curiosity; for from these dozen words I understood that the lives of all the honest men aboard depended upon me alone.

9 grog: unsweetened mixture of spirits and water.
10 duff: pudding.
11 broached: opened.
12 foc's'le: the forward part of the vessel where the sailors live.
13 trades: trade winds which, on the north side of the equator, blow continually from the northeast.
14 to . . . island: to get to the windward of the island.

15 luff: forward or weather edge of the sail which the helmsman watches to be sure the sails are full.

WHAT I HEARD IN THE APPLE BARREL

"No, NOT I," said Silver. "Flint was cap'n; I was quartermaster,[16] along of my timber leg. The same broadside I lost my leg, old Pew lost his deadlights.[17] It was a master surgeon, him that ampytated me—out of college and all—Latin by the bucket, and what not; but he was hanged like a dog, and sun-dried like the rest, at Corso Castle.[18] That was Roberts's men, that was, and comed of changing names to their ships—*Royal Fortune* and so on. Now, what a ship was christened, so let her stay, I says. So it was with the *Cassandra,* as brought us all safe home from Malabar, after England took the Viceroy of the Indies; so it was with the old *Walrus,* Flint's old ship, as I've seen a-muck with the red blood and fit to sink with gold."

"Ah!" cried another voice, that of the youngest hand on board, and evidently full of admiration, "he was the flower of the flock, was Flint!"

"Davis was a man, too, by all accounts," said Silver. "I never sailed along of him; first with England, then with Flint, that's my story; and now here on my own account, in a manner of speaking. I laid by nine hundred safe, from England, and two thousand after Flint. That ain't bad for a man before the mast—all safe in bank. 'Tain't earning now, it's saving does it, you may lay to that. Where's all England's men now? I dunno. Where's Flint's? Why, most on 'em aboard here, and glad to get the duff—been begging before that, some on 'em. Old Pew, as had lost his sight, and might have thought shame, spends twelve hundred pound in a year, like a lord in Parliament. Where is he now? Well, he's dead now and under hatches; but for two year before that, shiver my timbers! the man was starving. He begged, and he stole, and he cut throats, and starved at that, by the powers!"

"Well, it aint much use, after all," said the young seaman.

"'Tain't much use for fools, you may lay to it—that, nor nothing," cried Silver. "But now, you look here: you're young, you are, but you're as smart as paint. I see that when I set my eyes on you, and I'll talk to you like a man."

You may imagine how I felt when I heard this abominable old rogue addressing another in the very same words of flattery as he had used to myself. I think, if I had been able, that I would have killed him through the barrel. Meantime, he ran on, little supposing he was overheard.

"Here it is about gentlemen of fortune. They lives rough, and they risk swinging, but they eat and drink like fighting cocks, and when a cruise is done, why, it's hundreds of pounds instead of hundreds of farthings in their pockets. Now, the most goes for rum and a good fling, and to sea again in their shirts. But that's not the course I lay. I puts it all away,

16 quartermaster: an officer on a ship who attends to the helm, binnacle, signals, etc. On a pirate ship this officer had much authority over the crew.
17 deadlights: sailors' slang for *eyes.*
18 Corso Castle: a British fort on the western coast of Africa.

FAMOUS CHARACTERS

some here, some there, and none too much anywheres, by reason of suspicion. I'm fifty, mark you; once back from this cruise, I set up gentleman in earnest. Time enough, too, says you. Ah, but I've lived easy in the meantime; never denied myself o' nothing heart desires, and slep' soft and ate dainty all my days, but when at sea. And how did I begin? Before the mast, like you!"

"Well," said the other, "but all the other money's gone now, aint it? You daren't show face in Bristol after this."

"Why, where might you suppose it was?" asked Silver, derisively.

"At Bristol, in banks and places," answered his companion.

"It were," said the cook; "it were when we weighed anchor. But my old missis has it all by now. And the 'Spy-glass' is sold, lease and goodwill and rigging; and the old girl's off to meet me. I would tell you where, for I trust you; but it 'ud make jealousy among the mates."

"And can you trust your missis?" asked the other.

"Gentlemen of fortune," returned the cook, "usually trusts little among themselves, and right they are, you may lay to it. But I have a way with me, I have. When a mate brings a slip on his cable—one as knows me, I mean—it won't be in the same world with old John. There was some that was feared of Pew, and some that was feared of Flint; but Flint his own self was feared of me. Feared he was, and proud. They was the roughest crew afloat, was Flint's; the devil himself would have been feared to go to sea with them. Well, now, I tell you, I'm not a boasting man, and you seen yourself how easy I keep company; but when I was quartermaster, *lambs* wasn't the word for Flint's old buccaneers. Ah, you may be sure of yourself in old John's ship."

"Well, I tell you now," replied the lad, "I didn't half a quarter like the job till I had this talk with you, John; but there's my hand on it now."

"And a brave lad you were, and smart, too," answered Silver, shaking hands so heartily that all the barrel shook, "and a finer figure head for a gentleman of fortune I never clapped my eyes on."

By this time I had begun to understand the meaning of their terms. By a "gentleman of fortune" they plainly meant neither more nor less than a common pirate, and the little scene that I had overheard was the last act in the corruption of one of the honest hands—perhaps of the last one left aboard. But on this point I was soon to be relieved, for Silver giving a little whistle, a third man strolled up and sat down by the party.

"Dick's square," said Silver.

"Oh, I know'd Dick was square," returned the voice of the coxswain, Israel Hands. "He's no fool, is Dick." And he turned his quid and spat. "But, look here," he went on, "here's what I want to know, Barbecue: how long are we a-going to stand off and on like a blessed bumboat? I've had a'most enough o' Cap'n Smollett; he's hazed me long enough, by thunder! I want to go into that cabin, I do. I want their pickles and wines, and that."

"Israel," said Silver, "your head aint much account, nor ever was. But you're able to hear, I reckon; leastways, your ears is big enough. Now, here's what I say: you'll berth forward, and you'll live hard, and you'll speak soft, and you'll keep sober, till I give the word; and you may lay to that, my son."

"Well, I don't say no, do I?" growled the coxswain. "What I say is, when? That's what I say."

"When! by the powers!" cried Silver. "Well now, if you want to know, I'll tell you when. The last moment I can manage; and that's when. Here's a first-rate seaman, Cap'n Smollett, sails the blessed ship for us. Here's this squire and doctor with a map and such—I don't know where it is, do I? No more do you, says you. Well, then, I mean this squire and doctor shall find the stuff, and help us to get it aboard, by the powers. Then we'll see. If I was sure of you all, sons of double Dutchmen, I'd have Cap'n Smollett navigate us halfway back again before I struck."

"Why, we're all seamen aboard here, I should think," said the lad Dick.

"We're all foc's'le hands, you mean," snapped Silver. "We can steer a course, but who's to set one? That's what all you gentlemen split on, first and last. If I had my way, I'd have Cap'n Smollett work us back into the trades at least; then we'd have no blessed miscalculations and a spoonful of water a day. But I

know the sort you are. I'll finish with 'em at the island, as soon's the blunt's on board, and a pity it is. But you're never happy till you're drunk. Split my sides, I've a sick heart to sail with the likes of you!"

"Easy all, Long John," cried Israel. "Who's a-crossin' of you?"

"Why, how many tall ships, think ye, now, have I seen laid aboard? and how many brisk lads drying in the sun at Execution Dock?"[19] cried Silver, "and all for this same hurry and hurry and hurry. You hear me? I seen a thing or two at sea, I have. If you would on'y lay your course, and p'int to windward, you would ride in carriages, you would. But not you! I know you. You'll have your mouthful of rum tomorrow, and go hang."

"Everybody know'd you was a kind of a chapling,[20] John; but there's others as could hand and steer as well as you," said Israel. "They liked a bit o' fun, they did. They wasn't so high and dry, nohow, but took their fling, like jolly companions every one."

"So?" says Silver. "Well, and where are they now? Pew was that sort, and he died a beggarman. Flint was, and he died of rum at Savannah. Ah, they was a sweet crew, they was! on'y, where are they?"

"But," asked Dick, "when we do lay 'em athwart, what are we to do with 'em, anyhow?"

---

19 Execution Dock: place in London where buccaneers were hanged.
20 chapling: chaplain.

"There's the man for me!" cried the cook, admiringly. "That's what I call business. Well, what would you think? Put 'em ashore like maroons? That would have been England's way. Or cut 'em down like that much pork? That would have been Flint's or Billy Bones's."

"Billy was the man for that," said Israel. " 'Dead men don't bite,' says he. Well, he's dead now hisself; he knows the long and short on it now; and if ever a rough hand come to port, it was Billy."

"Right you are," said Silver, "rough and ready. But mark you here: I'm an easy man—I'm quite the gentleman, says you; but this time it's serious. Dooty is dooty, mates. I give my vote—death. When I'm in Parlyment, and riding in my coach, I don't want none of these sea-lawyers in the cabin a-coming home, unlooked for, like the devil at prayers. Wait is what I say; but when the time comes, why let her rip!"

"John," cries the coxswain, "you're a man!"

"You'll say so, Israel, when you see," said Silver. "Only one thing I claim—I claim Trelawney. I'll wring his calf's head off his body with these hands, Dick!" he added, breaking off, "you just jump up, like a sweet lad, and get me an apple, to wet my pipe like."

You may fancy the terror I was in! I should have leaped out and run for it, if I had found the strength; but my limbs and heart alike misgave me. I heard Dick begin to rise, and then some one seemingly stopped him, and the voice of Hands exclaimed:

"Oh, stow that! Don't you get sucking of that bilge, John. Let's have a go of the rum."

"Dick," said Silver, "I trust you. I've a gauge on the keg, mind. There's the key; you fill a pannikin²¹ and bring it up."

Terrified as I was, I could not help thinking to myself that this must have been how Mr. Arrow got the strong waters that destroyed him.

Dick was gone but a little while, and during his absence Israel spoke straight on in the cook's ear. It was but a word or two that I could catch, and yet I gathered some important news; for, besides other scraps that tended to the same purpose, this whole clause was audible: "Not another man of them'll jine." Hence there were still faithful men on board.

When Dick returned, one after another of the trio took the pannikin and drank—one "To luck;" another with a "Here's to old Flint;" and Silver himself saying, in a kind of song, "Here's to ourselves, and hold your luff, plenty of prizes and plenty of duff."

Just then a sort of brightness fell upon me in the barrel, and, looking up, I found the moon had risen, and was silvering the mizzentop and shining white on the luff of the foresail; and almost at the same time the voice of the lookout shouted, "Land ho!"

21 pannikin: cup.

Understanding Literature

1. Find evidence in the story indicating that Jim at first thought Long John Silver to be brave, respected, kind, and charming; in general, "the best of men."

2. What words might Jim have used to describe Silver after he overheard the conversation while in the apple barrel?

3. At the beginning of the chapter called "What I Heard in the Apple Barrel" how many people are talking? Who are they? What is the purpose of Long John's talk? What is it that Jim learns in the apple barrel that makes him realize that "the lives of all the honest men aboard depended upon me alone"?

4. Silver is a pirate and a leader of those who will endanger the lives of all honest men aboard the ship. But what good qualities do you see in his character?

5. Long John Silver and Jim Hawkins are the two main characters in the book, as they are in these two chapters. But there are, of course, many other characters in the book who are interesting and who help carry the story along to its outcome. Two of these minor characters are Captain Smollett and Israel

Hands, the coxswain. (*a*) How would you characterize Captain Smollett? What in the story causes you to describe him in this way? (*b*) How would you characterize Israel Hands? Explain what in the story causes you to describe him in this way. (*c*) How do you think Captain Smollett would act if the pirate members of the crew mutinied? (*d*) What role can you imagine Israel Hands playing in such a mutiny?

6. How does Stevenson create a feeling of suspense in the apple-barrel episode?

7. How is the transition made from the discussion of the loss of the ship's mate to a description of Long John Silver? How is the transition made from the captain's statement that the foc's'le hands are being spoiled to the story of Jim's being trapped in the apple barrel?

Kenneth Grahame said that he wrote for children because they are "the only really living people." But the many readers of his masterpiece, *The Wind in the Willows,* have understood that he was writing not only for children but also for all those people who are really interested in life itself. The Rat and the Mole, living in Rat's hole by the river bank, the Toad in his magnificent Toad Hall, and the Badger, who lives in the Wild Wood nearby, are the main characters in this book. In this chapter you will see how Mr. Toad lures Rat and Mole away from their beloved river to the open road and the beginning of some of their adventures.

from The Wind in the Willows

Kenneth Grahame

IMPROVING YOUR READING: Rat, Mole, Toad, Badger, and the other animals in *The Wind in the Willows* are not only animals; they are something more. They are distinctly individual characters with many of the characteristics of the people you know. In fact, each of them seems to be much more of a real "person" than many fictional people you will meet in your reading. By this fanciful treatment of animals, giving them the traits of human beings, Kenneth Grahame has enchanted children and adults while commenting on people and the way they behave.

THE OPEN ROAD

"RATTY," SAID THE Mole suddenly, one bright summer morning, "if you please, I want to ask you a favor."

The Rat was sitting on the river bank, singing a little song. He had just composed it himself, so he was very taken up with it, and would not pay proper attention to Mole or anything else. Since early morning he had been swimming in the river in company with his friends the ducks. And when the ducks stood on their heads suddenly, as ducks will, he would dive down and tickle their necks just under where their chins would be if ducks had chins, till they were forced to come to the surface again in a hurry, spluttering and angry and shaking their feathers at him, for it is impossible to say quite *all* you feel when your head is under water. At last they implored him to go away and attend to his own affairs and leave them to mind theirs. So the Rat went away, and sat on the river bank in the sun, and made up a song about them, which he called

"DUCKS' DITTY."

All along the backwater,
Through the rushes tall,
Ducks are a-dabbling,
Up tails all!

Ducks' tails, drakes' tails,
Yellow feet a-quiver,
Yellow bills all out of sight
Busy in the river!

Slushy green undergrowth
Where the roach swim—
Here we keep our larder,
Cool and full and dim.

Everyone for what he likes!
We like to be
Heads down, tails up,
Dabbling free!

High in the blue above
Swifts whirl and call—
We are down a-dabbling
Up tails all!

"I don't know that I think so *very* much of that little song, Rat," observed the Mole cautiously. He was no poet himself and didn't care who knew it; and he had a candid nature.

"Nor don't the ducks neither," replied the Rat cheerfully. "They say, '*Why* can't fellows be allowed to do what they like *when* they like and *as* they like, instead of other fellows sitting on banks and watching them all the time and making remarks and poetry and things about them? What *nonsense* it all is!' That's what the ducks say."

"So it is, so it is," said the Mole, with great heartiness.

"No, it isn't!" cried the Rat indignantly.

"Well then, it isn't, it isn't," replied the Mole soothingly. "But what I wanted to ask you was, won't you take me to call on Mr. Toad? I've heard so much about him, and I do so want to make his acquaintance."

"Why, certainly," said the good-natured Rat, jumping to his feet and dismissing poetry from his mind for the day. "Get the boat out, and we'll paddle up there at once. It's never the wrong time to call on Toad. Early or late he's always the same fellow. Always good-tempered, always glad to see you, always sorry when you go!"

"He must be a very nice animal," observed the Mole, as he got into the boat and took the sculls, while the Rat settled himself comfortably in the stern.

"He is indeed the best of animals," replied Rat. "So simple, so good-natured, and so affectionate. Perhaps he's not very clever—we can't all be geniuses; and it may be that he is both boastful and conceited. But he has got some great qualities, has Toady."

Rounding a bend in the river, they came in sight of a handsome, dignified old house of mellowed red brick, with well-kept lawns reaching down to the water's edge.

"There's Toad Hall," said the Rat; "and that creek on the left, where the notice-board says, 'Private. No landing allowed,' leads to his boathouse, where we'll leave the boat. The stables are over there to the right. That's the banqueting hall you're looking at now—very old, that is. Toad is rather rich, you know, and this is really one of the nicest houses in these parts, though we never admit as much to Toad."

They glided up the creek, and the Mole shipped his sculls as they passed into the shadow of a large boathouse. Here they saw many handsome boats, slung from the crossbeams or hauled up on a slip, but none in the water; and the place had an unused and a deserted air.

The Rat looked around him. "I understand," said he. "Boating is played out. He's tired of it, and done with it. I wonder what new fad he has taken up now? Come along and let's look him up. We shall hear all about it quite soon enough."

They disembarked, and strolled across the gay flower-decked lawns in search of Toad, whom they presently happened upon resting in a wicker garden-chair, with a preoccupied expression of face, and a large map spread out on his knees.

"Hooray!" he cried, jumping up on seeing them, "this is splendid!" He shook the paws of both of them warmly, never waiting for an introduction to the Mole. "How *kind* of you!" he went on, dancing round them. "I was just going to send a boat down the river for you, Ratty, with strict orders that you were to be fetched up here at once, whatever you were doing. I want you badly— both of you. Now what will you take? Come inside and have something! You don't know how lucky it is, your turning up just now!"

"Let's sit quiet a bit, Toady!" said the Rat, throwing himself into an easy chair, while the Mole took another by the side of him and made some civil remark about Toad's "delightful residence."

"Finest house on the whole river," cried Toad boisterously. "Or anywhere else, for that matter," he could not help adding.

Here the Rat nudged the Mole. Unfortunately the Toad saw him do it, and turned very red. There was a moment's painful silence. Then Toad burst out laughing. "All right, Ratty," he said. "It's only my way, you know. And it's not such a very bad house, is it? You know you rather like it yourself. Now, look here. Let's be sensible. You are the very animals I wanted. You've got to help me. It's most important!"

"It's about your rowing, I suppose," said the Rat, with an innocent air. "You're getting on fairly well, though you splash a good bit still. With a great deal of patience, and any quantity of coaching, you may——"

"O, pooh! boating!" interrupted the Toad, in great disgust. "Silly boyish amusement. I've given that up *long* ago. Sheer waste of time, that's what it is. It makes me downright sorry to see you fellows, who ought to know better, spending all your energies in that aimless manner. No, I've discovered the real thing, the only genuine occupation for a lifetime. I propose to devote the remainder of mine to it, and can only regret the wasted years, that lie behind me, squandered in trivialities. Come with me, dear Ratty, and your amiable friend also, if he will be so very good, just as far as the stable yard, and you shall see what you shall see!"

He led the way to the stable yard accordingly, the Rat following with a most mistrustful expression; and there, drawn out of the coach house into the open, they saw a gypsy caravan, shining with newness, painted a

canary-yellow picked out with green, and red wheels.

"There you are!" cried the Toad, straddling and expanding himself. "There's real life for you, embodied in that little cart. The open road, the dusty highway, the heath, the common, the hedgerows, the rolling downs! Camps, villages, towns, cities! Here today, up and off to somewhere else tomorrow! Travel, change, interest, excitement! The whole world before you, and a horizon that's always changing! And mind, this is the very finest cart of its sort that was ever built, without any exception. Come inside and look at the arrangements. Planned 'em all myself, I did!"

The Mole was tremendously interested and excited, and followed him eagerly up the steps and into the interior of the caravan. The Rat only snorted and thrust his hands deep into his pockets, remaining where he was.

It was indeed very compact and comfortable. Little sleeping-bunks— a little table that folded up against the wall—a cooking stove, lockers, bookshelves, a bird cage with a bird in it; and pots, pans, jugs and kettles of every size and variety.

"All complete!" said the Toad triumphantly, pulling open a locker. "You see—biscuits, potted lobster, sardines—everything you can possibly want. Soda water here—baccy there —letter paper, bacon, jam, cards and dominoes—you'll find," he continued, as they descended the steps again, "you'll find that nothing whatever has been forgotten, when we make our start this afternoon."

"I beg your pardon," said the Rat slowly, as he chewed a straw, "but did I overhear you say something about 'we,' and 'start,' and 'this afternoon'?"

"Now, you dear good old Ratty," said Toad imploringly, "don't begin talking in that stiff and sniffy sort of way, because you know you've *got* to come. I can't possibly manage without you, so please consider it settled, and don't argue—it's the one thing I can't stand. You surely don't mean to stick to your dull fusty old river all your life, and just live in a hole in a bank, and *boat*? I want to show you the world! I'm going to make an *animal* of you, my boy!"

"I don't care," said the Rat doggedly. "I'm not coming, and that's flat. And I *am* going to stick to my old river, *and* live in a hole, *and* boat, as I've always done. And what's more, Mole's going to stick to me and do as I do, aren't you, Mole?"

"Of course I am," said the Mole loyally. "I'll always stick to you, Rat, and what you say is to be—has got to be. All the same, it sounds as if it might have been—well, rather fun, you know!" he added wistfully. Poor Mole! The Life Adventurous was so new a thing to him, and so thrilling; and this fresh aspect of it was so tempting; and he had fallen in love at first sight with the canary-colored cart and all its little fitments.

The Rat saw what was passing in his mind, and wavered. He hated disappointing people, and he was fond of the Mole, and would do almost anything to oblige him. Toad was watching both of them closely.

"Come along in and have some lunch," he said diplomatically, "and we'll talk it over. We needn't decide anything in a hurry. Of course, *I* don't really care. I only want to give pleasure to you fellows. 'Live for others!' That's my motto in life."

During luncheon—which was excellent, of course, as everything at Toad Hall always was—the Toad simply let himself go. Disregarding the Rat, he proceeded to play upon the inexperienced Mole as on a harp. Naturally a voluble[1] animal, and always mastered by his imagination, he painted the prospects of the trip and the joys of the open life and the roadside in such glowing colors that the Mole could hardly sit in his chair for excitement. Somehow, it soon seemed taken for granted by all three of them that the trip was a settled thing; and the Rat, though still unconvinced in his mind, allowed his good nature to override his personal objections. He could not bear to disappoint his two friends, who were already deep in schemes and anticipations, planning out each day's separate occupation for several weeks ahead.

When they were quite ready, the now triumphant Toad led his companions to the paddock and set them to capture the old gray horse, who, without having been consulted, and to his own extreme annoyance, had been told off by Toad for the dustiest job in this dusty expedition. He frankly preferred the paddock, and took a deal of catching. Meantime Toad packed the lockers still tighter with necessaries, and hung nose bags, nets of onions, bundles of hay, and baskets from the bottom of the cart. At last the horse was caught and harnessed, and they set off, all talking at once, each animal either trudging by the side of the cart or sitting on the shaft, as the humor took him. It was a golden afternoon. The smell of the dust they kicked up was rich and satisfying; out of thick orchards on either side the road, birds called and whistled to them cheerily; good-natured wayfarers, passing them, gave them "Good day," or stopped to say nice things about their beautiful cart; and rabbits, sitting at their front doors in the hedgerows, held up their fore paws, and said, "O my! O my! O my!"

Late in the evening, tired and happy and miles from home, they drew up on a remote common far from habitations, turned the horse loose to graze, and ate their simple supper sitting on the grass by the side of the cart. Toad talked big about all he was going to do in the days to come, while stars grew fuller and larger all around them, and a yellow moon, appearing suddenly and silently from nowhere in particular, came to keep them company and listen to their talk. At last they turned into their little bunks in the cart; and Toad, kicking out his legs, sleepily said, "Well, good night, you fellows! This is the real life for a gentleman! Talk about your old river!"

1 **voluble:** talkative.

KENNETH GRAHAME

"I *don't* talk about my river," replied the patient Rat. "You *know* I don't, Toad. But I *think* about it," he added pathetically, in a lower tone: "I think about it—all the time!"

The Mole reached out from under his blanket, felt for the Rat's paw in the darkness, and gave it a squeeze. "I'll do whatever you like, Ratty," he whispered. "Shall we run away tomorrow morning, quite early—*very* early—and go back to our dear old hole on the river?"

"No, no, we'll see it out," whispered back the Rat. "Thanks awfully, but I ought to stick by Toad till this trip is ended. It wouldn't be safe for him to be left to himself. It won't take very long. His fads never do. Good night!"

The end was indeed nearer than even the Rat suspected.

After so much open air and excitement the Toad slept very soundly, and no amount of shaking could rouse him out of bed next morning. So the Mole and Rat turned to, quietly and manfully, and while the Rat saw to the horse, and lit a fire, and cleaned last night's cups and platters, and got things ready for breakfast, the Mole trudged off to the nearest village, a long way off, for milk and eggs and various necessaries the Toad had, of course, forgotten to provide. The hard work had all been done, and the two animals were resting, thoroughly exhausted, by the time Toad appeared on the scene, fresh and gay, remarking what a pleasant easy life it was they were all leading now, after the cares and worries and fatigues of housekeeping at home.

They had a pleasant ramble that day over grassy downs and along narrow by-lanes, and camped, as before, on a common, only this time the two guests took care that Toad should do his fair share of work. In consequence, when the time came for starting next morning, Toad was by no means so rapturous about the simplicity of the primitive life, and indeed attempted to resume his place in his bunk, whence he was hauled by force. Their way lay, as before, across country by narrow lanes, and it was not till the afternoon that they came out on the high road, their first high road; and there disaster, fleet and unforeseen, sprang out on them —disaster momentous[2] indeed to their expedition, but simply overwhelming in its effect on the aftercareer of Toad.

They were strolling along the high road easily, the Mole by the horse's head, talking to him, since the horse had complained that he was being frightfully left out of it, and nobody considered him in the least; the Toad and the Water Rat walking behind the cart talking together—at least Toad was talking, and Rat was saying at intervals, "Yes, precisely; and what did *you* say to *him?*"—and thinking all the time of something very different, when far behind them they heard a faint warning hum, like the drone of a distant bee. Glancing back, they saw a small cloud of dust, with a dark center of energy, advancing on them at incredible speed, while

2 momentous: of great importance.

from out the dust a faint "Poop-poop!" wailed like an uneasy animal in pain. Hardly regarding it, they turned to resume their conversation, when in an instant (as it seemed) the peaceful scene was changed, and with a blast of wind and a whirl of sound that made them jump for the nearest ditch, it was on them! The "poop-poop" rang with a brazen shout in their ears, they had a moment's glimpse of an interior of glittering plate glass and rich morocco, and the magnificent motor car, immense, breath-snatching, passionate, with its pilot tense and hugging his wheel, possessed all earth and air for the fraction of a second, flung an enveloping cloud of dust that blinded and enwrapped them utterly, and then dwindled to a speck in the far distance, changed back into a droning bee once more.

The old gray horse, dreaming, as he plodded along, of his quiet paddock, in a new raw situation such as this simply abandoned himself to his natural emotions. Rearing, plunging, backing steadily, in spite of all the Mole's efforts at his head, and all the Mole's lively language directed at his better feelings, he drove the cart backwards toward the deep ditch at the side of the road. It wavered an instant—then there was a heart-rending crash—and the canary-colored cart, their pride and their joy, lay on its side in the ditch, an irredeemable wreck.

The Rat danced up and down in the road, simply transported with passion. "You villains!" he shouted, shaking both fists, "You scoundrels,

you highwaymen, you—you—road hogs!—I'll have the law on you! I'll report you! I'll take you through all the Courts!" His homesickness had quite slipped away from him, and for the moment he was the skipper of the canary-colored vessel driven on a shoal by the reckless jockeying of rival mariners, and he was trying to recollect all the fine and biting things he used to say to masters of steam launches when their wash, as they drove too near the bank, used to flood his parlor carpet at home.

Toad sat straight down in the middle of the dusty road, his legs stretched out before him, and stared fixedly in the direction of the disappearing motor car. He breathed short, his face wore a placid, satisfied expression, and at intervals he faintly murmured "Poop-poop!"

The Mole was busy trying to quiet the horse, which he succeeded in doing after a time. Then he went to look at the cart, on its side in the ditch. It was indeed a sorry sight. Panels and windows smashed, axles hopelessly bent, one wheel off, sardine tins scattered over the wide world, and the bird in the bird cage sobbing pitifully and calling to be let out.

The Rat came to help him, but their united efforts were not sufficient to right the cart. "Hi! Toad!" they cried. "Come and bear a hand, can't you!"

The Toad never answered a word, or budged from his seat in the road; so they went to see what was the matter with him. They found him in a sort of trance, a happy smile on his face, his eyes still fixed on the dusty wake of their destroyer. At intervals he was still heard to murmur "Poop-poop!"

The Rat shook him by the shoulder. "Are you coming to help us, Toad?" he demanded sternly.

"Glorious, stirring sight!" murmured Toad, never offering to move. "The poetry of motion! The *real* way to travel! The *only* way to travel! Here today—in next week to-morrow! Villages skipped, towns and cities jumped—always somebody else's horizon! O bliss! O poop-poop! O my! O my!"

"O *stop* being an ass, Toad!" cried the Mole despairingly.

"And to think I never *knew!*" went on the Toad in a dreamy monotone. "All those wasted years that lie behind me, I never knew, never even *dreamt!* But *now*—but now that I know, now that I fully realize! O what a flowery track lies spread before me, henceforth! What dust clouds shall spring up behind me as I speed on my reckless way! What carts I shall fling carelessly into the ditch in the wake of my magnificent onset! Horrid little carts—common carts—canary-colored carts!"

"What are we to do with him?" asked the Mole of the Water Rat.

"Nothing at all," replied the Rat firmly. "Because there is really nothing to be done. You see, I know him from old. He is now possessed. He has got a new craze, and it always takes him that way, in its first stage. He'll continue like that for days now, like an animal walking in a happy dream, quite useless for all practical purposes. Never mind him. Let's go and see what there is to be done about the cart."

A careful inspection showed them that, even if they succeeded in righting it by themselves, the cart would travel no longer. The axles were in a hopeless state, and the missing wheel was shattered into pieces.

The Rat knotted the horse's reins over his back and took him by the head, carrying the bird cage and its hysterical occupant in the other hand. "Come on!" he said grimly to the Mole. "It's five or six miles to the nearest town, and we shall just have to walk it. The sooner we make a start the better."

"But what about Toad?" asked the Mole anxiously, as they set off to-gether. "We can't leave him here, sitting in the middle of the road by himself, in the distracted state he's in! It's not safe. Supposing another Thing were to come along?"

"O, *bother* Toad," said the Rat savagely; "I've done with him!"

They had not proceeded very far on their way, however, when there was a pattering of feet behind them, and Toad caught them up and thrust a paw inside the elbow of each of them; still breathing short and staring into vacancy.

"Now, look here, Toad!" said the Rat sharply: "as soon as we get to the town, you'll have to go straight to the police station, and see if they know anything about that motor car and who it belongs to, and lodge a complaint against it. And then you'll have to go to a blacksmith's or a wheelwright's and arrange for the

536

cart to be fetched and mended and put to rights. It'll take time, but it's not quite a hopeless smash. Meanwhile, the Mole and I will go to an inn and find comfortable rooms where we can stay till the cart's ready, and till your nerves have recovered their shock."

"Police-station! Complaint!" murmured Toad dreamily. "Me *complain* of that beautiful, that heavenly vision that has been vouchsafed[3] me! *Mend* the *cart!* I've done with carts forever. I never want to see the cart, or to hear of it, again. O, Ratty! You can't think how obliged I am to you for consenting to come on this trip! I wouldn't have gone without you, and then I might never have seen that—that swan, that sunbeam, that thunderbolt! I might never have heard that entrancing sound, or smelt that bewitching smell! I owe it all to you, my best of friends!"

The Rat turned from him in despair. "You see what it is?" he said to the Mole, addressing him across Toad's head: "He's quite hopeless. I give it up—when we get to the town we'll go to the railway station, and with luck we may pick up a train there that'll get us back to River Bank tonight. And if ever you catch me going a-pleasuring with this provoking animal again!"—He snorted, and during the rest of that weary trudge addressed his remarks exclusively to Mole.

On reaching the town they went straight to the station and deposited Toad in the second-class waiting room, giving a porter twopence to keep a strict eye on him. They then left the horse at an inn stable, and gave what directions they could about the cart and its contents. Eventually, a slow train having landed them at a station not very far from Toad Hall, they escorted the spellbound, sleepwalking Toad to his door, put him inside it, and instructed his housekeeper to feed him, undress him, and put him to bed. Then they got out their boat from the boathouse, sculled down the river home, and at a very late hour sat down to supper in their own cozy riverside parlor, to the Rat's great joy and contentment.

The following evening the Mole, who had risen late and taken things very easy all day, was sitting on the bank fishing, when the Rat, who had been looking up his friends and gossiping, came strolling along to find him. "Heard the news?" he said. "There's nothing else being talked about, all along the river bank. Toad went up to Town by an early train this morning. And he has ordered a large and very expensive motor car."

3 **vouchsafed:** granted; given.

Understanding Literature

1. Describe the first scene of this chapter. What do you learn about Rat and Mole from what they say? from what they do?

2. You learn a good deal about Toad before you meet him. What do you learn about him from what Rat says? What do you learn about him from the description the author gives of his house, grounds, and boathouse?

3. As soon as you meet Toad, you learn even more about him from his own words and his way of talking. What does Toad's conversation before lunch reveal about his character?

4. Toad watches Mole and Rat closely after he proposes a trip in his new gypsy cart. Why does he suggest having some lunch before anything is decided?

5. How have you been prepared earlier in the story for the shift in Toad's passion for his cart to his new craze, cars?

6. Read again the description of the motor car's approach and passing. Notice the sounds that the car makes. What does it sound like in the distance? How are the sounds of the car described as it gets closer and passes? What sound do you hear again as it goes off into the distance? Notice that the author uses the name of the thing he is describing, a motor car, only once. Why do you think he uses the word just when he does in the description?

7. Why does the author capitalize the words Rat, Mole, and Toad throughout the selection?

8. Considering a real toad's appearance, why is it appropriate that the type of person which Mr. Toad resembles should be characterized in the form of a toad?

9. Turn back to Rat's song about the ducks. What does his song say about ducks? What does it imply about "everyone"? How does this song apply to the Rat and the Toad as well as to ducks? How can it apply to people as well?

Further Activities

1. ". . . that swan, that sunbeam, that thunderbolt! I might never have heard that entrancing sound, or smelt that bewitching smell!"

   Those are the words Toad uses to describe his new interest. They do *not* represent the point of view of Rat or Mole. Have you known anyone who has taken such an exaggerated interest in a new hobby, a sport, or another activity? Write a paragraph describing this interest or hobby from the point of view of the enthusiastic person.

2. The good-natured Rat did not want to go on the trip with Toad. He knew he would rather be on, in, or near the river, but he went to please his friends. If you have ever done something or gone somewhere just to please a friend, write about it, explaining why you went and the results of your doing so.

Focusing on Words

The italicized adjectives and adverbs in the following sentences all help to characterize one of the animals or the way he says something. First try to decide what you think the italicized words mean, judging from what you know of the situation being described and the character to whom they refer. Then look up each word in the glossary or a dictionary and choose the meaning which seems best suited to the use of the word in the sentence.

Words used to characterize Mole:
1. "He was no poet himself and didn't care who knew it; and he had a *candid* nature."
2. " 'Come with me, dear Ratty, and your *amiable* friend also, if he will be so very good. . . .' "
3. " 'All the same, it sounds as if it might have been—well, rather fun, you know!' he added *wistfully*."

Words used to characterize Rat:
4. " 'I don't care,' said the Rat *doggedly*. 'I'm not coming, and that's flat.' "
5. " 'Come on!' he said *grimly* to the Mole."

Words used to characterize Toad:
6. " '. . . it may be that he is both boastful and *conceited*.' "
7. " 'Finest house on the whole river,' cried Toad *boisterously*."
8. " 'Come along in, and have some lunch,' he said *diplomatically*, 'and we'll talk it over.' "
9. "Naturally a *voluble* animal, and always mastered by his imagination, he painted the prospects of the trip and the joys of the open life and the roadside in such glowing colors that the Mole could hardly sit in his chair for excitement."

Alone on an uninhabited island after a shipwreck, Robinson Crusoe faces the problem of how to survive. The adventures of Crusoe on the island are only a part of a whole book, but the island episode is the central part of the book and the best known. *The Life and Strange Surprising Adventures of Robinson Crusoe* was first published in 1719 and very soon became popular.

In the section of the book included here you will read about the first days on the island after the shipwreck. The first night ashore Crusoe slept in a tree. You meet him on the morning of the second day as he begins to solve the problems of his situation. Consider why Robinson Crusoe's nature well equips him to solve these problems.

from Robinson Crusoe

Daniel Defoe

IMPROVING YOUR READING: Robinson Crusoe's story is *fiction;* it is Defoe's imaginative account of a man's adventures. He based some of Robinson Crusoe's experiences on those of Alexander Selkirk, a sailor who did, in fact, live on an uninhabited island from 1704 to 1709. But the way that Defoe wrote his story leads the reader to believe that Robinson Crusoe's experiences actually did happen. Decide, as you read, how Defoe makes his story believable.

WHEN I WAKED it was broad day, the weather clear, and the storm abated, so that the sea did not rage and swell as before: but that which surprised me most, was, that the ship was lifted off in the night from the sand where she lay, by the swelling of tide, and was driven up almost as far as the rock which I first mentioned, where I had been so bruised by the dashing me against it; this being within about a mile from the shore where I was, and the ship seeming to stand upright still, I wished myself on board, that, at least, I might have some necessary things for my use.

When I came down from my apartment in the tree, I looked about me again, and the first thing I found was a boat, which lay as the wind and the sea had tossed her up upon the land, about two miles on my right hand. I walked as far as I could upon the shore to have got to her, but found a neck or inlet of water between me and the boat, which was about half a mile broad, so I came back for the present, being more intent upon getting at the ship, where I hoped to find something for my present subsistence.

A little after noon I found the sea very calm, and the tide ebbed so far out, that I could come within a quarter of a mile of the ship; and here I found a fresh renewing of my grief, for I saw evidently, that if we had kept on board, we had all been safe, that is to say, we had all got safe on shore, and I had not been so miserable as to be left entirely destitute of all comfort and company, as I now was; this forced tears from my eyes again, but as there was little relief in that, I resolved, if possible, to get to the ship, so I pulled off my clothes, for the weather was hot to the extremity, and took the water; but when I came to the ship, my difficulty was still greater to know how to get on board, for as she lay aground, and high out of the water, there was nothing within my reach to lay hold of. I swam round her twice, and the second time I spied a small piece of a rope, which I wondered I did not see at first, hang down by the fore-chains so low, as that with great difficulty I got hold of it, and by the help of that rope, got up into the forecastle of the ship; here I found that the ship was bulged, and had a great deal of water in her hold, but that she lay so on the side of a bank of hard sand, or rather earth, that her stern lay lifted up upon the bank, and her head low almost to the water; by this means all her quarter was free, and all that was in that part was dry; for you may be sure my first work was to search and to see what was spoiled and what was free; and first I found that all the ship's provisions were dry and untouched by the water, and being very well disposed to eat, I went to the bread-room and filled my pockets with biscuit, and eat it as I went about other things, for I had no time to lose; I also found some rum in the great cabin, of which

I took a large dram, and which I had indeed need enough of to spirit me for what was before me. Now I wanted nothing but a boat to furnish myself with many things which I foresaw would be very necessary to me.

It was in vain to sit still and wish for what was not to be had, and this extremity[1] roused my application; we had several spare yards, and two or three large spars of wood, and a spare topmast or two in the ship. I resolved to fall to work with these, and flung as many of them overboard as I could manage for their weight, tying every one with a rope that they might not drive away; when this was done I went down the ship's side, and pulling them to me, I tied four of them fast together at both ends as well as I could, in the form of a raft, and laying two or three short pieces of plank upon them crossways, I found I could walk upon it very well, but that it was not able to bear any great weight, the pieces being too light; so I went to work, and with the carpenter's saw I cut a spare topmast into three lengths, and added them to my raft, with a great deal of labor and pains, but hope of furnishing myself with necessaries encouraged me to go beyond what I should have been able to have done upon another occasion.

My raft was now strong enough to bear any reasonable weight; my next care was what to load it with, and how to preserve what I laid upon it

1 **extremity:** necessity.

from the surf of the sea. But I was not long considering this: I first laid all the plank or boards upon it that I could get, and having considered well what I most wanted, I first got three of the seamen's chests, which I had broken open and emptied, and lowered them down upon my raft; the first of these I filled with provisions, viz.:[2] bread, rice, three Dutch cheeses, five pieces of dried goat's flesh, which we lived much upon, and a little remainder of European corn which had been laid by for some fowls which we brought to sea with us, but the fowls were killed; there had been some barley and wheat together, but, to my great disappointment, I found afterwards that the rats had eaten or spoiled it all; as for liquors, I found several cases of bottles belonging to our skipper, in which were some cordial waters,[3] and in all about five or six gallons of rack:[4] these I stowed by themselves, there being no need to put them into the chest, nor no room for them. While I was doing this, I found the tide began to flow, though very calm, and I had the mortification to see my coat, shirt, and waistcoat, which I had left on shore upon the sand, swim away; as for my breeches, which were only linen and open-kneed, I swam on board in them and my stockings. However, this put me upon rummaging for clothes, of which I found enough, but took no more than I wanted for present use, for I had other things which my eye was more

upon, as first tools to work with on shore, and it was after long searching that I found out the carpenter's chest, which was indeed a very useful prize to me, and much more valuable than a shiploading of gold would have been at that time. I got it down to my raft, even whole as it was, without losing time to look into it, for I knew in general what it contained.

My next care was for some ammunition, and arms: there were two very good fowling pieces[5] in the great cabin, and two pistols; these I secured first, with some powder horns, and a small bag of shot, and two old rusty swords: I knew there were three barrels of powder in the ship, but knew not where our gunner had stowed them, but with much search I found them, two of them dry and good, the third had taken water; those two I got to my raft, with the arms, and now I thought myself pretty well freighted, and began to think how I should get to shore with them, having neither sail, oar, or rudder, and the least capful of wind would have overset all my navigation.

I had three encouragements, 1. A smooth calm sea, 2. The tide rising and setting in to the shore, 3. What little wind there was blew me towards the land; and thus, having found two or three broken oars belonging to the boat, and besides the tools which were in the chest, I found two saws, an ax, and a hammer, and with this cargo I put to sea. For a mile, or thereabouts, my raft

2 **viz.:** *videlicet*, Latin word meaning "namely."
3 **cordial waters:** spiritous liquors.
4 **rack:** arrack, an Eastern liquor made from rum and flavored with fruits and plants.

5 **fowling pieces:** lightweight guns.

went very well, only that I found it drive a little distant from the place where I had landed before, by which I perceived that there was some indraft of the water, and consequently I hoped to find some creek or river there, which I might make use of as a port to get to land with my cargo.

As I imagined, so it was, there appeared before me a little opening of the land, and I found a strong current of the tide set into it, so I guided my raft as well as I could to keep in the middle of the stream: but here I had like to have suffered a second shipwreck, which, if I had, I think verily would have broke my heart, for knowing nothing of the coast, my raft run aground at one end of it upon a shoal,[6] and not being aground at the other end, it wanted but a little that all my cargo had slipped off toward that end that was afloat, and so fallen into the water. I did my utmost by setting my back against the chests, to keep them in their places, but could not thrust off the raft with all my strength, neither durst I stir from the posture I was in, but holding up the chests with all my might, stood in that manner near half an hour, in which time the rising of the water brought me a little more upon a level, and a little after, the water still rising, my raft floated again, and I thrust her off with the oar I had, into the channel, and then driving up higher, I at length found myself in the mouth of a little river, with land on both sides, and a strong current or tide running up. I looked on both sides for a proper place to get to shore, for I was not willing to be driven too high up the river, hoping in time to see some ship at sea, and therefore resolved to place myself as near the coast as I could.

At length I spied a little cove on the right shore of the creek, to which with great pain and difficulty I guided my raft, and at last got so near, as that, reaching ground with my oar, I could thrust her directly in, but here I had liked to have dipped all my cargo into the sea again; for that shore lying pretty steep, that is to say sloping, there was no place to land, but where one end of my float, if it run on shore, would lie so high, and the other sink lower as before, that it would endanger my cargo again: all that I could do was to wait till the tide was at highest, keeping the raft with my oar like an anchor to hold the side of it fast to the shore, near a flat piece of ground, which I expected the water would flow over; and so it did: as soon as I found water enough, for my raft drew about a foot of water, I thrust her on upon that flat piece of ground, and there fastened or moored her by sticking my two broken oars into the ground; one on one side near one end, and one on the other side near the other end; and thus I lay till the water ebbed away, and left my raft and all my cargo safe on shore.

My next work was to view the country, and seek a proper place for my habitation, and where to stow my goods to secure them from whatever might happen; where I was I yet

<hr>

6 **shoal:** sand bank where the water is shallow.

knew not, whether on the continent or on an island, whether inhabited or not inhabited, whether in danger of wild beasts or not: there was a hill not above a mile from me, which rose up very steep and high, and which seemed to overtop some other hills which lay as in a ridge from it northward; I took out one of the fowling pieces, and one of the pistols, and an horn of powder, and thus armed I traveled for discovery up to the top of that hill, where, after I had with great labor and difficulty got to the top, I saw my fate to my great affliction, (viz.) that I was in an island environed[7] every way with the sea, no land to be seen, except some rocks which lay a great way off, and two small islands less than this, which lay about three leagues to the west.

I found also that the island I was in was barren, and, as I saw good reason to believe, uninhabited, except by wild beasts, of whom however I saw none, yet I saw abundance of fowls, but knew not their kinds, neither when I killed them could I tell what was fit for food, and what not; at my coming back, I shot at a great bird which I saw sitting upon a tree on the side of a great wood: I believe it was the first gun that had been fired there since the creation of the world; I had no sooner fired, but from all the parts of the wood there arose an innumerable number of fowls of many sorts, making a confused screaming, and crying every one according to his usual note; but not one of them of any kind that I knew: as for the creature I killed, I

7 environed: surrounded.

took it to be a kind of a hawk, its color and beak resembling it, but had no talons or claws more than common: its flesh was carrion, and fit for nothing.

Contented with this discovery, I came back to my raft, and fell to work to bring my cargo on shore, which took me up the rest of that day, and what to do with myself at night I knew not, nor indeed where to rest; for I was afraid to lie down on the ground, not knowing but some wild beast might devour me, though, as I afterwards found, there was really no need for those fears.

However, as well as I could, I barricadoed[8] myself round with the chests and boards that I had brought on shore, and made a kind of a hut for that night's lodging; as for food, I yet saw not which way to supply myself, except that I had seen two or three creatures like hares run out of the wood where I shot the fowl.

I now began to consider, that I might yet get a great many things out of the ship, which would be useful to me, and particularly some of the rigging, and sails, and such other things as might come to land, and I resolved to make another voyage on board the vessel, if possible; and as I knew that the first storm that blew must necessarily break her all in pieces, I resolved to set all other things apart, until I got everything out of the ship that I could get; then I called a council, that is to say, in my thoughts, whether I should take back the raft, but this appeared impracticable; so I resolved to go as before, when the tide was down, and I did so, only that I stripped before I went from my hut, having nothing on but a checkered shirt, and a pair of linen drawers, and a pair of pumps on my feet.

I got on board the ship, as before, and prepared a second raft, and having had experience of the first, I neither made this so unwieldy, nor loaded it so hard, but yet I brought away several things very useful to me; as first, in the carpenter's stores I found two or three bags full of nails and spikes, a great screw jack,[9] a dozen or two of hatchets, and above all, that most useful thing called a grindstone; all these I secured together, with several things belonging to the gunner, particularly two or three iron crows,[10] and two barrels of musket bullets, seven muskets, and another fowling piece, with some small quantity of powder more; a large bag full of small shot, and a great roll of sheet lead: but this last was so heavy, I could not hoist it up to get it over the ship's side.

Besides these things, I took all the men's clothes that I could find, and a spare fore-topsail, a hammock, and some bedding; and with this I loaded my second raft, and brought them all safe on shore, to my very great comfort.

I was under some apprehensions during my absence from the land, that at least my provisions might be

---

9 screw jack: hoisting machine worked with a screw.
10 crows: bars of iron.

8 barricadoed: barricaded; fortified.

devoured on shore; but when I came back, I found no sign of any visitor, only there sat a creature like a wild-cat upon one of the chests, which when I came towards it, ran away a little distance, and then stood still; she sat very composed, and unconcerned, and looked full in my face, as if she had a mind to be acquainted with me; I presented my gun at her, but as she did not understand it, she was perfectly unconcerned at it, nor did she offer to stir away; upon which I tossed her a bit of biscuit, though by the way I was not very free of it, for my store was not great: however, I spared her a bit, I say, and she went to it, smelled of it, and ate it, and looked (as pleased) for more, but I thanked her, and could spare no more; so she marched off.

Having got my second cargo on shore, though I was fain[11] to open the barrels of powder, and bring them by parcels, for they were too heavy, being large casks, I went to work to make me a little tent with the sail and some poles which I cut for that purpose, and into this tent I brought everything that I knew would spoil, either with rain or sun, and I piled all the empty chests and casks up in a circle round the tent, to fortify it from any sudden attempt, either from man or beast.

When I had done this I blocked up the door of the tent with some boards within, and an empty chest set up on end without, and spreading one of the beds upon the ground, laying my two pistols just at my head, and my gun at length by me, I went to bed for the first time, and slept very quietly all night, for I was very weary and heavy, for the night before I had slept little, and had labored very hard all day, as well as to fetch all those things from the ship, as to get them on shore.

I had the biggest magazine[12] of all kinds now that ever were laid up I believe, for one man, but I was not satisfied still; for while the ship sat upright in that posture, I thought I ought to get everything out of her that I could; so every day at low water I went on board, and brought away something or other: but particularly the third time I went, I brought away as much of the rigging as I could, as also all the small ropes and rope-twine I could get, with a piece of spare canvas, which was to mend the sails upon occasion, the barrel of wet gunpowder: in a word, I brought away all the sails first and last, only that I was fain to cut them in pieces, and bring as much at a time as I could; for they were no more useful to be sails, but as mere canvas only.

But that which comforted me more still, was, that at last of all, after I had made five or six such voyages as these, and thought I had nothing more to expect from the ship that was worth my meddling with, I say, after all this, I found a great hogshead[13] of bread, and three large runlets[14] of rum or spirits, and a box

---

11 **fain:** obliged; compelled.

12 **magazine:** stock of provisions and goods.
13 **hogshead:** large cask or barrel.
14 **runlets:** casks holding about eighteen gallons.

of sugar, and a barrel of fine flour; this was surprising to me, because I had given over expecting any more provisions, except what was spoiled by the water; I soon emptied the hogshead of that bread, and wrapped it up parcel by parcel in pieces of the sails, which I cut out; and in a word, I got all this safe on shore also.

The next day I made another voyage; and now having plundered the ship of what was portable and fit to hand out, I began with the cables; and cutting the great cable into pieces, such as I could move, I got two cables and a hawser[15] on shore, with all the ironwork I could get; and having cut down the spritsail-yard, and the mizzen-yard, and everything I could to make a large raft, I loaded it with all those heavy goods, and came away. But my good luck began now to leave me; for this raft was so unwieldy, and so overladen, that after I was entered the little cove, where I had landed the rest of my goods, not being able to guide it so handily as I did the other, it overset, and threw me and all my cargo into the water; as for myself it was no great harm, for I was near the shore; but as to my cargo, it was great part of it lost, especially the iron, which I expected would have been of great use to me: however, when the tide was out, I got most of the pieces of cables ashore, and some of the iron, though with infinite labor; for I was fain to dip for it into the water, a work which fatigued me very much.

After this I went every day on board, and brought away what I could get.

I had been now thirteen days on shore, and had been eleven times on board the ship; in which time I had brought away all that one pair of hands could well be supposed capable to bring, though I believe verily, had the calm weather held, I should have brought away the whole ship piece by piece: but preparing the twelfth time to go on board, I found the wind begin to rise; however, at low water I went on board, and though I thought I had rummaged the cabin so effectually, as that nothing more could be found, yet I discovered a locker with drawers in it, in one of which I found two or three razors, and one pair of large scissors, with some ten or a dozen of good knives and forks; in another I found about thirty-six pounds[16] of value in money, some European coin, some Brazil, some pieces of eight,[17] some gold, some silver.

I smiled to myself at the sight of this money. O Drug! said I aloud, what art thou good for? thou art not worth to me, no not the taking off of the ground: one of those knives is worth all this heap: I have no manner of use for thee, e'en remain where thou art, and go to the bottom as a creature whose life is not worth saving. However, upon second thoughts, I took it away, and wrapping all this in a piece of canvas, I began to think of making another raft, but while I was preparing this, I

---

15 **hawser:** large rope used for securing a ship.

16 **pounds:** English monetary units.
17 **pieces of eight:** large silver coins of Spain.

FAMOUS CHARACTERS

found the sky overcast, and the wind began to rise, and in a quarter of an hour it blew a fresh gale from the shore; it presently occurred to me, that it was in vain to pretend to make a raft with the wind offshore, and that it was my business to be gone before the tide of flood began, otherwise I might not be able to reach the shore at all. Accordingly I let myself down into the water, and swam across the channel, which lay between the ship and the sands, and even that with difficulty enough, partly with the weight of the things I had about me, and partly the roughness of the water, for the wind rose very hastily, and before it was quite high water, it blew a storm.

But I was gotten home to my little tent, where I lay with all my wealth about me very secure. It blew very hard all the night, and in the morning when I looked out, behold no more ship was to be seen; I was a little surprised, but recovered myself with this satisfactory reflection, viz.: that I had lost no time, nor abated no diligence[18] to get everything out of her that could be useful to me, and that indeed there was little left in her that I was able to bring away if I had had more time.

I now gave over any more thoughts of the ship, or of anything out of her, except what might drive on shore from her wreck, as indeed divers[19] pieces of her afterwards did; but those things were of small use to me.

My thoughts were now wholly em-

18 nor abated no diligence: nor lessened my efforts.
19 divers: various.

ployed about securing myself against either savages, if any should appear, or wild beasts, if any were in the island; and I had many thoughts of the method how to do this, and what kind of dwelling to make, whether I should make me a cave in the earth, or a tent upon the earth: and, in short, I resolved upon both, the manner and description of which, it may not be improper to give an account of.

I soon found the place I was in was not for my settlement, particularly because it was upon a low moorish ground near the sea, and I believed would not be wholesome, and more particularly because there was no fresh water near it, so I resolved to find a more healthy and more convenient spot of ground.

I consulted several things in my situation which I found would be proper for me. 1st, health, and fresh water I just now mentioned. 2dly, shelter from the heat of the sun. 3dly, security from ravenous creatures, whether men or beasts. 4thly, a view to the sea, that if God sent any ship in sight, I might not lose any advantage for my deliverance, of which I was not willing to banish all my expectation yet.

In search of a place proper for this, I found a little plain on the side of a rising hill, whose front toward this little plain was steep as a house-side, so that nothing could come down upon me from the top; on the side of this rock there was a hollow place worn a little way in like the entrance or door of a cave, but there was not really any cave or way into the rock at all.

On the flat of the green, just before this hollow place, I resolved to pitch my tent; this plain was not above an hundred yards broad and about twice as long, and lay like a green before my door, and at the end of it descended irregularly every way down into the low-grounds by the seaside. It was on the N.N.W. side of the hill, so that I was sheltered from the heat every day, till it came to a W. and by S. sun, or thereabouts, which in those countries is near the setting.

Before I set up my tent, I drew a half circle before the hollow place, which took in about ten yards in its semidiameter from the rock, and twenty yards in its diameter, from its beginning and ending.

In this half circle I pitched two rows of strong stakes, driving them into the ground till they stood very firm like piles, the biggest end being out of the ground about five foot and a half, and sharpened on the top: the two rows did not stand above six inches from one another.

Then I took the pieces of cable which I had cut in the ship, and I laid them in rows one upon another, within the circle, between these two rows of stakes, up to the top, placing other stakes in the inside, leaning against them, about two foot and a half high, like a spur to a post, and this fence was so strong, that neither man or beast could get into it or over it. This cost me a great deal of time and labor, especially to cut the piles in the woods, bring them to the place, and drive them into the earth.

The entrance into this place I

made to be not by a door, but by a short ladder to go over the top, which ladder, when I was in, I lifted over after me, and so I was completely fenced in, and fortified, as I thought, from all the world, and consequently slept secure in the night, which otherwise I could not have done, though as it appeared afterward, there was no need of all this caution from the enemies that I apprehended danger from.

Into this fence or fortress, with infinite labor, I carried all my riches, all my provisions, ammunition and stores, of which you have the account above, and I made me a large tent, which, to preserve me from the rains that in one part of the year are very violent there, I made double, viz., one smaller tent within, and one large tent above it, and covered the uppermost with a large tarpaulin which I had saved among the sails.

And now I lay no more for a while in the bed which I had brought on shore, but in a hammock, which was indeed a very good one, and belonged to the mate of the ship.

Into this tent I brought all my provisions, and everything that would spoil by the wet, and having thus enclosed all my goods, I made up the entrance, which till now I had left open, and so passed and repassed, as I said, by a short ladder.

When I had done this, I began to work my way into the rock, and bringing all the earth and stones that I dug down out through my tent, I laid them up within my fence in the nature of a terrace, that so it raised the ground within about a foot and a half; and thus I made me a cave just behind my tent, which served me like a cellar to my house.

It cost me much labor, and many days, before all these things were brought to perfection, and therefore I must go back to some other things which took up some of my thoughts. At the same time it happened after I had laid my scheme for the setting up my tent, and making the cave, that a storm of rain falling from a thick dark cloud, a sudden flash of lightning happened, and after that a great clap of thunder, as is naturally the effect of it; I was not so much surprised with the lightning as I was with a thought which darted into my mind as swift as the lightning itself. O my powder! My very heart sunk within me, when I thought, that at one blast all my powder might be destroyed, on which, not my defense only, but the providing me food, as I thought, entirely depended; I was nothing near so anxious about my own danger, though had the powder took fire, I had never known who had hurt me.

Such impression did this make upon me, that after the storm was over, I laid aside all my works, my building, and fortifying, and applied myself to make bags and boxes to separate the powder, and keep it a little and a little in a parcel, in hope that whatever might come, it might not all take fire at once, and to keep it so apart that it should not be possible to make one part fire another. I finished this work in about a fortnight,[20] and I think my powder,

20 a fortnight: two weeks.

which in all was about 240 lb. weight, was divided in not less than a hundred parcels; as to the barrel that had been wet, I did not apprehend any danger from that, so I placed it in my new cave, which in my fancy I called my kitchen, and the rest I hid up and down in holes among the rocks, so that no wet might come to it, marking very carefully where I laid it.

In the interval of time while this was doing I went out once at least every day with my gun, as well to divert myself, as to see if I could kill anything fit for food, and as near as I could to acquaint myself with what the island produced. The first time I went out I presently discovered that there were goats in the island, which was a great satisfaction to me; but then it was attended with this misfortune to me, viz.: that they were so shy, so subtile, and so swift of foot, that it was the difficultest thing in the world to come at them. But I was not discouraged at this, not doubting but I might now and then shoot one, as it soon happened, for after I had found their haunts a little, I laid wait in this manner for them: I observed if they saw me in the valleys, though they were upon the rocks, they would run away as in a terrible fright; but if they were feeding in the valleys, and I was upon the rocks, they took no notice of me, from whence I concluded, that by the position of their optics,[21] their sight was so directed downward, that they did not readily see objects that were above them; so

afterward I took this method, I always climbed the rocks first to get above them, and then had frequently a fair mark. The first shot I made among these creatures, I killed a she-goat which had a little kid by her which she gave suck to, which grieved me heartily; but when the old one fell, the kid stood stock still by her till I came and took her up: and not only so, but when I carried the old one with me upon my shoulders, the kid followed me quite to my enclosure, upon which I laid down the dam, and took the kid in my arms, and carried it over my pale,[22] in hopes to have bred it up tame; but it would not eat, so I was forced to kill it and eat it myself: these two supplied me with flesh a great while, for I eat sparingly, and saved my provisions (my bread especially) as much as possibly I could. Having now fixed my habitation, I found it absolutely necessary to provide a place to make a fire in, and fuel to burn; and what I did for that, as also how I enlarged my cave, and what conveniences I made, I shall give a full account of in its place. But I must first give some little account of myself, and of my thoughts about living, which it may well be supposed were not a few.

I had a dismal prospect of my condition, for as I was not cast away upon that island without being driven, as is said, by a violent storm quite out of the course of our intended voyage, and a great way, viz. some hundreds of leagues, out of the

---

21 **optics:** eyes.

22 **pale:** fence.

FAMOUS CHARACTERS

ordinary course of the trade of mankind, I had great reason to consider it as a determination of Heaven, that in this desolate place, and in this desolate manner, I should end my life; the tears would run plentifully down my face when I made these reflections, and sometimes I would expostulate with myself, why Providence should thus completely ruin its creatures, and render them so absolutely miserable, so without help abandoned, so entirely depressed, that it could hardly be rational to be thankful for such a life.

But something always returned swift upon me to check these thoughts, and to reprove me; and particularly one day walking with my gun in my hand by the seaside, I was very pensive upon the subject of my present condition, when reason as it were expostulated with me the other way, thus: Well, you are in a desolate condition it is true, but pray remember, where are the rest of you? Did not you come eleven of you into the boat? Where are the ten? Why were not they saved and you lost? Why were you singled out? Is it better to be here or there? and then I pointed to the sea. All evils are to be considered with the good that is in them, and with what worse attends them.

Then it occurred to me again, how well I was furnished for my subsistence, and what would have been my case if it had not happened, which was an hundred thousand to one, that the ship floated from the place where she first struck and was driven so near the shore that I had

time to get all these things out of her. What would have been my case, if I had been to have lived in the condition in which I at first came on shore, without necessaries of life, or necessaries to supply and procure them? Particularly, said I aloud (though to myself), what should I have done without a gun, without ammunition, without any tools to make anything, or to work with, without clothes, bedding, a tent, or any manner of covering? and that now I had all these to a sufficient quantity, and was in a fair way to provide myself in such a manner as to live without my gun when my ammunition was spent; so that I had a tolerable view of subsisting without any want as long as I lived; for I considered from the beginning how I would provide for the accidents that might happen, and for the time that was to come, even not only after my ammunition should be spent, but even after my health or strength should decay.

I confess I had not entertained any notion of my ammunition being destroyed at one blast, I mean my powder being blown up by lightning, and this made the thoughts of it so surprising to me when it lightened and thundered, as I observed just now.

And now being to enter into a melancholy relation of a scene of silent life, such perhaps as was never heard of in the world before, I shall take it from its beginning, and continue it in its order. It was, by my account, the 30th of Sept. when, in the manner as above said, I first set foot upon this horrid island, when the sun being, to us, in its autumnal equinox,[23] was almost just over my head, for I reckoned myself, by observation, to be in the latitude of 9 degrees 22 minutes north of the line.[24]

23 equinox: the time when day and night are of equal length all over the earth. The autumnal equinox now occurs about September 22.

24 line: equator.

Understanding Literature

1. Crusoe's first move is to get to the ship for supplies. What kind of things does he first load into the chests on the raft? Are these the things you would expect him to take first? Why? What does he load next? Why is it a very useful prize to him?

2. How does Robinson Crusoe manage to get his raft to shore without sail, oar, or rudder? What characteristics of the man are shown by his being able to do so?

3. What factors does Robinson Crusoe take into consideration in choosing a permanent location for his home?

4. Thinking of his companions who were lost needlessly and of his own loneliness, Robinson Crusoe says, "this forced tears from my eyes again, but as there was little relief in that, I resolved, if possible, to get to the ship. . . ." What does this reaction show about Crusoe's character?

5. Cite evidence from the selection which shows that Robinson Crusoe is (a) foresighted, (b) resourceful, (c) levelheaded. Describe some of his other character traits. What makes you believe he had these traits?

6. Why would some men, given the supplies Robinson Crusoe had, have difficulty surviving on the island?

7. What things does Robinson Crusoe have which are unnecessary to support life? Name some of the modern equipment of everyday living which most people feel they cannot do without. Are these really necessities of life?

8. Why does Defoe enumerate so many of the items that Robinson Crusoe rescues from the ship? Point out other instances of Defoe's careful attention to detail.

9. Why is it particularly appropriate that the reader should see everything through Robinson Crusoe's eyes, that is, from his point of view? How does this point of view help to make the story believable?

Further Activity

Read again Defoe's description of the construction of the raft which Robinson Crusoe used to carry his first load of supplies to shore. Then reread his description of the construction of his permanent headquarters. Notice how the author explains each step in the building process so clearly and carefully that, given Crusoe's equipment, physical strength, and manual skill, you could build such a raft or home by following the steps Defoe describes.

Write a short paragraph in which you explain the way you have made something, such as a dress, a birdhouse, a cake, or a model airplane. Be sure that the explanation of your methods is so clear that someone reading your paper would be able to make the same object.

Focusing on Words

Some groups of words are seldom used except by those whose work or hobby calls for these words. Anyone, for instance, who is familiar with sailing ships and the sea would know the following italicized words used in *Robinson Crusoe*. If a reader is to understand fully stories relating to ships and the sea, he too must know these words. Which of the following italicized words do you know? Look up the meanings of those you do not know.

Words, of course, can have entirely different meanings when used in different ways. When you look up these words in the dictionary, be sure that you choose the appropriate meaning; in this case the appropriate meaning will sometimes be preceded by the abbreviation *Naut.* What does *Naut.* mean?

1. ". . . the tide *ebbed* so far out, that I could come within a quarter of a mile of the ship."
2. "[I] got up into the *forecastle* of the ship."
3. ". . . all her *quarter* was free. . . ."
4. ". . . we had several spare *yards*, and two or three large *spars* of wood. . . ."
5. My next care was "how to preserve what I laid upon [my raft] from the *surf* of the sea."
6. "[I] began to think how I should get to shore with them, having neither sail, oar, nor *rudder*. . . ."
7. ". . . my raft run aground . . . upon a *shoal*. . . ."
8. "I now began to consider, that I might yet get a great many things out of the ship . . . particularly some of the *rigging*, and sails. . . ."
9. ". . . I took all the men's clothes that I could find, and a spare *fore-topsail*, a hammock, and some bedding. . . ."

The Bad Boy of this story lived over a hundred years ago in a small seaport in northern New England. Thomas Bailey Aldrich based the story on his own boyhood, and the "I" of the story is frequently the author himself remembering the town he calls Rivermouth, his friends of that time, and what they did. The author looks back with fondness to his 19th-century New England boyhood, but whether or not it was so very different in spirit from a 20th-century boyhood remains for you to decide as you read this excerpt from *The Story of a Bad Boy*.

from The Story of a Bad Boy

Thomas Bailey Aldrich

IMPROVING YOUR READING: In telling the main story of the chapter—how the boys astonished Rivermouth—the author includes a great deal of the history of the cannons. At times he even treats them as people. When a writer describes inanimate objects as if they were human beings, he is using *personification*. Notice how the cannons are personified in this story.

How We Astonished
the Rivermouthians

Among the few changes that have taken place in Rivermouth during the past twenty years there is one which I regret. I lament the removal of all those varnished iron cannon which used to do duty as posts at the corners of streets leading from the river. They were quaintly ornamental, each set upon end with a solid shot soldered into its mouth, and gave to that part of the town a picturesqueness very poorly atoned for by the conventional wooden stakes that have deposed them.

These guns ("old sogers" the boys called them) had their story, like everything else in Rivermouth.

When that everlasting last war—the War of 1812, I mean—came to an end, all the brigs, schooners, and barks fitted out at this port as privateers were as eager to get rid of their useless twelve-pounders and swivels as they had previously been to obtain them. Many of the pieces had cost large sums, and now they were little better than so much crude iron—not so good, in fact, for they were clumsy things to break up and melt over. The government didn't want them; private citizens didn't want them; they were a drug in the market.

But there was one man, ridiculous beyond his generation, who got it into his head that a fortune was to be made out of these same guns. To buy them all, to hold on to them until war was declared again (as he had no doubt it would be in a few months), and then sell out at fabulous prices—this was the daring idea that addled the pate of[1] Silas Trefethen, "Dealer in E. & W. I. Goods and Groceries," as the faded sign over his shop door informed the public.

Silas went shrewdly to work, buying up every old cannon he could lay hands on. His back yard was soon crowded with broken-down gun carriages,[2] and his barn with guns, like an arsenal. When Silas's purpose got wind, it was astonishing how valuable that thing became which just now was worth nothing at all.

"Ha, ha!" thought Silas; "somebody else is tryin' tu git control of the market. But I guess I've got the start of *him*."

So he went on buying and buying, oftentimes paying double the original price of the article. People in the neighboring towns collected all the worthless ordnance[3] they could find, and sent it by the cartload to Rivermouth.

When his barn was full, Silas began piling the rubbish in his cellar, then in his parlor. He mortgaged the stock of his grocery store, mortgaged his house, his barn, his horse, and would have mortgaged himself, if anyone would have taken him as security, in order to carry on the grand speculation. He was a ruined man, and as happy as a lark.

Surely poor Silas was cracked, like the majority of his own cannon. More or less crazy he must have been always. Years before this he purchased an elegant rosewood coffin, and kept it in one of the spare rooms in his residence. He even had his name engraved on the silver-plate, leaving a blank after the word "Died."

The blank was filled up in due time, and well it was for Silas that he secured so stylish a coffin in his opulent days, for when he died his worldly wealth would not have bought him a pine box, to say nothing of rosewood. He never gave up expecting a war with Great Britain. Hopeful and radiant to the last, his dying words were, *England—war— few days—great profits!*

It was that sweet old lady, Dame Jocelyn, who told me the story of Silas Trefethen; for these things happened long before my day. Silas died in 1817.

At Trefethen's death his unique collection came under the auctioneer's hammer. Some of the larger guns were sold to the town, and planted at the corners of divers[4] streets; others went off to the iron foundry; the balance, numbering twelve, were dumped down on a deserted wharf at the foot of Anchor Lane, where, summer after summer, they rested at their ease in the grass and fungi, pelted in autumn by the rain and annually buried by the winter snow. It is with these twelve guns that our story has to deal.

---

1 **addled . . . of:** confused; unbalanced.
2 **gun carriages:** wheeled bases for guns.
3 **ordnance:** artillery.

4 **divers:** several.

The wharf where they reposed was shut off from the street by a high fence—a silent, dreamy old wharf, covered with strange weeds and mosses. On account of its seclusion and the good fishing it afforded, it was much frequented by us boys.

There we met many an afternoon to throw out our lines, or play leap-frog among the rusty cannon. They were famous fellows in our eyes. What a racket they had made in the heyday of their unchastened youth! What stories they might tell now, if their puffy metallic lips could only speak! Once they were lively talkers enough; but there the grim sea dogs lay, silent and forlorn in spite of all of their former growlings.

They always seemed to me like a lot of venerable disabled tars,[5] stretched out on a lawn in front of a hospital, gazing seaward, and mutely lamenting their lost youth.

But once more they were destined to lift up their dolorous[6] voices—once more ere they keeled over and lay speechless for all time. And this is how it befell.

Jack Harris, Charley Marden, Harry Blake, and myself were fishing off the wharf one afternoon, when a thought flashed upon me like an inspiration.

"I say, boys!" I cried, hauling in my line hand over hand, "I've got something!"

"What does it pull like, youngster?" asked Harris, looking down at the taut line and expecting to see a big perch at least.

"Oh, nothing in the fish way," I returned, laughing; "it's about the old guns."

"What about them?"

"I was thinking what jolly fun it would be to set one of the old sogers on his legs and serve him out a ration of gunpowder."

Up came the three lines in a jiffy. An enterprise better suited to the disposition of my companions could not have been proposed.

In a short time we had one of the smaller cannon over on its back and were busy scraping the green rust from the touchhole.[7] The mold had spiked the gun so effectually, that for a while we fancied we should have to give up our attempt to resuscitate the old soger.

"A long gimlet[8] would clear it out," said Charley Marden, "if we only had one."

I looked to see if Sailor Ben's flag was flying at the cabin door, for he always took in the colors when he went off fishing.

"When you want to know if the Admiral's aboard, jest cast an eye to the buntin', my hearties," says Sailor Ben.

Sometimes in a jocose mood he called himself the Admiral, and I am sure he deserved to be one. The Admiral's flag was flying, and I soon procured a gimlet from his carefully kept tool chest.

5 **tars:** sailors.
6 **dolorous:** sorrowful.

7 **touchhole:** vent in the cannon through which fire was communicated to the powder.
8 **gimlet** (gĭm′lĭt): tool for boring holes.

FAMOUS CHARACTERS

Before long we had the gun in working order. A newspaper lashed to the end of a lath[9] served as a swab to dust out the bore.[10] Jack Harris blew through the touchhole and pronounced all clear.

Seeing our task accomplished so easily, we turned our attention to the other guns, which lay in all sorts of postures in the rank grass. Borrowing a rope from Sailor Ben, we managed with immense labor to drag the heavy pieces into position and place a brick under each muzzle to give it the proper elevation. When we beheld them all in a row, like a regular battery, we simultaneously conceived an idea, the magnitude of which struck us dumb for a moment.

Our first intention was to load and fire a single gun. How feeble and insignificant was such a plan compared to that which now sent the light dancing into our eyes!

"What could we have been thinking of?" cried Jack Harris. "We'll give 'em a broadside,[11] to be sure, if we die for it!"

We turned to with a will, and before nightfall had nearly half the battery overhauled and ready for service. To keep the artillery dry we stuffed wads of loose hemp into the muzzles, and fitted wooden pegs to the touchholes.

At recess the next noon the Centipedes[12] met in a corner of the school yard to talk over the proposed lark.

The original projectors, though they would have liked to keep the thing secret, were obliged to make a club matter of it, inasmuch as funds were required for ammunition. There had been no recent drain on the treasury, and the society could well afford to spend a few dollars in so notable an undertaking.

It was unanimously agreed that the plan should be carried out in the handsomest manner, and a subscription to that end was taken on the spot. Several of the Centipedes hadn't a cent, excepting the one strung around their necks; others, however, were richer. I chanced to have a dollar, and it went into the cap quicker than lightning. When the club, in view of my munificence, voted to name the guns Bailey's Battery I was prouder than I have ever been since over anything.

The money thus raised, added to that already in the treasury, amounted to nine dollars—a fortune in those days; but not more than we had use for. This sum was divided into twelve parts, for it would not do for one boy to buy all the powder, not even for us all to make our purchases at the same place. That would excite suspicion at any time, particularly at a period so remote from the Fourth of July.

There were only three stores in town licensed to sell powder; that gave each store four customers. Not to run the slightest risk of remark, one boy bought his powder on Monday, the next boy on Tuesday, and so on until the requisite quantity was in our possession. This we put into a

9 **lath:** thin, narrow strip of wood.
10 **bore:** interior of a cannon muzzle.
11 **give . . . broadside:** fire all the guns at once.
12 **Centipedes:** the name of the boys' club. Each of the twelve members wore a cent-piece on a cord around his neck.

THOMAS BAILEY ALDRICH

keg and carefully hid in a dry spot on the wharf.

Our next step was to finish cleaning the guns, which occupied two afternoons, for several of the old sogers were in a very congested state indeed. Having completed the task, we came upon a difficulty. To set off the battery by daylight was out of the question; it must be done at night; it must be done with fuses, for no doubt the neighbors would turn out after the first two or three shots, and it would not pay to be caught in the vicinity.

Who knew anything about fuses? Who could arrange it so the guns would go off one after the other, with an interval of a minute or so between?

Theoretically we knew that a minute fuse lasted a minute; double the quantity, two minutes; but practically we were at a standstill. There was but one person who could help us in this extremity—Sailor Ben. To me was assigned the duty of obtaining what information I could from the ex-gunner, it being left to my discretion whether or not to entrust him with our secret.

So one evening I dropped into the cabin and artfully turned the conversation to fuses in general, and then to particular fuses, but without getting much out of the old boy, who was busy making a twine hammock. Finally, I was forced to divulge the whole plot.

The Admiral had a sailor's love for a joke, and entered at once and heartily into our scheme. He volunteered to prepare the fuses himself,

and I left the labor in his hands, having bound him by several extraordinary oaths—such as "Hope-I-may-die" and "Shiver-my-timbers"—not to betray us, come what would.

This was Monday evening. On Wednesday the fuses were ready. That night we were to unmuzzle Bailey's Battery. Mr. Grimshaw saw that something was wrong somewhere, for we were restless and absent-minded in the classes, and the best of us came to grief before the morning session was over. When Mr. Grimshaw announced "Guy Fawkes"[13] as the subject for our next composition, you might have knocked down the Mystic Twelve with a feather.

The coincidence was certainly curious, but when a man has committed, or is about to commit, an offense, a hundred trifles, which would pass unnoticed at another time, seem to point at him with convicting fingers. No doubt Guy Fawkes himself received many a start after he got his wicked kegs of gunpowder neatly piled up under the House of Lords.

Wednesday, as I have mentioned, was a half holiday, and the Centipedes assembled in my barn to decide on the final arrangements. These were as simple as could be. As the fuses were connected, it needed but one person to fire the train. Hereupon arose a discussion as to who

13 **Guy Fawkes:** a conspirator in the Gunpowder Plot, a scheme to destroy the King, Lords, and Commons of England by blowing them up on the day of the opening of Parliament. On November 5, 1605, Fawkes was about to fire the barrels of gunpowder under the House of Lords when he was seized.

560

was the proper person. Some argued that I ought to apply the match, the battery being christened after me, and the main idea, moreover, being mine. Others advocated the claim of Phil Adams as the oldest boy. At last we drew lots for the post of honor.

Twelve slips of folded paper, upon one of which was written "Thou art the man," were placed in a quart measure, and thoroughly shaken; then each member stepped up and lifted out his destiny. At a given signal we opened our billets. "Thou art the man," said the slip of paper trembling in my fingers. The sweets and anxieties of a leader were mine the rest of the afternoon.

Directly after twilight set in Phil Adams stole down to the wharf and fixed the fuses to the guns, laying a train of powder from the principal fuse to the fence, through a chink of which I was to drop the match at midnight.

At ten o'clock Rivermouth goes to bed. At eleven o'clock Rivermouth is as quiet as a country churchyard. At twelve o'clock there is nothing left with which to compare the stillness that broods over the little seaport.

In the midst of this stillness I arose and glided out of the house like a phantom bent on an evil errand; like a phantom I flitted through the silent street, hardly drawing breath until I knelt down beside the fence at the appointed place.

Pausing a moment for my heart to stop thumping, I lighted the match and shielded it with both hands until it was well under way, and then dropped the blazing splinter on the slender thread of gunpowder.

A noiseless flash instantly followed, and all was dark again. I peeped through the crevice in the fence, and saw the main fuse spitting out sparks like a conjurer. Assured that the train had not failed, I took to my heels, fearful lest the fuse might burn more rapidly than we calculated, and cause an explosion before I could get home. This, luckily, did not happen. There's a special Providence that watches over idiots, drunken men, and boys.

I dodged the ceremony of undressing by plunging into bed, jacket, boots, and all. I am not sure I took off my cap; but I know that I had hardly pulled the coverlid over me, when "Boom!" sounded the first gun of Bailey's Battery.

I lay as still as a mouse. In less than two minutes there was another burst of thunder, and then another. The third gun was a tremendous fellow and fairly shook the house.

The town was waking up. Windows were thrown open here and there and people called to each other across the streets asking what that firing was for.

"Boom!" went gun number four.

I sprung out of bed and tore off my jacket, for I heard the Captain feeling his way along the wall to my chamber. I was half undressed by the time he found the knob of the door.

"I say, sir," I cried, "do you hear those guns?"

"Not being deaf, I do," said the Captain, a little tartly—any reflection

THOMAS BAILEY ALDRICH

on his hearing always nettled him; "but what on earth they are for I can't conceive. You had better get up and dress yourself."

"I'm nearly dressed, sir."

"Boom! Boom"—two of the guns had gone off together.

The door of Miss Abigail's bedroom opened hastily, and that pink[14] of maidenly propriety stepped out into the hall in her nightgown—the only indecorous thing I ever knew her to do. She held a lighted candle in her hand and looked like a very aged Lady Macbeth.[15]

"O Dan'el, this is dreadful! What do you suppose it means?"

"I really can't suppose," said the Captain, rubbing his ear; "but I guess it's over now."

"Boom!" said Bailey's Battery.

Rivermouth was wide awake now, and half the male population was in the streets, running different ways, for the firing seemed to proceed from opposite points of the town. Everybody waylaid everybody else with questions; but as no one knew what was the occasion of the tumult, people who were not usually nervous began to be oppressed by the mystery.

Some thought the town was being bombarded; some thought the world was coming to an end, as the pious and ingenious Mr. Miller had predicted it would; but those who couldn't form any theory whatever were the most perplexed.

In the meanwhile Bailey's Battery bellowed away at regular intervals. The greatest confusion reigned everywhere by this time. People with lanterns rushed hither and thither. The town-watch had turned out to a man, and marched off, in admirable order, in the wrong direction. Discovering their mistake, they retraced their steps, and got down to the wharf just as the last cannon belched forth its lightning.

A dense cloud of sulphurous smoke floated over Anchor Lane, obscuring the starlight. Two or three hundred people, in various stages of excitement, crowded about the upper end of the wharf, not liking to advance farther until they were satisfied that the explosions were over. A board was here and there blown from the fence, and through the openings thus afforded a few of the more daring spirits at length ventured to crawl.

The cause of the racket soon transpired. A suspicion that they had been sold gradually dawned on the Rivermouthians. Many were exceedingly indignant, and declared that no penalty was severe enough for those concerned in such a prank; others—and these were the very people who had been terrified nearly out of their wits—had the assurance to laugh, saying that they knew all along it was only a trick.

The town-watch boldly took possession of the ground, and the crowd began to disperse. Knots of gossips lingered here and there near the place, indulging in vain surmises[16] as

14 pink: excellent example.
15 Lady Macbeth: In a scene from Shakespeare's play *Macbeth*, Lady Macbeth sleepwalks with a lighted candle in her hand.

16 surmises: guesses.

FAMOUS CHARACTERS

to who the invisible gunners could be.

There was no more noise that night, but many a timid person lay awake expecting a renewal of the mysterious cannonading. The Oldest Inhabitant refused to go to bed on any terms, but persisted in sitting up in a rocking chair, with his hat and mittens on, until daybreak.

I thought I should never get to sleep. The moment I drifted off in a doze I fell to laughing and woke myself up. But toward morning slumber overtook me, and I had a series of disagreeable dreams, in one of which I was waited upon by the ghost of Silas Trefethen with an exorbitant bill for the use of his guns. In another, I was dragged before a court-martial and sentenced by Sailor Ben, in a frizzled wig and three-cornered cocked hat, to be shot to death by Bailey's Battery—a sentence which Sailor Ben was about to execute with his own hand, when I suddenly opened my eyes and found the sunshine lying pleasantly across my face. I tell you I was glad!

That unaccountable fascination which leads the guilty to hover about the spot where his crime was committed drew me down to the wharf as soon as I was dressed. Phil Adams, Jack Harris, and others of the conspirators were already there, examining with a mingled feeling of curiosity and apprehension the havoc accomplished by the battery.

The fence was badly shattered and the ground plowed up for several yards round the place where the guns formerly lay—formerly lay, for now they were scattered every which way. There was scarcely a gun that hadn't burst. Here was one ripped open from muzzle to breech, and there was another with its mouth blown into the shape of a trumpet. Three of the guns had disappeared bodily, but on looking over the edge of the wharf we saw them standing on end in the tide-mud. They had popped overboard in their excitement.

"I tell you what, fellows," whispered Phil Adams, "it is lucky we didn't try to touch 'em off with punk.[17] They'd have blown us all to flinders."[18]

The destruction of Bailey's Battery was not, unfortunately, the only catastrophe. A fragment of one of the cannon had carried away the chimney of Sailor Ben's cabin. He was very mad at first, but having prepared the fuse himself he didn't dare complain openly.

"I'd have taken a reef in the blessed stovepipe," said the Admiral, gazing ruefully at the smashed chimney, "if I had known as how the Flagship was agoin' to be under fire."

The next day he rigged out an iron funnel, which, being in sections, could be detached and taken in at a moment's notice. On the whole, I think he was resigned to the demolition of his brick chimney. The stovepipe was a great deal more shipshape.

The town was not so easily appeased.[19] The selectmen determined

17 **punk:** slow-burning material used for such purposes as lighting fireworks.
18 **flinders:** pieces.
19 **appeased:** satisfied; calmed.

THOMAS BAILEY ALDRICH

to make an example of the guilty parties, and offered a reward for their arrest, holding out a promise of pardon to any one of the offenders who would furnish information against the rest. But there were no faint hearts among the Centipedes. Suspicion rested for a while on several persons—on the soldiers at the fort; on a crazy fellow, known about town as "Bottle-Nose"; and at last on Sailor Ben.

"Shiver my timbers!" cried that deeply injured individual. "Do you suppose, sir, as I have lived to sixty year, an' ain't got no more sense than to go for to blaze away at my own upper riggin'? It doesn't stand to reason."

It certainly did not seem probable that Mr. Watson would maliciously knock over his own chimney, and Lawyer Hackett, who had the case in hand, bowed himself out of the Admiral's cabin convinced that the right man had not been discovered.

People living by the sea are always more or less superstitious. Stories of specter ships and mysterious beacons, that lure vessels out of their course and wreck them on unknown reefs, were among the stock legends of Rivermouth; and not a few people in the town were ready to attribute the firing of those guns to some supernatural agency. The Oldest Inhabitant remembered that when he was a boy a dim-looking sort of schooner hove to in the offing one foggy afternoon, fired off a single gun that didn't make any report, and then crumbled to nothing, spar, mast, and hulk, like a piece of burnt paper.

The authorities, however, were of the opinion that human hands had something to do with the explosions, and they resorted to deep-laid stratagems to get hold of the said hands. One of their traps came very near catching us. They artfully caused an old brass fieldpiece to be left on a wharf near the scene of our late operations. Nothing in the world but the lack of money to buy powder saved us from falling into the clutches of the two watchmen who lay secreted for a week in a neighboring sail loft.

It was many a day before the midnight bombardment ceased to be the town talk. The trick was so audacious and on so grand a scale that nobody thought for an instant of connecting us lads with it. Suspicion at length grew weary of lighting on the wrong person, and as conjecture—like the physicians in the epitaph—was in vain, the Rivermouthians gave up the idea of finding out who had astonished them.

They never did find out, and never will, unless they read this veracious[20] history. If the selectmen are still disposed to punish the malefactors,[21] I can supply Lawyer Hackett with evidence enough to convict Pepper Whitcomb, Phil Adams, Charley Marden, and the other honorable members of the Centipede Club. But really I don't think it would pay now.

---

20 **veracious:** truthful.
21 **malefactors** (măl′ə făk′tərs): criminals.

FAMOUS CHARACTERS

Understanding Literature

1. What part does Tom Bailey, the narrator, play in the planning and execution of the cannon incident? What do you learn about his character from this role?
2. How are the boys extremely lucky in their escapade?
3. You are often able to learn something about the character of the author himself from the way he writes about others. In other words, an author sometimes reveals his personality when he is describing someone else. From his descriptions of Silas and the Oldest Inhabitant do you get the impression that Thomas Bailey Aldrich has a sense of humor? Explain your answer.
4. The boys call the cannons "old sogers." When a writer describes objects as if they were human beings or gives to objects the characteristics of human beings, he is using *personification*.

    By calling the cannons "sogers," the boys are personifying the cannons, describing them in terms of people. Why is "old sogers" an appropriate name for the cannons? List all the instances in which the author compares the cannons to people, and explain why these are good comparisons.

Further Activity

In your reading you will often find a statement or an idea you immediately agree with because you yourself have had some personal experience which has led you to the same conclusion.

Consider the following statements or themes from *The Story of a Bad Boy*. Write a paragraph or two on one of these. In your paper prove the truth of the theme or statement by describing one of your own personal experiences. On the other hand, if your own experience has proved the opposite to be true, write a paragraph or two explaining why.

1. ". . . when a man has committed, or is about to commit, an offense, a hundred trifles, which would pass unnoticed at other times, seem to point at him with convicting fingers."
2. "The sweets and anxieties of a leader. . . ." (Be sure to explain what this phrase means before you proceed to agree or disagree with it.)
3. "There's a special Providence that watches over idiots, drunken men, and boys."
4. "People living by the sea are always more or less superstitious."

Sherlock Holmes, the detective hero of this story and of many others by Sir Arthur Conan Doyle, is one of the best-known characters in English literature. His stories have been made into movies and plays, and the image of the tall, thin Mr. Holmes with his double-peaked hat and his pipe has become familiar to millions of people even if they have not read the stories themselves.

This story, "The Redheaded League," is from *The Adventures of Sherlock Holmes,* which was published in 1891. *The Adventures* is a book of stories about Sherlock Holmes, each complete in itself. Here in this story you will meet Mr. Holmes and his friend and assistant, Dr. Watson, as Holmes's keen, analytical mind cuts through the confusion surrounding the Redheaded League to stop the plans of a dangerous criminal.

The Redheaded League

Sir Arthur Conan Doyle

IMPROVING YOUR READING: Notice who tells the story, from whose *point of view* you learn what happens. Why do you think the author chose to tell the story from this point of view?

Each detail and each small event should be important to every story's outcome and to the story's total effect on the reader. It is especially important in a detective story such as this that all the details, all the events, all the conversations included are there because they do contribute to the outcome of the story. Read carefully and try to predict the outcome of the mystery; that is, try to guess from everything you learn how the story will end.

I HAD CALLED upon my friend, Mr. Sherlock Holmes, one day in the autumn of last year and found him in deep conversation with a very stout, florid-faced, elderly gentleman with fiery red hair. With an apology for my intrusion, I was about to withdraw when Holmes pulled me abruptly into the room and closed the door behind me.

"You could not possibly have come at a better time, my dear Watson," he said cordially.

"I was afraid that you were engaged."

"So I am. Very much so."

"Then I can wait in the next room."

"Not at all. This gentleman, Mr. Wilson, has been my partner and helper in many of my most successful cases, and I have no doubt that he will be of the utmost use to me in yours also."

The stout gentleman half rose from his chair and gave a bob of greeting, with a quick little questioning glance from his small, fat-encircled eyes.

"Try the settee," said Holmes, relapsing into his armchair and putting his finger tips together, as was his custom when in judicial moods. "I know, my dear Watson, that you share my love of all that is bizarre and outside the conventions and humdrum routine of everyday life. You have shown your relish for it by the enthusiasm which has prompted you to chronicle,[1] and, if you will excuse my saying so, somewhat to embellish so many of my own little adventures."

"Your cases have indeed been of the greatest interest to me," I observed.

"You will remember that I remarked the other day, just before we went into the very simple problem presented by Miss Mary Sutherland, that for strange effects and extraordinary combinations we must go to life itself, which is always far more daring than any effort of the imagination."

"A proposition which I took the liberty of doubting."

"You did, Doctor, but none the less you must come round to my view, for otherwise I shall keep on piling fact upon fact on you until your reason breaks down under them and acknowledges me to be right. Now, Mr. Jabez Wilson here has been good enough to call upon me this morning, and to begin a narrative which promises to be one of the most singular which I have listened to for some time. You have heard me remark that the strangest and most unique things are very often connected not with the larger but with the smaller crimes, and occasionally, indeed, where there is room for doubt whether any positive crime has been

1 chronicle: record.

committed. As far as I have heard, it is impossible for me to say whether the present case is an instance of crime or not, but the course of events is certainly among the most singular that I have ever listened to. Perhaps, Mr. Wilson, you would have the great kindness to recommence your narrative. I ask you not merely because my friend Dr. Watson has not heard the opening part but also because the peculiar nature of the story makes me anxious to have every possible detail from your lips. As a rule, when I have heard some slight indication of the course of events, I am able to guide myself by the thousands of other similar cases which occur to my memory. In the present instance I am forced to admit that the facts are, to the best of my belief, unique."

The portly client puffed out his chest with an appearance of some little pride and pulled a dirty and wrinkled newspaper from the inside pocket of his great-coat. As he glanced down the advertisement column, with his head thrust forward and the paper flattened out upon his knee, I took a good look at the man and endeavored, after the fashion of my companion, to read the indications which might be presented by his dress or appearance.

I did not gain very much, however, by my inspection. Our visitor bore every mark of being an average commonplace British tradesman, obese, pompous, and slow. He wore rather baggy gray shepherd's check trousers, a not overclean black frock coat, unbuttoned in the front, and a drab waistcoat with a heavy brassy Albert chain, and a square pierced bit of metal dangling down as an ornament. A frayed top hat and a faded brown overcoat with a wrinkled velvet collar lay upon a chair beside him. Altogether, look as I would, there was nothing remarkable about the man save his blazing red head, and the expression of extreme chagrin and discontent upon his features.

Sherlock Holmes's quick eye took in my occupation, and he shook his head with a smile as he noticed my questioning glances. "Beyond the obvious facts that he has at some time done manual labor, that he takes snuff, that he is a Freemason,[2] that he has been in China, and that he has done a considerable amount of writing lately, I can deduce nothing else."

Mr. Jabez Wilson started up in his chair, with his forefinger upon the paper, but his eyes upon my companion.

"How, in the name of good fortune, did you know all that, Mr. Holmes?" he asked. "How did you know, for example, that I did manual labor? It's as true as gospel, for I began as a ship's carpenter."

"Your hands, my dear sir. Your right hand is quite a size larger than your left. You have worked with it, and the muscles are more developed."

"Well, the snuff, then, and the Freemasonry?"

"I won't insult your intelligence by telling you how I read that, especially as, rather against the strict rules of your order, you use an arc-and-compass breastpin."

"Ah, of course, I forgot that. But the writing?"

"What else can be indicated by that right cuff so very shiny for five inches, and the left one with the smooth patch near the elbow where you rest it upon the desk?"

"Well, but China?"

"The fish that you have tattooed immediately above your right wrist could only have been done in China. I have made a small study of tattoo marks and have even contributed to the literature of the subject. That trick of staining the fishes' scales of a delicate pink is quite peculiar to China. When, in addition, I see a Chinese coin hanging from your watch chain, the matter becomes even more simple."

Mr. Jabez Wilson laughed heavily. "Well, I never!" said he. "I thought at first that you had done something clever, but I see that there was nothing in it, after all."

"I begin to think, Watson," said Holmes, "that I make a mistake in explaining. 'Omne ignotum pro magnifico,'[3] you know, and my poor little reputation, such as it is, will suffer shipwreck if I am so candid. Can you not find the advertisement, Mr. Wilson?"

"Yes, I have got it now," he answered with his thick red finger planted halfway down the column. "Here it is. This is what began it all. You just read it for yourself, sir."

---

2 **Freemason:** member of a well-known, secret society.

3 *Omne . . . magnifico:* "Whatever is unknown is magnified."

FAMOUS CHARACTERS

I took the paper from him and read as follows:

To the Redheaded League:

On account of the bequest of the late Ezekiah Hopkins, of Lebanon, Pennsylvania, U.S.A., there is now another vacancy open which entitles a member of the League to a salary of £ 4 a week for purely nominal services. All redheaded men who are sound in body and mind, and above the age of twenty-one years, are eligible. Apply in person on Monday, at eleven o'clock, to Duncan Ross, at the offices of the League, 7 Pope's Court, Fleet Street.

"What on earth does this mean?" I ejaculated after I had twice read over the extraordinary announcement.

Holmes chuckled and wriggled in his chair, as was his habit when in high spirits. "It is a little off the beaten track, isn't it?" said he. "And now, Mr. Wilson, off you go at scratch and tell us all about yourself, your household, and the effect which this advertisement had upon your fortunes. You will first make a note, Doctor, of the paper and the date."

"It is *The Morning Chronicle* of April 27, 1890. Just two months ago."

"Very good. Now, Mr. Wilson?"

"Well, it is just as I have been telling you, Mr. Sherlock Holmes," said Jabez Wilson, mopping his forehead; "I have a small pawnbroker's business at Coburg Square, near the City. It's not a very large affair, and of late years it has not done more than just give me a living. I used to be able to keep two assistants, but now I only keep one; and I would have a job to pay him but that he is willing to come for half wages so as to learn the business."

SIR ARTHUR CONAN DOYLE

"What is the name of this obliging youth?" asked Sherlock Holmes.

"His name is Vincent Spaulding, and he's not such a youth, either. It's hard to say his age. I should not wish a smarter assistant, Mr. Holmes; and I know very well that he could better himself and earn twice what I am able to give him. But, after all, if he is satisfied, why should I put ideas in his head?"

"Why, indeed? You seem most fortunate in having an employee who comes under the full market price. It is not a common experience among employers in this age. I don't know that your assistant is not as remarkable as your advertisement."

"Oh, he has his faults, too," said Mr. Wilson. "Never was such a fellow for photography. Snapping away with a camera when he ought to be improving his mind, and then diving down into the cellar like a rabbit into its hole to develop his pictures. That is his main fault, but on the whole he's a good worker. There's no vice in him."

"He is still with you, I presume?"

"Yes, sir. He and a girl of fourteen, who does a bit of simple cooking and keeps the place clean—that's all I have in the house, for I am a widower and never had any family. We live very quietly, sir, the three of us; and we keep a roof over our heads and pay our debts, if we do nothing more.

"The first thing that put us out was that advertisement. Spaulding, he came down into the office just this day eight weeks, with this very paper in his hand, and he says:

"'I wish to the Lord, Mr. Wilson, that I was a redheaded man.'

"'Why that?' I asks.

"'Why,' says he, 'here's another vacancy on the League of the Redheaded Men. It's worth quite a little fortune to any man who gets it, and I understand that there are more vacancies than there are men, so that the trustees are at their wits' end what to do with the money. If my hair would only change color, here's a nice little crib all ready for me to step into.'

"'Why, what is it, then?' I asked. You see, Mr. Holmes, I am a very stay-at-home man, and as my business came to me instead of my having to go to it, I was often weeks on end without putting my foot over the door mat. In that way I didn't know much of what was going on outside, and I was always glad of a bit of news.

"'Have you never heard of the League of the Redheaded Men?' he asked with his eyes open.

"'Never.'

"'Why, I wonder at that, for you are eligible yourself for one of the vacancies.'

"'And what are they worth?' I asked.

"'Oh, merely a couple of hundred a year, but the work is slight, and it need not interfere very much with one's other occupations.'

"Well, you can easily think that that made me prick up my ears, for the business has not been overgood for some years, and an extra couple of hundred would have been very handy.

" 'Tell me all about it,' said I.

" 'Well,' said he, showing me the advertisement, 'you can see for yourself that the League has a vacancy, and there is the address where you should apply for particulars. As far as I can make out, the League was founded by an American millionaire, Ezekiah Hopkins, who was very peculiar in his ways. He was himself redheaded, and he had a great sympathy for all redheaded men; so when he died it was found that he had left his enormous fortune in the hands of trustees, with instructions to apply the interest to the providing of easy berths to men whose hair is of that color. From all I hear it is splendid pay and very little to do.'

" 'But,' said I, 'there would be millions of redheaded men who would apply.'

" 'Not so many as you might think,' he answered. 'You see it is really confined to Londoners, and to grown men. This American had started from London when he was young, and he wanted to do the old town a good turn. Then, again, I have heard it is no use your applying if your hair is light red, or dark red, or anything but real bright, blazing, fiery red. Now, if you cared to apply, Mr. Wilson, you would just walk in; but perhaps it would hardly be worth your while to put yourself out of the way for the sake of a few hundred pounds.'

"Now, it is a fact, gentlemen, as you may see for yourselves, that my hair is of a very full and rich tint, so that it seemed to me that if there was to be any competition in the matter I stood as good a chance as any man that I had ever met. Vincent Spaulding seemed to know so much about it that I thought he might prove useful, so I just ordered him to put up the shutters for the day and to come right away with me. He was very willing to have a holiday, so we shut the business up and started off for the address that was given us in the advertisement.

"I never hope to see such a sight as that again, Mr. Holmes. From north, south, east, and west every man who had a shade of red in his hair had tramped into the city to answer the advertisement. Fleet Street was choked with redheaded folk, and Pope's Court looked like a coster's[4] orange barrow. I should not have thought there were so many in the whole country as were brought together by that single advertisement. Every shade of color they were—straw, lemon, orange, brick, Irish-setter, liver, clay; but, as Spaulding said, there were not many who had the real vivid flame-colored tint. When I saw how many were waiting, I would have given it up in despair; but Spaulding would not hear of it. How he did it I could not imagine, but he pushed and pulled and butted until he got me through the crowd, and right up to the steps which led to the office. There was a double stream upon the stair, some going up in hope, and some coming back dejected; but we wedged in as well as we could and soon found ourselves in the office."

4 **coster:** fruit seller.

SIR ARTHUR CONAN DOYLE

571

"Your experience has been a most entertaining one," remarked Holmes as his client paused and refreshed his memory with a huge pinch of snuff. "Pray continue your very interesting statement."

"There was nothing in the office but a couple of wooden chairs and a deal table, behind which sat a small man with a head that was even redder than mine. He said a few words to each candidate as he came up, and then he always managed to find some fault in them which would disqualify them. Getting a vacancy did not seem to be such a very easy matter, after all. However, when our turn came the little man was much more favorable to me than to any of the others, and he closed the door as we entered, so that he might have a private word with us.

" 'This is Mr. Jabez Wilson,' said my assistant, 'and he is willing to fill a vacancy in the League.'

" 'And he is admirably suited for it,' the other answered. 'He has every requirement. I cannot recall when I have seen anything so fine.' He took a step backward, cocked his head on one side, and gazed at my hair until I felt quite bashful. Then suddenly he plunged forward, wrung my hand, and congratulated me warmly on my success.

" 'It would be injustice to hesitate,' said he. 'You will, however, I am sure, excuse me for taking an obvious precaution.' With that he seized my hair in both his hands, and tugged until I yelled with the pain. 'There is water in your eyes,' said he as he released me. 'I perceive that all is as it should be. But we have to be careful, for we have twice been deceived by wigs and once by paint. I could tell you tales of cobbler's wax which would disgust you with human nature.' He stepped over to the window and shouted through it at the top of his voice that the vacancy was filled. A groan of disappointment came up from below, and the folk all trooped away in different directions until there was not a redhead to be seen except my own and that of the manager.

" 'My name,' said he, 'is Mr. Duncan Ross, and I am myself one of the pensioners upon the fund left by our noble benefactor. Are you a married man, Mr. Wilson? Have you a family?'

"I answered that I had not.

"His face fell immediately.

" 'Dear me!' he said gravely, 'that is very serious indeed! I am sorry to hear you say that. The fund was, of course, for the propagation and spread of the redheads as well as for their maintenance. It is exceedingly unfortunate that you should be a bachelor.'

"My face lengthened at this, Mr. Holmes, for I thought that I was not to have the vacancy after all; but after thinking it over a few minutes he said that it would be all right.

" 'In the case of another,' said he, 'the objection might be fatal, but we must stretch a point in favor of a man with such a head of hair as yours. When shall you be able to enter upon your new duties?'

" 'Well, it is a little awkward, for I have a business already,' said I.

" 'Oh, never mind about that, Mr. Wilson!' said Vincent Spaulding. 'I should be able to look after that for you.'

" 'What would be the hours?' I asked.

" 'Ten to two.'

"Now a pawnbroker's business is mostly done of an evening, Mr. Holmes, especially Thursday and Friday evening, which is just before payday; so it would suit me very well to earn a little in the mornings. Besides, I knew that my assistant was a good man, and that he would see to anything that turned up.

" 'That would suit me very well,' said I. 'And the pay?'

" 'Is £4 a week.'

" 'And the work?'

" 'Is purely nominal.'⁵

" 'What do you call purely nominal?'

" 'Well, you have to be in the office, or at least in the building, the whole time. If you leave, you forfeit your whole position forever. The will is very clear upon that point. You don't comply with the conditions if you budge from the office during that time.'

" 'It's only four hours a day, and I should not think of leaving,' said I.

" 'No excuse will avail,' said Mr. Duncan Ross; 'neither sickness nor business nor anything else. There you must stay, or you lose your billet.'⁶

" 'And the work?'

" 'Is to copy out the Encyclopedia Britannica. There is the first volume of it in that press. You must find your own ink, pens, and blotting paper, but we provide this table and chair. Will you be ready tomorrow?'

" 'Certainly,' I answered.

" 'Then, good-by, Mr. Jabez Wilson, and let me congratulate you once more on the important position which you have been fortunate enough to gain.' He bowed me out of the room, and I went home with my assistant, hardly knowing what to say or do, I was so pleased at my own good fortune.

"Well, I thought over the matter all day, and by evening I was in low spirits again; for I had quite persuaded myself that the whole affair must be some great hoax or fraud, though what its object might be I could not imagine. It seemed altogether past belief that anyone could make such a will, or that they would pay such a sum for doing anything so simple as copying out the *Encyclopaedia Britannica*. Vincent Spaulding did what he could to cheer me up, but by bedtime I had reasoned myself out of the whole thing. However, in the morning I determined to have a look at it anyhow, so I bought a penny bottle of ink, and with a quill pen, and seven sheets of foolscap paper, I started off for Pope's Court.

"Well, to my surprise and delight, everything was as right as possible. The table was set out ready for me, and Mr. Duncan Ross was there to see that I got fairly to work. He started me off upon the letter *A*, and

5 **nominal:** trifling.
6 **billet:** position.

then he left me; but he would drop in from time to time to see that all was right with me. At two o'clock he bade me good day, complimented me upon the amount that I had written, and locked the door of the office after me.

"This went on day after day, Mr. Holmes, and on Saturday the manager came in and planked down four golden sovereigns for my week's work. It was the same next week, and the same the week after. Every morning I was there at ten, and every afternoon I left at two. By degrees Mr. Duncan Ross took to coming in only once of a morning, and then, after a time, he did not come in at all. Still, of course, I never dared to leave the room for an instant, for I was not sure when he might come, and the billet was such a good one, and suited me so well, that I would not risk the loss of it.

"Eight weeks passed away like this, and I had written about Abbots and Archery and Armor and Architecture and Attics, and hoped with diligence that I might get on to the B's before very long. It cost me something in foolscap, and I had pretty nearly filled a shelf with my writings. And then suddenly the whole business came to an end."

"To an end?"

"Yes, sir. And no later than this morning. I went to my work as usual at ten o'clock, but the door was shut and locked, with a little square of cardboard hammered on to the middle of the panel with a tack. Here it is, and you can read for yourself."

He held up a piece of white card-board about the size of a sheet of note paper. It read in this fashion:

THE REDHEADED LEAGUE
IS
DISSOLVED.
October 9, 1890.

Sherlock Holmes and I surveyed this curt announcement and the rueful face behind it, until the comical side of the affair so completely overtopped every other consideration that we both burst out into a roar of laughter.

"I cannot see that there is anything very funny," cried our client, flushing up to the roots of his flaming head. "If you can do nothing better than laugh at me, I can go elsewhere."

"No, no," cried Holmes, shoving him back into the chair from which he had half risen. "I really wouldn't miss your case for the world. It is most refreshingly unusual. But there is, if you will excuse my saying so, something just a little funny about it. Pray what steps did you take when you found the card upon the door?"

"I was staggered, sir. I did not know what to do. Then I called at the offices round, but none of them seemed to know anything about it. Finally, I went to the landlord, who is an accountant living on the ground floor, and I asked him if he could tell me what had become of the Red-headed League. He said that he had never heard of any such body. Then I asked him who Mr. Duncan Ross was. He answered that the name was new to him.

" 'Well,' said I, 'the gentleman at No. 4.'

" 'What, the redheaded man?'

" 'Yes.'

" 'Oh,' said he, 'his name was William Morris. He was a solicitor and was using my room as a temporary convenience until his new premises were ready. He moved out yesterday.'

" 'Where could I find him?'

" 'Oh, at his new office. He did tell me the address. Yes, 17 King Edward Street, near St. Paul's.'

"I started off, Mr. Holmes, but when I got to that address it was a manufactory of artificial kneecaps, and no one in it had ever heard of either Mr. William Morris or Mr. Duncan Ross."

"And what did you do then?" asked Holmes.

"I went home to Saxe-Coburg Square, and I took the advice of my assistant. But he could not help me in any way. He could only say that if I waited I should hear by post. But that was not quite good enough, Mr. Holmes. I did not wish to lose such a place without a struggle, so as I had heard that you were good enough to give advice to poor folk who were in need of it, I came right away to you."

"And you did very wisely," said Holmes. "Your case is an exceedingly remarkable one, and I shall be happy to look into it. From what you have told me I think that it is possible that graver issues hang from it than might at first sight appear."

"Grave enough!" said Mr. Jabez Wilson. "Why, I have lost four pound a week."

"As far as you are personally concerned," remarked Holmes, "I do not see that you have any grievance against this extraordinary league. On the contrary, you are, as I understand, richer by some £30, to say nothing of the minute knowledge which you have gained on every subject which comes under the letter A. You have lost nothing by them."

"No, sir. But I want to find out about them, and who they are, and what their object was in playing this prank—if it was a prank—upon me. It was a pretty expensive joke for them, for it cost them two and thirty pounds."

"We shall endeavor to clear up these points for you. And, first, one or two questions, Mr. Wilson. This assistant of yours who first called your attention to the advertisement— how long had he been with you?"

"About a month then."

"How did he come?"

"In answer to an advertisement."

"Was he the only applicant?"

"No, I had a dozen."

"Why did you pick him?"

"Because he was handy and would come cheap."

"At half wages, in fact."

"Yes."

"What is he like, this Vincent Spaulding?"

"Small, stout-built, very quick in his ways, no hair on his face, though he's not short of thirty. Has a white splash of acid upon his forehead."

Holmes sat up in his chair in considerable excitement. "I thought as much," said he. "Have you ever observed that his ears are pierced for earrings?"

"Yes, sir. He told me that a gypsy had done it for him when he was a lad."

"Hum!" said Holmes, sinking back in deep thought. "He is still with you?"

"Oh, yes, sir; I have only just left him."

"And has your business been attended to in your absence?"

"Nothing to complain of, sir. There's never very much to do of a morning."

"That will do, Mr. Wilson. I shall be happy to give you an opinion upon the subject in the course of a day or two. Today is Saturday, and I hope that by Monday we may come to a conclusion."

"Well, Watson," said Holmes when our visitor had left us, "what do you make of it all?"

"I make nothing of it," I answered frankly. "It is a most mysterious business."

"As a rule," said Holmes, "the more bizarre a thing is the less mysterious it proves to be. It is your commonplace, featureless crimes which are really puzzling, just as a commonplace face is the most difficult to identify. But I must be prompt over this matter."

"What are you going to do, then?" I asked.

"To smoke," he answered. "It is quite a three pipe problem, and I beg that you won't speak to me for fifty minutes." He curled himself up in his chair, with his thin knees drawn up to his hawklike nose, and there he sat with his eyes closed and his black clay pipe thrusting out like the bill of some strange bird. I had come to the conclusion that he had dropped asleep, and indeed was nodding myself, when he suddenly sprang out of his chair with the gesture of a man who has made up his mind and put his pipe down upon the mantelpiece.

"Sarasate[7] plays at the St. James's Hall this afternoon," he remarked. "What do you think, Watson? Could your patients spare you for a few hours?"

"I have nothing to do today. My practice is never very absorbing."

"Then put on your hat and come. I am going through the City first, and we can have some lunch on the way. I observe that there is a good deal of German music on the program, which is rather more to my taste than Italian or French. It is introspective, and I want to introspect. Come along!"

We traveled by the Underground as far as Aldersgate; and a short walk took us to Saxe-Coburg Square, the scene of the singular story which we had listened to in the morning. It was a poky, little, shabby-genteel place, where four lines of dingy two-storied brick houses looked out into a small railed-in enclosure, where a lawn of weedy grass and a few clumps of faded laurel bushes made a hard fight against a smoke-laden and uncongenial atmosphere. Three gilt balls and a brown board with

7 **Sarasate:** a brilliant violinist.

FAMOUS CHARACTERS

"JABEZ WILSON" in white letters, upon a corner house, announced the place where our redheaded client carried on his business. Sherlock Holmes stopped in front of it with his head on one side and looked it all over, with his eyes shining brightly between puckered lids. Then he walked slowly up the street, and then down again to the corner, still looking keenly at the houses. Finally he returned to the pawnbroker's, and, having thumped vigorously upon the pavement with his stick two or three times, he went up to the door and knocked. It was instantly opened by a bright-looking, clean-shaven young fellow, who asked him to step in.

"Thank you," said Holmes, "I only wished to ask you how you would go from here to the Strand."

"Third right, fourth left," answered the assistant promptly, closing the door.

"Smart fellow, that," observed Holmes as we walked away. "He is, in my judgment, the fourth smartest man in London, and for daring I am not sure that he has not a claim to be third. I have known something of him before."

"Evidently," said I, "Mr. Wilson's assistant counts for a good deal in this mystery of the Redheaded League. I am sure that you inquired your way merely in order that you might see him."

"Not him."

"What then?"

"The knees of his trousers."

"And what did you see?"

"What I expected to see."

"Why did you beat the pavement?"

"My dear doctor, this is a time for observation, not for talk. We are spies in an enemy's country. We know something of Saxe-Coburg Square. Let us now explore the parts which lie behind it."

The road in which we found ourselves as we turned round the corner from the retired Saxe-Coburg Square presented as great a contrast to it as the front of a picture does to the back. It was one of the main arteries which conveyed the traffic of the City to the north and west. The roadway was blocked with the immense stream of commerce flowing in a double tide inward and outward, while the footpaths were black with the hurrying swarm of pedestrians. It was difficult to realize as we looked at the line of fine shops and stately business premises that they really abutted on the other side upon the faded and stagnant square which we had just quitted.

"Let me see," said Holmes, standing at the corner and glancing along the line, "I should like just to remember the order of the houses here. It is a hobby of mine to have an exact knowledge of London. There is Mortimer's, the tobacconist, the little newspaper shop, the Coburg branch of the City and Suburban Bank, the Vegetarian Restaurant, and McFarlane's carriage-building depot. That carries us right on to the other block. And now, Doctor, we've done our work, so it's time we had some play. A sandwich and a cup of coffee, and then off to violin-land, where all is sweetness and delicacy and harmony, and there are no redheaded clients to vex us with their conundrums."[8]

My friend was an enthusiastic musician, being himself not only a very capable performer but a composer of no ordinary merit. All the afternoon he sat in the stalls wrapped in the most perfect happiness, gently waving his long, thin fingers in time to the music, while his gently smiling face and his languid, dreamy eyes were as unlike those of Holmes, the sleuth-hound, Holmes the relentless, keen-witted, ready-handed criminal agent, as it was possible to conceive. In his singular character the dual nature alternately asserted itself, and his extreme exactness and astuteness represented, as I have often thought, the reaction against the poetic and contemplative mood which occasionally predominated in him. The swing of his nature took him from extreme languor to devouring energy; and, as I knew well, he was never so truly formidable as when, for days on end, he had been lounging in his armchair amid his improvisations and his black-letter editions. Then it was that the lust of the chase would suddenly come upon him, and that his brilliant reasoning power would rise to the level of intuition, until those who were unacquainted with his methods would look askance at him as on a man whose knowledge was not that of other mortals. When I saw him that afternoon so enwrapped in the music at St. James's Hall I felt that an evil

8 vex . . . conundrums: annoy us with their riddles or puzzles.

time might be coming upon those whom he had set himself to hunt down.

"You want to go home, no doubt, Doctor," he remarked as we emerged.

"Yes, it would be as well."

"And I have some business to do which will take some hours. This business at Coburg Square is serious."

"Why serious?"

"A considerable crime is in contemplation. I have every reason to believe that we shall be in time to stop it. But today being Saturday rather complicates matters. I shall want your help tonight."

"At what time?"

"Ten will be early enough."

"I shall be at Baker Street at ten."

"Very well. And, I say, Doctor, there may be some little danger, so kindly put your army revolver in your pocket." He waved his hand, turned on his heel, and disappeared in an instant among the crowd.

I trust that I am not more dense than my neighbors, but I was always oppressed with a sense of my own stupidity in my dealings with Sherlock Holmes. Here I had heard what he had heard, I had seen what he had seen, and yet from his words it was evident that he saw clearly not only what had happened but what was about to happen, while to me the whole business was still confused and grotesque. As I drove home to my house in Kensington I thought over it all, from the extraordinary story of the redheaded copier of the Encyclopedia down to the visit to Saxe-Coburg Square, and the omi-

nous words with which he had parted from me. What was this nocturnal expedition, and why should I go armed? Where were we going, and what were we to do? I had the hint from Holmes that this smooth-faced pawnbroker's assistant was a formidable man—a man who might play a deep game. I tried to puzzle it out, but gave it up in despair and set the matter aside until night should bring an explanation.

It was a quarter past nine when I started from home and made my way across the Park, and so through Oxford Street to Baker Street. Two hansoms[9] were standing at the door, and as I entered the passage I heard the sound of voices from above. On entering his room I found Holmes in animated conversation with two men, one of whom I recognized as Peter Jones, the official police agent, while the other was a long, thin, sadfaced man, with a very shiny hat and oppressively respectable frock coat.

"Ha! our party is complete," said Holmes, buttoning up his pea jacket and taking his heavy hunting crop from the rack. "Watson, I think you know Mr. Jones, of Scotland Yard? Let me introduce you to Mr. Merryweather, who is to be our companion in tonight's adventure."

"We're hunting in couples again, Doctor, you see," said Jones in his consequential way. "Our friend here is a wonderful man for starting a chase. All he wants is an old dog to help him to do the running down."

---

9 hansoms: horse-drawn two-wheeled carriages; cabs.

"I hope a wild goose may not prove to be the end of our chase," observed Mr. Merryweather gloomily.

"You may place considerable confidence in Mr. Holmes, sir," said the police agent loftily. "He has his own little methods, which are, if he won't mind my saying so, just a little too theoretical and fantastic, but he has the makings of a detective in him. It is not too much to say that once or twice, as in that business of the Sholto murder and the Agra treasure, he has been more nearly correct than the official force."

"Oh, if you say so, Mr. Jones, it is all right," said the stranger with deference. "Still, I confess that I miss my rubber.[10] It is the first Saturday night for seven-and-twenty years that I have not had my rubber."

"I think you will find," said Sherlock Holmes, "that you will play for a higher stake tonight than you have ever done yet, and that the play will be more exciting. For you, Mr. Merryweather, the stake will be some £30,000; and for you, Jones, it will be the man upon whom you wish to lay your hands."

"John Clay, the murderer, thief, smasher, and forger. He's a young man, Mr. Merryweather, but he is at the head of his profession, and I would rather have my bracelets on him than on any criminal in London. He's a remarkable man, is young John Clay. His grandfather was a royal duke, and he himself has been to Eton and Oxford. His brain is as cunning as his fingers, and though we meet signs of him at every turn, we never know where to find the man himself. He'll crack a crib in Scotland one week, and be raising money to build an orphanage in Cornwall the next. I've been on his track for years and have never set eyes on him yet."

"I hope that I may have the pleasure of introducing you tonight. I've had one or two little turns also with Mr. John Clay, and I agree with you that he is at the head of his profession. It is past ten, however, and quite time that we started. If you two will take the first hansom, Watson and I will follow in the second."

Sherlock Holmes was not very communicative during the long drive and lay back in the cab humming the tunes which he had heard in the afternoon. We rattled through an endless labyrinth of gaslit streets until we emerged into Farrington Street.

"We are close there now," my friend remarked. "This fellow Merryweather is a bank director, and personally interested in the matter. I thought it as well to have Jones with us also. He is not a bad fellow, though an absolute imbecile in his profession. He has one positive virtue. He is as brave as a bulldog and as tenacious as a lobster if he gets his claws upon anyone. Here we are, and they are waiting for us."

We had reached the same crowded thoroughfare in which we had found ourselves in the morning. Our cabs were dismissed, and, following the guidance of Mr. Merryweather, we

10 rubber: round of whist, a card game.

passed down a narrow passage and through a side door, which he opened for us. Within there was a small corridor, which ended in a very massive iron gate. This also was opened, and led down a flight of winding stone steps, which terminated at another formidable gate. Mr. Merryweather stopped to light a lantern, and then conducted us down a dark, earth-smelling passage, and so, after opening a third door, into a huge vault or cellar, which was piled all round with crates and massive boxes.

"You are not very vulnerable from above," Holmes remarked as he held up the lantern and gazed about him.

"Nor from below," said Mr. Merryweather, striking his stick upon the flags which lined the floor. "Why, dear me, it sounds quite hollow!" he remarked, looking up in surprise.

"I must really ask you to be a little more quiet!" said Holmes severely. "You have already imperiled the whole success of our expedition. Might I beg that you would have the goodness to sit down upon one of those boxes, and not to interfere?"

The solemn Mr. Merryweather perched himself upon a crate, with a very injured expression upon his face, while Holmes fell upon his knees upon the floor and, with the lantern and a magnifying lens, began to examine minutely the cracks between the stones. A few seconds sufficed to satisfy him, for he sprang to his feet again and put his glass in his pocket.

"We have at least an hour before us," he remarked, "for they can hardly take any steps until the good pawnbroker is safely in bed. Then they will not lose a minute, for the sooner they do their work the longer time they will have for their escape. We are at present, Doctor—as no doubt you have divined—in the cellar of the City branch of one of the principal London banks. Mr. Merryweather is the chairman of directors, and he will explain to you that there are reasons why the more daring criminals of London should take a considerable interest in this cellar at present."

"It is our French gold," whispered the director. "We have had several warnings that an attempt might be made upon it."

"Your French gold?"

"Yes. We had occasion some months ago to strengthen our resources and borrowed for that purpose 30,000 napoleons from the Bank of France. It has become known that we have never had occasion to unpack the money, and that it is still lying in our cellar. The crate upon which I sit contains 2,000 napoleons packed between layers of lead foil. Our reserve of bullion is much larger at present than is usually kept in a single branch office, and the directors have had misgivings upon the subject."

"Which were very well justified," observed Holmes. "And now it is time that we arranged our little plans. I expect that within an hour matters will come to a head. In the meantime, Mr. Merryweather, we must put the screen over that dark lantern."

"And sit in the dark?"

"I am afraid so. I had brought a pack of cards in my pocket, and I thought that, as we were a *partie carrée*,[11] you might have your rubber after all. But I see that the enemy's preparations have gone so far that we cannot risk the presence of a light. And, first of all, we must choose our positions. These are daring men, and though we shall take them at a disadvantage, they may do us some harm unless we are careful. I shall stand behind this crate, and do you conceal yourselves behind those. Then, when I flash a light upon them, close in swiftly. If they fire, Watson, have no compunction about shooting them down."

11 *partie carrée:* foursome.

I placed my revolver, cocked, upon the top of the wooden case behind which I crouched. Holmes shot the slide across the front of his lantern and left us in pitch darkness—such an absolute darkness as I have never before experienced. The smell of hot metal remained to assure us that the light was still there, ready to flash out at a moment's notice. To me, with my nerves worked up to a pitch of expectancy, there was something depressing and subduing in the sudden gloom, and in the cold dank air of the vault.

"They have but one retreat," whispered Holmes. "That is back through the house into Saxe-Coburg Square. I hope that you have done what I asked you, Jones?"

"I have an inspector and two officers waiting at the front door."

"Then we have stopped all the holes. And now we must be silent and wait."

What a time it seemed! From comparing notes afterwards it was but an hour and a quarter, yet it appeared to me that the night must have almost gone, and the dawn be breaking above us. My limbs were weary and stiff, for I feared to change my position; yet my nerves were worked up to the highest pitch of tension, and my hearing was so acute that I could not only hear the gentle breathing of my companions, but I could distinguish the deeper, heavier inbreath of the bulky Jones from the thin, sighing note of the bank director. From my position I could look over the case in the direction of the floor. Suddenly my eyes caught the glint of a light.

At first it was but a lurid spark upon the stone pavement. Then it lengthened out until it became a yellow line, and then, without any warning or sound, a gash seemed to open and a hand appeared; a white, almost womanly hand, which felt about in the center of the little area of light. For a minute or more the hand, with its writhing fingers, protruded out of the floor. Then it was withdrawn as suddenly as it appeared, and all was dark again save the single lurid spark which marked a chink between the stones.

Its disappearance, however, was but momentary. With a rending, tearing sound, one of the broad, white stones turned over ·upon its side and left a square, gaping hole, through which streamed the light of a lantern. Over the edge there peeped a clean-cut, boyish face, which looked keenly about it, and then, with a hand on either side of the aperture, drew itself shoulder-high and waist-high, until one knee rested upon the edge. In another instant he stood at the side of the hole and was hauling after him a companion, lithe and small like himself, with a pale face and a shock of very red hair.

"It's all clear," he whispered. "Have you the chisel and the bags? Great Scott! Jump, Archie, jump, and I'll swing for it!"

Sherlock Holmes had sprung out and seized the intruder by the collar. The other dived down the hole, and I heard the sound of rending cloth as Jones clutched at his skirts. The light flashed upon the barrel of a revolver, but Holmes's hunting crop came down on the man's wrist, and the pistol clinked upon the stone floor.

"It's no use, John Clay," said Holmes blandly. "You have no chance at all."

"So I see," the other answered with the utmost coolness. "I fancy that my pal is all right, though I see you have got his coattails."

"There are three men waiting for him at the door," said Holmes.

"Oh, indeed! You seem to have done the thing very completely. I must compliment you."

"And I you," Holmes answered. "Your redheaded idea was very new and effective."

"You'll see your pal again presently," said Jones. "He's quicker at climbing down holes than I am. Just hold out while I fix the derbies."[12]

"I beg that you will not touch me with your filthy hands," remarked our prisoner as the handcuffs clattered upon his wrists. "You may not be aware that I have royal blood in my veins. Have the goodness, also, when you address me always to say 'sir' and 'please.'"

"All right," said Jones with a stare and a snigger. "Well, would you please, sir, march upstairs, where we can get a cab to carry your Highness to the police station?"

"That is better," said John Clay serenely. He made a sweeping bow to the three of us and walked quietly off in the custody of the detective.

"Really, Mr. Holmes," said Mr. Merryweather as we followed them from the cellar, "I do not know how the bank can thank you or repay you. There is no doubt that you have detected and defeated in the most complete manner one of the most determined attempts at bank robbery that have ever come within my experience."

"I have had one or two little scores of my own to settle with Mr. John Clay," said Holmes. "I have been at some small expense over this matter, which I shall expect the bank to refund, but beyond that I am amply repaid by having had an experience which is in many ways unique, and by hearing the very remarkable narrative of the Redheaded League."

"You see, Watson," he explained in the early hours of the morning as we sat over a glass of whisky and soda in Baker Street, "it was perfectly obvious from the first that the only possible object of this rather fantastic business of the advertisement of the League, and the copying of the Encyclopedia, must be to get this not overbright pawnbroker out of the way for a number of hours every day. It was a curious way of managing it, but, really, it would be difficult to suggest a better. The method was no doubt suggested to Clay's ingenious mind by the color of his accomplice's hair. The £4 a week was a lure which must draw him, and what was it to them, who were playing for thousands? They put in the advertisement, one rogue has the temporary office, the other rogue incites the man to apply for it, and together they manage to secure his absence every morning in the week. From the time that I heard of the assistant having come for half wages, it was obvious to me that he had some strong motive for securing the situation."

"But how could you guess what the motive was?"

"Had there been women in the house, I should have suspected a mere vulgar intrigue. That, however, was out of the question. The man's business was a small one, and there was nothing in his house which could account for such elaborate preparations, and such an expenditure as they were at. It must, then, be something out of the house. What could it be? I thought of the

12 derbies: handcuffs.

assistant's fondness for photography, and his trick of vanishing into the cellar. The cellar! There was the end of this tangled clue. Then I made inquiries as to this mysterious assistant and found that I had to deal with one of the coolest and most daring criminals in London. He was doing something in the cellar—something which took many hours a day for months on end. What could it be, once more? I could think of nothing save that he was running a tunnel to some other building.

"So far I had got when we went to visit the scene of action. I surprised you by beating upon the pavement with my stick. I was ascertaining whether the cellar stretched out in front or behind. It was not in front. Then I rang the bell, and, as I hoped, the assistant answered it. We have had some skirmishes, but we had never set eyes upon each other before. I hardly looked at his face. His knees were what I wished to see. You must yourself have remarked how worn, wrinkled, and stained they were. They spoke of those hours of burrowing. The only remaining point was what they were burrowing for. I walked round the corner, saw the City and Suburban Bank abutted on our friend's premises, and felt that I had solved my problem. When you drove home after the concert I called upon Scotland Yard and upon the chairman of the bank directors, with the result that you have seen."

"And how could you tell that they would make their attempt tonight?" I asked.

"Well, when they closed their League offices that was a sign that they cared no longer about Mr. Jabez Wilson's presence—in other words, that they had completed their tunnel. But it was essential that they should use it soon, as it might be discovered, or the bullion might be removed. Saturday would suit them better than any other day, as it would give them two days for their escape. For all these reasons I expected them to come tonight."

"You reasoned it out beautifully," I exclaimed in unfeigned admiration. "It is so long a chain, and yet every link rings true."

"It saved me from ennui,"[13] he answered, yawning. "Alas! I already feel it closing in upon me. My life is spent in one long effort to escape from the commonplaces of existence. These little problems help me to do so."

"And you are a benefactor of the race," said I.

He shrugged his shoulders. "Well, perhaps, after all, it is of some little use," he remarked. " 'L'homme c'est rien—l'oeuvre c'est tout,'[14] as Gustave Flaubert wrote to George Sand."[15]

---

13 **ennui** (än′wē): boredom.
14 **L'homme . . . tout:** "Man is nothing; his work is everything."
15 **Gustave Flaubert . . . George Sand:** 19th-century French writers.

Understanding Literature

1. From whose *point of view* is the story told?
2. The author plunges the reader immediately into the story and gives much information very quickly. What do you learn about the three characters and what they are doing in the first six short paragraphs?
3. How does Holmes's inspection of the client, Mr. Wilson, differ from Watson's? What does this difference in the way Holmes and Watson see Wilson point out about Sherlock Holmes?
4. After Holmes and Watson hear all the facts of Wilson's story and go to the pawnbroker's shop, Watson is still confused, whereas Holmes has obviously understood the whole affair and its results. Find the passage in which Watson remarks about his failure to understand the case whereas Holmes evidently has understood it completely. Considering what Watson says about himself in this passage, why do you think his *point of view* is a good one from which to tell the story? How would the story be different if Holmes had told it?
5. After you have finished the story, you understand the significance of some remarks or details that you had not understood previously. Point out in the early part of Wilson's story about himself and his business some details that Holmes makes mental note of and which help him solve the case. How do they help him solve the problem?
6. What in Mr. Wilson's description of the advertisement for the vacancy in the Redheaded League and his acceptance into the League aroused your suspicion as you read it—or that you see now *should* have aroused your suspicion?
7. At what point in the story do you first know that Sherlock Holmes has some clue as to the meaning of Wilson's story?
8. At what point were you able to begin to predict the outcome of the story? Explain what clues led you to your solution.
9. Why does Sherlock Holmes, according to his own words, work on such cases?
10. Describe Sherlock Holmes in your own words, basing your description on what Watson says about him, on what Holmes himself says, and on the way he acts. Be sure that you are able to prove all your statements about Sherlock Holmes from evidence in the story.

Focusing on Words

Read aloud Sherlock Holmes's words in the paragraph beginning "Try the settee" (p. 566).   His way of speaking is certainly far different from the way Tom Sawyer, Jim Hawkins, or even Robinson Crusoe would speak.   The language has a different ring to it.   Holmes uses words which Tom Sawyer would probably not know or, if he did, would consider affected or, as Tom might say, "show-off."   However, for both Sherlock Holmes, a mature, scholarly gentleman, and for Watson, a learned doctor, these words are not affected; they are natural to them.   Many of the words they use came originally to the English language from the Latin or Greek languages.

Look up in the Glossary or a dictionary the italicized words in the quotations below.

Copy what the dictionary tells you about the derivation of each word, that is, in what language it appeared first, the spelling of the word in that language, and what it meant.   In many dictionaries you will find this information in brackets directly after the pronunciation and the part of speech of the word you are looking up.

Example: *precaution:* from Latin, *praecavere,* "to be on one's guard."

Also try to find for each word a synonym which you think simpler.   (It may not always be possible to find one word which would mean exactly the same thing.)

1. "With an apology for my *intrusion.* . . ."
2. ". . . he said *cordially.*"
3. ". . . *relapsing* into his armchair. . . ."
4. ". . . putting his finger tips together, as was his custom when in *judicial* moods."
5. ". . . to *chronicle,* and . . . somewhat to *embellish* so many of my own little adventures."
6. "A *proposition* which I took the liberty of doubting."
7. ". . . you would have the great kindness to *recommence* your *narrative.*"

Author Biographies

AESOP (about 620-560 B.C.). (Pronounced ē′səp, ē′sŏp.) Although there is no positive proof that Aesop ever existed, most Greek scholars believe that a Greek slave with that name became famous for his witty retellings of Oriental animal stories. Aesop himself probably never wrote down any of these fables, but about 320 B.C. a ruler named Demetrius of Athens assembled the first known collection of Aesop's fables.

ALCOTT, LOUISA MAY (1832-1888). Louisa May Alcott wrote her first book, *Flower Fables,* for a friend's daughter. But she first became well known as a writer with *Hospital Sketches,* which first appeared in 1863. These sketches were letters which she had written to her family when she was a nurse for six weeks in a Washington hospital during the Civil War. In *Little Women* (1868) Louisa May Alcott herself appears as Jo. *Little Men* (1871) and *Jo's Boys* (1886) followed after *Little Women* and were equally popular.

ALDRICH, THOMAS BAILEY (1836-1907). Aldrich wrote about his own boyhood in Portsmouth, New Hampshire, in *The Story of a Bad Boy.* As he tells in that book, he had intended to go to college, but because of his father's death he went into business in New York. He left business for journalism, eventually returning to New England, where he was editor of *The Atlantic Monthly,* a famous magazine.

BALDWIN, JAMES (1841-1925). As he grew up in a backwoods Quaker settlement in Indiana, Baldwin developed a great affection for books and reading. At twenty-four he became a teacher; a few years later he moved up to the superintendency of the public schools of Indiana. Later he became an editor of school texts, and in his free time he wrote about fifty books, such as *The Story of Siegfried* and *The Story of Roland.*

BENÉT, ROSEMARY CARR (1898-   ). *See* **BENÉT, STEPHEN VINCENT.**

BENÉT, STEPHEN VINCENT (1898-1943). (Pronounced bĭ nā′.) Benét's family was quite literary: his brother, William Rose Benét, was a very successful poet and novelist, as was his sister-in-law, Elinor Wylie; his wife, Rosemary Carr Benét, was a reporter for the *Chicago Tribune* when he first met her. Benét's most famous works deal with American history: *John Brown's Body* is a narrative poem about the Civil War; "The Devil and Daniel Webster" has become a classic short story.

BLAKE, WILLIAM (1757-1827). William Blake's father recognized his son's artistic talent and sent him to a London art school when the boy was ten. From fourteen to twenty-one Blake was apprenticed to an engraver from whom he learned the techniques which allowed him to earn his living as one of England's notable engravers and water-colorists. Even as a boy,

Blake had shown the same flair for writing poetry that he had for art, and some of his well-known poems were written when he was less than fifteen. Because he was not business-minded, but preferred to work independently, Blake was poor during his adult life. Although his poetry was not understood during his lifetime, it is now famous for its imaginative qualities.

BRADBURY, RAY (1920-   ). Best known as a writer of science fiction and fantasy, Bradbury writes of subjects which have interested him most of his life. At fifteen he decided that someday he should have a story of his own in a collection of *Best American Short Stories*. After graduation from high school, Bradbury sold newspapers for three years, while he wrote daily in his free time. His first published story appeared in a magazine when he was nineteen. After a few years of writing primarily for science fiction and detective-story magazines, his earlier dream was realized when his story "The Big Black and White Game" was included in *The Best American Short Stories of 1946*.

BROWNING, ROBERT (1812-1889). Browning grew up in a London suburb, where he was given a thorough education by his intelligent, cultured parents. His early ambition was to be a poet; by the age of twelve he had written a book of poems. In 1846 Browning married Elizabeth Barrett, also a poet. Because of her poor health and the displeasure of her strong-willed father, they lived in Italy for fifteen years, until her death. Returning to England, Browning finally gained recognition for his poetry when he published *Dramatis Personae* and *The Ring and the Book*.

BULFINCH, THOMAS (1796-1867). One of eleven children of a famous architect, Bulfinch was born in Newton, Massachusetts. After graduation from Harvard in 1814, he was a teacher for a year. In 1818 the entire family moved to Washington, D.C., because the father, Charles Bulfinch, had been appointed architect of the United States Capitol. Thomas Bulfinch tried business several times, never with much success, and finally was satisfied to be a bank clerk because the job allowed so much time for study and writing. His best-known work is *The Age of Fable*, a collection of myths.

BURNS, ROBERT (1759-1796). The child who was to become the greatest of Scottish poets was born to a poor but respectable farm family in Ayrshire. Robert Burns had only a few years of formal schooling, and by the age of thirteen he was doing a man's work on the farm. Most of his life was spent in poverty, which probably contributed to his early death. Although Burns received a minimum of education in schools, he was educated, it has been said, by the traditional ballads and folk songs of Scotland. In poems like "The Cotter's Saturday Night" and songs like "Auld Lang Syne" he captures the moods and language of the Scottish people.

CAMPBELL, THOMAS (1777-1844). Born and educated in Glasgow, Scotland, Campbell became famous when he published *The Pleasures of Hope*. His best poems, such as "Ye Mariners of England," were written while he toured Germany and witnessed several battles and battle scenes. Eventually he settled in London and spent the rest of his life in various literary activities.

CARTER, RUSSELL GORDON (1892-1957). New Jersey-born Russell Gordon Carter attended Harvard, from which he graduated in 1916. He worked on several magazines and wrote numerous books based on scouting and American history.

CANE, MELVILLE (1879-   ). Cane received his bachelor's degree from Columbia University in 1900, and a law degree in 1903. While at Columbia he edited its literary magazine. He then engaged in law practice, specializing in copyright law. Cane's interest in writing has ranged from the light verse of his early years to more recent serious poetry, articles, and short stories.

CLEMENS, SAMUEL LANGHORNE. *See* **TWAIN, MARK.**

COLETTE (1873-1954). The child who was to become one of France's greatest women writers was named Gabrielle Claudine Colette when she was born in a village in Burgundy. At the age of twenty she married a

music critic and novelist who used the pen name "Willy," and together the couple wrote a highly successful series of gay novels. During World War I Colette converted an estate into a hospital where she worked as a nurse. Over the years she turned out an impressive list of novels and short stories, always distinguished by her ability to describe scenes, sounds, odors, and other sensations with great clarity and realism.

COLUM, PADRAIC (1881-   ). (Pronounced pô'drik kol'em.) A native of Ireland, Padraic Colum did not migrate to the United States until he had achieved moderate success as a poet and playwright in Dublin, although the vast majority of his published works have appeared since he came to America in 1914. Many of Colum's stories and plays are based on folk tales which he learned in Ireland, and in 1923 he visited Hawaii to record and reshape some of the folk stories of the Polynesians.

COWPER, WILLIAM (1731-1800). (Pronounced koo'per, kou'per.) Cowper's life contained a series of unfortunate events. Six years after his birth in Hertfordshire, England, his mother died. In "Tirocinium" he describes how he was bullied by the boys in his first school. He was unhappy in his London law practice and disappointed when his uncle forbade his marriage to his cousin Theodora. Throughout the rest of his life he lived with various families and wrote poetry and hymns. He is known for a humorous ballad, "John Gilpin," and a long poem, *The Task*.

590

CRANE, STEPHEN (1871-1900). Born in Newark, New Jersey, Stephen Crane lived in a great variety of circumstances during his short life before he died of tuberculosis in Germany. For five years he lived in New York City, sometimes among students, sometimes in the Bowery slums. Crane's first novel, written under a pseudonym, was a realistic description of the hard life of the slums. His ability to depict the terrors of war was a feature of his famous novel, *The Red Badge of Courage*, although when he wrote it, Crane had no personal experience with war.

DAVIS, FRANK MARSHALL (1905-). Born in Kansas, Frank Marshall Davis attended school there and studied journalism at Kansas State College, where he also began writing poetry. During the summers he worked on farms and on street construction crews. Much of his adult life has been spent in newspaper work—he began one paper and was its editor—and he has lived, besides Kansas, in Georgia and Hawaii. Three volumes of his poetry are *Black Man's Verse, I Am the American Negro,* and *47th Street.* He has also been a lecturer on the history of jazz.

DAY, CLARENCE S. (1874-1935). The parents of Clarence Day, Jr., are well known, not because they were famous by their own efforts, but because they are so thoroughly described in two of their son's widely read books, *Life with Father* and *Life with Mother.* Day's father was a very successful financier in the New York Stock Exchange, and after Clarence, Jr., graduated from Yale University in 1896, he joined his father's stocks and bonds brokerage. He left to join the Navy during the Spanish-American War, during which he began to be crippled by arthritis. Although confined to bed much of the time, he continued to write essays and books.

DEFOE, DANIEL (1660-1731). During the early part of his life Defoe was a London merchant. His business success ended abruptly in 1692 when he went bankrupt. He then turned to writing pamphlets, books, and newspapers. In 1719 he published *Robinson Crusoe,* his first novel. Later he produced such other well-known books as *A Journal of the Plague Year* and *Moll Flanders.*

DICKINSON, EMILY (1830-1886). Born in Amherst, Massachusetts, Emily Dickinson was the daughter of the community's leading lawyer, Edward Dickinson. After a brief formal education and an unhappy love affair, Emily Dickinson spent most of her time at home, seeing only a limited circle of friends. Her poetry was written in secret on scraps of paper and tucked away in bureau drawers. Only three or four Dickinson poems were published during her lifetime, but a collection of her poems published several years after her death was a great success. Ever since then her poetry has been admired for its sharp wit and graceful, though often irregular, rhythm.

DOYLE, SIR ARTHUR CONAN (1859-1930). Sherlock Holmes, one of the most famous characters in English literature, might never have existed if Arthur Conan Doyle, a Scottish doctor, had not needed money to supplement a meager medical practice. Doyle created Holmes as the fictional sleuth who solved crimes scientifically by careful observation and diagnosis of situations and people. The Sherlock Holmes stories were such a success that Doyle eventually gave up the practice of medicine to devote his full time to writing. The first Holmes story was *A Study in Scarlet,* published in 1887. *The Adventures of Sherlock Holmes,* a cycle of stories each complete in itself, was published in 1891.

DUNSANY, EDWARD JOHN MORETON DRAX PLUNKETT, LORD (1878-1957). Born in London, of Irish parentage, Dunsany became the 18th Baron Dunsany. He was educated at Sandhurst, the English equivalent of West Point, and applied his military training in the Boer War and World War I. His first literary ventures were in drama, but he also wrote poetry and short stories. His works often use fantasy.

EATON, JEANETTE. Born in Columbus, Ohio, Jeanette Eaton earned her master's degree from Ohio State University in that city in 1910 after receiving her first degree from Vassar College in 1908. She is known chiefly as a biographer for young readers, and her books include *Young Lafayette, Jeanne d'Arc,* and *Betsy's Napoleon.*

FIELD, EUGENE (1850-1895). Field, born in St. Louis, Missouri, was sent to Massachusetts to live with relatives after his mother died when he was six. He attended several colleges, but never received a degree. Most of his adult life was spent as a newspaper reporter and columnist in several cities of the Midwest. He is known chiefly for a few children's poems which have been very popular.

FLACK, AMBROSE (1902?-). Flack was raised in Syracuse, New York, where he had a chance meeting with his family's idol, Theodore Roosevelt, described in a short story called "Theodore Roosevelt and My Green-Gold Fountain Pen." Flack has always enjoyed writing about children in his magazine stories.

FRANCE, ANATOLE (1844-1924). (Pronounced à nà tôl' fräNs.) The son of a Paris bookseller, Jacques Anatole François Thibault was given a thorough education in the Greek and Roman classics, although he perhaps learned even more from his father's library and the discussions of artists in the family home. Throughout his life he preferred reading to writing, and the prodding of his friends was needed to make him work steadily. France's short stories and novels, such as *The Revolt of the Angels* and *Penguin Island,* are known for their insight into human nature. His observations of the good and evil in people show a keen vision and reflect his skeptical, satiric point of view.

GALE, ZONA (1874-1938). Born in Portage, Wisconsin, Zona Gale spent most of her life in her native state and used it, along with other Mid-western states, as the setting for some of her best-known writings. She was employed by newspapers in Milwaukee and New York until 1904 when she returned to Portage, where she remained for the rest of her life. She wrote novels, short stories, and plays; and for her dramatization of *Miss Lulu Bett* in 1920 she won a Pulitzer prize.

GARLAND, HAMLIN (1860-1940). Born on a farm in Wisconsin, Hamlin Garland spent his school years in Iowa, graduating from the Cedar Valley Seminary in Osage, Iowa. He farmed a homestead in North Dakota for a year, and then sold it so that he could move to Boston to prepare for a career as a teacher of American literature. After nine years in Boston, during which he wrote a number of short stories and his first novel, *A Spoil of Office*, he returned to Wisconsin, and later lived in Chicago, New York, and Los Angeles. He is best known for his real-istic description of the frontier Mid-west in *A Son of the Middle Border*. Hamlin Garland was one of the first writers to describe the American Indian with accuracy, realism, and understanding.

GRAHAME, KENNETH (1859-1932). Grahame was born in Edinburgh, Scotland, but grew up in England. He did not consider writing of first importance in his life, being more concerned with his family and his work as a banker. He wrote *The Wind in the Willows* for his one son, Alistair. Except for one book of essays and a collection of writing published after his death, Grahame wrote only three books, *The Golden Age, Dream Days*, and *The Wind in the Willows*.

GREGORY, ISABELLA, LADY (1852-1932). In Roxborough, County Galway, Ireland, the twelfth child of Dudley Persse was named Isabella Augusta. In 1881 she married Sir William Gregory, a member of Parliament; thereafter she was known as Lady Gregory. Through her friend-ship with William Butler Yeats she became involved in the Irish literary revival, and together they made a success of the famous Abbey Theatre in Dublin. She collaborated with Yeats on a few plays and wrote more than thirty plays of her own, such as *Spreading the News, The Workhouse Ward*, and *The Rising of the Moon*.

GUITERMAN, ARTHUR (1871-1943). (Pronounced gĭt'ər mən.) Guiter-man's family lived in New York City, and he was educated at the City College of New York. In college he was active in sports, and even when he was past sixty he engaged in mountain climbing, tennis, and skating. He began his literary ca-reer as a reporter and editor, and then became a free-lance writer of poetry. He ventured into drama briefly and wrote the story and words for an opera, *A Man Without a Country*. He is perhaps best known, however, for his humorous poems, such as those in *The Laughing Muse*.

HALE, NANCY (1908-   ). Born in Boston, the only child of parents who were both painters, Nancy Hale studied art for a brief period. At age eleven her first publication was a short story in *The Boston Herald*. In New York City she wrote numerous magazine articles, eventually becoming assistant editor of *Vogue* and *Vanity Fair* and the first woman reporter on *The New York Times*. Her best-known writings are her short stories, which are collected in *The Earliest Dreams* and *Between the Dark and the Daylight*.

HAMILTON, EDITH (1867-1963). Although she was born in Dresden, Germany, her parents were American citizens, and Edith Hamilton grew up in Fort Wayne, Indiana. With her father's encouragement, Miss Hamilton became a recognized authority on Greek, Roman, and Hebrew culture; she graduated from Bryn Mawr College in Pennsylvania. She also studied at the Universities of Leipzig and Munich in Germany, although no woman had ever before enrolled at Munich. When she returned to America, she became headmistress of the Bryn Mawr School in Baltimore. In *The Greek Way, The Roman Way*, and a collection of the Greek myths, she combined extensive knowledge with an entertaining style of writing which has made these books extremely popular.

HENRY, O. (1862-1910). William Sydney Porter, who used the pen name O. Henry, was born in Greensboro, North Carolina. When he was fifteen, he left school to go to work in an uncle's drugstore for five years. In 1882 he went to Texas, working on a ranch for two years and then becoming a bank teller. The remaining quarter-century of his life was spent in a great variety of settings—Texas, New Orleans, Honduras, Mexico, South America, and New York City. Many of his short stories were written while he was in prison in Ohio, after being convicted of embezzling funds when he was a bank teller. O. Henry is considered a master of the short story, especially those with a surprise twist at the end. Some of his short-story collections are *The Four Million, The Voice of the City, Sixes and Sevens*, and *Waifs and Strays*.

HORGAN, PAUL (1903-   ). Horgan lived in Buffalo, New York, until the age of eleven, when his family moved to Albuquerque, New Mexico. After studying music in Rochester, New York, he returned to New Mexico to join the staff of the New Mexico Military Institute. His most successful literary effort is a two-volume history of the Rio Grande, entitled *Great River*, which won a Pulitzer prize and the Bancroft prize for history after its publication in 1954. Horgan has also written novels and short stories.

HOVEY, RICHARD (1864-1900). After completing Dartmouth College, Hovey studied art and theology, worked as a reporter and actor, and traveled about Europe and northeastern America. He became acquainted with the Canadian poet Bliss Carman, and together they wrote a number of poems which comprise three volumes of *Songs of Vagabondia.*

HOUSMAN, A. E. (1859-1936). The oldest of seven children, Alfred Edward Housman grew up in Worcestershire, England. He received a good formal education, including four years at Oxford University. After a decade in the civil service he became professor of Latin, first at University College, London, and later at Trinity College, Cambridge. During his lifetime he was a respected and feared literary critic and translator, but his greatness rests on his books of poetry, especially *A Shropshire Lad.*

HUGHES, LANGSTON (1902-   ). Langston Hughes, born in Missouri, was the class poet at Central High School in Cleveland, Ohio; and even before he graduated from Lincoln University, in 1929, he was recognized as a professional writer. His first book of poems, *The Weary Blues,* appeared in 1926, and since then he has also written a novel, short stories, and nonfiction. *The Langston Hughes Reader* contains various works; and *The Big Sea* and *I Wonder as I Wander* are the first two volumes of his autobiography, which he is writing in three volumes. With Arna Bontemps he has collected *The Poetry of the Negro.*

HUNT, LEIGH (1784-1859). (Pronounced lē.) Born in Middlesex, England, (James Henry) Leigh Hunt was the son of parents who were driven from the United States shortly after the Revolutionary War because of their sympathy with the English monarchy. Whereas his father had favored the English rulers, Leigh Hunt and his brother John eventually got into difficulty when they criticized the English government in their weekly *Examiner.* Throughout his life Hunt spoke out in favor of freedom of speech and belief. He edited and published a variety of papers and magazines. His great contributions to literature were his campaigns to draw attention to the excellence of the writings of Keats and Shelley.

JACOBS, WILLIAM WYMARK (1863-1943). Born in London and educated in English private schools, W. W. Jacobs was employed as a civil service clerk during his early adult years. He began writing as a hobby, but when he was thirty-six he resigned from the Civil Service to devote full time to writing. Jacobs's work was chiefly of two types: gentle humor and mystery. The majority of his stories concern seamen and the tales they have to tell. His spine-chilling "The Monkey's Paw" is one of the most famous short stories in English.

JONSON, BEN (1573-1637). Jonson, a great 17th-century poet-dramatist, was born in Westminster, the district of London in which his body is now buried in the famous Westminster

Abbey. The boy received formal education, but it apparently did not include university training, and he took on his stepfather's trade as a bricklayer as soon as he left school. Because bricklaying did not appeal to him, he became a soldier and served in Flanders. Jonson later was employed as an actor, but he seems to have lacked acting talent and so drifted into playwriting. His best work appeared between 1605 and 1615, just about the time of Shakespeare's plays. Jonson's best-known plays are the comedies *Volpone, The Alchemist,* and *Every Man in His Humor.*

KIPLING, RUDYARD (1865-1936). Kipling was born in Bombay, India, of English parentage and he was educated in England. He wrote mainly about the British soldiers, government officials, and Indian natives whom he knew from personal experience. Kipling had great faith and trust in the ideals of the British Empire, and his writing often glorifies the British soldiers or officials. After marrying an American, Kipling lived in the United States for four years, and during that period he published *Many Inventions,* the book which introduced Mowgli, the boy who is raised by jungle animals. Among his well-known books are the poems of *Barrack Room Ballads* and the lively adventure stories of *Just So Stories, The Jungle Books, Puck of Pook's Hill,* and *Captains Courageous.*

LINDSAY, VACHEL (1879-1931). (Pronounced vā'chəl lǐnd'zǐ.) Lindsay's home town, Springfield, Illinois, gave him an interest in Abraham Lincoln, whose life was closely associated with Springfield. Lindsay originally expected to be an artist, and after three years at Hiram College, he entered the Chicago Art Institute. Because he was unable to sell any of his art work, he eventually began a wanderer's tour of the country, during which he recited his poems in exchange for meals. Through much of his life he continued to recite his dramatic poetry, even after he was receiving income from several volumes of published poetry. The strong rhythms of "The Congo" and "General William Booth Enters into Heaven" were always popular with his audiences.

LONGFELLOW, HENRY WADSWORTH (1807-1882). The son of a Maine lawyer, Longfellow was the second of eight children in a family which traced its ancestors to the Pilgrims of early America. As a boy he read much from his father's excellent library, and his first poem was published when he was only thirteen. At Bowdoin College, from which he was graduated in 1825, one of his classmates was Nathaniel Hawthorne. By the time Longfellow was twenty-two he was a professor of languages at Bowdoin and had traveled in France, Spain, Germany, and Italy. In 1836 he accepted a position at Harvard, where he remained until 1854. *The Song of Hiawatha, Evangeline,* and "Paul Revere's Ride" are among his most famous poems.

LOWELL, JAMES RUSSELL (1819-1891). Son of a distinguished family in Cambridge, Massachusetts, James Russell Lowell was born in the colonial house in which he lived most of his life. He attended Harvard College, and at Harvard Law School prepared for his law career. He achieved his first public recognition with the publication of antislavery poems and articles and the *Biglow Papers*, which contained witty political comments about the Mexican War. After journeys to Europe in 1851 and 1855, he succeeded Longfellow as professor of modern languages at Harvard. He was the first editor of *The Atlantic Monthly*, and was also appointed as United States minister to Spain and England.

MACAULAY, THOMAS BABINGTON (1800-1859). Macaulay, who was born in Leicestershire, England, showed his brilliance at an early age. He could read at the age of three, and before he was eight he had written a *Compendium of Universal History*. Macaulay became involved in political and governmental matters; he went to India in 1834, where he wrote a new code of criminal law for that country. In 1838 he returned to England and resumed both political and literary activities. His major literary work was the compiling of a detailed *History of England*.

McGINLEY, PHYLLIS (1905-   ). Phyllis McGinley grew up in Oregon, Colorado (on a ranch), and Utah. After graduating from the University of Utah, she began teaching in Utah and New York, writing poetry when time permitted. After four or five years she left teaching to give fuller attention to writing. In 1944 her first children's book, *The Horse Who Lived Upstairs*, was published. Phyllis McGinley's light verse for adult readers has appeared in *The New Yorker* magazine. Selections from three decades of her verse appear in *Times Three*.

McKAY, CLAUDE (1891-1948). Claude McKay, born in Jamaica, was the eleventh child of a farmer. He himself studied agriculture for a time, at Tuskegee Institute and at Kansas State University, but then became interested in a literary life and moved to New York City. He had already published in Jamaica two books of poetry in the Jamaica dialect. Now he began to contribute poems to American magazines, and a collection of his poems, *Harlem Shadows*, appeared in 1922. Later he turned to short stories and novels but still wrote enough verse for another volume, *Selected Poems*, published in 1953, after his death.

MILLER, JOAQUIN (1841-1913). (Pronounced wä kēn'.) While there is some uncertainty about his birth date and his middle name, there is assurance that Cincinnatus Heine (or Hiner) Miller was born in Indiana into a Quaker schoolteacher's family. The name "Joaquin" was attached to him years later when he wrote a defense of a Mexican bandit, Joaquin Murietta. After moving to Oregon with his family, Miller ran away to the California gold mines in 1855, and for most of the remainder of his life he was a wanderer who followed a great variety of temporary interests, such as law, newspaper editing, and traveling. His poetry is known for its pictures of life on the Pacific coast and various types of American people.

MILNE, A. A. (1882-1956). Born in London, Alan Alexander Milne lived in England nearly all his life. After graduation from Cambridge University, he worked as a free-lance writer for about three years; then he became assistant editor of the British magazine called *Punch*. He kept the position with *Punch* until he entered the army during World War I. When he left the service, he decided not to return to the magazine but to devote his time to writing. A. A. Milne was known through the English-speaking world as the author of a series of children's books such as *Winnie the Pooh, The House at Pooh Corner*, and *When We Were Very Young* (poetry). In fact, his fame as an author of fanciful children's stories was so great that he found it difficult to gain attention as a writer of serious plays and essays for adults.

MORISON, SAMUEL ELIOT (1887-). Morison, a descendant of distinguished educators on both sides of his family, received a Ph.D. from Harvard in 1913. He taught at the University of California for one year, then returned to Harvard, where he taught American history until his retirement in 1955. Although he is an excellent writer and has won several prizes for his books, including a Pulitzer prize in 1942, Morison thinks of himself as a historian more than as a literary figure. His specialties are the history of seafaring activities and the history of early New England.

NASH, OGDEN (1902-). America's leading writer of humorous verse was born in Rye, New York. He was employed for several years in the editorial and publicity departments of two New York publishing companies. In 1931 he published his first two volumes of verse and eventually turned to writing full time. Among his books of poetry are *Versus, I'm a Stranger Here Myself*, and *Family Reunion*.

NATHAN, ROBERT (1894-). Born in New York City, Nathan attended a private school in Geneva, Switzerland, and then went to Phillips Exeter Academy and Harvard University. After working in advertising and teaching journalism, he became a full-time writer. In addition to his several volumes of poetry and more than two dozen novels (*Portrait of Jennie* is the best-known), he has written several plays and motion-picture dramas.

O'CONNOR, FRANK (1903-1966). Even though his family was too poor to provide him with a college education, Michael O'Donovan, whose pen name was Frank O'Connor, began writing in the Gaelic language (which he learned by listening to his grandmother) when he was very young. His work as a librarian, first in his native County Cork, Ireland, and later in Dublin, provided him with the opportunity to extend his education and to improve as a writer. With Yeats and Lady Gregory, he was one of the directors of the famous Abbey Theatre. His first book of stories was published in 1931 under the title *Guests of the Nation*.

POE, EDGAR ALLAN (1809-1849). The son of traveling actors, Edgar Poe was orphaned at the age of two. He was cared for until his late teens by Mr. and Mrs. John Allan, whose name he took for his own middle name. Poe entered the University of Virginia in 1826, but stayed for only one term. When his foster father then wished him to study law, Poe quarreled with him and went off to Boston. From that time, Edgar Allan Poe's life was a tragic one. All his romances took unhappy twists, his business and literary ventures failed to reward him in spite of his hard work, and alcoholism added to his miseries. Poe is often referred to as father of the modern detective story; among his stories are "The Gold Bug," "The Purloined Letter," and "The Murders in the Rue Morgue." He also wrote poetry ("The Raven," "Annabel Lee") and was a capable critic of literature during the 1830's and 1840's.

PORTER, WILLIAM SYDNEY. *See* **HENRY, O.**

PYLE, HOWARD (1853-1911). Although he achieved his greatest recognition as an author and illustrator of children's books, Howard Pyle was for most of his professional life chiefly an artist and art teacher. Born in Wilmington, Delaware, Pyle was guided and encouraged to an artistic career by his mother. From 1894 to 1900 he taught art at Drexel Institute in Philadelphia and then returned to Wilmington to start an art school of his own. In both his art and writing, Pyle featured chivalric characters (such as Robin Hood), adventure, and the sea.

ROSSETTI, CHRISTINA (1830-1894). The youngest of the amazing children in the Rossetti family, Christina was born in a northern section of London, where she remained for most of her life. She was educated entirely at home by her mother, and soon became a very capable writer in both Italian and English. Her first book of poems was published privately by her grandfather when she was twelve, but her first real publication was carried by a magazine when she was nineteen. She remained single, although almost marrying twice, largely because her suitors did not share her Anglican religious views. She withdrew from society eventually, partly because of prolonged illness.

SANDBURG, CARL (1878-   ). Born in Galesburg, Illinois, Sandburg worked at a variety of jobs (including that of dishwasher) before becoming known as a newspaperman, poet, historian, and biographer. His poetry is down-to-earth, sometimes hard-hitting in its language and sometimes very folksy. He is equally well known for his six-volume biography *Abraham Lincoln*.

Scott, Sir Walter (1771-1832). As a lad in Edinburgh, Scotland, Walter Scott was often unable to participate in athletic activities because he was lame. Fortunately he enjoyed listening to and telling adventure stories, and thus he developed the background which helped him to become the favorite romantic poet and adventure novelist of his day. His most well-known novels of romantic adventure are *Ivanhoe, Rob Roy,* and *Kenilworth.*

Scoville, Samuel (1872-1950). Born in Norwich, New York, Samuel Scoville, Jr., was the son of a Congregational minister. He attended Yale University, graduating in 1893. At Yale he was a boxer and track star, and also wrote for the college newspaper and magazine. Scoville spent most of his adult life in law practice; however, his writing provided most of his fame. Among his books are *Wild Folk* and *Boy Scouts of the Wilderness.*

Service, Robert W. (1874-1958). Few authors or poets traveled as widely as Robert W. Service, who was born in England, educated formally in Scotland, trained in the difficulties of life on the Pacific coast of Canada, employed as a war correspondent and ambulance driver on the mainland of Europe in World War I, and driven from France back to Canada by the Nazis in World War II. After the war he returned to France, where he continued writing until his death. His most recited and imitated poem is "The Shooting of Dan McGrew," which in style is very much like "The Cremation of Sam McGee."

Shakespeare, William (1564-1616). Literary critics agree that the greatest playwright the world has yet produced was William Shakespeare, who was born in Stratford-on-Avon about eighty miles from London, England. The facts of his early life are not known because few records were kept in the 16th century, but it is recorded that he married Anne Hathaway in 1582 and that they had three children. No one knows how he began his career as an actor and dramatist, but by 1592 he enjoyed a reputation as an actor and playwright in London, where he was then living. Among his more famous plays are *Hamlet, Macbeth, The Merchant of Venice, Twelfth Night,* and *Romeo and Juliet.*

Steffens, Lincoln (1866-1936). Born in San Francisco, Lincoln Steffens spent his boyhood on a ranch near Sacramento. He attended the University of California and then studied for three years at several European universities. When he returned to the United States, he was employed first as a newspaper reporter and later as editor of various newspapers and magazines. His books *The Shame of the Cities* (1904) and *The Struggle of Self-Government* (1906) show his concern for social injustices. Steffens was a very direct, honest writer who asked straightforward questions and gave straight-from-the-shoulder answers; many critics consider him one of the best reporters that America has produced.

AUTHOR BIOGRAPHIES

STEVENSON, ROBERT LOUIS (1850-1894). Stevenson's life was a restless one. It was not until six years before he died that he found a place to settle down: he lived in Samoa in the South Sea Islands from 1888 until his death. As a young man he first planned to become an engineer, but he soon left the study of engineering for that of law. After he had finished his studies, poor health sent him on frequent journeys about the world as he searched for a suitable climate. Throughout his lifetime of traveling, he continued to write essays, novels, stories, and poems. Besides *Treasure Island,* he wrote *The Strange Case of Dr. Jekyll and Mr. Hyde, Kidnapped, The Master of Ballantrae, The Black Arrow,* and a famous book of poems, *A Child's Garden of Verses.*

SYMONS, ARTHUR (1865-1945). Born in Wales and educated mainly in French and Italian private schools, Arthur Symons had command of three languages from childhood. When he was twenty-one, his first book was published, but he was already recognized as an editor and literary critic. His vast knowledge of literature was demonstrated by the range of authors he edited.

TEASDALE, SARA (1884-1933). Born in St. Louis, Sara Teasdale received her education through home tutoring, attendance at a private school, and extensive travel in Europe and the Near East. She wrote several volumes of poetry and edited two anthologies of poetry for young people, *Rainbow Gold* and *Stars Tonight.* Her own poetry is known for its delicate lyric quality and careful rhythm.

TENNYSON, ALFRED, LORD (1809-1892). The fourth of seven sons of a clergyman, Alfred Tennyson was born in Lincolnshire, England. He entered Trinity College, Cambridge, in 1827, but left without a degree in 1831 when his father died. However, he had already decided that poetry writing would be his life's work, and thus he was not interested in training for any other profession. In 1850, after the death of Wordsworth, he was appointed poet laureate. In 1884 Tennyson was given a seat in the House of Lords; hence the inclusion of "Lord" in his name. Among his many famous poems are "Ulysses," *Idylls of the King* (about King Arthur), "Break, Break, Break," and *In Memoriam.*

TWAIN, MARK (1835-1910). Samuel Langhorne Clemens grew up in the small river town of Hannibal, Missouri. He used the name Mark Twain (river-boat language for two fathoms of water, or safe water) when he began to write later in life. He went to school in Hannibal until he was twelve years old; then his father died and he went to work in a printing office. Twain was a river-boat pilot on the Mississippi for several years and then he followed his brother west to Nevada during the Civil War. Here Twain began his writing career on the Virginia City *Enterprise,* making the pen name Mark Twain famous for the comic anecdotes of frontier life which culminated in "The Celebrated Jumping Frog of Calaveras County." Twain's fame was further extended by the dry humor of his platform lectures about places where he had traveled. *Roughing It* is Twain's account of life in the West; other books are *Tom Sawyer, The Prince and the Pauper, A Connecticut Yankee in King Arthur's Court,* and *Huckleberry Finn.*

ULLMAN, JAMES RAMSEY (1907-). New York-born James Ramsey Ullman graduated from Princeton University in 1929. After a trip abroad he returned to New York and became a reporter and playwright. Then he turned his attention to a different field, writing *High Conquest,* a history of mountaineering. *The White Tower* is a novel about the attempt to conquer a mountain in the Alps. Ullman has himself done much mountaineering and thus writes from firsthand experience.

WEST, JESSAMYN (1907-). Although she was born in Indiana, Jessamyn West has lived in California since the age of six. Her first major book, *The Friendly Persuasion,* concerned a Quaker family in Indiana during the Civil War. It was made into a very successful movie in 1956. Miss West has written her autobiography, entitled *To See the Dream.*

WORDSWORTH, WILLIAM (1770-1850). Wordsworth was born into a pros-

perous landowning family in Cumberland, England, a beautiful region of lakes and mountains. For nine years he attended school at Hawkshead in the Esthwaite Valley, and because he was able to spend much time outdoors he developed a love of nature which became the subject of many of his poems. After graduating from Cambridge University, Wordsworth became acquainted with Samuel Taylor Coleridge, and the two poets decided to work together. In 1798 they published *Lyrical Ballads;* these poems were treated unfavorably by the critics because they were written in a new style. Wordsworth's influence later became very great when this new style of poetry led the Romantic movement. Wordsworth's ideas—particularly his faith in the power of nature and his admiration for the spontaneous and creative life of the child—were also very influential.

YEATS, WILLIAM BUTLER (1865-1939). (Pronounced yāts.) The son of a renowned Irish painter, William Butler Yeats was born in Dublin and educated in that city and in London. Following the family tradition, Yeats studied art but soon realized that his creative talents were more effective with words than with paints. Besides writing poetry, he was interested in drama and Irish politics. Yeats wrote a number of excellent plays and, with Lady Gregory, organized the Irish Literary Theatre, later called the Abbey Theatre, which attracted to it many of the best writers of the 20th century.

Literary Terms

Definitions for literary terms used in this book and also for certain fairly common terms not used in the text itself are given below. Page references in parentheses indicate that a term is further discussed on the pages listed. An asterisk after a word within a definition indicates that the word is defined under its own heading.

Acting Edition: An edition of a play which gives detailed instructions about staging and properties. This edition would be used by the director and actors who were putting on a play. "The Ghost of Jerry Bundler" is presented in an acting edition. (See p. 369.)

Alliteration: *See* Sound Devices.

Allusion: A reference to a person or place which the author expects the reader to recognize. Emily Dickinson's poem "Elysium" (p. 468) is based on an allusion to a place in Greek mythology. (See pp. 246, 468.)

Anecdote: A brief narrative* of a single incident. (See p. 26.)

Assonance: *See* Sound Devices.

Autobiography: An account of a person's life written by the person himself. "A Miserable, Merry Christmas" (p. 94) is part of *The Autobiography of Lincoln Steffens.*

Ballad: A narrative poem,* often meant for singing, using very simple language. Ballads usually deal with basic subjects such as love, honor, or death. The action is brief; it is often explained in dialogue,* with very little description* and characterization.* (See pp. 419, 435, 437, 452.)

The BALLAD STANZA usually consists of four lines, with the second and fourth lines rhyming. The rhythm of each line is usually iambic meter.* Often ballads contain a refrain,* a line that is repeated at the end of each stanza. (See p. 419.)

The POPULAR BALLAD, or FOLK BALLAD, comes from the people; it is passed down by word of mouth for generations and has no single known author. The LITERARY BALLAD has most of the characteristics of a ballad, but it has a single known author. "Bonny Barbara Allan" (p. 424) is a popular ballad; Tennyson's "The Revenge" (p. 452) is a literary ballad.

Beast Fable: A story presenting some useful truth or moral and narrated or acted by animals. (See p. 297.)

Biography: An account of a person's life written by another person. Some biographies are nonfictional; that is, they are based only on historical facts. Others, such as "That Lively Man, Ben Franklin" (p. 187), contain some fiction; that is, the author has added imaginary events or details.

Characterization: The technique of showing what a person is like. An author characterizes a person by telling what the person says, thinks, or does; by telling what others say or think about him; and by providing details of his dress and appearance. (See pp. 53, 358.)

Choice of Words: The words a writer chooses in order to create a particular mood* or feeling in the reader.

Climax: The point of greatest emotional impact in a story or drama. The climax is a turning point because it leads on to a resolution of the conflict* upon which the work is based. (See pp. 357, 26.)

Comparison: The technique of showing the likenesses between two things. In "On the Loss of the *Royal George*" (p. 450) Cowper compares a ship to a plow since a ship cuts a path into the sea in the same way a plow cuts a path into the ground. Two kinds of comparisons are the metaphor* and the simile.* (See pp. 452, 479.)

Conflict: A struggle of some kind, on which drama and fiction are based. Conflict in literature may involve a struggle of man against man or man against nature; it may also be an inner conflict, in which a character attempts to understand a situation, overcome a fear, make a decision, etc. Several conflicts may be present in one work of literature. (See pp. 81, 357.)

Connotation (kŏn′ə tā′shən): The emotional associations of a word, beyond the dictionary meaning of the word. For example, in describing a pleasant shade of green we might say "moss green," but we would probably not say "algae green" even though the latter might be a true description. A good writer chooses words with connotations ap-propriate to the subject he is describing. (See p. 228.)

Context: The words or passages surrounding a term or passage in speech or writing. The meanings of words or passages should always be determined in context. For example, the word *match* means something quite different in these two contexts: "He beat me in the tennis *match*" and "The wet *match* would not strike easily." (See p. 93.)

Contrast: The technique of showing the differences between two things. A work of literature is often based on a contrast between characters or settings or ideas.

Dialogue (dī′ə lôg′): Conversation between two or more characters in a story, drama, or poem. Often the story of a ballad* is told entirely through dialogue. Some writers, like Mark Twain in *The Adventures of Tom Sawyer* (p. 501), are skillful in using dialogue to characterize the people in a story and to present the events of the plot.* (See p. 358.)

Downstage: The front part of a stage; the part nearest the audience. (See diagram on p. 369.)

End Rhyme: *See* Sound Devices.

Epic: A long narrative poem* which tells of the adventures and achievements of a hero important to the history of his race or nation. The *Iliad* and *Odyssey* (p. 307) are Greek epics believed to have been written by Homer; Roland is an epic hero of France (*The Song of Roland*, p. 320). Since the epic hero is the principal element of an epic, an epic may also be called a hero tale.

Episode: An incident. A plot* is made up of a series of episodes, all closely related and each leading logically from one to the next. For example, the chapter from *Robinson Crusoe* (p. 541) is one episode in a series of adventures.

Exposition: Writing which explains something. The background for the plot of a short story or drama is called the exposition. In the exposition, characters are introduced and information about their backgrounds and their present situations is given. (See p. 357.)

Extended Metaphor: A metaphor,* or implied comparison between two objects, that is continued for several lines of a poem (as in Ben Jonson's "Oak and Lily," p. 482).

Fable: Short story which teaches some useful truth or moral. Often fables contain animals which speak and act like humans; these fables may be called beast tales.* Aesop is an important writer of fables. (See pp. 246, 297.)

Falling Action: The action following the climax* of a plot;* the outcome, or resolution, of a plot. The falling action presents the solutions to the problems raised, and it resolves the conflicts* in the story or play. (See p. 357.)

Farce: A kind of play which puts very simple types of characters into ridiculous situations in order to make the audience laugh. (See p. 382.)

Fiction: Imaginative writing, rather than factual reporting of real events. The term *fiction* usually refers to

novels like *Robinson Crusoe* (p. 541) and short stories like "The Gift of the Magi" (p. 113).

First Person Point of View: *See* Point of View.

Flashback: An episode* which suddenly interrupts the action of a story by shifting the scene back to an earlier time. The flashback usually explains something necessary to understanding the characters or plot. Nancy Hale uses flashback in "You Never Know" (p. 106).

Focus: The point of interest. An author will often concentrate on one character who then becomes the focus of the narrative. Ray Bradbury focuses on one character in "Good-by, Grandma" (p. 101).

Folk Ballad: *See* Ballad.

Free Verse: Poetry which does not have a uniform pattern of rhythm.* Carl Sandburg discusses free verse in his essay "Short Talk on Poetry" (p. 411).

Hero Tales: *See* Epic.

Iambic Meter: A rhythm used in poetry. It consists of an unaccented sound followed by an accented sound. For example, the word *Elaine* has iambic meter since the sound "E" is unaccented and the sound "laine*" is accented. Ballads are usually written in iambic meter. (See p. 419.)

Image: A word that appeals to one of the five senses. An image creates a picture or suggests a sensation of sound, smell, taste, or touch. For example, in "Good-by, Grandma" (p. 101) Ray Bradbury associates Grandma with many images: broom, dustpan, mixing spoon, baked pies, croquet mallets, chewing gum.

Imagery (ĭm′ĭj rĭ): The collection of images in a work of literature. In "The Wind" (p. 469) Stevenson makes the reader feel the effect of the wind even though no one can actually see the wind. He does this by using imagery. (See p. 295.)

Internal Rhyme: *See* Sound Devices.

Irony: A contrast between what appears to be so and what really is. Irony of statement occurs when a writer or speaker appears to be saying one thing but is really saying the opposite, as in "Crazy Horse" (p. 226). Irony of situation occurs when the outcome of a situation is the opposite of what one would expect, as in "The Idealist" (p. 147) where the little boy's expectations about school prove to be the opposite of reality.

Legend: A narrative,* sometimes based on historical people or events, handed down from the past. The stories about Robin Hood (p. 333) are called legends; King Arthur (p. 312) is a legendary hero. (See p. 246.)

Light Verse: Short, lyric poems that are written to entertain but often have a serious, instructive purpose. They often use rhyme to gain a humorous effect. (See p. 498.)

Literary Ballad: *See* Ballad.

Lyric (lĭr′ĭk): A poem with a single speaker who expresses personal thoughts or emotions about a subject. For example, in "Song" (p. 477) Christina Rossetti expresses a personal point of view about death. (See p. 466.)

Melodrama: A kind of play which generally has the following characteristics: (1) the characters are either extremely good or extremely bad; (2) the ending is happy (the villain is defeated, the hero marries the heroine, etc.); (3) the plot* depends on coincidences, or chance occurrences; (4) a strong appeal is made to the audience's emotions, although in a rather shallow way (that is, the audience is supposed to like or dislike the various characters strongly, although these characters are not very realistic). Dunsany's *A Night at an Inn* (p. 359) is a melodrama.

Metaphor (mĕt′ə fər): An implied comparison of two basically different objects that are alike in at least one way. For example, in the poem "He Wishes for the Cloths of Heaven" (p. 481) Yeats compares the heavens to embroidered cloths: the silver and gold on the cloths are like the stars and sun in the sky. Both the cloths and the sky shine. (See p. 479).

Mood: The feeling that a work of literature produces in the reader, viewer, or hearer. In "Robin Hood and Alan a Dale" (p. 430) the mood is bright and gay; in "The Telltale Heart" (p. 33) the mood is dark and mysterious. (See p. 434.)

Moral: The lesson or truth about life that a fable draws as its conclusion. The moral of Aesop's "The Fox and the Crow" (p. 299) is "Do not trust flatterers." *See* Theme. (See pp. 246, 297.)

Motivation: The reasons for a character's behavior. If an author skillfully motivates a character, the reader will believe that the character's behavior is not only possible but also probable. (See p. 53.)

Myth: A story of gods and goddesses that often explains unusual occurrences in nature. The Greeks had myths that explain the creation of the universe and the creation of man. (See pp. 245-246, 282.)

Mythology: The total collection of myths told by a group of people. (See p. 246.)

Narrative: A story. A narrative may be brief (see Fable) or very long, as a novel is.

Narrative Poem: A poem which tells a story and has a plot.* The ballad is one kind of narrative poem. (See pp. 39, 443.)

Narrator (nă rā′tər): A person who tells a story. A little boy is the narrator of "The Idealist" (p. 147); the author is the narrator of "Bill" (p. 2). *See* Point of View.

Nonfiction: Factual reporting of real events. *See* Fiction.

Omniscient Author's Point of View: *See* Point of View.

One-Act Play: *See* pp. 357-358.

Personification: The poetic device of giving animals, objects, or qualities the characteristics of a human being. For example, in "City: San Francisco" (p. 478) Langston Hughes describes the city as going to bed and "Hanging lights/About its head."

Play: *See* pp. 357-358.

Plot: The sequence of events in a story or play. In organizing a series of incidents into a plot, the author shows the relationship between one incident and the next. (See p. 1.)

Poetry: *See* pp. 411-418, 419, 443, 466, 498.

Point of View: The vision through which a narrative is presented; the person through whom the reader sees the action of the story. An author may handle point of view in several ways. Among these are the following:

The OMNISCIENT ("All-knowing") AUTHOR'S POINT OF VIEW, in which the author is the narrator* and can supply any information about motivation, character, or theme; can move from one place and time in the action to another; and can reveal the thoughts of any character. Most of the stories in this book are written from the omniscient author's point of view. (See p. 476.)

The FIRST PERSON POINT OF VIEW, in which the first person, "I," is narrator. The narrator may be a character in the story (Dr. Watson in "The Redheaded League," p. 566), or the narrator may be an uninvolved observer. What the first-person narrator tells is limited to what he himself would be able to see. (See p. 476.)

Popular Ballad: *See* Ballad.

Refrain: A line that is repeated at the end of the stanzas of a ballad.* "Lord Randal" (p. 435) makes use of the refrain to show the reader what has happened. (See p. 437.)

Resolution: *See* Falling Action.

Rhyme: *See* Sound Devices.

Rhyme Scheme: *See* Sound Devices.

Rhythm (rĭth′əm): The beat of prose

or poetry. *See* Iambic Meter.

Rising Action: That section of a plot in which the conflict* is developed. The rising action leads to the climax* of the story or play. (See p. 357.)

Satire (săt'ĭr): A technique used to ridicule or make fun of human failings (such as cruelty, greed, jealousy). "The Idealist" (p. 147) satirizes the failings of a particular kind of teacher.

Scene: An episode* in a story, or a division within an act of a play.

Selection of Detail: An author's choice of details to include in a work. Because a writer cannot possibly include every fact about his subject, he must decide which to include and which to exclude. The details he selects should help to reveal his theme.* (See pp. 138, 156.)

Setting: The time and place of the action. Setting often contributes directly to the feelings aroused in the reader or to the reader's understanding of character. "The Reef" (p. 43) shows the importance of setting. (See p. 358.)

Short Story: A brief work of fiction,* designed to produce a single effect. Short stories vary in length: a short story is longer than an anecdote* and shorter than a novel. A short story shows characters (usually only a few characters) in a setting;* it develops a conflict* and reveals a theme* through its plot.*

Simile (sĭm'ə lē'): A stated comparison between two basically different objects. It uses the word *as* or *like* to make the comparison. In "Columbus" (p. 449) Miller says that "The words leapt as a leaping sword." Though words are basically different from swords, they are similar in issuing a sharp, commanding challenge. (See p. 452.)

Sound Devices: Techniques for producing a musical or pleasing effect in literature, used especially in poetry. Some of the most common sound devices are the following:

ALLITERATION: The repetition of the same beginning sound in closely linked words. For example, in "Ariel's Song" (p. 470) the line "*Full fathom five* thy *father* lies" has alliteration in the repeated *f* sound.

ASSONANCE (ăs'ə nəns): The repetition of similar vowel sounds in words that have different consonants. For example, in "Full fathom *five* th*y* father l*ie*s" the *i* sound is repeated to produce assonance. (See p. 470.)

RHYME: The repetition of similar or identical sounds at the ends of two words, such an h*and* and l*and*. (See p. 452.)

INTERNAL RHYME occurs when the rhyming words are in the same line of poetry. (See p. 452.)

END RHYME occurs when the rhyming words appear at the ends of lines of poetry. (See p. 452.)

RHYME SCHEME: The repeated patterns of end rhyme in the stanzas* of a poem.

Stage Directions: Instructions in a play, telling a director or actor about the arrangement of the stage, the physical location of characters and their movements, and the manner in which the actors should deliver their speeches (as *loudly, angrily*). (See p. 358.)

Stanza: A division of a poem in which each unit is usually like the others in number of lines and rhyme scheme. The beginning of a new stanza is usually indicated by skipping a line. *See* Ballad Stanza.

Surprise Ending: An unexpected ending to a short story or play. A good surprise ending should startle the reader but also satisfy him. O. Henry's "The Gift of the Magi" (p. 113) has an effective surprise ending. (See p. 118.)

Suspense: The curiosity aroused in a reader as to what will happen next. A skillful writer will try to introduce the element of suspense early in the story or drama, so that the reader will be eager to read on. Zona Gale uses suspense skillfully in "Bill" (p. 2). (See p. 357.)

Symbol: Something which stands for, or represents, something else, as a school mascot stands for the school or as the American flag represents the United States. In "The First Snowfall" (p. 494) Lowell makes the falling snow a symbol of his sorrow.

Theme: The central idea of a work of literature. All parts of the work (characterization, plot, setting, mood) should contribute to the theme in some way. The theme is not usually stated directly, but the reader can determine it by analyzing the various elements of the work after he has finished reading it. (See p. 171.)

A moral* is the lesson which a fable teaches to the reader and is directly stated at the end of the fable. The theme, on the other hand, does not necessarily teach a lesson and is not usually directly stated. The moral of Aesop's "The Fox and the Crow" (p. 299) is "Do not trust flatterers." The theme of Scott's "My Native Land" (p. 488) is love of country.

Tone: The expression of an author's attitude toward his subject. The tone is revealed partly through the selection of detail* and words chosen to express ideas. Tone in literature corresponds to the tone of voice a speaker uses: a work may have an angry tone, a humorous tone, an apologetic tone.

Topic Sentence: A sentence expressing the main idea of a paragraph. The topic sentence is often the first sentence in a paragraph.

Transition: A movement from one idea or event to another. When a writer wishes to shift from one episode* to another, he must use a transitional device to help the reader follow clearly the progress of ideas or events and see the connection between them. As Jim Hawkins narrates *Treasure Island* (p. 517), he connects the various events and descriptions with transitional devices: the sound of a song in the present may remind him of a similar scene in the past, or an object like the apple barrel may appear in two episodes and link them together.

Upstage: The rear of the stage; the part farthest from the audience. (See diagram on p. 369.)

Glossary

The glossary is provided as a convenient means for looking up unfamiliar words used in this book. It may also be used in doing the *Focusing on Words* exercises. The words are defined according to their use in the book, although additional meanings of the words are also given often. Words that are footnoted in the text have not usually been included in the glossary.

The order and kinds of information to be found in an entry are shown below. Reading this information will help in using the glossary quickly and accurately.

Information given in the entry:

1. The word to be defined, divided into syllables. Example: **chro·nom·e·ter.**
2. Pronunciation of the entry. When two pronunciations are common for a word, both are usually given. Example (ä′rĭ ə, âr′ĭ ə).
3. Part of speech and, when useful, information concerning the singular or plural form.
4. Clarifying labels. These may be usage labels (example: **scriv·en** . . . *Archaic*), geographical labels (example: **set·tle** . . . *Chiefly British*), or special subject labels (example: **yard** . . . *Nautical*).
5. Definition of the entry. Where appropriate, examples may be given (as for *chimney*) or the use of the word may be illustrated (as for *abolish*).
6. Derivative parts of speech. Other parts of speech derived from nouns, verbs, or adjectives are sometimes given. Syllable divisions and accent marks for these derivative forms are always given; phonetic pronunciations are given whenever they would not be obvious. Example: **be·seech** . . . **—be·seech′ing,** *adj.* **—be·seech′ing·ly,** *adv.*

The following abbreviations are used:

adj.	adjective	l.c.	lower case
adv.	adverb	n.	noun
cap.	capital	pl.	plural
Colloq.	colloquial	prep.	preposition
conj.	conjunction	pron.	pronoun
Fr.	French	sing.	singular
Ger.	German	v.	verb

Pronunciation Key*

ă act	ī ice	ou out	y yes
ā able	j just	p page	z zeal
â air	k kept	r read	zh vision
ä art	l low	s see	ə a in *alone*
b back	m my	sh shoe	e in *system*
ch chief	n now	t ten	i in *easily*
d do	ng sing	th thin	o in *gallop*
ĕ ebb	ŏ box	th that	u in *circus*
ē equal	ō over	ŭ up	à as in Fr. *ami*
f fit	ô order	ū use	KH as in Ger. *ach*
g give	oi oil	û urge	N as in Fr. *bon*
h hit	o͝o book	v voice	œ as in Ger. *schon*
ĭ if	o͞o ooze	w west	Y as in Ger. *uber*

a·bate (ə bāt′), *v.* to become less in amount or force.

ab·duct (ăb dŭkt′), *v.* to take away a person illegally and by force; kidnap.

a·bol·ish (ə bŏl′ish), *v.* to get rid of completely; put an end to: as, *to abolish slavery.*

ab·sorb·ing (ăb sôr′bĭng, ăb zôr′bĭng), *adj.* very interesting; holding the attention; compelling.

ac·com·plice (ə kŏm′plĭs), *n.* someone who helps another violate the law; a partner in crime.

ad·mon·ish (ăd mŏn′ish), *v.* 1. to warn or advise against. 2. to scold gently; remind a person of something he should or should not do: as, *to admonish the class to be on time.*

ag·gra·vate (ăg′rə vāt′), *v.* 1. to make worse or more severe. 2. *Colloq.* to irritate, bother, or annoy; to make impatient. —**ag′gra·vat′ing,** *adj.*

aim·less (ām′lĭs), *adj.* without purpose or direction.

al·lude (ə lo͞od′), *v.* to mention in a general way; refer to, but not directly. (Followed by *to.*)

al·lur·ing (ə lo͞or′ĭng), *adj.* 1. very attractive; quite appealing or tempting. 2. charming.

al·ter (ôl′tər), *v.* to change; modify; make different, at least to some extent.

a·mi·a·ble (ā′mĭ ə bəl), *adj.* having a good disposition; friendly; agreeable.

an·guish (ăng′gwĭsh), *n.* great mental or physical suffering; agony.

an·tag·o·nist (ăn tăg′ə nĭst), *n.* a person who fights or competes with another; opponent.

an·tic·i·pa·tion (ăn tĭs′ə pā′shən), *n.* 1. a looking forward to; expectation. 2. a previous notion or idea.

an·ti·so·cial (ăn′tĭ sō′shəl), *adj.* 1. wishing to avoid, or avoiding, the company of other people: as, *a hermit is antisocial.* 2. harmful to the welfare of people in general.

ap·pa·ri·tion (ăp′ə rĭsh′ən), *n.* 1. something which appears suddenly and unexpectedly. 2. a phantom; ghost. 3. any act of appearing.

ap·pre·hen·sive (ăp′rĭ hĕn′sĭv), *adj.* 1. fearful about what may happen; uneasy. 2. quick to understand; learning easily or rapidly. —**ap′pre·hen′sive·ly,** *adv.* —**ap′pre·hen′sion,** *n.*

ap·pren·tice (ə prĕn′tĭs), *n.* 1. a person who is learning a craft or trade by helping a skilled master of that craft. 2. any beginner. —*v.* 3. to appoint to a position as an apprentice.

ar·dent (är′dənt), *adj.* 1. glowing; beaming. 2. glowing with enthusiasm or eagerness.

---

*The pronunciation system of *The American College Dictionary,* © Copyright 1947, 1963, Random House, Inc., New York. Used by permission.

ar·du·ous (är′jŏŏ əs), *adj.* **1.** laborious; hard to do. **2.** working hard; using much energy. **3.** difficult to climb; steep.

a·ri·a (ä′rĭ ə, âr′ĭ ə), *n.* *Music.* a melody in an opera or oratorio, sung as a solo.

a·skance (ə skăns′), *adv.* **1.** with a glance to the side. **2.** with suspicion, doubt, or mistrust.

as·sent (ə sĕnt′), *v.* to agree; consent. —*n.* agreement.

a·stride (ə strīd′), *adj., adv.* **1.** with one leg on each side: as, *sitting astride a horse.* **2.** with about half lying on each side of something; straddling.

a·tone (ə tōn′), *v.* to make up for one's mistakes or sins; pay, in money, goods, or deeds, for wrong done. —**a·tone′ment**, *n.*

at·tain (ə tān′), *v.* **1.** to achieve; reach; gain. **2.** to come to; arrive at: as, *to attain the age of twenty-five.*

au·dac·i·ty (ô dăs′ə tĭ), *n.* **1.** bold courage; reckless daring. **2.** rude boldness; impolite forwardness. —**au·da·cious** (ô dā′shəs), *adj.*

aus·tere (ô stĭr′), *adj.* **1.** very strict or stern in one's view of morals or behavior. **2.** severe; harsh: as, *the austere living standard of the early pioneers.* **3.** plain; simple; without decoration.

av·a·lanche (ăv′ə lănch′), *n.* **1.** a large mass, usually of snow, that suddenly falls down a mountainside. **2.** anything like an avalanche in being sudden, swift, and inescapable.

a·ver·sion (ə vûr′zhən, ə vûr′shən), *n.* **1.** a dislike; avoidance of something or someone disliked. **2.** the object which is disliked.

awe (ô), *n.* a feeling which is a mixture of fear and respect, often caused by religious inspiration or great wonders of nature: as, *the view of the Grand Canyon filled the tourists with awe.*

bale·ful (bāl′fəl), *adj.* evil; harmful.

ban·ish (băn′ĭsh), *v.* **1.** to force one out of the country as a punishment. **2.** to get rid of; put out of one's mind.

be·drag·gled (bĭ drăg′əld), *adj.* wet and dirty; worn and limp.

bel·fry (bĕl′frĭ), *n.* the part of a tower or steeple in which a bell is hung.

be·seech (bĭ sēch′), *v.* to ask in a pleading manner; beg; request eagerly. —**be·seech′ing**, *adj.* —**be·seech′ing·ly**, *adv.*

bick·er·ing (bĭk′ər ĭng), *n.* minor argument or quarrel.

bi·zarre (bĭ zär′), *adj.* extremely odd; queer; unusual in appearance or manner; fantastic; marked by odd contrasts.

bleak (blēk), *adj.* **1.** unsheltered; barren; exposed to wind: as, *the bleak winter prairie.* **2.** bitterly cold and penetrating: as, *a bleak wind.* **3.** cheerless; unhappy; gloomy.

blithe (blīth, blīth), *adj.* cheerful; lighthearted; gay; carefree. —**blithe′ly**, *adv.*

bois·ter·ous (boi′stər əs), *adj.* **1.** rough; violent. **2.** noisy; loud and lively.

boo·ty (bōō′tĭ), *n.* goods taken from an enemy or a conquered people; any goods taken by force.

bra·zen (brā′zən), *adj.* **1.** like brass, as in color. **2.** bold; shameless in word or act.

bul·wark (bŏŏl′wərk), *n.* **1.** a wall used for defense against attack. **2.** a sea wall, used to break the force of the waves. **3.** any defense or protection.

buoy·ant (boi′ənt, bōō′yənt), *adj.* **1.** tending, or having the ability, to float. **2.** able to support a floating object. **3.** gay; cheerful; light-spirited.

burgh·er (bûr′gər), *n.* a citizen of a town or borough.

bur·nished (bûr′nĭsht), *adj.* polished.

can·did (kăn′dĭd), *adj.* **1.** saying directly just what one feels or thinks; honest; frank. **2.** not biased; fair.

cas·cade (kăs kād′), *n.* **1.** a small waterfall or a series of waterfalls. **2.** anything which falls or showers down, such as sparks, lace, drapery, etc. —*v.* **3.** to fall like a waterfall.

ce·les·tial (sə lĕs′chəl), *adj.* **1.** concerning the sky or heavens. **2.** of heaven; heavenly. **3.** ideal or perfect: as, *celestial happiness.*

cha·grin (shə grĭn'), *n.* a feeling of disappointed embarrassment or humiliation caused by failure or the upsetting of plans.

chas·ten (chā'sən), *v.* 1. to correct behavior by punishment: as, *we chasten an unruly child.* 2. to subdue; to control the spirited emotions of (someone).

cher·ish (chĕr'ĭsh), *v.* 1. to value highly; to hold dear. 2. to treat with great care; to deal with carefully or tenderly.

chim·ney (chĭm'nĭ), *n.* 1. a structure by which smoke is carried off. 2. anything resembling a chimney (for example, the opening of a volcano or narrow rock passage).

chiv·al·ry (shĭv'əl rĭ), *n.* 1. a band of knights or noble gentlemen. 2. knighthood of the Middle Ages. 3. the code of noble behavior required of knights, such as courage, fairness, respect for women, etc.

chron·i·cle (krŏn'ə kəl), *n.* a record of events in the order that they occurred; a history. *—v.* to keep such a history.

chro·nom·e·ter (krə nŏm'ə tər), *n.* an instrument for measuring time with great precision; a very accurate watch.

ci·vil·ian (sĭ vĭl'yən), *n.* a person who is not in the armed services.

clout (klout), *n.* 1. *Archaic.* a piece of cloth or leather used for mending. 2. an archery target; a shot that hits the target. 3. *Colloq.* a blow with the hand. *—v.* 4. *Colloq.* to strike with the hand.

com·mend (kə mĕnd'), *v.* 1. to praise; mention with approval. 2. to put into the care of someone else: as, *to commend the patient to the nurse's care.*

com·pli·ance (kəm plī'əns), *n.* 1. act of carrying out, or giving in to, a wish, request, or demand. 2. a tendency to give in easily to the wishes of others.

com·pose (kəm pōz'), *v.* 1. to assemble into a combination: as, *to compose paste from flour and water.* 2. to put

in proper order. 3. to calm or settle (oneself or one's mind). 4. to write or create.

com·pute (kəm pūt'), *v.* to determine; figure by arithmetic; calculate. *—com'·pu·ta'tion, n.*

con·ceit·ed (kən sē'tĭd), *adj.* vain; having too high an opinion of oneself.

con·fi·dant (kŏn'fə dănt', kŏn'fə dănt'), *n.* a trusted friend with whom secrets are shared.

con·fis·cate (kŏn'fĭs kāt'), *v.* 1. to seize property with official authority. 2. to seize; take and keep. *—con'fis·ca'tion, n.*

con·found·ed (kŏn foun'dĭd, kən foun'dĭd), *adj.* 1. cursed; damned; brought to ruin. 2. confused; mixed up.

con·gest·ed (kən jĕs'tĭd), *adj.* 1. blocked; obstructed; plugged up. 2. overcrowded; overfilled.

con·se·quent (kŏn'sə kwĕnt'), *adj.* coming as an effect; resulting.

con·spir·a·cy (kən spĭr'ə sĭ), *n.* 1. a secret plot by two or more persons to do something harmful, dishonest, or illegal. 2. a working together of forces. 3. a plot or plan of a group. 4. the group making such a plan.

con·spire (kən spīr'), *v.* 1. to plan secretly as a group, especially to do something evil or illegal. 2. to work together to some purpose or effect: as, *the weather and insects may conspire to ruin our picnic.*

con·stan·cy (kŏn'stən sĭ), *n.* the quality of remaining firm, steady, and unchanging; steadiness of purpose; loyalty.

con·ster·na·tion (kŏn'stər nā'shən), *n.* paralyzing fear or astonishment; dread or amazement which makes one speechless or helpless.

con·tem·plate (kŏn'təm plāt', kən tĕm'plāt), *v.* 1. to think about; consider seriously. 2. to look at thoughtfully; gaze: as, *to contemplate a sunset.* 3. to expect; to look forward to. *—con'tem·pla'tion, n.*

con·temp·tu·ous (kən tĕmp'chŏŏ əs), *adj.*

ăct, āble, dâre, ärt; ĕbb, ēqual; ĭf, īce; hŏt, ōver, ôrder, oil, bŏŏk, ōōze, out; ŭp, ūse, ûrge; ə = a in *alone*; ch, chief; g, give; j, judge; ng, ring; sh, shoe; th, thin; th, that; zh, vision. See the full key at the beginning of this glossary.

showing a lack of respect; scornful; expressing the feeling that someone or something is cheap, unworthy, or evil.

con·tort (kən tôrt'), *v.* to twist or bend out of the usual shape.

con·trive (kən trīv'), *v.* **1.** to think up; plan; scheme. **2.** to design or invent: as, *to contrive a three-passenger bicycle.* **3.** to bring about in some way; manage to do even though difficult.

con·ven·tion (kən věn'shən), *n.* **1.** a meeting of members or delegates. **2.** a custom; usual way of doing something; standard usage. —**con·ven'tion·al**, *adj.*

con·vic·tion (kən vĭk'shən), *n.* **1.** act or process of proving or declaring the guilt of an offender. **2.** a firm belief: as, *he stuck to his conviction that the lost explorers would be found.*

cor·dial (kôr'jəl), *adj.* **1.** hearty; warm. —*n.* **2.** anything stimulating. **3.** a strong, sweet liquor. —**cor'dial·ly**, *adv.*

coun·te·nance (koun'tə nəns), *n.* **1.** the expression on the face. **2.** the face. —*v.* **3.** to approve; give support to.

coun·ter·act (koun'tər ăkt'), *v.* to check or neutralize by a contrary action.

cour·age (kûr'ĭj, kŭr'ĭj), *n.* the quality of spirit or mind that enables a person to meet danger, pain, etc., with firmness; fearlessness; bravery.

Cov·en·try (kŏv'ən trĭ, kŭv'ən trĭ), *n.* a city in England. —**send to Coventry**, refuse to associate with; ostracize. [The origin of this phrase is unknown.]

cov·et (kŭv'ĭt), *v.* to desire something very much, especially something that belongs to someone else. —**cov·et·ous** (kŭv'ə təs), *adj.*

cre·mate (krē'māt), *v.* to burn a corpse.

cre·vasse (krə văs'), *n.* a deep crack or crevice in the ice of a glacier.

cudg·el (kŭj'əl), *n.* **1.** a short, thick stick; a club. **2.** (*pl.*) the sport of dueling with such clubs. —*v.* **3.** to hit with a club.

curt (kûrt), *adj.* short; rudely brief; too abrupt to be polite. —**curt'ly**, *adv.*

cut·wa·ter (kŭt'wô'tər, kŭt'wŏ'tər), *n.* the front part of the bow of a ship that cuts through the water.

dar·ing (dâr'ĭng), *n.* **1.** adventurous courage; boldness. —*adj.* **2.** bold; adventurous. —**dar'ing·ly**, *adv.*

daunt (dônt, dänt), *v.* to frighten or discourage.

de·cap·i·tate (dĭ kăp'ə tāt'), *v.* to behead.

de·ceive (dĭ sēv'), *v.* to delude by a false appearance or statement; beguile; mislead. —**de·ceiv'er**, *n.*

de·file (dĭ fīl'), *v.* **1.** to make dirty; soil. **2.** to discredit the name of.

deign (dān), *v.* **1.** to consider as being beneath one's dignity; lower oneself slightly. **2.** to condescend.

de·ject·ed (dĭ jĕk'tĭd), *adj.* discouraged; low in spirit; downhearted. —**de·jec'tion**, *n.*

dem·o·li·tion (dĕm'ə lĭsh'ən, dē'mə lĭsh'ən), *n.* act of destroying or tearing down; destruction.

de·pose (dĭ pōz'), *v.* to remove from office; remove from a position of power: as, *to depose the king.*

de·pressed (dĭ prĕst'), *adj.* **1.** sad; gloomy; downhearted; discouraged. **2.** pushed down.

dep·ri·va·tion (dĕp'rə vā'shən), *n.* **1.** condition in which one no longer possesses certain things which have been taken away. **2.** a loss.

de·ser·tion (dĭ zûr'shən), *n.* **1.** the act of leaving one's post or duty without permission. **2.** abandonment of one's military duty with no intention of returning.

des·o·late (*adj.* dĕs'ə lĭt; *v.* dĕs'ə lāt'), *adj.* **1.** lonely; feeling friendless; without hope. **2.** deserted; without population. **3.** barren; ruined; not suitable for human residence. —*v.* **4.** to lay waste; to make unfit for human habitation. —**des'o·late·ly**, *adv.*

de·spoil (dĭ spoil'), *v.* to take away from by force; rob; plunder.

des·ti·ny (dĕs'tə nĭ), *n.* **1.** the series of events which is bound to occur; fate; (one's) fortune, good or bad. **2.** the force which seems to make things happen.

dev·as·tate (dĕv'ə stāt), *v.* to destroy; ruin: as, *World War III might devastate the earth.*

dic·tum (dĭk′təm), *n.* a forceful statement; a saying or opinion given with authority.

di·lap·i·dat·ed (dĭ lăp′ə dā′tĭd), *adj.* 1. broken down; falling to pieces. 2. shabby; not having as good appearance or value as in earlier times.

di·min·ish (dĭ mĭn′ĭsh), *v.* 1. to become smaller. 2. to make less in number or smaller in size.

dip·lo·mat·ic (dĭp′lə măt′ĭk), *adj.* able to manage negotiations with skill; suave; tactful. —**dip′lo·mat′i·cal·ly,** *adv.*

dire (dīr), *adj.* dreadful; fearful; horrible.

dis·cre·tion (dĭs krĕsh′ən), *n.* 1. wise caution about what is said or done. 2. the power or freedom to make decisions and to carry them out.

dis·dain·ful (dĭs dān′fəl), *adj.* feeling or showing the attitude that something is inferior, unworthy, or unimportant; scornful; aloof.

di·shev·eled (dĭ shĕv′əld), *adj.* untidy and in disorder; mussed up; not neat.

dis·mal (dĭz′məl), *adj.* 1. causing sadness or gloom. 2. gloomy; cheerless. 3. dreadful.

dis·suade (dĭ swād′), *v.* to advise against something; deter.

dis·tor·tion (dĭs tôr′shən), *n.* 1. state of being twisted out of shape. 2. anything twisted out of shape or appearance.

dis·tract (dĭs trăkt′), *v.* 1. to draw thoughts away to a different subject; divert attention. 2. to confuse; mix up mentally.

di·vin·i·ty (dĭ vĭn′ə tĭ), *n.* 1. godlike quality. 2. a god; divine being. 3. the study of religion. 4. a soft, creamy candy.

doc·ile (dŏs′əl), *adj.* 1. easy to manage, train, or teach. 2. easy to control or discipline; quietly obedient.

dog·ged (dôg′ĭd, dŏg′ĭd), *adj.* having the stubbornness of a dog; determined;

tenacious. —**dog′ged·ly,** *adv.*

dole (dōl), *n.* 1. money or food given to the poor or the unemployed. 2. anything given out in small amounts. 3. *Archaic.* sorrow; grief.

dom·i·nate (dŏm′ə nāt′), *v.* 1. to control or rule; exercise power over. 2. to tower over: as, *the new skyscraper will dominate the downtown area.*

drudge (drŭj), *n.* one who does tiresome, hard, unpleasant work.

ear·mark (ĭr′märk′), *n.* 1. a mark or brand put on an animal's ear to show who owns it. 2. any identifying mark or sign. —*v.* 3. to put an identifying mark on.

ebb (ĕb), *n.* the receding of the tide. —*v.* flow back; to decline; fall from a better state to a worse state; waste away.

e·la·tion (ĭ lā′shən), *n.* a feeling of joy or pride; high-spirited gladness.

el·o·quent (ĕl′ə kwənt), *adj.* 1. forceful, arousing, graceful, or persuasive, usually in speech. 2. expressing much feeling.

em·bark (ĕm bärk′), *v.* 1. to board a ship; put on board a ship. 2. to begin a journey or some other venture.

em·bel·lish (ĕm bĕl′ĭsh), *v.* 1. to decorate; adorn; add ornaments to. 2. to improve (a story) by adding to it, especially fictional details.

en·dure (ĕn dyŏŏr′, ĕn dŏŏr′), *v.* 1. to last or remain firm under suffering, pain, or misfortune without yielding; tolerate. 2. to continue to exist.

en·gross (ĕn grōs′), *v.* to occupy the entire attention of; interest keenly and completely so that other things are not noticed.

en·ter·pris·ing (ĕn′tər prī′zĭng), *adj.* venturesome; willing to try new schemes; daring to take risks; bold and active.

e·nu·mer·ate (ĭ nū′mə rāt′, ĭ nŏŏ′mə rāt′), *v.* to list one by one, as if counting.

ep·i·logue (ĕp′ə lôg′, ĕp′ə lŏg′), *n.* 1. the final part of a story or a series of events.

ăct, āble, dâre, ärt; ĕbb, ēqual; ĭf, īce; hŏt, ōver, ôrder, oil, bŏŏk, ōōze, out; ŭp, ūse, ûrge; ə = a in *alone*; ch, chief; g, give; j, judge; ng, ring; sh, shoe; th, thin; th, that; zh, vision. See the full key at the beginning of this glossary.

2. a speech, usually in verse, given by an actor after the end of a play.

es·ca·pade (ĕs′kə pād′, ĕs′kə pād′), *n.* a prank; wild adventure.

e·ter·ni·ty (ĭ tûr′nə tĭ), *n.* an endless period of time without beginning or end.

e·vac·u·a·tion (ĭ văk′yōō ā′shən), *n.* **1.** an emptying; a removal of the contents. **2.** withdrawal of persons from an area.

ex·ag·ger·ate (ĭg zăj′ə rāt′), *v.* to magnify an event beyond the truth; overstate.

ex·em·pli·fy (ĭg zĕm′plə fī′), *v.* to be an example of.

ex·ile (ĕg′zīl, ĕk′sīl), *v.* to force a person to leave his home territory, often as a legal punishment. —*n.* an enforced residing away from one's community.

ex·pos·tu·late (ĭk spŏs′chə lāt′), *v.* to argue with vigor; attempt to convince; reason with a person, especially to change his actions or intentions: as, *to expostulate with the referee.* —**ex·pos′tu·la′tion,** *n.*

ex·qui·site (ĕks′kwĭ zĭt, ĭk skwĭz′ĭt), *adj.* **1.** very beautiful, delicate, or lovely. **2.** carefully done or painstakingly made: as, *an exquisite watch.* **3.** of highest quality.

ex·traor·di·nar·y (ĭk strôr′də nĕr′ĭ), *adj.* **1.** very unusual; remarkable. **2.** exceeding the usual; quite exceptional.

ex·trem·i·ty (ĭk strĕm′ə tĭ), *n.* **1.** the farthest part; the end. **2.** the greatest degree or extent. **3.** a condition of great need or danger. **4.** a severe course of action.

ex·ul·ta·tion (ĕg′zŭl tā′shən, ĕk′sŭl tā′shən), *n.* proud rejoicing; great joy; triumphant happiness.

fa·çade (fə säd′, fă säd′), *n.* **1.** the front of a building. **2.** the front of anything, especially a front which has been made more attractive than the less visible parts of the object.

fac·ul·ty (făk′əl tĭ), *n.* **1.** any of the natural abilities of animals: as, *the faculty of hearing.* **2.** a special skill or talent: as, *a faculty for making money.* **3.** all the members of a teaching staff or other professional group.

fal·ter (fôl′tər), *v.* **1.** to hesitate; proceed in an unsure way; give way to opposition or discouragement. **2.** to walk unsteadily; stumble. **3.** to stumble in speech; stammer.

fa·tigue (fə tēg′), *n.* tiredness caused by hard work.

fer·vent (fûr′vənt), *adj.* **1.** hot; glowing. **2.** having or showing great warmth of feeling; extremely earnest.

flor·id (flôr′ĭd, flŏr′ĭd), *adj.* **1.** rosy in color; flushed with color, as the face. **2.** much decorated; showy.

fore·bod·ing (fōr bō′dĭng), *n.* a prediction of something evil or harmful; a feeling that something bad is soon to happen.

fore·cas·tle (fōk′səl, fōr′kăs′əl), *n. Nautical.* the forward section of a ship where the seamen have their quarters.

fore·top·sail (fōr′tŏp′səl), *n. Nautical.* a sail set on a forward mast of a ship.

for·lorn (fôr lôrn′), *adj.* lost; abandoned; deserted; miserable.

for·mi·da·ble (fôr′mĭ də bəl), *adj.* **1.** to be feared or dreaded; of alarming size or power. **2.** difficult to overcome; hard to handle.

for·ti·tude (fôr′tə tūd′), *n.* courage in the face of pain or disaster; patient endurance.

fur·tive (fûr′tĭv), *adj.* **1.** done in a secret, hidden way. **2.** sly; sneaky; shifty. —**fur′tive·ly,** *adv.*

gait (gāt), *n.* **1.** a manner of walking or running; as, *he had a stumbling gait.* **2.** any of the specific foot movements of horses: gallop, trot, pace, etc.

gar·ret (găr′ĭt), *n.* attic; unfinished room or space just under the sloping roof of a house.

ges·ta·tion (jĕs tā′shən), *n.* the act or period of carrying the unborn young in the body.

gild (gĭld), *v.* **1.** to cover with gold or a gold color. **2.** to give a bright, shiny appearance (to something). **3.** to make (something) appear more desirable than it is.

gin·ger·ly (jĭn′jər lĭ), *adv.* carefully; cautiously; timidly.

gla·cier (glā′shər), *n.* a huge mass of ice,

616

usually in high mountains, formed by many years of snowfall and moving slowly.

gorge (gôrj), *n.* **1.** a narrow valley between steep cliffs. **2.** the throat. —*v.* **3.** to stuff oneself with food; eat in a greedy way.

gra·di·ent (grā′dĭ ənt), *n.* **1.** a slope or incline. **2.** the degree of slanting in an incline.

graft (grăft, gräft), *v.* to set a stem or bud from one plant into a cut on another plant, where it continues to grow. —*n.* the dishonest use of a job, especially in government, to acquire money for oneself.

gren·a·dier (grĕn′ə dĭr′), *n.* **1.** originally, a soldier who fought by throwing grenades. **2.** a member of a special regiment in the British Army.

griev·ance (grē′vəns), *n.* **1.** a cause for complaint; an actual or imagined wrong or hardship. **2.** complaint; resentment.

grim (grĭm), *adj.* dreadful; stern; fierce. —**grim′ly,** *adv.*

gris·ly (grĭz′lĭ), *adj.* horrible; ghastly; gruesome.

gro·tesque (grō tĕsk′), *adj.* **1.** having a wildly odd or fantastic appearance. **2.** so twisted in appearance as to be funny; ridiculous. **3.** combining in a confused, unnatural way, as in certain types of art.

ha·lo (hā′lō), *n.* **1.** a ring of light around the moon or other body in the sky. **2.** a ring of light around the head of an angel or other saintly being.

heave (hēv), *v.* **1.** to hoist; raise. **2.** *Nautical.* to haul, draw, or pull, as by a cable (for example, *to heave up the anchor, to heave a ship*). (Past tense **heaved** or **hove.**)

hi·lar·i·ty (hĭ lăr′ə tĭ, hī lăr′ə tĭ), *n.* noisy laughter and fun.

hol·land (hŏl′ənd), *n.* a cotton or linen cloth used for children's clothing.

hos·pi·ta·ble (hŏs′pĭ tə bəl), *adj.* **1.** entertaining guests in a friendly, warm manner. **2.** inclined to be friendly and generous to guests or neighbors. **3.** open-minded; willing to consider new ideas.

hove, *see* **heave.**

hull (hŭl), *n.* the frame or shell of a ship.

hys·te·ri·a (hĭs tĭr′ĭ ə, hĭs tĕr′ĭ ə), *n.* **1.** a state of extreme emotional excitement, often with some loss of self control. **2.** uncontrolled wild laughing or crying.

im·meas·ur·a·ble (ĭ mĕzh′ər ə bəl), *adj.* too large or too much to be measured; vast; boundless.

im·per·turb·a·ble (ĭm′pər tûr′bə bəl), *adj.* unable to be disturbed or upset; not excitable; calm.

im·pet·u·ous (im pĕch′oŏ əs), *adj.* **1.** moving with a wild force; rushing: as, *the impetuous flood waters.* **2.** acting quickly, without much thought; acting on impulse.

im·pro·vi·sa·tion (ĭm′prə vī zā′shən, ĭm′prŏv ə zā′shən), *n.* act of preparing, composing, or making without preparation; process of doing something on the spur of the moment with the materials or facts at hand.

im·pu·dent (ĭm′pyə dənt), *adj.* lacking respect; shameless in boldness or rudeness. —**im′pu·dence,** *n.*

im·pulse (ĭm′pŭls), *n.* a sudden urge to action: as, *to act on impulse.*

in·ar·tic·u·late (ĭn′är tĭk′yə lĭt), *adj.* **1.** not (expressed) in speech that is understandable: as, *an inarticulate moan.* **2.** not able to speak clearly.

in·au·di·ble (ĭn ô′də bəl), *adj.* not capable of being heard.

in·cal·cu·la·ble (ĭn kăl′kyə lə bəl), *adj.* **1.** too numerous or too great to be counted or measured. **2.** too uncertain to be predicted; unpredictable.

in·cred·u·lous (ĭn krĕj′ə ləs), *adj.* **1.** unable or unwilling to believe; doubting.

ăct, āble, dâre, ärt; ĕbb, ēqual; ĭf, īce; hŏt, ōver, ôrder, oil, boŏk, ōoze, out; ŭp, ūse, ûrge; ə = a in *alone*; ch, chief; g, give; j, judge; ng, ring; sh, shoe; th, thin; th, that; zh, vision. See the full key at the beginning of this glossary.

2. showing one's doubt or disbelief. —in·cred'u·lous·ly, *adv.*

in·dec·o·rous (ĭn děk'ə rəs, ĭn'dĭ kôr'əs), *adj.* not proper; lacking good taste.

in·dif·fer·ent (ĭn dĭf'ər ənt), *adj.* **1.** having no interest; not caring; unconcerned. **2.** having no bias, favorite, or choice; being neutral. **3.** average; neither good nor bad. **4.** not very good; poor.

in·dig·nant (ĭn dĭg'nənt), *adj.* angry or scornful because of unfair, mean, or ungrateful treatment.

in·dis·pen·sa·ble (ĭn'dĭs pĕn'sə bəl), *adj.* absolutely necessary.

in·dom·i·ta·ble (ĭn dŏm'ə tə bəl), *adj.* not easily conquered or overcome; unyielding; not giving in to defeat or discouragement.

in·duce (ĭn dūs', ĭn dōōs'), *v.* **1.** to lead to some action or state of mind: as, *to induce a citizen to change his vote.* **2.** to cause; bring about. **3.** to arrive at a conclusion based on certain facts.

in·ev·i·ta·ble (ĭn ĕv'ə tə bəl), *adj.* bound to happen; unavoidable.

in·ex·pli·ca·ble (ĭn ĕks'plə kə bəl), *adj.* not to be accounted for or understood; unexplainable.

in·fa·mous (ĭn'fə məs), *adj.* **1.** of bad reputation; in dishonor or disgrace. **2.** causing or deserving evil reputation; shameful; wicked.

in·fil·tra·tion (ĭn'fĭl trā'shən), *n.* the act or process of passing into or through: as, *infiltration of a secret club by outsiders.*

in·gen·ious (ĭn jēn'yəs), *adj.* **1.** clever; inventive; original; skillful at designing or contriving. **2.** cleverly done; showing inventiveness.

in·ge·nu·i·ty (ĭn'jə nū'ə tĭ, ĭn'jə nōō'ə tĭ), *n.* **1.** the quality of cleverness, inventiveness, or clever skillfulness. **2.** knack for clever design or construction. **3.** a cleverly made device.

in·let (ĭn'lĕt), *n.* **1.** a narrow body of water running into land; a small bay. **2.** a strip of water between two islands.

in·sig·nif·i·cant (ĭn'sĭg nĭf'ə kənt), *adj.* not important; too small or of too little value to matter.

in·so·lent (ĭn'sə lənt), *adj.* lacking respect for customs or authorities; rude; insulting.

in·su·per·a·ble (ĭn sōō'pər ə bəl), *adj.* unable to be overcome or passed over; unconquerable.

in·ter·ces·sion (ĭn'tər sĕsh'ən), *n.* the process of asking, pleading, or praying for someone else.

in·ter·vene (ĭn tər vēn'), *v.* **1.** to come between. **2.** to come between in order to settle or adjust.

in·tol·er·a·ble (ĭn tŏl'ər ə bəl), *adj.* unbearable; too painful, cruel, or awful to be endured. —in·tol'er·a·bly, *adv.*

in·tol·er·ant (ĭn tŏl'ər ənt), *adj.* **1.** having no patience with beliefs or ideas different from one's own. **2.** making no allowance or adjustment for the ideas or needs of others.

in·tro·spect (ĭn'trə spĕkt'), *v.* **1.** to examine one's own thoughts and feelings; to look into one's own mind. **2.** to observe or analyze oneself. —in'tro·spec'tive, *adj.*

in·tru·sion (ĭn trōō'zhən), *n.* an awkward forcing in or interruption.

in·ven·to·ry (ĭn'vən tôr'ĭ), *n.* **1.** a complete list of all the goods or properties on hand. **2.** a stock of goods on hand. —*v.* **3.** to compile or make a list of goods; to make note of possessions.

in·vol·un·tar·y (ĭn vŏl'ən tĕr'ĭ), *adj.* not intentional; accidental; not done by choice. —in·vol'un·tar'i·ly, *adv.*

im·plore (ĭm plôr'), *v.* to ask with great feeling; beg.

ir·rel·e·vant (ĭ rĕl'ə vənt), *adj.* not to the point; having nothing to do with the subject.

jour·ney·man (jûr'nĭ mən), *n.* a person who has already been an apprentice at a trade but continues to work at the trade under another person.

joust (jŭst, joust), *n.* **1.** a fight with lances by two knights on horseback. **2.** (*pl.*) a tournament of such fights. —*v.* **3.** to take part in such a fight.

jo·vi·al (jō'vĭ əl), *adj.* playful and good-humored; cheerful and jolly.

ju·di·cial (jōō dĭsh'əl), *adj.* **1.** having to

618

do with judges, courts, or their functions. **2.** carefully considering the facts; careful in making decisions.

knick·er·bock·ers (nĭk'ər bŏk'ərz), *n.* short trousers gathered at or just below the knee.

lab·y·rinth (lăb'ə rĭnth), *n.* a series of winding passages in which it is difficult to find one's way.

lam·en·ta·tion (lăm'ən tā'shən), *n.* an outward expression of grief or sorrow; wailing; weeping.

land·fall (lănd'fôl'), *n.* **1.** the sighting of land from a vessel at sea. **2.** a landing by plane or ship.

lan·guid (lăng'gwĭd), *adj.* **1.** lacking energy, vitality, or spirit; drooping; weak. **2.** lacking interest; indifferent.

lan·guor (lăng'gər), *n.* **1.** a lack of spirit or vigor; weakness; sluggishness. **2.** a lack of interest; dullness. **3.** a tender mood.

lee (lē), *n.* **1.** the sheltered side, which the wind does not strike. **2.** a shelter. —*adj.* **3.** of or on the side which is protected from the wind.

lithe (līth), *adj.* limber; flexible; bending easily.

lit·er·al (lĭt'ər əl), *adj.* exactly true to fact; having no exaggeration or distortion.

mag·ni·tude (măg'nə tūd', măg'nə tōōd'), *n.* largeness; importance; extent or greatness of power.

mal-, *prefix.* bad, wrongful, evil: as, *maladjustment, malpractice, malodorous.*

ma·li·cious (mə lĭsh'əs), *adj.* **1.** wishing to harm others; evil-intentioned. **2.** deliberately harmful or mischievous. —**ma·li'cious·ly,** *adv.*

mal·o·dor·ous (măl ō'dər əs), *adj.* having a bad odor.

mar·vel (mär'vəl), *n.* an amazing or wonderful thing. —*v.* to be astonished; wonder.

mate (māt), *n.* *Nautical.* an officer of a merchant ship who is lower in rank than the captain.

max·im (măk'sĭm), *n.* a short statement of some general truth about life.

med·i·tate (mĕd'ə tāt'), *v.* **1.** to think deeply, quietly. **2.** to plan; consider; intend.

mel·an·chol·y (mĕl'ən kŏl'ĭ), *adj.* **1.** sad; gloomy; depressed. **2.** causing sadness or gloom: as, *a melancholy fog at night.* —*n.* **3.** a state of sadness or gloom.

mol·ten (mōl'tən), *adj.* **1.** melted by heat. **2.** made by being melted and poured in a mold.

mo·nas·tic (mə năs'tĭk), *adj.* **1.** having to do with monasteries. **2.** relating to monks or nuns.

mort·gage (môr'gĭj), *n.* **1.** a claim to property, given to the lender of money as security for payment of the loan. **2.** the legal document for such a claim to property. —*v.* **3.** to pledge property when borrowing money.

mor·ti·fy (môr'tə fī), *v.* **1.** to embarrass or make ashamed; injure the pride. **2.** to subdue the body by fasting or severe self-discipline. —**mor'ti·fy'ing,** *adj.*

mul·ti·tu·di·nous (mŭl'tə tū'də nəs), *adj.* numerous; happening, or existing, in great numbers.

mut·ed (mū'tĭd), *adj.* **1.** silent; quiet. **2.** silenced; made more quiet.

mu·ti·ny (mū'tə nĭ), *n.* a fighting or rebelling against the officers or leaders of a group; revolt of sailors or soldiers against their officers. —*v.* to take part in such a revolt. —**mu'ti·nous,** *adj.*

nar·ra·tive (năr'ə tĭv), *n.* an account or story of events.

neg·lect·ed (nĭ glĕkt'ĭd), *adj.* not cared for; disregarded.

noc·tur·nal (nŏk tùr'nəl), *adj.* **1.** concerning the night. **2.** active at night; done or occurring at night. **3.** having flowers that open only at night.

ăct, āble, dâre, ärt; ĕbb, ēqual; ĭf, īce; hŏt, ōver, ôrder, oil, bŏŏk, ōōze, out; ŭp, ūse, ûrge; ə = a in *alone*; **ch**, chief; **g**, give; **j**, judge; **ng**, ring; **sh**, shoe; **th**, thin; **th**, that; **zh**, vision. See the full key at the beginning of this glossary.

nup·tials (nŭp′shəlz), *n.* a marriage ceremony; wedding.

o·blige (ə blīj′), *v.* 1. to exert a moral or legal force (on someone) to do (or not to do) something. 2. to make (a person) feel indebted because of a favor done for him.

ob·liv·i·on (ə blĭv′ĭ ən), *n.* 1. the state of being forgotten. 2. the forgetting, or the tendency to forget, something.

ob·scene (əb sēn′, ŏb sēn′), *adj.* 1. indecent; shockingly immodest. 2. filthy; disgusting.

ob·scure (əb skyoŏr′), *v.* 1. to hide from view; conceal. 2. to overshadow; confuse: as, *a bad argument can obscure the truth.* —*adj.* 3. not easily seen; hidden. 4. not easily understood. —**ob·scure′ly,** *adv.*

ob·sti·nate (ŏb′stə nĭt), *adj.* 1. stubborn; not willing to change one's mind. 2. difficult to overcome or cure: as, *an obstinate head cold.* —**ob′sti·nate·ly,** *adv.*

ob·vi·ous (ŏb′vĭ əs), *adj.* 1. easily seen; open to view. 2. easy to understand.

off·ing (ôf′ĭng), *n.* 1. a distant position at sea, as seen from the shore. 2. a distant, but still visible, spot.

om·i·nous (ŏm′ə nəs), *adj.* threatening; suggesting approaching evil or disaster.

om·nip·o·tent (ŏm nĭp′ə tənt), *adj.* all-powerful; having all possible power or authority.

op·er·a (ŏp′ər ə, ŏp′rə), *n.* a long musical production with singers, orchestra, and scenery.

op·u·lent (ŏp′yə lənt), *adj.* 1. wealthy; rich. 2. plentiful; abundant.

or·a·cle (ôr′ə kəl), *n.* 1. a place or person from which the early Greeks and Romans learned the will of the gods. 2. a message from such a place or person. 3. a very wise person.

or·dain (ôr dān′), *v.* 1. to arrange; cause to happen; establish. 2. to appoint or order by official decree.

out·crop·ping (out′krŏp′ĭng), *n.* a protrusion above the surface, as rocks which stick up above the ground.

pad·dock (păd′ək), *n.* a small field near a stable for exercising horses.

par·a·phrase (păr′ə frāz′), *v.* to restate the meaning of a passage in one's own words or in simpler words. —*n.* the words which restate the meaning of a passage.

pare (pâr), *v.* 1. to cut off an outer layer: as, *to pare an apple.* 2. to diminish; reduce; make smaller.

pas·sion (păsh′ən), *n.* a strong emotion such as intense hate or love.

pa·thet·ic (pə thĕt′ĭk), *adj.* causing one to feel pity, sympathy, or sadness.

pawn (pôn), *n.* 1. something given as security for a debt. 2. the state of being pledged as security: as, *her jewelry was in pawn.* —*v.* 3. to deposit as security.

pen·e·tra·li·a (pĕn′ə trā′lĭ ə), *n.* 1. the most inner part, as of a temple. 2. private or secret things.

pen·i·tent (pĕn′ə tənt), *adj.* sorry for a wrong done and willing to make things right.

pen·non (pĕn′ən), *n.* 1. a long, thin flag carried on the lance of a knight. 2. any pennant or flag.

pen·sive (pĕn′sĭv), *adj.* thinking deeply, seriously, or sadly; deeply thoughtful.

per·se·cute (pùr′sə kūt′), *v.* to constantly injure or distress; treat cruelly, especially because of the victim's religion, race, or politics.

per·se·ver·ance (pùr′sə vĭr′əns), *n.* persistence; quality of sticking to a task until it is completed.

per·sist (pər sĭst′, pər zĭst′), *v.* 1. to continue in spite of resistance or opposition; refuse to give up. 2. to say or do repeatedly: as, *to persist in teasing a younger brother.*

per·sist·ence (pər sĭs′təns, pər zĭs′təns), *n.* 1. stubborn, unyielding continuation in a course of action or thought; steady, determined pursuit of a purpose. 2. continuous going on: as, *the persistence of a heat wave.*

phe·nom·e·non (fĭ nŏm′ə nŏn′), *n.* 1. any happening or situation that can be observed and described: as, *an earthquake is a phenomenon of nature.* 2. anything that is very remarkable or unusual; a very unusual person.

pin·nace (pĭn'ĭs), *n.* a small boat which attends a large ship.

pin·na·cle (pĭn'ə kəl), *n.* a high peak, as of a mountain.

pi·ous (pī'əs), *adj.* 1. showing religious devotion; devoted to one's religion and its procedures. 2. pretending to be religious.

plac·id (plăs'ĭd), *adj.* calm; quiet; peaceful; undisturbed. —**plac·id·ly**, *adv.*

plague (plāg, plĕg), *n.* 1. a deadly, epidemic disease. 2. anything that causes trouble or pain. —*v.* 3. to torment, trouble, annoy, irritate, or bother.

plume (plōōm), *n.* 1. a large feather. 2. one or more feathers in an ornamental arrangement. 3. a token of honor. —*v.* 4. to decorate with feathers. 5. to smooth the feathers. 6. to feel proud; take credit.

pomp (pŏmp), *n.* 1. stately, splendid, or dignified display. 2. vain or showy display.

pon·der·ous (pŏn'dər əs), *adj.* 1. bulky and heavy. 2. unwieldy or clumsy because of large size or weight. 3. dull or tiresome. —**pon'der·ous·ly**, *adv.*

pos·sessed (pə zĕst'), *adj.* influenced or governed by an evil spirit or by an overwhelming idea or emotion; crazed; mad.

prec·i·pice (prĕs'ə pĭs), *n.* a high cliff with a steep or vertical face.

pred·e·ces·sor (prĕd'ə sĕs'ər, prĕd'ə sĕs'ər), *n.* 1. one who held a job or performed a task previous to another. 2. a forefather or ancestor.

pre·lim·i·nar·y (prĭ lĭm'ə nĕr'ĭ), *adj.* coming before or leading up to; preparatory; introductory.

pres·tige (prĕs tēzh', prĕs'tĭj), *n.* respect, status, fame, or good reputation based on approved traits or achievements.

pri·va·teer (prī'və tĭr'), *n.* 1. a privately-owned ship which is authorized by the government to attack enemy vessels. 2.

the commander or a crew member of such a ship.

pri·va·tion (prī vā'shən), *n.* lack of usual necessities and comforts of life.

pro·claim (prō klām'), *v.* to announce publicly; make public an official act or decision. —**proc·la·ma·tion** (prŏk'lə mā'shən), *n.*

pro·found (prə found'), *adj.* 1. indicating great knowledge or deep wisdom. 2. deep; far down; much below the surface. 3. intense; deeply felt: as, *the sailors showed profound joy when rescued.*

prop·o·si·tion (prŏp'ə zĭsh'ən), *n.* an idea, plan, or explanation presented for consideration.

Prov·i·dence (prŏv'ə dəns), *n.* God; one who guides or watches over human events.

pru·dence (prōō'dəns), *n.* 1. wisdom in practical matters; wise concern for one's own interest. 2. sensible caution; good judgment.

pub (pŭb), *n.* *British slang.* 1. a tavern. 2. an inn or hotel. [Short for *Public House.*]

punc·tu·al (pŭngk'chōō əl), *adj.* on time; prompt.

quar·ry (kwôr'ĭ, kwŏr'ĭ), *n.* an open pit from which stone is taken.

quar·ter (kwôr'tər), *n.* *Nautical.* the region around the stern of a ship.

quar·tet (kwôr tĕt'), *n.* 1. a group of four persons. 2. *Music.* a musical composition for four voices or instruments.

rar·e·fy (râr'ə fī), *v.* to become less dense; become thinner: as, *rarefied air.*

re·cess (rĭ sĕs', rē'sĕs), *n.* 1. a hollow or indented place in a wall or surface. 2. a hidden, withdrawn, or inner place. 3. a brief stopping of work or study. —*v.* 4. to set back. 5. to halt work or study for a short time.

re·coil (rĭ koil'), *v.* 1. to jump back or

ăct, āble, dâre, ärt; ĕbb, ēqual; ĭf, īce; hŏt, ōver, ôrder, oil, bŏŏk, ōōze, out; ŭp, ūse, ûrge; ə = *a* in *alone*; **ch**, chief; **g**, give; **j**, judge; **ng**, ring; **sh**, shoe; **th**, thin; **t̶h̶**, that; **zh**, vision. See the full key at the beginning of this glossary.

draw back, as in fear or surprise. **2.** to fly back when released or fired, as with a spring or a gun.

re·com·mence (rē′kə mĕns′), *v.* to begin again; start over.

rec·on·cile (rĕk′ən sīl′), *v.* **1.** to make friendly again. **2.** to make fit; to bring into harmony: as, *to reconcile two descriptions of an accident.* **3.** to become willing to put up with the situation.

re·con·nais·sance (rĭ kŏn′ə səns), *n.* a survey or examination of an area with some purpose in mind.

re·deem (rĭ dēm′), *v.* **1.** to get back or buy back. **2.** to pay off, as a debt. **3.** to set free or ransom. **4.** to save or rescue from sin. **5.** to carry out a promise. **6.** to make up for (mistakes or errors).

reek (rēk), *v.* to have a strong, unpleasant smell; to stink. *—n.* a strong, bad odor.

ref·er·ence (rĕf′ər əns), *n.* **1.** a statement or symbol which refers the listener or reader to something. **2.** a source, usually printed, of specialized information, such as an encyclopedia. **3.** a statement about the ability or character of a person; recommendation. **4.** the person who can provide such a statement or recommendation.

re·frain (rĭ frān′), *v.* to keep (oneself) from doing or saying something; hold back.

ref·uge (rĕf′ūj), *n.* **1.** protection from danger; shelter. **2.** person, place, or thing which provides safety, shelter, or comfort.

re·lapse (rĭ lăps′), *v.* to fall back.

re·lent (rĭ lĕnt′), *v.* to become less stern, harsh, or stubborn; become more tender or forgiving.

re·morse (rĭ môrs′), *n.* a deep, punishing feeling of guilt or sorrow because of a wrong one has done. **—re·morse′ful,** *adj.* **—re·morse′ful·ly,** *adv.*

re·pose (rĭ pōz′), *v.* **1.** to lie at rest. **2.** to lie in a grave. **3.** to lay to rest. *—n.* **4.** a state of rest or sleep. **5.** calmness; peace of mind.

re·prove (rĭ proōv′), *v.* to criticize; find fault with; scold; rebuke.

re·pulse (rĭ pŭls′), *v.* **1.** to drive back: as, *to repulse enemy forces.* **2.** to turn (someone) back rudely or coldly: as, *to repulse one's former friends.*

re·pul·sion (rĭ pŭl′shən), *n.* feeling of distaste or dislike.

re·sign (rĭ zīn′), *v.* **1.** to accept what happens calmly, patiently, and without complaint. **2.** to yield; give in. **—re·signed** (rĭ zīnd′), *adj.* **—re·sign·ed·ly** (rĭ zī′nĭd lĭ), *adv.*

res·o·lute (rĕz′ə loōt′), *adj.* determined; not giving in; firm in holding to a purpose.

re·solve (rĭ zŏlv′), *v.* **1.** to decide; make up one's mind. **2.** to decide by voting; make a formal group decision. **3.** to provide an explanation or a solution. **4.** to break up into basic parts or elements. *—n.* **5.** determination or definite, firm intention.

re·sus·ci·tate (rĭ sŭs′ə tāt′), *v.* to revive; bring back to consciousness or life.

rev·e·la·tion (rĕv′ə lā′shən), *n.* **1.** the act of making known or revealing (something). **2.** something made known or disclosed, especially something surprising.

re·volt·ing (rĭ vōl′tĭng), *adj.* **1.** rebellious; taking part in a revolt. **2.** disgusting; horribly distasteful.

rid·i·cule (rĭd′ə kūl′), *v.* to make fun of; force people to laugh at. *—n.* words which make fun of something.

rig·ging (rĭg′ĭng), *n.* *Nautical.* the ropes and chains which keep the masts and sails of a ship in place.

rig·or·ous (rĭg′ər əs), *adj.* **1.** strict; harsh; severe. **2.** extremely accurate or precise: as, *rigorous control of the experiment.*

rogue (rōg), *n.* **1.** a wandering beggar; tramp. **2.** a rascal; dishonest or scheming person. **3.** a playful, mischievous person. **4.** an animal that lives apart from its kind and becomes unusually savage or destructive.

ro·man·tic (rō măn′tĭk), *adj.* pertaining to a world of fancy and pleasant dreams, rather than the world of unpleasant reality.

rud·der (rŭd′ər), *n.* a movable device for steering a boat or ship.

ru·mi·nate (rōō′mə nāt′), *v.* 1. to chew again. 2. to chew the cud, as a cow does. 3. to turn over in the mind; think quietly; keep thinking about (something). —**ru′mi·na′tion,** *n.*

sac·ri·le·gious (săk′rə lij′əs, săk′rə lē′jəs), *adj.* showing disrespect for things considered sacred.

same·ness (sām′nĭs), *n.* a lack of variation; boredom; monotony.

sanc·ti·ty (săngk′tə tĭ), *n.* 1. holiness; saintliness. 2. the state of being reserved for religious purposes; sacredness.

sa·vor (sā′vər), *n.* 1. a certain taste or smell; flavor. —*v.* 2. to smell or taste with pleasure. 3. to have a particular taste, smell, or quality.

sa·vor·y (sā′və rĭ), *adj.* 1. pleasant to taste or smell. 2. morally correct; respectable.

scab·bard (skăb′ərd), *n.* the cover or sheath for the blade of a sword.

scav·en·ger (skăv′ĭn jər), *n.* 1. an animal that eats garbage or decaying matter. 2. a person who collects things that others have discarded.

scep·ter (sĕp′tər), *n.* rod or wand held by a king as a symbol of his power over his country.

scriv·en (skriv′ən), *v. Archaic.* to write.

scull (skŭl), *n.* an oar; one of a pair of oars for a boat. —*v.* to row a boat with oars.

seethe (sēth), *v.* 1. to boil, bubble, or foam, as a liquid. 2. to be extremely excited, disturbed, or angry.

sen·ti·men·tal (sĕn′tə mĕn′təl), *adj.* appealing to the emotions, especially in an excessive way.

set·tle (sĕt′əl), *n. Chiefly British.* a long wooden bench with a high back.

sham·ble (shăm′bəl), *v.* to walk slowly and awkwardly.

shoal (shōl), *n.* 1. a shallow area in a body of water. 2. a sand bar in a river, lake, etc.

sin·is·ter (sĭn′ĭs tər), *adj.* 1. toward the left-hand side. 2. threatening the approach of evil, disaster, etc. 3. wicked or dishonest.

smug (smŭg), *adj.* satisfied with oneself; pleased with one's own goodness, cleverness, etc.

so·lem·ni·ty (sə lĕm′nə tĭ), *n.* 1. a serious, formal, or sacred ceremony. 2. a formal, serious feeling; a grave, earnest, or sacred quality.

sol·i·tude (sŏl′ə tūd′, sŏl′ə tōōd′), *n.* the state of being alone, isolated, or lonely.

som·ber (sŏm′bər), *adj.* 1. dark; dull. 2. sad; gloomy; in low spirits.

sor·did (sôr′dĭd), *adj.* 1. dirty; disgusting; trashy. 2. selfish; greedy: as, *a sordid plan to bribe officials.*

spar (spär), *n. Nautical.* a strong pole such as would be used for the mast of a ship.

spec·u·la·tion (spĕk′yə lā′shən), *n.* 1. a thought, especially of a wondering or guessing nature. 2. the process of seeking to make money by buying and selling stocks, bonds, or other valuables.

spir·it·ed (spĭr′ĭt ĭd), *adj.* lively; energetic. —**spir′it·ed·ly,** *adv.*

squeam·ish (skwē′mĭsh), *adj.* 1. easily upset by crude words or ugly sights; too particular. 2. having a stomach that is easily upset; easily made sick.

strat·a·gem (străt′ə jəm), *n.* 1. a scheme or trick used to fool an enemy. 2. any trick or device used to deceive.

sub·sist (səb sĭst′), *v.* 1. to continue to exist. 2. to continue to live; stay alive.

sub·sis·tence (səb sĭs′təns), *n.* existence; the act or state of remaining alive.

sub·tile (sŭt′əl, sŭb′tĭl), *adj.* 1. subtle. 2. crafty; sly; cunning. 3. delicate; fine; difficult to see or understand.

ăct, āble, dâre, ärt; ĕbb, ēqual; ĭf, īce; hŏt, ōver, ôrder, oil, bŏŏk, ōōze, out; ŭp, ūse, ûrge; ə = a in *alone*; **ch**, chief; **g**, give; **j**, judge; **ng**, ring; **sh**, shoe; **th**, thin; **th**, that; **zh**, vision. See the full key at the beginning of this glossary.

suit·or (sōō′tər), *n.* **1.** a man who seeks the love of a woman. **2.** a person who sues or asks for something.

sul·len (sŭl′ən), *adj.* **1.** showing anger or hurt feelings by keeping to oneself and looking gloomy. **2.** sad; gloomy. — **sul′len·ly**, *adv.*

sup·press (sə prĕs′), *v.* **1.** to force or push down; to crush. **2.** to keep back; hide: as, *to suppress a smile.* **3.** to prevent or block: as, *to suppress a news story.*

sum·mit (sŭm′ĭt), *n.* the highest point that can be reached.

su·per·fi·cial (sōō′pər fish′əl), *adj.* **1.** touching only the surface meaning; shallow. **2.** concerning only that which is easily seen or on the surface; lacking in thoroughness; not penetrating. **3.** apparent or seeming, but not real.

su·per·nat·u·ral (sōō′pər năch′ə rəl), *adj.* outside or beyond the view or experience of ordinary men; beyond the laws of nature.

sup·ple (sŭp′əl), *adj.* **1.** limber; flexible; bending easily; not rigid. **2.** easily adjustable; adaptable to new conditions or needs: as, *a supple mind.*

surf (sŭrf), *n.* the foamy waves on the surface of an ocean or lake.

sward (swôrd), *n.* a grassy area; the grass-covered earth.

sym·met·ri·cal (sĭ mĕt′rə kəl), *adj.* balanced in design; having a regular form or arrangement, so that opposite sides are matched.

sym·pho·ny (sĭm′fə nĭ), *n.* *Music.* a long musical composition written for an orchestra.

syn·o·nym (sĭn′ə nĭm), *n.* a word which has the same, or almost the same, meaning as another.

tal·ly (tăl′ĭ), *v.* **1.** to count. **2.** to record a count of. —*n.* **3.** anything used to record a count or keep a score.

te·di·ous (tē′dĭ əs, tē′jəs), *adj.* long and tiresome; boring.

tem·per·a·ment (tĕm′pər ə mənt, tĕm′prə-mənt), *n.* **1.** disposition; frame of mind; usual mood or attitude. **2.** a nature that is moody or easily upset.

ten·or (tĕn′ər), *n.* *Music.* a male singer who can sing a high range of notes.

tink·er (tĭngk′ər), *n.* **1.** a traveling worker who mends pots and pans. **2.** a general repairman; jack-of-all-trades. **3.** a clumsy worker. —*v.* **4.** to work as an unskilled repairman. **5.** to fuss and putter around.

tol·er·a·ble (tŏl′ər ə bəl), *adj.* **1.** bearable; able to be endured. **2.** not too bad; fairly good.

tol·er·ant (tŏl′ər ənt), *adj.* **1.** willing to let others think, say, and do what they wish, even if in conflict with one's own views. **2.** free from bias or prejudice.

tran·quil (trăng′kwĭl), *adj.* **1.** calm; steady; quiet; motionless. **2.** mentally undisturbed; peaceful. —**tran′quil·ly**, *adv.* —**tran·quil′li·ty**, *n.*

trans·fix (trăns fĭks′), *v.* **1.** to pierce through, as with something pointed. **2.** to make unable to move, as though pierced through: as, *he was transfixed with fear.*

trap·pings (trăp′ĭngz), *n. pl.* **1.** decorated covering for a horse. **2.** ornamented clothing; adornments.

trav·erse (trăv′ərs, trə vûrs′), *v.* to pass over, through, or across; cross (something). —*n.* the act of crossing over, through, or across.

trem·u·lous (trĕm′yə ləs), *adj.* **1.** shaking; quivering; trembling. **2.** timid; fearful.

trib·ute (trĭb′ūt), *n.* **1.** a payment that a nation is forced to make to a stronger, or victorious, nation. **2.** any forced payment. **3.** a gift, act, or comment offered to show thanks or respect.

triv·i·al·i·ty (trĭv′ĭ ăl′ə tĭ), *n.* **1.** an unimportant thing or idea. **2.** the quality of unimportance.

ul·ti·mate·ly (ŭl′tə mĭt lĭ), *adv.* finally; in the end.

un·as·sum·ing (ŭn′ə sōō′mĭng), *adj.* not bold; not pushing oneself forward; modest.

un·bri·dled (ŭn brī′dəld), *adj.* **1.** without a bridle. **2.** not under control; ungoverned.

un·chas·tened (ŭn chā′sənd), *adj.* **1.** not

restrained; not subdued; somewhat un-disciplined. **2.** not punished or corrected, but allowed to do what one wishes.

un·daunt·ed (ŭn dôn′tĭd), *adj.* **1.** retaining one's courage; not afraid. **2.** not hesitating or retreating in the face of a threat or discouragement.

un·fath·om·a·ble (ŭn făth′əm ə bəl), *adj.* **1.** too deep to be measured. **2.** not understandable; impossible to comprehend.

un·feigned (ŭn fānd′), *adj.* genuine or real; not made up or pretended.

un·wit·ting (ŭn wĭt′ĭng), *adj.* **1.** not knowing; unaware. **2.** not intended; not done purposely: as, *an unwitting insult.*

ur·chin (ûr′chĭn), *n.* a small boy; a mischievous child.

ve·he·ment (vē′ə mənt), *adj.* **1.** intense; full of strong feeling. **2.** violent; forceful. —**ve′he·ment·ly**, *adv.*

vex (vĕks), *v.* **1.** to annoy, disturb, or irritate. **2.** to worry or torment: as, *her nagging vexes her husband.*

vex·a·tion (vĕks ā′shən), *n.* **1.** state of being annoyed, irritated, or provoked, usually by a small problem. **2.** something that annoys or disturbs.

vice (vīs), *n.* **1.** a bad or immoral habit: as, *gambling is his worst vice.* **2.** general evil conduct.

vi·cious (vĭsh′əs), *adj.* **1.** involved in evil. **2.** spiteful; dangerously evil.

vict·ual (vĭt′əl), *n.* **1.** *Archaic or Dialect.* food or provisions, especially for human use. **2.** *(pl.) Dialect or Colloq.* articles of prepared food.

vi·per (vī′pər), *n.* a dangerous snake.

vir·tu·al (vûr′chσο əl), *adj.* being something in effect or power, though not in name: as, *the prime minister is a virtual king.*

vol·u·ble (vŏl′yə bəl), *adj.* talkative; fluent.

wist·ful (wĭst′fəl), *adj.* thoughtfully sad, often because of longing for something. —**wist′·ful·ly**, *adv.*

yard (yärd), *n.* *Nautical.* a long, tapered piece of wood which holds the square sails of a ship crosswise to the mast.

yeo·man (yō′mən), *n.* **1.** *Archaic.* a servant or helper in a noble household. **2.** *Archaic.* an assistant to an official. **3.** *Archaic.* a farmer who owns his small farm. **4.** a petty officer assigned as a clerk in the U.S. Navy.

ăct, āble, dâre, ärt; ĕbb, ēqual; ĭf, īce; hŏt, ōver, ôrder, oil, bŏŏk, ōōze, out; ŭp, ūse, ûrge; ə = a in *alone*; **ch**, chief; **g**, give; **j**, judge; **ng**, ring; **sh**, shoe; **th**, thin; **th**, that; **zh**, vision. See the full key at the beginning of this glossary.

Contents by Types

Index of Authors and Titles

The number in italics after an author's name indicates the page on which a short biographical sketch of that author appears.

ABCDEFGHIJ   06987
PRINTED IN THE UNITED STATES OF AMERICA